PRACTICAL ENQUIRE WITHIN

A Practical Work that will Save Householders and Houseowners Pounds and Pounds Every Year

Volume I

DIY

'Do It Yourself', also known as DIY, is the method of building, modifying, or repairing something without the aid of experts or professionals. It is undertaken by a wide variety of people, for many different reasons – but what links them all, is a desire to improve their material surroundings and skills.

The term 'do-it-yourself' has been associated with consumers since at least 1912, primarily in the domain of home improvement and maintenance activities. It only came into common usage around the 1950s however. Back in the mid-twentieth century, DIY referred specifically to the new trend for people undertaking home improvements and various other small craft and construction projects, both as a creative-recreational and as a cost saving activity.

In the present day, DIY can also refer to music, radio, magazines and the arts and crafts movement – in that it offers an alternative to modern consumer culture's emphasis on relying on others, to satisfy needs. It also includes crafts such as knitting, crochet, sewing, handmade jewellery and ceramics, as well as the general environmental movement towards 'Recycle, Reuse and Reduce.' Painting and decorating is also a particularly prevalent form of home and aesthetic improvement.

Aside from its appearance in 1912, DIY as a broader concept has a much longer history. Italian archaeologists unearthed the ruins of a sixth century BCE Greek structure in southern Italy that came with detailed assembly instructions. It has since become known as an 'ancient IKEA building'! The find was a temple-like construction discovered at Torre Satriano, near the southern city of Potenza; a region where local people mingled with Greeks who settled along the southern coast of Sicily from the eighth century BCE onwards. Professor Christopher Smith, director of the British School at Rome, said that the discovery was 'the clearest example yet found of mason's marks of the time. It looks as if someone was instructing others how to mass-produce components and put them together in this way.'

Much like the instruction booklets, various sections of the luxury building were inscribed with coded symbols showing how the pieces slotted together. The characteristics of these inscriptions indicate they date back to around the sixth century BCE, which tallies with the architectural evidence suggested by the decoration. Although close to the modern conception of DIY, this find cannot properly be termed a 'do it yourself' though – as the building was actually built by Greek artisans coming from the Spartan colony of Taranto in Apulia (Southern Italy).

The DIY movement is a re-introduction (often to urban and suburban dwellers) of the old pattern of personal involvement and use of skills in upkeep of a house or apartment, making clothes; maintenance of cars, computers, websites; or any material aspect of living. In the 1970s, DIY spread through the North American population of college and recent-graduate age groups. In part, this movement involved the renovation of affordable, rundown older homes. But it also related to various projects expressing the social and environmental vision of the 1960s and early 1970s. The young visionary Stewart Brand, working with friends and family, and initially using the most basic of typesetting and page-layout tools, published the first edition of *The Whole Earth Catalogue* (subtitled *Access to Tools*) in late 1968.

The first *Catalogue*, and its successors, used a broad definition of the term 'tools'. There were informational tools, such as books (often technical in nature), professional journals, courses, classes, and the like. There were specialized, designed items, such as carpenters' and masons' tools, garden tools, welding equipment, chainsaws, fibreglass materials and so on; even early personal computers. Often copied, the *Catalogue* appealed to a wide cross-section of people in North America and had a broad influence.

For decades, magazines such as *Popular Mechanics* and *Mechanix Illustrated* offered a way for readers to keep current on useful practical skills and techniques. DIY home improvement books began to flourish in the 1970s, first created as collections of magazine articles. *Time-Life*, *Better Homes and Gardens*, and other publishers soon followed suit. In the mid-1990s, DIY home-improvement content began to find its way onto the World Wide Web. HouseNet was the earliest bulletin-board style site where users could share information. Beyond magazines and television, the scope of home improvement DIY continues to grow online, and in the true spirit of DIY, many homeowners blog about their experiences – taking knowledge away from organisations, and into the hands of individual people.

As is evident from this short introduction to the practice of DIY, it is an aspect of human endeavour with a surprisingly long history. We will always need to make and improve the spaces in which we live and work, and DIY provides the means with which everyday people can do just this. It is hoped that the current reader enjoys this book on the subject – and it encouraged to undertake some DIY of their own.

Woodworking

Woodworking is the process of making items from wood. Along with stone, mud and animal parts, wood was one of the first materials worked by early humans. There are incredibly early examples of woodwork, evidenced in Mousterian stone tools used by Neanderthal man, which demonstrate our affinity with the wooden medium. In fact, the very development of civilisation is linked to the advancement of increasingly greater degrees of skill in working with these materials.

Examples of Bronze Age wood-carving include tree trunks worked into coffins from northern Germany and Denmark and wooden folding-chairs. The site of Fellbach-Schmieden in Germany has provided fine examples of wooden animal statues from the Iron Age. Woodworking is depicted in many ancient Egyptian drawings, and a considerable amount of ancient Egyptian furniture (such as stools, chairs, tables, beds, chests) has been preserved in tombs. The inner coffins found in the tombs were also made of wood. The metal used by the Egyptians for woodworking tools was originally copper and eventually, after 2000 BC, bronze - as ironworking was unknown until much later. Historically, woodworkers relied upon the woods native to their region, until transportation and trade innovations made more exotic woods available to the craftsman.

Today, often as a contemporary artistic and 'craft' medium, wood is used both in traditional and modern styles; an excellent material for delicate as well as forceful artworks. Wood is used in forms of sculpture, trade, and decoration including chip carving, wood burning, and marquetry, offering a fascination, beauty, and complexity in the grain that often shows even when the medium is painted. It is in some ways easier to shape than harder substances, but an artist or craftsman must develop specific skills to carve it properly. 'Wood carving' is really an entire genre itself, and involves cutting wood generally with a knife in one hand, or a chisel by two hands - or, with one hand on a chisel and one hand on a mallet. The phrase may also refer to the finished product, from individual sculptures to hand-worked mouldings composing part of a tracery.

The making of sculpture in wood has been extremely widely practiced but survives much less well than the other main materials such as stone and bronze, as it is vulnerable to decay, insect damage, and fire. It therefore forms an important hidden element in the arts and crafts history of many cultures. Outdoor wood sculptures do not last long in most parts of the world, so we have little idea how the totem pole tradition developed. Many of the most important sculptures of China and Japan in particular are in wood, and the great majority of African sculptures and that of Oceania also use this medium. There are various forms of carving which can be utilised; 'chip carving' (a style of carving in which knives or chisels are used to remove small chips of the material), 'relief carving' (where figures are carved in a flat panel of wood), 'Scandinavian flat-plane' (where figures are carved in large flat planes, created primarily using a carving knife - and rarely rounded or sanded afterwards) and 'whittling' (simply carving shapes using just a knife). Each of these techniques will need slightly varying tools, but broadly speaking, a specialised 'carving knife' is essential, alongside a 'gouge' (a tool with a curved cutting edge used in a variety of forms and sizes for carving hollows, rounds and sweeping curves), a 'chisel' and a 'coping saw' (a small saw, used to cut off chunks of wood at once).

Wood turning is another common form of woodworking, used to create wooden objects on a lathe. Woodturning differs from most other forms of woodworking in that the wood is moving while a stationary tool is used to cut and shape it. There are two distinct methods of turning wood: 'spindle turning' and 'bowl' or 'faceplate turning'. Their key difference is in the orientation of the wood grain, relative to the axis of the lathe. This variation in orientation changes the tools and techniques used. In spindle turning, the grain runs lengthways along the lathe bed, as if a log was mounted in the lathe. Grain is thus always perpendicular to the direction of rotation under the tool. In bowl turning, the grain runs at right angles to the axis, as if a plank were mounted across the chuck. When a bowl blank rotates, the angle that the grain makes with the cutting tool continually changes between the easy cuts of lengthways and downwards across the grain to two places per rotation where the tool is cutting across the grain and even upwards across it. This varying grain angle limits some of the tools that may be used and requires additional skill in order to cope with it.

The origin of woodturning dates to around 1300 BC when the Egyptians first developed a two-person lathe. One person would turn the wood with a rope while the other used a sharp tool to cut shapes in the wood. The Romans improved the Egyptian design with the addition of a turning bow. Early bow lathes were also developed and used in Germany, France and Britain. In the Middle Ages a pedal replaced hand-operated turning, freeing both the craftsman's hands to hold the woodturning tools. The pedal was usually connected to a pole, often a straight-grained sapling. The system today is called the 'spring pole' lathe. Alternatively, a two-person lathe, called a 'great lathe', allowed a piece to turn continuously (like today's power lathes). A master would cut the wood while an apprentice turned the crank.

As an interesting aside, the term 'bodger' stems from pole lathe turners who used to make chair legs and spindles. A bodger would typically purchase all the trees on a plot of land, set up camp on the plot, and then fell the trees and turn the wood. The spindles and legs that were produced were sold in bulk, for pence per dozen. The bodger's job was considered unfinished because he only made component parts. The term now describes a person who leaves a job unfinished, or does it badly. This could not be more different from perceptions of modern carpentry; a highly skilled trade in which work involves the construction of buildings, ships, timber bridges and concrete framework. The word 'carpenter' is the English rendering of the Old French word *carpentier* (later, *charpentier*) which is derived from the Latin *carpentrius;* '(maker) of a carriage.' Carpenters traditionally worked with natural wood and did the rougher work such as framing, but today many other materials are also used and sometimes the finer trades of cabinet-making and furniture building are considered carpentry.

As is evident from this brief historical and practical overview of woodwork, it is an incredibly varied and exciting genre of arts and crafts; an ancient tradition still relevant in the modern day. Woodworkers range from hobbyists, individuals operating from the home environment, to artisan professionals with specialist workshops, and eventually large-scale factory operations. We hope the reader is inspired by this book to create some woodwork of their own.

NEWNES
PRACTICAL
ENQUIRE WITHIN

A PRACTICAL WORK THAT WILL SAVE HOUSEHOLDERS AND HOUSEOWNERS POUNDS AND POUNDS EVERY YEAR

INTRODUCTION

AS a practical man you have, no doubt, already carried out many small jobs in connection with your house, and doubtless in doing so you have acquired a fair amount of practical knowledge of the best ways of tackling certain types of work.

No doubt there are many other things which you would like to tackle if you just had a little expert advice as to the best method of setting about the work. This is the kind of information which you will obtain in the pages of this work.

The House Repair and Renovation articles appearing in the pages of the PRACTICAL ENQUIRE WITHIN are written, in every case, by men who have had years of experience in the particular class of work with which they deal. In these articles our contributors have generously placed the fruits of their experience at your disposal so that you can add their practical knowledge to that which you already possess.

Whether you are going to erect a fence, paint a front door, repair a leaking ball cock, re-enamel a bath, lay some crazy paving, or fit an extra switch in your bedroom, it is most important that the work shall be started in a proper manner. For instance, before erecting a fence post it is important to make sure that the lower part of the post has been rendered thoroughly rot-proof. This is best done by immersing the lower end of the post in hot creosote and allowing it to cool whilst still in creosote. Merely painting the end of the post with creosote is practically useless as a rot proofing method.

Here is a very good example of how a little expert knowledge, added to your own common sense, may make all the difference between an amateur job and one done in the best professional style. This is why the PRACTICAL ENQUIRE WITHIN has a very definite financial value to the practical man, because it ensures that all the work he undertakes as a result of reading the articles will be well begun and well finished.

SHELVES FOR ALL PURPOSES
IN THE KITCHEN, DRAWING-ROOM, DINING-ROOM AND BEDROOM

THE shelf is probably the simplest kind of fitment the householder can undertake to erect, and it is one of the most useful. In most cases only the cheapest timber is needed, deal, and the tools required are few, since the material can be obtained ready prepared. This applies not only to the shelves themselves, but also to the battens and other parts needed.

The method of procedure depends mainly upon the position in which the shelves are to be fixed, and the purpose for which they are required. The latter point is decided by the reader in accordance with his particular requirements. Their form, however, must be decided by their position. For instance, in the case of a recess, the walls themselves offer all the necessary support, a series of battens only being needed. If no side walls are available, either uprights of timber must be provided, or brackets.

Most Suitable Wood to Use.

For most purposes, $\frac{7}{8}$-inch deal is suitable for the work. This can be obtained ready planed in various widths, from $5\frac{1}{2}$ inches or so up to $11\frac{1}{2}$ inches. It is sold at so much per foot run, not by the square foot. For instance, 12 feet of 9-inch by $\frac{7}{8}$-inch deal at 6d. per foot would cost 6s.

LIVING ROOM SHELVES

A suggestion for a useful set of bookshelves for the living room is given in Fig. 1. They can be anything from 2 feet 6 inches to 3 feet in height, and can either be arranged along one wall, or around the whole room. Before beginning, the reader should measure up his books so that the vertical depths can be arranged to suit. It is advisable to have at least $1\frac{1}{2}$ inches clearance between the tops of the books and the shelf above, because the shelves are supported by battens, as shown. The books should clear these.

These shelves are a case in which the walls do not give any support. Consequently, uprights are required. In fact, the whole thing is made up in the form of a complete fitment, and is merely placed against the wall. The

*Fig. 2.—*Handy Fitment suitable for Bedroom or Hall.

addition of metal plates through which screws can be driven may be desirable, but they serve merely to prevent any tendency for the shelves to fall forward.

Construction.

Fig. 1A shows how to make the fitment. The two lower shelves fit between the uprights, and the top one lies above. The length has to be considered. If they are to be more than 4 feet or so long, it is desirable to fix an intermediate upright to prevent them from sagging under the weight of the books.

*Fig. 3.—*Plate Shelf fixed above Picture Rail.

Cut the uprights to length, making this about 1 inch less than over-all height to allow for the top. If there is a skirting to the room, a long notch must be cut away at the bottom of the back edge, so that the whole will fit flush against the wall. Battens of $1\frac{1}{2}$-inch by $\frac{7}{8}$-inch deal are nailed across the inner faces, as shown. If these were omitted, the shelves would be liable to drag the nails. A neat finish is given by cutting off the front corners. The bottom batten stops short $\frac{7}{8}$ inch, to allow the plinth piece to be fitted.

When cutting off the shelves, remember that the top is $1\frac{3}{4}$ inches longer than the others, because it reaches to the outer edges of the uprights. Fix the lower shelves to the last-named first and punch in the nails. The whole is then stood on its feet and the top added. To obtain the maximum strength the nails should be driven in in alternate directions, as shown in Fig. 1B. This gives them a "dovetail" grip. The plinth should be tried in position when the shelves are in place, because it may be necessary to take off a shaving to allow for any irregularities in the floor.

If a stained finish is desired, the staining should be done before the shelves are put together, as it is much easier to stain a plain board than a fitment which has many angles. For a glossy finish varnish stain can be used, a preliminary coat of size being first applied. This size must dry thoroughly before the varnishing is begun.

PLATE SHELVES

A particularly attractive form of plate shelf is shown in Fig. 3. It is fixed immediately above the picture rail, the latter providing the necessary support. Brackets of wood are fixed beneath at intervals. These brackets are obtainable in various shapes ready cut, though it may be necessary to cut away part to allow them to clear the picture rail.

The exact sizes are first calculated, and the positions of the brackets marked out as required. They are fixed before the shelves are placed in

*Fig. 1.—*Attractive Book Shelves suitable for a Living Room.

Fig. 4.—Useful Oddment Rack fixed against two Walls.

position, nails being driven in askew, as shown in Fig. 3A. Glue also is advisable. The important point is to keep the free ends square with the inner edge of the shelf. This is done as in Fig. 3A, by holding a square against the shelf whilst nailing. Another important addition is a plate bead to the top surface to prevent the plates from sliding forward. A ¼-inch square bead is big enough for most plates. It should be about 2 inches from the edge—more if large plates are to stand on the shelf.

Fixing the Plate Shelf.

If possible, allow the shelf to run the whole length of one wall. If this is impracticable, fix one piece first, and fit the other to it, driving in a nail askew to hold them together. Fig. 3A shows how nails are driven downwards into the picture rail. Not many nails are needed, as there is no great strain.

The shelf on the adjoining wall is fitted up to it in the same way, and so on all round. Any staining is done, of course, before fixing.

OTHER USEFUL SHELVES

Bedroom or Hall Shelves.

Fig. 2 shows a fitment handy in either bedroom or hall. Its construction is given in Fig. 2A. The two uprights are prepared first. The height is not important to an inch or so. That shown is 6 feet high. The lower ends are cut away at the back to fit over the skirting. Battens are nailed across to support the shelf.

The latter fits between the uprights, whilst the top lies upon them. The top has therefore to be 1¾ inches longer than the shelf. Nail the shelf in position and add the top. A frieze piece about 5 inches wide also is nailed in, this serving to conceal the curtain rail. To give clearance for the curtain, the shelf should be about 1 inch narrower than the top. The addition of a moulding around the top gives a neat finish.

To hold the whole thing to the wall, metal plates are screwed to the back edges at the top. Screws can then be driven into the wall. At the bottom, angle plates can be screwed either to the floor or to the skirting, as in Fig. 2A. Curtain rails with special brackets are obtainable. Hooks can be screwed in as desired.

Shelves in Recesses.

A shelf is easily fitted to a recess by nailing battens to the sides to form supports. The chief thing to watch is that these are fixed at the same height at both sides, and that they are square. Fig. 2B shows how squareness is ensured by drawing a pencil line with the square on the wall. Fix one batten along this line, and rest a

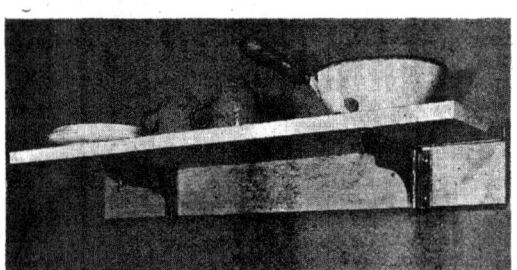

Fig. 5.—Folding Shelf supported by Bracket Hinges.
The photograph is taken from below to show the bracket hinges.

temporary batten upon it, as in Fig. 2C. A spirit-level is placed on the batten, and the latter adjusted at the free end until it is level. A mark made on the wall gives the height at the opposite side.

Should the shelf be extra long, or be required to sustain considerable weight, an additional batten along the back is desirable, as in Fig. 2D. The edges should be bevelled to give a neat finish.

Kitchen or Scullery Shelves.

These offer considerable variety, from the simple oddments shelf to the full plate dresser. An example of the former is shown in Fig. 4. Being at an angle, one end can be supported by a batten nailed to the wall. At the other end is a metal bracket. To give the screws a good grip the wall should either be plugged, or rawlplugs should be used.

Fig. 4A shows the method of plugging with wood. A hole is made in the wall with a small cold chisel, the hole being inclined downwards, as this lessens the tendency for the weight to pull it out. The strongest form of plug has a series of cuts made in it, as shown, this giving it a slight screwing tendency when it is hammered in. It is cut off flush afterwards. Rawlplugs have the advantage of making a small hole, and are very strong. Special tools for making the hole are provided.

Folding Shelf or Table.

In a scullery where space is limited, a shelf to fold flat when not in use is an advantage. Fig. 5 is an example. It should be fixed at table height, or a trifle higher. It is shown from below in Fig. 5 to reveal the metal bracket hinges which support it. Fig. 5A shows it closed. The provision of a back piece is necessary, partly to give a good fixing to the wall, and partly to bring the top hinges forward so that the shelf clears the bracket hinges when lowered. Fig. 5B shows these details.

Two pieces are nailed together at right angles. The lower, which stands upright, has holes bored in it to allow the fixing screws to be driven through into the wall. That at the top must project sufficiently to clear the hinges. In other words, the distance X in Fig. 5B must be greater than the thickness of the bracket hinges when closed, otherwise the shelf would foul the hinges. One other point to watch is that the hinges which pivot the shelf must be placed so that the bracket hinges clear them when being folded. The projecting knuckles would otherwise prevent the bracket from opening.

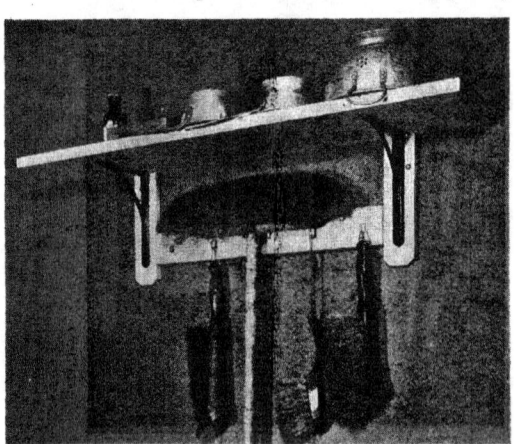

Fig. 6.—Combined Saucepan Shelf and Brush Rack.

SHELVES FOR ALL PURPOSES

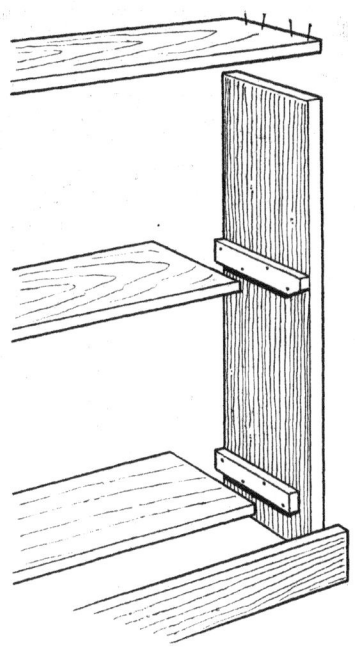

Fig. 1A.—Method of Construction of Living Room Bookshelves.

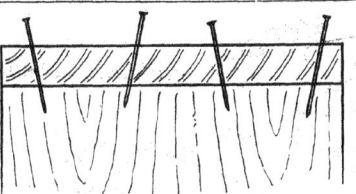

Fig. 1B.—How Nails should be "Dovetailed" to give Maximum Strength.

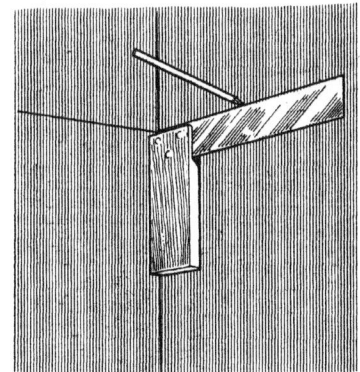

Fig. 2B.—Squaring Line of Shelf Battens.

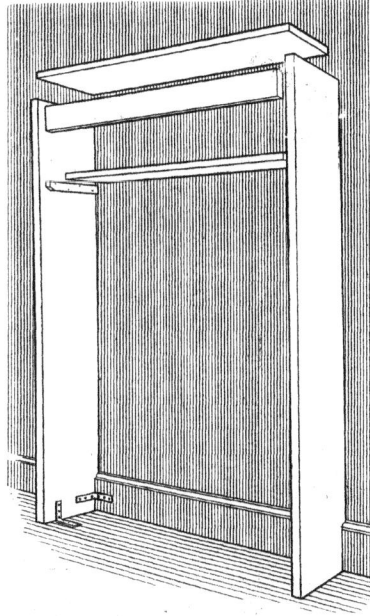

Fig. 2A.—How the Bedroom Fitment is made.

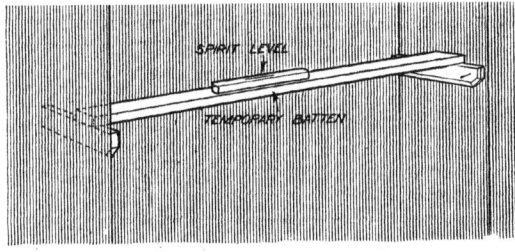

Fig. 2C.—How to ensure the Shelves being Horizontal.

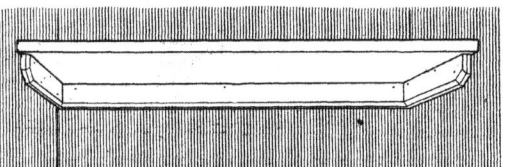

Fig. 2D.—Additional Batten at Back of Long Shelf to give Increased Support.

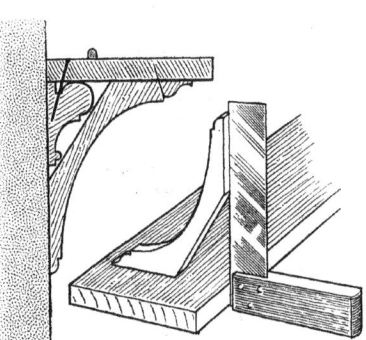

Fig. 3A.—Section through Plate Shelf, showing how Brackets are fixed Square.

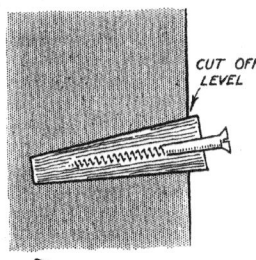

Fig. 4A.—Method of Plugging. Note the downward slope, also shape of plug.

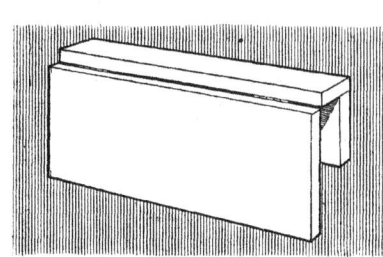

Fig. 5A.—The Folding Shelf in Closed Position.

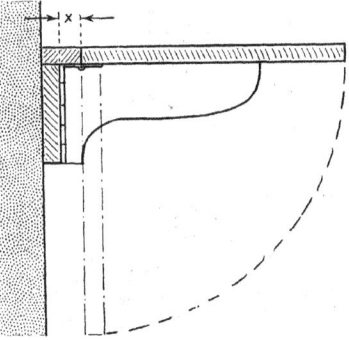

Fig. 5B.—Section through Folding Shelf. The distance X must be greater than the thickness of the folded bracket hinge.

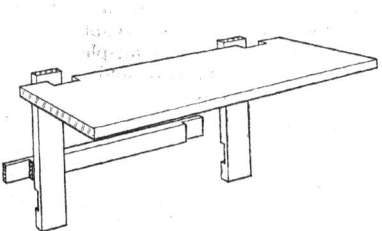

Fig. 6A.—Construction details of the combined Saucepan Shelf and Brush Rack

5

SHELVES FOR ALL PURPOSES

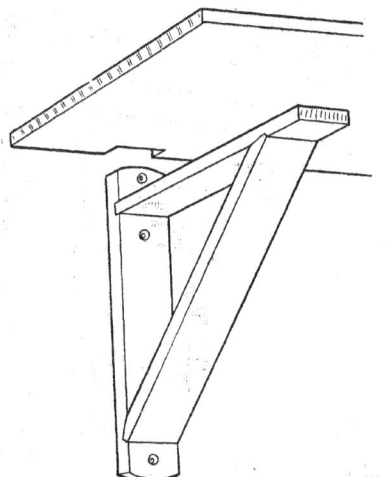

Fig. 6B.—EXTRA STRONG BRACKET FOR SHELF TO TAKE GREAT WEIGHT.

It is a good plan to allow the uprights to project 2 inches or so above the shelf. Screws driven in these projections give more support than those driven in below.

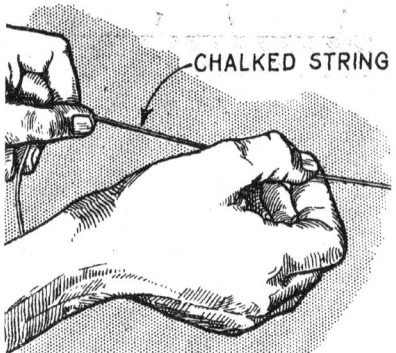

Fig. 7.—CONVENIENT METHOD OF MARKING THE WALL.

A chalked string is fixed at the desired height at one end. The other end is held between finger and thumb. The alignment is tested by means of a spirit level and the string is then plucked so that it will leave a line upon the wall.

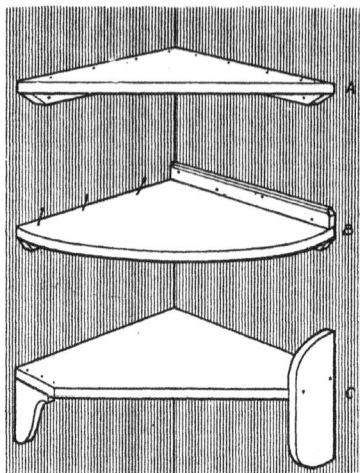

Fig. 6C.—SOME CORNER SHELVES.

A, Battens are fixed to underside only. B Battens fixed to both sides for shelf with curved front. C, Front brackets for shelf with projecting front edge.

Saucepan Shelf and Brush Rack.

Fig. 6 is a handy rack. Its accommodation could be amplified to almost any extent. It is made as shown in Fig. 6A. Notches are cut in the back edges to take the uprights, the last-named being screwed to them. The batten to hold the brush hooks should preferably be fitted to the uprights with halved joints, as shown. A simpler alternative is to screw it straight to the surface. In this case it must be placed to clear the metal brackets. If great weight is to be placed on the shelf, or if the wall is of plaster, it is a good plan to allow the uprights to project 2 inches or so above the shelf. Screws driven in these projections give more support than those driven in below.

This detail is shown in Fig. 6B, which is intended for extra strong shelves. The brackets are of wood, the cross member fitting in notches cut in the upright and horizontal pieces. Notice that the shelf is notched at the back. Screws are driven through the uprights into these notches. When putting the whole together, the brackets are made up complete in themselves, and the shelf fixed to them. If desired, a double tier set of shelves could be made on the same principle by continuing the uprights and adding brackets above.

Corner Shelves.

For light shelves, it is usually necessary only to fix battens to the wall, and nail the triangular shelf down on to them as at A, Fig. 6c. Should the front edge of the shelf require to be rounded, however, additional battens at the top are desirable, because any weight placed at the front might cause the back to rise. These battens are shown at B.

A third form of corner shelf is given at C. In this, either shape of front bracket could be used. The battens beneath the back edges are required, as in the other examples.

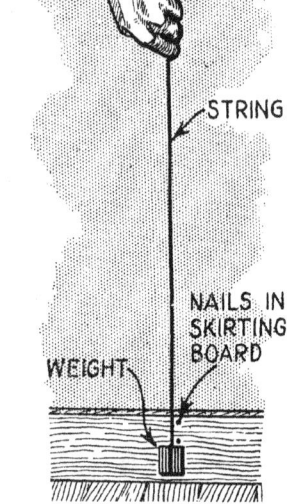

Fig. 8.—HOW TO FIND BEAMS IN A WALL.

It is generally reliable to take a line from a nail in the skirting board.

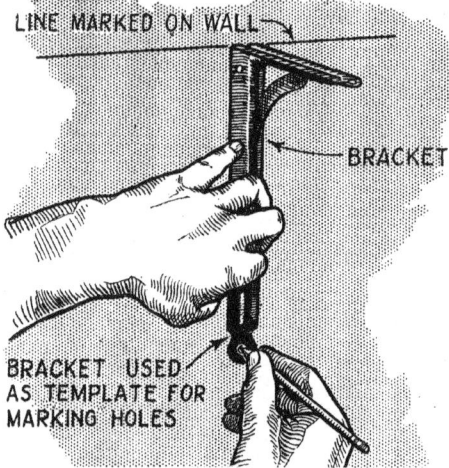

Fig. 9.—MARKING THE HOLES FOR THE BRACKET. Using the bracket as a template.

MARKING THE WALL FOR SHELVES

A convenient method of marking the wall is shown in Fig. 7. First fix a chalked string at one end at the desired height for the shelf. Now hold the other end of the string between the finger and thumb, and test the alignment by means of a spirit level.

Now pluck the string against the wall when it will be found that a chalk line is left on the wall.

How to find the solid uprights in a Lath and Plaster Wall.

When it is desired to find the solid uprights in a lath and plaster wall, the first thing to do is to examine the skirting board. This is fixed in position with nails, and it is generally safe to assume that wherever the nails occur there is an upright, and if marks are made vertically above these nails it is usually safe to drive in the nails for fixing the shelves at these marks. Fig 8 shows the method of marking a vertical line above the skirting board, and it will be seen that this consists of a weight attached to a piece of string and used as a plumb line.

Using Iron Brackets.

When using iron brackets to support a shelf, it is a good idea to use the bracket as a template.

Repairing Cracks in Plaster

Cracks in plaster arise from various causes. Minor cracks are usually the result of the shrinkage of the wood which the plaster surrounds. In a ceiling, the drying out of the beams and the laths generally results in a number of small cracks. These are not serious if the ceiling has been properly plastered in the first place, but when the ceiling is so bad that it is divided into small areas, complete replastering may be necessary.

Cracks radiating from door and window frames are common. These are caused by the wood shrinking or swelling with changing atmospheric conditions. Another kind of crack is found over fireplaces. The heat from the gases rising in the chimney breast assist the drying of the wood in the floor or roof above, and this causes cracks to appear at the junction of the ceiling and the wall over the fireplace. Cracks caused by the subsidence of a wall are beyond the scope of ordinary repairs, because this involves underpinning the foundations.

When to Repair.

Repairs to plaster walls and ceilings should be undertaken immediately prior to decorating, so that a proper finish may be given to the surface. After stripping a wall for papering, it is examined for cracks and holes. These are filled up before hanging the new paper, so as to provide a perfect surface, which eliminates the possibility of the paper being torn during the hanging, or afterwards if the paper is pressed over a hole.

Examine the Crack First.

The first step in repairing a crack is to examine the soundness of the plaster immediately surrounding it. All loose plaster round the crack must be broken away or the mend will be unsatisfactory. If the crack is over a doorway, it is probable that a similar crack may be on the other side of the wall, but may have passed unnoticed because of a picture or other hanging.

Cutting out the Crack.

If the crack is long and thin, it is necessary to cut away some of the existing sound plaster on either side of it to enable the new cement to be worked into the cleft. If the crack is not opened out in this way, the filling will not penetrate sufficiently to hold securely in place.

The old plaster on either side of the crack is cut away with a straight thin steel knife for about ¼ inch on either side of the crack. The more experienced man may prefer to chip out the plaster with a broad thin chisel. On ceilings great care must be taken when hammering the chisel or other cracks in the plaster will be started.

Undercutting.

When the crack has been cut out in this fashion, it is undercut so as to form a dovetail-shaped ridge for the new plaster. This provides a method of keying the filling into the crack and

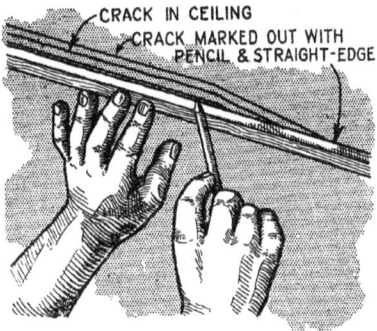

Fig. 1.—To Save Time and Make a Neat Job the Crack should be Marked Out with a Pencil and Straightedge.

First mark the course of the crack by means of a series of straight lines. Then draw parallel lines on each side at a distance of about ¼ inch.

also prevents it from falling out if it should not adhere properly to the sides of the crack.

Very Important.

No repair, however carefully done, will be satisfactory unless the hole or crack and the surrounding plaster are thoroughly wetted before applying the filling. However wet the new plaster may be, it will not adhere to the old plaster unless it is first properly wet. The crack to be repaired is moistened before mixing the plaster for the job, and again after mixing, immediately before the application of the filling. The crack is watered twice, because most of the water first applied soaks right into the surrounding plaster. A distemper or whitewash brush is the most effective tool for wetting the crack. With this, the water can be thrown well into the crack as well as brushed in.

The Plaster.

The material for filling consists of Keene's cement. This is very pale pink in colour. A mixture of equal parts of plaster of paris and Keene's cement produces a whiter mixture, but is more difficult to handle, because it sets quicker. Do not attempt to use plaster of paris alone. This sets very rapidly; in fact, it is sometimes impossible to mix it properly before it has set. A stronger and slower setting mixture, used for setting tiles and pointing glazed brickwork, is made of a mixture of equal parts of Portland and Keene's cements. Keene's cement alone is recommended for plaster repairs.

Mixing the Plaster.

If a large amount of plastering is to be done, do not mix enough for the whole lot at once. Mix as much as you think you can use up in five minutes. The portion of plaster for mixing is heaped on a board and a crater is made in the middle with the point of the trowel. Water is then poured slowly into the crater until it no longer soaks into the mass. The plaster is then fed into the middle from the sides, taking care not to let the water break through. When all the water has been absorbed in this way, a fresh cavity is formed and more water added until an easily workable consistency is obtained.

If the mixture is made too wet at first, add more plaster and mix again. The plaster must be mixed quickly and used at once, before it commences to harden. When the right consistency has been obtained, no more water may be added when the mixture begins to harden during the application. As soon as the plaster on the board becomes too stiff to apply easily a fresh lot is made up. It is advisable

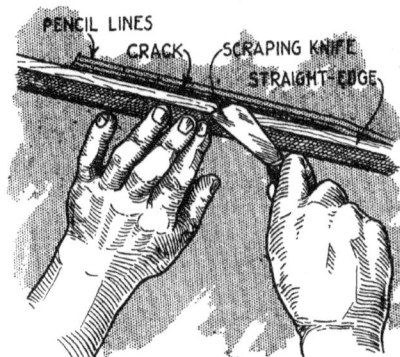

Fig. 2.—After marking out scrape away the Plaster along the two Outside Lines.

A scraping knife should be used.

Fig. 3.—The remainder of the Plaster can now be removed with a Chisel and Hammer.

REPAIRING CRACKS IN PLASTER

Fig. 4.—THE NEXT OPERATION IS TO UNDER-CUT THE PLASTER TO FORM A KEY TO HOLD THE PLASTER FILLING.

This is done by widening the back of the slot with the chisel.

safe if done while the first part of the plaster is still wet. It is important to work the plaster into the base of the crack before filling it flush with the wall or ceiling. If it is attempted to fill a deep hole with a single application of the trowel, an air-pocket will be formed which will prevent the plaster from keying properly to the sides of the crack.

Finishing the Surface.

When the crack is filled with plaster it is smoothed off as evenly as possible with the trowel and left proud rather

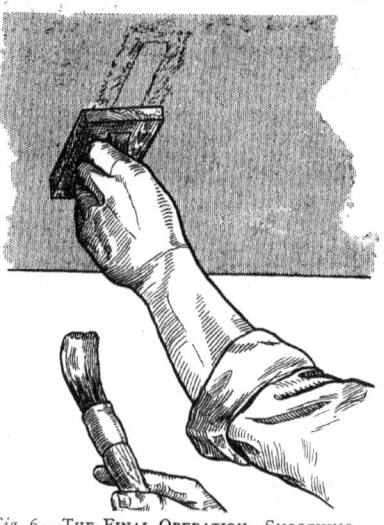

Fig. 6.—THE FINAL OPERATION—SMOOTHING THE PLASTER.

As soon as the crevice is completely filled, rub the plaster over with the wooden tool, keeping the cement moist and soft with further applications of water from the brush.

to remix the plaster on the board once or twice during use, because it tends to harden first on the surface.

Filling the Crack.

The best tool for applying the Keene's cement is a small pointed trowel, like that used by bricklayers for pointing work. The plaster is taken from the board in small quantities, on the underside of the tip of the trowel and worked into the crack. If the hole is large or deep it may be necessary to make two applications to complete the filling. This is quite

Fig. 5.—AFTER THOROUGHLY WETTING THE CREVICE THE PLASTER CAN BE APPLIED.

Use a small trowel and press a bit at a time into the back of the "key." Keep applying water with the brush while you do this.

than hollow. The trowel is now quickly cleaned of plaster and wetted. The surface of the damp plaster is then brushed with water and the trowel again used to even up the surface. This is repeated if necessary until the repaired portion is level with the surrounding surface. If any difficulty is experienced in levelling the surface properly, owing to the rapid setting of the cement, allow the filling to set slightly proud of the wall or ceiling. Afterwards, the surface is levelled off with a glass-paper block before whitewashing or papering.

MAKING FRAMELESS MIRRORS

SMALL or medium-size mirrors of modern or simple design can readily be purchased and with them and a few clips it is possible to make numerous shapes and styles of frameless mirrors.

The procedure is simple. First decide upon the size and style of mirror and obtain one, which of course will be unmounted.

Next obtain a piece of plywood slightly larger than the mirror and at least ⅜ inch thick for small mirrors up to 12 inches greatest measurement, ½ inch thick for mirrors up to 24 inches and ¾ inch for larger mirrors.

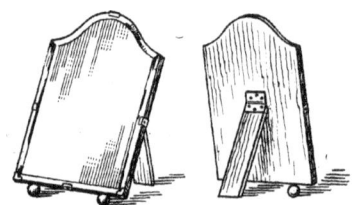

Fig. 1.—FRONT AND BACK VIEW OF FRAMELESS MIRROR.

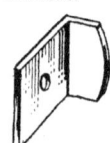

Fig. 1A.—THE SIDE CLIP USED FOR THE FRAMELESS MIRROR.

Lay the mirror flat on the plywood and run a pencil around the edges, then cut the plywood to shape and make the edges quite smooth with a plane, sandpaper or chisel and paint or stain the edges of the wood.

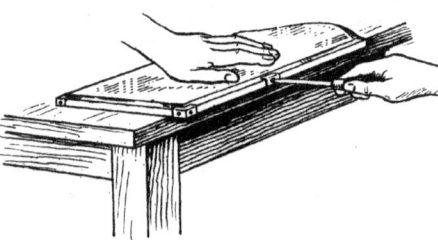

Fig. 2.—HOW TO FIX ON THE CLIPS.

Place the mirror and the wood backing so that they just overhang the table, and allow the screwdriver to be manipulated.

Obtain a few "side" frameless mirror clips as in Fig. 1A, and two or more "corner" clips, as in Fig. 1B, one being required for each square corner.

Put the mirror on the wood backing and set both on the table so that an edge projects about ½ inch beyond the table, as in Fig. 2, and screw the clips into place. Space them out nicely and fasten them with round-headed nickel-plated screws so that the "lip" or turned-over edge of the clip bears on the bevelled edge of the mirror.

The clips must be tight enough to hold the glass securely, but must not strain it at all.

Provide two hooks or "glass plates" if the mirror is to be suspended, or fit two "caddy feet" to the bottom and a strut (as in Fig. 1) if a table mirror is wanted.

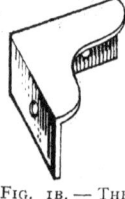

Fig. 1B.—THE CORNER CLIP.

Practical Methods of Distempering

DISTEMPERING is probably the easiest and cheapest form of decoration, and it is specially suitable for new walls and ceilings where other and more expensive treatments might be damaged by the still active lime in the plaster.

The Tools and Equipment Required.

The chief tool required is a large flat distemper brush from 6 to 8 inches wide. If a part-worn one can be purchased or borrowed, so much the better, for a new brush is apt to cause excessive splashing.

If a "broken-in" brush is not available and a new one has to be purchased, one of the special types made for household use is best. These have shorter bristles than the standard patterns and are therefore more suitable and cheaper.

A small brush for cutting in the distemper to the edges of the woodwork, etc., is a useful accessory. Either a 1-inch "flat" fitch, a No. 4 "tool," or a 2-inch flat varnish brush would serve, and would be useful afterwards for many other purposes.

At least two buckets, a large sponge, a small trowel, and, if there is old wallpaper to be stripped off, a painter's scraper costing about a shilling will be required.

Except in the case of very low rooms, where a chair might be sufficient to enable the top of the room to be reached, a step-ladder will be required; and, when a large ceiling has to be done, it is much better to have two step-ladders and a plank.

Preparation of the Room.

If possible, all furniture and carpets should be removed from the apartment under treatment. If that is impracticable, any large article left in should be well covered so as to protect it from splashing. If the ceiling only is to be done, the walls should be protected by means of sheets of some kind hung from the picture mould or tacked to the top of the wall.

How to Make Distemper.

Place a quantity of whiting (about 3½ lbs. for a ceiling, 5 lbs. for a ceiling and frieze space combined, or 7 lbs. for the walls of an average-sized room) in a bucket. Add water and allow the whiting to soak for two or three hours. Then pour off the surplus water, which will leave a thick white paste.

In another bucket place some concentrated size powder. This is merely pulverised glue, and is generally sold in ½-lb. and 1-lb. packets. For a ceiling, ¼ lb. of this concentrated size will be sufficient, but if both walls and ceiling are to be done, ¾ lb. is an appropriate quantity.

Fig. 1.—To avoid unsightly Streaks when the Distemper is applied it is essential to Stir it thoroughly both while Mixing and during Use.

This is best done with a piece of wood which can be kept in the distemper pot and used for stirring at frequent intervals while the work is in progress.

First add just sufficient water to soak the powder. After a few minutes has elapsed, add boiling water in the proportion of 1 quart to each ¼ lb. of the powder. Stir the mixture until the powder is completely dissolved.

The solution thus produced is what is called "size," and, when it has cooled somewhat, it is added to the whiting paste and well stirred. The result is white distemper.

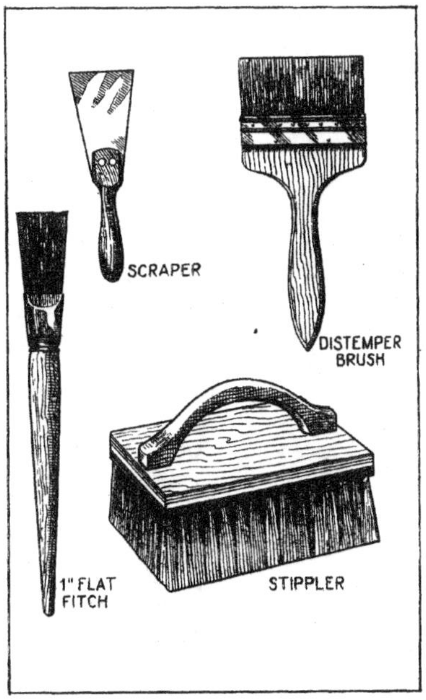

Adding Colour.

If a very pure white is required, a little lime blue, say, 1 oz. to each 3½ lbs. of whiting, is generally added. Or, if a cream is required, a little dry ochre or lime yellow is used instead of the blue.

For deeper shades, any of the following dry colours are obtainable and are suitable for use in distemper, either singly or in combination : Lime Blue, Lime Green, Yellow Ochre, Umber, Venetian Red, Lime Yellow, etc.

Colours should be thoroughly soaked in water before they are added to the distemper, and there should be a thorough stirring to distribute them completely. Otherwise, unsightly streaks will appear when the distemper is applied.

Testing the Colour

To find out whether the right depth and shade of colour has been obtained, a little of the distemper should be brushed on to a piece of white paper and dried. It will be noticed that distemper always dries out considerably lighter than it appears when wet. When the colour has been satisfactorily adjusted, the distemper can be put aside for a few hours, after which it will be found to work better than if it is used immediately after it is made.

Ready Prepared Distempers.

The foregoing particulars apply where it is desired to make up the distemper in the traditional way. But, happily, much of this trouble can be avoided, for many of the manufacturers of decorating materials now put up dry distempers in packet form. These specially prepared powder distempers contain all the necessary ingredients in correct proportions. They are quite inexpensive, they are made in a variety of colours, and they require nothing but the addition of water to make them ready for use.

Preparing the Surface.

If this is of new or previously untreated plaster, all that is required is a light brushing down to remove surface dust and the repair of any cracks or other defects. These repairs may be done either with Keene's cement, which is a particularly hard plaster, or with plaster of paris mixed with water. If plaster of paris is used, only small quantities should be mixed at one time, as it sets very rapidly. The present writer has found that if, instead of using water, some of the liquid size previously described be mixed with the plaster of paris, the hardening is

Fig. 2.—Some of the Tools required for Distempering.

The distemper brush should be from 6 to 8 inches wide. The scraper will be required if old wallpaper has to be stripped off.

PRACTICAL METHODS OF DISTEMPERING

Fig. 3.—The Quickest Way of Removing Old Distemper from a Wall is to soak it thoroughly with Water and then Scrub with a Distemper Brush.

The "puddle" produced can be conveyed to a bucket, a brushful at a time.

Fig. 4.—The Wrong Way to leave the Brush.

Note that the brush has been left with the bristles immersed in the distemper. This is very bad for the brush, and also tends to overload it with distemper.

Fig. 5.—The Correct Way to leave the Brush.

Here it will be seen that the brush has been placed across the top of the pail. This photograph also shows how only the tip of the brush should be placed in the distemper.

slightly retarded, which makes application easier. All holes and cracks to be filled must first be thoroughly wetted, otherwise the new plaster will not adhere to the old (see also page 7).

Removing Old Wallpaper.

If the wall or ceiling to be treated has previously been papered, the old paper will need to be removed. It must first be thoroughly soaked, and this is best done by means of the large distemper brush, which is repeatedly dipped in water and applied in brushing fashion to the whole surface. It is best to soak one wall all over and then soak it again, a square yard or two at a time. The stripping knife will then remove the old paper in long strips quite easily.

Removing Old Distemper.

If the ceiling or wall has been previously distempered and is thickly covered with old material, this should be removed by thoroughly soaking it with water and scrubbing off the "puddle" so produced with a distemper brush, and conveying it, a brush full at a time, to a bucket.

If no change of colour is intended, it may be sufficient merely to reduce the thickness of the old colour, but if a complete change of tint is required, the old distemper should be completely removed.

If there are any bad stains on the ceiling or wall, a treatment often successful is to coat them over with a mixture of fine plaster of paris and water and allow this to dry before proceeding with the distempering.

When a Preliminary Coating of Size is Advisable.

New plaster walls, and old walls which have been bared, often need a preliminary coating before the dis-

Fig. 6.—The Secret of Successful Distempering of a Ceiling is to proceed in a Steady Progression of Short Strips of a Foot or so.

Avoid more brushing than is necessary. Completely cover the surface, and use short strokes, using the brush lightly.

Fig. 7.—Always work towards the Darker end of the Room, *i.e.*, from the Window.

This will make it easier to see that no portion of the surface is missed. There must be no interruption once the ceiling has been started, or the break will show.

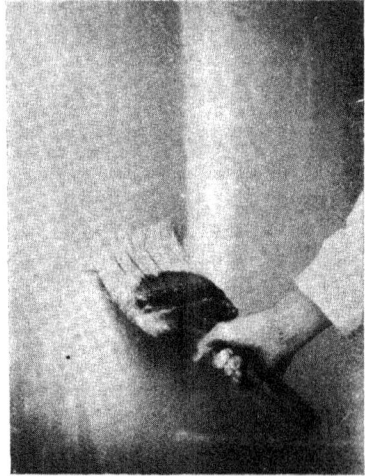

Fig. 8.—In the case of Walls coat a Strip of about 2 feet wide from top to bottom, laying the Distemper on with rapid Cross Strokes of the Brush and finishing off with long, lightly applied Vertical Movements.

Note how only the tip of the brush is being used.

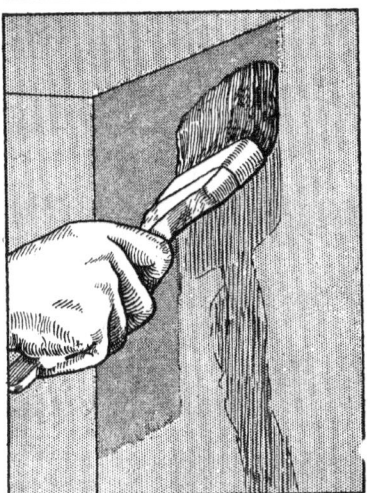

Fig. 9.—Distempering should always be started at a Top Corner, and Worked in Strips about 2 feet wide from Top to Bottom.
Treat each wall as a separate unit.

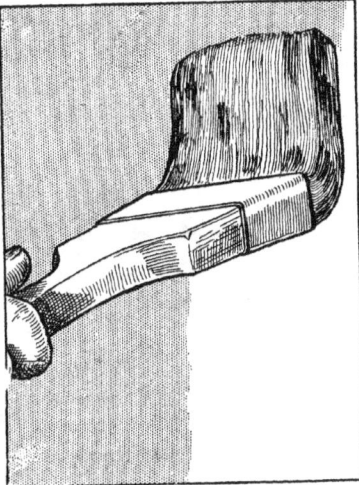

Fig. 10.—The Wrong Way of using the Brush.
The brush should be used lightly and not overloaded with material or the surplus will run down the handle.

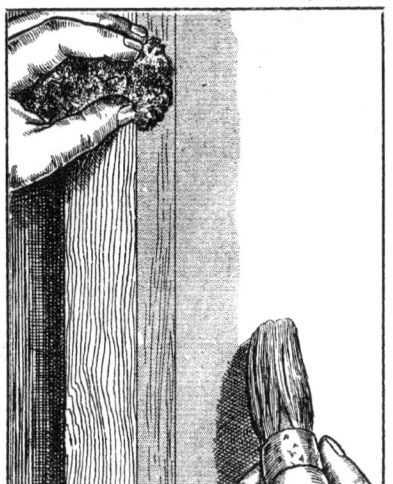

Fig. 11.—What to do if Woodwork is Splashed or Smeared.
The distemper should be wiped off while wet with a small sponge.

temper is applied. The plaster is sometimes too porous, and this can be corrected by giving a first coating of what is called "claircolle." This is simply prepared size, as described before, with a little whiting added. A coat of this applied to a plaster surface partially stops and helps to equalise the suction and thus renders it, when dry, a much more suitable surface upon which to apply the actual distemper.

Applying the Distemper to a Ceiling.

The following points should be observed in applying distemper to a ceiling. Put on plenty of material in short strokes, using the brush lightly. Work from the light; that is, the window, towards the darker end of the room. It is thus much easier to see that no part of the surface is missed, and this is highly necessary, as later touching-up is very difficult to do without producing a patchy effect.

Use the material as thick as can be conveniently worked. If it is too stiff, add a little cold water. And do not overload the brush with material or the surplus will run down the handle.

The Secret of Successful Distempering.

Do small portions at once, proceeding in a steady progression of short strips of a foot or so. When the ceiling has once been started upon, there must be no interruption. If there is such interruption, the break will show, owing to the strip done before the stoppage having dried.

This steady progress in short, easily worked strips without more brushing than is necessary completely to cover the surface with the distemper is the main secret of successful distempering.

While the work is in progress, do not have any fire in the room and keep the windows closed. This facilitates the work being done without drying under the brush and thus producing patchiness. But immediately the ceiling is coated, the windows should be opened so as to dry the whole surface equally and quickly.

Applying the Distemper to Walls.

The distempering of walls is a similar, but rather easier, process, so long as each wall is treated as a unit, to be completed without interruption. Begin

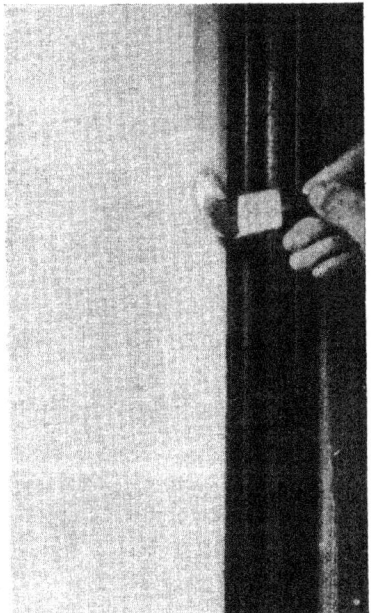

Fig. 12.—"Cutting-in" the Distemper to the Edge of Fixed Woodwork.
A 1-inch "flat" fitch, a No. 4 "tool" or a 2-inch varnish brush would be suitable.

at the top in one corner and coat a strip of about 2 feet wide from top to bottom. Lay the distemper on with rapid cross strokes of the brush, finishing off with long, lightly applied, vertical movements.

It is important that the "bands" of distempering should follow one another as quickly as can be managed. The main thing is to see that the edge is not dry before connecting the next "band" to it. This means that there must be no halt in working until a corner of the room is reached.

Cleaning Up.

Any splashes of distemper which may have fallen upon the fixed woodwork or floor of the room should be removed immediately the work is finished. A sponge dipped in water will effect this easily enough if the job is not delayed until the splashes have become dry and hard.

Water Paints and Washable Distempers.

Quite a number of these extremely useful materials are now on the market, and they are gradually supplanting the older type of distemper in public favour.

They cost rather more than whiting distempers, but are much superior in lasting quality and in their resistance to wear and tear. They are not more difficult to apply. Indeed, the reverse is the case, and the householder who decides to use any one of those now so widely advertised and well known may be assured that, if the directions of the maker printed on the tin are carefully followed, success is almost certain.

On New Plaster.

Water paints should be applied direct to new plaster, and no first coating of size is either necessary or desirable.

On a clean plaster surface two coats, applied according to the maker's directions, are generally sufficient, but sometimes three coats are preferable.

One advantage of this class of material is that it forms a satisfactory foundation, without any further preparation, for painting or paperhanging at a future date.

A Caution.

A word of warning is here necessary. Water paints and washable distempers should not be applied over old whiting distemper. This, if present, must be thoroughly removed by washing, otherwise subsequent cracking and flaking will probably occur.

But when applied to new or cleaned plaster walls and ceilings, water paints produce an entirely satisfactory and artistic result.

Stippling.

When a wall is finished with washable distemper or water paint, it sometimes reveals, when dry, some of the brush marks. If the material is properly applied at the consistency and in the way recommended by the makers, this should not occur or only in such a small degree as not to be objectionable to the eye. It can be entirely obviated, however, by means of stippling. The "stippler" is a square or oblong brush containing close-packed bristles and operated by means of a handle attached to its back.

These brushes are relatively expensive, and they are a luxury rather than an absolute necessity. The purchase of one might well be worth while if several, and those the most important, rooms in a house have to be done in water paint.

The stippler (preferably wielded by an assistant) is applied with a dabbing motion to each stretch of surface immediately after it has been coated, and while the distemper or water paint is still quite wet.

The result of this treatment is a complete absence of streakiness or brush marks, and the production instead of a finely granulated surface which considerably enhances the beauty of the finished work.

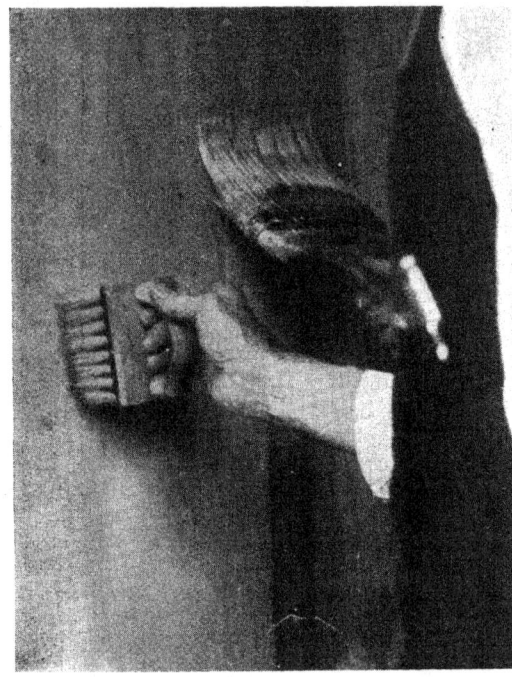

Fig. 13.—Brush Marks when the Distemper Dries can be Avoided by using a "Stippler."
This is applied with a dabbing motion to each stretch of surface immediately after it has been coated, and is best wielded by an assistant so that the distemper does not have time to dry.

CLEANING A SINK TRAP

Every sink is fitted with a trap, that is, a U-shaped pipe leading from the vent; normally it contains water in the two upright arms forming a gas-tight seal to the pipe leading from the drain. When water drains away slowly it shows that foreign matter has accumulated in the bend.

Remove the plug, which will be found at the base of the U tube, and the guard or grill at the bottom of the basin, which is usually held in place by a central screw.

A cane introduced through the plug vent will force solid matter in the pipe back into the sink as this arm tapers and is larger at the upper end.

If the Grill is cemented in place.

Older types have the grill cemented into the floor of the sink; in such cases, partially flood the sink, remove the plug and apply a rubber force pump immediately over the grill, pressing the handle sharply up and down. This will cause the obstruction to move towards the plug hole through which it can be removed.

The arm does not usually become blocked, but the gelatinous deposit coating the walls can be removed by the vigorous application of a cane.

When replacing the plug, grease the thread and see that there is a few turns of tow round the base to form a washer.

Dealing with a waste pipe that discharges over a gulley.

When dealing with a waste pipe that discharges over a gulley or hopper head and is consequently not very long, it can often be cleared by pouring a solution of common washing soda in hot water down the trap, after plugging the end of the waste pipe with a cork or wad, or piece of rag wrapped round a stick.

The solution should be poured down the trap until the waste pipe is filled. Leave the solution for about half an hour, then drain it off by removing the plugging.

Another good cleaning agent is spirits of salt, which might be tried if soda fails.

Fig. 1.—Remove the Plug at the base of the U Tube.
Then insert a cane through the plug vent.

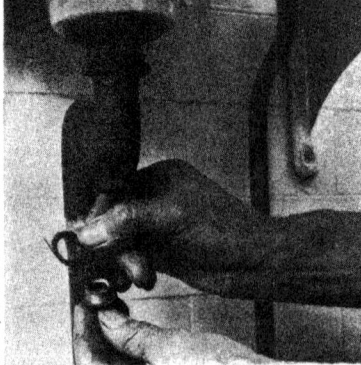

Fig. 2.—When replacing the Plug see that there are a few turns of Tow round the base to form a Washer.

Notes on Hard Soldering

Although soft soldering is used more frequently in the average home workshop than is the case with hard soldering, we believe many of our readers are familiar with the elements of simple soldering. The practical method of hard soldering is not so widely known, and as it can be used for repairing and making all kinds of small household appliances, we are including these notes before dealing with the general subject of soft soldering.

Hard soldering provides a convenient method of joining or repairing metal surfaces when a stronger join than that given by soft soldering is required. Hard soldering cannot be applied to metals with a low melting point, such as aluminium, lead or pewter; but silver, copper, steel, nickel-silver, gunmetal, etc., can all be worked with very successfully.

Materials Required.

For most home workers' requirements the following materials will be found quite sufficient:—

1 oz. of No. 2 silver solder (in the form of thin sheets).
¼ lb. of borax.
Bunsen burner with ⅜-inch tube.
Pair of pliers for holding the work.
Pair of tweezers for feeding the solder.
Piece of wire flattened at one end for applying the borax to the joint.

As it is important that the articles to be soldered are raised to red heat, a gas blow-pipe and a pair of foot bellows would be advisable for more elaborate work.

No soldering iron is used, the work itself being heated in the flame.

Preparing the Solder and Borax.

Unlike soft soldering, where the bar of solder is used direct on the work, silver solder is used in small pieces about ⅛ inch square. Cut a strip about ⅛ inch wide from the sheet of solder with scissors and break up the strip into small pieces with the pliers.

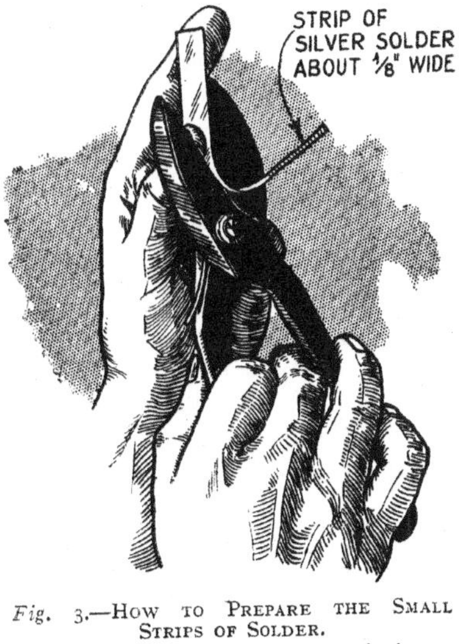

Fig. 1.—Here We See What Happens When the Heat is First Applied to the Join.
The borax swells up. As the work gets hotter it finally melts and assumes the appearance of molten glass when the metal is red hot. It is then ready for the solder.

Fig. 2.—The Solder is Applied to the Red Hot Join by Means of Tweezers.
Only a small piece of solder, about ⅛ in. square, should be used.

The borax should be made into a stiff paste with water.

First Clean the Join.

A good, clean-fitting surface for the join between the two pieces of metal is important in hard soldering. Use emery cloth or a file to obtain a clean surface. In the case of a very irregular join where a file might damage the fit of the join, clean with a rag moistened with nitric acid.

If an article has been previously soft soldered, all the soft solder must be removed, although soft soldering may be done on top of hard soldering.

Now Apply the Borax.

Apply the borax paste to both parts of the join to be soldered before assembling the parts. It will sometimes be found convenient to wire on the broken piece with soft iron wire, but the borax must first be applied to the two surfaces. Now hold the join in the flame until the borax begins to bubble and give off steam. Then apply more borax paste freely round the join, using the piece of wire specially prepared for this purpose, and heat up again.

Hold in the flame until the borax swells up and finally melts, assuming the appearance of molten glass when the metal is red hot.

Applying the Solder.

The work is now ready for the solder to be applied. A little piece should be picked up with the tweezers and applied to the join. Continue heating until the solder is seen to run over the surface. As soon as it has run and sufficient solder to make a good join has been applied, remove from the flame.

If the first attempt is unsuccessful, there is no need to pull the join apart. Apply more borax and reheat until the solder runs over the parts covered with the molten borax.

Cooling.

No attempt to cool the work with water should be made, or the join may crack.

Cleaning.

When cool, it will be seen that the surface around the join is covered with a glassy substance. This is only the result of the melted borax, and should be removed by

Fig. 3.—How to Prepare the Small Strips of Solder.
The solder can be cut with a pair of scissors.

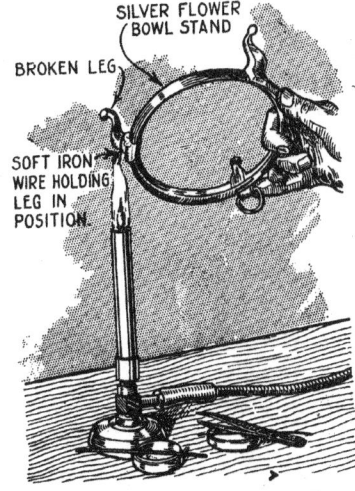

Fig. 4.—A Typical Job that can be Dealt with by Hard Soldering.
Showing a broken leg of a silver flower bowl stand being repaired. Note that the broken leg is held in position with soft iron wire.

chipping off with an old file kept specially for the purpose. Do not use any good tools for this operation, as the substance is extremely hard and would soon blunt them.

If difficulty is experienced in cleaning steel work after hard soldering, try pickling in a weak solution of sulphuric acid for a few hours. A satisfactory solution can be made by diluting acid from an old accumulator, with an equal amount of water.

Causes of Unsatisfactory Joins.

The most likely causes of unsatisfactory joins are insufficient heat, failure to cover the join properly with borax before the work gets hot, or a badly fitting join. A gap between the surfaces to be joined results in the solder merely covering the surface and not uniting them.

MORE ADVANCED WORK

Although rather outside the scope of the home worker, for larger jobs a gas blow-pipe and a pair of bellows are advisable. The best type of bellows to use is one having a rubber reservoir, as this gives a steadier flame.

An iron tripod will also be found useful on which to stand the work.

Fig. 6 shows a typical job where hard soldering could be used to advantage. This is soldering the water tubes into a model boiler.

Method of Working.

The tubes must be made a tight fit in the holes of the boiler shell and the borax smeared in the holes and round the tubes before they are pushed in the holes.

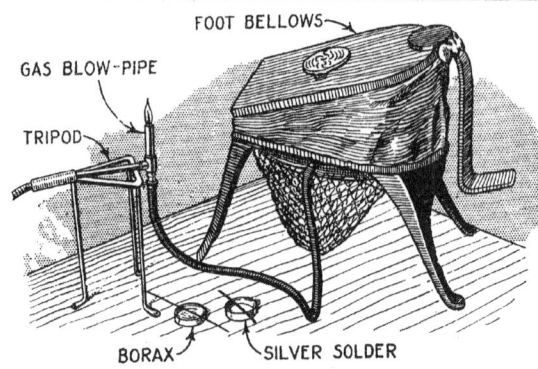

Fig. 5.—Suitable Apparatus for Hard Soldering Larger Work.

This consists of a pair of foot bellows, a gas blow-pipe, iron tripod, borax and hard solder.

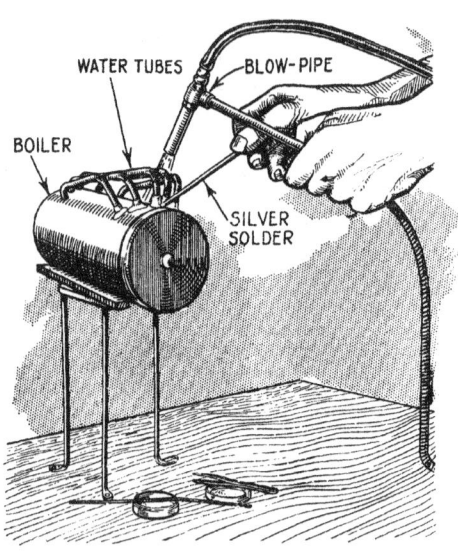

Fig. 6.—How Hard Soldering can be used for a Model-making Job.

Showing the water tubes of a model boiler being hard soldered. For work of this nature it would be more convenient to feed the solder by strip than by adding small pieces with tweezers.

Take care, however, not to get any borax in the holes or they will be blocked owing to the fact that after the borax has been melted it is insoluble in water.

Next heat round all five joins, applying plenty of borax. Then concentrate the flame round each tube in turn and run on the solder when the job is red hot.

Feeding the Solder.

In work of this nature it will be found more convenient to feed the solder in a narrow strip. Just touch the strip on the join and then remove it quickly so that it does not melt in the flame.

Fig. 6 shows how the strip of solder is held while the flame is kept continually playing on the join.

The other ends of the tubes can be hard soldered in without fear of remelting the joints.

No difficulty should be experienced with a copper boiler of this description, provided sufficient heat for the job is available, owing to the fact that copper takes the heat readily and that the molten borax readily removes any traces of copper oxide which form during the preliminary heating.

Brazing.

Brazing has no particular advantage over hard soldering except that it is cheaper. It is more applicable to jointing steel work than brass.

A higher temperature than that used for ordinary hard soldering is required, and brazing spelter is used instead of silver solder. The procedure is, however, exactly the same as that described for hard soldering.

WATERPROOFING CONCRETE FLOORS

ALTHOUGH concrete is particularly convenient for the floors of certain rooms, e.g., for cellars, sculleries, sheds and garages, it possesses the disadvantage of producing dust, owing to the disintegration of the surface particles. If the floor is subject to much usage, the formation of dust is apt to become a serious drawback.

In order to overcome this trouble, and at the same time to render the floor waterproof, the following method can be recommended.

Make up a solution of sodium silicate (otherwise known as waterglass and used for the preservation of new-laid eggs) in water and apply this to the surface of the concrete by means of a large flat brush of the type used for distempering or paperhanging.

About a quart of water-glass diluted down to a gallon with warm water will be found to be about the correct consistency. Mix the water-glass thoroughly with the water before applying the solution to the concrete surface. The solution takes only a few hours to dry and in the latter state leaves the surface somewhat darker than before and with a slightly polished appearance.

If necessary, more than one application of the water-glass solution may be made. Thus, in the case of concrete steps or gangways which are liable to more wear than other parts of the surface, several applications of the solution should be made.

Not only does this method prevent the formation of dust but it also waterproofs, thoroughly, the surface, so that if necessary the latter can be painted with ordinary oil paints. *Concrete walls, furniture and other domestic articles* can be painted satisfactorily after one or two applications of water-glass solution.

TIME, LABOUR AND MONEY SAVING IDEAS

AVOID DUSTY CORNERS.

A simple and effective way of dealing with corners that hold dust is to fill up the corner with a little fitment known as a brass dust shield (see below). These are slightly domed triangular-shaped brass plates measuring about 3 inches from point to point and having three fixing holes. They are finished either in bright copper, bronzed or

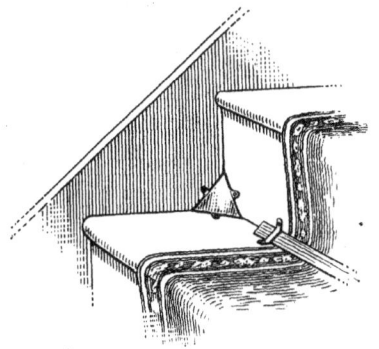

bright brass, are inexpensive and can be fitted to any corner, for example, on the staircase, in the corners of wainscots, in cupboards and larders, anywhere, in fact, where dust could lodge. They are fixed very easily with three small brass tacks, simply put the shield in place and nail it there.

PAINTING CORRUGATED IRON.

Corrugated galvanised iron is not an easy surface to take paint permanently, as the paint has a tendency to crack and peel off after a time.

In order to safeguard against this a good plan is first to clean the surface with a wire brush and then apply a liberal coating of boiled linseed oil, which has previously been well heated. The oil fills all the pores of the metal, forming an adhesive layer to which the paint will remain firmly fixed under all weather conditions.

TO CLEAN WHITE ENAMEL PAINT.

White enamel paint can be cleaned satisfactorily with warm soapy water to which a little powdered whiting has been added. If the paint is dirty or discoloured to any appreciable extent, the better method is to dip a piece of soft flannel in warm soapy water, wring it out and then dip it into the whiting. Rub the enamel paint until it is clean and then finish off with a piece of chamois leather which has previously been soaked in clean cold water and wrung out.

PREVENTING STEEL ARTICLES FROM RUSTING.

Domestic articles made of iron or steel, e.g., fire-irons, metal screens, fire-dogs and fenders, may be maintained in their original polished condition by giving them a liberal coating of a cellulose polishing wax, such as Belco or Johnson's wax, using a piece of soft rag to apply the wax. Afterwards well rub with a clean duster. The wax fills the fine interstices of the metal, and also gives a protective transparent film, which is proof against the effect of moisture or temperature changes in the room.

WATERPROOFING SAILCLOTH.

Sailcloth used for tents, haversacks, sleeping beds of the folding pattern, motor-car and cycle covers, etc., can be rendered thoroughly waterproof in the following manner.

Boil 72 parts, by weight, of linseed oil for two or three hours after adding to the boiling oil 6 parts of sulphate of iron and 4 parts of sulphate of zinc. When cool, mix with 60 parts of oil of turpentine and the necessary quantity of pigment, e.g., lamp black in the case of coloured canvases. The sailcloth is painted with this compound and then dried in the sun. After allowing a few days for the surface thoroughly to harden, the operation should be repeated.

RENOVATING LINOLEUM.

In order to restore worn or marked linoleum it should first be spread on the floor and washed thoroughly with a hot solution of water and washing soda in order to remove any grease; afterwards allow it to dry. The linoleum should then be stretched and tacked down in this condition. Next apply two thin coats of varnish, made by mixing together 6 parts of elastic oak varnish and 1 part of japan goldsize.

Let the first coat dry thoroughly before applying the next; about a fortnight should be allowed to elapse before placing anything heavy on the linoleum. The addition of the goldsize makes the varnish harder and causes it to dry quicker.

CEMENTING CLOTH TO WOOD.

To fasten cloth to wood, take equal parts of glue and isinglass made into a liquid glue-like consistency, and then thicken to the desired degree with tannin.

FIXING TACKS IN AWKWARD SPOTS.

A lot of time can be wasted in attempting to drive tacks into inaccessible places. If, however, the tack is forced through a piece of paper, of the appropriate length and width, the tack can be manœuvred into position, driven into the material and the paper removed by tearing it away. Wood-screws can usually be inserted into corners in the same way.

RE-POLISHING DULL PLATE GLASS.

The following is a satisfactory method for repolishing the surface of plate glass which has become dull.

Obtain some sponge, or mutton, cloths that have been well washed in soda water to remove grease. Take $\frac{1}{2}$ gallon of hot water and dissolve 1 oz. of Epsom-salt in it. Then in a separate $\frac{1}{2}$ gallon of water dissolve 2 oz. of common washing soda. When the former solution has become quite cold mix the two together. Put the cloths into this and bring to a boil and then, when the solution is cold again remove the cloths and hang out to dry. The cloths will then be charged with a fine precipitate of magnesium carbonate and they are then ready for use upon the dull plate glass.

A USEFUL POST HINT.

It frequently happens that posts used in the garden have a habit of working loose when subjected to any repeated side pressure. This often occurs with posts used for small gates, clothes lines, children's swings and similar fixtures.

In order to overcome this difficulty the post must be reinforced at its base so as to transmit any bending, or uprooting tendency to as large a mass of earth as possible.

One good method of achieving this end is to fix, securely, to the base of the post a sufficiently large piece of sheet metal or timber. If sheet metal is employed it should be screwed to the foot of the post in several places. If timber is used, long nails (4 to 6 inch wire nails) will be found to give satisfactory results.

The timber should be sufficiently thick to withstand any bending action. Thus, for a 4-inch square post a piece of 1-inch deal or pine of about 12 × 12 inches or 18 × 18 inches is recommended.

Well creosote the end of the post and also the wooden footing, and sink the post as deeply as possible. Tramp the earth around the post as you fill in the hole.

How to Lay Linoleum

The first thing to decide when you contemplate covering a floor with linoleum is the quantity required to cover a given space. All cork linos with the exception of bordered widths are made 6 feet wide.

A convenient method of determining the quantity required is to divide the width of the roll of linoleum into the shorter side of the room and multiply the answer by the longer side. To this add sufficient for any recesses. If the width of the lino does not divide exactly into the width of the floor it is advisable to count the fraction either as one or as a half, as shown in the following examples.

An Example.

Size of room, 11 × 14 feet. Size of lino, 6 feet wide.

Then 11 divided by 6 = 2 feet approx.

Multiplying by the length of the room, we get 2 × 14 = 28 feet.

This is just slightly more than actually required, but the extra will allow for wastage and matching the pattern.

Another Example.

If, however, the room were only 9 feet wide by 14 feet, one width of lino might be cut down the middle and there would be no wastage. This would be worked out as follows:—

9 ÷ 6 = 1½ feet. 1½ × 14 = 21 feet of lino required.

If the lino has a large pattern, some allowance must be made for matching. A 10 per cent. surplus will generally be found ample.

Estimating Quantity of Lino Required for Surrounds.

The simplest method of laying a surround is in right-angled strips. Reference to Fig. 10 will show a convenient method of measuring, and the following measurements should be taken:—

A to B and multiply by width

		B to H
D „ C	„	L „ C
E „ I	„	E „ F
H „ L	„	K „ F

Adding together the results obtained will give the required amount of linoleum. Allowance must, of course, be made for any recesses.

Preparing the Floor.

Great care must be taken before

Fig. 1.—Measuring off a Length of Linoleum.
This is best done while the linoleum is standing up.

Fig. 2.—Cutting the Linoleum.
Another method is to first make a groove along the intended line of separation, then raise the lino slightly, fold it upper side outwards, and run the knife along the fold, attacking it from underneath.

laying linoleum to see that the floor is in a good condition, otherwise the lino will wear through quickly. If the floor is an old one it will probably be found that the wood has either shrunk or worn below the nail heads. All projecting nail heads should be hammered level with the surface. If there are knots in the wood which stand above the surface, these must be made level with a plane or chisel.

Spaces Between the Boards.

If there are any uneven spaces between the boards, these should be packed with thick paper, as shown in Fig. 14. (See later article for method of treating badly shrunk boards.)

Holes in the Floor.

A hole in a floor must be filled up or covered over. A good method of doing this is to cut from a tin cigarette or tobacco box a piece of tin larger than the hole. Place this over the hole and tack it down.

It is well worth covering the whole floor with a cheap felt paper underlay which should be laid the opposite way to the run of the floorboards (see Fig. 15). This will help to give durability to the linoleum.

If laying lino on concrete or stone floors it is advisable to protect the floor covering by using a damp-resisting underlay which can be obtained quite cheaply.

LAYING THE LINO ON THE FLOOR

Materials Required.

Lino knife.

Strip of emery cloth for sharpening the knife.

Lino brads or gimp pins.

Hammer.

Tracer. This consists of a flat piece of wood, about 6 inches long and 1 inch wide, shaped as shown in Fig. 5. The hole in the point, which is ½ inch from the end, should be large enough to take the point of a lead pencil.

Laying the First Strip.

To unroll the lino, lay the roll on the floor and kneel on one end. It will be found best to start by laying the width the opposite side to the fireplace. The tracer is used to fit the lino accurately along the skirting board, if this is at all uneven. Place the pencil through the hole and the piece of wood against the wall skirting as shown in Fig. 6. The outline of the skirting board is then traced either direct on to the lino or on to a piece of brown paper which is then used as a template. By cutting the lino on these lines a perfect fit is ensured.

For fitting into awkward recesses and corners it is best to trace out on

HOW TO LAY LINOLEUM

Fig. 3.—FITTING THE LINOLEUM ALONG A STRAIGHT SKIRTING BOARD (1).
First make a coarse cut to somewhere near a fit.

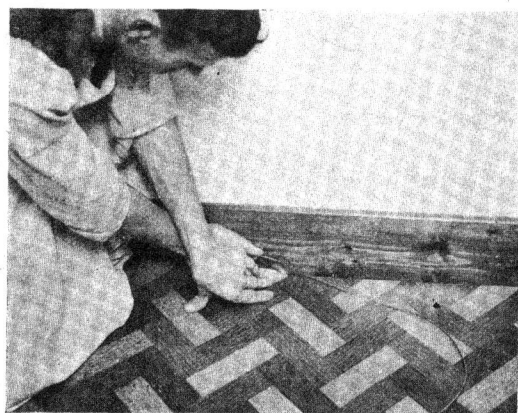

Fig. 4.—FITTING THE LINOLEUM ALONG A STRAIGHT SKIRTING BOARD (2).
Now make a fine cut to fit flush.

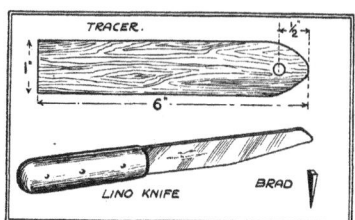

Fig. 5.—DETAILS OF THE TRACER FOR FITTING LINOLEUM TO AN UNEVEN SKIRTING BOARD.

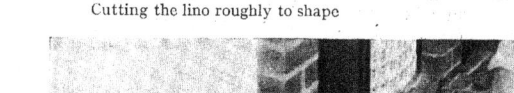

Fig. 6.—USING THE TRACER.

Fig. 7.—THE FIRST STAGE IN FITTING LINOLEUM ROUND A FIREPLACE CURB.
Cutting the lino roughly to shape

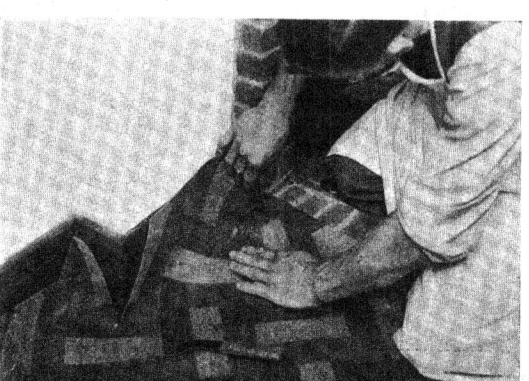

Fig. 8.—SECOND STAGE IN FITTING ROUND A FIREPLACE.
Fitting in the corners after cutting roughly to shape.

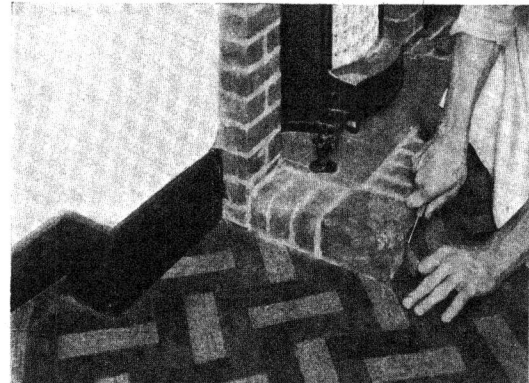

Fig. 9.—FINAL OPERATION IN FITTING ROUND A FIREPLACE.
Trimming up flush with the brickwork

HOW TO LAY LINOLEUM

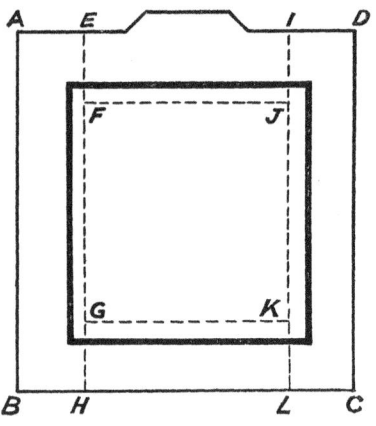

Fig. 10.—Diagram for Measuring the Quantity of Linoleum Required for Fitting a Surround.

Fig. 11.—Fitting Linoleum into a Doorway.

paper first and then cut the lino to the required shape.

Cutting.

The lino should be cut in two definite operations. With the point of the knife first make a groove along the intended line of separation, then raise the lino slightly, fold it upper side outwards, and run the knife along the fold, attacking it from underneath.

Laying the Second Strip.

Having got the first strip satisfactorily in position, the second width should be laid matching the pattern and allowing it to overlay the first strip by about ⅛ inch.

This overlap is to enable a perfect join to be obtained. The point of the knife should be run along the edge of the width that is overlapping, and when the cut has been finished and the trimmed off portion removed the two widths will be perfectly flush. The same method should be applied wherever a join occurs.

Fixing Down.

As new linoleum tends to spread as it becomes flattened down on the floor it is advisable to leave the final fixing for about ten days.

Headless brads should be used about 6 inches apart and about ¼ inch from the edge of the linoleum. Should buckling occur after fixing down, the brads will have to be removed and the lino left unfixed for a further week or so until the buckles finally disappear.

If, however, the linoleum has already seen previous use no further spreading out is likely to occur.

Fig. 12.—Any Projecting Nails in the Floor should be Hammered Down before Laying Lino.

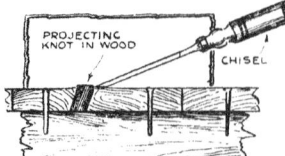

Fig. 13.—Remove any Knots in the Wood with a Chisel or Plane.

Fig. 14.—How Thick Paper is Used to Fill up Spaces between Floor Boards.

Fig. 15.—Correct Method of Placing Overlay.

Special attention is drawn to the series of photographs which accompany this article and which show

Fig. 16.—A Convenient Method of Fitting Lino into Awkward Corners

First make a template from paper. Lay the paper over the lino and cut to required shape.

clearly the approved methods of fitting linoleum.

It may be mentioned that although an expert with some years of experience in fitting linoleum may not find it necessary to use a template when fitting into awkward places, such as the fireplace shown in Figs. 7, 8 and 9, the man who is tackling the job for the first time will probably find he will get a better fit by adopting the method shown in Fig. 16.

CARE AND TREATMENT OF LINOLEUM

With regard to care and treatment, linoleum may be kept with either a matt or polished surface. If the surface is matt, it should be washed over once or twice a week. Warm soapy water should be used, but not soda, as the latter dries out the oil in the material and causes it to crack. The application of a little linseed oil after washing will act as a preservative.

Wash only a small patch at a time, and avoid making the surface too wet. Each patch should be well rinsed and dried as thoroughly as possible with a clean floorcloth.

Applying Bees' Wax for the First Time.

In applying bees' wax to linoleum for the first time between 2 and 3 lbs. of bees' wax should be sufficient for an average-size floor. The wax should first be dissolved in warm turpentine and should be well rubbed in. If the job is done thoroughly it should not need re-waxing for about ten years. A weekly application of liquid polish will be all that is needed.

With printed linoleum an alternative course is to apply a coat of varnish.

Dealing With a Leaking Ball Cock

Persistent running at the overflow pipe of a water cistern or water closet flush tank is an indication of the faulty working of the ball cock. Steps should be taken at once to remedy the fault, especially in cold weather, when there is danger of the overflow pipe becoming frozen up and preventing the water from getting away.

Faults to Look for.

The most likely causes of trouble are :—
 (1) Bent ball lever.
 (2) Ball punctured
 (3) Faulty washer.

Fig. 3 shows the general arrangement of a flush tank, while Figs. 11 and 12 show two types of ball valve in general use.

Bent Ball Lever.

The first thing to do is to remove the cover over the tank and move the ball up and down by holding the arm. There should be no flow whatsoever when in the up position. If the ball lever is bent the result will be that the level of the water in the tank comes too high, allowing the water to leak out through the overflow pipe. The lever must, therefore, be bent to bring the ball slightly lower into the tank.

This lever is generally made of soft brass and is quite easy to bend. Hold the end of the lever near the body firmly in one hand, taking care not to press the plug hard on its seat or it may be damaged. With the other hand hold the lever close to the ball and bend it down slightly as shown in Fig. 10. On no account bend the lever by pressing on the ball itself, as this is only soldered to the lever and any pressure on it would probably cause it to break off.

Correct Position for the Ball.

The correct position for the ball is such that when the level of the water

Fig. 1.—If the Cistern is in an Inaccessible Place it may be Advisable to Remove the Ball and Valve Complete.
First turn off the water supply, then remove the union nut.

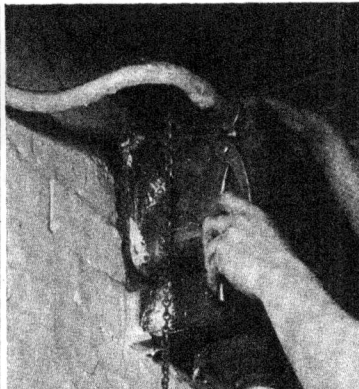

Fig. 2.—Now Remove the Back Nut.
The ball and valve can then be lifted out for examination.

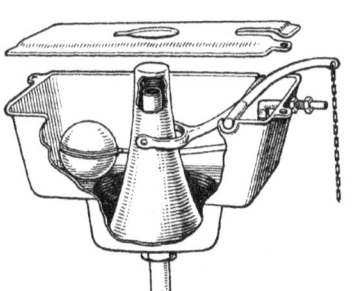

Fig. 3.—How to Obtain Access to the Ball Valve for Repair.
Lift off the lid of the tank; the syphon cowl can then be lifted right out.

is just below the overflow pipe, the ball has risen sufficiently for the valve to shut off the water. Bending the lever too far down will shut off the water too soon and prevent sufficient water entering the tank to start syphonage. It is best to bend a little at a time and keep on testing until the correct angle is obtained.

Ball Punctured.

Another cause of leakage is due to the sinking of the ball through it having punctured and filled with water so that it no longer has sufficient buoyancy to lift the lever as the tank fills with water. By shaking the ball slightly it will be easy to determine whether there is any water inside. In a very bad case, of course, the ball may be completely submerged.

To remedy a punctured ball, the ball and lever must be removed. First turn off the water at the main or at the tank, as the case may be. Then withdraw the split pin which holds the arm in place and remove the ball and its lever. If the valve is of the "Croydon" type (see Fig. 11) hold the fingers over the end of the plug so as to prevent it falling to the bottom of the tank. In the case of the "Portsmouth" type, the plug can be withdrawn after removing the lever.

Now shake the ball to make quite sure that water is the trouble.

Locating the Puncture.

If the puncture in the ball is very small, it may be difficult to locate it. The best way is to make two small holes, one on each side, either by using a drill or "stabbing" with a file tang.

Fig. 4.—Removing the Ball and Valve from the Cistern.
Showing also the various parts of the cistern.

Fig. 5.—If a Faulty Washer is Suspected, Remove the Split Pin from the Valve.
This will enable the plunger to be withdrawn

DEALING WITH A LEAKING BALL COCK

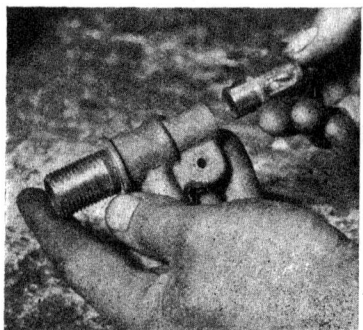

Fig. 6.—AFTER REMOVING THE SPLIT PIN, THE PLUNGER CAN BE EXTRACTED.
A Portsmouth type valve is shown here.

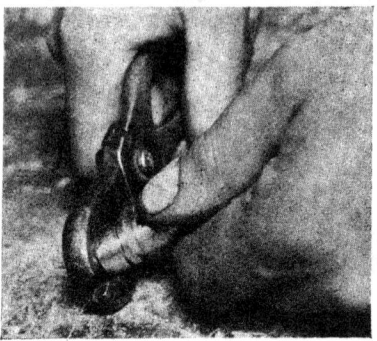

Fig. 7.—TO EXPOSE THE WASHER, THE CAP MUST BE UNSCREWED FROM THE PLUNGER.

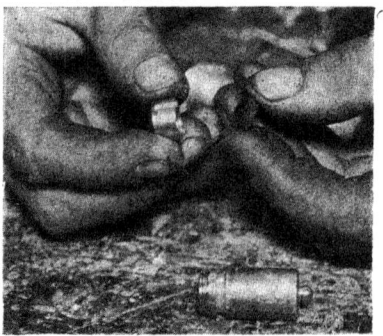

Fig. 8.—FITTING A NEW WASHER.
A rubber washer should be used, and not a leather one.

Now blow through one hole with the other hole downwards. This will cause the water to squirt out. Stop up one hole with a finger and hold the ball under water with the other hole at the bottom, and the leakage will be betrayed by air bubbles escaping. Scratch a mark with a sharp point to indicate the position of the leak. The ball must now be completely dried by holding over a flame, taking care not to hold it too close or the soldered joints may be melted.

When dry, scrape the metal round the leak and round the two holes until quite bright and solder up in the usual way, using killed spirits of salts as a flux, or one of the proprietary fluxes (see the article on "Soldering").

Testing the Repair.

To test whether the ball is now free from leakages it can either be immersed in hot water to make sure that no air bubbles appear, or else sunk in a pail of water for a few hours to see if any water leaks in.

When you are satisfied that the ball is sound it can be replaced by inserting the lever through the slot in the plug and replacing the cotter pin.

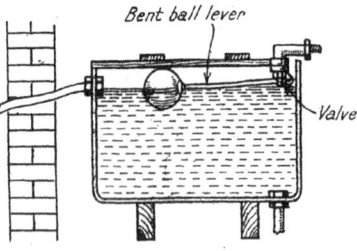

Fig. 9.—DIAGRAM SHOWING WHY A BENT BALL LEVER CAUSES THE WATER TO OVERFLOW.
The water rises to the overflow pipe before the valve closes.

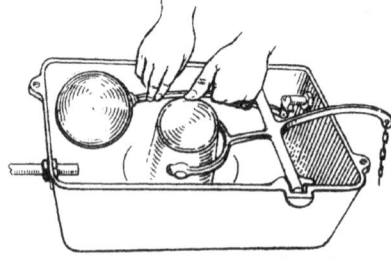

Fig. 10.—HOW TO BEND THE BALL LEVER WITHOUT REMOVING FROM CISTERN.
Do not press on the ball itself, but press the lever at the ball end.

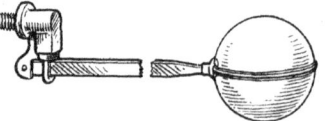

Fig. 11.—CROYDON TYPE BALL VALVE.
The plunger, which is operated by the ball float lever, works vertically.

Fig. 12.—PORTSMOUTH TYPE BALL VALVE.
In this type, the plunger works horizontally instead of vertically.

Fig. 13.—DETAILS OF THE PLUG OR PLUNGER.

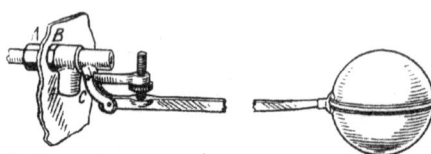

Fig. 14.—A HIGH PRESSURE BALL VALVE USED IN MAIN CISTERNS.
To fit a new washer, unscrew nut A and take the valve and ball out of the cistern. Then remove nut B, pull out split pin C so that the lever can be extracted. This will release the plug.

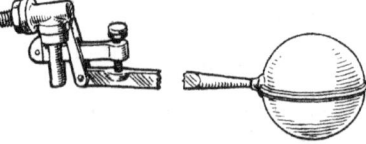

Fig. 15.—ANOTHER TYPE OF HIGH PRESSURE BALL VALVE.
The construction is similar to the ordinary Croydon, but the leverage is multiplied, as shown.

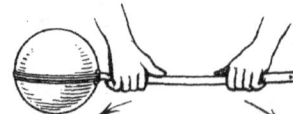

Fig. 16.—ANOTHER METHOD OF BENDING BALL VALVE LEVER.

Faulty Washer.

If, when testing the action of the ball and lever it is found that raising the lever does not stop the water trickling out of the valve, the trouble is most likely due to a faulty washer.

The ball and lever must be removed as previously described after turning off the water. Examination of the plug may reveal that a bit of dirt, straw, etc., carried through by the water has lodged on the seat and is preventing it closing, but it is more likely that the washer will be found at fault.

The plug is in two parts, the top part unscrewing from the part that has the hole for the lever. Unscrew the top part (anti-clockwise) and the washer will be revealed (see Fig. 7). This is a solid piece of rubber, and the fault will probably be that the centre has worn away due to constant pressure against the seat nozzle.

To fit a new rubber washer push the new washer into the cap and reassemble. The level of the water in the tank may need adjusting by bending the lever as previously described.

Easy Methods of Rug Making

DEALING WITH SHORT PILE, LONG PILE AND CROSS-STITCH METHODS

RUG making is one of the most popular, and often profitable, of home handicrafts. The materials and tools required are simple and inexpensive and, in addition, the rug can be made to any particular shape required or to suit any particular colour scheme with which it is desired to tone.

The Question of Design.

Before considering the various methods of making a rug, it is necessary to have some idea of how to make up a suitable design. The beginner will probably find it best to start by making a plain rug either in one colour or with a fairly wide border of about 6 inches. A good plan is to work the centre of the rug in a rather lighter shade than that of the border.

For more advanced work charts of designs can be obtained from any fancy-work shop at a cost of from 2d. to 6d. each. If you wish to make up your own design, this is best done by drawing it out on squared paper, each square counting as one stitch. Crayons can be used to represent the various colours, so that you can see exactly what the rug will look like before you start it. It is also possible to buy canvas with the design stencilled on in the correct colours. One of the advantages of buying a ready-made design is that the exact quantity of wool required for each colour will be found on the chart.

The Canvas.

The special canvas to use for rug making can be obtained either plain or with a coloured line dividing it up into large squares of eight holes to correspond with the charts. The advantage of the latter is that it makes the counting of the squares a very simple matter and, as paper ruled out in the same manner can also be obtained, patterns may easily be worked out.

Various widths of canvas are available, the sizes being 12, 18, 27, 36, 40 and 45-inch widths, the price varying from 1s. 6d. to 2s. 11d. per yard, according to the width and quality.

The canvas should be bought the exact width that you need, so that the selvedge will serve as the rug edge without having to turn in any of the canvas, except at the ends, for which purpose it is necessary to allow about 4 inches extra.

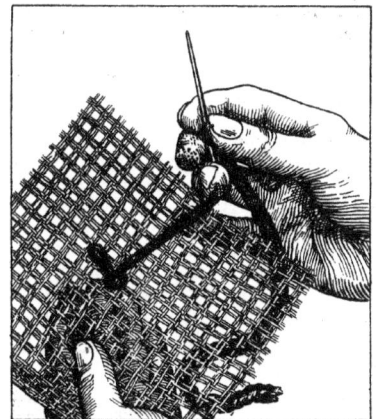

Fig. 2.—The Second Stage.
The wool is now drawn through and pulled tightly to form the knot, as shown above.

The Wool.

The most suitable wool to use is six-ply yarn, which can be obtained in a wide variety of colours. It is always advisable to buy the whole amount of wool required straight away so that no difficulty will be experienced in matching the exact shade should you find that you have insufficient.

What to do if you run out of Wool.

If it should happen that when the rug is half made you find you have not brought enough and cannot obtain any more of the right shade, the nearest shade should be used and the cut pieces mingled with the others. The slight difference will not notice in the finished rug. Alternatively, it may be possible to substitute one colour for another in the subordinate parts of the design if you find that you have too little of one colour and too much of another.

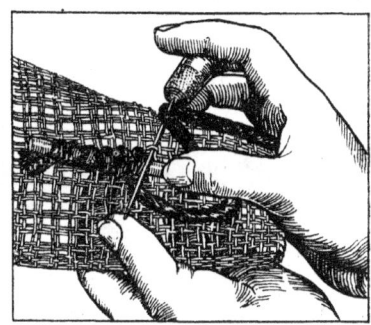

Fig. 3.—The Third Stage.
Having formed the first knot, the gauge is placed on the canvas and the wool brought under and over it. The needle is inserted under the lower strand of the next mesh and then under the top strand.

Quantity of Wool Required.

The exact quantity of wool required for a complicated design is given on the design itself. A rug 56 × 26 inches would take 7 lbs. of wool in all. Thus if you were working a rug in four colours and there was an equal amount of each colour in the design you would require 1¾ lb. of each colour wool.

It is always best to buy a good quality wool, for although cheaper kinds of wool may seem thicker, they generally contain more loose fluff than the dearer kinds, and are therefore more liable to lose their body quickly.

Three Methods of Rug Making.

There are three methods of making rugs in general use.

(1) Short pile rug, worked with a needle.
(2) Long pile rug, worked with some form of hook.
(3) Cross-stitch rug, worked with a needle.

As the short pile rug is in many ways more economical in time and material, we will deal with this method first.

SHORT PILE RUG.

Materials Required.

Canvas. This should be a little coarser and with rather thicker strands than that used for other methods.

Wool. Six-ply.

Needle. This should be a coarse wool needle with an eye large enough to carry the wool easily.

Gauge. A pencil will be found suitable.

Webbing for binding if desired.

What to do First.

The canvas should be placed on a table and held there in position with a weight, so that the row to be worked

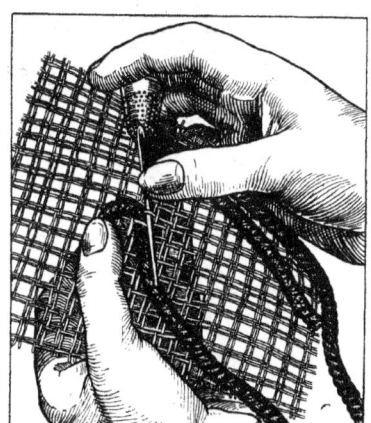

Fig. 1.—The First Stage in making a Short Pile Rug.
Thread the needle with a convenient length of wool, and pass it downwards through the lower of the two horizontal strands. Then pass the needle downwards underneath the upper strand.

EASY METHODS OF RUG MAKING

lies exactly on the edge. Thread into the needle a length of wool about a yard long. Begin working about 2 inches from the edge and work from left to right.

The needle should be passed downwards through the lower of the first two horizontal threads, leaving the free end about as long as the width of the gauge. Holding the free end firmly with the thumb of the left hand, pass the needle downwards underneath the upper of the two strands. The wool is now drawn through and pulled tightly to form the knot.

Now place the gauge on the canvas, pass the needle under and over it, and then under the lower thread of the next mesh, so that the wool is on the left of the needle. Now draw it through and insert the needle under the upper thread of the same mesh, so that the wool is on the right. Pull the wool through and draw up tight. Repeat this to the end of the row.

Beginning and Ending Threads.

When one length of wool is finished, or it is desired to start another colour, cut the end of the wool in use so that

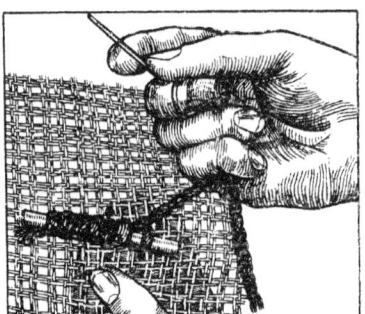

Fig. 4.—THE FOURTH STAGE IN MAKING A SHORT PILE RUG.
Draw the wool through ready for bringing it under and over the gauge again.

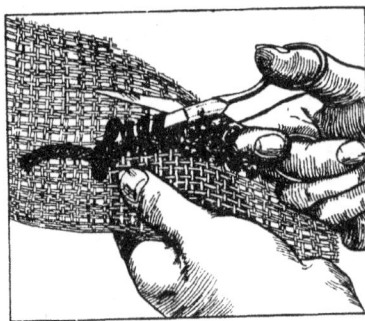

Fig. 5.—THE FINAL OPERATION.
Showing the gauge removed and the loops being cut with scissors.

it is the same length as the width of the gauge. Thread the needle with the new length of wool and start again, as already described.

The gauge will probably be shorter than the length of the rows, so that when you are approaching the end of the gauge it will be necessary to slip off some of the loops on the left and push the gauge along.

Cutting the Loops.

The next operation is to cut the loops, and scissors should be used for this purpose. It is really immaterial whether the loops are cut after a length or so of the gauge has been worked, or after a row has been completed, or even after all the rows have been finished. If, however, the work is only being done in odd moments, it is advisable to cut the loops each time the work is left, otherwise they are liable to be pressed out of position and make cutting difficult.

Finishing Off.

The surface of the rug should be trimmed with scissors to remove any irregular strands and then rubbed over and shaken thoroughly to remove the fluff. The ends of the canvas should be turned back and sewn down. Unless the rug is to be used on a stone or tiled floor there is no need to line the underneath with webbing.

A Hint for Saving Time while Working.

As each different colour occurs in the design it is begun by the same stitch as at the beginning of a row. Considerable time can be saved by using as many needles as there are colours in the design. This will save constantly threading the same needle, as in some patterns the separate lengths may be quite short.

After completing an outside border, it is a good plan to work straight across the canvas from left to right. This helps to keep the work even and

Fig. 6.—PREPARING THE WOOL FOR AN ORDINARY PILE RUG.
As each strand of wool must be of equal length, the wool is wound round a wooden gauge, as shown.

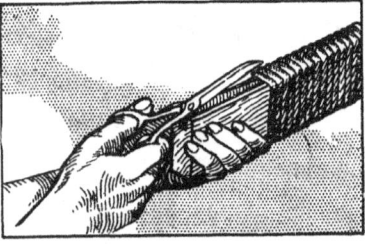

Fig. 7.—CUTTING THE WOOL AFTER WINDING ROUND THE GAUGE.
Cut the strands either with scissors or an old razor blade along the groove.

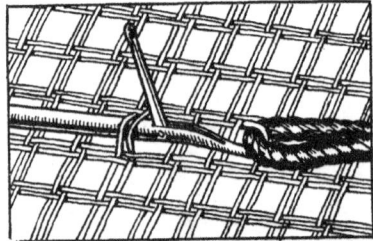

Fig. 8.—THE FIRST STAGE IN MAKING AN ORDINARY PILE RUG.
The hook is inserted in the canvas and the doubled strand of wool placed in the hook. Note the position of the catch.

Fig. 9.—THE SECOND STAGE.
The hook is drawn back, thus pulling the loop of wool with it under the canvas mesh. The catch will drop down and prevent the hook catching in the mesh.

Fig. 10.—THE THIRD STAGE.
After pushing the hook forward through the loop and catching the two ends of wool, the two ends are pulled through the loop.

Fig. 11.—THE FINAL OPERATION.
The tuft is completed by removing the hook and pulling up the ends of the wool tightly to make a secure knot.

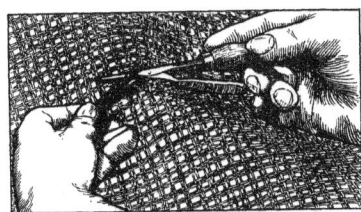

Fig. 12.—Another Method of Making an Ordinary Pile Rug—First Step.

Spring nippers can be used instead of a hook. Pass the end of the nippers through the loop of a doubled wool strand and then through two holes in the mesh of the canvas.

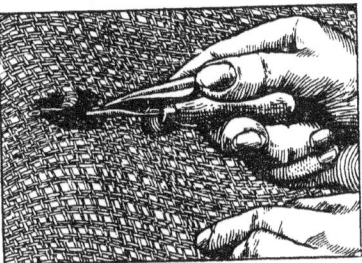

Fig. 13.—Second Stage.

Catch hold of the two ends of the wool in the jaws of the nippers ready for pulling through the loop.

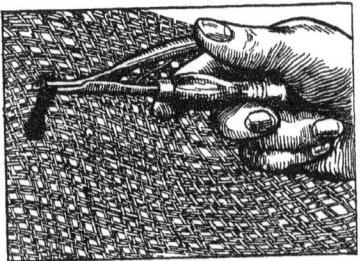

Fig. 14.—Completion of the Tuft.

The two ends of the wool are pulled through the loop and pulled up tight. This will knot the tuft to the canvas.

the canvas straight. Another method is to work out the pattern completely and then fill in the background.

A LONG PILE RUG

Materials Required.

Canvas.
Wool. Six-ply.
Catch hook or spring nippers.
Gauge.

What to do First—Cutting the Wool.

The first thing to do is to cut the wool to the required size. This is done with a wooden gauge about 8½ inches long, and 1 inch wide, one edge being grooved. Wind the wool on to the gauge from end to end, taking care not to pull or stretch the wool or overlap any strands. Then cut along the groove with a pair of scissors or a sharp knife. This will result in a number of short pieces of wool all the same length. The size of gauge used determines the height of the pile in the rug, but the size given above will be found satisfactory in most cases.

As a considerable number of strands will be required it is a good plan to keep the strands of different colours in shallow boxes, so that the stock can be renewed at odd moments.

Having decided on a particular design and prepared sufficient strands of wool for immediate needs, the canvas should be placed conveniently on the knees or on a table with one end immediately in front. First turn up about 1 inch of the canvas at one end on the right side and work the border through the double canvas, thus making the wrong side quite neat.

How to Use the Hook.

The first stage in knotting the strands of wool consists of pushing the hook through a mesh in the canvas so that the catch is carried past a double strand through a hole in the next row. Leave the catch standing up and take a strand of wool in the left hand, double it and slip the loop end over the hook and draw tight.

Now draw the hook towards you, keeping the cut ends of the strand of wool in the left hand. Pull the hook through the two holes for about half the length of the strand. The catch will, of course, be pushed down and cover the point of the hook, thus allowing it to pass the strands of the canvas. Now push the hook through the loop in the wool and hook up the two loose ends. A firm and steady pull on the hook will enable the double strands to be pulled through the loop which can be held in the fingers of the left hand.

Remove the hook and tighten the knot firmly by pulling up the two cut ends.

The sequence of operations described above, although sounding very involved, soon become entirely automatic and a high speed will easily be attained.

How to Work the Pattern.

It is best to work the rows from right to left. When one row is completed work another row, inserting the hook in the hole of the last one. Thus every hole is used, the stitches being formed on the horizontal ridges of the canvas.

Some workers prefer to work across the horizontal rows and fill in the colours of the pattern as they come for a depth of 2 or 3 inches and then complete the background. Others work from the centre and outline the pattern, one knot all round. The space inside the outline is then filled row by row.

When the other end of the canvas is reached, turn back the edge as at the beginning and work the border. It is easier to work the last row of all by doing it before the two or three rows which are next to it.

Remember to work always in the same direction, that is, from one end to the other, or the pile will lie unevenly.

Special Note on Oval or Circular Rugs.

When working an oval or circular rug, about 2 inches of canvas should be left all round, and this should not be doubled back for working. Instead, when the rug is finished, the canvas should be turned back and the raw edges covered with welting.

Finishing Off.

Very little clipping with scissors should be required if the two ends of

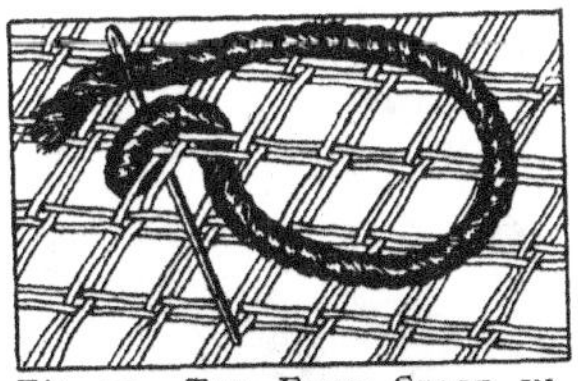

Fig. 15.—The First Stage in Making a Cross Stitch Rug.

Pass the needle from underneath through the square and down again through the square above it on the right. Bend the canvas as the needle is passed down so as to allow the needle point to come up through the square immediately below.

Fig. 16.—Second Stage.

The stitch is completed by crossing over to the square above the first square, pushing the needle down and back to the third square. A completed stitch is shown above. (See also Fig. 17.)

Fig. 17.—Making Stitches in a Row.

Time and energy can be saved when making a number of cross stitches in a row by filling the row with half stitches and returning along the row to complete with the cross-over stitch.

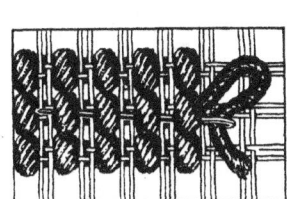

Fig. 18.—How to Finish Off the Stitches.

When you come to the end of the wool or want to start a new colour, turn over the canvas and finish off by passing the needle under four or five of the loops made by the cross stitches.

each loop have been kept fairly level during the doubling process. There is one point to remember; it will probably have been found that while the rug has been in progress some loose material has constantly been coming up to the surface. This is inseparable from the production of a pile fabric, and the tips of some of the fibres which have been cut are almost sure to come out. Therefore the rug must have a very thorough rubbing with the hand across its surface. Some experts use a comb, but care is needed to avoid straining the fibres.

It is not necessary to line the rug, but a strip of webbing may be sewn flatly all round the edge on the underside if desired. A lead weight sewn at each corner will ensure the rug lying flat without curling at the edges.

Using the Spring Nippers.

Exactly the same result as that with a hook is obtained by using spring nippers, and the method is as follows:—

First pick up a doubled strand of wool in the left hand, and pass the end of the nippers through the loop. The point of the nippers is then pushed through one hole of the canvas to the next, the loop of wool being behind and on top of the canvas.

Now open the jaws of the nippers and insert the cut ends of the strand of wool. Release the pressure on the spring so that the wool is securely held in the jaws. Draw the tool backwards through the hole and the loop and pull tight to form the knot.

CROSS-STITCH RUGS

Materials Required.
Canvas.
Wool. Six-ply.
Rug needle.

Rugs made with cross stitch are much flatter than those already described, and are therefore more suitable for bedrooms. Less wool will be required.

Method of Working.

The canvas is best held on the knee, and in order to bring your hands to the part you are stitching it is advisable to fold the canvas over.

Now thread the wool through the needle and pass the needle from underneath through the first square and down again through the square above it on the right (see Fig. 15). As the needle is passed down, bend the canvas so as to allow the needle point to come up through the square immediately below. The stitch is completed by crossing over to the square above the first square, and pushing the needle down and back to the third square.

A complete cross stitch is shown in Fig. 16, but where there are a number of cross stitches to be made in a row much time will be saved by filling in the row with half stitches and then work back along the row, completing with the cross-over stitch, as shown in Fig. 17.

How to Finish Off.

When the end of the wool is reached, or it is desired to start another colour, the canvas should be turned over and the stitch finished off at the back. Pass the needle under four or five of the loops made by the cross stitches. When the rug is completed the edges of the canvas are turned back and sewn down in a similar manner as with tufted rugs.

ARE YOUR WALLS DAMP?

WHILST there are many causes of a wall being damp, such as the need for re-pointing, a faulty damp course, bad ventilation, etc., one frequent cause that is easy to remedy is that shown in the diagram.

It will be seen that the earth outside the wall has been banked up too high in order to improve the appearance of the flower bed, with the result that the earth is higher than the damp course, which surrounds the wall rendering the course ineffective.

The dampness enters above the damp course and "creeps" up the wall. If this state of affairs is allowed to continue for long, the skirting board, floorboards and floor joists will soon be affected as well, and will in time rot away.

The remedy, of course, is to remove some of the earth until the level is at least 6 inches below that of the damp course, as will be seen in the diagram.

Although we have only dealt here with one of the simplest causes of damp walls, it is worth while suspecting it as the source of the trouble as soon as damp walls are noticed, for the very obviousness of it might otherwise cause it to be overlooked.

If, however, it is found that the damp course is well clear of the level of the earth, some more serious cause must be suspected and a later article will deal thoroughly with the tracing and remedying of damp walls due to other causes.

Damp Walls mean Continual Expense.

In addition to their unsightly appearance, damp walls are a cause of much bad health. They also mean continual expense due to the need for repeated decorating and replacing of plaster and decayed wood. Whenever timber is in contact with dampness it is certain to decay in time. Dampness is also destructive to brickwork, especially during a frost.

Faulty Damp Course.

A faulty damp course is probably the most common and at the same time the most serious cause of damp walls, and often the only remedy is to insert a new course, which necessitates removing the bricks through the wall. Only small portions of the wall are removed at a time and the removed brickwork made good before the next portion is removed, otherwise the wall may collapse. A later article will deal thoroughly with the correct method of inserting a new damp course.

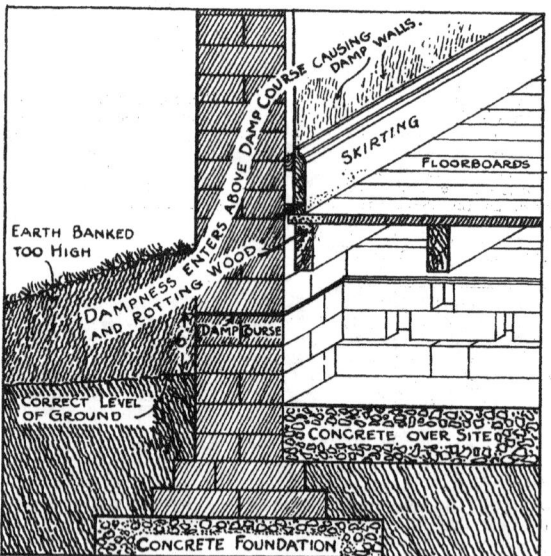

SHOWING HOW DAMPNESS CAN BE CAUSED BY EARTH BEING BANKED TOO HIGH AGAINST THE WALL.

Uses of Corrugated Iron

GALVANIZED corrugated iron is a useful material with innumerable applications. It is inexpensive, is readily obtainable and easy to handle.

Quality, Price and Size.

There are many qualities and grades of corrugated galvanized iron on the market. When comparing prices make sure of the " gauge " or thickness that is offered.

Small quantities are priced by the sheet, larger quantities are priced and sold by the ton. The following are the nominal stock sizes and weights:—

Corrugated Galvanized Sheets.

Approximate Weight per Sheet in Lbs.

Length of Sheet.	4'	5'	6'	7'	8'	9'	10'
Gauge, 18	22	27	32	37	44	49	54
,, 20	16	20	24	28	32	36	40
,, 22	13½	17	20	23	27	31	34
,, 24	11	13½	16	18½	22	24½	27
,, 26	8	10	12	14	16	18	20

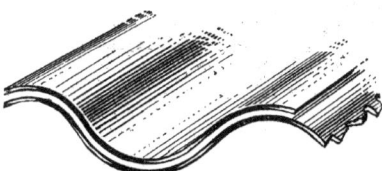

Fig. 1.—The Edge Joint.
The hollow of the under sheet is covered by the ridge of the upper sheet, thus forming a watertight joint.

The normal width of a sheet is 2 feet 3 inches, but when reckoning the covering power allow 2 feet only, as the odd 3 inches is required to overlap the top and edge of the next sheet.

Jointings and Fixings.

The sheets are joined together by overlapping the edges, as shown in Fig. 1, this arrangement ensuring a watertight joint because the under sheet always has a hollow which acts as a gutter beneath the cover sheet, this being the correct procedure when joining the edges or in whatever job the metal is used.

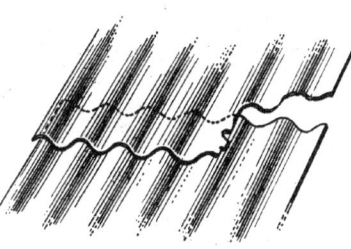

Fig. 2.—End Joints.
At the ends the top sheet overlaps the lower by about 6 inches, and at the side by one corrugation.

End joints are made as in Fig. 2 by overlapping the sheets about 6 inches or more so that the corrugations interlock. The sheets are easily fastened to substantial wooden frames by means of cone-head galvanized screws and washers—as shown in Fig. 3—taking care to set the screw head at the uppermost part of the ridge, not in the valley, as in that position it would let the water through.

Every sheet should have at least six fixing screws, two at each end and two about the centre. Instead of driving screws it is possible to use special galvanized nails with cone heads. Use washers beneath them as when using screws; in any case always use galvanized fastenings to avoid rusting.

Fig. 3.—Four Methods of Fixing Corrugated Iron.
Top, left: Fixing to woodwork by means of cone head screws through hole punched in the top of the corrugations, with a washer under the head of each screw. Top, right: Fixing to iron frame by bolts and nuts through holes drilled in metal frame. Bottom, left: Showing use of hook bolt. Bottom, right: Joining overlapping edges with short cone head bolts, nuts and washers.

Fixing to Metal Framework.

If the sheets have to be fixed to metal framework—such as one of the complete skeleton frames that are supplied for building small garages and the like, the correct procedure is to use galvanized bolts and nuts as in Fig. 3, or, if the frame is not drilled, use hook bolts and nuts as shown in Fig. 3, with the nuts on the outside.

Overlapping joints between sheets should be fastened with short bolts, nuts and washers—as shown in Fig. 3—for mutual strength and support.

Roofing.

Roofs of small buildings can be covered efficiently with galvanized corrugated sheets. The method is

Table of Scantlings.

Length of building	5'	8'	10'	12'	15'
Width of roof from eaves to ridge	3'	4'	4'	5'	6'
Purlins and size.	2"×2" 1	3"×2" 1	3"×2" 2	4"×2" 1	4"×2" 2
Rafters and size	—	3"×2" 1	4"×2" 1	4"×2" 2	4"×2" 3

clearly depicted in Fig. 4. The sheets rest upon wall plates fixed to the walls and to purlins supported on the end walls and intermediately by stout rafters.

The size of the purlins depends on the span or unsupported length. The table above gives average sizes for normal small buildings.

The above sizes are not arbitrary but can be modified according to circumstances, but they form a guide for new work.

At the ends or " verges " the sheets should be supported by

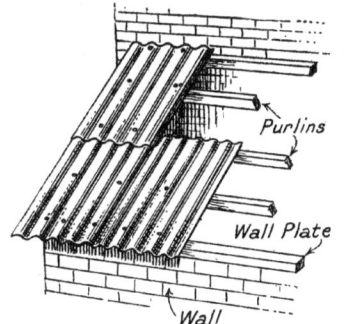

Fig. 4.—Corrugated Iron Roof.
The sheets are laid from the eaves upwards and are fastened to the wall plates and purlins.

the over-hanging ends of the purlins and wall plates. A Barge board can be fitted —as shown in Fig. 5—if a good-class finish is desired, the board should be about 6 inches deep and ⅞ inch thick and screwed or nailed in place with galvanized fasteners.

Finishing a Ridge.

The ridge or apex of a span roof is completed with a special ridge capping shown in place in Fig. 6, which is merely screwed to the wooden ridge board or to the purlins. The usual length of the ridge capping is 6 feet. The lengths can be cut as required and joints should overlap at least 4 inches. When the roof rests against the side wall of a brick building the junction between the two should be made good

USES OF CORRUGATED IRON

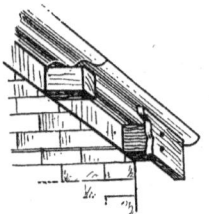

Fig. 5.—Detail at Verge.
Purlins extend beyond the wall to support the roofing and may be finished with a Barge board.

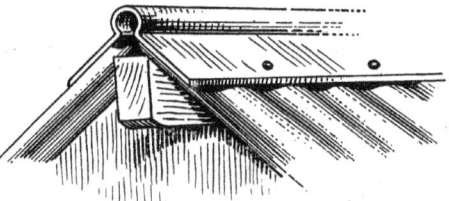

Fig. 6.—Ridge Capping.
The apex of a span roof is covered with a special ridge capping fastened through the roofing sheets to the framing.

Fig. 7.—Metal Flashing.
When the roof butts against a brick wall a metal flashing or covering over the joint should be provided. The flashing is fixed into one of the brick courses.

with a zinc or lead "flashing" as shown in Fig. 7. The strip of metal should be about 12 inches wide and be bent to shape, and it is fixed into a joint in the brickwork.

The mortar has first to be raked out, then the metal fitted into it and secured with metal wedges, and subsequently the joint is filled in with cement mortar.

In the case of rough cast walls the junction can be effected with a good fillet of cement mortar made with good sharp sand gauged 1 part of Portland cement to 2 parts sharp sand.

Cutting Corrugated Sheets.

Corrugated iron is awkward material to cut, and the job can best be done with special cutting snips made for the purpose or with a "Shetack" saw.

In the latter case the saw is used in the same way as a hack saw—as indicated in Fig. 8—the sheet must be firmly supported on trestles or the like and a piece of board should be pressed on the sheet, near the saw, to hold the sheet secure and check vibration.

An effective mould for making a concrete column for a sundial or similar purposes can be extemporized by rolling a sheet of corrugated iron into cylindrical form and fastening it with wire.

Place it upright on a board, coat the interior freely with grease, paraffin or creosote, then pour the concrete into

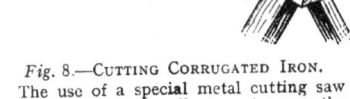

Fig. 8.—Cutting Corrugated Iron.
The use of a special metal cutting saw enables the novice easily to cut across the sheet, provided it is firmly supported.

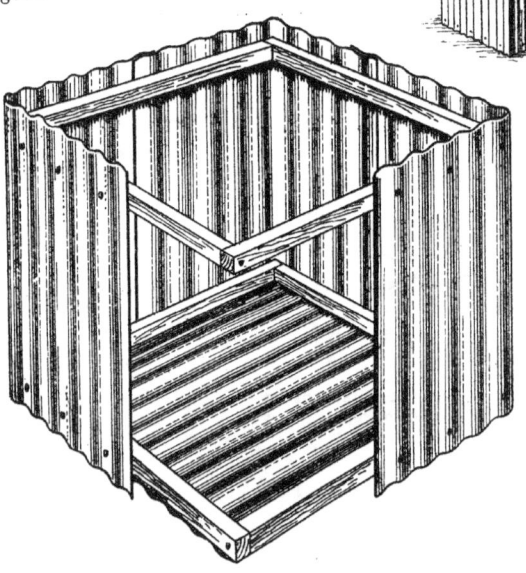

Fig. 9.—Rat-proof Corn Bin.
Poultry keepers will find this rat-proof grain store a distinctly profitable production.—it is readily made as described in the text. Inset shows completed bin.

place, let it set for a day or so, then unwrap the sheet and leave the concrete untouched to harden.

Storage Bin.

An inexpensive storage bin can be made with pieces of corrugated sheet. The scheme is practically self-evident from Fig. 9, but the best way to proceed is to bend four sheets of corrugated iron down the centre of their length. These bends form the corners of the bin, the joints come at the middle of each side. Measure the exact inside size when the sheets are in place, then make two plain rectangular wooden frames from 1½ inch square deal. Screw the sheets to them, cut a piece to fit on the bottom outside the frames and another on the inside.

Make a third similar frame to slip easily into the top and rest flush on the upper fixed frame. Cover the loose frame with a piece of the corrugated iron so that it overlaps on all sides. The result is a strong, weatherproof and rat-proof storage bin.

Such a storage bin as that described would be particularly suitable for poultry keepers, for the storing of grain.

CARE OF VARNISH BRUSHES

A GOOD many brushes are spoilt through neglect to store them in the correct manner. Varnish brushes are by no means inexpensive items, so that it behoves the user to look after them.

Once a varnish brush has been allowed to dry in the air it is very difficult, if not impossible, to restore the hairs, or bristles, to their original soft and pliable condition.

An excellent way to store spirit varnish brushes, after use, is to keep the bristles immersed in methylated spirits in such a manner that the bristles do not touch the bottom of the vessel in which the spirits are stored. Further, it is essential to prevent the latter from evaporating so that it must be confined in a closed vessel.

A satisfactory method of storing varnish brushes is to use a long, narrow type of bottle similar to a milk or pickle bottle. This should be fitted with an air-tight lid made of wood, and the brush suspended from a hook screwed into the lid of the bottle.

An alternative method, suitable for use with screwed metal-capped bottles, is to drill a hole in the metal cap so that it will fit over the tapered part of the brush handle. If the cap be driven on to the brush handle and a little pitch or Chatterton's compound be melted around the junction of the two, an air-tight fit will be assured.

How to Enamel a Bath

THE modern house is often fitted with a bath, the inside surface of which is porcelain finished. Such surfaces do not require painting, and thus a recurring expense and trouble is avoided.

But in an enormous proportion of homes the bath is still of the older type, with a painted interior that requires renewal from time to time.

The Reason Why.

Paint on the inside of a bath has to stand a more severe test than almost any other kind of painting.

When it is not in use, the conditions are not exceptional. But at more or less regular intervals water, varying in temperature from quite cold to almost boiling point, is run into it. Even where the original enamel has been given an extremely hard finish it is liable in time to become worn owing to the severe conditions which it has to meet. Re-enamelling, to be successful, must be done thoroughly, otherwise the enamel will peel off after a few weeks wear.

Preparation.

Nothing is more detrimental to existing paint, or a greater hindrance to successful repainting, than a dripping tap, and, therefore, if a new washer or other repair is required to either or both of the taps, this should be seen to before the actual renovation begins.

If for any reason the drip cannot be entirely stopped, a tin or jar should be tied to each tap so as to catch any possible leakage of water.

Fig. 1.—Preparing the Brush for the First Coat of Enamel.

The same brush as that used for the preliminary priming can be used again. Wash thoroughly in turpentine, then in warm soapy water.

Smoothing the Surface.

If the old paint is merely discoloured or only partly worn away, it should be well scoured with medium-grade waterproof sandpaper, using water in which a little common washing soda has been dissolved as a lubricant. Every part of the surface should be carefully gone over in this way, so that a perfectly smooth and dull groundwork for repainting is produced.

The bath should then be thoroughly swilled down with plenty of cold water, making sure that every trace of dirt and grit is carried away. Operations must now be suspended until the whole surface is bone dry.

First Coating.

Now examine the bath again. It may be that the bottom is more discoloured than the sides, or even that there are bare patches showing the iron. Should that be so, these parts should have a preliminary priming of paint, consisting of white lead and a very small proportion of japan gold size, which will act as a drier and hardener. Ordinary paint driers are not suitable for this purpose.

This paint will require thinning with three parts turpentine and one part raw linseed oil.

Fig. 3.—If the Old Enamel is in a Bad State it is Advisable to Remove it Entirely.

This can be done by using an enamel removing mixture applied by means of a rag secured to the end of a stick. A trowel or a fibre brush could be used instead if preferred.

Fig. 2.—Gently Squeeze out the Soapy Water as Shown.

Then rinse in clean water and dry the brush.

When this priming is thoroughly dry and hard, the whole of the bath, both those parts primed and those not, should receive a coat of the paint just described. It should be applied as evenly and be as well brushed out as possible. As in all other kinds of painting, thin coats (which means paint brushed out thinly, not too thin paint) are much better than thick ones. This is especially true in the case of bath painting, where the complete hardening of the successive coatings is imperative. Too thick coats would be fatal to durability, causing cracking and curdling of the final enamel.

Undercoating.

The first coat having become dry and thoroughly hard, it is lightly sand-papered with a fine grade of paper, and any dust so produced must be carefully removed. Then the enamel undercoating must be applied in the same well-brushed and laid-off manner as the first coat. But, this time, the composition of the material requires alteration.

An excellent undercoating can be made by taking three parts of the paint previously described and one part of the enamel to be used in finishing. The undercoating having been applied, another interval of at least twenty-four hours should elapse before operations are resumed.

Enamelling.

Now we come to the most delicate operation of all—the application of the

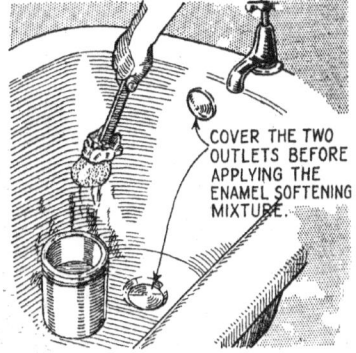

Fig. 4.—Applying the Enamel Solvent.

The solvent can be made by dissolving some potash or pearl ash in boiling water and adding lime to the dissolved mixture. Several pieces of ash about as big as one's fist will be sufficient, with enough lime to make the mixture into a moderately thick paste.

final enamel coat. Ordinary enamel, even of the very finest quality, is not suitable for this particular purpose, and a ½-pint tin of special bath enamel should be procured.

The same brush (a flat enamel or paint brush, 2 inches wide, is probably the best tool) that has been used for the earlier painting will do, provided that it has been thoroughly washed out (first in turpentine, then in warm soapy water, then in clean water) and completely dried.

The Start.

First, very lightly sandpaper the surface of the undercoating all over, and get rid of any dust so formed. And, for the final process of enamelling at any rate, the worker should not wear a sleeved garment. In fact, the arms and hands should be both bare and clean. As we have already pointed out, dust is the enemy at every stage, but never so much so as during the application of the enamel.

Keep the Contents of the Tin well mixed.

It is important that the contents of the enamel tin should be well mixed and that there should be no settled matter at the bottom, involving too thin material at the top.

Stirring with a clean knife or stick will ensure this, but the writer prefers to turn the tin upside down an hour or two before opening it. If this is done and the tin is shaken just before removing the lid, the contents will be in the right consistency for use.

Applying the Enamel.

Once the application of the enamel has begun, it should proceed without interruption with as much speed as is consistent with good workmanship. In short, there should be neither delay nor flurry.

Care must be observed to make sure that the whole surface is covered with a consistent coating of the enamel, without missing any portion, however small.

Apply each brushful in one direction and lay it off in the other. If the enamel is a good one and it is laid on in anything like an even coating, we need not worry about the brush marks. They will flow out by themselves in a moment or two.

The important thing is to allow no wet edge of the enamel to remain unconnected with the next portion applied for longer than a moment or two, and these connections must be made by strong but brief brush work.

It is on the manner in which these joinings are made that much of the success of enamelling depends. An edge of material left too long before being joined is the most common cause of defects in the final coating of baths.

The Right Sequence.

To plan out the best way of keeping the edges joined is worth a few moments' thought before beginning, and this will depend to some extent upon the position in which the bath is fixed.

Many baths are fixed close up to a wall. Therefore, it is probably the best procedure to begin at the back top edge in the middle and work alternately downward and toward each end.

Gradually the whole farther side will become coated from top to bottom and end to end.

Then continue round each end, doing a portion of both ends alternately. Next do the bottom of the bath, and finally work, again in alternate sections from the two ends, along the nearer side until the last gap is joined.

Next survey the whole of the work, and, if it has been carefully done, no part should have been missed. If such a "miss" has occurred, the only thing to do is to stipple it with the tip of the brush very lightly charged with enamel. If this is very carefully done and the patch is lightly crossed again with the tip of the brush, this touching up may not be perceptible when the enamel has dried. But the necessity for this turning back is best avoided, if possible.

After Precautions.

The task is now completed, but it remains to ensure that the finished work is protected against possible mishap.

Leaving the room quietly, wedge the door just a little ajar so that air may be admitted, but the risk of dust entering will be minimised. And if the use of the room can be entirely suspended for the following twenty-four hours, so much the better. It is not always realised that even ordinary movements create fine dust even in the cleanest apartment.

Hardening Time.

After one night has elapsed the bathroom may be used in the ordinary way, except that the longer the bath itself can remain out of action the better. A week is not too long a period for the complete hardening of the enamel, which is one reason why the days immediately preceding the family holiday is a good time for undertaking the work of renovation.

Completing the Hardening.

A good plan for expediting and completing the hardening process is to fill the bath with cold water and allow this to remain for twelve hours or so just before putting the bath back into use.

After Care.

As stated previously, perhaps the factor most detrimental to the life of the paint and enamel on a bath is the sudden impact of very hot water. This evil effect can be largely minimised if, when a bath is to be taken, the cold-water tap is first opened for a moment before the hot water is turned on.

The inch or so of cold water in the bottom of the bath prevents the jet of hot water from striking the paint in a particular spot, and, although the temperature of the water is quickly raised, the effect is more gradual and diffused. This

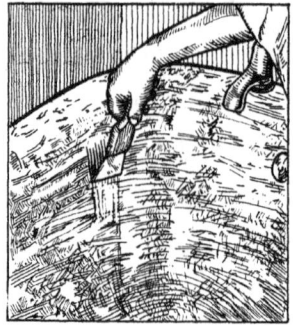

Fig. 5.—After applying the Solvent, the Soft Enamel can be scraped off.

A broad knife should be used on the flat parts.

Fig. 6.—When dealing with the Corners use a Narrow Knife with the End Slightly Rounded.

A shavehook will be found suitable.

Fig. 7.—All Trace of Old Enamel should now be removed with Glass Paper.

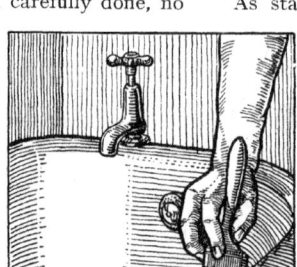

Fig. 8.—The Bath is now Ready for the First of the Undercoats.

HOW TO ENAMEL A BATH

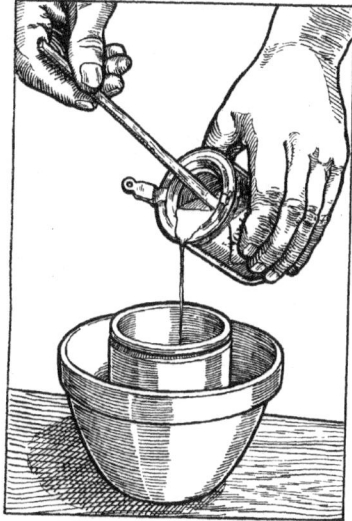

Fig. 9.—How to make the Enamel more Fluid.

If the enamel is too thick pour it into an earthenware pot standing inside a bowl, after a thorough stirring. (See also Fig. 11.)

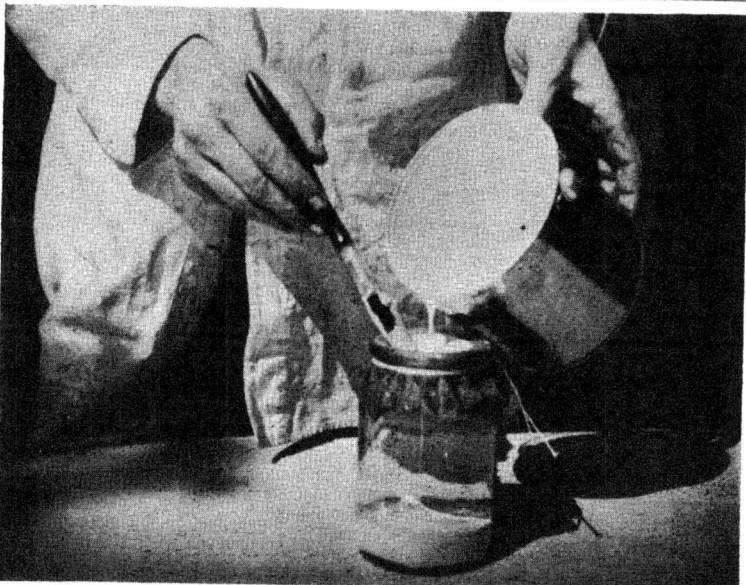

Fig. 10.—Make sure there are no Lumps, Skin or Grit in the Paint used for Undercoating by Straining it through Muslin stretched and tied over the Top of a Jar. Straining should not be necessary with the enamel.

precaution alone will probably double, at least, the period that will elapse before the bath will need repainting.

The Badly Neglected Bath.

It sometimes occurs that the repainting of a bath is so long deferred that the old paint becomes badly perished. It may have peeled off in places or have cracked and crazed. Or it may be that, owing to the use of poor material or workmanship on a previous occasion, the paint has softened and curdled.

In such a case, no other course is open than to remove the whole of the old paint down to the metal.

Removing the Old Paint.

The strongest and quickest paint remover is a mixture of lime and caustic potash, moistened with water and applied, in the form of a thick paste, to the surface by means of a trowel or fibre (not bristle) brush. After this compound has been left on for a time, it will be found that the old paint has softened so that it can be removed with a scraper.

But this process has the disadvantage that, if any of the caustic material comes into contact with clothing, carpets, or even the human skin, burning and damage take place. If this can be avoided, well and good.

Fig. 11.—How to make the Enamel more Fluid.

After pouring into a pot as shown in Fig. 9, pour hot water into the bowl. Take great care not to let any water get into the enamel. If the mouth of the tin is large enough to take the brush easily there is no need to pour the enamel out into a pot. The tin can be stood in the bowl instead.

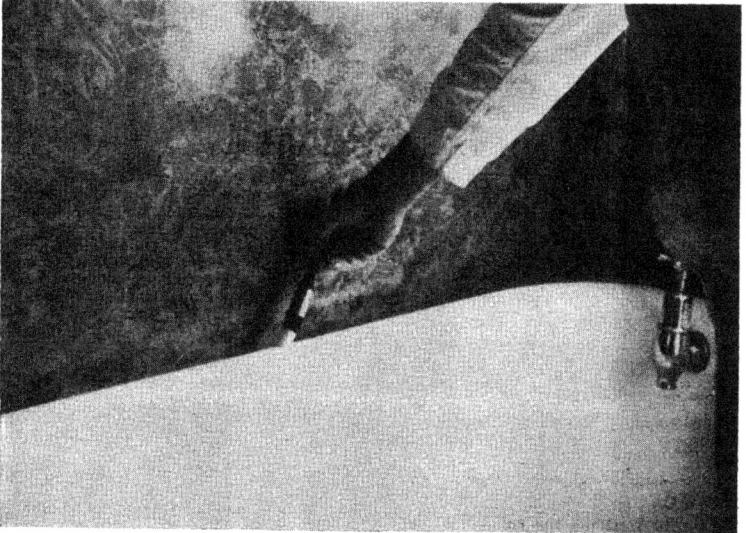

Fig. 12.—It will generally be found advisable to start painting at the Back Top Edge in the Middle.

Then work alternately downward and toward each end. The important thing is to allow no wet edge of enamel to remain unconnected with the next portion applied for longer than a moment or two.

HOW TO ENAMEL A BATH

Perhaps the best course to adopt is to pick up the sludge of softened paint and caustic by means of the scraper, and transfer it to a bucket placed in the bath.

If this method is adopted, the bared surface of the metal must be well swilled down, first with a mixture of vinegar and water and then again with clean water.

Alternative Methods.

A rather cleaner and safer, but slightly more expensive, method of removing old paint is to use one of the spirituous paint removers sold for this purpose, following the maker's instructions printed on the tin. (The ½-pint size may be sufficient.)

Using "Sugar Soap."

An even more economical method is to use "Sugar Soap." This material, used in weak solution, is an excellent paint cleaner. Used in very strong solution, according to the maker's instructions printed on the carton,

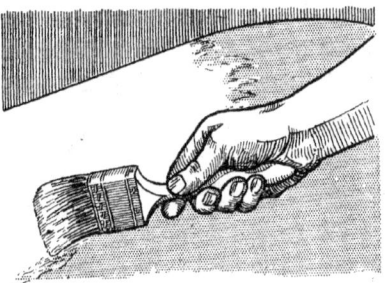

Fig. 13.—Apply each Brushful in One Direction and lay it off in the Other.

Sugar Soap becomes a quite effective paint remover.

Clean the Surface Thoroughly.

Whatever method is adopted, there should be a very thorough cleansing, smoothing and drying of the surface before any paint is applied.

The actual painting and enamelling will be exactly as we have previously described, except that an additional coat of paint similar to, and following, the first coat may be necessary.

Final Hints.

It will be seen that the main necessity in renovating a bath is for scrupulous cleanliness at every stage. Especially is it necessary to see that there are no lumps, skin or grit in the paint used. This can be guarded against by straining the material through a piece of muslin stretched and tied over the top of a jar. This straining, so necessary in the case of the paint, should not be required with the enamel if it is used from and immediately after opening the tin.

Coloured Effects.

So far the description of the various stages of renovating a bath has been upon the assumption that a white finish is required. Should a coloured effect be desired, the only changes in procedure called for are the purchase of a coloured enamel instead of a white one and the addition to the undercoating material of sufficient oil colour to produce the same shade as the finishing enamel.

WEATHERBOARD FIXING HINTS

WHEN fixing weatherboard, single-handed, to the framework of a shed or similar building, some difficulty may be experienced in holding up one end of a long length of weatherboard, whilst the other is being nailed to the framework.

Start from the Bottom.

To overcome this difficulty an excellent plan is to start from the bottom, next to the ground, nailing the first board in position, with the exception of the last nail (shown at the left in Fig. 1), which is only just driven in so as to enter the framework member, leaving most of the nail projecting. Now take up the next length of weatherboard and rest one end on this nail, lifting the other end to its correct position (see diagram) and then nailing it in position with a single nail. Then proceed to the other end, lift the board to its correct position and secure with three or more nails. The other projecting nail previously used as a support can then be driven home.

Leave One Nail Projecting.

Finally nail up the other end, leaving one nail projecting to act as a support for the next piece of weatherboard. The object of driving only one nail in at first, at the end that is not supported, is to enable the board to be rotated slightly when it is lifted

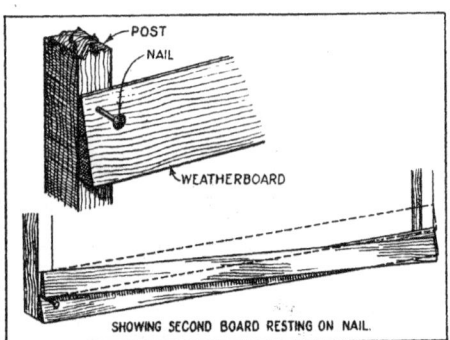

Fig. 1.—A Convenient Method of fixing Weatherboard Single-handed.
Showing how a nail is left projecting at one end, to provide a support for the next length of weatherboard.

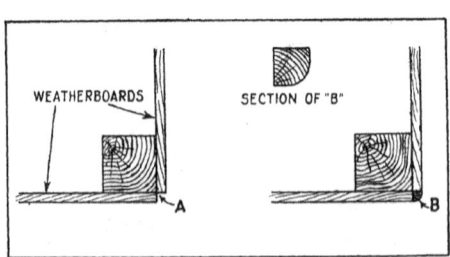

Fig. 2.—How to finish off Weatherboard so that the Ends are not left exposed to the Weather.

from the supporting nail. If more than one nail was used the end would be made rigid and there would then be a risk of splitting the board in lifting the other end off its support.

A Neat Weatherboard Finishing Idea.

Sheds that have been built up with weatherboard sides suffer from the disadvantage of leaving the ends of the boards exposed. These are not only unsightly, but rain or moisture from the atmosphere will attack these ends—which are the most vulnerable parts of the timber—so that rot may occur after the structure has been erected for a year or two.

To overcome both of these objections the ends of the weather boards should be fixed square in the first place, or sawn afterwards, so that they form an angle at the corner of the post to which they are attached, as shown at A in Fig. 2.

Next, a piece of wood—that can be sawn from a spare length of weatherboard—is planed down to a quarter round section, i.e., is first planed square and then one edge is rounded off. This strip is then nailed into the corner, as shown at B, Fig. 2. The edges of the weatherboard should be well painted or creosoted before the strip B is nailed into position.

Simple Woodwork Joints

THE amateur woodworker often comes up against the problem of making joints in framework, where two or three members meet or cross. Unless he is particularly skilled in the art of making some of the more or less intricate mortise, tenon and dovetail joints of the professional worker he may find it difficult to undertake any serious woodworking operations.

Fortunately for the amateur there are some effective alternative methods of joint making that we shall describe, requiring little skill, but giving thoroughly sound joints without the aid of the tenon or dovetail joints.

Right-angle or Butt Joint.

The most common joint met with in home carpentry is the right angle or butt joint, where one member has to be fastened securely at right angles to another—as in the framework of small sheds, poultry-houses, etc.

In the ordinary way the member B (Fig. 1) would have a rectangular hole or mortise cut through it, whilst the other member A would be suitably cut down to form a tenon and driven into the mortise.

A simple method, obviating the mortise and tenon joint, is to cut a recess in the piece B for the end of A to butt into so as to locate A sideways. The piece B is then held firmly to A by one or more long wood screws, or wire nails. The wood screws should be equal in length to at least twice the width of B. It will be observed that the recessing of A into B takes all side strain off the screws, or nails.

The Half-joint Method.

When it is desired to join two pieces of timber to one another at right angles, at their ends, the half-joint method, illustrated in Fig. 2, is particularly convenient for the amateur woodworker. It is only necessary to make two saw cuts with a tenon saw down and across each end to remove one-half of the wood, so that the two ends fit flush, as shown in Fig. 2. The abutting faces should then be brushed over with carpenter's glue and screwed together in at least two places; this gives a strong joint.

Where two pieces of timber have to cross one another the same method of halved joints can be employed with equally effective results.

These joints will be found most useful in the construction of timber frames for sheds, using 2 × 2-inch or 2 × 3-inch deal for the purpose.

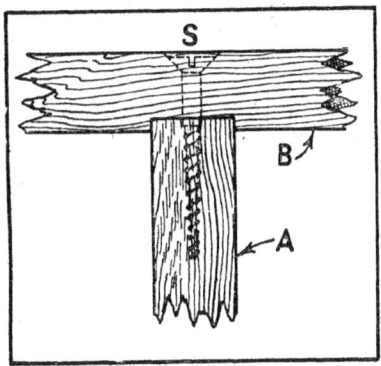

Fig. 1.—The Most Common Joint met with in Home Carpentry—the Right Angle or Butt Joint.

This is used for fastening one piece of wood at right angles to another, and the simple method above shows how this can be done without using the mortise and tenon joint.

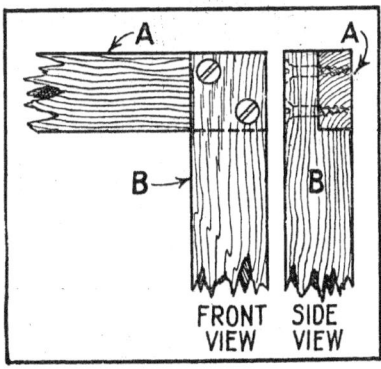

Fig. 2.—A Simple Half-joint Method of Joining Two Pieces of Timber to One Another at Right Angles at Their Ends.

Two saw cuts are made down and across each end to remove one-half of the wood, so that the two ends fit flush. The abutting faces should then be glued and screwed together in at least two places.

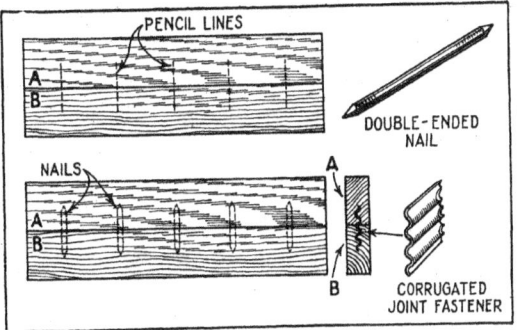

Figs. 3 and 4.—A Simple Method of Jointing Two Pieces of Wood Edgewise.

(Top), showing how pencil lines are drawn across the two boards to locate the positions of the double-ended nails. (Bottom), when the two pieces of wood have been joined with nails a corrugated metal joint fastener should be driven into each end.

Jointing Two Boards Edgewise.

It is sometimes necessary to joint two boards together edgewise, as shown in Figs. 3 and 4. In this case, if the two boards are first laid together and a number of pencil lines drawn across, double-ended nails similar to that shown can be driven in the centres of the edges opposite the pencil marks, on the one board, and holes can be started with a bradawl in the corresponding centres of the other board's edge.

The two edges to be joined should then each be given a coating of glue, and the board that has not the nails fastened in a carpenter's vice with the glued edge horizontal. The other board should then be carefully arranged over it so that the points of the nails just enter the corresponding holes in the fixed board; it may sometimes be necessary to adjust the nails a little sideways, by tapping with a hammer until they all coincide with their holes.

Finally, with a mallet, tap the upper board evenly so that the nails are forced into the holes, the edges of the boards remaining parallel all the time. When the two edges are in contact and the surplus glue has been squeezed out a corrugated metal joint fastener should be driven into each end, as shown in the bottom sketch in Figs. 3 and 4. With a certain amount of care a number of flat boards can be joined together edgewise, in this manner, to form a wide board. This method gives a waterproof and light-tight joint and can be used in connection with the construction of table-tops, pastry boards, drawing boards, panels, partitions and similar constructions.

Three Pieces of Timber Joint at Right-angles.

In the erection of framework for sheds, garages, poultry and summer-houses, as well as for various inside structures in connection with household alterations and improvements, the home carpenter frequently has to join three pieces of timber together, each at right angles to the other. Moreover, the joint in question must be quite strong and rigid in every direction.

One fairly simple method of accomplishing this is shown in Fig. 5, where two of the wooden frame members, P and Q, butt up against the third member R, and are secured to each other by means of two large and long wood screws at A and B. This gives a fairly strong joint, but it is not altogether an easy matter to assemble the members in position single handed.

A More Convenient Method.

It is usually more convenient first to assemble two of the three members separately and then to fix this assembly to the third member. Thus, in Fig. 5, the two timbers D and E are fastened together by the halved-joint method, using the two screws *a* and *b* to secure them. The framework thus built is brought up against the third member F and secured to it by means of the long screw G.

Wire Nails can be Used instead of Woodscrews.

In place of these long wood screws, which are expensive and take a certain amount of extra time to screw into place, long wire nails can be used to give at least as strong a joint. Thus, in the case of 2 × 2-inch timber, round wire nails measuring 5 × $\frac{3}{16}$ inches will be found to provide ample security. For 3 × 3-inch timber, the 6-inch size of nail is generally employed. One long and two shorter nails will give a stronger joint than a single long nail alone; the shorter nails prevent any twisting of the timber about the axis of the longer nail.

It should be remembered that most frameworks are covered with boards, or patent composition sheets that automatically strengthen them, so that the completed structure is considerably stronger than the framework itself.

A Secret Wooden Joint.

An interesting type of joint that is sometimes used in cabinet work and for some furniture joints is that known as the "secret screw joint." It is used to join two pieces of timber together—usually edge-on—so that when assembled there is no external indication of the manner in which the joint is made; it is used almost entirely for secret butt joints.

Referring to Fig. 6, a wood screw is driven into one member B until only part of the plain portion of its shank projects. A circular hole of the same diameter as the head of the wood screw is drilled in the other member B, using a flat-bottom bit. The slotted part marked S is then removed with a thin chisel, so as to leave a kind of key-hole shaped cavity.

To fasten the joint first glue the surfaces A and B, and then press A over the screw head. Next, when the two surfaces A and B are in contact, tap the upper member in the direction shown by the arrow R, until the shank of the wood screw comes hard up against the left-hand side of the slot S. In this operation the head of the wood screw actually cuts through the wood

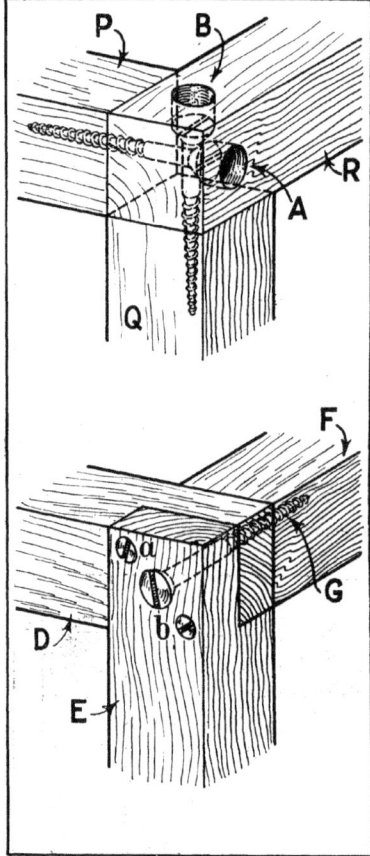

Fig. 5.—WHEN ERECTING FRAMEWORK FOR SHEDS, GARAGES, ETC., IT IS OFTEN NECESSARY TO JOIN THREE PIECES OF TIMBER TOGETHER, EACH AT RIGHT ANGLES TO THE OTHER.

Two methods of doing this are shown in the above illustration.

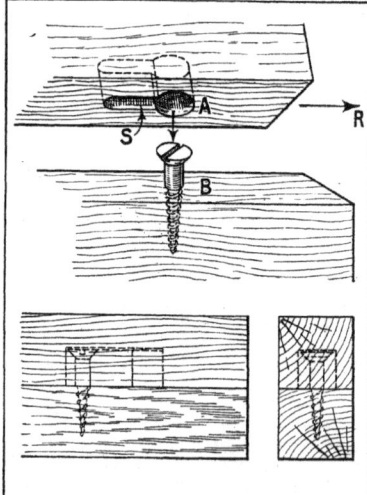

Fig. 6.—A SECRET WOODEN JOINT SOMETIMES USED IN CABINET WORK AND FOR SOME FURNITURE JOINTS.

on either side of the slot, and thus makes a firm joint.

Several screws and "key-holes" are required for long joints of this type; in this case more care is needed in marking off the positions of the holes, so that they all correspond with the wood screw heads.

In Fig. 6 are given sectional views through the completed joint showing how the screw head embeds itself in the wood. It should be pointed out that the hole in member A is sunk a trifle deeper than the projecting length of the screw head to ensure the surfaces A and B making proper contact.

Preparing Wood for Glueing.

Timber that is to be glued should be perfectly dry before the glue is applied, otherwise there will be shrinkage at the joint and a deterioration of the glue itself.

The surfaces to be joined should be planed perfectly true and then sandpapered smooth. In order to make the glue adhere firmly it is necessary to roughen the surfaces by making a number of scratches or scores in the direction of the grain; these should only be made after the sandpapering operation previously mentioned.

A special plane on the market, known as a "toothing plane," has an iron provided with a number of teeth of 60 degrees angles, for scoring wooden surfaces. It is an easy matter, however, to make a scraper for this purpose, out of a piece of sheet steel—old sawblade answers admirably. File the teeth after bending the blade over at right angles. A suitable wooden handle should be fitted afterwards. With such a tool it will be found that large areas of wood can be scored for glueing very quickly.

Glueing Soft Woods.

If the wood to be glued is one of the soft woods, such as deal, whitewood or pine, it should first be sized, to prevent it from soaking up too much glue. It is usual to employ a thin, or well watered glue for this purpose, allowing this to soak well into the grain and to dry thoroughly before the final coat of thicker glue is applied. The latter must be spread evenly over the whole surface and any solid matter removed before the surfaces are placed under pressure to set.

Making Glue Size.

This is made by taking about 4 ozs. of best white glue and soaking it in cold water until it becomes soft, a process occupying about four hours. Next heat the softened glue in sufficient water to cover it until it has quite dissolved. Finally, add warm water, stirring until the solution is of a thin syrupy consistency; it is then right for sizing purposes.

Practical Methods of French Polishing

The art of french polishing consists of applying a thin film of shellac over a properly prepared surface of wood with the object of beautifying the grain and producing dull, semi-dull and bright finishes. The handicraft offers to amateurs many baffling perplexities, but with a little careful thought and practice good results may be obtained. The operations or stages of work must be carefully performed and the groundwork or base of the job must receive as much attention as the polishing.

The Three Chief Furniture Woods: Walnut, Mahogany and Oak.

Three kinds of hardwoods are principally used in the construction of furniture, viz., walnut, mahogany and oak, with each having a different treatment through the various stages to the finish, hence the difficulties confronting the amateur. When the construction of a piece or article has been decided on, obtain timber of the same class as far as possible, in order to obviate the difficulty of colouring to match one particular colour. This art requires experience, and is not recommended as an operation to be successfully employed by the amateur.

Preparing the Wood.

In preparing the wood for polishing it is essential to remove plane marks, which should be done by using a wood-scraper and then smoothing down with grade No. 0 glass-paper; otherwise all marks and bruises will be accentuated when polished.

To Stain Mahogany.

The next stage is staining, and we will first take mahogany. Make up a solution of bichromate in the following proportions, ½ lb. to 1 gallon of water. The best method is to boil about ¼ gallon of water, place in an earthenware jar, add the bichromate and stir until dissolved. When a solution has been made, run in water to make up 1 gallon and allow to cool. (A word of warning—this solution is poisonous and should be marked as such.) Never apply the stain while hot, as crystallisation will take place in the grain after drying, which, if not removed, will perish the polish.

Fig. 1.—How to Use the Woodscraper.
In preparing the wood for polishing it is essential to remove plane marks. This can be done by using a woodscraper and then smoothing down with No. 0 glass-paper

To stain the wood apply with a flat brush, and set aside for a few hours to dry. Should colour be too light, give a further coat or coats until the desired shade is obtained; allow to dry. With grade No. 1 glass-paper lightly paper the raised grain; the work is now ready for the next stage of filling in.

Filling in Grain.

In this operation two methods are in general use: (*a*) plaster; (*b*) woodfiller. Both give satisfactory results according to experience of handling.

Plaster Filling.

Fine plaster of paris should be used, into which is mixed a little rose pink, the object of this being to colour the plaster so that when applied and the grain filled no white marks appear, the filling toning with the redness of the stain. Put the rose-pink plaster of paris mixture into a shallow wooden box, take a piece of coarse rag, soak with water and dip into mixture, rub

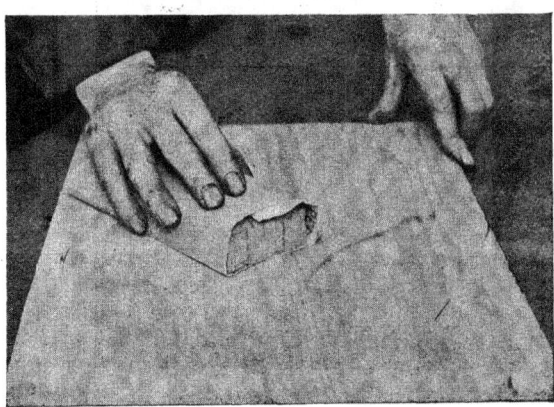

Fig. 2.—When Using the Glass-paper for Smoothing, it should be Wrapped round a Cork Block.
Use No. 0 glass-paper and work with the grain of the wood.

freely and with pressure across the grain, continuing the operation until the job is well covered. Carefully wipe off across the grain all superfluous plaster and set aside for twenty-four hours. Now oil with linseed oil by means of a piece of rag, then thoroughly glass-paper with grade No. 1 until all surface plaster has been removed. You will notice that the oil renders the plaster transparent and brings out the colour of the stained wood. When well papered or cleaned wipe the surface until all oil has been cleared. The job is now ready for applying the first coat of polish, known as fadding.

Here it would be as well to mention the grades of french polish used. Assuming the stained wood is of a dark red shade, and that this colour is desired, garnet polish is used for preference; this, having a red tone, keeps the work to a uniform colour. Button polish should be used only when colour of a light shade is required; remember that button polish is of a medium to light yellow colour, which, when applied to dark red groundwork, is apt to reflect when finished a foggy or greenish effect. A mixture of half and half of these two polishes can be made if a colour of a medium red shade is desired.

Woodfiller Filling: An Alternative Method.

Woodfiller may be obtained in all shades in a stiff paste condition, which may be thinned with genuine American turpentine or woodfiller thinners as supplied by the manufacturers to a cream-like consistency. Apply with coarse rag, rubbing across the grain, wipe off superfluous filler, also against the grain, and allow twenty-four hours or longer to harden.

Smooth Off After the Filler has been Applied.

Then well paper with glass-paper, grade No. 1; no oil must be used. If this operation is not well performed, muddiness in the grain will result. Now proceed with the fadding-in.

Next the Fadding-in.

Obtain a quantity of cotton wool or wadding, and with either proceed to make up a portion into a pear-shaped pad; cover this with a piece of moder-

PRACTICAL METHODS OF FRENCH POLISHING

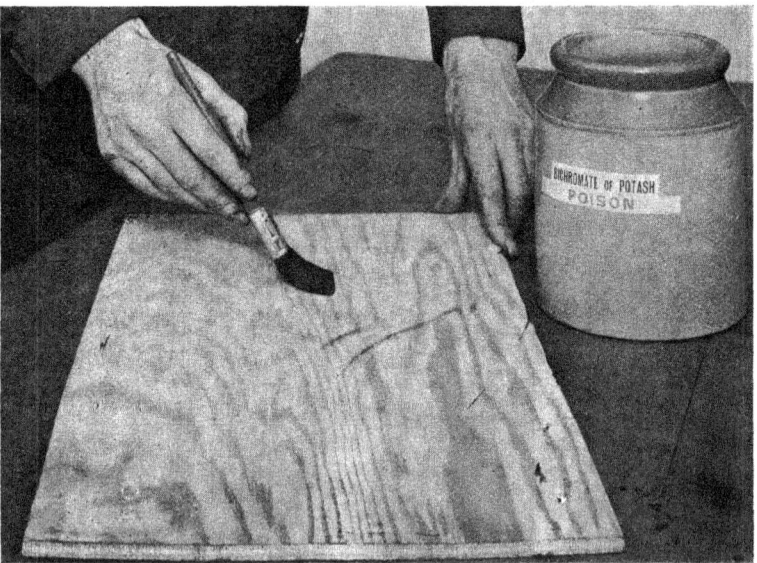

Fig. 3.—THE FIRST APPLICATION IN STAINING MAHOGANY.
Use a solution of b chromate, ¼ lb. to 1 gallon of water. Boil about ½ gallon of water, place in an earthenware jar and add the bichromate. Stir until dissolved and add enough water to make up a gallon. When cold, apply to wood with a flat brush.

ately woven white rag, which gives the rubber. Keep the polish in a glass bottle with a small channel cut in the side of the cork, which will allow the polish to be shaken out. Take the rag off the rubber and shake polish on to the wool pad until partially saturated, replace rag to make a smooth base, then with light, even pressure work up and down with the grain; as work proceeds it will be noticed that the surface develops a semi-gloss appearance; at this stage set aside for a few hours to harden. (Work rubber until nearly dry, remove rag and recharge pad; never apply polish to the covering of the pad.)

Now Prepare Work for Bodying-in.

Paper job with grade No. 0 glass-paper, taking care to remove the cutting edge by rubbing two faces of glass-paper together, smear a little linseed oil over the paper and proceed to level down with light, even pressure the semi-gloss surface. This operation removes any raised grain and smooths down the fad-in surface.

Applying the Body Coat.

Recharge rubber and on the base of pad cover smear a drip of linseed oil. Now begin to work over the surface in a series of circling strokes, which must cover the work without the removal of the rubber. As work proceeds it shows greasy marks or smears. Continue the operation of recharging the rubber when dry, using oil only when rubber shows signs of sticking, and after a little time a layer or body of shellac will have been applied. Allow it to stand until the surface has hardened, again paper down as already described, follow with the rubbering and so on until a good, sound body results.

Finishing.

The work now has a smeary, dull appearance due to the oil being worked to the surface, which, before a bright finish can be obtained, must be removed. Varying methods are employed by the craftsman, but the easiest course recommended for amateurs is just to dampen the rubber with polish and use in straight strokes, working with the grain as in fadding-in; continue the operation until all oil has been removed and the bright finish obtained.

Polishing Walnut.

Walnut may be polished natural colour or stained with walnut water stain to varying depths of shade.

To polish unstained walnut, fill in with either fine plaster of paris or transparent woodfiller and proceed as already explained. After woodfilling, apply white french polish, following the same method as used on mahogany.

How to Stain Walnut.

To stain, obtain a quantity of walnut crystals, make up stain solution using 1 lb. to 1 gallon.

Prepare by dissolving the crystals in about half the quantity of water (if possible, boil the mixture, as this assists solubility). Water is now added until desired shade or colour is obtained. It

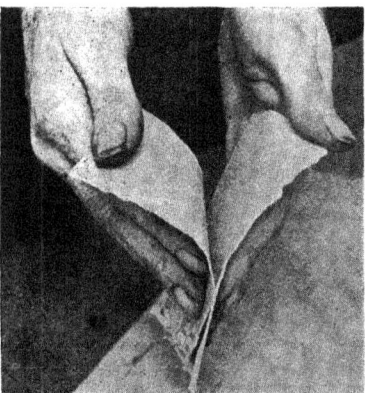

Fig. 4.—AFTER FADDING-IN, THE WOOD MUST BE RUBBED DOWN.
This is done with glass-paper, after the cutting edge of the paper has been taken off by rubbing two sheets together.

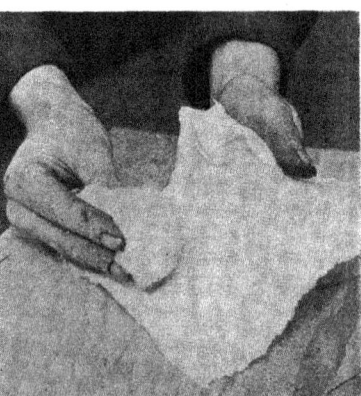

Fig. 5.—HOW TO MAKE THE RUBBER FOR APPLYING THE BODY COAT.
Showing the cotton-wool pad and rag for covering.

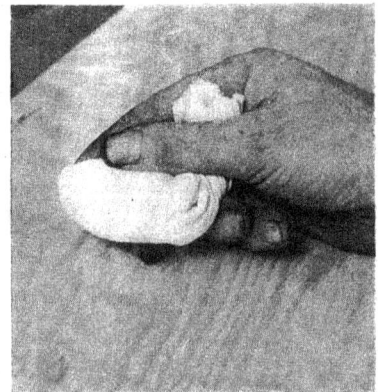

Fig. 6.—HOW TO HOLD THE RUBBER.
Note the flattened surface for applying the body coat to the wood.

is advisable to test the colour on a piece of spare wood before applying to job.

Apply stain with a piece of rag, well rubbing across the grain, allow to dry, paper and prepare for filling-in. If plaster is used, colour with a little brown umber and proceed as for mahogany. Either of the following three polishes may be used according to the finish required : button polish, garnet polish or white french polish. The polishing process should follow the same routine as for mahogany.

Working on Oak.

Oak, of the three hardwoods, gives the best and easiest means of obtaining good results for the amateur ; owing to the finish and the texture of the wood few difficulties arise which are beyond the beginner, assuming an average amount of intelligence.

Stains that Can be Used.

Oak is world-wide, and providing the wood is selected and of the white variety excellent finishes of all types can be produced. Varying finishes are now on the market ; as, for example, waxed, limed, flat-stained, semi-gloss and bright, which may be open-grained or filled. Oak, on account of its texture and grain, lends itself to the ready application of various stains, viz., spirit, water, oil and naphtha, each giving a range of shades of a pleasing character.

With spirit stains permanency is not definite, this being objectionable to the craftsman, which is accentuated by the difficulty of fixing the stain before polishing. Water stains may be produced by dissolving water-soluble anilines, which may be obtained in a wide variety of colours ; fading is their weak point.

The material in general use is Vandyke in a crystal form, which, when dissolved in water (mixture as in the case of walnut crystals), gives an excellent range of shades from Jacobean to light oak, according to the amount of water added. Naturally, when spirit or water stains are used, the raising of the grain must follow.

Oil and Naphtha Stains.

Oil and naphtha stains are a class of stains which have come into general use in more recent years, both being more or less permanent with a range of pleasing shades through light oak to black, including, if desired, red or mahogany colour. Special thinners are made by the manufacturers which can be used to thin a particular colour to a weaker tone, thereby greatly helping the craftsman to match or produce given shades ; again, stains of these classes may be intermixed without doing any material harm to the stains or colour, also little or no raising of the grain results.

Use Vandyke Crystal Solution First.

The amateur is well advised to begin staining this class of wood with Vandyke crystal solution thereby assuring himself of continuity of colour, this stain being easily applied and giving a satisfactory finish. As experience grows the use of oil or naphtha stains may be experimented with, and if care be taken the results will recompense the user for his extra trouble.

Waxed Open-grain Oak.

For waxed open-grain oak, proceed as follows. For natural colour give the work a fad coat of white polish as described for mahogany and walnut, set

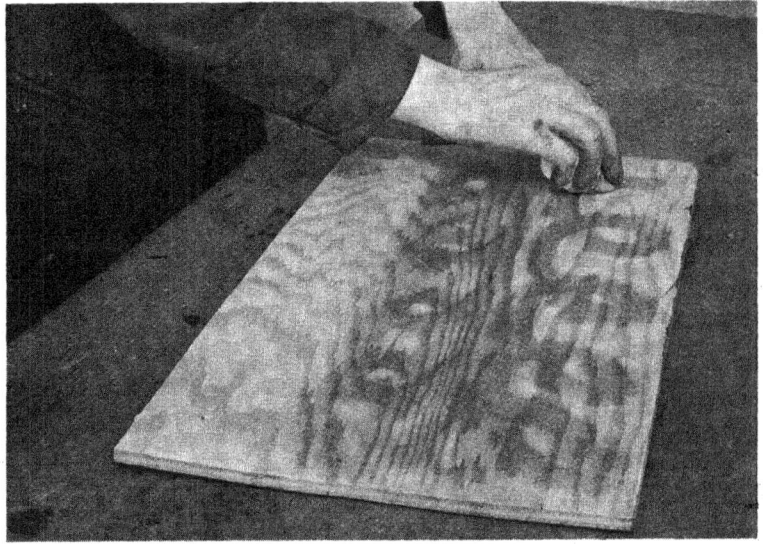

Fig. 7.—The Polishing Stroke.
Note the continuous loops of the stroke. The professional polishers often develop this into the figure eight movement, which, however, requires considerable practice.

Fig. 8.—A Useful Tip.
Cut a channel in the cork of the polish bottle so as to allow polish to be easily sprinkled on the rubber

Fig. 9.—Shaking the Polish on the Rubber.
After cutting the cork, as shown in the previous illustration.

PRACTICAL METHODS OF FRENCH POLISHING

aside to harden, paper with grade No. 0 glass-paper, then apply a thin smear of a hard, light wax polish (such as Harracks), give a good rubbing, after which finish off with a clean duster. A semi-dull or wax finish is then obtained.

For stained open-grained waxed finishes, follow the same procedure after the stain has been applied and allowed to dry, only use garnet polish for dark, and button polish for medium to light yellow, shades.

Semi-bright finishes are produced on open grain by applying a full fad coat, set aside to harden, paper, apply further fad coats until the desired finish is obtained. The work may be waxed at the discretion of the craftsman.

For bright open-grained finishes, proceed to fad in, then follow the instructions given for polishing walnut and mahogany.

How to Polish Filled Grain Oak.

To polish oak, filled grain, use fine plaster of paris and colour according to shade required with either yellow ochre, brown umber, burnt Turkey umber, etc., or mixtures as may be desired. Polish in the same manner as described for walnut and mahogany.

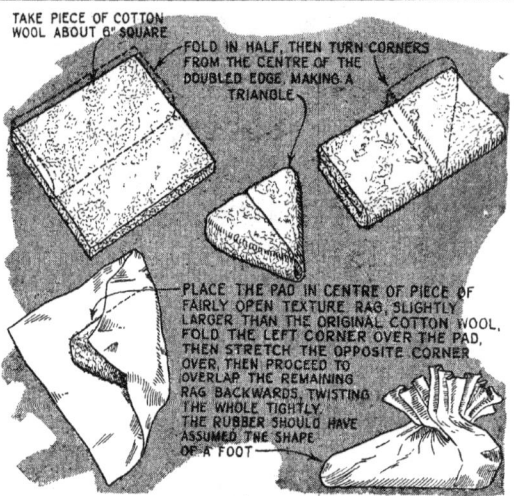

Fig. 10.—HERE CAN BE SEEN CLEARLY THE VARIOUS STAGES IN THE CONSTRUCTION OF A SUITABLE RUBBER.

Dull Finished Oak.

The method employed for dull finished oak is first to obtain a bright surface, and when hard, sprinkle over a little fine pumice powder, grade 400, then by using a dulling or shoe brush lightly rub over the polished surface; the object in view is to brush the pumice powder until a degree of dullness is obtained, then clean the work with a piece of soft rag.

Staining Oak.

When staining oak apply with a piece of coarse rag, rubbing across the grain, giving a free application. Allow to stand for a few minutes, wipe off superfluous stain and set aside for twenty-four hours or longer before proceeding.

Limed Oak.

A new finish known as limed oak has been offered to the public during the last year, and has been much sought after by amateurs with, we are afraid, poor results and disappointments, but if the following procedure is given careful attention, the worker can and will perform jobs above criticism.

The work having been properly cleaned must be first treated with a water stain if the natural colour is not desired. Any colour may be obtained from first-class polish and varnish manufacturers. After staining, allow the work to stand for twenty-four hours, lightly paper with grade No. 0 glass-paper, then with a stiff wire brush open up the grain, using moderate pressure with strokes running with the grain so that all the soft grain is opened up. At this stage it will be noticed that the stain shows a lighter shade due to the brushing, and a

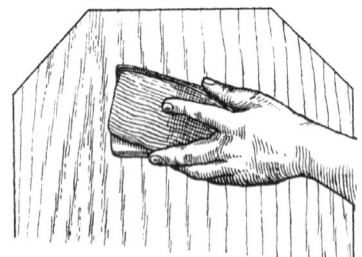

Fig. 11.—CLEANING UP THE TIMBER.
In the case of solid oak or mahogany, it may be necessary to damp the wood with warm water and, when dry, rub with very fine glass-paper. This is in addition to the preliminary cleaning-up shown in Fig. 1.

Fig. 12.—APPLYING THE STAIN.
If possible it is a good plan to stand the wood in an upright position, as shown. The brush can then be held so as to allow the stain to run on to the work from the brush.

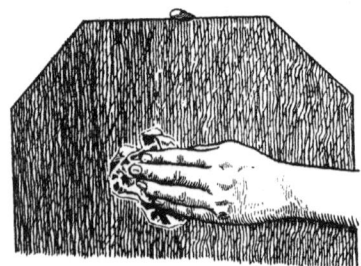

Fig. 13.—TO PREVENT BRUSH MARKS SHOWING AFTER APPLYING THE STAIN IT IS A GOOD PLAN TO WIPE THE SURFACE WITH A CLEAN RAG.
This should be done immediately after applying the stain.

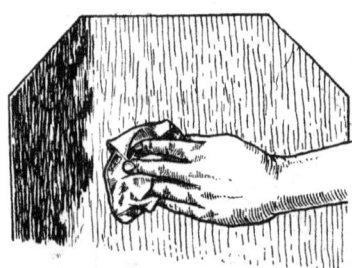

Fig. 14.—FILLING IN THE SURFACE.
After the stain has dried the grain of the wood is filled by rubbing in damp plaster of paris with a rag.

Fig. 15.—FILLING IN THE SURFACE.
When the plaster is dry, rub gently with glass-paper to an even surface. Then rub with linseed oil to remove surplus plaster.

Fig. 16.—DIAGRAM SHOWING HOW THE POLISH IS APPLIED WITH A CIRCULAR MOTION. See also Fig. 7.

further weak stain solution should be applied if required. When dry apply a mixture of half white polish and half methylated spirit with a flat varnish brush. This application fixes the stain, and work is now ready for the filling of the opened-up grain with the liming wax.

The Liming Wax.

Use a piece of soft rag, apply a free coating, rubbing with moderate pressure across the grain, repeating the operation until all open grain has been filled. Leave for about fifteen minutes, wipe off superfluous liming wax, set aside for two or three hours, take off the cutting edge of a piece of grade No. 0 glass-paper, and proceed to paper the surface, rubbing with the grain in order to clean off all liming wax which is not in the grain. Work should now show the grain filled with the hard grain or pebble free from all foreign matter. Apply thin film of a hard light wax polish (as previously described); give a good rubbing, finally finishing with a piece of soft clean rag.

If a brighter finish is required, make up a french polishing rubber, half soak with white polish, and pass lightly over the waxed surface with the grain as in fadding.

Liming wax may be obtained in a number of colours, viz., white, broken white, cream, deep cream, grey, blue, gold, etc., and are only manufactured together with Harracks light wax polish by Henry Flack, Ltd.

Dealing with Plywood.

So far only timber of a solid nature has been dealt with, but if plywood veneered mahogany, walnut or oak are used the operations described are followed although plywood of this class may, or may not, according to quality, require extra colouring or shading; our advice to the amateur or novice when using plywood is always

Fig. 17.—Liming Oak.
Using the wire brush before or after staining oak to open the grain for the liming effect.

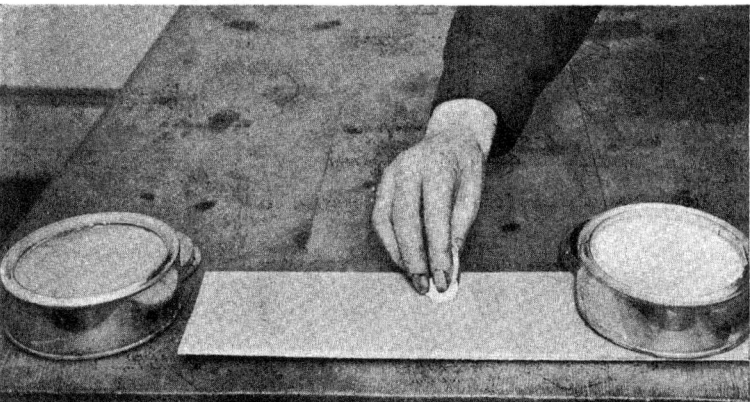

Fig. 18.—Liming Oak.
Apply the liming wax, rubbing across the grain, and afterwards finish with light wax polish.

Fig. 19.—Dulling the Highly Polished Surface.
Here we see the method of using the pumice powder and dulling brush to remove the high polish and to give the dull finish which is used so much in modern furniture.

to stain to a dark colour, thereby greatly reducing the risk of having to colour down a job and so avoiding disappointments. Remember always that french polishing is a skilled art, never rush the various stages of operation, and, above all, satisfy yourself that the groundwork of a job is perfect, otherwise hours of labour and material are wasted. In a later article we shall deal with birch, beech and various soft woods, ply and solid, in order to obtain finishes of a varying nature, especially with oil and spirit varnishes.

Summary of the Hardwoods.

It may be of interest to the amateur if a list or summary of the hardwoods as dealt with in this article are summarised.

Mahogany.

Firstly, Mahogany; this particular timber is fairly distributed through the tropical zone, varying naturally in its hardness and beauty of grain, which is due to the conditions of growth. The outstanding varieties are Spanish, Cuban, Honduras and, lastly, a variety known as Caboon, which should be rigidly avoided, for only the skilled craftsman can deal with this class of timber.

Walnut.

Walnut has principally two sources—English and Italian. The latter gives the better variety of grain and is in general use; although that known in the trade as Burr Walnut is the outstanding grade.

Oak.

As already mentioned, Oak is known world-wide. The various sources are as follows: English, Polish, Austrian, Japanese and American; each having its own characteristics, for it will be noted that the nearer this class of timber is grown to the Equator, the redder becomes the oak. This variety should be avoided if colours of a light to medium oak are desired.

Repairing China and Pottery

Fig. 1.—To start the Drill through the Glaze, scratch away the Shiny Surface with a Glass Cutter.

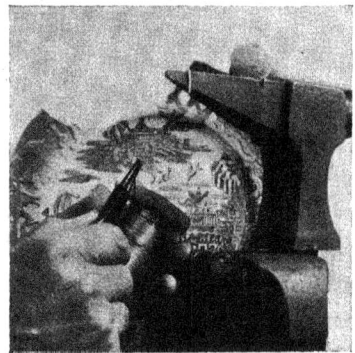

Fig. 2.—Making a Rivet from a Piece of $\tfrac{1}{16}$-inch Brass Tinned Wire.

Fig. 3.—Knocking in the Rivet with a Small Hammer.

Broken pottery can be repaired by sticking with cement or by riveting. The latter method, although not so neat, is undoubtedly the best.

One of the best cements can be made at home. Crush some calcine oyster shell and grind it to a fine powder with a stone on a flat slab; when reduced to the consistency of flour, mix into a paste with the raw white of an egg. Smear the edges to be joined, press the pieces firmly together for seven minutes, when a perfect joint will be made which will resist both heat and water.

Drilling the Rivet Holes.

When riveting, the holes should be $\tfrac{1}{4}$ inch from the edge of the fracture and slope slightly inwards towards the bottom; they must be at least as deep as half the thickness of the china. To start the drill through the glaze, the hardest part of the pottery, scratch away the shiny surface with a diamond or glass cutter. The hole is bored with a $\tfrac{3}{32}$-inch bit, having a diamond-shaped point; an Archimedean drill is most suitable for holding the bit, as it rotates in both directions; the point should be lubricated with turpentine.

For drilling very hard ware a copper bit impregnated with emery is very useful. Take a piece of copper wire $\tfrac{3}{32}$ inch diameter, $1\tfrac{1}{2}$ inches long and stiffen it by sweating on the outside a tubular piece of tin, so that only $\tfrac{3}{16}$ inch of the copper is exposed. Now drill down into a piece of boxwood, withdraw the bit and put some fine emery powder in the hole, then give a few turns in the powder until the emery becomes embedded in the copper; this bit will then pierce the hardest pottery, and by repeating the above process more emery can be worked into the copper.

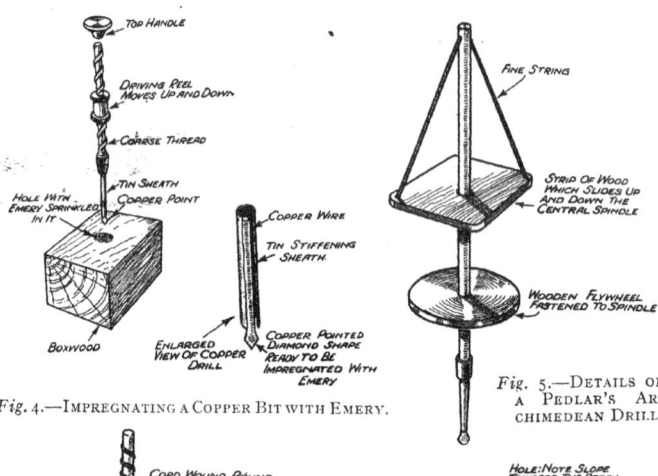

Fig. 4.—Impregnating a Copper Bit with Emery.

Fig. 5.—Details of a Pedlar's Archimedean Drill.

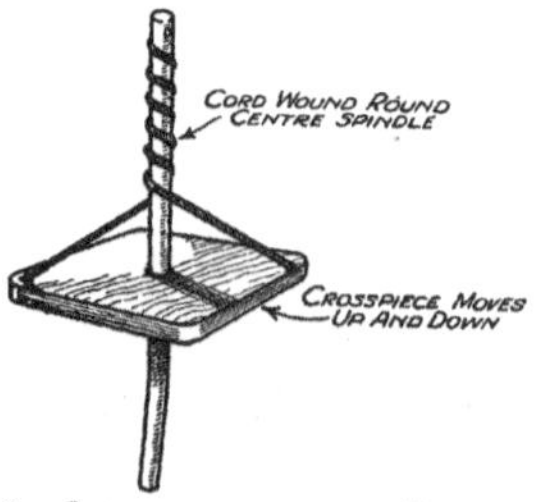

Fig. 6.—Showing how the Cross-piece of Archimedean Drill Moves Up and Down.

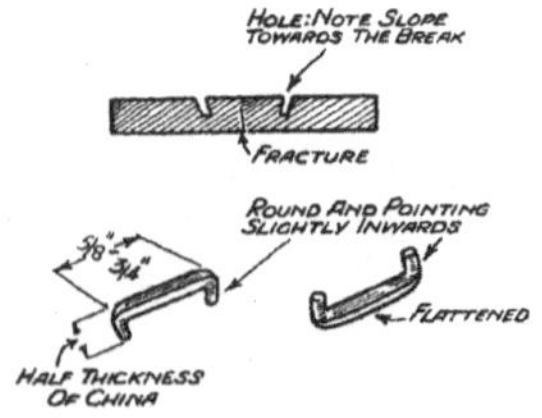

Fig. 7.—Details for making Rivets.

Making the Rivets.

These are bent to shape out of $\tfrac{1}{16}$-inch brass wire, tinned for sake of appearance; they are $\tfrac{5}{8}$ inch to $\tfrac{3}{4}$ inch long and the two ends slope slightly inwards, while the central portion is flattened on an anvil to make it lie close to the surface of the china. It must be made just too small to drop into the holes, but so that it can be sprung in with a slight rap from a small hammer or mallet, or it may be expanded by heating, when it will easily tap in and tighten up on cooling. If the rivets are put in hot a little shellac should be run into the holes.

Final Hints.

When the job is completed fluid plaster of Paris must be brushed into the crack to make it watertight. The position of the rivets should be so arranged that they form the corners of a triangle, when the strongest result is obtained.

As a general rule not less than three rivets should be used to each broken piece. Small pieces of clay fastened round the edges form a useful expedient for holding the broken fragment while springing the rivet in place.

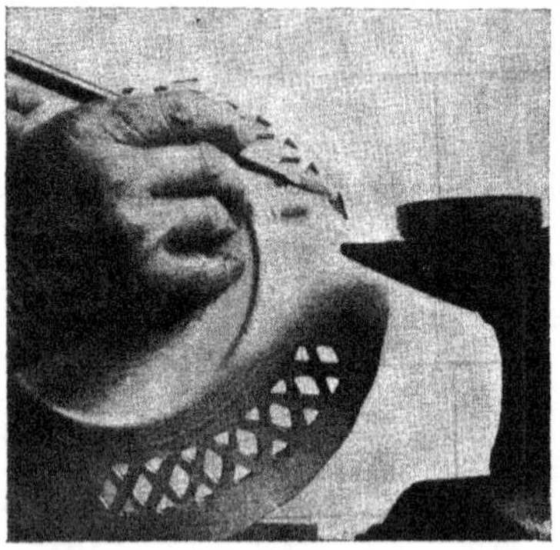

Fig. 8.—When the Job is completed Fluid Plaster of Paris must be brushed into the Crack to make it Watertight.

Care of the Home Billiards Table

WITH PRACTICAL NOTES ON THE USE OF THE TABLE

BILLIARDS is the one and only indoor game which combines physical exercise with mental relaxation. It is an ideal game for the family at home.

An Undersize Table is often Preferable for Home Use.

In the majority of homes, a full-size table is out of the question. It really requires a billiard room built on purpose for it, or part of a very large ground floor room. Because of this, however, it is altogether a mistake to assume that billiards, real billiards, cannot be played and enjoyed because there is no room in the house for a full-size table. If anything, the reverse is more true in a family sense, as a table below standard size is a piece of furniture, part of the home, not something housed apart for the express purpose of billiard playing.

There is also the consideration that, because the balls are always nearer to the player, it is rather easier to score on the undersize table. This increases the zest for the game in the family circle. It is difficult enough to reward skill, but not so difficult that playing is rather a bore unless one is something of an adept. Every shot in the game is playable on a small table, there is not the slightest diminution of recreative value in this important respect.

Deciding where to put the Table.

But, to ensure really enjoyable billiards on an undersize table, the first thing is to decide where the table is to be put when it arrives from the manufacturers. A room on the ground floor is always preferable, but an upstairs room, particularly in a well-built flat, will be quite satisfactory. The essential thing is sufficient solidity of construction to enable the table to stand true and free from vibration.

Fig. 1.—The Billiard-diner is a very convenient Table for Household Use.

Here we see a dining table top being removed. This and the accompanying photographs are by courtesy of Messrs. Thurstons.

Fig. 2.—The Height of the Playing Table can be raised by means of a Screw at the end of the Table.

The Question of Light and Ventilation.

Light and ventilation should also be considered before the table is brought home. Play by daylight is only rarely feasible, a top-light being necessary for perfect play. Artificial light, usually electric, is the general thing, but gas with good mantles gives a capital light for billiards. Ventilation is well worth more thought than it often receives. Billiard playing brings company into the room, there may be a good deal of smoking. It is then both healthful and pleasant if you can switch on one of the many electrical appliances which will clear out the smoke and foul air.

What Size Room is Wanted?

It all depends on the size of the table you would like. This is where the undersize table scores over the standard size. You fit your table to your room, not the room to the table, as must be done for the full size. The following measurements will serve as a reliable general guide:—

Overall size of table.	Room.
5' 6" × 3'	13' × 10' 6"
6' 6" × 3' 6"	14' × 11'
7' 6" × 4'	15' × 11' 6"
8' 6" × 4' 6"	16' × 12'
9' 6" × 5'	17' × 12' 9"

Advantages of the Billiard-diner.

When deciding upon the size of the room available, the main point is

Fig. 3.—Brushing the Cloth.
The cloth should be brushed with the "nap" of the cloth if woollen; there is no "nap" to bother about on cotton cloth.

Fig. 4.—Ironing a Woollen Table with the Nap.
To test heat of iron rub over a piece of old white rag. If it is singed even in the slightest, the iron is too hot.

CARE OF THE HOME BILLIARDS TABLE

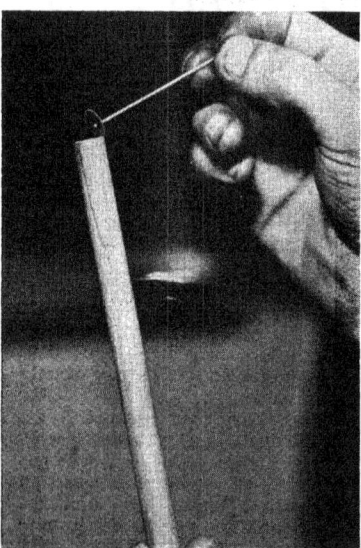

Fig. 5.—Re-tipping a Cue—First Operation, Fixing the Wafer in Position.

Fig. 6.—Re-tipping a Cue. Second Operation, Showing the Tip being Fixed in Position.

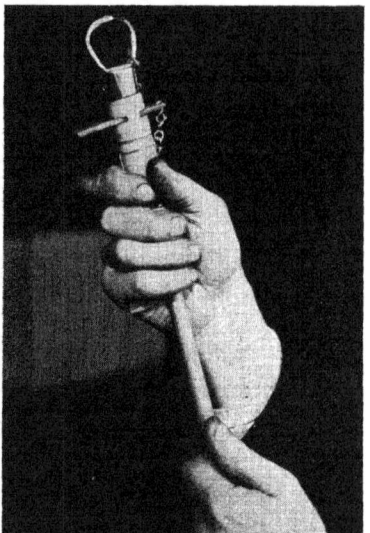

Fig. 7.—Rasping the Top of the Cue to Make it Level.

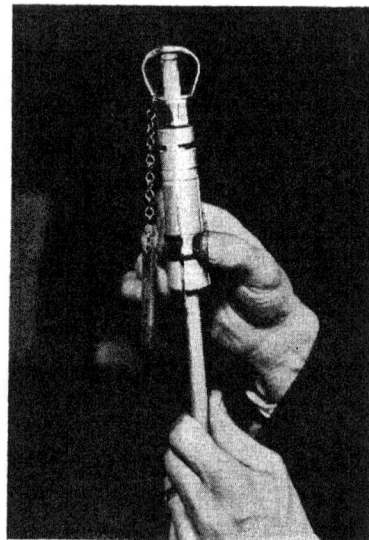

Fig. 8.—Pressing the Tip.

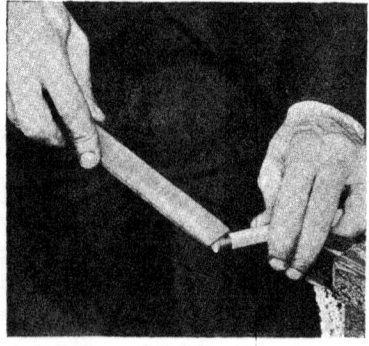

Fig. 9.—Filing the Tip when it has Set.

whether the room is to be used for billiards only. Some houses may have a spare room available, but the vast majority will find that the most suitable room for billiards in point of size is the dining-room. This brings that most useful invention, the billiard-diner into use. Any size of small table can be supplied for use as a dining table and billiard table combined.

Types of Tables to Choose from.

To give the whole range of choice, the following list is complete:—

(1) The Billiard-diner.

The description of this is self-explanatory.

(2) An Undersize Table for Billiards only.

This is suitable when a room can be set apart for play.

(3) Portable Billiard Table.

This is strictly a billiard table top made to stand on an ordinary table. These, if well made and carefully adjusted, will serve for play, but the table top is rather an awkward thing to find room for when not in use; levelling-up for play is not always a success, and the billiard-diner is decidedly preferable.

(4) Undersize Tables with Full-size Standard Pockets.

These are best in a room for billiards. They are occasionally made to specification when two corner pockets are fitted. A modern development, the M.I.P. table, has four pockets. This table measures 6 feet by 4 feet 6 inches, and would require a room about 13 feet 6 inches by 12 feet.

Buying the Table—the Question of Price.

Having selected your general type from the above, the next question is the actual purchase of your table. Remember this, before you part with sixpence, a "cheap" billiard table, big or little, is not worth house room. Billiards demands a solid playing surface on which, year in and year out, the balls will run truly. The table must provide this surface, it must be strongly built of selected material and put together by craftsmen who know their job. Otherwise, it soon gets out of true, becomes an eyesore, you are ashamed to show it to your friends, and when it gets shabby, as it very soon will, you wish you had never seen the thing.

Get your Table from a Firm of Established Reputation.

There is no "cheap" substitute for the indispensable quality of material and workmanship. These must be paid for, or you get something which looks like a billiard table, but does not happen to be one. Therefore, go to a billiard house of standing and reputation and pay a fair price for your table. Deferred terms can be arranged, and you will have a table worth the money. The making of such reliable tables is no monopoly. There are several good firms of long standing in the business. The thing to do is to get price lists from several billiard houses, and please your fancy at a figure which entitles you to have a table you will be proud and pleased to own.

Two Kinds of Cloth.

Cloth is very important. There are two kinds; the woollen cloth, known as West of England cloth, and the cotton cloth, known as the Janus cloth.

CARE OF THE HOME BILLIARDS TABLE

Woollen Cloth.

The woollen cloth offers a playing surface fit for the best of billiards when British made, as most of it is, but there are "cheap" imported woollen cloths, about which the least said the better. A woollen cloth must be brushed and ironed to be kept fit for play. It tends to become loose after a little play and requires "stretching," after which it needs no further expert attention until worn out. When the upper surface is worn out, a woollen cloth cannot be "turned," as the under surface is not the same for playing purposes, and you cannot play real billiards on a "turned" woollen cloth.

Cotton Cloth.

The Janus cotton cloth is also fit for the best of billiards. It has to be brushed, but requires no ironing, a point worth considering, as heating a billiard iron is not a popular job in the house, and dire results are certain if the iron happens to be too hot. The cotton cloth is less subject to accidental damage than the woollen. It is next to impossible to cut it with a cue-tip. It does not "stretch," and can be washed if soiled. When the upper surface is worn out, the cotton cloth is reversible, offering a new cloth for every playing purpose.

Balls and Cues.

Composition balls are now practically universal. The safe choice is between bonzoline, crystalate, or vitalite; beware of "cheap" composition balls, particularly if of foreign origin. Cues are sure to be good if you buy your table from a firm of repute, but not otherwise. Remember this: table, cushions, cloth, balls and cues are all links in a chain of quality and accuracy. One "cheap" link in the chain spoils your billiards.

Care of the Table.

Care of the table and accessories comes next. You do not want your troubles to begin from the moment the outfit comes into the home, but they assuredly will if you regard your billiard table as capable of taking care of itself. The cloth should be brushed, with the "nap" of the cloth if woollen; there is no "nap" to bother about on the cotton cloth. Composition balls pick up dirt and chalk and should be washed and rubbed with a dry cloth. Everything necessary to make your table a pleasure to play on can be done in under ten minutes unless a woollen cloth has to be ironed, when the job naturally takes longer.

Fig. 10.—HERE WE SEE THE CORRECT STANCE.
Stand easily at the table with the left leg foremost and the knee a little bent, the right leg should be kept as straight as possible.

Using the Iron.

When ironing a woollen cloth take care that it is well brushed with the "nap" before using the iron. To test the correct heat of the iron rub it over a piece of old white rag. If it is hot enough to singe that rag in the slightest, even to make the least brown mark on it, it is too hot to iron your billiard table. Having made sure of this important point, proceed to iron quickly in swathes running straight up the table, again with the "nap" of the cloth. This completes the ironing and it is only necessary to dust the woodwork of the table to have everything ready for play. The above, it is very necessary to note, does not apply to the "Janus" cotton cloth, which requires no ironing.

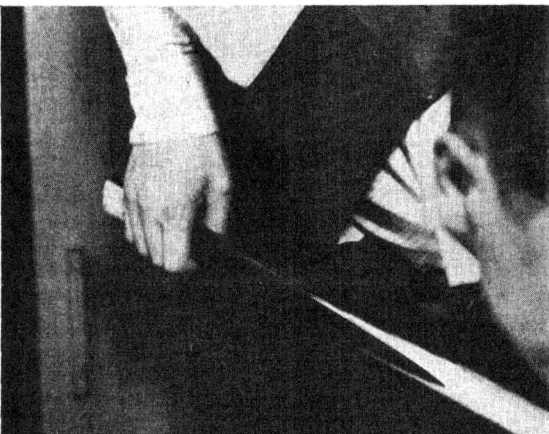

Fig. 11.—METHOD OF HOLDING THE CUE IN THE RIGHT HAND.
Hold the cue firmly but easily in a loop formed by the fingers and thumb. Do not grip it hard.

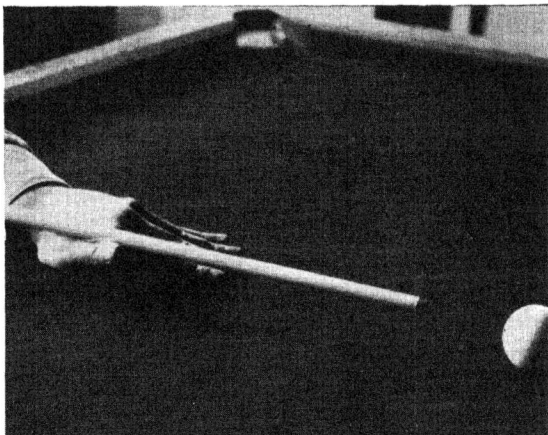

Fig. 12.—HOW TO MAKE THE BRIDGE FOR THE CUE.
The left arm should be thrown well forward. Arch the fingers of the hand, keeping the thumb firm against the forefinger.

CARE OF THE HOME BILLIARDS TABLE

What to do with Cues.

Cues should be rubbed with an old newspaper. Never sandpaper a cue. When not in use, do not allow them to lean against a wall or they will soon become too crooked to play with. A little cue-rack is the proper place for them. Tipping cues is a task the average householder must know something about when a tip flies off a cue. The job is simple enough.

Our photographs show very clearly how to manipulate the various operations connected with tipping a cue. Actually, the job is by no means difficult if our photos are followed. But it is a neat fingered job and it is fatal to be in a hurry with it. When the tip is fixed and dry, be very careful not to nib the woodwork of the cue if any sandpapering is necessary to make the tip fit.

Be careful, when tipping a cue, to get a tip which fits as nearly as possible, the less filing and sandpapering there is to do to make the tip fit neatly, the better it will be to play with.

First Steps in Playing Billiards.

Having bought your billiard table and learned how to take care of it, the next step is to know something about how to play billiards. Mark this, you can play real billiards on an undersize table. Do not listen to those who say that billiards is only playable on a full-size table. That is nonsense, but you must remember that billiards is a very beautiful and scientific game, demanding such accuracy and touch that the more you practise and study the game, the more you will enjoy it. Just knocking the balls about is not billiards, but it is all you can do unless an insight into the game is provided.

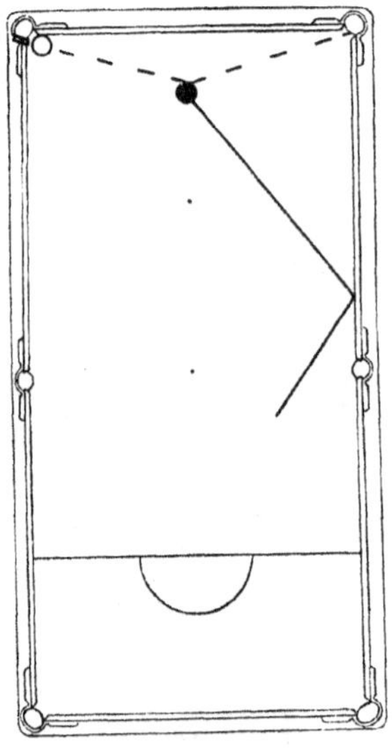

How to Hold the Cue.

The rules supplied with your outfit tell you all you want to know about scoring values, foul shots, and the general layout of the game. When you first begin to play, remember that anything stiff, rigid, or awkward is bad for billiards. The game is essentially graceful and effortless to the eye. Therefore study comfort in every action. Hold your cue firmly but easily in a loop formed by the fingers and thumb. Do not grip it hard or you

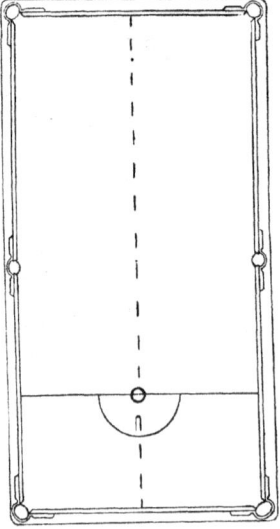

Fig. 13.—THE FIRST PRACTICE SHOT—TO LEARN HOW TO HIT THE BALL IN ITS CENTRE.

Place the ball on the middle spot on the baulk-line and play straight up the table over the central line of spots.

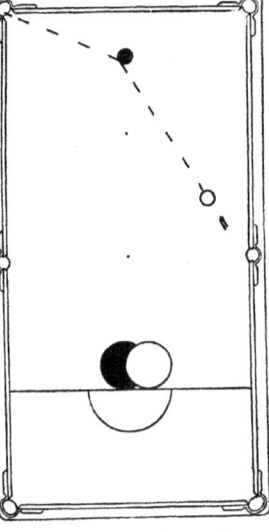

Fig. 14.—THE HALF-BALL STROKE—THE KEY-SHOT IN BILLIARD PLAYING.

Scored by making the centre of your ball hit the outside edge of the object-ball.

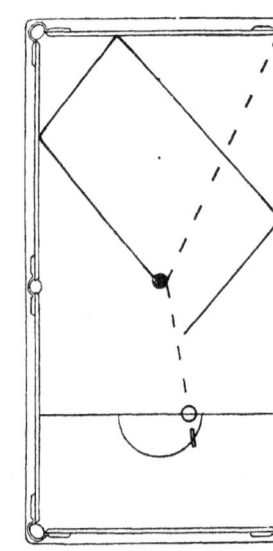

Fig. 15.—ANOTHER HALF-BALL SHOT OFF THE SPOTTED RED, THIS TIME INTO THE FACING TOP POCKET.

Fig. 16.—ANOTHER EXAMPLE OF THE SAME SHOT.

The "long one" played from baulk off the red on the centre spot.

will set up a muscular tremor which makes billiards impossible.

The Correct Stance.

Stand easily at the table with the left leg foremost and the knee a little bent; the right leg should be kept as straight as possible. Obviously there must be a wide margin of permissible variation to allow for tall people or short. But ease of pose, allied to steadiness, is the unvarying requirement. As a rough guide, you can say that if you would be firm on your feet if the table was taken away suddenly as you shape at your stroke, your stance is good for ordinary shots which do not demand reaching over to play.

Position of Arms and Hands.

Your left arm should be thrown well forward and your left hand made into a "bridge" for the cue to slide over. If you lay your hand flat on the table and gradually arch your fingers, keeping the thumb firm against the forefinger, you will make a groove between thumb and forefinger through which the cue will slide without effort. The "bridge" must be free from wobble; the least unintentional movement is transmitted to the cue, with the inevitable result that you hit your ball incorrectly.

Hitting the Ball.

The correct delivery of the cue is a straight swing, always a swing, never a push or jab. You have to impart rotation to a moving ball, which cannot be done except by a cue delivery free and virile enough to impart whatever spin may be wanted. It will pay you to think over stance, the making of your "bridge," and the manner of your cue delivery. These, to billiards, are, like the scales a beginner has to practise in music, indispensable preliminaries to success.

What to do if the Cue-tip Wears Smooth.

Do not forget to chalk your cue lightly at intervals. It is wrong, bad for play and messy for the cloth, to smother your cue-tip with a thick smear of chalk. All you need is as much as can be put on by a light whisk, like an artist using a crayon. If your cue-tip is shiny through wear, it is wasting time to try to chalk it.

CARE OF THE HOME BILLIARDS TABLE

Roughen it by the gentle application of very coarse sandpaper against the grain of the leather. This will "prick up" a new surface on which the chalk will hold and act to perfection. But do not let the sandpaper touch the wood of the cue; sandpapering cues, a common practice, is the quickest way to spoil them.

Playing the Ball—How to Hit it in the Centre.

Now, in proper sequence, we come to the playing of shots. Usually there is a great hurry to do this without troubling over the things which should be taken first if the game is to be really worth while. The first practice shot is designed to teach you to hit your ball in its centre. Place it on the middle spot of the baulk-line, as shown in Fig. 13, and play straight up the table over the central line of spots. If you have struck your ball truly in the middle, it will return over the same line from the top cushion. You will soon discover how extremely unlikely it is to do this owing to the unintentional side imparted because you are hitting your ball to the right or left instead of in the middle. Correct this fault by practice and observation, and you will make progress, but you cannot expect to advance while you are hazy about where you are actually striking your ball.

The Half-ball Stroke.

Fig. 14 introduces the half-ball stroke, the key-shot to billiard playing. It is scored by making the centre of your ball hit the outside edge of the object-ball. The actual half-ball contact is shown by the two big balls at the bottom of the diagram, the result is shown by the stroke at the top of the diagram. This is an in-off red. To make it, place the coloured ball on its spot. Arrange your ball as indicated by continuous line in diagram, which runs from the spot to the shoulder of the middle pocket. Strike your ball as taught by Fig. 13, hit the red as shown at the baulk end of Fig. 14, your ball will then travel over the dotted line at the top-end of Fig. 14 and enter the corner pocket every time. Nothing else can possibly happen unless you play with stupid force. This stroke should be played at strength to leave red as indicated by the line from the top cushion towards baulk.

Another Half-ball Shot.

Fig. 15 shows another half-ball shot off the spotted red, this time into the facing top pocket. Fig. 16 presents another example of the same shot, the "long one" played from baulk off the red on the centre-spot. When playing this stroke, you have to place your ball in the "D" and gauge the angle yourself. The previous strokes from "set" positions will help you to do this, and when you can play this "long one" reasonably well in addition to the shots shown in the other diagrams, you will be able to progress on sound lines to any degree of proficiency.

Do not dismiss these shots as elementary. They are in constant demand in every championship; the "long one" in Fig. 15 has settled the fate of more than one championship. If you play them well, they teach you to recognise a multitude of other half-ball shots which may be left, and, much more important, how to place your ball in the "D" for half-ball shots when your ball is in hand. This half-ball shot, played as described, is the one known quantity in billiards. You reckon from it to solve innumerable playing problems. Practising it, particularly at first, is the one road to proficiency.

PREPARING A GROUND BRUSH FOR PAINTING CEMENT

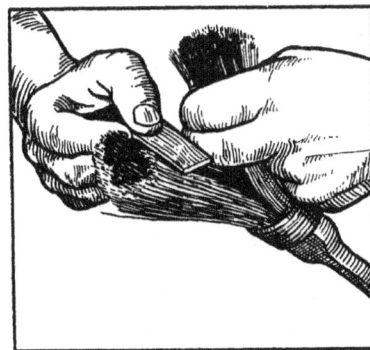

Fig. 1.—Part the Brush in the Centre and Insert a Piece of Wood of Veneer Thickness and of the same Width as the Brush, against the End of the Handle.

Fig. 2.—Make an Ordinary Parcel Slip-knot with a Piece of Strong String. Do not Draw too Tightly. Lay Short End of String along Handle and Tie Firmly.

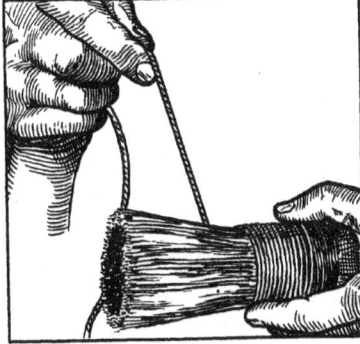

Fig. 3.—Now Wind the String Round the Bristle until about One-third of the Length of Bristle is encircled. This is termed the Bridle.

Fig. 4.—Make a Half-loop and lay the String along the Handle on the Opposite Side to the Other End.

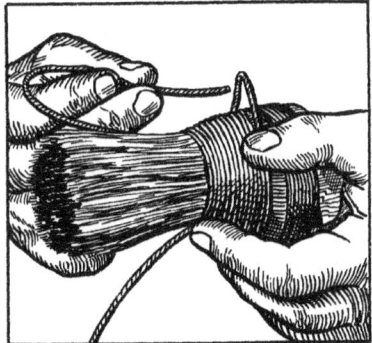

Fig. 5.—Make a Loop by slightly lifting up the First Bind of String and pass the End under to hold it firmly.

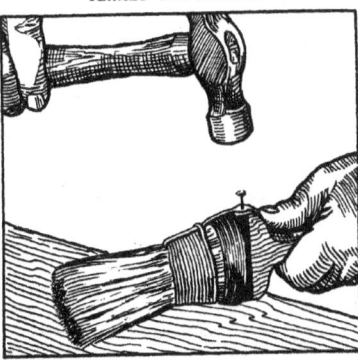

Fig. 6.—Secure the Two Ends with ⅜-inch Tacks. Immerse the Brush in Water to Swell the Timber and Shrink the String.

TIME, LABOUR AND MONEY SAVING IDEAS

RENOVATING GRASS SHEARS.

The life of grass shears can be prolonged greatly by replacing the bolt that acts as a hinge pin. Special "grass shear bolts and nuts" can be had from most ironmongers. The bolt has a round head with square shank (as shown below), and is supplied with a spring washer and nut.

Remove the old nut, then try the new one in place to see that it fits; if not, a few rubs with a file or a piece of emery paper will remedy matters.

Smear the bolt with grease or thick oil, put the blades together, then put the bolt into place, slip the spring washer over the bolt and screw up the nut as tightly as possible.

Apply some oil to the blades and working surfaces near the bolt, and the shears will cut almost as well as before.

INSOLUBLE GLUE.

A glue that does not melt under the action of water can be made by dissolving 20 grains of bichromate of potash in water and adding it to 2 ounces of ordinary melted glue. The resulting mixture is not quite so strong as pure Scotch glue, but once it has set it cannot be re-melted.

FROSTING GLASS WINDOWS.

Ordinary plain glass windows can be given an imitation frosted appearance by brushing them over with a saturated solution of Epsom-salt. As the solution dries the crystalline effect is produced.

A more permanent method is to thin down a little, some ordinary white oil paint and to apply it to the previously cleaned surface of the glass by means of a flat-ended, or stipple, brush so as to obtain a uniform grained effect over the whole surface. Windows frosted on the inside by this method appear very similar to sandblasted or acid etched glass when viewed from the outside.

CLEANING STAINED PORCELAINED IRON.

Porcelained iron vessels, such as bowls, baking dishes, cups and saucers, which have become stained may be cleaned by soaking a piece of cloth in potassium bichromate solution, and rubbing over the stained areas. In bad cases ordinary household Vim powder should be used in addition.

A HOME-MADE PAINT REMOVER.

As the removal of dried paint from surfaces by the methods of scraping or burning is sometimes a tedious process, it is often more convenient to employ a paint-removing solution.

Although there are, of course, several good proprietary makes of paint remover on the market, it is quite an easy matter to make up one's own solution, as follows:—

Take a strong solution of ordinary washing soda in boiling water and add a quantity of soft soap which has been made into a stiff paste with lime. The resulting mixture should be applied to the painted surface with a brush, two or three applications frequently being necessary. It will then be found that the paint is softened so that it can readily be rubbed or scraped off. The surface should then be washed clean with warm water.

SPRING CATCHES.

Useful little fitments known as "French catches," costing only a penny or so, can add greatly to the comfort of the home. The catch consists of two parts, one containing a spring-pressed catch. The other part called the striking plate has a slot in it to receive the catch. The plate is fixed to the door frame and the catch to the door, with the result that when pushed, the door closes, presses the catch back as it passes the striking plate and then springs outwards into the slot in the plate and holds the door in position. The device works in either direction and is consequently

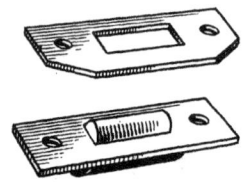

effective on swing doors; it can also be used on drawers.

To fit the device, cut shallow recesses in the wood to take the plates, then cut out the wood (as above) to clear the catch. The plates should finish flush with the surface of the wood.

MAKING THE PUNCH HOLD THE NAIL.

The home handyman will find that he uses the nail punch quite a lot when making wooden articles having separate parts nailed together.

In this connection a good deal of time and trouble may be saved by means of an ordinary fountain pen clip slipped over the plain part of the punch. The nail to be used is then held by means of the clip, so that the fingers are quite clear of the hammer

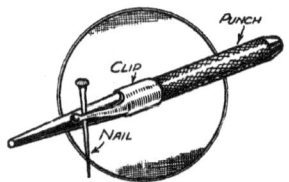

blow. Once the nail has entered the wood sufficiently to be held by the latter the clip can be sprung clear and the nail driven right into position with the hammer.

FANCY RUBBER TABLE MATS.

Coloured rubber sheeting in various thicknesses and many attractive colourings can now be purchased for sixpence from various shops. It is very useful for making table mats; it has only to be cut to any desired shape, either with very strong scissors or a sharp knife. Cutting is quite easy if the blades are kept wet with cold water. Simple geometrical outlines, such as squares, oblongs and triangles, are the best to adopt.

Ornaments placed on rubber mats are not liable to accidental displacement by vibration.

A GOOD FLOOR STAIN.

One of the cheapest and most effective stains for white deal or pine floors is made by dissolving potassium permanganate crystals in warm water. The stronger the solution the deeper will be the colour of the stained surface, although several applications of a less strong solution will give the same result. One advantage of the solution in question is its strong deodorising and disinfecting property.

DETECTING LEAKAGE OF GAS.

A small leakage of gas that cannot be traced by ordinary methods can quickly be located if the pipe is smeared over with soap suds, or with oil. Bubbles will continue to appear at the seat of the leakage, which, if slight, can probably be remedied by turning off the gas, cleaning the pipe and thoroughly painting it with red lead paint, applied fairly thickly. Do not turn on the gas until the paint has hardened, then test as before.

DEALING WITH FLOORS

SOME PRACTICAL NOTES ON REPAIRING, STAINING AND POLISHING

THE best treatment for a floor depends upon its condition, whether new or old. In the former case one can stain and polish it straightway, but an old floor usually calls for some preliminary attention. As repairs are always dealt with first, we will begin with this part of the work, with a few notes on various other jobs which the householder sometimes finds necessary, and which should be done before attempting to stain or polish.

RAISING A FLOOR BOARD

When electrical work has to be done it is sometimes required to raise a board in order that a ceiling rosette can be fitted to the room beneath. It may also be that a board has rotted, necessitating a new one. Most readers realise that boards are laid crosswise on stout supports known as joists. The ends of the boards, when they occur away from the walls, are always arranged over one of the joists so that both ends are supported. If this were not done they would merely hang loose. This point should always be remembered, and the same plan followed when a new board is fitted.

When the end of the board is visible it is usually possible to prise it up by punching in the nails so that they no longer grip, and inserting an instrument with which to lever the board. A cold chisel is suitable. Do not hammer too vigorously or the plaster of the ceiling beneath may suffer. Naturally, the wood is bound to be bruised to a certain extent whilst being levered, though it can be minimised by holding a thin piece of metal beneath the chisel whilst the latter is being forced over. Any damage can be made good with stopping as described later. When partly levered up a batten can be placed beneath it as shown in Fig. 1 to hold it whilst the nails in the next joist are being attended to.

What to do if End of Board cannot be reached.

If the end of the board cannot be reached it has to be cut. The same thing applies when part of it has to be renewed. It is here that the point about the ends being supported by the joists has to be remembered. The cut has to be made at the joist. It is obvious, however, that the cut cannot

Fig. 1.—When prising up the End of a Floorboard, have a Batten handy to place beneath the Board to hold it whilst the Nails in the Next Joist are being attended to.

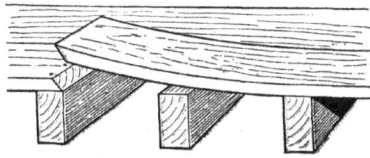

Fig. 2.—Showing Cut made at Angle immediately above Joist when End of Board cannot be reached.
The bend of the board is exaggerated for clearness.

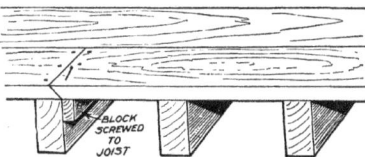

Fig. 3.—Block screwed to Joist to support Replaced Board.

be made downwards in the middle of the joist because it would be impossible to work the saw. The method shown in Fig. 2 is followed. A cut is made

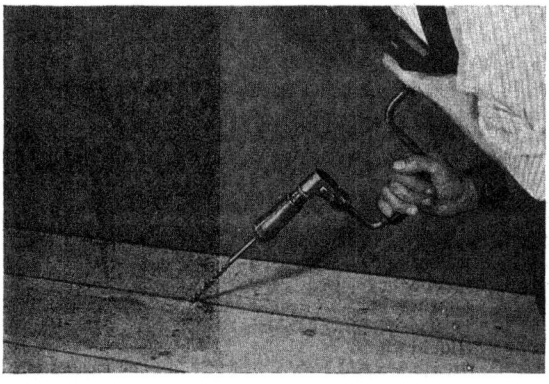

Fig. 4.—How to start the Cut when dealing with a Board the End of which cannot be reached.
First drill a hole at an angle so that the bit emerges beneath at the edge of the joist.

at an angle as shown, so that when it is replaced the end is still supported. In any case, it is as well to screw on a block to the joist as shown because the thickness of the saw-cut makes a certain amount of give inevitable (see Fig. 3).

Starting the Cut.

To start the cut a hole must be bored at the angle as shown in Fig. 4. The bit should emerge beneath at the edge of the joist. As most joists are 2 or 3 inches thick, it is simple to calculate the position at which to start the bit, taking the nails as approximately the centre of the joists. The hole is made at the edge of the board, and a keyhole saw used to make the cut. Fig. 5 shows this being used. When a short section has to be removed, a second similar cut is made as in Fig. 6. If the angle runs in the opposite direction, blocks can be screwed on to the joists at both joints as shown.

SHRUNK BOARDS

In old houses the boards have often shrunk badly, leaving unsightly gaps. To fill these in a number of tapered strips of wood should be prepared. These are fitted to the cracks and planed down. It is a somewhat laborious job, aggravated by the awkward stooping posture the worker has to adopt. However, as the centre is usually covered by a carpet, only the border need be done.

Preparing the Tapered Strips.

The simplest way of preparing the tapered strips is to obtain a thin board of deal (slightly thicker than the width of the gaps), and taper off one side as shown in Fig. 9. A cutting gauge is set to about 1 inch, and this used to slice off the piece. It will be found that the wood easily snaps off after a single cut with the gauge each side.

The pieces are glued and hammered in, as in Fig. 7. When the glue has set the surface can be levelled with the plane. For working near the skirting a bull-nose plane is handy. Failing this a chisel is used. A thorough glass-papering follows.

FILLING IN NAIL HOLES

Nails always look unsightly, especially when only a slight darkening of the boards is intended. The best thing to do is to punch them

DEALING WITH FLOORS

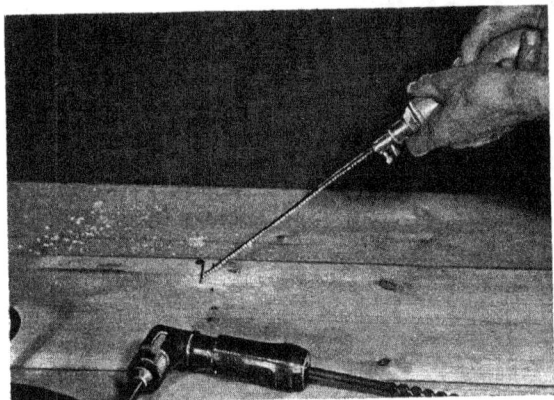

Fig. 5.—Cutting the Board at an Angle with the Keyhole Saw.
It is quite easy to calculate the position at which to start the bit and hold the saw. Most joists are 2 or 3 inches thick, so, by taking the nails as approximately the centre of the joists, the position can be gauged fairly accurately.

Fig. 6.—When a Short Section of Board has to be Removed a Second Cut is made.
Note the supporting blocks screwed to joists, ready for replacing the board.

in and fill in the holes. Putty can be used. It can be darkened with powder colour obtained from an oil and colourman's store. Burnt umber is a useful shade. It is worked well into the putty, a little linseed oil being added if the latter has become dry.

Plaster of paris mixed with powder colour and water also can be used. If a water stain is being used for the floor, a little of this can be used to mix with the plaster instead of water, this rendering it of about the right shade.

Using Wax.

For an oak floor it is better to use wax. This again is mixed with a suitable powder colour, the wax being melted first. A little resin can be added to harden the wax. A simple way of using it is to roll it into a stick whilst still warm. A pointed piece of iron is then heated and held over the nail hole. The wax stick is placed against the iron, when it will melt and drop into the hole. Fig. 8 shows the process. It is levelled afterwards with glass-paper, the bulk being first taken down with a chisel.

Plastic Wood.

Plastic wood is used a great deal nowadays for filling in. It works out rather more expensive, but has the advantage that it can be stained afterwards like the surrounding wood. When a bruise is being filled in with it, the surface is first scraped to form a key. It is heaped slightly as it shrinks somewhat when setting.

Secret Nail.

When one has a specially clean floor into which it is desired to drive a nail, a good plan is to nail it, as shown in Fig. 10. With a chisel a cut is made to raise a shaving about 1½ inches long. It is raised, and the nail driven in and punched. The shaving is then glued and pressed tightly back.

STAINING A FLOOR

There are various stains that can be used. First is water stain, the chief advantage of which is its cheapness. It takes rather long to dry out, however, and is liable to raise

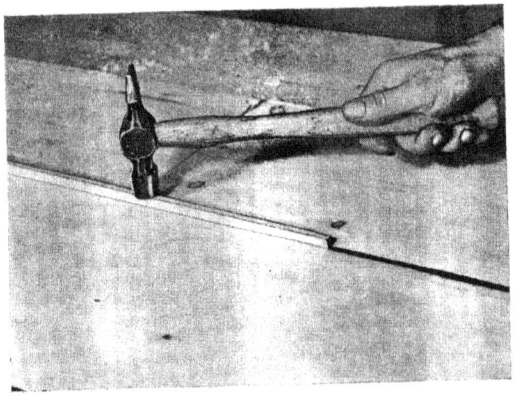

Fig. 7.—Unsightly Gaps in a Floor, caused by Shrunk Boards, are best filled in with Tapered Strips of Wood.
Obtain a thin board of deal, slightly thicker than the width of the gaps, and taper off one side (see also Fig. 9). The pieces are then glued and hammered in, and when the glue has set the surface can be levelled with a plane.

the grain. A better stain is that ground in oil. It costs more, but is much more durable and does not raise the grain. Various proprietary stains of both kinds are available, or they can be made up. It is not advisable to use what is known as varnish stain because, although it gives a quick gloss, it does not wear well. If the reader for one reason or another should decide to use it, however, he should first give the floor a coat of size and allow it to dry out thoroughly. Otherwise the stain will "grab" into the wood, making it very difficult to make clean joins.

WATER STAIN

A good colour can be obtained from vandyke brown crystals. Mix these with warm water and allow to stand for several hours. To each quart of mixture add about 1 oz. of ammonia. Warm it and add a little glue size. The colour can only be ascertained by actually trying on a spare piece of deal. One point to remember is that when the floor has been rubbed down with coarse glass-paper it is liable to become darker than when fine glass-paper has been used.

Use a fairly wide, flat brush for staining, beginning at one wall by the skirting and working along each board, as shown in Fig. 11. It has been already mentioned that water stain is liable to raise the grain. To minimise the trouble it is a good plan to go over the whole floor first with clean water and allow it to dry out. It will dry with a rough surface, and this should be glass-papered smooth. When the stain is applied it will dry fairly smooth,

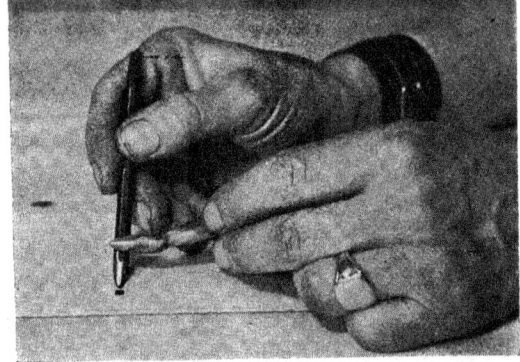

Fig. 8.—For filling in Nail Holes in an Oak Floor it is best to use Wax.
Heat up a pointed piece of iron and hold it over the nail hole. Then place the piece of wax against the iron so that it melts and drops into the hole. It is levelled afterwards with glass-paper.

DEALING WITH FLOORS

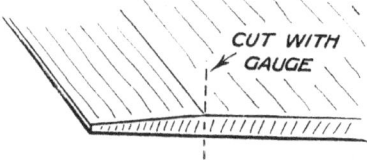

Fig. 9.—SHOWING HOW THE TAPERED PIECES ARE PREPARED FOR FILLING IN WIDE GAPS BETWEEN BOARDS.
A cutting gauge is set to about 1 inch, and used to slice off the piece.

though a rubbing down with fine glass-paper will probably be desirable. The important point in connection with water staining is that the surface must be free from grease, as water stain cannot penetrate this. Such places should be cleaned first with soda water and swilled afterwards with clear water.

OIL STAIN

A colour such as burnt umber can be used for the stain. When obtaining it remember to ask for a colour which has been ground in oil. It is thinned with linseed oil and turpentine, and a little drier added. Here again the colour should be tested on the actual wood.

Before it is applied make sure that the floor is perfectly dry. It is applied with a brush, in the same way as the water stain. It is fixed afterwards with spirit varnish. Make sure that the stain has dried out thoroughly before applying the varnish.

POLISHING WITH WAX

This is a job that is liable to be somewhat disheartening in that the results it gives do not seem compatible with the amount of work put into it. It usually does take several applications before a good eggshell sheen appears. The polish is made up with beeswax. Shred this out into a tin, and cover it with turps. It will gradually dissolve. To hasten the process the wax can be melted, the turps added, and the mixture stirred well. Be sure, if this is done, to remove the wax from any naked flame whilst the turps is being added. A few lumps of resin can be added with advantage.

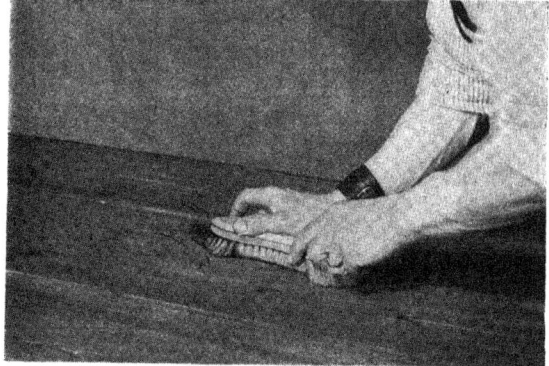

Fig. 12.—WAX POLISH SHOULD BE APPLIED WITH A BRUSH.
Use a brush with fairly stiff bristles, and drive the wax well into the grain. Polish after twenty-four hours with a softer brush and finish off with a rubber worked into a suitable pad.

Fig. 11.—WATER STAINING SHOULD ALWAYS BE STARTED AT ONE WALL BY THE SKIRTING AND WORKED ALONG EACH BOARD.
Use a fairly wide, flat brush for staining, and work with the grain. The surface of the floor must be free from grease, any marks being first removed with soda water and swilled afterwards with clear water.

This will harden the wax and give a better shine.

Apply the mixture with a brush, as shown in Fig. 12. Any brush with fairly stiff bristles is suitable. Use plenty of elbow grease, driving the wax well into the grain. Allow it to remain overnight before polishing. This allows the turps to evaporate. Polishing is done first with a brush with rather softer bristles, and finished off with a rubber worked into a suitable pad. There are polishers available which are provided with a long handle, this saving a great deal of stooping. After an interval of a week or so the process should be repeated.

OLD FLOORS

When a floor has been previously varnished and has got into bad condition, the most satisfactory plan is to strip off the old varnish with one of the proprietary strippers obtainable at an oil and colourman's store. Afterwards it can be stained with an oil stain and either varnished or waxed. A quicker alternative is to go over the whole thing with a dark varnish stain, though the result is not so durable.

REMEDIES FOR SPRINGY FLOORS

Floors that vibrate are generally due to lack of support of the joists at the walls. When joists are laid it is usual to pack under the ends to make them level. These packings very often work out of position, hence the end of the joist has no support, but is suspended by the nails in the floorboards. The excessive shrinking of one joist will also cause the trouble.

It is best to replace the packings for ground floor joists from under the floor if possible, and the joists should be packed with slate or tile bedded in cement. If wood packings are used they must be nailed when in position. For upper floors, remove a little of the plaster just under the ceiling and under the joist that requires packing. If this method is not convenient, or if several joists require attention, a floorboard may be taken up near the wall and the packing done from above.

Driving in solid struts between each joist right across the room will probably cure vibration in an upstairs room. The struts should be nailed to prevent them from working out of position.

Fig. 10.—METHOD OF NAILING A FLOOR SO THAT THE NAILS DO NOT SHOW.
A convenient method of hiding a nail in a floor is to raise a shaving about 1½ inches long with a chisel, drive the nail in and punch it, and then glue back the shaving.

WIRING A HOUSE F(

Many occasions arise when it is a decided advantage to be able to operate a loud speaker in some room in the house far removed from the location of the set.

By far the most satisfactory and convenient scheme is to arrange permanent wiring from the set to plug points in each room where the loud speaker is likely to be needed.

The arrangement of such wiring depends to a large extent on the type of set in use and on the requirements of the household, that is to say, whether multi-room listening or single-room listening will be indulged in regularly, and whether the set is provided with facilities for the use of extra loud speakers.

The method that will be found most satisfactory is by means of plugs and jacks wired in parallel with the output terminals of the receiver, as shown in Fig. 1.

Tools.

The tools required to carry out the work will probably be found in the tool chest of any handyman, with the exception of a bell hanger's gimlet, which is in every respect like the ordinary gimlet, except that its **length** may be anywhere from 15 inches to 24 inches. This implement is essential where the wire is to be run through the floorboard and the ceiling of the room underneath, without the inconvenience and upset entailed in taking up floorboards.

Those unaccustomed to the use of staples may find the finger ends occasionally get in the way of the hammer and a handy tool recently introduced for this purpose will probably be a welcome addition to the outfit. This instrument consists of a hollow tube, shaped at one end to hold the staple in position, whilst a special punch inside the tube, when struck with a light hammer, drives home the staple without difficulty.

Use Rubber Insulated Bell Wire.

Rubber insulated bell wire consisting of two strands of 20 or 22 gauge wire laid side by side and enclosed in a tough rubber sheath will be found suitable, or use can be made of the special wire marketed by several of the leading firms specifically for the purpose. Avoid using ordinary twisted flex, it is definitely not the best medium for the purpose.

Remember that two wires laid closely together function in the same way as a condenser and possess capacity. This in the case of poor wire or very long leads will be sufficient appreciably to affect the reproduction from the speaker. The wires should lay side by side in their insulation and be of fairly stout gauge.

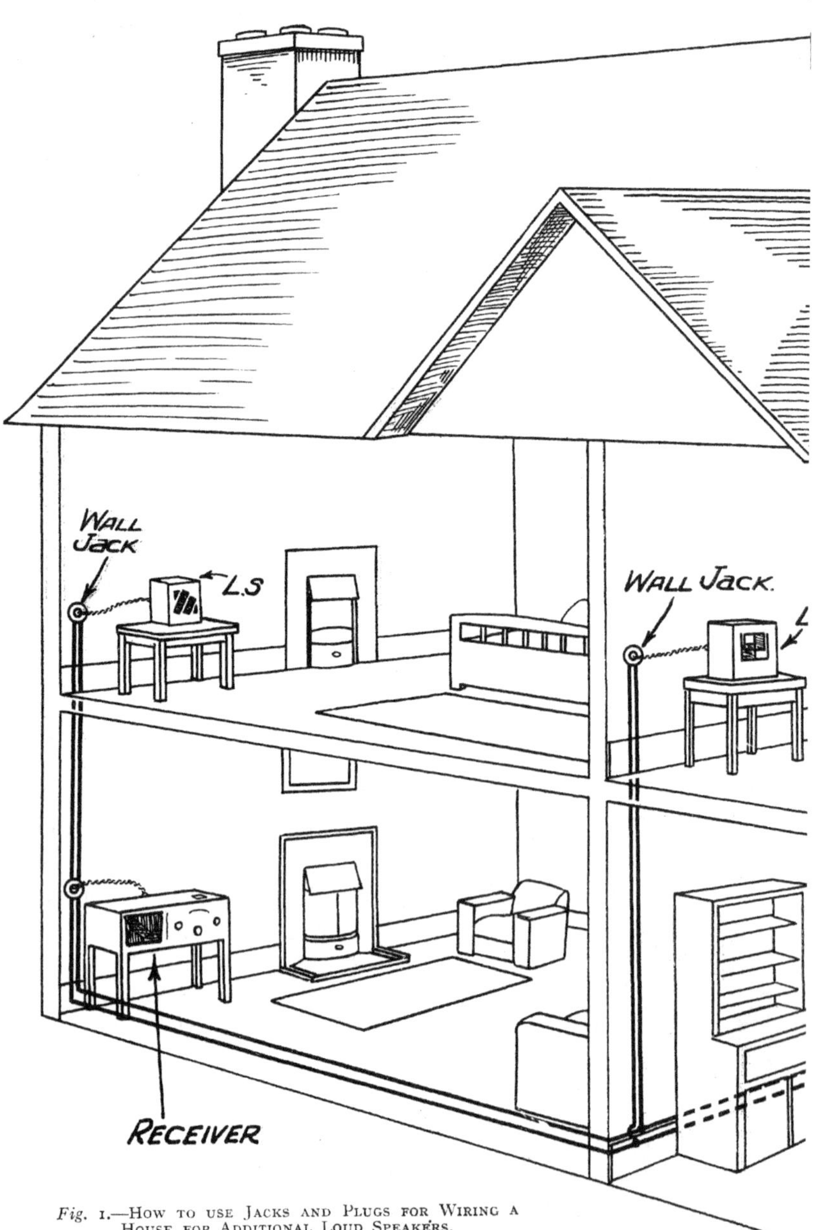

Fig. 1.—How to use Jacks and Plugs for Wiring a House for Additional Loud Speakers.

The method shown here is that known as the parallel wiring system. The output terminals of the receiver are connected to a wall jack placed just above the receiver. From this jack wires are taken to other wall jacks in the various rooms in which a loud speaker is required. When it is desired to use a loud speaker in any of the rooms it is only necessary to insert the plug which is attached to the loud speaker leads, into the jack.

ADDITIONAL LOUD SPEAKERS

Jacks and Plugs.

Telephone type jacks are to be preferred rather than two-pin plugs, as the latter are usually reversible, thus enabling the polarity of the wiring to be reversed, and this is not advisable as some speakers are sensitive to polarity. Messrs. Bulgin offer an excellent selection of these jacks in various finishes to suit the decoration of the rooms. Note that these are made in two types, one for series connection, the other for parallel connection.

When series connection to several points is contemplated, the telephone jack should be used in conjunction with a special socket so that removal of the plug completes the circuit, otherwise the system will only work when speakers are plugged in to every point.

Position of the Plug Points.

When contemplating the wiring of the house careful consideration of the run of the wiring and the location of the plug-points in each room will be well repaid. Two main considerations must be kept in mind; firstly, the run of the wiring to each plug-point must be kept as short as possible, and, secondly, that the plug-points should be so positioned that the loud speaker can be placed in the best acoustic position in each particular room. Excessively long runs of wire to the loud speaker generally lead to a reduction in the strength of the high notes, and thus to a change in the tone of reproduction of the loud speaker as it is moved from room to room, so that slightly different results are to be expected from different rooms.

Finding Best Position for Loud Speaker.

It is advisable first to try the speaker in all the alternative positions which present themselves in each room, by running a temporary lead from the set, before finally deciding where the plugs should be placed and the run of the permanent leads.

One of the most effective positions for the loud speaker is across a corner of the room. Here it is out of the way, gives good acoustic results, and is usually fairly easily wired so that long exposed leads are avoided.

Planning the Run of the Wires.

When running an extension on the parallel wiring system the best plan is to run the double wire by the most direct route to the farthest plug-point, and then employ small junction boxes outside each room from which additional leads in parallel can be run to each individual plug.

An item which should be given close attention is the correct connection of the wire to each plug-point so that the

WIRING A HOUSE FOR ADDITIONAL LOUD SPEAKERS

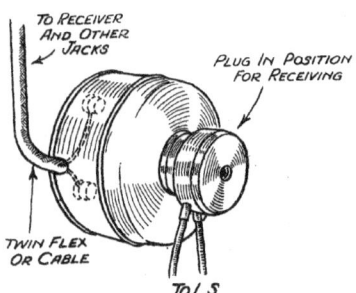

Fig. 2.—HERE CAN BE SEEN CLEARLY THE CONNECTIONS AT THE WALL JACK.

The wires should be connected before the jack is fixed in position.

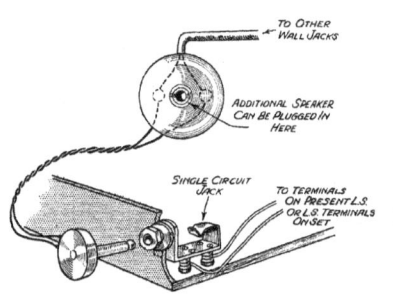

Fig. 3.—If there is a loud speaker incorporated in the receiver it will probably be found convenient to fit a single circuit jack to the panel.

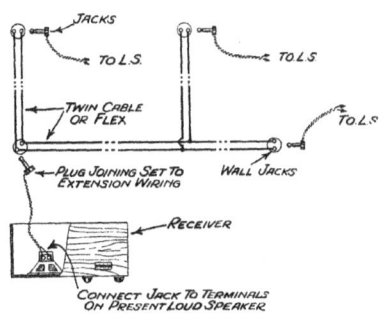

Fig. 4.—Showing how the leads to the extension wiring plug can be connected direct to the loud speaker in the receiver.

polarity is not reversed in different rooms. As already mentioned, some speakers are susceptible to polarity and give better results when connected to the set one way round, particularly the moving-iron type.

Fixing the Wires.

The run of the wires should be carefully considered in order to avoid unnecessary disfigurement of the walls and woodwork. In many cases it is easy to carry the wire through the floor into the basement, coming up again in the room where the connection is desired. Where this form of wiring is employed the connecting points may, with advantage, be fixed to the skirting.

In running conductors in upper floors where lath and plaster walls are usually found, it is often easier and neater to pass the wire under these

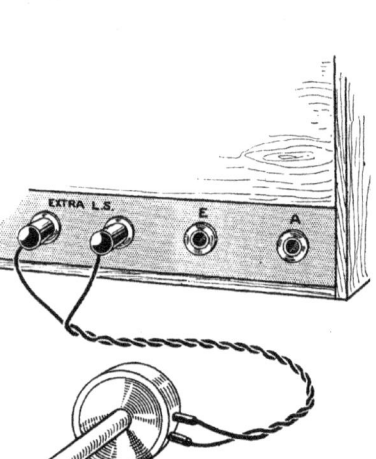

Fig. 5.—Where terminals are provided in the receiver for extra loud speakers, these should of course be used.

walls, rather than through them. If, however, it is desired to pass the wire through a lath and plaster wall, the wall should be sounded and one of the timbers located, the bell hanger's gimlet then being used to make a neat hole as near as possible to the timber, the plug sockets may then be screwed one on each side of the wall to the same timber, the wire being only visible on one side.

Picture rails and door casings often form a convenient run for wiring, whilst in many houses it is often found possible to carry the wire from the attic to the cellar, the whole run being concealed by wardrobes and cupboards.

Remember that gas pipes and electric light wiring are often found under plaster and care should be taken not to drive staples where there is any likelihood of these being present.

Remember when arranging the run of the wire to position it so that it is out of danger from damage by brooms or vacuum cleaners carelessly manipulated during the household cleaning

DOUBLE-CONTROL PUSH

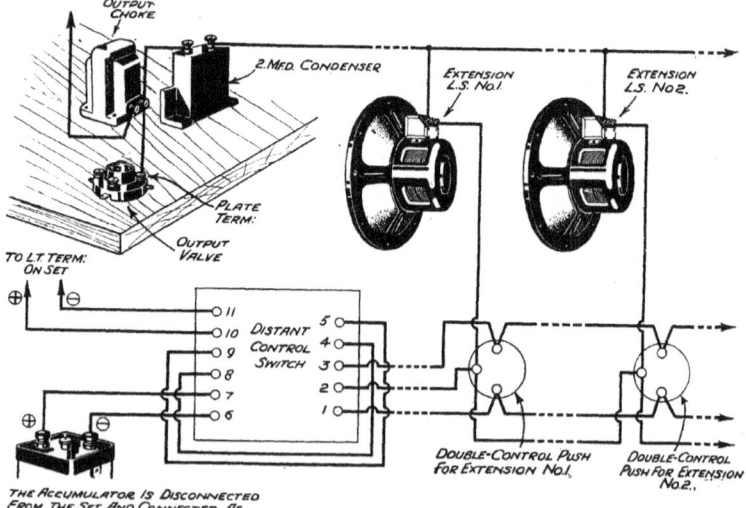

DISTANT CONTROL SWITCH WITH COVER REMOVED SHOWING TERMINAL CONNECTIONS

Fig. 6.—DETAILS OF THE BULGIN DISTANT CONTROL RELAY WHICH ENABLES THE RECEIVER TO BE SWITCHED ON AND OFF FROM A DISTANCE.

It will control battery, A.C. or D.C. sets and the method of connecting it is shown in Figs. 7, 8 and 9.

Fig. 7.—USING THE DISTANT CONTROL RELAY FOR BATTERY SETS.

WIRING A HOUSE FOR ADDITIONAL LOUD SPEAKERS

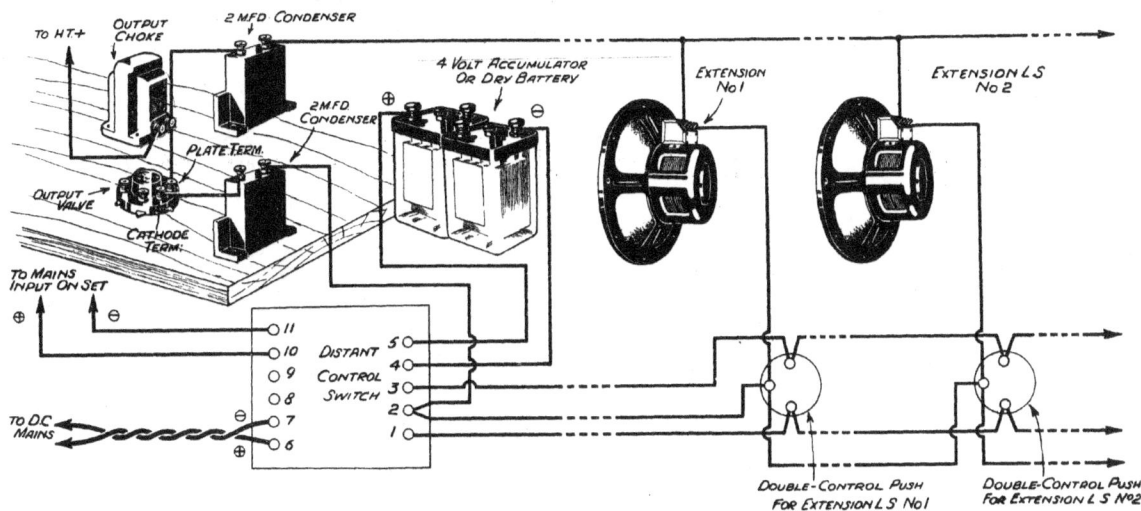

Fig. 8.—Using the Distant Control Relay for a D.C. Mains Driven Set.

process. For this reason the angle between the skirting and the floorboards is by no means an ideal position for the wire.

The wire should be firmly secured at intervals by insulated staples, and if neatly and carefully laid in the first place should remain unobtrusive and free from damage for a long period.

Isolate the Leads from the H.T. Current.

The modern wireless set is usually provided with an output valve carrying a large anode current, and it is advisable to make sure that the set is provided with a choke-condenser or transformer output to isolate the leads from the high tension current or unpleasantness may result.

What to do if there is a Loud Speaker in the Set.

In the case of a receiver in which the loud speaker is incorporated in the cabinet there may often be occasions when it is not desired to have this loud speaker operating when a loud speaker is being used in another room.

Fit an on-off Switch.

The simplest way of overcoming this difficulty is to disconnect one of the wires which connect the internal loud speaker in circuit and attach it to one side of a simple on-off switch. A wire is then taken from the other side of the switch back to the loud speaker. The switch can quite conveniently be mounted on the side of the receiver and will enable the loud speaker to be switched on or off as required, irrespective of the extensions to other rooms.

Volume Control.

This can be effected by the use of 50,000-ohm potentiometers at each plug point where high impedance speakers are to be used. The potentiometer can be conveniently mounted on a 6 × 3-inch block, such as is used for mounting electric light switches, ample space being available for mounting the plug socket on the same block. The extension lines should be connected directly across the outside terminals of the potentiometer, whilst the loud speaker socket should be connected between one side and the slider.

Where logarithmic controls are used, the tapered end of the resistance is connected to the terminal to which the loud speaker socket should not be wired, if a gradual reduction of volume is required. In straight line controls, the changing of the outer connection between one terminal and the other merely alters the direction in which the volume control knob must be rotated to produce a given effect.

REMOTE CONTROL

Once the house is wired for permanent extensions the need will undoubtedly be felt for improved means for controlling the set so that it may be switched on and off from any of the rooms without going to the trouble of walking to the set and switching off. Remote control devices of this nature are on the market and do not add appreciably to the difficulty of wiring the house, as this only entails the use of two twin wire instead of one, or a single four-wire cable, examples of which can be obtained having each wire braided with a different coloured sleeving for identification.

These remote control devices consist of a relay which is wired to the switches in each room and arranged to cut off or switch off the low tension supply to the set. The method of wiring up a distant control, relay for battery, A.C. or D.C. mains sets, is shown in Figs. 7, 8 and 9

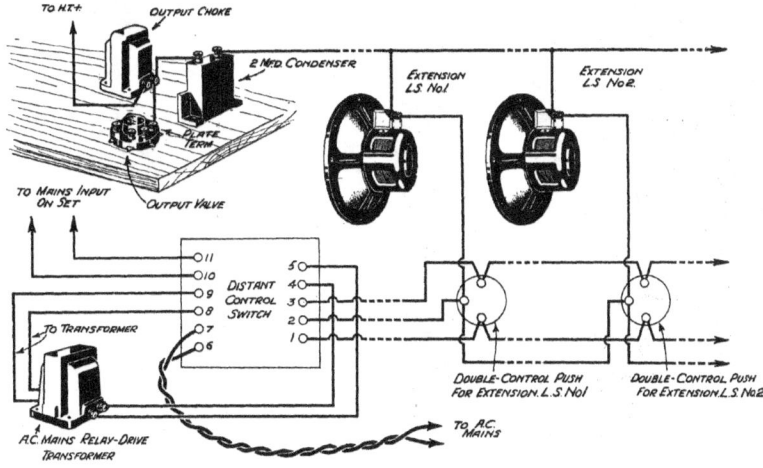

Fig 9.—Using the Distant Control Relay for an A.C. Mains Driven Set.

51

A Compact Shoe-Rack

THE idea of this shoe-rack is that it holds the shoes of a small family within the space of a shallow cupboard or wardrobe, while allowing the maximum of air around the shoes so that they will keep dry.

Important Dimensions.

The actual dimensions of the rack shown are 31 inches high by 26 inches wide, the feet being 8 inches long. This will take six pairs of shoes. These sizes can be varied to suit individual requirements. The actual size or thicknesses of wood used is not important. The essential detail is the spacing of the bars, as shown in Fig. 3. A second important point is to have not less than 6½ inches between the top projecting bar and the lower frame bar, and not less than 4 inches between the bottom projecting bar and the foot. Those are the smallest spaces that can be used conveniently.

The third and last important point is that the frame bars (that is to say, those which carry the shoe-heels) are more than a ½-inch thick; they must be bevelled or rounded off on the back edge, so that the heels hang on the saw-teeth and not on the wood.

The Frame Bars.

The length of these is just 26 inches. Allowing for the joints to the uprights, this leaves 24 inches clear. On these bars are tacked three 8-inch hacksaw

Fig. 1.—The Completed Shoe-rack.

blades. The teeth of the saws should project above the wood as much as possible, and their ends can be overlapped, so that there is no gap between sets of teeth (see Fig. 4). Larger racks should be made by adding extra spaces of 8 inches, that being the length of the saw-blade (less the bit that overlaps), and an 8-inch blade just takes comfortably one pair of average-sized shoes.

The top back edges of these bars are chamfered off if they exceed ½ inch in thickness, to allow the shoe-heels to engage with the saw-teeth.

Projecting Bars.

These are of dowel sticks held by simple brass plates with screws through them. They should be approximately 5 inches below the saw-edge, and project 2 inches from the saw.

A strip of thin wood screwed on over the saws helps to hold them in place, and produces a finished appearance.

Feet.

The feet need not be more than 8 inches long. The frame is fixed well back on them partly to allow of taking up the minimum of space in the cupboard, and partly because practically all the weight, when loaded with shoes, is at the front.

A shoe rack of this design enables shoes of all sizes to be placed on it without any special trouble or exactness and without fear of their slipping off.

The size can, of course, be varied to suit individual requirements, or to fit into a cupboard or recess already in existence.

Saw Teeth do not harm the Heels.

No harm is done to the heels of the shoes by the saw teeth. All they do is to give the necessary grip that keeps the shoes in place, and it is this use of a fretsaw blade that enables the shoes to be held in such a narrow space.

Fig. 2.—Here can be seen the simple Construction of the Rack.

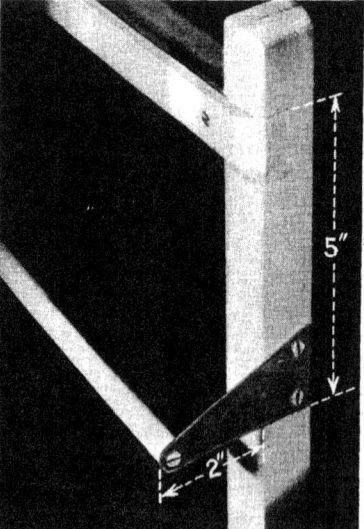

Fig. 3.—The only Essential Measurements are those shown above.

Fig. 4.—Tack the Saw-blades as close to the Top Edge of the Rail as Possible.

RIGHT AND WRONG WAYS OF USING WALLPAPER

To make the most of wallpapers requires at least a knowledge of the many types available and a wide experience of their use. The object of this article is to state as concisely as possible the problems which usually have to be faced in connection with wall decoration, and to indicate briefly principles which experience has shown can be relied upon to guide individual taste.

Wallpapers are produced to serve the most simple needs of utility, and can be purchased at a very low price; and, at the other extreme, they are so elaborated that rooms can be decorated with panoramic landscapes and gardens with realistic representations of flowers and flowering shrubs.

It has been said that decoration begins where utility ends. In the case of wallpaper, however, even the simple patterned paper which may be chosen to furnish the bare walls of attic or boxroom not only makes less obvious the inevitable effect of usage, but if wisely chosen gives interest and a cheerful appearance to the otherwise ordinary and even dingy room.

How to give the Appearance of Increased or Reduced Height.

Well-proportioned rooms have an initial advantage over those which are faulty in this respect and need the application of such treatment as may make the faults less evident. Decoration based upon certain accepted principles will do much to improve appearances. Emphasis laid on horizontal wall divisions, such as dado, picture rail and cornice, will have the effect of reducing height, whilst the appearance of increased height will be given by the emphasis of vertical features, such as pilasters and narrow panels or striped patterns. It is well to remember that vertical emphasis suggests growth, activity, support; diagonal emphasis is restless and suggests movement, whilst horizontal lines indicate balance, repose, or even security.

Fig. 1.—An Attractive Scheme of Panelling for a Dining-room.
Arranged by using two wallpapers and a stile border. One paper is cut into lengths 10½ inches wide and is used for the decorative panel, the other for the large panels.

Making Small Rooms appear large.

Where space is restricted, it is often desired that the appearance of greater dimensions should be given by decoration than actually exist. Although such illusion may seem to be impossible, it is certain that if two rooms of equal dimensions are decorated, one with light walls and ceiling, and the other with dark colours, the light room will appear to be the larger.

Colour: Blue for Distance, Red for Warmth, Yellow for Light.

The subject of colour should be carefully considered in this connection. Blue is a receding colour, whilst red is an aggressive colour. To the extent that blue dominates in the wall colour, whether in a uniform tint or a pattern, the wall will appear to be at greater or less distance. Red being what can be called an aggressive colour, it has a greater furnishing quality as compared with the colder colours, and suggests warmth and comfort. Yellow is light-giving, in contrast to the light-absorbing character of green, brown, violet, etc.

Pattern.

The value of patterned paper with distinct design is generally appreciated for rooms of considerable size, and, whilst ornamental treatment on a large scale increases the important appearance, well-drawn and refined detail will add still further to the apparent size. For small rooms, patterns of proportionately small scale should be adopted, and vivid contrasts avoided. Undefined pattern will assist in giving the illusion of space, where this is restricted.

Contrasts make a Room appear lighter.

Where there is insufficient light, sharp contrasts will help to give the impression of light by assisting the eyes to realise form and colour. This principle should be applied not only to decorative work, but to floor covering, upholstery and furniture.

THE STAIRCASE

The frequent use of stairways and the fact that they are rarely wide enough to prevent walls being easily marked should be taken into account when staircase papers are chosen.

Fig. 2.—How to Treat an Angle with a Doorway.
An attractive arrangement, panelled with a stiling border.

Fig. 3.—Method of using a Leather Paper decorated with "Stud" Border.
Double width is used vertically, forming effective panels. Hand-finished leather papers representing hide and skins of various kinds, as well as imitations of the hand-tooled patterns of antique leather hangings, are particularly suitable.

Fig. 4.—A Typical Example of Panelling and Appliqué used for a Staircase.

Fig. 5.—A Panel of Landscape Paper of this Type might be used for One Wall of a Hall only.

Fig. 6.—A Simple Panelling Scheme for use in a Bedroom. This attractive arrangement gives a feeling of repose and peacefulness.

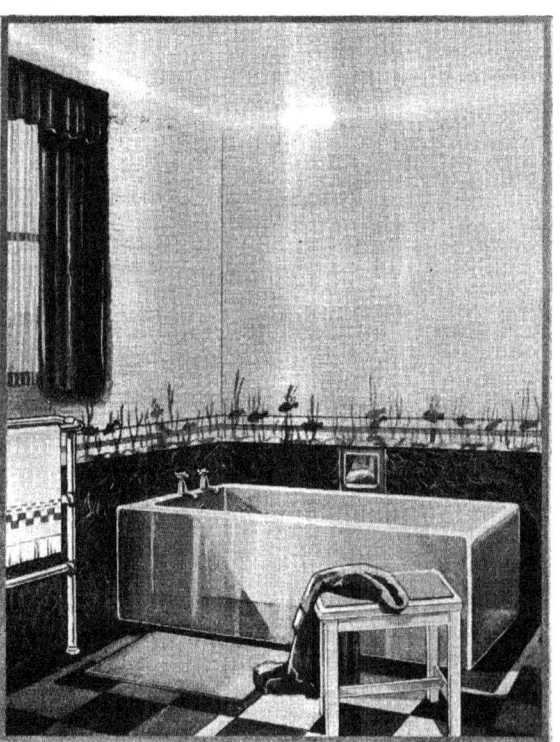

Fig. 7.—An Example of Successful Bathroom Treatment. Showing the use of a frieze which blends into the paper and varnished marble paper dado.

RIGHT AND WRONG WAYS OF USING WALLPAPER

Avoid Plain Papers in Delicate Tints.

Quite plain papers in delicate tints should be avoided unless there is a dado of sufficient height to take the wear. For dado decoration a number of excellent designs are executed in relief material, some completely decorated, others which after hanging are painted and varnished or enamelled, which gives a surface of great durability.

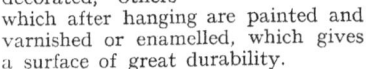
Showing a bedroom with heavily patterned wallpaper, patterned bedspread, patterned curtains and patterned rugs. Compare with Fig. 8B.

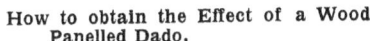
This shows the same bedroom and the same furniture, but having plain painted or distempered walls and plain bedspread. Patterned rugs and curtains only.

How to obtain the Effect of a Wood Panelled Dado.

The effect of a wood panelled dado can be obtained either by the use of an embossed paper having the grain of wood and the panels formed with Lincrusta bordering or by panelling completed in Lincrusta. By either of these methods a series of panels can be formed to fit exactly into the wall spaces and stained to any tint desired.

There are a number of wallpapers designed particularly for staircase walls, some of the best do not show to advantage in pattern books, and should be seen, therefore, in the roll, if possible, before decision is made.

Staircase Walls.

For staircase walls, patterns with a slightly horizontal emphasis will be found pleasant, especially if there are several flights of stairs, the horizontal lines apparently lessening the height and making progress upward seem less arduous, whereas patterns having vertical emphasis have the opposite effect, increasing the apparent height and consequent labour in the ascent.

PICTURE RAILS

A rail from which pictures can be hung is often fixed at the level of the top of the door. This is a good division of the wall if the ceiling is 9 feet or less. If the room is higher, a rail at door-head level will seem to be rather low and will need to be raised by 6 or 8 inches so that a pleasant space shall be between door-head and rail.

There is no actual need for a picture rail so far as decorative effect is concerned, and wallpaper can be well hung up to the cornice or ceiling. If a division is desired, but for some reason a rail or moulding cannot be fixed, a border can take the place.

With unpatterned papers, borders are frequently used below the picture rail and as a means of emphasising colour are very effective.

The Frieze.

Above the picture rail the space is usually termed the "frieze." Here a tint of the colour of the paper below but slightly lighter looks well with the ceiling a shade lighter still of the same colour.

From floor to ceiling the relations of the tints can be from darkest at the skirting to lightest on the ceiling.

THE ENTRANCE HALL

It is probably the intention of everyone who has to decorate an entrance hall that it shall give a cheerful and hospitable impression at first sight. To secure this, floor space, height and light must be carefully considered.

What to do if Light is Poor.

If light is poor, the walls must not be covered with any paper that will absorb what little light there is. Usually there is much woodwork in halls—the staircase, several doors, skirtings, etc.—which in superficial area is sometimes equal to the wall space.

If the woodwork is stained and polished it cannot have much light-reflecting value, but if painted it can, of course, be in a light and bright colour. If a bright colour is desired, it must be related to the wallpaper, floor covering and stair carpet, otherwise the most carefully chosen wallpaper will lack its intended effect.

A hall can be decorated with more features which arrest attention than rooms in which one remains for more lengthy periods. Appliqué motifs are very serviceable for this purpose and can be obtained for using in several different positions.

If woodwork is in oak or similar warm tones, cream or yellow walls look well. The darker the woodwork the stronger and purer the colour can be.

An Effective Colour Scheme for Hall and Staircase.

An unusual but successful scheme for a hall and staircase can be done in the following manner. Walls bright warm yellow, woodwork in a burnt orange colour with newel posts and handrail in polished black. The rise and tread of the staircase steps can be stained to the shade of dark oak; with this a deep rich blue or dark green carpet would be very pleasing.

DINING-ROOMS

There is good reason for handsome wall treatment for dining-rooms on account of the excellent contrast which can thus be given to the dining-table display of beautiful linen, glass and silver, as well as the customary cut flowers which are made such an attractive feature.

Types of Wallpaper.

Certain types, such as hand-finished leather papers representing hide and skins of various kinds as well as imitations of the hand-tooled patterns of antique leather hangings are particularly suitable. There are also a number of embossed effects in richly varied colours touched with gold which are of great decorative value.

Tapestry and Oak Panelling.

Tapestry and oak panelling are traditionally associated with dining-rooms, and both of these methods of decoration have their

Fig. 9.—How to obtain a Low Ceiling Effect.
Horizontal panels placed above a dado make a ceiling seem lower and can often be used with advantage in a tall room.

Fig. 10.—How to obtain Effect of Height.
Narrow panels on the walls give the effect of height.

counterparts in modern homes. Walls can be panelled with Lincrusta, which is hung like wallpaper and can be adapted to fit any wall space stained to match any shade of oak.

Reproductions of Antique Panelling.

There are excellent reproductions of antique panelling made in Lincrusta both of Tudor carving and simpler Jacobean examples. Tapestry patterned papers can be hung all over the walls or enclosed in panels formed with stiling borders, which can be obtained in several different widths to suit rooms of different sizes.

Dining-room Frieze and Ceiling.

The freize and ceiling of the dining-room should receive consideration, for not only is this in accordance with historical custom, but there is an abundance of excellent material made in wallpaper suitable for the purpose, notably rough cast papers and plaster effects produced by embossing, also ceiling designs in relief—which can be coloured after being hung to suit the wall decoration.

LOUNGE, SITTING-ROOM, DRAWING-ROOM

These designations indicate slight differences in the character of rooms, which are also termed "reception rooms."

Suitable decoration for such rooms depends on their most frequent use, whether for formal or informal purposes or for general usage including both purposes.

Quality.

It may be helpful to point out that the quality of the wallpaper should be in accordance with the furniture and other contents, so that a sense of unity should prevail. Papers which are slightly embossed and almost plain in colour look well in small rooms, for larger rooms heavier embossing and more colours introduced blended and interwoven; some of these papers are touched with gold.

By using a stile over plain or semi-plain papers, panels can be formed. This is a simple method of giving a room an important appearance. Additional interest and colour can be added by appliqué motifs which are made suitable for every type of room and for almost every position where they can be used effectively.

Colour.

The importance of colour cannot be over-emphasised, and its distribution throughout the room so that a well-balanced relationship exists between floor covering, upholstery, curtains and walls is by no means easily accomplished even by the most experienced.

Colours approaching prismatic purity can only be used on small areas in decoration, otherwise their value is lost and eye strain results instead of the pleasurable effect intended.

The colour which it is intended shall dominate should appear in its purest tint in small areas only of the wallpaper design, border stiling or appliqué portion in curtains and motif. It can be larger in cushions. Lighter and darker shades of the same colour throughout the room will give support and a rich appearance. The general colour of the walls should be in harmony or gentle contrast with the dominating tint.

An Example.

As an example, if orange is chosen as the dominating colour its brightest tint can be in cushions, curtains, wall-

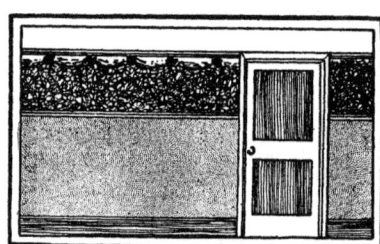

*Fig. 11.—*Two more Methods of obtaining Height Effects.
Top.—Vertical lines to increase effect of height. Bottom.—Horizontal treatment to lessen effect of height. Both these effects would be quite easily obtainable with wallpaper.

paper border or small portions of the pattern; deeper shades of the same colour in the carpet, lighter shades also in the wallpaper and well distributed throughout the room. The general effect of the walls can be a dull gold. To give rest to the scheme black should be introduced. Deep blue is a valuable contrast for orange and can be introduced in vases or pottery, but is needed only on small areas. The ceiling should be in a lighter tint of the wall colour.

Panelling.

Panelling either by mouldings or by borderings is a valuable decorative device. A well-arranged scheme of panels will give arresting character to an otherwise unimportant room and will also be of considerable assistance in producing the effect of unity where there are structural features which break walls unpleasantly.

Angle Pieces, Centre Pieces, etc.

Plain panels can be enriched by the use of appliqué ornaments, which are made in great variety of types and colourings. There are angle pieces and centre pieces of less formal types, such as sprays and branches, there are pendants for use on stiles, also crowns and base ornaments.

By means of these features colour can be introduced where desired and interest concentrated; their use also lessens the formal appearance which a screen of plain panels may impress. In large rooms it is possible to arrange furniture or pictures so that they occupy the centre or other definite positions in relation to panels. In a bedroom the bedstead can be enclosed in a panel, the wardrobe and dressing table up against a wall can be similarly surrounded.

The surround to panels should be considered in relation to the size of the "field" of the panel.

Simplest Method of Panelling.

The simplest method of panelling is to use a "stile" or "stiling border," which is applied after the wallpaper has been hung.

Stilings are made in several widths, 5 inches, 7 inches and 10 inches being the most popular. The greater part of the width is usually plain or stippled; both edges are emphasised either with lines of colour or elaborated to form a border. A stile of 10 inches width can be divided through the centre and hung around the room below the picture rail or cornice above the skirting. Then the same can be done vertically at the four corners, the result being that four large panels are formed, one on each wall. These may be divided vertically.

Hanging the Stile.

Start by hanging the stile at the chimney-breast at both the internal and external angles. The opposite wall can be divided in the same proportions, but the plain centre of the stile should be reduced to half its width so that there is equal plain space surrounding each panel.

Panelling in Large Rooms.

In large rooms the 10-inch stile can be used full width instead of half width. The narrower stiles can be used for smaller rooms. If a stile is to be used full width one edge should be trimmed off except where it is used to divide panels on the same wall surface. Decorated edges should never meet at angles.

The wall decoration schemes shown in Figs 4, 5, 6 and 7 are based on designs by the well-known firm of Arthur Sanderson & Sons Ltd.

How to Make a Needlework Cabinet Screen

This is a very handy cabinet for needlework, because, in addition to holding without confusion quite a quantity and variety of articles, its shape allows it to be stood away, where it will occupy a minimum of space. As a fire-screen, in summer, it is admirable.

Materials.

One board of ¼-inch oak (or oak-ply) 6 × 2 feet will make the sides and the inside trays, and one board of ½-inch oak 6 feet × 6 inches will make the tops and bottoms of the trays, and the rails for the legs. A few feet of quarter-round glueing-block strips are required, in addition to the two pairs of legs, and some veneer " plant carvings " for ornamentation of the front face.

Note that legs of this Jacobean style, or the " cabriole " shape which is usually associated with mahogany articles, are sold in pairs for correct balance of shape.

As the cabinet is fairly plain on the flat front surface, it is desirable to select a nicely grained wood, in addition to having a small amount of added ornament.

Make Both Halves in One.

Both for convenience in making, and so that the two halves will close properly, the body of the cabinet is made as one box, which is then cut in halves (Fig. 3). Two squares of the ¼-inch wood are cut carefully to 21½ × 22½ inches. Two strips of the same for the upright sides are cut 22½ × 4½ inches. The top and the bottom, for strength, are of the ½-inch wood. The thinner pieces are carefully mitred at the edges, so that the joints coincide with the angles, and are consequently invisible, but the tops and bottoms are fixed, for strength, flush inside the sides.

Mitreing Edges.

This is done by carefully marking a line on the back surface of the wood, preferably with a gauge, at ¼ inch from the edges. With a small sharp plane chamfer off the wood between the two lines, and the edges will then fit together as the section shown in Fig. 4. If any hesitation is felt at attempting this perhaps advanced joint, ordinary lapped joints should be made, to show on the narrow sides of the box. In this case ply should not be used, owing to the layers which would make the joints noticeable. The parts of the box are fixed together with thin, hot glue and fine panel pins, which are punched home just below the surface, as is usual in this kind of work (see Fig. 5.).

Separating the Boxes.

Marking a straight line in the centre

Fig. 2.—How the Cabinet opens. Showing how a large number of articles can be accommodated in orderly fashion.

of all four edges of the box, this line is cut with a sharp tenon saw (Fig. 3), and then the inside corners are strengthened with the aid of pieces of the glueing strip, as in Fig. 6. The reason for fixing this strip in sections, instead of just glueing in a long strip for each angle, is that by this method each piece can be rubbed to and fro into position—which process, as is well known, greatly increases the stickiness, and when dry, the strength, of the glue.

When these strips are all set perfectly hard and dry, glass-paper the cut edges of the separated halves (Fig. 7). In doing this do not do more than is essential, and check the work repeatedly by laying the two halves together, so as to ensure a perfect fit.

Veneer Ornaments.

At this stage it will be convenient to fix the veneer ornaments. These should first be glass-papered smooth, and the edges chamfered down in the same operation (Fig. 8), so that they do not stand up too sharply. They can then be glued into place. Glue is applied to the under-surface of the

Fig. 1.—The completed Needlework Cabinet described in this article.
It will be seen that it occupies the minimum of space when out of use. It can be used as an admirable fire-screen in the summer.

HOW TO MAKE A NEEDLEWORK CABINET SCREEN

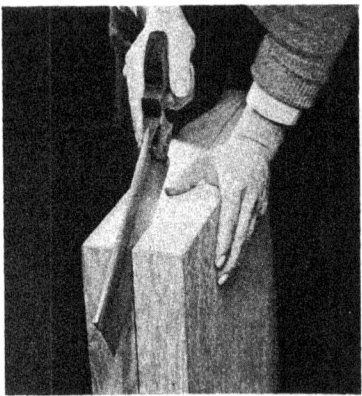

Fig. 3.—The Box is made in one and then sawn in half.

The body of the cabinet is made as one box, so that the two halves will close properly.

Fig. 4.—A section of the Mitred Angle of the Box.

The sharp arris is taken off with glass-paper and produces an invisible rounded joint. If this joint is felt to be too difficult, ordinary lapped joints should be made, to show on the narrow sides of the box. In this case do not use plywood.

Fig. 5.—Fine Panel Pins are used to join the Sides of the Box.

A pointed punch will drive the heads just below the surface.

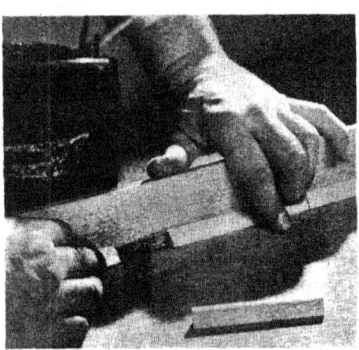

Fig. 6.—Strengthen the Insides of the Box with Glued Blocks.

Each short piece is worked to and fro into position so as to increase adhesion of the glue.

Fig. 7.—Glass-paper the Cut Edges of the Box carefully.

Test the two halves together frequently, so as to ensure retaining a close fit.

Fig. 8.—Glass-papering the Plant Carvings.

The edges should be slightly chamfered down so that they do not stand up too sharply.

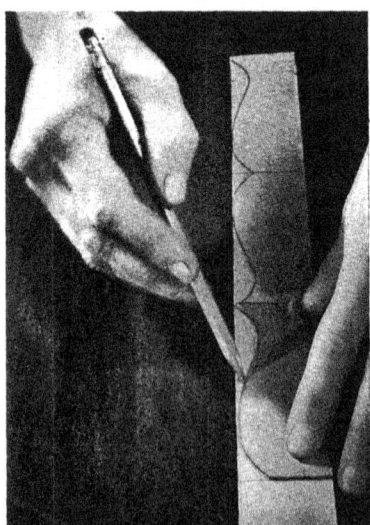

Fig. 9.—A Cardboard Template is used to Mark the Pattern for the Top Rail.

Fig. 10.—The Legs and Rails are Mortised together and strengthened with Glue Blocks.

Fig. 11.—When completed, the Stand is Sawn Apart at the Centre at Each End.

58

HOW TO MAKE A NEEDLEWORK CABINET SCREEN

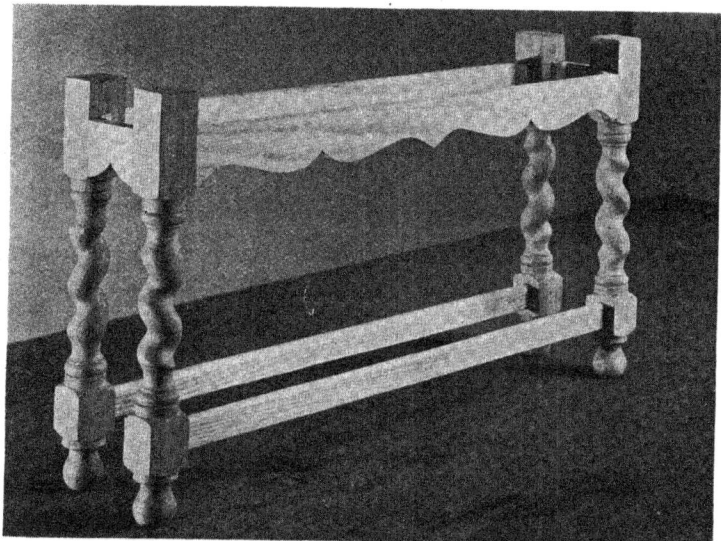

Fig. 12.—Here we see the Stand before the Two Halves are Separated. By constructing the stand in one piece, it is easier to get the legs to stand true.

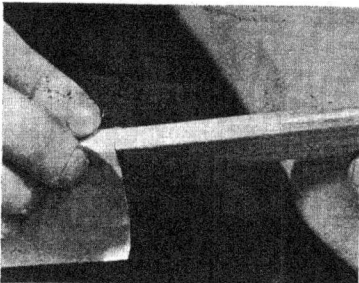

Fig. 13.—The Rounded Top Edge is obtained by Planing Off the Angles and then Rounding with Glass-paper.

Fig. 14.—Glue in Strips at the Long Sides of the Box to take the Screws of the Hinges and Fastenings.

Fig. 15.—When the Tops of the Legs have been Cut Off and Planed Level with the Rails, they are fixed to the Halves of the Box with Glue and Blocks.

veneer, which is then pressed down into place, and kept there by a heavy flat weight. A piece of paper should be kept between weight and paper in case glue oozes out.

Stand is also Built in One Piece.

The rails are mortised into the legs, with the aid of glue, in the usual way. The bottom rail, $\frac{1}{2} \times 1$ inch, has its top surface rounded, by first planing off the angles, and then by the use of glass-paper (see Fig. 13). The top rails are cut from plain $\frac{1}{2} \times 1\frac{1}{2}$ inch strips and the ornament is introduced by the following method:—

First divide the space between the legs (length of rail) into four equal parts. Then draw the curve shown in Fig. 9 (or any other to fancy) in one part, noting that one point of the curve comes to the bottom of the rail. Then cut a card template to the curve, and with this mark the other three sections, reversing the template for alternate sections. Cut the rail with a fret- or a bow-saw. The whole stand is put together, as the box was, in one piece, but is strengthened with glue blocks and allowed to set hard before cutting apart (see Figs. 11 and 12).

Hinge Strips.

As the wood of which the box is built is not of itself strong enough to take the strain of the hinges, etc., it is advisable here to fix strips to thicken the edges of the long sides, as in Fig. 14. Fix these with glue flush with the edges.

Fixing Box to Legs.

The best way to do this is temporarily to reassemble and tie the halves of the box and of the stand together with strong twine. Turning both upside down, the stand can then be easily glued to the underside of the box, inserting at the same time a number of glue-blocks (Fig. 15). When these have set hard, and the outer edges of the box have been slightly rounded off with glass-paper, the outside of the box is complete except for French polishing (see page 33).

Tray Strips.

The trays inside the box are formed of simple flat strips of the $\frac{1}{4}$-inch wood. The front edges are rounded, but the back edges are chamfered. The lower strips are chamfered as in Fig. 17, and the same illustration shows how the ends should be cut to make a tight fit against the inside of the box and the hinge-strips when inserted, as in the previous photograph No. 16. The chamfer thus fits on the bottom, but in the case of the upper trays the chamfer is planed at the reverse angle to be glued against the wall of the cabinet. It may be found advisable to glue in a small strip or two as an extra support for the tray.

HOW TO MAKE A NEEDLEWORK CABINET SCREEN

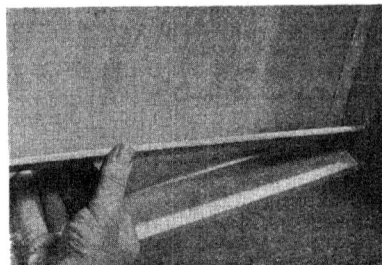

Fig. 16.—How the Tray Strips are put in.
The method of cutting the ends to give an exact fit is shown in Fig. 17.

Fig. 17.—The Front Edge of the Tray Strips is Rounded and the Back Edge Chamfered.
The ends are cut so as to fit the box.

for holding cotton-reels and other similar oddments.

Bag Strips.

Further strips are glued in at this stage on which to fix the bags. It will be noticed that these are staggered, so that the fulness of each bag has the full depth of the cabinet to accommodate it. In this way articles in process of making are not squeezed up when the cabinet is closed. The bags are made of printed linen or cretonne, with a fair amount of fulness at the fronts, which is taken up with elastic. The bags are fixed to the box, when the latter has been polished, by means of small screws with washers under their heads.

Reference to Fig. 2 will show how very convenient are these simple trays

MAKING A MANTELPIECE

MANY mantelpieces fitted about twenty years ago, although sound, solid and made of excellent materials, were decorated with innumerable dust-catching brackets, ornamented profusely with raised festoons of flowers and fruit, and each provided with a mirror that has probably grown spotty and corroded. Consequently it may be decided to replace it with a more modern one.

The first thing to do is to remove the old mantelpiece. By forcing the tip of a packing-case opener between the woodwork and the wall it can be loosened in its moorings and lifted out of position. It will probably be found that it is only held to the wall by four ordinary nails.

Erecting the New Mantelpiece.

First, some long lengths of wood, 2 × 2 inches in section, should be obtained. These are cut into twelve strips and fitted as shown in the first diagram. As will be seen, the pieces are braced together by means of a dozen notched joints and six halved joints, while each individual piece is perforated with two countersunk holes, through which long nails are driven into the bricks of the wall. When this skeleton is finished, it will hold as firm as a rock.

To avoid the trouble of repairing

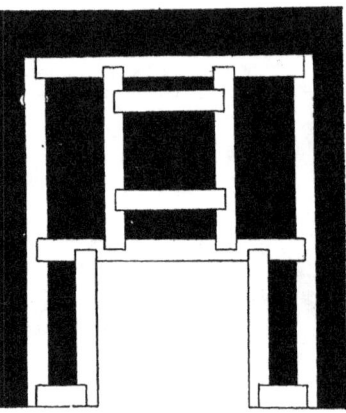

Fig. 1.—Showing the Skeleton Frame fixed to the Wall.

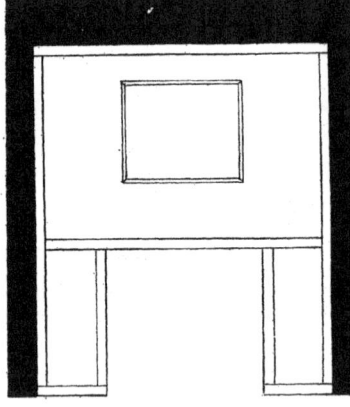

Fig. 2.—The New Mantelpiece fixed to the Skeleton Frame.

the walls it is a good idea to make the new mantelpiece exactly cover the space occupied by the old one.

Covering the Skeleton Frame with Plywood.

The next step is to obtain sufficient plywood to cover the skeleton frame. Material, ¼ inch in thickness, serves very well for the purpose. As it will probably not be possible to obtain it large enough to cover the whole area in one piece, the large upper panel should be fixed in one section and the two small lower panels fitted separately. They are nailed to the skeleton by means of 1-inch panel pins, which go through the plywood readily and without causing splits.

After that, some laths, 1 inch wide and ¼ inch thick, should be fixed all round the edge of the plywood, as shown in the second diagram. This provides a neat finish and serves to hide the places where the pieces of plywood are joined together.

Fitting the Mirror.

A mirror is now fitted centrally on the large panel. When the piece of glass is obtained, its position should be marked out on the wood and some very narrow picture-frame moulding, without a trace of pattern, screwed on to hold the glass.

Naturally, the screws require more support than could be afforded by a thin sheet of plywood, and that is why the two horizontal and two vertical short pieces of 2 × 2 in. are fixed in the centre of the skeleton. They serve to hold the mirror firmly.

Very little now remains. Nails and screws are forced below the surface of the wood, either by the aid of a punch or a screw-driver, the heads covered over with plastic wood and the entire erection given a thorough sandpapering.

Enamelling the New Mantelpiece.

Lastly, the new mantelpiece should be given three coats of colour, the last one being a good enamel. For the main surfaces, a shade of enamel coming between dove and oyster-grey might be chosen, while the raised edges can be done in the same colour, but of a slightly darker tint. The edge of the mirror is given two coats of jade enamel.

Replacing a Gramophone Spring

THE clockwork gramophone motor is still most efficient as a driver for the turntable, even when a pick-up is being used instead of the old-fashioned soundbox.

When the spring breaks no time should be lost in removing the motor-board and placing it face downwards on an empty box covered with a duster. This leaves the motor ready to dissemble without scratching the motor-board or spreading grease all over the table.

Look for Washers.

Take care to note the presence of all thin metal washers when taking the screws out, for these have been placed there to perfect the bearings and make the motor silent. Owing to the excess of grease, these washers are often hidden and lost during dismantling. If it is likely that some time will elapse before the new spring can be procured, it is worth while to put the motor together again so that nothing will be lost during the period of waiting.

New Spring must be of Correct Size.

Having found which of the two barrels has the broken spring, mark the cover and the barrel with a file, in order that it can be replaced in exactly the same position later on. Then remove the cover (which may or may not be screwed) and examine the spring. Even if it is broken quite near to one of the ends, it is hardly worth while to tinker with it and make fresh holes. Send the barrel with spring still inside it to a shop where springs are obtainable, and the salesman there will see to it that you get a replacement of similar length and width. Over-long springs fill the barrel, and so prevent full-time running, which is a bad fault in a motor. Over-wide springs graze against the cover and give rise to irregular bumping as the motor runs down.

When the new spring arrives try to realise that much energy lies held by the wire round the circumference and that care must be taken to avoid accidents at this stage.

Removing the Old Spring.

Examine the broken spring and see whether it lies curling clockwise or anti-clockwise in the barrel. Covering the left hand with a piece of thick rag, hold the

Fig. 1.—Method of Removing Spring Barrel from a Single Spring Motor.

First make sure that the spring is fully unwound. Then release the spring clip, withdraw the main spindle and the barrel can be easily detached.

barrel in the fingers and place another rag over the spring. Then grip the

Fig. 2.—Method of Removing Spring Barrels from a Double Spring Motor.

First release the four screws in the motor bottom plate. Then remove bottom plate (see Fig. 5).

centre with a pair of strong pliers and pull steadily without letting go of

Fig. 3.—Withdrawing the Spring from the Barrel.

The barrel should be covered with a large rag before gripping the centre of the spring with a pair of pliers. Now pull steadily until the whole of the spring is out. On no account must either the pliers or the barrel be released while this is being done (see also Fig. 6).

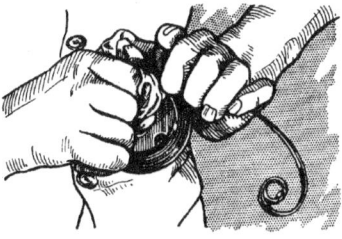

Fig. 4.—Another Method of Removing the Spring from the Barrel.

This method is rather slower than that shown in Figs. 3 and 6. The spring is uncoiled from the barrel, starting from the centre. When the spring is out clean the barrel thoroughly, softening any hardened graphite with paraffin oil.

the pliers until the whole spring has quietly left the barrel (Figs. 3 and 6).

Clean the barrel thoroughly, softening any hardened graphite with paraffin oil. Spread motor grease over the bottom of the barrel, and all is then ready to insert the new spring.

The New Spring—Using a Special Spring Clip.

If possible, borrow a special spring clip and attach it to the new spring, carefully pushing its binding wire to the edge. As soon as the clip is holding every turn of the spring securely, cut the binding wire. The spring can then be lowered into the barrel so that its outer end engages the hook in the side of the barrel. The clip is then gently released and the spring is snugly in position. With a piece of wood in contact with the edge of the spring, carefully tap it down to the bottom of the barrel in every part. Then replace the axle and see if the inner end of the spring is so shaped as to grip it readily. If not, adjust it with a screwdriver pushed in between the coils. Then replace the well-greased cover and the barrel is ready for assembly in the motor.

What to do if a Special Clip is not available.

Should the special clip not be available, place the spring on a piece of sacking on the floor. With one foot on the spring, cut the binding wire and let the spring open up as gradually as possible. After wiping any dirt from the spring, hook its outer end in position (holding the barrel in the left hand) and feed the whole length into the barrel gradually, taking care that at no time is the spring allowed to fly out. If a large vice is at hand, place the barrel in it, as this allows both hands to be free for feeding the spring into the barrel.

Re-winding the Motor after inserting New Spring.

When first rewinding the motor, listen for adjustments of the springs inside. Should the end slip off the axle it will be heard to do so several times and the barrel must be opened up. One big and noisy adjustment is sometimes heard, and this is due to the spring engaging with the barrel

HOW TO REPLACE A GRAMOPHONE SPRING

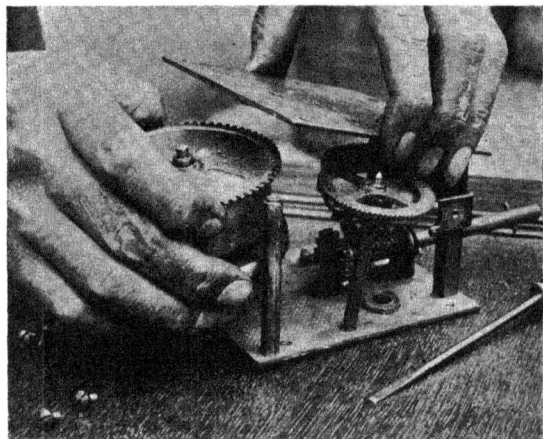

Fig. 5.—After taking off the Bottom Plate, as shown in Fig. 2, the Spring Barrel can be removed.

Fig. 6.—Grip the Centre of the Spring with Round-nosed Pliers (see also Fig. 3).
The rag is not shown covering the spring, for the sake of clearness.

Fig. 7.—Fitting the New Spring into the Barrel.
Wipe the barrel first to prevent it slipping out of the grasp. Grip firmly in the left hand. Hold the spring in the right hand and carefully hook on to the peg of the barrel.

Fig. 8.—Keep a Firm Grip on the Spring when fitting it into the Barrel.
It can then easily be wound into the barrel. Take care that at no time is the spring allowed to fly out.

hook, which it probably "jumped" when first inserted. As soon as the springs are partly wound, tighten all pillar screws, because the main load falls on them, and, if not properly tightened, the framework twists and makes the running noisy.

Should the winding be noisy, the thin metal washers have probably been forgotten, and these must be found and replaced.

Buy a Powerful Motor.

A gramophone motor cannot be too powerful, because the governing device will keep it to its proper speed, but the addition of extra springs will enable it to run for much longer without the exertion of re-winding. The silence of a good multi-spring motor can literally be felt rather than heard. By holding the motor in one hand any vibration period can be distinctly traced, and the best motor is that which lies quietly without any signs of vibration whatever. Correct adjustment of all the bearings can reduce vibration enormously, and insulating the motor from the board by means of rubber washers inside the screw-holes as well as above and below them, prevents the residual vibration acting on the casework and making it into an unwanted amplifier.

Refinements to Look For.

An easily removable aluminium casting makes the modern motor dust and shaving proof, and when the winding handle is being operated a cam works a little pumping device which distributes oil to all the necessary parts (except the barrel springs). Moreover, the oil which settles at the bottom of the casing is collected in a "sump" ready for re-circulation, thus rendering it unnecessary to oil-up more than once a year. These motors also have metal platforms which give a first-class finish to any cabinet work which the amateur has made. All that has to be done is to cut out a hole in the old motor-board and lay the body of the motor into it. The metal platform can then be screwed down without any adjustment to the working parts, speed regulator or automatic brake.

How to Stop "Bumping."

When, more especially in cold weather, the gramophone motor emits a startling "bump" while the record is playing, the noise is due to the fact that one of the springs has been stationary for several turns of the axle, whereas both springs ought to run gradually down together. This leaves one spring to do all the work until suddenly the other one is able to overcome the friction which is holding it back. The jump forward of the coils jerks the whole motor badly and the noise can be heard all over the room.

Clotted graphitic grease becomes as hard as metal after a time and has sufficient substance to hold the spring back. The remedy is to remove the springs and scrape away the graphite, and to use none in lubricating the barrel afterwards. Occasionally, however, it is the spring itself which is at fault. If the hole at the ends of the spring is not centrally cut the edge of the spring may scrape heavily on the top or bottom of the barrel as soon as tension is applied by winding.

Making Old Furniture Look Like New

In the average home there are many pieces of furniture which are not wanted because they do not fit in with the others surrounding them. Accordingly, they are pushed aside in boxrooms and attics, where they soon fall into decay. Simultaneously with this process, it often happens that a suite is wanted for a boy's bedroom, a study or, perhaps, a smoking den. Obviously the economic thing to do is to collect together the odd pieces, to repair whatever defects they may possess, and to give them all a coat of enamel paint, which transforms them from a set of shabby oddments into an attractive suite, capable of adorning any but the very best rooms of the house.

Repairing Small Defects.

When such an assembly of furniture has been brought together the first step is to go over the pieces carefully and to note what repairs are needed. Hinges on wardrobe doors may need tightening, chair-legs may have to be strengthened by fixing angle-brackets on the underside, drawers are perhaps suffering from missing handles which require replacing, the carcasses of chests and cupboards may need pinning here and there, castors on chair-legs are, as likely as not, in a condition that calls for some skilful manipulation, and in a dozen other instances the glue-pot will be needed to stick something that has cracked or fallen apart. None of the jobs will be of much magnitude, but, when they have been attended to, the pieces of furniture will be as strong again as they were on the day of purchase.

Modernising Out-of-date Furniture.

Before putting away the tools, it is advisable to survey the pieces critically to see if any of them need bringing into line with modern shapes and patterns.

Dealing with Wardrobe Cornices.

For instance, the cornice of a wardrobe may be suffering from an excess of florid Victorian curves. Usually, this ornamentation is merely tacked on to the body-part and can be removed by means of a screwdriver. In its place a simple upstanding edge of plain wood can be provided, or the wardrobe may even be left without any embellishment at all.

On such pieces of furniture as cupboards or dressing-tables there may be trivial festoons of raised Adams work or crude panels of machine-made carving. If these offend the eye, strip them off or cover them up with plain panels of wood, the edges of which have been simply mitred. In several other ways it will be easy to transform an article that is obviously old fashioned into one that is pleasingly up to date.

Smoothing the Surfaces.

When all these preliminaries have been attended to, the next thing will be to take some medium grade of glass-paper and rub all the surfaces, finishing off the work with paper of a much finer grade. This rubbing is done not only to smooth the surfaces, and to take out bruises or other imperfections, but also to get rid of whatever coating was originally applied.

Having done this, the furniture is carefully dusted in order to remove all the powder formed by the rubbing. After that, the painting is begun.

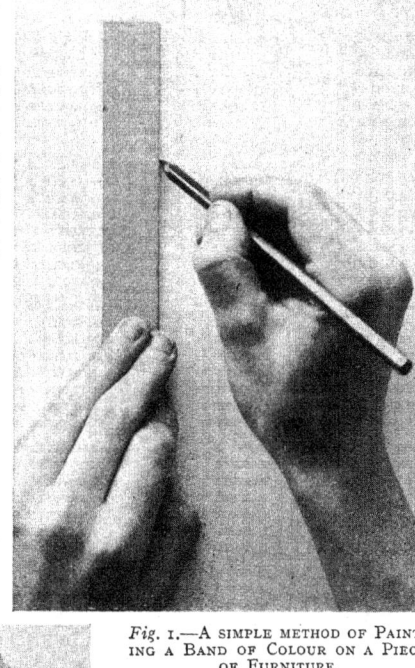

Fig. 1.—A simple method of Painting a Band of Colour on a Piece of Furniture.

First cut a lath equal to the length and width of the required band. Then place the lath where the band is required and mark with a pencil all round it.

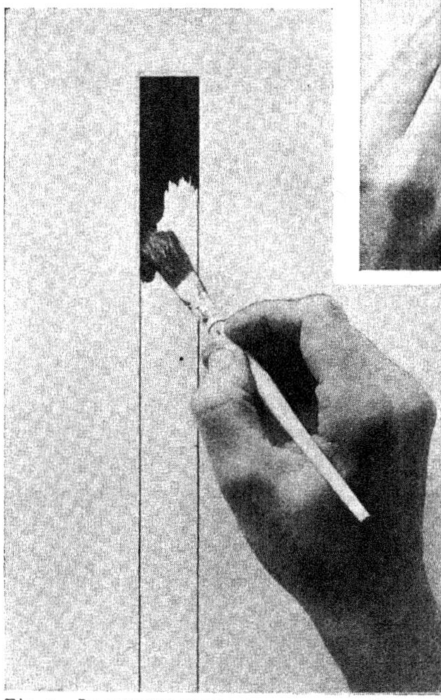

Fig. 2.—It is then easy to fill in the Colour by using the Pencil Lines as a Guide.

Choosing the Paint.

In selecting the paint it is inadvisable to choose a sombre colour, and even white is not as pleasing as might be supposed. Furniture, unlike the doors, windows and other woodwork in a room, will look best when its colour strikes a note of liveliness; it then serves to brighten up the surroundings. Of course, the colour must be chosen with due regard for the floor covering, the wallpaper, the curtains, etc.

Applying the Paint.

The painting is carried out in three coats, the first two are done in a flat paint or enamel, and the last in a high-gloss enamel. As it is not always possible to buy a flat paint which matches the glossy enamel that has been chosen for the final coat, it may be necessary to buy white flat paint and then tint it to suit the enamel.

The paint should be applied in thin coats, which are laid on as smoothly and as evenly as possible. Two brushes are generally needed, one about 2 inches wide for doing the large expanses, and another, much smaller, for going neatly into the angles and corners.

The flat paint will dry in a few hours, but a day at least should be allowed before a subsequent coat is put on. When the first and second applications have dried quite hard, it is advisable to take a clean piece of the finest grade of glass-paper and rub lightly over the surfaces. This will remove any raised points that may have formed or settled on the paint, and it will be the means of imparting a much smoother and a more glazed finish to the final coat of enamel.

Fig. 3.—How to make a Chest of Drawers look Attractive.

First give it a coat of biscuit-coloured enamel and then paint the handles and feet in pillar-box red. Line the edges of the drawers in the same colour and the result will look very attractive.

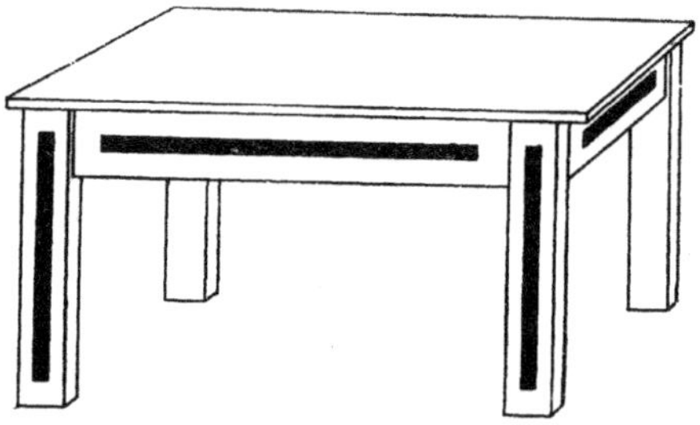

Fig. 4.—A Successful Method of Treating an Ordinary Wooden Table.

Quite an attractive appearance can be given by the addition of bars, painted in a second colour, as shown above.

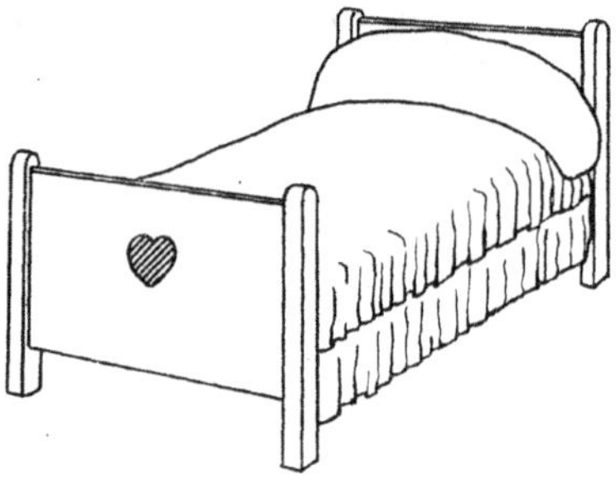

Fig. 5.—The appearance of a Wooden Bedstead can be greatly enhanced with a little Paint.

Enamelled in jade or bottle-green and with a heart-shaped ornamentation in heliotrope the result will be very pleasing.

The enamel will take two or three days to harden. In applying it, care must be taken to spread it evenly and without a great deal of brushing.

Ornamentation.

When a piece of furniture has been painted it may be thought that a small amount of ornamentation will improve its appearance. This is likely to be the case with large articles possessing considerable flat expanses. If it is decided to attempt anything in this nature, it is advisable to keep the amount of decoration to its smallest limits and only simple effects should be attempted.

How to deal with a Chest of Drawers.

For instance, a chest of drawers may have the face of each drawer outlined with a band of colour ½ inch wide, or the panel of a cupboard door may be given a similar band which runs down its longest dimension, but does not quite reach either end. Naturally,

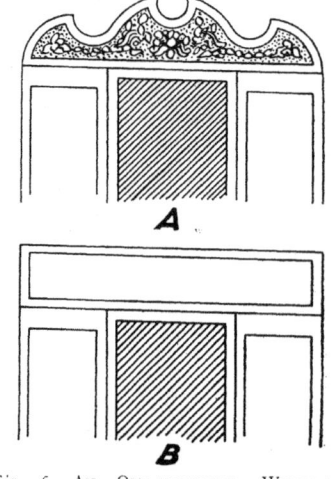

Fig. 6.—An Old-fashioned Wardrobe brought up-to-date.

Before starting to paint an old wardrobe, remove the florid ornament in A and fit something more suitable as in B.

the colour chosen for the band will be one that contrasts with that used for the groundwork.

How to Paint the Band.

In painting the band it is useless to trust to the eye or to do the work by freehand. One good plan is to trim up a thin lath which is exactly the same length and width as the band of colour is to be. The lath is then placed exactly where the band is to come and a pencil is run all round it. After that it is fairly easy to fill in the second colour by using the pencil lines as a guide.

Diamond, Heart and Circle Shapes.

Of course, it should not be forgotten that any desired shape may be cut out of tough paper and used as a stencil. A diamond, a heart, a circle, etc., may look very well in the centre of a panel. In employing a stencil it is imperative that both sides of the paper should be wiped free of all paint before being used a second time, or smears will be imparted to the ground paint.

PAINTING OR VARNISHING CREOSOTED WOOD

MANY householders, especially those who have purchased new houses, are often confronted with the difficulty of either re-painting or varnishing wood-work, both interior and exterior, which has been treated by the builders with creosote.

This material being a by-product of coal is associated with other chemicals of a destructive nature, hence, when treated wood-work has been painted or varnished the householder after a short time is surprised to find brown patches appearing on the surface of the paint, or that the varnished surface has become tacky or sticky.

Further, if the coated surfaces are allowed to remain, complete destruction takes place, ending more or less with the creosoted wood-work exposed.

Never apply Creosote to a Surface intended for Further Treatment.

Creosote is essentially a wood preservative and should never be applied to wood-work that is intended for further decorative treatment; its use is limited to fencing and all wood subjected to atmospheric conditions.

The Treatment of Creosoted Wood.

No outstanding application or method of a permanent nature can be advised but only of a temporary kind, which may last for from one to two years, but if the following method is employed a good or reasonable result may be expected.

First, well wash the creosoted wood-work with warm soda water, rinsing with plenty of cold water so as to remove all traces of soda, then allow to dry, follow with No. 1 glass-paper and well paper the work, smoothing all raised grain; wipe the surface with a piece of clean rag. Obtain from the local stores a quantity of **pure** shellac knotting and apply with a flat varnish brush freely over the surface and allow to dry, when it will now be noticed that the shellac solution has been absorbed by the wood.

A further free coat may be applied or until a shellac film appears. The work is now ready for the application of paint drying with a gloss, or which is intended for varnishing.

A Word of Warning.

Only pure shellac knotting with a margin of about 5 per cent. of rosin can be used, otherwise chemical action affects the rosin thereby rendering the shellac coating open to immediate destruction, after which the painted or varnished surface is affected. The object of applying a pure shellac solution is to form a protective film which will withstand any chemical action for a reasonable time.

Making Shellac Solution.

For those who prefer to make their own shellac solution the following should be used :—

1 gallon methylated spirit.
6 lb. finest orange shellac, or pure button shellac.

Or again,

3 lb. finest orange shellac,
3 lb. pure button shellac.

Painting a Front Door

Of all the parts of a house that require painting from time to time the front entrance door is generally the most prominent.

It welcomes the caller and speeds the parting guest, and, therefore, it has to stand a frequent and close inspection. Let us suppose that the time has come for repainting and that the householder has decided to tackle the job himself. How shall he proceed?

Getting Ready.

The first thing to do is to remove the door fittings: the knob, letter box cover, knocker, etc., and put them safely away. It is a great mistake to try to paint a door with these fittings in position, and in the majority of cases it is quite easy to remove them, the method of doing so being obvious on examination.

Preparing for Painting.

If the door has only been painted once and the surface is in good condition, entirely free from cracks, blisters or other defects, it may be safe to proceed without removing the old paint and varnish.

In that case the door should be dry dusted and then washed down with water, in which a little common soda has been dissolved. This must be thoroughly washed off with clean water and then the rubbing down can proceed.

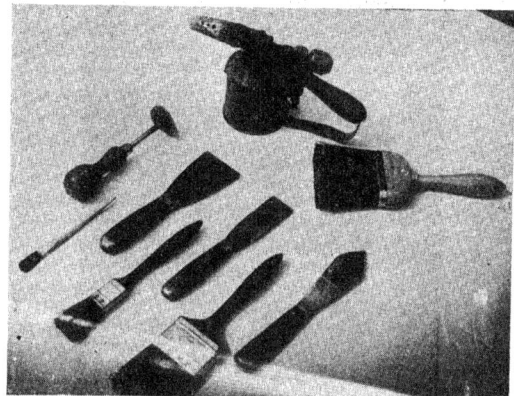

Fig. 1.—The Tools and Brushes required for Painting a Front Door.
These include a painter's scraper, a square-bladed putty knife, a shavehook, a burner and brushes of various sizes.

Rubbing Down.

This is best done with either pumice stone and water or waterproof sandpaper and water.

If pumice is used, two pieces will be required, one rather large piece rubbed first to a smooth face on a flat stone, and a smaller, shaped piece, which will be convenient for getting into the mouldings. If waterproof sandpaper is used, the same sheet will do for both level and curved surfaces, as the paper is quite pliable and will bend to fit the hollows and curves.

This rubbing down should be carefully done, keeping the parts under treatment well wetted, as the water acts as a lubricant to the abrasive. Special care should be taken to clean those parts of the panels immediately adjacent to the mouldings, as, owing to the shrinkage of the wood, ridges of old paint are sometimes found there.

It should be noted that the object of this rubbing down is not only to smooth the surface, but to kill the gloss on the old material, and thus provide a satisfactory base for the new paint. The rubbing being completed, the whole of the door should be swilled down to remove all traces of the sludge created.

Stopping Up.

If there are any open joints or other inequalities, these should now be stopped up. First brush a little paint into these places, allow this to dry, and then fill the openings with a putty made as described later and smooth off with the knife. When this is quite hard, sandpaper the whole surface of the door and dust off.

Removing Old Paint.

In the majority of cases, however, it is necessary, before repainting, to remove the old paint.

If there is any cracking or blistering apparent, or if the door has been repainted more than once without removal of the old paint, complete

Fig. 2.—The First Step in preparing the Surface for repainting.—Rubbing down with Pumice Stone.
Two pieces of pumice will be required, one rather large piece rubbed first to a smooth surface on a flat stone and a smaller shaped piece for getting into the mouldings. Keep the surface well wetted when using the stone.

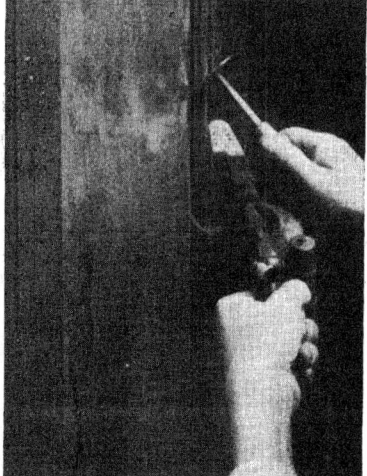

Fig. 3.—Burning off Old Paint from Moulding.
When dealing with curved or hollow mouldings and the fine recesses use the shavehook. The paint will probably need rather more softening than that on the broad parts. The mouldings should therefore be tackled first.

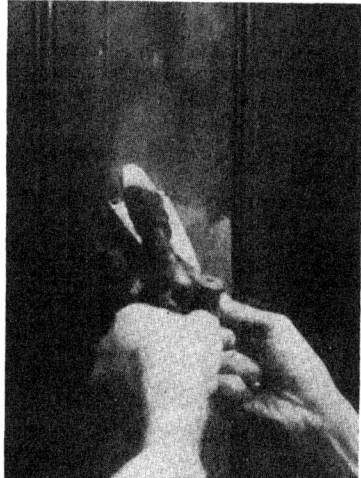

Fig. 4.—Burning off Old Paint from a Flat Surface.
The flame should be regulated to a strong jet, and brought close to the old paint, which will be crinkled and softened by the heat and then removed by the scraper. The burning should begin at the bottom, working upwards, as the heat of the flame rises.

removal will now be advisable, and, indeed, is generally quite necessary if a good result is to be obtained. The safe rule is: when in doubt, remove.

There are two alternative methods of doing this.

Burning Off.

This is done by means of the paraffin, petrol or benzol lamp. These lamps are exceedingly useful tools for many repair and other purposes, and if the householder possesses one, it can be used as the most inexpensive method.

The other tools required are a painter's scraper (cost 1s., or less), a square-bladed putty knife (cost the same, or less) and a shavehook (similar in cost) of the heart-shape pattern.

The scraper is for stripping the broad flat surfaces, the putty knife for narrower flats, and the shavehook for the curved and hollow mouldings and the fine recesses, which are called "quirks."

Using the Lamp.

The lamp having been lighted and the flame regulated to a strong jet, it is held in the left hand, and the appropriate stripping tool in the right.

The flame is brought close to the old paint, which will be crinkled and softened by the heat, and the tool is used for scraping off the softened material. The best way of disposing of the scrapings is to scrape the tool on the edge of a bucket containing water. Thus the formation of dry paint dust, both a nuisance and, if breathed, a danger, is avoided.

It is generally found that the paint in the hollows and mouldings needs rather more softening than that on the broad parts. Therefore it is best to tackle these places first. If that is done, the paint on the adjacent stile or panels protects those surfaces from the charring that otherwise would occur.

Start burning at the Bottom and work up.

Whatever part of the door is being treated, the burning should begin at the bottom, working upwards. The reason for this is that the heat of the flame rises, and, if work was proceeding downwards, the bared wood above would be charred. By working from the bottom, the paint above the spot upon which the flame is directly applied will be softening, but will remain as a shield against charring.

The precautions to be taken, then, are two. First, to remove completely all old paint. Second, to do this with as little scorching of the wood as possible.

Paint Removers.

If you do not, however, possess a lamp, and are unwilling to incur the cost (from 10s. 6d. upwards) of pur-

Fig. 5.—Applying the First Coat of Paint.

Note that the knots have been coated with shellac knotting to prevent the exudation of sap. The paint should be well brushed out. Start with the panels and fill them all in, then in turn the mouldings, the upright centre stile, the cross rails and the upright side stiles.

chasing one, it will be necessary to use one of the chemical paint removers, of which there are several makes on sale in small and large tins. A half-pint tin costs, usually, about 1s. to 1s. 6d.

These removers are rather more expensive in use than the lamp, but they are cleaner and also easier in

Fig. 6.—Crossing the Brush Strokes to ensure even distribution of Paint.

application. There are two types, the caustic and the spirituous, and, although the spirituous type is the dearer of the two, it is the safest.

Using Paint Removers.

It is best to use paint removers when the temperature is low (the evening is generally a good time), for they are apt to evaporate rather quickly in the presence of heat, and this may necessitate repeated applications.

The compound is applied in a fairly thick film and left for a short time to exert its effect. The softened paint is then removed by means of the tools previously described.

It is especially necessary to ensure that the rebate of the door casing and the edge of the door fitting into it when the door is closed should be well cleared of their accumulations of old paint. Otherwise, when the new paint is added the thickness is so great that, when the door is closed and then re-opened, there may result a tearing of the paint on the edge. This is most unsightly.

However carefully and completely the mixture of old paint and remover is removed, some trace of grease will probably be left behind. A sponge down with turpentine or benzol will remove this.

Brushes.

The tools required, in addition to those already mentioned, are a painter's duster (cost about 1s.) a large size flat paint brush (not less than 2½ inches wide), and a smaller brush (say 1 inch) of the same type.

After every time of use in paint, the two last mentioned should be well rinsed out in oil, washed with warm water and soap, and allowed to dry before being used again. It is of great importance that brushes should be kept scrupulously clean.

Priming.

The now bared surface of the door should next be well sandpapered until it is perfectly smooth. All knots require to be coated with shellac knotting to prevent the exudation of sap, and, even if the door is an old one, this is quite necessary. A small brush costing about a penny can be used for the purpose, and the coating of knotting must be evenly applied so as to extend slightly beyond the actual area of the knot.

The whole of the door should then be "primed," which is the word applied to the first coating of a new or bared surface.

Use White Lead Paint for Priming.

The best paint for priming, and indeed for many other purposes, is a genuine white lead paint, and the ready mixed form is the most convenient.

Assuming that a 2-lb. tin of this

ready-mixed paint has been purchased and opened, it will be found that part of the oil has risen to the top. This should be carefully poured off into another vessel and saved for later use.

Sufficient of the paint for the priming coat should be poured into the paint kettle, and a very little turpentine added. The object of this turpentine is to enable the priming coat partially to penetrate into the wood. The first or priming coat should then be applied.

Stopping.

When, and not until, the priming is thoroughly dry and hard, the next thing to be done is the stopping. This means the filling up of all cracks and other inequalities with hard stopping or putty. Ordinary glaziers' putty is sometimes used for this purpose, but it is not the best material, as it is too soft and oily. A mixture of stiff white lead and putty is better, and if this is too soft and sticky, a little dry whiting may be kneaded with it to give the right consistency. This mixture is forced into the orifices with the putty knife and left as smooth and level with the surrounding surface as possible. When it is thoroughly hard, the whole surface of the door again requires sandpapering. First damp it and then smooth it with a fine grade of waterproof sandpaper. Then sponge the door down with clean water and allow to dry off.

Second Coating.

So much of the white lead paint as was not used for priming may be used for this coat, adding, if too stiff, the oil previously poured off. This second coat and indeed all paint coats should be well brushed out, as thin coats are always better than thick ones. That does not mean that the paint itself must be too thin, but that it should be spread as evenly and as far as it will go. This coat, too, must have ample time to harden before we proceed further. Twenty-four hours is the minimum, and thirty-six would be better.

We have now brought up the burned-off door to the same stage where we left the process of simply smoothing old paint to receive new. The subsequent treatment is now the same in either case.

First Finishing Coat.

The further processes will depend upon the kind of finish required, and the number of possible treatments is legion. But assuming that a plain colour scheme with a glossy surface is required, it remains to choose the colour.

It is impossible in the space of one or even a dozen articles to describe the appropriate colour formulas for all the individual choices of our readers.

Fig. 7.—The Final "Laying-off" of the Paint.
This should be done very lightly, using the tip of the brush.

That being so, the most practicable course is to visit the paint stores and get the paints mixed to your requirements as to colour and shade.

White lead as the basis should be specified, and the first finishing coat should consist, so far as the medium is concerned, of linseed oil and genuine turpentine in the proportions of two-thirds oil to one-third turpentine by measure.

This coat should be carefully applied, and when dry and hard, must be sandpapered as previously described.

Final Paint Coat.

The final paint coat may be of the same composition as the previous one, but if it is to be afterwards varnished, it should be more "flat," which means that the proportions of oil and turpentine must be reversed; viz., two-thirds turpentine to one-third of oil. Also the paint should be very well strained so as to avoid skins or grit.

This having been applied and allowed to dry, the door is now ready for varnishing.

Varnishing.

The varnish to be used will depend somewhat upon the colour of the paint used. If the colour is dark, the most suitable varnish will be either an outside copal front door varnish or an outside quality carriage varnish. If the colour is pale, a pale decorative varnish (outside quality) is called for.

The main secret of successful varnishing is scrupulous cleanliness. The work, after a light sandpapering with a very fine-grade paper, must be well dusted off so that not a trace of grit remains. Also, no varnishing should be done if there is dust about. The air should be still, and if a time immediately after a shower of rain can be chosen, so much the better. On the other hand, foggy or damp weather should be avoided.

The Same Brushes can be used.

The brushes previously used for painting may be used for varnishing, always provided that they have been thoroughly cleaned and dried.

The vessel from which we work must also be perfectly clean. A 2-lb. jam jar will be found very satisfactory.

Loading the Brush.

Having carefully poured the varnish into the jar, the brush should be dipped for about an inch of the length of the bristles into the varnish. Whereas, in painting, the brush is sometimes patted against the side of the kettle to distribute the paint among the bristles, this should be avoided in varnishing.

Working.

The brush with its charge of varnish should be applied straight to the door. In varnishing the panels, first brush downward, then across, and then finish up and down to spread the varnish evenly. The cross stiles should be done in a different order of strokes finished lengthways. The upright stiles should be done as the panels. Varnish should not be applied sparingly like paint. As much should be applied as will "stay put" without running.

If the door is a panelled one, the panels should be done first, then the mouldings, thirdly, the upright centre stile, fourthly, the cross rails and finally, the upright side stiles.

If the above-described processes and precautions are observed, the entrance door should be a thing of beauty and an adornment to the house.

Gloss Paints.

If a simpler process is desired, this is made possible by using one of the gloss enamel or hard gloss paints now available, instead of the final paint and the varnish coats.

These gloss paints are really compounds of pigment and varnish, and by using them, we perform the two final operations in one.

Although their lasting quality is not quite so great as that resulting from the traditional method of separate paint and varnish coats, they are possessed of a considerable degree of durability and they enjoy a well-deserved vogue in many quarters.

Re-heeling High-heel Shoes
A SIMPLE MONEY-SAVING REPAIR

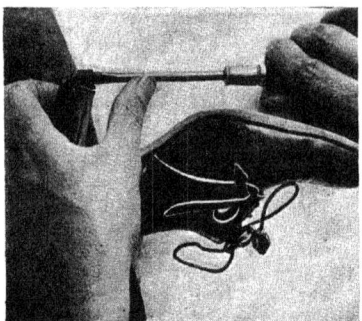

Fig. 1.—The First Operation is to Remove the Worn Heels.
This can be done by levering them off with a screwdriver. Rest the shoe on a pad of cloth, grip the heel with the left hand, extend the left thumb and use it as a fulcrum for the screw-driver.

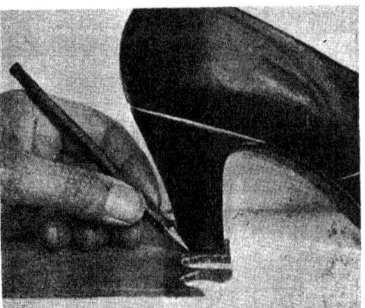

Fig. 2.—After Removing the Old Heel, Rest the Heel on the Leather with the Sole on the Table.
Now mark on the leather the outline of the heel, using a pencil for the purpose.

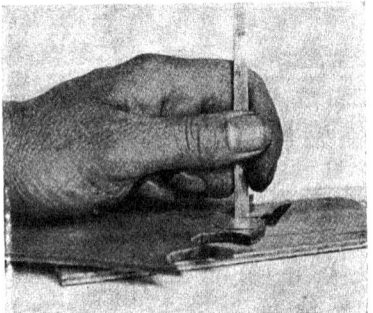

Fig. 3.—Now Cut Out the Leather with a Chisel.
Hold the chisel upright with the flat part of the blade on the outside of the curve. Drive the chisel through the leather with a mallet.

A FEW pence expended on leather and a penny for small brass tacks provides sufficient material to re-heel a pair of ladies' high-heel shoes about a dozen times.

Doing the work at home saves a perceptible amount for repairs, but has the greater advantages that the shoes last very much longer if new heels are fitted directly the leather has worn, and if the repairs are carried out with very thin nails.

The method illustrated has proved its efficiency and worth during several seasons.

It should be clearly understood that the repairs dealt with here only refer to cases where the leather has worn and not to heels in which the wood has also worn away. In the latter case, repairs are rather outside the scope of home treatment. Thus it will be realised that by dealing with the heel as soon as the leather has worn a great deal of expense can be saved.

Most Suitable Leather to Use.

The best leather to use is good English "sole bend," about $\frac{3}{16}$ inch thick, and this can be obtained from any leather shop or boot repairers. Obtain also some brass "fretwork pins," and use them for nailing on the heels.

Remove the Worn Heels.

First remove the worn heels —as shown in Fig. 1—by levering them off with a screwdriver, rest the shoe on a pad of cloth, grip the heel with the left hand, extend the left thumb and use it as a fulcrum for the screwdriver.

The heels can be readily levered off in this way without damage to the shoe heel.

Rest the heel on the leather with the sole on the table, as in Fig. 2, and mark on the leather the outline of the heel.

Cutting the Leather.

As only a very small piece of leather has to be cut, a chisel can be used for the purpose.

Hold the chisel upright with the flat part of the blade on the outside of the curve, as shown in Fig. 3, and drive the chisel through the leather with a mallet. Have a piece of plywood under the leather to protect the table top while chiselling.

Next lay the shoe flat on its side and hold it down with the palm of the left hand. With the finger and thumb hold the leather heel, as shown in Fig. 4, and fasten it with the pins.

Driving in the Pins.

One pin in the centre, three at the back, and one each side near the front corners will be ample. Wet the pins before driving them in, and use a small light-weight hammer. No trouble will then be experienced.

Trim the Edges with a Pocket Knife.

Trim the edges with a sharp pocket knife moistened with water, taking care not to cut the covering leather on the shoe heel. When trimming off the leather round the heel it is advisable to hold the shoe in an upright position so as to see whether the leather is being cut to the exact shape of the heel, at the same time giving an outward bevel, that is a very desirable feature.

If the shoe is turned with the sole upwards when trimming it is not so easy to see whether the correct outline is being maintained.

Smooth the edge with a few strokes of a piece of sandpaper, then stain the leather to match the colour of the shoes— as shown in Fig. 5 — using ink specially sold for this purpose, and applying it with a small brush. Finish by a liberal application of shoe cream or polish.

Shoes can be re-heeled in this way dozens of times without damage to the wooden heel.

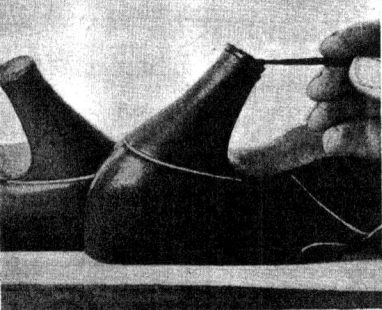

Fig. 4.—Fixing the New Leather Heel in Position.
Small brass fretwork pins should be used. Insert one pin in the centre, three at the back and one each side near the front corners. Wet the pins before driving them in.

Fig. 5.—Finishing Off the Heel.
Smooth the edge with a few strokes of sandpaper, then stain the leather to match the colour of the shoes. Finish by a liberal application of shoe cream or polish.

Practical Methods of Repairing Furniture

It is a golden rule in connection with the breakages that occur in furniture that repair should follow as soon as possible after the damage has taken place. If the damage is structural, a broken chair leg, for instance, the remaining parts are submitted to a great deal of strain, which in time will probably result in their being weakened.

As an example, suppose that one castor has either come off or has become so bent over that the legs do not stand squarely on the floor. To continue to use the table whilst in this condition means that every time any pressure is exerted on it, the rails beneath the top are forced out of truth owing to there being no support beneath the faulty leg. This would soon result in the joints between the rails and legs starting open.

Then again, minor troubles, such as a broken strip of moulding, should be put right straightway, because loose pieces are liable to be lost. In any case, the sharp edges of the breakages are soon rubbed over, making it impossible to make a really clean job of the repair, even when the broken piece is available.

REPAIRING A CHEST OF DRAWERS

Naturally enough, every repair job is different from all others in one way or another, so that each has to be considered on its own merits. There are, however, certain similarities common in breakages of a class. The simplest way of explaining the best procedure is to take an actual case of an article needing repair. The reader can then adapt the information to suit his own particular case.

A typical item is that shown in Fig. 1. It is an old mahogany chest of drawers damaged in the way that most chests are damaged after a period of use. Structurally, except for the broken foot, there is not a great deal to be done. The majority of chests are dovetailed together at the corners, and if these are loose they should be re-glued. It is not always necessary to knock the whole thing apart unless it is in a very bad state. Glue can usually be inserted from the inside after tapping the parts slightly apart. The advantage of this is that it saves unduly loosening the joints, and obviates the rather awkward job of reassembling the whole.

Fixing the Broken Foot.

In the present case the first job is to fix the broken foot. In actual practice it is usual to glue on all missing or new parts at the same time, so that the glue can be setting. Here, however, we are taking each job in its entirety for clearness. As a rule the old joints are covered with dried-up glue, and this must be removed, because it would prevent the parts from fitting closely together. In any case, the new glue would not grip well over the old. Scraping is the best method of cleaning. Professional cabinet-makers use a toothing iron which is like a plane iron, but has a serrated edge which makes a series of fine scores on the wood. Fig. 2 shows the toothing iron being used. A chisel can be used quite well for the purpose, though it is advisable afterwards to score the surface to form a sort of key to which the glue can grip.

The parts being clean, the broken foot can be fixed. Generally it is possible to drive a screw through the thin part into the bottom of the main carcase. As a rule, however, it is better to glue the parts and drive in the screw after the glue has set, as the screw may tend to draw the part out of place. It just depends. Some-

Fig. 1.—A Typical Repair Job that can quite easily be tackled in the Home Workshop.
The correct treatment for the various faults shown above is described in this article.

Fig. 2.—How to repair a Broken Foot (1).
The first thing to do is to remove the old glue, and this is done by scraping with a toothing iron as shown. If this tool is not available, use a chisel, but the surface must be scored afterwards to form a sort of key to which the glue can grip.

Fig. 3.—How to repair a Broken Foot (2).
Put glue on both joining surfaces and rub the loose piece back and forth once or twice to squeeze out any surplus glue. A glue block placed as shown will be found useful for strengthening the join.

PRACTICAL METHODS OF REPAIRING FURNITURE

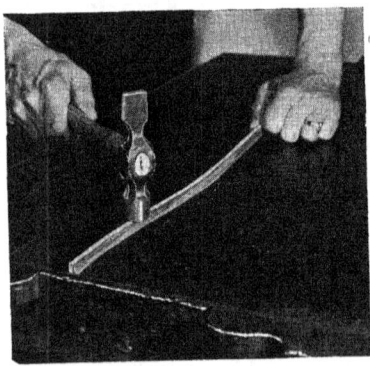

Fig. 4.—How to fill in a Crack in the Side of a Chest or Cabinet.
A thin strip of wood slightly tapered in its width should be used. Glue both the new piece and the crack and tap it in until it fits tightly. Most of the surplus wood can be chiselled away when the glue is dry.

one side. Most cracks are wider at one end than at the other. This necessitates planing the strip more at one end than at the other.

To enable the new piece to be inserted, the point of a saw should be inserted in the crack and worked along the length. The strip can then be cut to length and tried in. Glue both the crack and the shiver, and tap in the latter, as in Fig. 4, until it fits tightly. Make sure that the surface of the wood is level on both sides as any unevenness makes levelling off an awkward job. Thin wood especially is liable to be knocked down one side more than the other.

Allow the job to stand overnight before cleaning up. Most of the surplus wood can be chiselled away, care being taken not to remove more of

thicker than the old so that it can be cleaned down level afterwards. Thicker wood can often be used—say ⅛ inch. This can have a couple of veneer pins driven in to hold it whilst the glue sets. In addition to the veneer, any other damaged parts can be made good. The lower piece in Fig. 6 is an example. The side is cut back at an angle with the saw, and the waste wood chiselled away. This allows the new piece to be inserted. Notice that its outer shape at this stage is immaterial.

The levelling is done with a chisel. The wood is chiselled practically level and finished off with the plane. Scraping and glass-papering follows. In the case of the veneer, the edges can be chiselled, but the surface must be scraped and glass-papered only.

Replacing Broken Mouldings.

When the broken moulding is available it can be glued in position with little trouble. A cramp of one kind or another can generally be applied. If there is no suitable surface to which a cramp can be fixed, a pair of home-made springs can be applied. These can be cut from any spring wire (such as an old chair spring) and strained over so that they exert a pressure on the moulding. Fig. 7 shows a pair used for a top moulding. A block is cramped down as shown to provide a gripping

times it is an advantage to put in the screw straightway so that it pulls the parts firmly together.

Heat the Joint before applying Glue.

In any case, always heat the joints before applying the glue. This is important, as it prevents the glue from being chilled by the cold wood. Attention to this will add tremendously to the strength of the repair. Put glue on both joining surfaces, and, placing the loose piece in position, rub it back and forth once or twice with a firm pressure. This squeezes out the surplus glue.

Fig. 5.—A Useful Hint for forcing the two Parts of a Panel Together.
Two small blocks are fixed, one at each side of the split. A hand screw can then be fixed over the blocks, so forcing the parts together.

Glue blocks can often be added with advantage. These are prepared in a long length, and cut off to suit the particular position in which they are required. Fig. 3 shows three blocks glued in. They are square in section with the outer corner bevelled off. They are glued and rubbed back and forth in the way already described.

A Precaution regarding Use of Nails.

When nails have to be driven in, it should be remembered that a great deal of old mahogany is brittle and liable to split. As a precaution fine holes should be drilled first. Allow several hours before attempting to set the job on its feet. If the joint is moved before the glue has set, it will be robbed of most of its strength.

Filling in Cracks.

To fill in the crack in the side, what is known as a shiver is used. This is a thin strip of wood slightly tapered in its width, as shown in Fig. 4. A piece of ⅛-inch wood about 1 inch wide is selected, and planed down on

the surrounding polished surface than is essential. Sometimes a plane can be used afterwards. The final cleaning is done with a wood-scraper and glass-paper. Use middle 2 glass-paper first and finish with No. 1½.

Some chests have panelled ends, and when these have split it is sometimes difficult to force the two parts of the panel together. A useful hint is given in Fig. 5. Two small blocks are fixed one at each side of the split. A handscrew can then be fixed over the blocks, so forcing the parts together.

Patching the Drawer Rails.

Many old chests are veneered along the drawer rails, and the continual opening of the drawers causes the veneer to be chipped off. To fit new pieces the splintered edges must be cut away to a clean edge. It is better to cut them at an angle.

Fig. 6 shows the new pieces glued in. The back flat part of a hammer can be used to press in the veneer after gluing. Use veneer which is

Fig. 6.—Patching a Veneered Drawer Rail.
Before fitting new pieces, the splintered edges must be cut away to a clean edge, preferably at an angle. The new veneer should be thicker than the old, so that it can be cleaned down level after gluing in place.

PRACTICAL METHODS OF REPAIRING FURNITURE

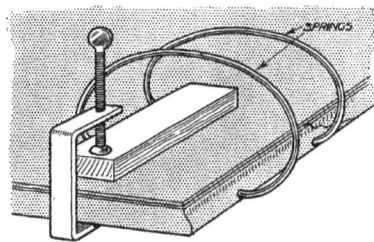

Fig. 7.—SHOWING HOW SPRINGS CAN BE USED TO CRAMP ON BROKEN PIECES WHEN THE USE OF A PROPER CRAMP IS IMPRACTICABLE.

Fig. 8.—FITTING A NEW PIECE TO A BROKEN MOULDING.

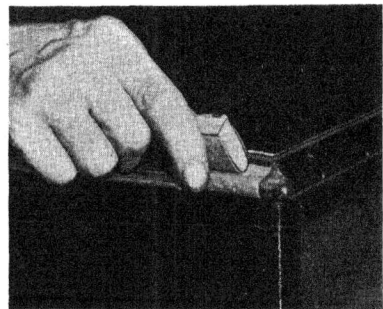

Fig. 9.—LEVELLING DOWN NEW PIECE IN MOULDING WITH GLASS-PAPER WRAPPED ROUND RUBBER.

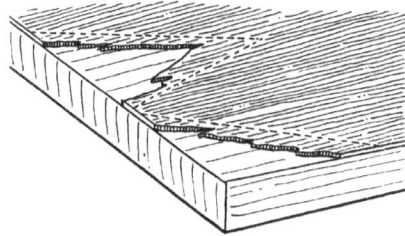

Fig. 10.—THE CORRECT METHOD OF CUTTING AWAY DAMAGED PARTS OF VENEER WHEN FITTING NEW PIECES.

Fig. 12.—CUTTING THROUGH A BUBBLE IN VENEER.

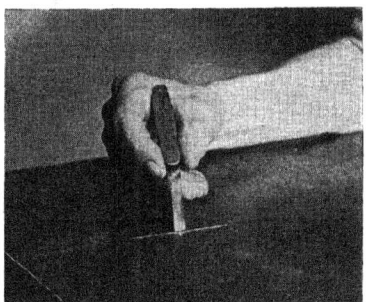

Fig. 13.—INSERTING GLUE BENEATH BUBBLE IN VENEER.

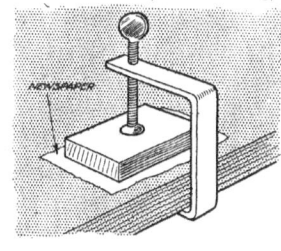

Fig. 11.—CRAMPING DOWN A BUBBLE IN VENEER AFTER INSERTING GLUE (see Figs. 12, 13 and 14).

Fig. 14.—PRESSING DOWN BUBBLE AFTER GLUE HAS BEEN FORCED IN.

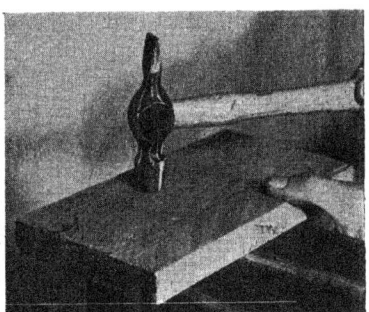

Fig. 15.—KNOCKING UP DRAWER DOVETAILS. Note the block of wood under the hammer.

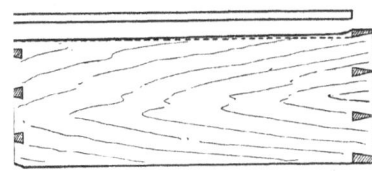

Fig. 16.—HOW A NEW PIECE IS FITTED TO BOTTOM EDGES OF WORN DRAWER SIDES.

Fig. 17.—SIMPLE METHOD OF FIXING OLD WOOD KNOB.

Fig. 18.—METHOD OF STRENGTHENING SPLIT IN DRAWER BOTTOM WITH CANVAS.

Fig. 19.—INSERTING NEW PIECE IN BROKEN COCKED BEAD.

surface for the springs. Nails, too, can be used if they are afterwards punched in and the holes filled in.

When the broken part is missing, a patch becomes necessary. The edges of the moulding are sawn to give a straight surface to which a new piece can be fixed. After chiselling the back flat the new piece is fitted and glued in as in Fig. 8. Here again the outer shape is unimportant. Afterwards it is levelled down with chisel and gouge to conform to the section of the moulding. To finish it off cleanly a block of wood is rounded to form a rubber, and the glass-paper wrapped around it. Rubbing this back and forth, as in Fig. 9, soon makes the whole thing level.

In cases where the majority of the moulding is missing, it is quicker completely to remove what is left and fix on an entirely new strip.

Filling in Small Indentations and Cracks.

We have mentioned the use of stopping for filling in nail holes. It also comes in handy for small indentations and cracks. It can be made from wax coloured with suitable powder colours obtainable from an oil shop; red ochre and burnt umber for mahogany, and burnt umber alone for oak. The wax is melted in a tin and the powder dropped in and stirred well. A little resin can be added to harden the mixture. In use, the wax is heated and dropped into the hole with a pointed match stick, and afterwards levelled with glass-paper. The surfaces of small bruises should be scratched to form a key to which the wax can grip. Certain proprietary brands of plastic wood, too, can be used. The advantage of this is that it can be stained like ordinary wood.

Dealing with Large Bruises.

Large bruises can often be raised by placing a damp rag over them and applying a hot iron. This is only possible in solid wood, however. If it is veneered, such treatment would merely cause the veneer to peel away.

Repairing Veneer.

Chipped veneer can be made good, as shown in Fig. 10. As in previous cases, the broken edges are cut away cleanly with the chisel. New pieces are then fitted in and glued. The flat back edge of a hammer is the best instrument to use to force the veneer down. The overhanging edges are chiselled level, and the surface made flat with scraper and glass-paper.

A frequent source of trouble is that of bubbles. These are usually the result of the glue having deteriorated, or of a hot substance having been placed upon the veneer, causing it to rise. The remedy is to force in some new glue and rub the veneer down. With a keen knife a cut is made *with*

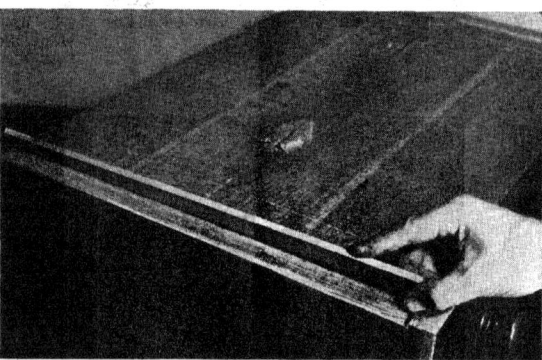

Fig. 20.—AFTER LONG USE, DRAWERS OFTEN WEAR BADLY ALONG THE BOTTOM EDGES.

This can be cured by adding a strip of wood beneath the drawer side. The strip is glued on and a few nails driven in and punched well in so that the plane can be used afterwards when fitting the drawer (see also Fig. 16).

Fig. 21.—LEVELLING DOWN THE NEW STRIP BENEATH THE DRAWER SIDE.

After fitting, all bearing edges should be rubbed with a piece of candle grease.

the grain along the bubble, as in Fig. 12. The knife is the dipped in glue and worked in the crack beneath the veneer, as in Fig. 13. Force in the glue generously, but avoid damaging the cut edges of the veneer. Fig. 14 shows how it is rubbed down afterwards with the hammer. Wipe off all surface glue before it sets.

If the veneer springs badly and will not lie flat, a block of wood with a piece of newspaper beneath can be cramped down as in Fig. 11. It is easy to tell when the veneer is springing by tapping it with the finger-nails. Veneer properly laid gives a solid feeling.

Making Good the Drawers.

The main corner joints of the drawers call for first attention. These are invariably dovetails, and they must be made firm. Do not take the easy (but thoroughly unsatisfactory) path of driving in nails. They look unsightly, and they do not make a good job. The better plan is to re-glue them. If they are only slightly loose glue can be worked into the joints from inside with a knife after tapping them open sufficiently. If in a bad state it is better to knock them apart and re-assemble. In this case chalk marks should be made at the corners, so that they can be put together again in the same positions. As much as possible of the old dried glue should be scraped away.

When knocking up the joints after glueing do not strike the dovetails direct with the hammer. It bruises the wood, and, the pressure being local, it is liable to cause the wood to split. The better plan is to hold a waste piece of wood across the whole joint and strike this, as in Fig. 15. It is obviously necessary to see that the drawer is square before setting aside. A good plan is to slip it into the main carcase. Wipe away all surplus glue with a rag damped in warm water.

Worn Drawer Sides.

After being in use for a long time, the drawers wear badly along the bottom edges, especially towards the back. It is desirable to fit strips to the underside to make good the wear. These strips cannot be glued straight on because of the uneven shape of the bottom edges. It is necessary to cut away the wood towards the front, as shown by the dotted line in Fig. 16. Much of it can be chiselled, and the finishing off done with the plane. The latter can be used as near to the front as possible, and the awkward corner finished either by chiselling or with the bull-nose plane, if one is available.

Fig. 20 shows the new strip being fitted. It should be about $\frac{7}{8}$ inch wide, and slightly thicker than the amount cut away from the side. It is glued on and a few nails driven in. The nails must be punched well in, so that the plane can be used afterwards when

PRACTICAL METHODS OF REPAIRING FURNITURE

Fig. 22.—A Typical Breakage in an Old Chair.

The top rail has been knocked off, a sudden blow probably having caused the dowels with which it was fixed to break. Redowelling will be necessary.

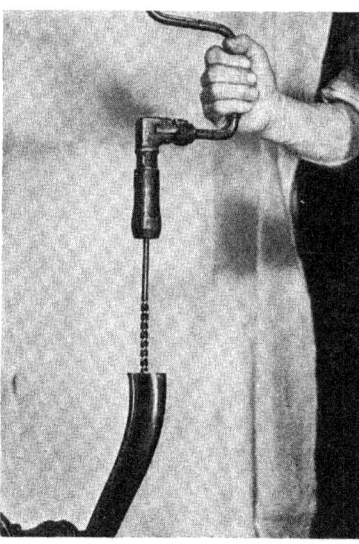

Fig. 23.—When boring the Hole for the Dowel, hold the Brace in a Line with the general Shape of the Leg.

This means that it is at right angles with the shoulder or the joint.

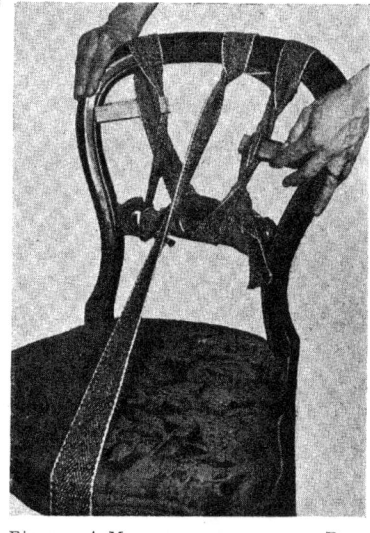

Fig. 24.—A Method of glueing the Back in Position.

Pieces of webbing are looped round tightly as shown, and strips of wood inserted and turned round in the form of a tourniquet.

fitting the drawer. Fig. 21 shows the plane being used to make the drawer a comfortable fit. Notice that the back corner of the slip is cut off at an angle. Though not a necessity, it certainly gives a neat finish. After fitting, all bearing edges should be rubbed with a piece of candle grease. This is a good lubricant, and is not liable to soil articles accidentally brought into contact with it. Oil should not be used.

Drawer Bottoms.

In old chests, the drawer bottoms were made of thin solid wood, which is bound to shrink in time. To allow for this they were made extra wide, a projecting part being allowed at the back. The idea of this was that after shrinkage had taken place the fixing screws or nails at the back could be withdrawn, and the bottom pushed forward and re-fixed. The projection at the back can be seen in Fig. 18, and the gap caused by shrinkage at the front. It is a simple matter to push the bottom forward into the groove at the front and re-fix it at the back.

Sometimes the

Fig. 25.—A Corner Bracket added to Seat Rails strengthens the Joint considerably.

bottom is split, and the best way to repair it is to withdraw it, plane the joint and glue it. A simpler way is to press the parts together and glue a strip of canvas to the underside, as in Fig. 18.

Broken Cocked Beads.

The cocked bead was a favourite decoration for drawers, and small pieces are invariably knocked off. To make them good the broken edges must be sawn across to make a square edge to which a new piece can be fitted. Usually the saw can only cut partially through the bead. It is finished off with a cut with the chisel and mallet. The surplus is then pared cleanly away.

The new pieces should be slightly thicker and wider than the old. They are fitted in as in Fig. 19, and fixed with glue and veneer pins. A plane and glass-paper will clean them up afterwards. Take special care that they are down level as otherwise they are liable to be knocked off again when the drawer is pushed in and out.

Wooden handles frequently cause trouble owing to the wooden thread

Fig. 26.—The Back Being cramped up.
Note the blocks of wood beneath the cramp shoes to prevent the surface from being damaged.

PRACTICAL METHODS OF REPAIRING FURNITURE

by which they are fixed becoming stripped. Merely to glue them in is unsatisfactory. A good plan is to fix a small piece of wood inside the drawer, as in Fig. 17. A screw can be driven through this into the knob.

REPAIRING CHAIRS

In many old chairs considerable use was made of shaped work, and this is often the source of trouble to the repairer. An example is that in Fig. 22. The top rail has been knocked off, a sudden blow probably having caused the dowels with which it was fixed to break. Re-dowelling is the only way to deal with it.

Method of Boring.

The method of boring depends upon whether the stumps of the dowel are firm in the wood. If they are loose the best plan is to withdraw them. A hole can be bored right in the dowel with a small bit. With a bradawl or similar tool the dowel can then be gradually splintered away until the original hole is left quite clean. A bit of the same size as the hole can be used to remove any irregularities. The advantage of this method is that, the original holes being used, the dowels are bound to fit accurately.

Re-boring the Dowels.

When the dowels cannot be moved in this way the only plan is to re-bore them. Begin by cutting the ragged ends of the dowel smooth and level with the joint. Select a bit of the same size as the dowel and place the point exactly in the centre of the dowel. When boring take care to hold the brace in a line with the general shape of the leg. This means

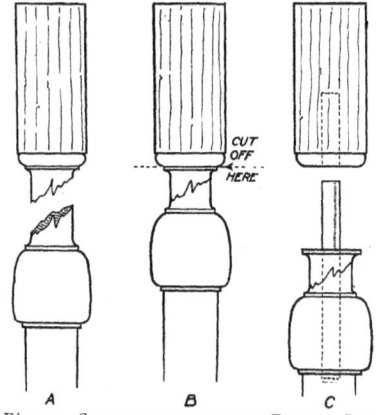

Fig. 27.—Stages in dowelling a Broken Leg.

that it is at right angles with the shoulder or the joint. Fig. 23 shows the hole being bored. Use a twist bit as shown. A centre bit is liable to run out of truth.

The dowel should be glued first into the upright of the back, the top rail

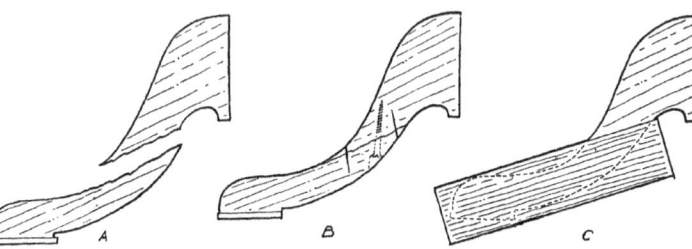

Fig. 28.—Dealing with a Broken Tripod Table Leg.
A, the broken leg; B, how the two parts are fixed together; C, splicing on a new piece.

being added after the glue has set. This enables the dowel to be filed a trifle if it is at all out of truth. A saw cut should be made along the length of the dowel. This is to enable the surplus glue to escape when the dowel is hammered in. If this is not done the glue at the bottom, being unable to get away, may split the wood.

Gluing the Back.

Difficulty is often experienced in gluing the back, since its shape makes it practically impossible to use cramps. Often it is sufficient to glue it and force it on, giving a few blows with a hammer with a piece of waste wood held over the top rail to prevent its being bruised. If it tends to spring, however, the method shown in Fig. 24 can be followed. Pieces of webbing are looped round tightly as shown, and strips of wood inserted and turned round in the form of a tourniquet. If there is a tendency for the rail to be bent backwards, another strip of webbing can be taken from the top to the front of the seat as shown.

What to do if whole Chair is Rickety.

When the whole chair is thoroughly rickety the only plan is to knock it apart completely and re-glue it. If a hammer has to be used to knock the joints apart, put a block over the surface and strike this. It is often the case that nails have been driven into the joints in an effort to strengthen them. These must be withdrawn first, as to attempt to force the joints whilst they are still in will probably result in the wood splitting out. Scrape away the old glue before applying the new.

The parts should be reassembled in sections as this saves having to deal with many joints in one operation. For instance, the back should be put together as a whole; also the front. The side rails can be added after the glue has set. Fig. 26 shows the back being cramped up. Notice the blocks of wood beneath the cramp shoes to prevent the surface from being damaged. If the joints of the seat rails are in a bad condition, they can be strengthened considerably by the addition of corner brackets, as in Fig. 25. These are planed to the required angle and are fixed with three screws, these being driven one in the centre into the leg, and the others at each side into the rails.

Broken Legs.

When a turned leg is broken off, the best way of repairing it is to dowel it on. The difficulty here is in centreing the bit, owing to the ragged nature of the break. A simple way out of the difficulty is given in Fig. 27. A shows the leg broken at the thin part of the turning. It is glued together just as it is, a cramp being used if possible. It is then sawn off either just above or below the break at one of the corners of the turning. This gives two clean

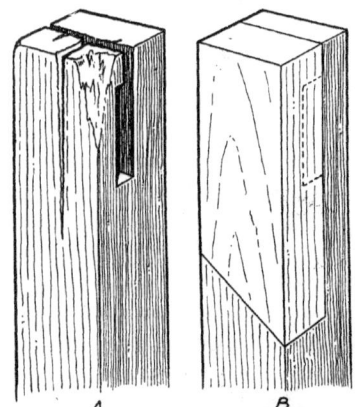

Fig. 29.—Method of splicing Piece to Top of Leg to Strengthen Joint.

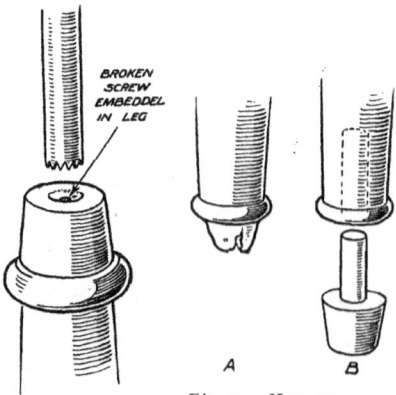

Fig. 30.—Removing the Screw from a Broken Castor.

Fig. 31.—How to fit a Cup Castor when the End of the Leg has Broken Away.

PRACTICAL METHODS OF REPAIRING FURNITURE

joining surfaces which can easily be centred by making a series of marks from the edge with a pair of compasses or dividers. The holes are then bored, these passing in deeply enough to go well through the original break. It is as well to ask a friend to stand at one side to indicate whether the brace is being held upright whilst boring. When gluing and cramping, turn the leg round to its original position. The joint will then be clean.

Tripod Table Legs.

Another form of leg liable to fracture is that used on tripod tables, shown in Fig. 28. When the broken piece is available it can usually be glued straight back. After the glue has set, a screw can be driven in as at B, and one or two nails put in near the edges. If the broken piece is missing, a new piece must be spliced on. The break is planed square, and the new piece jointed to it as at C. The shape is marked out after the sides have been levelled, and sawn with a bow-saw. After trimming up with spokeshave, scraper, and glass-paper, a strengthening screw can be put in as at B.

After a chair or table has been taken to pieces for re-gluing, it is often found that the joints of the legs are split as at A (Fig. 29). Merely to re-glue these would make but a weak repair. The better plan is to cut away the broken part to well below the joint, and glue on a new piece. Generally, one or two strengthening screws can be driven in from the back to make it firm. These, however, must clear the place where the mortise is to be re-cut. B shows the new piece spliced on.

Broken Castors.

A frequent source of trouble when fitting a new castor is that of removing the old screw which has broken off short in the wood. The end is usually well below the surface, and rust prevents it from being turned even when it can be gripped with pincers. A special tool to bore it out is easily made by the amateur. A piece of ⅜-inch barrelling is cut off about 4 inches long, and a series of teeth filed in it, as in Fig. 30. It is put in the brace and the teeth placed over the screw. It will rapidly bore a hole, leaving a centre core in which the screw is embedded. This is easily broken away and withdrawn. A piece of dowel is glued in the hole, and the new castor screwed on.

When a cup castor breaks off, it generally happens that the end of the leg is broken away as at A (Fig. 31). This should be sawn off, and a new piece turned to fit the castor cup as at B. It has a projecting dowel at the top. If a turner is preparing the new piece, it is as well to supply him with the castor so that he can make the new piece accordingly. A hole is bored in the end of the leg and the new piece glued on.

HOW TO FIT BATH PANELS

AN attractive treatment for baths that will considerably enhance their appearance is to surround them with decorated asbestos sheets as shown in the illustrations. The sheets are available in a wide range of colours. The maximum size of panel obtainable is 6 × 7 feet, but suitable sheets can be cut as desired.

How to Fix the Panels.

The best method of fitting the panels is to screw them to a wooden frame made from 1½ × 1½-inch wood. The framework is first fixed in position by screwing to the floor and walls.

Use chromium-plated head screws for fixing the panels to the frame. The method of fixing at the corner of the frame is shown at the bottom left in Fig. 1.

The splash surround can either be fixed direct to wall plugs or supported in rebated strips of 1½ ×

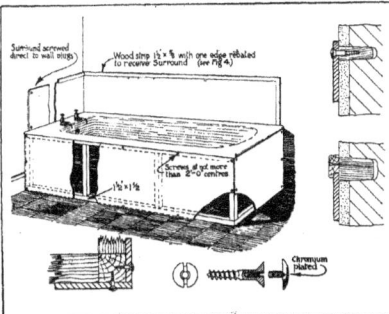

Fig. 1.—Details for fixing Panels round a Bath.

⅝-inch wood. The details are clearly shown at the right in Fig. 1.

Moulded Panels.

An alternative treatment to decorated sheets is the use of moulded asbestos-cement panels. These are supplied in a natural grey colour, ready for painting in any desired colour.

The panel should first be given two coats of sichel grounding and then finished with enamel in the ordinary way.

Fixing Moulded Panels.

Moulded panels can be screwed to wood corner pieces and to wood blocks fixed to walls and skirting boards. Nail blocks to the floor at intervals to locate the bottom edges of the sheets, but the panels need not be fixed to these blocks (see Fig. 2).

The framing can be similar to that used for fixing decorated sheets, with the exception that the intermediate posts should be left out so as not to foul the projecting back of the panels.

Splash Backs for Hand Basins.

A convenient method of preventing damage from splashes on the wall above a hand basin is to fix a splash back, as shown in Fig. 3. This is a stipple-gauze decorated sheet, obtainable in various colours.

The sheets are obtainable in the following sizes: dimension "A," 22 inches, 25 inches, or 27 inches. Dimension "B," 18 inches. The shelf is 1 inch shorter than the splash back and 4 inches wide. The four holes for fixing are ready drilled.

The splash back should be screwed direct to plugs driven in the wall, using detachable chromium-plated head screws. It can be cleaned by wiping with a damp cloth. The panels referred to can be obtained from The Asbestos Cement Building Products Ltd., Trafford Park, Manchester.

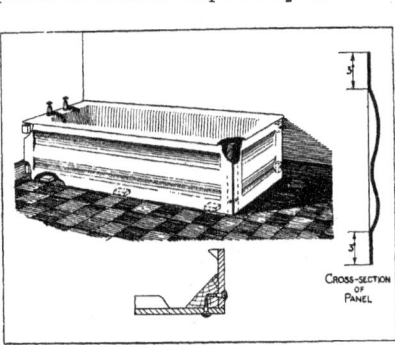

Fig. 2.—Details for fixing Moulded Panels.

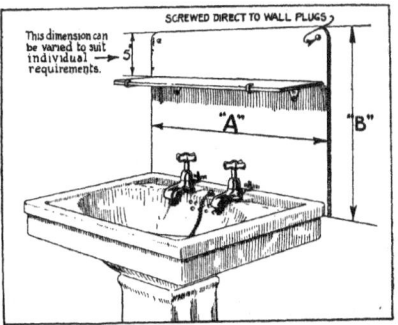

Fig. 3.—A Splash Back for a Hand Basin.

Making a Padded Top Ottoman

The handyman can readily construct a cretonne-covered ottoman with a padded top (Fig. 1), and utilise for it a good many pieces of wood from unwanted packing cases and other sources of inexpensive material.

Useful sizes are 5 feet long, 18 to 20 inches wide and 15 to 18 inches deep, but there is considerable latitude in the matter of dimensions; available space, convenience of material at hand and other kindred considerations will no doubt be deciding factors.

The most practical way of going about the work is to look over the materials that are available and use them to the best advantage.

Fig. 1.—The Finished Ottoman.
Made from pieces of odd wood, and covered inside and out with cretonne, with a nicely padded top.

How Short Pieces of Wood can be Utilised.

It is possible to use up a quantity of comparatively short pieces of wood by cutting them to uniform length and nailing them to long battens about $1\frac{1}{2}$ inches wide and $\frac{3}{4}$ inch thick. The two long sides, the top and the bottom, can all be prepared in this way if the battens are placed on the insides, as shown in Fig. 2.

Making the Box.

Begin making the box proper by screwing three cross-battens, about 4 inches wide and 1 inch thick, to what will be the underside, that is, the smooth side opposite to the long battens. Fix one cross piece at the middle of the length, as in Fig. 3, and the other two at an inch or so inwards from either end. Then nail the two ends to the faces of the bottom battens and to the sides.

Cut and fit upright pieces about 2 inches wide and 1 inch thick to fit neatly into the corners, notching the wood so that it fits snugly over the top and bottom battens. Then cut a number of pieces of board to reach from front to back, and nail them to these corner pieces and to the ends of the other boards.

The sides, bottom and top boards may be from $\frac{1}{2}$ to $\frac{3}{4}$ inch thick, the ends are preferably somewhat thicker, say, $\frac{3}{4}$ to 1 inch. If all the said joints are glued before they are nailed, the result will be a much more rigid and durable affair, and is certainly worth the little extra time and trouble involved.

A word of caution must be given, and that is to keep all the work square and flat, otherwise the ottoman will not look at all workmanlike.

Fitting Castors.

When the box is thus far completed, as shown in Fig. 4, it should be turned

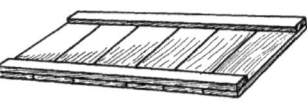

Fig. 2.—Construction of Sides.
Short pieces of old packing case wood are nailed to battens to form the sides, ends and bottom of the ottoman.

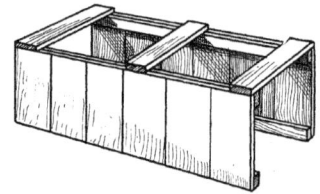

Fig. 3.—Assembling Sides and Bottom Battens.
Three cross-pieces are screwed to the sides.

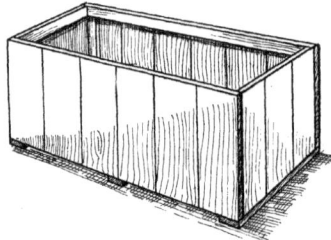

Fig. 4.—Ottoman Carcase completed.
The bottom, ends and sides assembled and ready for fitting the hinged top.

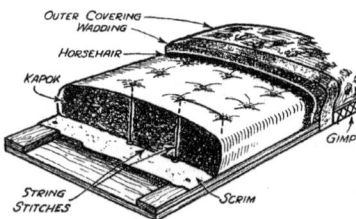

Fig. 5.—Section of Padded Top.
The kapok stuffing is held firm with stitches of string, the outer padding of horsehair is added and the whole covered with linen and a chintz or cretonne outer cover.

upside down and a set of four flat type castors fitted near the corners of the end battens, and the underside given a coat of any good paint.

The Lid.

The next thing to do is to hinge the lid to the box, which can most practically be done with three or four tee hinges. Set the smooth side of the lid downwards and see that it closes easily and truly at all points.

Lining the Interior.

The interior should now be lined with any good hard-wearing material, such as a strong linen or casement cloth. This should be fixed while it is slightly damp, so that it will tighten up when it dries. It is a good plan to remove the lid while the interior is being lined, as this enables the box to be placed on its side or end as is most convenient.

Line the underside of the lid in the same way, and, if the wood is rough, cover the exterior with any old material.

Padding.

Now fix a piece of stout canvas on to the top of the box, and nail it down here and there in the middle. The purpose of this canvas is to take the stitches which fashion and hold the padding in place.

Now nail a piece of scrim or coarse canvas to one edge and cover one end of the top of the lid for a depth of 3 or 4 inches with kapok or other stuffing. Fold over the scrim and nail it to the opposite edge, commencing at one end.

Get some strong thin string and with a packing needle stitch through the scrim—as shown in Fig. 5—to draw it down and hold the stuffing in place. Work along gradually until the whole is covered, then nail the scrim to the ends. Spread a layer of horsehair or other stuffing over the scrim, shape the roll or rounded edge, and cover the whole with canvas.

Complete the work by fixing the ornamental chintz or other covering to the top and to the outsides of the box. Fix the check straps at the ends to prevent the lid opening backwards too far, and finally tack a narrow edging of gimp or ribbon over all the corners and joints, thus completing a comfortable and capacious ottoman that will give years of useful service.

The ottoman can always be freshened up or changed in appearance by re-covering with a different material, while the addition of a gaily coloured cushion will prove welcome when using the ottoman for reclining.

How to Fit a New Tap Washer

Fig. 1.—The First Thing to do After Turning the Water Off at the Main is to Unscrew the Spindle of the Tap.

The tap should be turned full on before unscrewing.

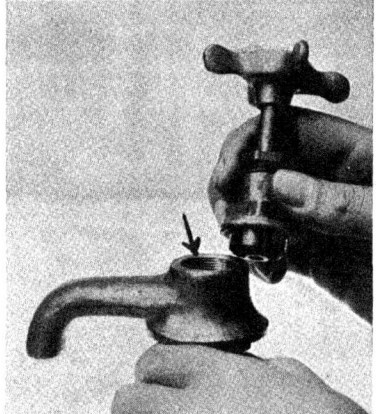

Fig. 2.—Now Lift off the Spindle.

The jumper will probably remain in the cavity marked by the arrow, unless the tap is of the type shown in Fig. 4.

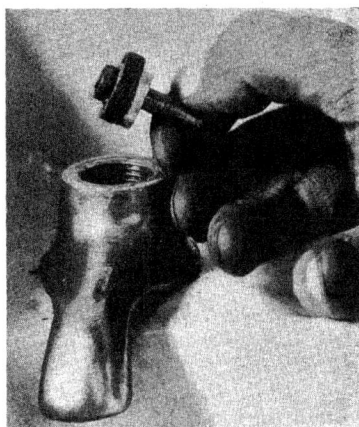

Fig. 3.—The Jumper being Lifted out after the Top of the Tap has been Removed.

The nut seen on the left must be taken off to enable the new washer to be placed on.

IF a water-tap goes wrong and takes to dripping, the first thing is to obtain three or four washers of different sizes. Half-inch washers are those most frequently used, but as one cannot be certain of the exact dimensions until the water is cut off and the tap dismantled, it is just as well to be prepared with alternative washers measuring ⅜ inch and ¾ inch.

Hot and Cold Washers.

Red fibre and treated leather washers are used for cold-water taps. Both kinds give good service. Leather and fibre must never be used for hot taps because these rapidly deteriorate under the action of hot water. Rubber-composition washers are used for hot-water taps. Do not attempt to make washers; they may be purchased at any ironmonger's.

Turn off the Water—the Main Cock.

Before anything is done to the tap the water should be cut off. What this entails depends on the tap itself. If the water flows direct from the main, it is necessary to turn off the main cock and wait a few moments for the connecting pipes to empty themselves. Sometimes this cock is near the kitchen sink, but frequently there is no other main cock except one in the front garden or in the street pavement. When the main cock is below the ground, it will be necessary to make a wood fork to fit the tap if it is too low to be reached by the hand.

Water Supply from a Tank.

If the supply comes from a tank, one of two things must be done. Either the ball valve has to be shut off by lifting the ball arm and tying it up, and then waiting for the tank to empty itself; or the outlet in the tank must be plugged so that the water cannot flow from the tank into the pipes. A good way to do this is to trim the end of a broom-handle to a point, to wrap some rag around the point, and to force it into the outlet hole. In the case of hot-water taps the source of heat must be removed or an explosion is possible.

A Useful Tip.

A hot-water tap, or a tap fed from the cold cistern, can be unscrewed without stopping the water supply if one is ready with a large wet cloth to cover the hole as soon as the cap is withdrawn from the tap. It is not safe to attempt re-washering a main tap by this method because the force behind the water is too great.

Unscrewing the Tap.

Taps are frequently difficult to unscrew, especially when they have

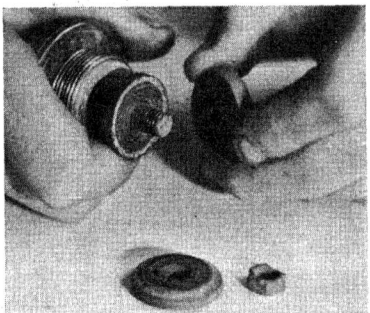

Fig. 4.—Fitting the New Washer on to the Jumper.

Some taps, usually those for hot water, have a fixed jumper to prevent the washer sticking down. The operations for renewing the washer are exactly the same, the only difference being that the jumper comes away with the top of the tap, and does not have to be lifted out as in Fig. 3.

been undisturbed for some time. A large adjustable spanner is the most suitable tool for unscrewing the tap in the absence of a plumber's wrench. The essential thing is to turn the spanner the correct way. Some taps have right-hand threads, that is to say, they undo when the cap is turned anti-clockwise, as seen from the top of the tap. A larger proportion of taps have left-hand threads. If it is not known whether a tap is left- or right-handed—try both ways before using too much force on the spanner.

Take extra care when unscrewing a tap which is wiped into a lead pipe or the joint may be damaged. The tap is firmly held in the left hand while the spanner is being turned. Care must also be taken in this way when the tap is backed with a tiled wall. Always unscrew away from the wall so that a sudden slip of the spanner will not damage it. Basin and bath taps are easiest to deal with because their seating is firmer.

Chromium-plated Taps.

In the case of chromium-plated taps and others of an expensive nature, there is often a domed covering, fitted over the nut, and the nut is therefore invisible. All that is necessary with them is to unscrew the dome, to lift it up and then the nut is revealed.

When the nut has been loosened the upper part of the tap can be lifted out of the fixed body, revealing the jumper.

The Jumper.

The jumper is the portion of the tap to which the washer is fixed. Its object is to prevent the rotation of the washer when the tap is turned. If the washer were to rotate with the tap, it would soon wear out on the seating. Some taps are made with the jumper

HOW TO FIT A NEW TAP WASHER

Fig. 5.—Showing How the Barrel of the Jumper Fits into the Tube Running through the Centre of the Spindle.

Fig. 6.—Here we see Two Jumpers, One Fitted with a New Washer, the Other with a Worn Washer.

separate from the cap of the tap,; others are separate because the retaining-pin has broken. When the jumper remains in the tap when the cap is lifted off, it should then be possible to lift it out as shown in Fig. 2.

Trouble with the Jumper.

Sometimes the jumper will not lift out of the tap because the washer has spread, or because too large a washer has been used on a previous occasion. The jumper spindle is then strongly gripped in a pair of pliers, with a protecting piece of leather in the jaws of the pliers. The jumper is then forced out with the old washer attached. Care must be taken not to damage the jumper spindle; it is made of copper and is easily scored with the pliers.

Removing the Old Washer.

The washer is held on to the jumper with a small nut. This unscrews anti-clockwise, looking down on the nut. If the washer nut is very tight it will be necessary to grip the flange of the jumper in a second pair of pliers in order to unscrew it. Hot-water taps frequently become corroded at this point, and are usually difficult to unscrew. The thread of the jumper may be so badly corroded that it breaks off. For this reason it is advisable to keep a spare jumper as a standby.

Replacing the Tap.

When the new washer has been fitted to the jumper, examine the washer, which provides a water-tight joint between the cap and the body of the tap. This washer is renewed if necessary. It is made of leather. Fibre should not be used for this, because it is liable to fray when the tap is screwed

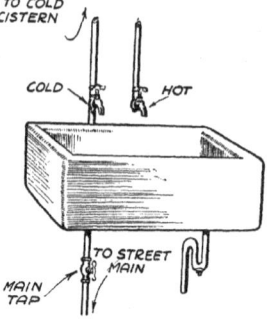

Fig. 7.—In some cases it will be Found Possible to Turn the Cold Water off at the Main by a Tap placed Close to the Sink.

If there is no such tap, the water will have to be turned off from the main cock, which will probably be found in the front garden.

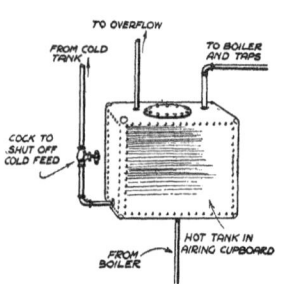

Fig. 8.—When Dealing with a Hot-water Tap, it will be Necessary to Turn Off the Cock from the Cold Feed and Allow the Tank to Empty.

The fire in the kitchen must not be alight when this is done, or an explosion is possible.

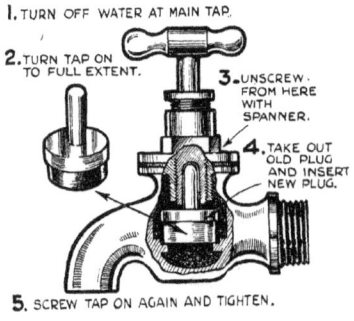

Fig. 9.—The Type of Washer shown above Obviates the Necessity of Fitting a New Washer to the Old Jumper.

The old jumper is simply removed and the new one complete with washer inserted in its place.

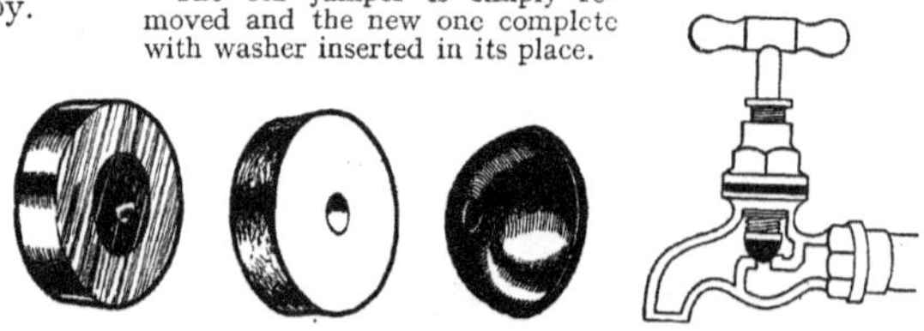

Fig. 10.—Three Types of Washers.

That on the left is of rubber, and is suitable either for hot or cold or bad seated taps. Next to it is a leather washer suitable for cold water taps. The third type is self-fixing, and is screwed direct to the end of the jumper, as shown on the right.

up. Do not put any paint or red lead on the cap thread with the object of making the joint water-tight, because this will contaminate the water supply. Make sure that the jumper rotates freely in the cap of the tap before putting the tap together again.

OTHER FAULTS WITH TAPS

It may be that when the water is turned on, the tap is no better than it was at the outset. This will be due to one of three reasons:—

(a) The washer has not been properly fitted. There is only one thing to do when this is suspected, and that is to go through the whole process again. Take particular care this time that the washer is pushed in perfect contact with the metal circle against which it is fitted.

(b) The washer is not the proper size. In such cases it is usually too small. It should be of exactly the same dimensions as the metal circle mentioned in (a).

(c) The tap is worn out. This happens after a considerable amount of wear, especially in areas where the water is gritty. In such cases the inside of the tap becomes roughened, and the soft washer cannot shut down in absolute contact with it. Hence the water is able to trickle through, although the spindle is shut down to its fullest extent. There are ways of regrinding the inside of the tap, but much the most satisfactory method is to fit an entirely new tap in place of the old one. This may seem a somewhat precarious job, but it is quite simple and straightforward.

Make sure the new tap has the right size thread, so that it will fit.

WINDOW TREATMENTS

There are two main varieties of curtains:—

(1) Screening curtains of fine net stretched across the lower half of the window.

(2) Hanging curtains which are drawn across at night and are mainly decorative during the day.

Net Curtains.

Net curtains can be obtained in many excellent designs and in softly tinted colours. If a net curtain is coloured with moderate brightness—if, say, it is cream, yellow or light blue—its daytime opacity will be greater from outside the house, and from indoors the colour will seem so subdued by the daylight as not to jar with almost any colour schemes.

Hanging Curtains.

It is, however, with hanging curtains that most readers will be concerned. Casement cloth, poplin, cretonne, shot artificial silk and artificial silk repps and damasks are among the most suitable materials for a house of moderate size.

Plain or Patterned Curtains?

Whether a plain or a patterned material will look best at your windows depends on the size of the room, and also on how much pattern is employed in other parts of the interior. If the room is small, plain curtains will look best; but a large room, if furnished with unpatterned fabrics and with plain painted or distempered walls, is liable to seem bare.

If patterned materials are chosen for small rooms, it is important that the design should be on a small scale, in proportion with the apartment and the furniture. The smaller pattern not only looks pleasing, but also gives a sense of spaciousness, whereas a large pattern catches the eye too emphatically, thereby breaking up the room and spoiling the effect.

If patterned wallpaper and patterned curtains are used, the chair coverings and carpet should be plain. Or you may have patterned chairs and patterned curtains with plain walls and carpet.

METHODS OF HANGING CURTAINS

In hanging curtains it was at one time considered satisfactory to hang a pole or rod across the top of the window architrave with sliding rings and curtain hooks which resembled safety-pins.

This method of hanging is still often used; but it is certainly not to be recommended, partly because the hooks are liable to shorten the life of the curtains, which may tear when being drawn across the window, and partly because curtains hung in this way are difficult to arrange in pleasing folds.

Fig. 1.—An Attractive Treatment that would be Suitable for Small Windows in a House of Moderate Size.

A window, the centre light of which is approximately twice the width of each side light, can be treated, as shown, with casement curtains and a pair of enclosing curtains. Although no valance is illustrated, it can be fitted if required, although the arrangement is quite satisfactory without one.

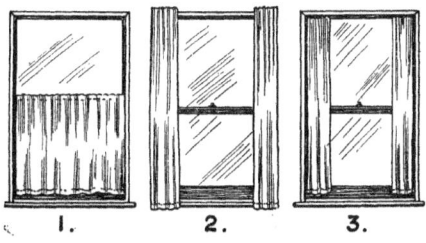

No. 1 is bad because it divides the window into halves and leaves the top part bare. Nos. 2 and 3 are pleasing. No. 2 just covers the woodwork, and No. 3 leaves an edge of wood just visible all round.

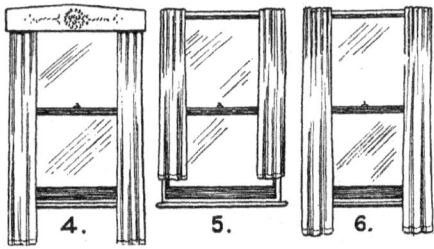

No. 4 is good if it is required to give an impression of greater height. The curtains in this treatment just reach the floor. In No. 5 the curtains are too short. No. 6 may be considered satisfactory, but when the bottom of the curtains fall half-way between the window sill and the floor they are unrelated to any structural line. If lengthened to the floor or shortened to the architrave the effect would be better.

Fig. 2.—An Expert's Advice.

By carefully studying the diagrams above and reading the expert criticism of each treatment you will find much to help you in arranging your curtains to the best advantage.

Metal Curtain Runners.

One of the several patent metal curtain runners now on the market will be found a great improvement on the old-fashioned curtain pole. It is possible to obtain an up-to-date curtain rod which is fixed in position with four screws and costs only 3s. 6d. complete, while some of the cheapest metal curtain runners cost only 1s. per foot.

Roller bearings are generally used with these runners, and the curtains are hung with curtain tape with detachable hooks, which are removed when the curtains are washed. They move easily to and fro at a touch, and, if preferred, the curtains can be drawn by pulling a cord.

A good curtain runner not only improves the appearance of the curtains, it greatly increases their length of life.

Valances and Pelmets.

A later article will deal thoroughly with the fitting and making of pelmets.

Choosing Curtains.

The wise home-maker will leave the choice of window curtains until last, "making do" with old curtains until the rooms are decorated and furnished. Purchasing curtains and furnishing fabrics of all kinds is one of the most delightful tasks in equipping the home, and as there is endless and bewildering variety from which to choose it is necessary to have a very clear idea of what would be best for each room before entering the shop. Then there should be little danger that you may afterwards regret your purchase.

NOTES ON MEASURING AND CUTTING CASEMENT CURTAINS

Determining Quantity of Material.

The difficulty of determining the lengths in yards of material for curtaining any particular casement window is that very often it is impracticable to say beforehand what width of material will be available when a choice has to be made at the shop.

The best way is first to measure the height of the window from the place where the curtain will be hung to the window board; then add to it an amount for "turning." This is usually taken as 1 inch for a narrow hem and 3 inches for a top turning, and a modest "heading."

Fig. 3.—How to deal with French Doors.
These have a lustre glass pelmet in blue and gold, with curtains of blue and gold brocade. (*Rowley Gallery.*)

Fig. 4.—An Attractive Bay-Window Treatment.
Curtains and pelmet of modern damask, in shades of green and golden-buff. (*Oliver Law, A.R.I.B.A.*)

Fig. 5.—Another Bay-Window Treatment.
This window has a pelmet in waxed French walnut wood, the same as the furniture. Curtains in silvery-white silk repp with hand-painted design in colours. (*Rowley Gallery.*)

For example, the distance from curtain rod to window-board may be 4 feet 10 inches to which adding 4 inches for turnings gives a total of 5 feet 2 inches, or 62 inches, or practically 1¾ yards.

Next measure the total width of the window and settle the number of separate curtains to cover it, and the amount of fullness in the curtains when drawn across the window.

An Example.

As an example, take a window which is 4 feet 10 inches high and 5 feet wide—dimensions that are often found in the modern small house.

This could be curtained with two lengths of material 48 inches wide, where the total overlap is 36 inches, and thus there is half a yard or 18 inches for "fullness" in each curtain —which would be about right.

Objections to this arrangement are that when opened the curtains bunch together rather clumsily at the sides and the centre of the window looks very bare.

When three curtains are used on any "three-light" window, the centre curtain never seems quite right and the "mullions" or upright divisions between the "sashes" or separate windows show up very prominently, but if this arrangement is used a suitable width of material would be 42 inches or thereabouts.

The best arrangement is to use four curtains for a three-light window, thus covering the mullions and leaving reasonable space between them.

Overlap and Fullness.

The amount of fullness is determined by the overlap, which is ascertained

Fig. 6.—How to deal with a Casement Window with three Equal Lights.
It is treated with four casement curtains and one pair of enclosing curtains, with a valance. Wide windows are generally improved in appearance by the addition of a valance extending about one-fifth to one-seventh of the drop of the curtains. The casement curtains at the sides of the windows are half the width of the centre curtains.

by multiplying the width of the material by the number of curtains; for example, width 27 inches, multiplied by 4, gives 108 inches. Subtract from this the total width of the window in inches, say 84, thus 108 − 84 equals 24 inches. Dividing this total overlap by 3 gives the overlap to be allowed to each of the centre pair of curtains and half the amount being allowed to each side curtain. In practice a little less fullness in the side curtains is desirable, because then their inner edges always remain in the same place, whereas the centre curtains have to be drawn both ways to close them.

It is desirable to reckon up in this way, because it is then quite easy to decide if, say, a 27-inch material will suit, or if some other width, say 32 inches, could be used successfully.

Fig. 7.—Treatment for a Narrow Window.
That on the left is quite pleasing, but that on the right is ugly and unattractive.

Fig. 8.—Attractive arrangement for French Doors.
The doors are treated with enclosing curtains and a pelmet surmounted by a cornice—a valance can be used if preferred.

WINDOW TREATMENTS

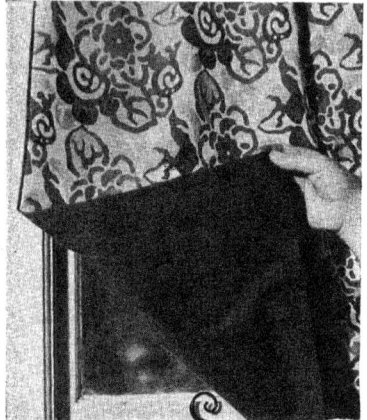

Fig. 9.—SHOULD CURTAINS BE LINED?
A house always looks best if the curtains, seen from the street, are alike. On the other hand, the housewife likes to study the ensemble of each room. A solution of this problem is to line all the curtains with a similar plain material, which will show from outside only.

Fig. 10.—WHY DO THESE CURTAINS LOOK TIDY?
Curtains for casement windows should be carefully measured, cut and sewn so that all are exactly the same length, and the rings put on at the same depth. The curtains will then all hang clear.

Fig. 11.—AN EASY WAY TO FIT A FRILL VALANCE.
To get the gathering regular and still to ha the frill exactly the right length, fix a narr board around the top of the window frame. shown. *See also* Figs. 15-17 for methods fixing the frill.

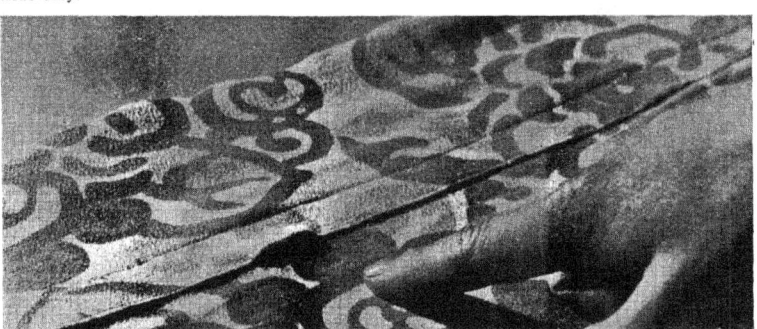

Fig. 12.—MAKING THE FRILL.
In hemming the frill, have the top hem on the face side, and leave a gap in the stitching at intervals of about half a yard.

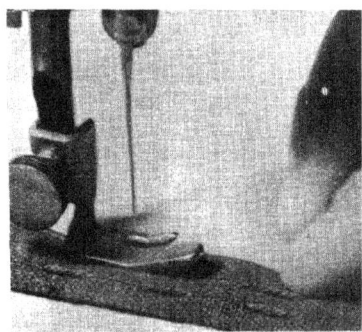

Fig. 13.—SEWING ON THE TAPE.
The upper tape in Fig. 16 is sewn quite fla on to the curtain material in the usual way

Fig. 14.—FITTING A CURTAIN FRILL.
Measure the edge of the board, shown in Fig. 11, and mark the correct length on the tape boldly. This makes it possible to do the gathering on the tape before fixing up, and still to be sure that the frill will fit the window.

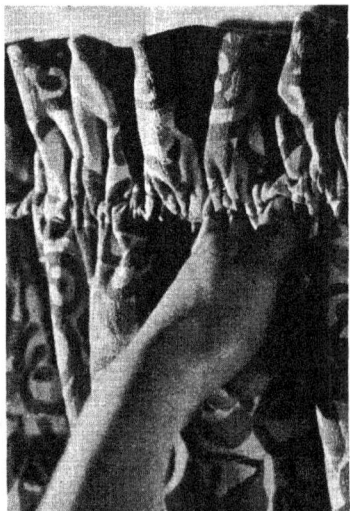

Fig. 15.—FITTING A CURTAIN FRILL.
Having secured the ends of the tape with a stitch or two, the frill is then attached in place with drawing-pins. The spaces left in hemming allow the heads of the pins to be hidden, although put in from the front.

Fig. 16.—THREE USEFUL TAPES.
The top tape shown in this picture, when attached to the curtain material, can be made to produce a gathered effect. The second tape is suitable for lace or muslin curtains. The lower tape will allow hooks to be attached.

WINDOW TREATMENTS

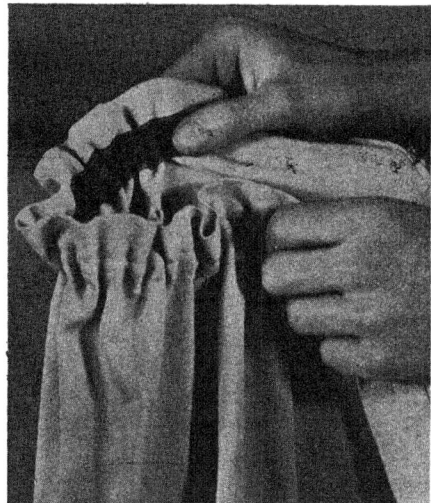

Fig. 17.—GATHERING UP.
The strings which run tightly through the tape will prevent the gathers from slipping loose when the ends have been tied.

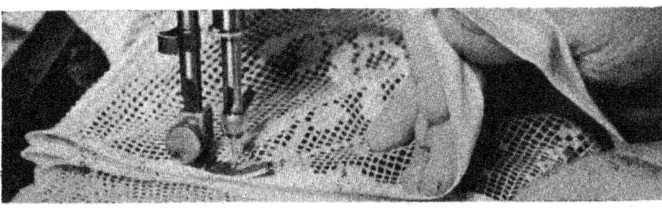

Fig. 18.—SEWING ON THE PLAIN TAPE.
Sew the plain tape *double* on to lace or muslin curtains. A strong hem will be produced.

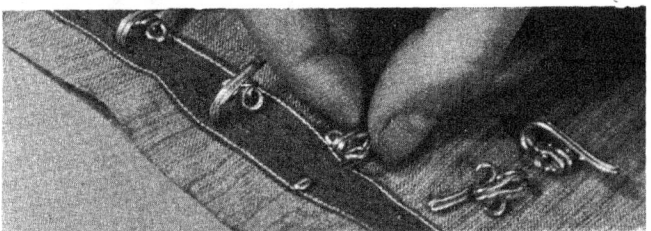

Fig. 19.—ANOTHER METHOD OF HANGING CURTAINS.
Two hooks are shown in the correct position for hanging, and the other in the act of slipping into or out of the pocket of the tape, whichever the case may be. They can be put in closely or any desired distance apart.

When actually purchasing, an attractive material at an agreeable price may be offered, but unless the buyer knows what widths are practicable it is a difficult matter to decide when in the shop.

Draw Tape.

As already mentioned the best way of hanging any draw curtain is to employ patent curtain rods and runners now on the market. The curtain is attached to the runners by means of small hooks inserted through loops formed in a woven material specially made for the purpose. This material includes a pair of thin cords or draw strings.

To use it, make the curtains, then machine the draw tape on to them, keeping everything flat. Fasten the draw strings at one end, then pull outwards the strings at the other end which gathers the curtain.

Draw up the curtain until it is a trifle wider than the desired "finished" width, then tie a knot in the draw strings to prevent them slipping back.

Fig. 20.—IF YOU USE RODS FOR HANGING SHORT CURTAINS.
It is a great help if the ends are rounded off with glasspaper. They will then slide smoothly through the hem of the curtain.

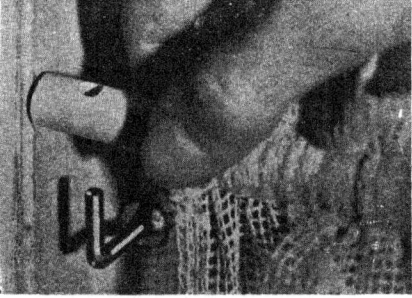

Fig. 21.—FOR SHORT CURTAINS.
This shows a simple and useful method of fixing when rods are used for short curtains. It consists merely of a dresser-hook in the window frame and a hole drilled in the rod.

Cutting Curtain Material.

Unroll the material, and spread it flat on the table with one selvedge flush with the long edge of the table.

Let the free end of the material overhang at the table end by the amount required for the top hem or heading; then lay on it a long strip of cardboard on thin wood with a straight-edge, hold it firm with the card edge flush with the table edge, then fold over the material and crease it with an iron. Turn in the hem, and tack it as usual, then draw sufficient of the material over the edge of the table, keeping the selvedge flush at the side as before, then fold over and crease the material as before and cut along the creased line.

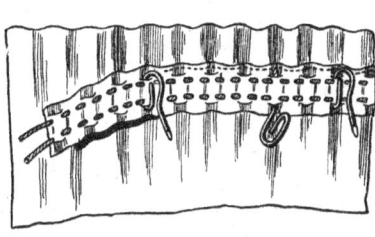

Fig. 22.—USEFUL TYPE OF CURTAIN HOOK.
Two hooks are shown in the correct position for hanging, and the other in the act of slipping in or out of the pocket.

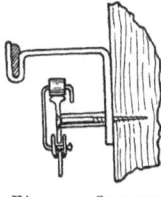

Fig. 23.—CURTAIN RUNNER FITTED TO RAIL.
Above the runner will be seen a bracket carrying valance rail.

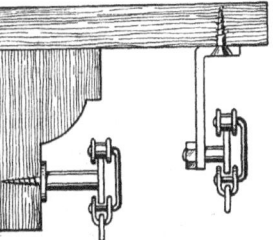

Fig. 24.—TWO METHODS OF FIXING CURTAIN RUNNERS.
A pelmet or valance board is used as the means of hanging one rail, while the other is screwed directly to the window frame.

How to Make Dowelled Joints

Uses of Dowelled Joints.

DOWELLING is a quick method of jointing wood. Few tools are necessary. A plane, brace and bits and a saw are the only essential tools. A properly designed dowelled joint is strong and reliable if certain precautions are taken when making. Not all kinds of work are suitable for dowelling. For any purpose where the joint is likely to be pulled apart, dowels are unsuitable. For example, the joints between the front and the sides of a drawer tend to be pulled apart each time the drawer is opened, so that dowelling cannot be used. The jointing of framework, generally, is the chief use of dowels. They are also used to strengthen any form of butt joint, such as the mitres of a picture frame or the edges of boards forming a table top.

The Dowels.

Dowels are made from hard wood; oak or beech. It is essential that the dowels are perfectly dry when they are used, otherwise the joint will loosen after it has been made. For general work three sizes of dowels are used, $\frac{1}{4}$, $\frac{3}{8}$ and $\frac{1}{2}$ inch. Dowels smaller than $\frac{1}{4}$ inch are used in cabinet work, but their manipulation is more difficult on account of the thin wood in which they are used.

How to make Dowels.

Although dowels are readily bought, the constructor may prefer to make his own. They are not difficult to make and home-made dowels are more satisfactory, because they can be made to suit the particular drilling bits in the tool kit, thus giving a better fit than could be obtained if the dowels are purchased.

The method of making dowels is shown in Fig. 1. A steel plate, $5 \times 1\frac{1}{2} \times \frac{3}{8}$ inches has three holes, $\frac{1}{4}$, $\frac{3}{8}$ and $\frac{1}{2}$ inch diameter. The holes are preferably tapered so that the underside is the larger. This makes it easier to drive the wood through.

Grooving the Dowels.

One of the advantages of making the dowels is that it is possible to groove them in the process of rounding. This is done by staking the dowel plate holes in four places with a cold chisel, so as to make four sharp projections in the holes, which cut grooves in the dowel as it is driven through the plate. These

Fig. 1.—How to make a Dowel from a Square Piece of Wood.
The dowel plate is made from a piece of tool steel $\frac{3}{8}$-in. thick.

grooves are necessary to allow the glue to flow out round the dowels when they are driven in. The wood for the dowels is split with a chopper, not cut with a saw. If the wood is sawn up, the grain in the dowels may not be straight. They are then more liable to split when driven in. After the wood has been split into square pieces approximately the size of the dowels and about 6 inches long, the ends are roughly rounded off with a knife or chisel, so as to give the sticks an entry into the dowel plate. The wood is now hammered through the hole to round them off the correct size.

Before using a dowel plate for the first time, test the holes for size with one piece of wood. If the dowels come out too small for the drill or centre bit, which is to be used for making the dowel holes, file out the holes to suit the bit. If the holes in the dowel plate are slightly oversize, causing the dowels to split the wood when driven in, the holes are made smaller by hammering round them so as to spread some of the metal into the top of the holes. In this way the dowels are made to suit the bit in the tool kit and good fitting dowels are assured for all subsequent jobs.

Preparing the Wood.

The joint faces of the wood to be dowelled must be carefully prepared to avoid gaps in the finished framework. This remark applies to any type of joint. Where dowels are to be inserted in the end grain of the wood, the ends are planed on a shooting board, as shown in Fig. 2.

Marking Off.

The strips forming a framework are all marked on the best side with a pencil, as shown in Fig. 3. The object of this is to show from which side to mark off the centre line of the dowels so as to ensure that all the joints will be flush on the face side. If the pieces of wood vary slightly in thickness and the lines are not all marked from one side, some of the joints will line up on the face side and some on the back.

The centre line of the dowels is scribed in the middle of the wood with a marking gauge. The distance between the dowels is marked on one half of the joint. The lines are copied on the second half of the joint by offering the two pieces together, as shown in Fig. 3. After squaring off the lines on the second half of the joint, make sure that the centre distance of the marks on each half are the same, so that no trouble is experienced in assembling the joint.

Size and Number of Dowels.

The size of dowels to use is one-half to one-third of the thickness of the wood into which they fit. Thus, for 1 inch wood $\frac{3}{8}$-inch dowels are used. The table on the facing page gives the best sizes of dowels to use for various thicknesses of wood.

When two pieces of wood of unequal thickness are to be jointed, the size of the dowels is judged by the thinner piece.

Certain exceptions must be observed, principally in framework consisting of square wood. Suppose a chair seat frame is made of wood $1\frac{1}{4}$ inch square.

Fig. 2.—Planing the End Grain of a Joint on a Shooting Board.

HOW TO MAKE DOWELLED JOINTS

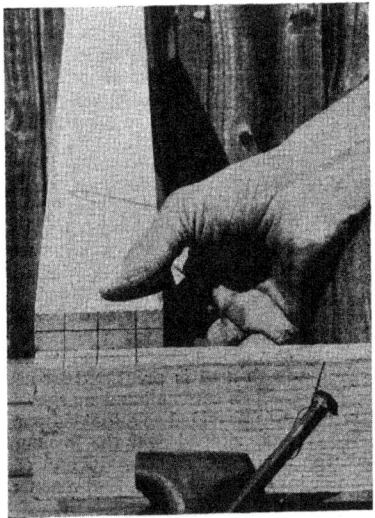

Fig. 3.—THE SECOND HALF OF THE JOINT IS COPIED FROM THE FIRST BY HOLDING THE TWO HALVES TOGETHER.

Fig. 4.—DRILLING THE HOLES IN THE FIRST HALF OF THE JOINT.

The depth of this part can be done by guesswork, but the depth of the holes in the second half must be gauged as described in the text.

twist bit, is to set a collar and grub screw at the required height so that the drilling is stopped when the correct depth is reached. The third way is to have a drill short enough for the drill chuck to form the stop. Which of the three methods is used will depend on the tools available.

Depth of Dowel Holes.

The actual depth of the holes is not important so long as they are sufficiently deep to give enough gluing surface for each half of the dowel. The table shows the depth of hole to use the various sizes of dowels. It is based on the principle that the dowel holes are three times as deep as the diameter of the dowels.

Inserting and cutting Dowels.

It is not advisable to cut the dowels to length before inserting them into the first half of the joint. The dowels are glued into the first half of the joint, then cut off to length, as shown in Fig. 5. This method avoids cutting the dowels up separately and accommodates the irregularity in the depth of the holes in one member of the joint.

The $\tfrac{7}{16}$ or even $\tfrac{3}{8}$-inch dowels would be too large, for they would either be too near the edge of the wood or too close together. The best arrangement for a joint of this size is to use four dowels $\tfrac{1}{4}$ inch diameter, spaced $\tfrac{1}{2}$ inch apart. Although two dowels suffice to prevent the members of the frame from twisting, four are used to give the necessary strength.

Drilling the Holes : Three Methods.

It is essential to keep the holes square when drilling, or trouble will be experienced when assembling the joint. Before starting to drill the holes, prick the centres deeply with an awl, so as to assist in picking up correctly the positions of the holes with the drill or centre bit. The second point is carefully to regulate the depth of the holes. This is done in one of three ways. If a plain centre bit is used, a piece of paper is stuck, to indicate the required depth, on the shank of the bit. The second method, for a long drill or a

Thickness of Wood. ins.	Diameter of Dowel. in.	Depth of Dowel Holes. ins.
2	$\tfrac{3}{4}$	$2\tfrac{1}{4}$
$1\tfrac{3}{4}$	$\tfrac{5}{8}$	$1\tfrac{7}{8}$
$1\tfrac{1}{2}$	$\tfrac{1}{2}$	$1\tfrac{1}{2}$
$1\tfrac{1}{4}$	$\tfrac{7}{16}$	$1\tfrac{5}{16}$
1	$\tfrac{3}{8}$	$1\tfrac{1}{8}$
$\tfrac{7}{8}$	$\tfrac{5}{16}$	1
$\tfrac{3}{4}$	$\tfrac{1}{4}$	$\tfrac{3}{4}$
$\tfrac{5}{8}$	$\tfrac{1}{4}$	$\tfrac{3}{4}$
$\tfrac{1}{2}$	$\tfrac{3}{16}$	$\tfrac{9}{16}$
$\tfrac{3}{8}$	$\tfrac{1}{8}$	$\tfrac{3}{8}$
$\tfrac{1}{4}$	$\tfrac{1}{8}$	$\tfrac{3}{8}$

Fig. 5.—AFTER GLUING CONVENIENT LENGTHS OF DOWELS IN ONE HALF OF THE JOINT, THEY ARE SAWN OFF TO LENGTH AS SHOWN HERE.

Fig. 6.—ASSEMBLING THE JOINT BETWEEN THE SIDE AND TOP RAIL OF A FIRE SCREEN

Gluing the Joint.

Before inserting the dowels, the holes are countersunk to remove any roughness from them and to provide a lead in for the dowels. Glue is put on the dowels, in the holes and also on the faces of the joint. When all the joints of the framework have been assembled with a mallet, it is advisable to cramp it up to prevent the joints opening up before the glue has set. If the dowels have been made a good fit, cramps will not be necessary.

Templates.

When several similar dowelled joints are to be made, the marking off is facilitated by the use of a template. This consists of a thin piece of wood or tinplate with small holes corresponding to the positions of the dowels. The template has locating flanges on two sides. The dowel holes are then marked off by pricking through the template holes with an awl or scriber. A template is an advantage for even two or three joints, because it assists in obtaining good alignment of the dowels.

Bad Alignment may cause Joint to Split.

In this connection it should be noted that bad alignment is just as likely to cause a joint to split as tight-fitting dowels, so that it is well worth the extra trouble of making a template.

An Improved Garden Chair

Whilst the ordinary type of folding deck chair is so widely used for deck and garden purposes, it is by no means as comfortable or convenient as it might be; it can only be regarded as a compromise between comfort and compactness.

The type of garden seat shown in Fig. 1 represents a marked improvement upon the ordinary type for the following reasons, namely: (1) It is much more comfortable. (2) It is provided with substantial arm-rests which can also be used to stand objects, such as books, glasses or cups, upon; and (3) it has a novel foot-rest arranged so as to give the correct reclining position; this item is adjustable in a moment to suit persons of different heights.

The seat in question can be folded flat, merely by releasing two brass pins held by chains to the framework. Further, by hinging the foot-rest members so as to enable them to be folded back on the arm-rest members, the folded length can be reduced considerably.

This type of seat has proved extremely comfortable in the garden, on liners and in the tropics.

Description.

The seat externally resembles the ordinary deck chair, but it is of rather heavier construction and larger dimensions. The upwardly sloping side members B (Fig. 2) are extended so as to form supports for the two flat horizontal members C, which act both as arm- and foot-rests. The two pairs of inclined side members A and B are pin-jointed at e, whilst the two flat members C are connected to the side members A, by means of pin-joints at f.

Sheet-metal brackets, or ordinary fork-end pieces are used to connect the front ends of the side members B to the horizontal members C, as shown at x. If necessary the inclinations of A and B can be varied merely by making the fixing bracket x adjustable along the member C.

Brass pins, or bolts of $\frac{1}{4}$-inch diameter are used to fasten the side members B to C. These pins should be provided with eyes and short lengths of brass chain, the ends of the latter being screwed to the lower surfaces of C, in order to prevent the pins from becoming lost when the seat is not in use. By removing these pins (at x) the seat folds flat. Further, as previously mentioned, if the portions of the horizontal members D, to the left of x (Fig. 2) are cut and hinged so as to fold over on to the top of the fixed portions C, a good deal of storage space will be saved.

Fig. 1.—This Type of Garden Seat is an Improvement on the Ordinary Type, as it Provides Comfortable Arm Rests together with an Adjustable Foot-rest.

The canvas band which forms the footrest is not shown in the photograph.

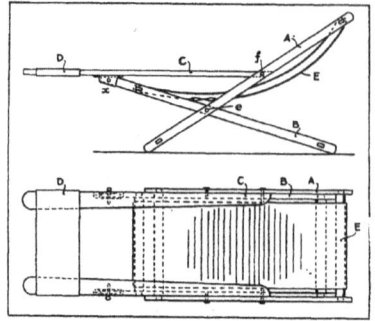

Fig. 2.—Side and Plan Views of the Completed Seat.

Showing the seat and foot canvases in position.

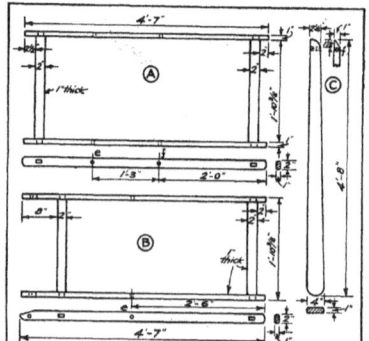

Fig. 3.—Dimensions and Constructional Details of the Seat Members.

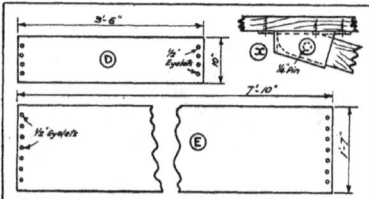

Fig. 4.—Showing the Foot and Seat Canvases, D and E.

The detail of the front fixture for the side member B in Fig. 2 is shown at x.

As in the case of the ordinary deck chair a canvas strip (or loop) E is connected between the upper and lower rails of the side members A and B. This canvas is of the standard size for deck chairs, and should preferably not be of the "tack-on" type, but of the eyelet and cord kind now sold for replacement purposes.

The latter type enables different parts of the canvas to be employed as wear or discolouration occur, for the canvas can be slid over the end rails so that a fresh area is presented for use.

The endless canvas band marked D in Fig. 2, is provided as a foot support. It is merely slipped over the free ends of the horizontal members C and can be adjusted to suit the foot-reach of the occupant of the seat.

Construction and Materials.

The inclined members A and B are made of 2 by 1 inch section timber, whilst the arms C are made from timber tapering in section from 4 inches at the foot-end to $2\frac{1}{4}$ inches at the other end.

The cross members of the frames containing the pairs A and B are of 2 by $\frac{3}{4}$-inch timber.

The two cross members holding the canvas, namely, at the top and bottom of A and B, are of circular section, about $1\frac{1}{4}$ inch diameter; broomsticks of ash or pine are quite suitable for these. They should be shouldered and driven into $\frac{7}{8}$-inch holes bored in the side members A and B; the joints should afterwards be pinned to prevent movement. Brass bolts of $\frac{1}{2}$-inch diameter are used for the pin joints at e and f.

The cross members of the seat frames must be mortised and tenoned into the side members, the ends being pinned with brass nails.

Teak is undoubtedly the best wood for outdoor, sea and colonial use. For occasional garden use, oak can be recommended, although it is rather heavy.

Where cheapness is the principal consideration, red pine or Oregon pine will be found quite satisfactory.

Constructional Details.

Constructional details and the dimensions of the framework, are given in Fig. 3. It will be observed that the lettering on the frames and members corresponds with that on the general arrangement shown in Fig. 2.

Particulars of the canvas for the seat E and the foot support D are given in Fig. 4, whilst a detail drawing of the joint x is given in the top right-hand corner of Fig. 4.

It is important to use brass screws, pins and other fittings throughout in order to resist corrosion effects.

TIME, LABOUR AND MONEY SAVING IDEAS

STRENGTHENING A GROUND POST.

Inclined ground posts which are subjected to a fair amount of side pressure, sometimes develop the habit of working loose in the ground under the strain. To overcome this difficulty a piece of board B should be nailed to the "pressure" side of the post

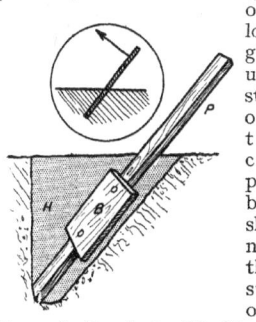

P, and the hole H filled in, and well rammed, with earth. The board B should be placed just below the surface so as to exert the greatest resistance. It should be well creosoted before placing in position.

SIMPLE HINGES FOR SCREENS AND CLOTHES HORSES.

Folding draught screens and clothes horses are designed so as to fold flat when not in use, for storage reasons.

Although the ordinary metal hinges are quite satisfactory for this purpose, they are apt to prove expensive to the home constructor; moreover, they take much longer to fit than the simple device shown in the illustration. In the latter case ordinary webbing, as used by upholsterers for chesterfields and easy chairs, is employed for the hinges.

The method of fixing the webbing so that the panels will fold flat is shown in the right-hand illustration.

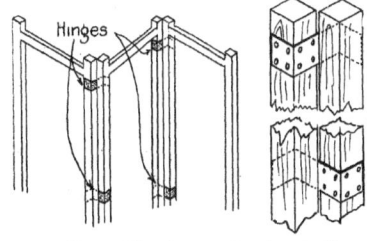

It will readily be understood if one imagines the ends are viewed from above. The webbing is secured to the vertical wooden members by means of upholsterers' or carpet tacks, four of the latter being necessary for each face.

A rather stronger joint can be made by first gluing the webbing to the wood, and, whilst the glue is still soft, driving in the tacks.

As shown in the left-hand illustration the webbing hinges are arranged, alternatively, right and left hand down each vertical member of the frames.

MAKING YOUR OWN WOOD FILLERS.

Holes in various kinds of timber can readily be filled with powdered white lead to which linseed oil is added so as to give it a putty-like consistency. Next add a small quantity of japan drier to bring the mixture to a more pasty state. It can then be applied as a wood filler to stop holes, cracks and similar defects. To colour the filler to match mahogany use powdered burnt sienna. For oak colour use raw sienna; for walnut, vandyke brown. By altering the proportions of pigment used any desired shade of colour can be obtained.

HOW TO SCORE WOODEN SURFACES.

When gluing two pieces of wood together the surfaces should be scratched or scored in the direction of

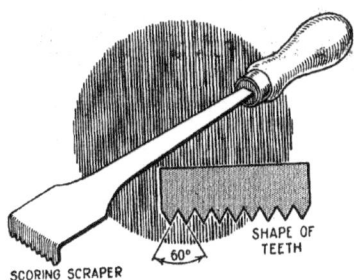

the grain. A scraper can be made out of a piece of sheet steel. The teeth are filed after bending the blade over at right angles, and a wooden handle fitted.

FURNITURE STEADIMENT.

Furniture standing on an uneven floor never stands steadily unless one or more of the legs are wedged up. The unsightliness of cardboard or wood slips can be avoided by using a piece of sheet rubber of a colour to harmonise with the carpet and cut to a shape only slightly larger than that of the foot of the furniture.

WHIPPING A ROPE END.

The end of a rope can be neatly finished off by "whipping," that is, binding it with twine or thin string.

First of all lay an end of the twine along the rope and secure it with several turns of twine then lay a loop of twine along the rope and let the "bight" or loop end project slightly. Continue the winding over the loop until the end of the rope is nearly reached; then slip the binding twine through the loop and draw the latter out of the binding, bring the latter with it. Cut off the end neatly and give the twine a rub with beeswax, thus completing the job.

PUTTY FOR STEEL-FRAMED WINDOWS.

Heat some glycerine to expel the water, then mix with it some finely powdered litharge to make a thick paste. Use it at once as it hardens very quickly. This putty can be used to fasten glass to iron or steel and is excellent for repairs to windows with metal frames.

USEFUL OUTDOOR WALL HOOKS.

Although it is customary to employ nails for the purpose of attaching ropes, cords, wires and similar items to the outside walls of buildings, these are by no means satisfactory; it is much better to use proper hooks. The only difficulty hitherto experienced with the latter has been to drive them into the walls without damaging the hooks.

Figs. 1 and 2 show two methods of overcoming this difficulty. In the former case a hook L is made, with the aid of a pair of pliers, out of $\frac{1}{16}$-inch copper wire, leaving an eyelet that will go under the head of the 1-inch galvanised nail N (sold for driving into the mortar of walls). The eyelet is slipped over the smaller part of the nail, and the latter is then driven into the wall. By suitably proportioning the hook L, this type can be used for training wall climbing plants, wall trees, etc., for the wire can be bent around the stems or branches to hold them in position.

The square-headed galvanised nail, shown in Fig. 2, having first been tapped to suit the screwed shank of

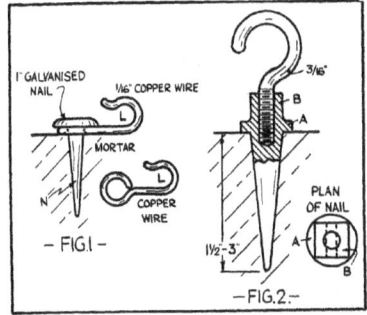

the hook, is driven into the wall, the hook being screwed in afterwards.

It is best to use a copper or hide-faced hammer to drive the nail into position, in order to avoid damaging the screw thread.

TO CLEAN TINWARE.

A simple and inexpensive method of cleaning tinware articles is to take some common washing soda and apply to the surface with a piece of moistened newspaper screwed into a ball. Afterwards use a dry piece of newspaper to polish the surface.

METHODS OF PRESERVING WOOD

DEALING WITH WOOD FENCING AND INTERIOR AND EXTERIOR WOODWORK FOR HOUSES

SINCE wood preservation by antiseptic treatment was first practised in this country a hundred or more years ago, research into its many problems has been continuously active, with the result that to-day, in spite of many methods and materials having been discarded as either useless or impracticable, there yet are many substances which can be used with confidence by those who wish to protect their wood against future attacks by its enemies, or who are determined to destroy them if they are already established. It is the aim of this article to describe as briefly and as nontechnically as possible the various methods which may be put into practice by the householder, the gardener, the farmer, the poultry-keeper and the furniture owner.

PRESERVATIVES.

Wood preservatives may be conveniently divided into (a) oil preservatives, (b) water soluble salts, (c) salts soluble in other materials than water.

The best known of the oil preservatives are coal tar and creosote. Most people are familiar with tar, which has been used extensively in the past for weatherboarding, sheds, roofs and posts; but in general, and particularly in posts, it is nothing like so good as creosote. It puts a sealing coat on the timber and does not allow the wood to dry out. Also, it does not penetrate as deeply as creosote.

The Creosote Compounds.

Creosote, which is distilled from coal tar, is a very much more satisfactory preservative. It is more easily applied, it is not sticky and messy, and it is extremely toxic to fungi and insects. For outside use, for timber in contact with the ground, it is unrivalled as a preservative for the treatment of wood against decay, chiefly because of its permanence in the wood. It is not washed out by water.

Under the heading Creosote come a number of proprietary brands of wood preservatives familiar to the public from advertisements. These are obtainable in small quantities from most ironmongers and stores, and in

Fig. 1.—THE DRILLING AND POURING METHOD OF TREATING OLD FENCING WITH CREOSOTE.
First drill a few holes with an auger, pointing downwards and slantwise towards the centre of the post.

a wide range of colours, some of them being comparatively odourless. Most of them are put up in decorated tins, and they are, for the most part, adapted for interior work, for staining and preserving floors, etc., and are suitable for brush application where this method can be satisfactorily adopted. They are, of course, slightly more expensive than crude creosote, and on that account are not so suitable for treating fencing material and posts by the open tank method, a description of which will be found on page 90.

Fig. 2.—THE DRILLING AND POURING METHOD OF TREATING OLD FENCING WITH CREOSOTE (2).
Now pour creosote in the holes. After one fill has soaked in, fill up again and close each auger hole with a plug of wood soaked in creosote.

A Word of Warning.

A word of warning is necessary against much socalled creosote which is being sold and which is but a spurious imitation of the real article. A very definite specification has been laid down by the British Standards Institution, and this specification is a safeguard of its purity. If purchasers will buy their creosote from a tar distiller or from other reliable sources, insisting that it shall comply with the British Standards Institution Specification, they need have no fear. The purchaser of creosote is warned against buying from unscrupulous firms and dealers who may be selling, as creosote, oils of doubtful origin or dilutions of creosote with petroleum.

Crude Creosote and its Limitations.

Among the disadvantages of creosote when used in its crude form, particularly in interior work, are its smell, its dark colour, and its liability to creep on to and to stain any adjacent timber or plaster. Another disadvantage is that it cannot be painted over.

Wood Preservatives suitable for Interior Work.

With regard to water-soluble salts, these have, generally speaking, the following advantages over creosote, particularly for interior use:—

(1) They are purchaseable in concentrated form, needing only dilution with water.

(2) They are odourless.

(3) They are comparatively colourless.

(4) They can be painted over.

(5) They do not creep and stain building material.

(6) Some of them—*e.g.*, zinc chloride—are mildly fire-retardant.

They are, of course, not so suitable for the treatment of outside woodwork unless this is afterwards painted over.

PRACTICAL METHODS OF PRESERVING WOOD FENCING.

We will deal first with practical methods for the protection of wood posts and fencing; because protection by antiseptic means will

METHODS OF PRESERVING WOOD

Fig. 3.—THE BRUSH METHOD OF TREATING OLD FENCING WITH CREOSOTE.

Remove some of the earth from round the ground-level line to a depth of about 6 inches. Then brush liberally with creosote, putting it on hot.

Fig. 4.—AFTER APPLYING A SECOND COAT OF CREOSOTE THE EARTH CAN BE REPLACED.

The earth should now be drenched with hot creosote to kill any traces of fungus which there may be in the soil.

Fig. 5.—SHOWING PENETRATION OF CREOSOTE AT GROUND LINE IN POSTS 5-INCH IN DIAMETER, OBTAINED BY THE HOT AND COLD PROCESS IN THE VERTICAL DRUM.

prevent replacement of posts and fencing becoming necessary.

Why Fence Posts decay at Ground Line and Joints.

The decay which is found in gate-posts, fence posts and pergola poles is due, in almost every case, to attack by one or more kinds of fungus. For a fungus to thrive on timber, four conditions must be present at one and the same time—moisture, air, food and a favourable temperature. If one or two conditions only are present, the wood may remain quite unharmed. In a post, the part at which these conditions most favourable to a fungus are likely to be found is the ground line, and a short distance just above and below. It is here that fungal attack usually develops, where, in fact, the post rots and breaks off. The point of the post, buried in soil and deprived of air, is usually unharmed. All mortises and tenons and other places where moisture can lodge are likely spots for development of attack by fungus. The top of the post will, as a rule, be unharmed unless cracks develop.

The Importance of Deep Penetration of the Preservative.

If the posts are to last, no cracks or crannies of untreated, naked wood into which fungus spores may be blown from a distance must be left when they are treated with the preservative solution. But wood is always liable to develop cracks, especially when it is unseasoned and in a climate such as ours, with extremes of heat and cold, and we must therefore be certain that when the preservative is applied it shall penetrate so deeply into the wood that it will go deeper than any cracks which may develop, so that if any cracks do appear during the drying out of the wood, they will be cracks in *treated* wood with no exposure of naked white wood.

"Does Brush Treatment give the Deep Penetration Necessary?"

The answer is No, it does not. By merely brushing over with preservative it is not possible to obtain that deep penetration of the antiseptic solution which is so absolutely necessary for timber which is to be in contact with the ground. (When we come to deal with outbuildings and household timbers, we shall see that brush treatment may be quite satisfactory—it is timber in contact with ground that we are here considering.)

Why Telegraph Poles are so Durable.

If a telegraph pole be cut across, a dark brown circular ring, 1½ to 2 inches wide, will be seen surrounding the inner core of natural-coloured wood, and this ring would show the depth of penetration of creosote required by the post office authorities. There is, with such a deep layer of preservative, no fear of fungus spores getting into the centre through holes made by the telegraph mechanics' climbing irons, or through bolt or screw holes. In the same way, we want to prevent spores getting into our posts through nail holes, etc., and if we wish to have a fence treated as effectively to resist decay as is the telegraph pole, it will, every time, be worth our while specifying, when we purchase our posts, rails, etc., that they be *pressure treated*—which is the name for the process by

CHARCOAL

Fig. 6.—ONE METHOD OF TREATING POSTS WHICH ARE TO GO IN THE GROUND IS TO CHAR THEM IN A FIRE.

which telegraph poles, railway sleepers and marine piling, etc., are impregnated with preservative, usually creosote.

The Best Method—Pressure Treatment.

Pressure treatment of timber consists, simply, of this operation: The timber is placed in a huge cylinder, which is hermetically sealed. A vacuum is applied to reduce the air pressure in the cylinder, then the preservative is introduced hot and a pressure up to about 100 lbs. to the square inch is applied and kept for a couple of hours or more, during which time the preservative is forced into the timber. After pressure is released, a final vacuum is applied to remove excess preservative, and the timber is then withdrawn from the cylinder. After being allowed to drain and dry, it is ready for use.

This pressure method is, above all other methods, the very best for securing proper and deep penetration of the preservative, and is the one which has been adopted in almost all the best-known records of the life of treated wood in service. As has already been said, it is a paying proposition to use only pressure treated wood for any permanent fencing.

It is not for one moment suggested that this is a method which can be carried out by anyone in his field or garden, for the necessary apparatus is very costly, but anyone can specify pressure treated wood when ordering timber.

The Least Efficient Method—Brush Treatment.

To go now from the best method to the least efficient—namely, treatment by the brush or brush application as it is usually called. This method is by no means useless for many classes of work, such as weatherboarding, wooden palings above ground, interiors of chicken houses, summer houses, and for interior work generally, but it is quite unsuitable for most external work in contact with the ground. It gives only a skin-

METHODS OF PRESERVING WOOD

Fig. 7.—THE OPEN TANK METHOD OF TREATING FENCING MATERIAL AND POSTS WITH CREOSOTE.

This consists of heating the timber in the preservative for a certain period and then allowing it to cool off. The drum is mounted on a rough and ready fireplace of bricks built up round a shallow hole in the ground.

Fig. 8.—THE OPEN TANK METHOD OF TREATING FENCING MATERIAL AND POSTS WITH CREOSOTE.

The creosote is heated to a temperature of about 180° F. and kept at that temperature for a little over an hour. A thermometer should be used to ensure that the temperature is kept constant. The posts are then allowed to cool for twenty-four hours.

Fig. 9.—THE OPEN TANK METHOD OF TREATING FENCING MATERIAL AND POSTS WITH CREOSOTE.

After removal from the cold bath, the posts should be up-ended in the drum for some hours, so that the tops of the posts are treated with a certain amount of preservative. Alternatively, brush the tops with hot creosote during treatment.

deep penetration, and for satisfactory results it is essential that a reasonable depth of impregnation of the antiseptic solution be obtained. If used, however, whether for interior or outdoor work, the preservative should be put on hot and liberally. When using creosote with the brush, or creosote preparations, it should be almost splashed on, not trying to make a little go a long way, as when using an oil paint. Also, and this is important, at least two coats should be given, allowing two or three weeks between the first and second coats.

A Satisfactory Half-and-half Method—The Open Tank.

There remains to be described a method which, although falling short of the pressure, or best, method, is yet very effective and very easily carried out. This is called the open tank method, and is one which can be recommended for the uprights of fences, or the bases of pergola poles, because it is possible, if instructions be followed carefully, to obtain a depth of penetration of the preservative which is not very much inferior to that which is given by the pressure method, especially if the poles be in the round and contain a certain amount of sapwood.

This method is infinitely superior to brush application. It should appeal to anyone who owns a small wood or spinney, or who is able to obtain posts in the round, for by treatment many species of timber can be used for fencing, etc., which would be quite useless untreated. For instance, many timbers, such as beech, alder, elm and birch, do not last more than a few years —six to seven at most—in an untreated state, but when treated by the open tank method they can be made to give good service for at least twenty-five years.

Details of the Open Tank Method.

In a few words, the process consists of heating the timber in the preservative for a certain time at a certain temperature, then allowing it to remain in the preservative until the latter has cooled down. During the preliminary heating a certain amount of air and moisture will be driven out of the timber, and a partial vacuum will be created. As soon as the preservative begins to cool, some of it will be drawn into the timber, to fill up the vacuum in the cells of the timber, and this absorption of preservative may continue for the best part of twenty-four hours' cooling.

It has been quite correctly described as a pressure process, it depending on atmospheric pressure to drive the liquid into the timber. It can be carried out, either in a large horizontal tank heated by a flue running the length underneath, and in which the posts are laid, flat, or in a very much simpler form in which the butt or base only of the post is treated, and this is amply sufficient for most fencing, for the vital part, the portion just above and below ground level, will be protected.

The operation of treating the butt-ends of posts is shown in the accompanying illustrations, where the tank is an old road-dressing drum of 90 gallons capacity in which a 40-gallon barrel of creosote has been emptied.

How the Drum is Mounted.

The drum is mounted on a rough and ready fireplace of bricks built up round a shallow hole in the ground and with a piece of piping for a chimney to ensure a good draught. In a plant of this kind excellent results can be obtained in the treatment of the butt-ends of posts, protection being given to that portion of the post which is liable to decay in service. It is advisable to treat the posts for at least 6 inches above ground line. Care should be taken to prevent the creosote boiling over, and its level should be kept well below the edge of the drum. The drum should never be used near buildings, stacks, etc.

Heat the Creosote to about 180° F.

The creosote is heated with the posts in it to a temperature of about 180° F. and kept at that temperature for a little over an hour. The fire should then be allowed to die down and the posts to remain in the creosote for twenty-four hours to cool. Absorption of creosote takes place during the cooling process.

Allowance must be made for Absorption.

During cooling, the level of the preservative will drop as it becomes absorbed by the posts and, therefore, liquid must be added from time to time to keep it to its original level.

Treating the Tops of the Posts.

During treatment the tops of the posts should be washed over with hot creosote, particular care being taken to brush hot liquid into the bottom of any cracks or shakes. As an alternative to washing over with hot preservative, which entails a certain amount of splashing and mess, the posts can, after removal from the cool bath, either be laid for some hours in an old trough filled with preservative, or up-ended in one of the drums.

Draining.

The posts should finally be put to drain in an empty drum. After treatment they should be carefully stacked until ready for erection, care being taken that the creosoted sapwood be not damaged by careless handling. Should it be necessary to saw or cut into the posts, the exposed untreated wood should be brushed over with hot creosote. It is very important that in setting the posts at least 6 inches of treated wood should be exposed above the surface of the ground, as already recommended.

Charring and Creosoting New Fence Posts.

There is another, and very old, method of treating posts which are to go into the ground, which, while not as reliable as the pressure or open-tank methods, does yet give a certain measure of protection—that is, charring them in a fire. This method was adopted, apparently, in prehistoric times by the builders of some of the forts on the South Downs, for traces of charred posts which seem to have formed part of a stockade have been found in more than one site. It is used to-day on several estates.

Much work has lately been done in Australia on this method, where an oxy-acetylene flame is used to char the post, which is afterwards dipped into a liquid preservative, such as creosote.

When the preservative is applied in this way, or by a spray, to the freshly charred post, a certain absorption takes place for the same reason that caused it to take place in the open tank—it is drawn into the wood to fill up the partial vacuum created by the expulsion of air due, in this case, to the heat during charring. If, therefore, this rough and ready method of charring be carried out, it should, to give the best results, be followed by immersion of the post in a small tank or drum of preservative.

TREATMENT OF OLD FENCING

By the Brush Method.

If it be desired to treat posts or fencing already erected of untreated wood, or to give extra protection to posts which have been merely brushed over with preservative, and which have received no special treatment at ground level, the best plan is to remove some of the earth from round the ground-level line, exposing about 6 inches of the post below that line, and then applying a liberal dose of creosote with the brush, putting it on hot. A second coat should be given in a few weeks' time, after which the earth may be replaced and itself drenched with hot creosote. This will kill any traces of fungus which there may be in the soil.

By Drilling and Pouring In.

Another method is to drill a few holes with an auger, pointing downwards and slantwise towards the centre of the post, and pouring creosote into these; after one fill of creosote has soaked in, fill up again and close each auger hole with a plug of wood soaked in creosote.

A Note on Oak Posts.

Even oak posts will decay in a few years if they contain any proportion of sap wood and are put in the ground after only brush treatment. The sap wood falls a ready prey to the attacks of fungi, and in a few years it may become eaten away to such an extent that a mere stick of the heartwood will be left, giving the post very small mechanical strength. It will be, therefore, a wise precaution to treat even oak posts at ground level in the way described in the last paragraph, especially if you are suspicious of the condition of other posts in the same fence or immediate neighbourhood. The stitch-in-time proverb is as true in the realm of wood-preserving as in any other field, and a little time and money spent on giving this extra treatment to posts will be found to be well invested.

OUTBUILDINGS, GARDEN EDGING AND STEPS

For the walls and roofs of tool sheds, garages, summer-houses, poultry-houses, etc., brush-application of a preservative is eminently suitable to any portion of them which will not be in contact with the ground. For any woodwork, however, which is to go into the ground, such as the uprights of the shed, or which will be resting on the ground or will be in contact with damp grass, it is essential that it be either pressure-treated or be treated in the open-tank by the heating-and-cooling method. At the risk of repetition it must be emphasised again that brush-treatment of timber at ground-level is not to be relied on to give proper protection.

When Creosoting a Poultry-house—a Word of Warning.

With regard to poultry-houses, a word of warning is necessary—birds should never be put into a house which has been freshly treated with any preservative, particularly those of coal-tar origin, such as creosote or some of the proprietary brands. The shed or house should be allowed to air thoroughly, and the timber to become quite dry after treatment, before birds can be safely put in.

Why Creosote is not Suitable for Greenhouse Interiors.

The same precaution should be taken when using treated wood for green houses or frame construction. Many plants, among which are tomatoes, seem to be very susceptible to even the fumes of creosote, and much damage has occurred through plants being stood on greenhouse staging which has been creosoted.

What to Use.

Some form of treatment of greenhouse and frame woodwork is very necessary, for in course of time wood is liable to rot under its coat of paint, through water finding its way under that coat, where it becomes broken or thin. For this purpose there are several preservatives quite suitable, as already described. They can be applied to the woodwork before painting, because they can be painted over quite satisfactorily, which creosote cannot be.

Garden Edging and Steps.

Before leaving the garden and outbuildings it may be mentioned that among the valuable uses to which pressure-creosoted wood can be put is that of garden edging and terrace steps. The decay of the ordinary untreated wooden edging is one of the most annoying things with which the gardener is faced, as also is the decay of steps in the path and steps holding up grass terraces or terraced flower-borders. If the wood be treated with creosote under pressure, it will not decay, and will last the proverbial lifetime.

Prolonging the Life of the Garden Barrow.

Also, the woodwork of a barrow or garden cart will be all the better for being treated with creosote under pressure, or treated with one of the non-creosote preservatives which, as will be described later, can be used out of doors without risk of their being washed out of the timber by rain and damp. We all know how, after some years' use, a barrow begins to get broken, first small pieces chipping off, then larger pieces, then a hole appears in the floor—this breaking up of the woodwork is due to decay caused by the comparatively damp life which the barrow leads. It is successively drenched with rain and scorched by sun—the wood opens, fungus spores get in, and, although masses of fungus and fruiting-bodies are not normally seen, fungus decay is going on all the time, insiduously, inside the woodwork. Proper treatment of the wood will stop this.

EXTERIOR WOODWORK OF A HOUSE

It is assumed here that this general heading does not include any timber which is to be in contact with the ground, and that there is no call for pressure-treatment or treatment by the open-tank method.

For Unpainted Woodwork.

Brushing on hot creosote will give adequate protection to doors, timbering or half-timbering, providing the woodwork is not to be painted after treatment.

If the owner likes the finish that a good oil paint will give, he is at once debarred from using crude creosote, and many, if not all, of the proprietary brands of coal-tar base preservatives, though there are colourless brands of some of the latter which are claimed by the makers to take paint without any harm to the paint coat.

Why Creosote Compounds are not suitable for Window Frames.

In the case of window frames, even though they may not have to be painted, there is the great difficulty that putty will not adhere to creosoted wood, and on this account creosote is no use for that purpose.

Use Salt Preservative.

There are, however, several water-soluble salt preservatives, such as those employing zinc chloride, sodium fluoride, copper sulphate, copper chromate, etc., and other preservatives employing copper salts in some solvent other than water, which can be used to advantage for window frames, for not only are they very toxic to fungi, but they can be painted over with any ordinary oil paint.

How to apply Preservative to Window Frames that have already been Painted.

Bore small holes downwards into the angles of the frame, and fill them up with the preservative in powder or crystalline form, and then paint over the wood. Any water which finds its way in course of time through the paint or into cracks which may develop in the woodwork will dissolve the salts and convey them into the interior of the wood.

Treating Doors which are to be Painted.

As to doors, if they are to be painted, the same salt preservatives can be used. If not, there is nothing better, from the point of view of both preservative value and appearance, than creosote or one of the coal-tar base preparations in their wide range of colours.

INTERIOR WOODWORK

Under this heading there naturally fall such uses of woodwork as floors and flooring, joists, rafters, skirting boards, etc., and imitation beams.

It is well known that much damage can be done by dry rot to floor boards and joists of houses, particularly when built on damp sites and of wood which is not properly dry.

Preventing Dry Rot.

Proper preservative treatment applied to the joists will prevent attacks of dry rot. Timber, pressure-treated preferably by the empty-cell process, is the best, if creosote be used, and if this be insisted upon at the time of building a house, the owner need fear no trouble from dry rot.

Curative Treatment.

If dry rot is suspected, have the floor boards up, in order to get at the joists, which should be thoroughly and copiously treated with hot creosote, or with one of the salt preservatives. The floor boards should be treated with a preservative, particularly on the underside, as also should be the backs of the skirting boards, for this is a situation very prone to fungal attacks.

Use Odourless Preservatives for Panelling and Imitation Beams.

Provided the under-floor construction be good, and the joists treated, there should be no need to treat panelling; but in doubtful cases and situations the panelling could be treated with one of the odourless and colourless salt or creosote preservatives of known toxic value. The same could be done to picture rails and other wooden fixtures, before construction, but it is extremely unlikely that a picture rail would be attacked by fungus without the householder having first become aware of the presence of the fungus in the floor. Imitation beams come rather under the same heading as picture rails, and should not need protection so long as there is no danger of their becoming damp through roof leakage or through the ascendency of moisture up a wall.

FURNITURE

So far we have dealt with fungal attacks on timber, and from them furniture may be said to be relatively immune in the average well-ordered household.

Three Furniture Pests.

But furniture, in common with other woodwork in a house, has other enemies than fungi—namely, the Common Furniture Beetle, the Powder Post Beetle and the Death Watch Beetle.

Use Paraffin and Turpentine.

With small lots of furniture much can be done with paraffin or turpentine as insecticides brushed on to unvarnished surfaces, backs of drawers, undersides of tables, and to joints, cracks and crevices. Repeat the process every three or four weeks during the spring and summer months for at least two years.

It is useless to expect one application of the most powerful insecticide to do the trick—it will kill some beetles and some grubs which happen to be near the surface of the wood, but will not touch those which are deeper down. These must be dealt with a few weeks later, when they will have moved nearer the surface.

There are many proprietary insecticide preparations on the market for treating timber and furniture attacked by the Furniture Beetle. Many of them give excellent results providing the treatment is persevered in, as explained in the paragraph above. The British Wood Preserving Association, 166 Piccadilly, W. 1, will on application supply the names of any of the proprietary brands of wood preservative, etc., referred to in this article.

REMOVING STAINS FROM CARPETS & LEATHER UPHOLSTERY

Stains on carpets, if tackled at once, generally yield to treatment. The following are some simple remedies for stains due to various causes.

Blacklead.

Blacklead stains can be removed with a paste made with fuller's earth and ammonia water, applied to the carpet, allowed to dry and then brushed off. The treatment must be repeated until the stains disappear.

Ink Stains.

Apply a thick layer of common salt. Leave it on for some minutes, brush off, and apply more salt until all the ink is absorbed. Now rub the carpet with lemon juice and wipe with clean water. If the lemon cannot be applied at once, the layer of salt should be kept moist until it is available.

General Discolouration.

General stains and discolouration can be treated with a lather of yellow soap applied with a flannel and rinsed with ammonia and water.

Leather Upholstery.

Warm water and vinegar applied with a clean sponge will remove most stains from leather, and the polish can be restored by rubbing with a cloth dipped in a mixture of turpentine and white of egg. Suitable proportions are one teaspoonful of turpentine to the white of one egg. Petrol and benzene are also effective in the renoval of stains. Any slight change in colour following this treatment can be remedied by using a suitably coloured leather reviver, or by adding a few drops of stain to a leather polish.

How to Fix Glass Shelves

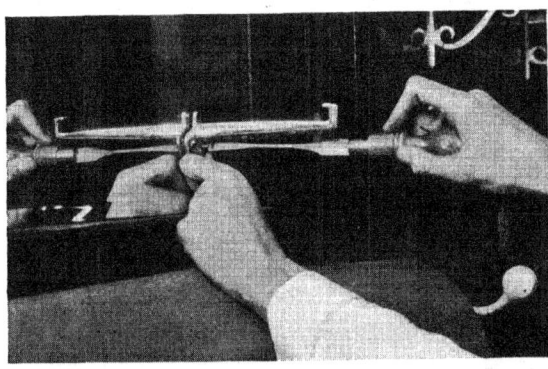

*Fig. 1.—*Fixing Ordinary Shelf Brackets to a Drilled Mirror.
This and the accompanying photographs were specially taken in Messrs. T. & W. Ide's showrooms.

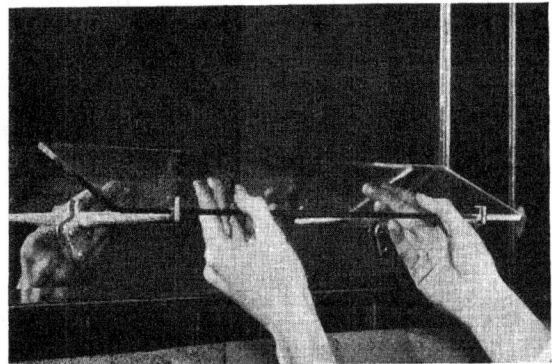

*Fig. 2.—*Placing the Shelf in Position.
Showing how the glass fits into the turned-over front lip of the bracket.

THE use of Glass Shelves in the home is of great importance, for they are hygienic, being very easy to keep clean and they are beautiful in appearance. In the bath room and the kitchen they are a great advantage, as wet sponges, brushes, etc., can be placed upon them without fear of staining the surface; the same applies in the other rooms of the house where a highly polished shelf can be ruined by placing a lighted cigarette or wine-glass upon it. This can be avoided if covered with transparent glass.

Types of Glass suitable for Shelves.

There are several types of glass suitable for the purpose. Transparent plate glass is the most popular, for with its perfectly flat polished surface it will fit in with any style or colour scheme. It is made ¼ inch thick, which is quite suitable for ordinary shelf work. Thicker substances can be had, but they are only necessary for extra large sizes or for carrying heavy articles. It can be had in various attractive tints.

Where an extra strong shelf is wanted, "Armourplate" glass should be used. This is specially strengthened and will hold a weight three or four times as heavy as ordinary plate glass; it will also resist a heat of molten lead at 620° F. It has the same appearance as plate glass and cannot be cut after manufacture.

Another transparent glass suitable for shelves is known as "Drawn" sheet glass of ¼-inch thickness. This is almost as strong as plate glass, but has not the same perfectly flat polished

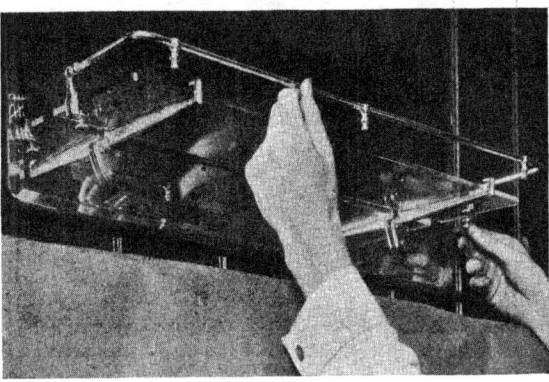

*Fig. 3.—*Fixing a Guardrail on to a Shelf.
Note how the rail is held in position with small thumb screws.

surface. It is much cheaper than plate glass when supplied in large sizes.

If a semi-opaque glass is wanted, ¼-inch rough cast glass is very attrac-

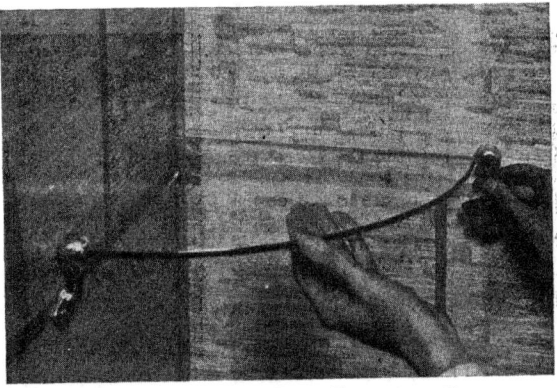

*Fig. 4.—*A Glass Corner Shelf Fitted with Brackets.

tive; this is a form of plate with a rimpled surface.

Coloured Glass.

There is also opal glass which is opaque and has a beautiful range of colours in both plain and marbled effects; it is made in two qualities known as Marmorite and Marmorene. The first named is the most expensive, and has the same polished surface as plate glass and a sanded back. It is made in several colours from ⅜ inch upwards in thickness. The Marmorene is made ¼ inch thick and is mainly used for shelving; it has a far greater range of colours which are very effective with the scintillating face that the glass possesses. This glass is finely ribbed on its back. These two glasses can be supplied in black or white ¼ inch thick with both surfaces polished.

Rubbing down the Rough Edges of Glass.

The rough edges of glass can always be rubbed down with a carborundum stone to avoid cutting, but if a highly finished edge is wanted a special stone is required, and any glass dealer will do the work quite reasonably.

Drilling Holes in Glass.

If it is necessary to drill holes in the glass, this also can be done at home if care is exercised. A small three-sided file with its end ground down to a fine point and fitted into an ordinary brace is used. During the process

HOW TO FIX GLASS SHELVES

the tip of the file must be kept moistened with turpentine, which acts as a cooling medium to both glass and drill. Just a little pressure is necessary and great care must be taken to prevent shelling the edge of the hole or splitting. When the drill is almost through, the glass should be turned over and the hole finished from the other side.

Methods of Fixing Glass Shelves.

There are several methods of fixing glass shelves, the main one being with brackets, which can be obtained in several styles in porcelain enamel and in metal chromium or nickel-plated.

Brackets.

Ordinary shelf brackets have a turned-over front lip to prevent the glass from slipping forwards; they are also made with a side lip which stops any movement whatever. Some are made with tumbler or toothbrush-holders complete. Another type simply has an upright support on which the shelf is laid, the glass being drilled and screwed down on to the bracket.

Bracket for Corner Shelves.

A special bracket is made for corner shelves, supplied in sets of three. Two of them are upright and grooved to take the glass, and the other is specially shaped for a corner fitting and has a flat top on which the glass rests. Special guardrails are made to prevent any possibility of articles slipping off, and these are quite simple to fix, being clipped on to the shelf. Rawlplugs should always be used for fixing any type of brackets.

Fixing Shelves to Tiles.

When fixing to tiles a special tool is necessary, namely, the Rawlplug jumping bit, which is a fluted tool. Gently tap this on the tiles, twisting the bit at the same time. It should penetrate quite easily, but as with glass great care is required to avoid any shelling or splitting.

Fixing Small Shelves in a Recess.

Fixing small shelves into a recess can be done in the same way as wooden shelves, i.e., with metal or wood fillets drilled and screwed each side of the opening and the glass allowed to rest on them. Another method is the use of metal strips about 4 inches long by $\frac{1}{2}$ inch wide and bent at right angles. One section is drilled and screwed to the wall and with two or more to each side of the shelf will give quite a good job. Grooves can also be used, being cut out to the thickness of the glass in which the shelves will slide.

Covering an Existing Shelf with Glass.

Where glass is required to cover an existing shelf it is hardly necessary to fix it as its own weight should hold it in position. If necessary, however, small clips are made for the purpose, known as "Nippy" clips, which are small pieces of metal about 1 inch long with a $\frac{1}{4}$-inch turnover. The long section is screwed to the edge of the existing shelf and the bent section holds the glass tight. The glass can be drilled and screwed to the existing shelf, but this is not recommended as the screws are inclined to collect the dirt.

Cutting Glass.

When cutting glass hold the cutter at an angle as shown in Fig. 5. The glass should be placed on a flat surface such as a table top. Make sure there are no loose objects or projections underneath, for unless this is done there is a risk of the glass breaking or cracking under pressure. If the diamond is held correctly it will make a clean scratch. Holding it incorrectly will result in a splintery or jagged scratch.

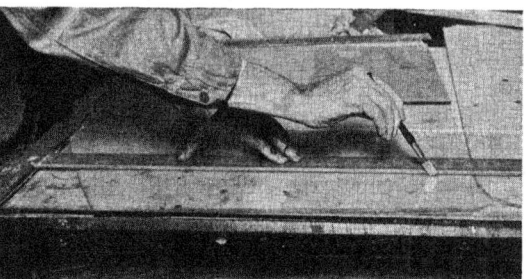

Fig. 5.—Here We see the Correct Angle for cutting Plate Glass with a Diamond Cutter.

Fig. 6.—Taking the Rough Edges off Glass with a Wet Carborundum Stone.

Fig. 7.—Drilling a Hole in Glass.
This should be done with a small three-sided file. The tip of the file must be kept moistened with turpentine.

Fig. 8.—Fitting a "Screw-on" Type Bracket.
Showing coloured Marmorene shelf.

Making and using Mortar

Mortar is used to bed and joint brickwork. It has several functions: primarily it distributes the pressures evenly throughout the brickwork; secondly, it holds the bricks in place, causes them to adhere, and prevents the transmission of moisture, sound and heat from one face of the wall to another.

Mortar is composed of two ingredients—one called the aggregate, the other the matrix. The strength and the method of preparing mortar depend upon the ingredients, as well as the purpose to which it is to be put.

Normally, mortar is made with lime or with Portland cement as the matrix, and with sand as the aggregate.

Cement Mortar.

As a general rule, cement mortar is the most convenient to prepare and use in small quantities, but lime mortar is cheaper and easier to work with.

Cement mortar is made with one part of Portland cement to three parts of sand. Portland cement can be bought in small quantities, but it is far more economical to purchase a "bag," that is, a large paper bag containing 1 cwt. (112 lb.). Provided the cement is kept bone dry, it will last for a year or more and always comes in handy for repair work and other purposes. The sand should be the ordinary grade of "building," that is, "sharp" or pit sand, not the kind sold for garden purposes and known as "horticultural" sand.

Several points should carefully be watched when doing such an apparently simple thing as making cement mortar.

Secrets of success are correct "gauging," that is, proportioning of the ingredients, thorough mixing, proper moistening and always keeping the mortar free from lumps, small stones or dirt.

Gauging and Mixing.

Begin by putting on the ground a large flat board—such as the bottom of a wooden box, and fix upright pieces at the back and two sides (as shown in Fig. 1) to act as a simple "banker" or board on which to mix the mortar; the raised edges are to keep the mortar in place and to protect it from dirt.

A banker about 3 by 2 feet will do for most amateur work, but, if a wheelbarrow load is to be mixed at a time, make the banker at least 6 feet long and 3 feet 6 inches wide, or larger if possible.

Always clean the banker after mixing to prevent the mortar hardening on it; if this happens the hard pieces will be knocked off and mixed in with the next batch of mortar and will spoil its usefulness, as the novice will speedily find when attempting to spread it smoothly with a trowel.

Gauge Box.

Next obtain an old bucket or a strong wooden box to use as a measure, one about 12 by 9 by 6 inches is a convenient size for small jobs. Obtain sufficient sand—have it deposited on a smooth hard surface, or in a large

Fig. 3.—Sifting Sand.
Shovel the sand into the sieve and shake it through into a box or bucket; reject all that remains in the sieve.

Fig. 2.—Preparations for Mortar Making.
Requirements are sand, cement, a mixing board, gauge box, sieve, shovel and water can.

box, so that dirt cannot get into it—also have at hand a fine mesh garden sieve, a shovel and a water can with rose head, all as sketched in Fig. 2.

Sift the Sand.

Unless it is certain the sand is clean and free from small bits of stone, it must be sifted, as shown in Fig. 3; this not only sorts out the foreign matter, but breaks up the sand, which often has a tendency to become lumpy if left untouched for some time.

Now Gauge the Ingredients.

The next step is to gauge the ingredients— so fill the gauge box three times with sand, then once with cement; fill the box loosely—do not beat it down.

Put the sand on one side of the banker, then pour the cement over it, add a second lot of sand, then the second lot of cement, and so on until sufficient has been measured out. Then mix the whole thoroughly by sliding the shovel into the heap and turning it over and shaking it out on the opposite side of the banker.

Mixing must be Very Thorough.

Do this, as indicated in Fig. 4, at least three times—shaking out the sand from the shovel each time, not merely turning it out; remember the object is to distribute all the cement evenly through the sand. Thorough mixing is vitally important, otherwise the mortar will be lumpy—some parts all cement, others nearly all sand.

When mixed, sprinkle lightly with clean fresh water, then turn over the mass to bring the dry parts to the surface, repeat the sprinkling and mix or "knock it up" until the whole is uniformly mixed and moistened.

How to Test whether Sufficient Water has been Added.

The proper amount of water to use can only be judged by experience—a reasonable test is to take a handful of mortar and squeeze it into a ball. If any water squeezes out it is too wet, if the mass crumbles it is too dry.

Cement mortar must be used directly it has been prepared—it soon goes

Fig. 1.—Banker or Mixing Board.
Place a large wooden board flat on the ground, and surround it on three sides with vertical pieces held in place with pegs and nails.

MAKING AND USING MORTAR

Fig. 4.—Mixing Mortar.
Place some sand first on the banker, then a proportion of cement, and so on. Mix by turning over from one heap to another until the cement is thoroughly distributed.

"green" or begins to set—and, although it is customary to sprinkle it with water and "knock up" again, the cement is never so strong as when used within half an hour or so of "knocking up."

How to carry the Mortar.

Use a bucket or a barrow to carry the mortar about. When at work on small jobs use a "hawk" to hold a small stock of cement. The hawk is shown in Fig. 5 and is simply a piece of board about 11 inches square with a vertical handle in the middle.

This is grasped by the left hand and is a great convenience when pointing—filling in cracks or doing similar jobs. Cement is spread and manipulated with a "bricklayer's" trowel (Fig. 6), about 10 inches long and 4 inches wide in the blade, also a small one called a "pointing" trowel.

Lime Mortar.

There are several kinds of limes used for mortar, but there are only two that call for consideration for average purposes. These are the ready ground limes—which are used substantially in the same way as Portland cement, but in proportions of 1 of lime to 2 of sand. The blue lias or semi-hydraulic limes are the best for making lime mortar for building work generally. An hydraulic lime is one that dries and hardens when mixed with water. Actually the water used to moisten the lime is converted by chemical action into hydrate of lime—the water remains as a solid, consequently it is essential to use clean water, because any vegetable or animal matter in the water will remain in the wall and might cause trouble. Similarly, the presence of salt either in the water or in the sand used for the aggregate will attract moisture from the atmosphere and would make a wall damp and unsightly.

Fig. 5.—How to carry the Mortar.
In carrying and holding small quantities of mortar, use a square board with a vertical handle.

Mixing Ready Ground Lime.

When mixing ready ground lime, proceed as described for cement, but use a "sharp" clean pit sand—proportioned or "gauged" 1 of lime to 2 of sand.

Use only as much water as necessary to ensure good combination, since any water that cannot turn into hydrate of lime must necessarily evaporate, hence it takes longer for the work to dry and harden properly if an excess of water is used.

Thorough mixing is all-important, because any lumpy pieces of unground or improperly mixed lime that escapes hydration when mixed will do so later on and will expand, cause blisters, and in bad cases break the work.

Hydraulic limes should be used within twenty-four hours of mixing, but slightly hydraulic limes—or "fat" limes—should be mixed and left to "temper" for a week or more.

Lump Lime or Quick-lime.

The ordinary lump lime or quick-lime must be prepared in a different manner. First the lumps are placed in a metal box—such as an old cistern—then water is sprinkled on it, just enough to moisten the lumps. The whole mass will then begin to heat up—it gets quite hot — and gradually disintegrates. The mass can be turned over from time to time and more water sprinkled on until the whole of the lime is "slaked" or has turned into a pasty mass—called lime putty.

This is then mixed with the sand as before, but in a pit or on a deep banker, and the whole is again moistened with water.

Fig. 6.—Two Useful Trowels.
One about 10 inches long and a small one for pointing will make a good outfit.

Leave for a Week before using.

The mass should be covered with wet sacks or with a rough roof of boards or corrugated iron, and left for a week or so to "temper," that is, to allow ample time for every particle of lime to hydrate, slack and become inert. This kind of mortar is not so strong as the hydraulic lime mortar—if used outdoors for brickwork the joints must be raked and pointed with cement mortar.

It is, however, excellent for use indoors—and, unlike other mortars, it expands on drying similarly to plaster—hence its value for wall surfacing and ornamental interior work, especially for the undercoatings, when hair is mixed with it, but this aspect of the work more properly belongs to the sphere of plastering.

Shrinkage of Mortar.

Lime and sand contracts when mixed and made into mortar. This is a desirable property, because in so doing the material becomes harder and more dense or solid.

For all ordinary purposes it can be assumed that this shrinkage is about one-third—that is to say, 3 cubic feet of cement and sand would be required to make enough mortar to fill a space of 2 cubic feet. Consequently, when purchasing materials, it is necessary first to ascertain the number of cubic feet of mortar needed, and then to add half as much again to the proportionate quantities of material.

An Example.

For example, 71 cubic feet of mortar are needed for a "rod" of brickwork —also a similar quantity would be needed to cover or "render" a wall measuring 850 square feet in area to a thickness of 1 inch—or about the area of the average small six-roomed house.

For this quantity of mortar the following materials would be required: 1½ cubic yards of lime, 3 yards of sharp sand or 1 cubic yard of cement, and 3½ cubic yards of sand. Roughly one-third the bulk of water would be needed for proper mixing.

Rendering.

This word is usually employed to describe the art of covering the surface of a wall with a thick layer of mortar. Two or sometimes three coats are applied separately, but in every case the mortar is spread with a rectangular trowel.

The mortar is picked up on the trowel and then thrown with a peculiar kind of flicking motion directly on to the wall, and is then pressed and flattened out with the trowel.

Fig. 7.—Slaking Lime.
The lump lime is put in a pit, or an old metal cistern, sprinkled with water and allowed to disintegrate slowly.

Building and Equipping a Small Poultry House

WE will assume that the house-owner contemplates keeping half a dozen laying pullets to supply new-laid eggs for the house—how best should he proceed to accommodate them?

Two Systems of Housing.

There is the choice of two systems of housing: (1) roost and covered run; (2) combined roost and run. In the former it is necessary to build a house in which the pullets will roost at night, and to attach thereto a covered-in run, with open or netted front, for use in the daytime as an exercising and scratching section. In the latter, both roost and scratching run are combined under the one roof, and this has real advantages, being more modern and taking up less room, also being more economical to build. The fowls roost at the back, on perches placed above a droppings board, and scratch in the litter on the floor.

The Intensive System.

The technical name for such a structure is an *intensive house*, and the system of keeping poultry, without any outside range, is termed *the intensive system*. It is necessary to know such matters, because there are certain important items in design, feeding and management which are essentials to maximum success where confined fowls are concerned.

Should you attempt to keep poultry confined in a house that has permanently closed windows of ordinary glass, they will not remain healthy, and will lay soft or thin-shelled eggs, suffer from leg weakness and be anæmic. Should you endeavour to keep fowls in dark confined places, they will be subjected to attacks from very many parasites and pests. If a house having such defects is ever used for rearing, then the young chickens will suffer from leg weakness, rickets, etc., and rearing will be a failure.

At any future date the house now accommodating laying pullets may be used for chick rearing, so that it is very sound in practice to select a proper design that fulfils all modern requirements, and for all classes or ages of poultry.

The Design for the Front.

The design of the *front* will make or mar the structure, and it must be planned to let in direct sunlight on to the floor, unimpeded too by ordinary glass. The latter keeps out the ultraviolet rays, which may be regarded as vitally essential to success with intensive poultry keeping or chicken rearing. One may, of course, fix specially prepared glass, like Vita glass, which admits the rays; or allow free entrance of direct sunlight through netting. Specially prepared material to admit the rays is also advertised.

Fig. 1.—Front of Poultry House for Intensive System. Showing hinged drop-down glass shutter over netting, and above that drop-in or hopper windows.

Warm Floor is Important in Winter.

It is not essential to have direct sunlight always penetrating the front of the house to the floor, as an hour daily will suffice. This is mentioned because in the winter months a warm floor is also important for good laying, when the period allowed daily for the rays to penetrate the netting will be enough. In the summer or during better weather there can be admittance of direct sunlight most of the day.

Fig. 2.—Here we see the Arrangement for watering the Fowls from Outside.

Dealing with the Front.

Usually a small poultry house measures 6 to 7 feet at the front, and slopes to 5 feet or 5 feet 6 inches at the back. Now for the ideal design of front! First board up the bottom of the front for about 2 feet, using 1-inch planed, tongued and grooved boards throughout. For a 2-foot depth above this have a hinged wooden or glass shutter that drops down on hinges and buttons up when closed. Beneath this shutter have 1-inch wire netting to keep the fowls in and wild birds out, also to admit the direct sunlight and the rays to the floor.

The Windows—Opening Inwards.

Directly above, one should arrange windows for the length of the house, which may open outwards or inwards. In opening inwards there is the disadvantage that the owner must enter the house to remove the window or open it, and the advantage that the window can be taken completely out to admit light, having netting in position. When thus removed, the glass can be placed out of the way on supports fixed to the underpart of roof.

Opening Outwards.

In opening outwards the windows can be attended to from outside the house, and can be propped well up to get all possible direct light into the structure. Netting should be fitted under the windows to keep the fowls in and wild birds out.

Aperture for Ventilation.

At the top of the front leave an aperture about 4 inches deep, covering this with perforated zinc, or having a hinged canvas shutter on the inside to check the ventilation, through netting. Also fix a wooden hood outside to keep the rain and snow from driving in. This is the ventilator and outlet at highest point, so is important.

Variations.

There are, of course, variations, although the principles remain the same. In a house 8 feet high, for instance, whether lean-to or span-roofed, the top ventilating aperture may be 6 or 8 inches deep, with larger hood. There can be two rows of windows above the drop-down shutter.

Find Out from Borough Surveyor's Office the Maximum Permitted Height.

Often one must conform to a given height for any building erected in the suburban garden, and the bye-law may be ascertained by application to the

BUILDING AND EQUIPPING A SMALL POULTRY HOUSE

borough surveyor's office. A height of 6 or 7 feet may be the accepted rule on some housing estates; and I have known the latter possess an approved design of house for poultry keepers where a poultry society has taken up the question of poultry keeping on an estate and agreed upon designs for plant, programme and rules.

The Drop-down Shutter.

The bottom boarding of the front may be 18 inches or so in the house only 6 feet high, and the drop-down shutter can be identical for depth. Again, this drop-down shutter may be of wood or glass, and I have seen the latter employed as a means when down of forming glass frames for young plants, the latter being put thereunder in boxes.

Flooring.

Flooring comes next in importance, and a wooden floor seems hygienic, as it can be scrubbed down with warm water and be scraped before fresh litter is put down. If, too, the house stands on bricks or supports, rats are discouraged and unable to enter the structure. There is also a free current of air below the house, and this keeps floor and scratching litter dry. Railway sleepers may be employed in support, or bricks or 3 × 1½-inch or 3 × 2-inch joists. Earth has the drawback that one is not always able to remove a good depth and renew it with fresh; in the summer months it can be very dusty; and in case of worms or disease earthen runs cannot as easily be cleaned as wooden floors.

Roofing.

For the roof there are advantages in favour of wood covered with felt. Many use corrugated sheeting, but this may be too warm in the summer and too cold in the winter months. As it is important to protect litter from wet, the roof should be thoroughly rainproof; and close boarding is suggested to prevent red mite and such pests from getting beneath the felt. Use tongued and grooved boarding which may be ¾ inch, although some may prefer 1 inch. The roofing felt may be one ply if of good quality, and it can be placed down after the roof has been tarred, and above the felt, nail felt laths to prevent the wind from turning it up.

Fig. 3.—ANOTHER EXAMPLE OF AN INTENSIVE POULTRY HOUSE.
With drop-down wooden shutter over netting, and above it hinged lift-up windows. Note the back glass windows under drop-board and to the right fly-up perch to nests fixed against partition. This also shows another style of watering or feeding from outside, the hinged netting opening to trough or water vessel on platform inside.

The floor and roof of any poultry house represent two very important sections of it. Place the felt lengthwise and the slats downwards, the latter at spaces of 2 feet or so. Use proper felt nails for the fixing, and take care to allow a suitable overlap of the felt to prevent rain from getting through; one may purchase a compound for joints.

Importance of Keeping Litter Dry.

A roof must keep out the rain, because if the litter should get wet the ammonia in the droppings is released, and that is harmful; in fact, deep and dry litter may be considered essential to good health. The floor must be dry underneath for a like reason, to keep the litter dry, and the sunlight through the netted parts of the front will also help in that direction. Flooring must be stout to take the weight of the owner, and also the boards should be close-fitting, so that grain does not pass through cracks to encourage rats or mice underneath. The roof will project a little at the back to take the rain clear of the house, and there can be a projection in the front.

Doors.

In a small house of but one section there will be one door at the end; in a building of two or more compartments there should be a door at each end. A hinged wooden door will do well for small houses, just as a sliding one suits large structures and the span-roofed types. A lock and key might be suggested, because it is quite a common occurrence for fowl thieves to steal poultry just as they are due to commence production, or at Christmas.

Outside Nest-boxes.

In the case of outside nest-boxes, a padlock may also be part of the equipment, so that no eggs can be stolen. Inside the ordinary wooden door it is practical to have a hinged netting door for use in the summer; in hot weather the wire-netting door can be closed to keep the fowls in, whilst the outer wooden door is buttoned back to let the air cool the interior of the house. With the same arrangement at each end of the house, and by the judicious opening of the front shutters, the fowls can be in better comfort and free from exhaustion during hot spells.

Droppings Board and Perches.

The droppings board and perches will be fixed at the rear of the house, and underneath in the back an aperture may be made and covered on the inside with netting of 1-inch mesh, and on the outside with a glass slide in grooves. This glass window in each compartment will throw light on to the floor and make the space beneath the dropboard light, thus discouraging the fowls from laying in the litter instead of in the nests, especially when they commence production.

The slide-along glass panel will also act as an inlet ventilator with the aperture at the top of the front as the exit or outlet. On warm summer nights it can be left open or partly so at discretion; on warm days there can be a current of fresh air coming through. Any such slide under the drop-board will make a good inlet, for inlets should be low and outlets at the highest points.

Dealing With the Outside Walls.

The outside walls of the house can be of planed

Fig. 4.—A LEAN-TO POULTRY HOUSE WITH CENTRE PARTITION, MAKING TWO SECTIONS.
There are glass windows at one end; perches and drop-board at back. The front is netted, but a wooden or canvas shutter can be placed against the lower part in the winter still further to protect the birds.

BUILDING AND EQUIPPING A SMALL POULTRY HOUSE

¾-inch tongued and grooved boards, or of 1-inch. Glass can be 21 oz. and clear. In large houses many use framework, purlins and joists of 3 × 2 inches, but for smaller plant, 2 × 2 inches, 2 × 1½ inches and 2 × 1 inch may be suggested for framework. One may always place two 2 × 1½-inch battens together and make the thickness of one 3 × 2 inches. Supports for floor and roof should be substantial enough to prevent sagging. In houses 20 × 12 feet I have seen 3 × 2-inch floor joists, but with both 2 × 2-inch and 3 × 2-inch framework and roof purlins. House in bolted sections can at any time be readily taken down.

Some Suggestions for Size.

The house we propose to build or purchase is not going to be a cumbersome affair, and here we had better decide upon the approximate measurements. Each confined fowl on the intensive system should have about 5 square feet of floor-space, so that if we are to keep six laying pullets they will need 30 square feet of flooring. We thus have a house 6 feet long by 5 feet deep, or 5 feet long and 6 feet deep.

Allow for Both Hens and Pullets.

If one intended to purchase each year half-a-dozen pullets for laying, that unit would not be complete, because by the time the new pullets were ready to arrive the others would still be laying. If the older hens were at once cleared out to make room for the new pullets, there would be a period when eggs would not be forthcoming. The best plan is to allow for both hens and pullets when making the original plans for housing. Fowls are usually kept on for two seasons of production, or at least the best ones, and as pullets are best for winter eggs each year, success depends upon having young birds, i.e., pullets hatched the same season. A two-compartment house would be much more satisfactory, for pullets could occupy one section, whilst the other was used for chick rearing—the one for pullets and the other for hens. Such a house then might be 12 feet long by 5 or 6 feet deep, being divided in the middle to make two compartments.

The Question of Extensions.

Poultry keeping catches one as a fever usually, and whatever ideas one may have at the start, they are often altered after the first year. It is well

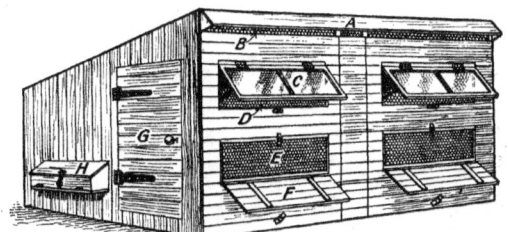

Fig. 5.—Constructional Details of an Intensive Poultry House

A, wooden hood over netted outlet ventilator B. C, hinged glass window over netting D. E, wire-covered aperture to admit direct sunlight. F, wooden (or glass) drop-down hinged shutter over E. G, door at end. H, outside nest-box.

The following should be noted:—F, buttons at top and is hinged at bottom; G, has lock; H, has padlock and front is hinged; C, buttons at bottom and is hinged at top; A is permanent hood of wood and with wooden ends; all the rest is match boarding.

to think of extensions when starting, and to plan housing accordingly. Take chicken rearing as an instance—it is best to separate the young cockerels from the pullets directly the sexes can be told; the pullets are able to get their proper share of food, and to make good development that way.

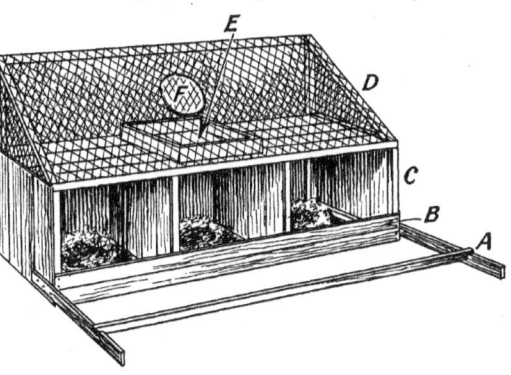

Fig. 6.—Details of Nest Box.

A, fly-up perch; B, board to keep nest material in C which is a three compartment nest box; D, netting slantwise to stop nesting on top; E, box for eggs; F, aperture or hole to take out or place in eggs as collected.

Where to place the cockerels? Some of course buy or build another house for them, but why not have a continuous but divided structure of several sections to make it an all-in-all unit? There are, or should be, two objectives, namely, eggs and table chickens. Confinement is ideal for

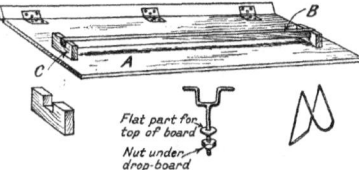

Fig. 7.—Details of Hinged Drop-board.

B is the perch and C the end support. Three methods of fixing perch are shown. On the left is a wooden support; in the centre a metal holder, on the right a stiff wire holder.

fattening young cockerels for table, and as we get 50 per cent. of cockerels in all broods, why not fatten them up and save the butcher's bill on joints?

Start with One Section and Extend Afterwards.

A house 18 feet long by 6 feet deep, divided into three sections, would see one fully equipped ready for stock of all ages, and with a place for rearing, and another for fattening cockerels. At first one house and section can be begun with, but in building or buying one can have the ultimate object in mind. Some screw together small houses, but every part can be so made to bolt together, and then by taking off one end the original one-compartment house may be extended to two, and even three. The end can be taken off and replaced on the extension.

Boarding Off the Compartments.

It will be necessary just to board off the compartments, and a light-boarded division will do, having a door therein. Such a partition should be boarded up from the ground to prevent birds in one section fighting with those in the other. One can dispense with the communicating door in the division for two-sectioned houses, making the partition the ideal support for the nest-boxes.

Details for Perches and Drop-board.

Along the back of the house one will need a drop-board, with perches above, the board to catch the droppings for hygiene and quick clearance. Hens need about 8 inches of space for perching, so that one perch will do for six pullets. There should be about a foot of drop-board behind and in front of the perch, and a foot between perches when two or more are erected. Have a good 3 × 2-inch batten screwed to the back to take the hinged 2-foot drop-board. In having this hinged to drop down and lift up it can be buttoned back to the wall when the house is being cleaned out. Also it is out of the way if a section is used for chick rearing. The perch should be movable and fit loosely into sockets at each end, for red mite often get into the sockets and can be guarded against where paraffin is applied to the ends. A solid metal stand can be bolted through each end of the drop-board to take the perch, this latter being about 2 × 1½ inches with the edges rounded off.

BUILDING AND EQUIPPING A SMALL POULTRY HOUSE

A Useful Tip.

A piece of linoleum may be fixed over the drop-board to facilitate cleaning, or asbestos sheeting; or a series of wire-covered boxes may be placed under the perch. Usually the cleaning outfit consists of a hard brush, a scraper and a bucket, and one may have handy near the perches a bucket of dry sand or earth to sprinkle the board after cleaning.

The Floor Litter.

The litter for the floor, if kept dry and deep, will last for months without needing renewal, although it can be raked over once monthly and hard pieces removed, and even sieved through if desired. Start with several inches of litter and add fresh until a good depth of 6 inches or more is obtained. Straw alone will do nicely, and the fowls will scratch it into small pieces. One may have a base of peat moss or sand and peat; and have chaff or chopped straw on top.

The droppings board should be 2 feet off the top of litter, as should all fitments, to conserve the floor-space.

Fitting up the Nest-boxes.

With a wooden partition it will be easy to fix up indoor nest-boxes, and three nesting sections will do nicely for each six birds. Each nest may be 15 inches deep, 10 or 12 inches wide, and 15 inches from front to back. There can be a low board at the bottom of the fronts, to keep the nesting material in position, this being straw or hay; or peat moss may be used as a base with chaff on top.

Wood shavings if obtainable locally can be used for nests and floor, and sawdust is excellent, although manurial value is here lost. A fly-up batten or board will be necessary at the base of the nests, and a piece of netting placed above the set of boxes slantwise will prevent the fowls from roosting on top.

An aperture for the hand will enable one to have a box inside to place the eggs in as collected. If a solid boarded back can thus be obtained for the nests, such as a partition, one need not have backs to the nests. The set can be hinged at the top so that the lot may be tilted up for the litter to be brushed out quickly. All fitments should be portable to remove for cleaning, and it will be found that hot water and soap make a fine cleanser.

Fig. 8.—How a Poultry House can be Hidden at the Bottom of a Garden by means of Ramblers, etc.

Collecting Eggs Without Going into the House.

Outside nests can be planned so that eggs may be collected without going into the house. They may be fixed 2 feet off the ground, with a fly-up perch at the end where there is no door, or under the drop-board to the left of the door. The roof can project into the house to keep out the rain, and the front will open as the door. Inside nests may be placed on legs, of course, and there can be a pop-hole and slide, giving access to birds from one compartment to the other, such slide to be operated from outside by a cord. The fly-up platform to nests may be hinged to pull up from the outside by a cord when not desiring the fowls to sleep in the boxes at night.

The Food Trough.

A food trough will be necessary, and can be the simple V-shaped one with ends, so that it will stand firmly on the litter. In this can be fed wet mash and grain, although some or all of the latter may be scattered in the litter, being raked in by a proper rake or a three-pronged tripod cut from a tree. The trough when not in use can be hung up to the underpart of roof out of the way. Conserve floor-space wherever possible.

Dry-mash Hopper.

A dry-mash hopper will be required,

Fig. 9.—Another Example showing the use of Foliage to Screen the Poultry House at the End of the Garden.

and this may be a small magazine type or a long trough pattern, one end being sectioned off for grit and limestone or shell, to which may be added charcoal. A trough pattern shaped as shown is very practical, and can be 2 or 3 feet long, with small end grit, etc., container. It has a small lip at the front to prevent waste, a 3-inch depth feeding aperture, and a top hinged part to open for filling. The hopper may be positioned directly under the drop-board, with fly-up batten at base, or on a table.

Water and Dry-mash Supply.

It is convenient to be able to supply water and dry mash without going into the house, and if one of the front netted sections is hinged and a table on four legs stands inside, the water and food troughs can be reached and filled from the outside. In fact there can be two such narrow tables off the ground, one for the trough of dry mash and the other for the water. It compels the birds to take more exercise if the utensils are apart.

An ordinary self-supply fountain may be used or a long narrow earthenware pig-trough pattern. The latter keeps the water cool, and medicines may be given in the water, being non-metal. One may hang the drinking fountain, also a small dry-mash hopper, on the wall.

Arrangement for Greenfood.

The greenfood may be given in a string bag suspended from the underpart of roof; or a piece of small-meshed netting may be nailed to the wall at sides and bottom, with slates also nailed over the edges, leaving the top open, pouch-like, for the raw greenfood, the fowls pecking it through the netting. The water vessel can be placed outside, the fowls placing their heads through spaces between slats; or an outside box will do with slatted arrangement on the inside.

How to Treat the Inside and Outside.

Usually houses are creosoted both outside and inside, but they may be tarred or painted on the outside and limewashed or distempered on the inside. There is no reason why paint should not be used to make the plant look nicer and whitewash makes for a light interior, which is an advantage.

BUILDING AND EQUIPPING A SMALL POULTRY HOUSE

A good colour scheme can easily be devised for outside painting, and there is no reason why the house should not be screened by foliage at the bottom of the garden. One may have rambler arches or sunflowers, the latter, when the seeds are ripe, being useful for the fowls. Loganberries might even be cultivated as a screen.

Broody-coop.

It is well to have at the side of the house a broody-coop into which any broody may be placed for a quick cure. The floor should be slatted to allow a current of cool air underneath the inmate, and the front should be slatted with the centre spar made removable. Roof and ends should be boarded, and the coop made rainproof, a wooden V-shaped trough being fixed at the base of the front, and a holder for the drinking vessel. The appliance can be attached to the house, or be on legs, and there can be several sections. In, out of seasons such a coop will be useful as an isolation place for individual hens with minor troubles.

How to Gain Additional Floor-space.

To gain additional floor-space one may build in the front of the house a sun balcony, or it can be made separately on legs to go against the front of the building. The bottom will be boarded and the rest wire netting, the front being hinged to open. Food and water may be placed within the balcony, which can be the length of the house and about 2 feet 6 inches to 3 feet deep, and about 2 feet high. Such a balcony allows the birds to get out into the sunshine, and is helpful for chick-rearing. With properly-designed fronts the balcony is not essential.

MODERNISING A CHEST OF DRAWERS

AN EFFECTIVE TREATMENT FOR AN OLD FASHIONED PIECE OF FURNITURE

MUCH can be done to improve the appearance of an old-fashioned chest of drawers by fitting new handles, escutcheons and ornamental plates.

First strip off the old handles and any applied ornaments, then thoroughly clean the surfaces and touch up any scratch marks or blemishes which may be visible at the places where the handles and other parts have been removed. Water stain of an appropriate colour should be used and be applied with a small brush; the stain will bite into the scratched part more quickly than it will over the undamaged surface, so directly the stain begins to dry, wipe it off with a piece of rag wrapped tightly around the finger. Repeat the process until the scratches are sufficiently darkened, then give the whole a brisk rub with furniture polish.

Any visible small screw holes should be "stopped" with coloured wax, or with a thick paste composed of whiting coloured with strong water stain.

Press the paste well into the hole, clean it off flush with the surface when quite dry and hard, then, if necessary, colour it to match the woodwork by the application of a spot of stain.

The next step is to select suitable new-style handles and escutcheon plates; those made of coloured "Erinoid" or one of the synthetic materials such as Bakelite, are particularly effective. Patterns are available at small cost in mottled brown, gold and black, blue, grey, green and other shades and in a

Fig. 1.—A Chest of Drawers Before and After Treatment.

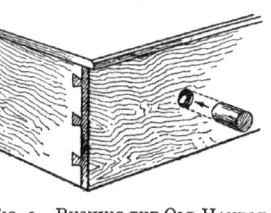

Fig. 2. Bushing the Old Handle Hole.

Insert a short plug of wood into the hole, after coating it with an adhesive. Then drill a hole to suit the new handle.

Fig. 3.—How to obtain Correct Alignment of Handle Holes.

Fig. 4.—An Example of a Modern Knob in Gold and Black.

This would look especially effective on light oak furniture.

Fig. 5.—A Modern Drawer Pull.

wide variety of patterns. Most of them are fixed by means of a bolt and nut of small size and it will be necessary to fit a wooden bush to fill up the original handle holes (as sketched in Fig. 2), then mark the exact whereabouts of the holes for the new handles.

Ensuring perfect alignment.

To ensure perfect alignment set the chest perfectly level, then drop a plumb line down the front of the chest, as sketched in Fig. 3, and make a mark across the face of each plug. The plumb line is just a piece of thin string with a small weight on the end, and can be held at the top by some books or any heavy object. Let it hang freely and clear of the ground, and use it as a guide when marking off the pegs.

Mark both sets of pegs then hold a straight-edge level across a pair at a time and mark off a horizontal line on each peg. This will ensure all the handles being correctly spaced and lined up. Drill the holes and fit the handles by tightening up the nut on the inside. Cut off any surplus from the bolt and cover with a neat disc of cloth glued over the nut to avoid any chance of its catching on clothing in the drawer.

The addition of ornamental plates of coloured "Erinoid" to match the handles or the application of a good "banding" transfer will complete the modernising of the old chest and give it a new lease of useful life.

Two specimens of modern handles are sketched in Figs. 4, and 5, and a complete transformation in Fig. 1, which will perhaps serve as a useful suggestion for the similar treatment of an old chest of drawers.

Best Methods of Lining Cupboard Shelves

It is safe to say that no comfortable house is ever without cupboards, and there are very few cupboards without at least one or two shelves. Even the hanging wardrobe cupboard generally has a shelf at the top for hats and similar items.

Shelves are intended not only for storage, but to enable things to be kept clean and free from dust. Most shelves, therefore, require some kind of lining, and the more thorough and conscientious we are about the lining of our shelves the better will they be, both in appearance and use.

Two Main Uses for Cupboard Shelves.

Broadly speaking, cupboard shelves fulfil two main uses in the home. Above stairs they are used for linen and various articles of clothing, and in the kitchen and scullery they are employed for foodstuffs and kitchen utensils.

Lining with Newspaper.

The simplest and most obvious course is to treat all these shelves alike by lining them with neatly folded lengths of newspaper. The newspaper costs nothing, it can be removed when

Fig. 1.—A Greatly Improved Appearance can be given to the Linen Cupboard by Panelling the Inside of the Door as shown.

dirty, and in the case of shelves or drawers which are used for clothing there is an advantage in that printing ink is a deterrent to clothes moth.

But if you want your shelves to look really nice, and if you would like to keep them spotlessly clean without having to be constantly folding new linings for them, they should be lined with some better, more durable, material.

Chintz, Cretonne or Casement Cloth Linings.

The best lining for the shelves of the linen cupboard is chintz or cretonne, or a white or coloured casement cloth. Kitchen shelves may be lined with American cloth or oilcloth, or they may be fitted with removable plate glass. Of course, if the shelves are glass to start with, or if they are tiled, no additional lining should be necessary. The shelves will only need a periodical wipe over.

LINEN CUPBOARD AND CLOTHING SHELVES.

To deal with linen cupboard and clothing shelves first, the material used for lining these should be cut to exactly the length of the shelves and rather more than twice their depth. The four edges of the lining should be neatly bound or hemmed. Then lay the linings smoothly on the shelves, with the patterned side downward in the case of cretonne, and secure firmly round the sides and back of the shelves with drawing-pins. Meanwhile, leave the front of the material, which, you will remember, has been made more than twice as wide as the depth of the shelf, hanging down in front.

Now place the contents of the shelf neatly in position, fold the lining over them, and tuck it in neatly at the top and back of the shelf. This not only results in a neat, orderly appearance; it protects the contents of the shelves from dust.

Another Method.

An alternative method is to pin or tack the lining to the front edge of the shelf and to bring the lining over the contents of the shelf from the back toward the front. This method will be found almost as serviceable as a protection against dust, and, of course, the contents of the shelf are more easily accessible. The appearance is also smart and attractive if the edges of the lining have been neatly bound with a contrasting colour, or the two edges visible along the front of the shelves may be trimmed with a border of lace.

Treatment for Panels inside the Door.

The appearance of the linen cupboard can be further improved if cretonne similar to that used for the lining of the shelves is pasted in the panels on the inside of the door. Alternatively, an ornamental wallpaper could be used, especially if casement cloth is used for the shelf linings. The cretonne or paper on the panels of the door should be finished by varnishing over.

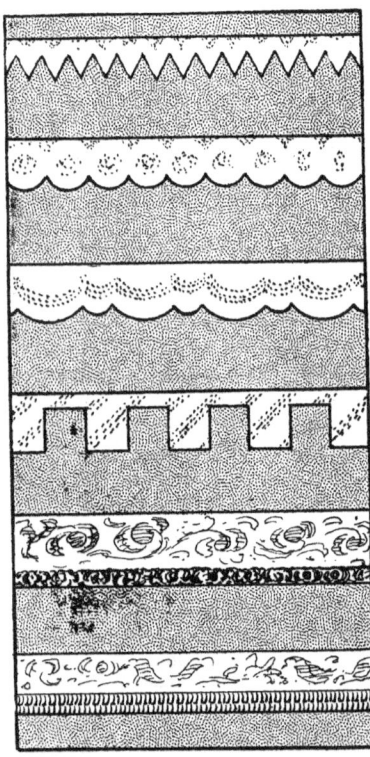

Fig. 2.—Some Suitable Shapes for Shelf Edgings.

The top four are suitable for American cloth; the bottom two for chintz or casement cloth. The edges should be bound with a contrasting colour and the edging left in a plain straight line or very simply scalloped.

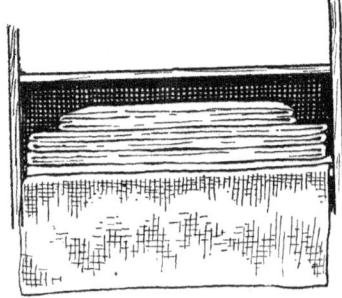

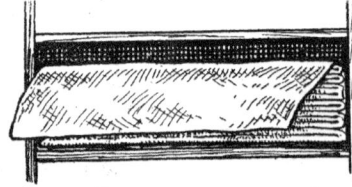

Fig. 3.—How to treat a Linen Shelf.

Top, shelf before lining is tucked in to protect contents of shelf; centre, how casement cloth is tucked in over the contents and secured with drawing-pins at the back; bottom, alternative method showing lining fixed at front of shelf and brought over forward from the back.

KITCHEN AND SCULLERY SHELVES.

Kitchen and scullery shelves should be lined either with linoleum or American cloth. The former has the advantage of being very durable, but American cloth is less expensive and lends itself to more decorative treatment. If, however, a length of linoleum or oilcloth should happen to be left over after laying any of the floors, an excellent use for it is as a lining for the shelves which support heavy saucepans, basins or the like. The linoleum should first be cut as nearly as possible to the required size, and should then be placed on the shelf and trimmed flush. For this you will need a proper lino-knife with a curved blade.

Finally, secure the front edge of the linoleum with tacks or lino-brads at intervals of 2 or 3 inches, placing them at points in the pattern where they are not easily noticed. The shelves can then be kept clean by wiping over with a damp cloth, the woodwork is protected, and there is no need for tiresome scrubbing.

American Cloth.

The advantages of American cloth are its cheapness, the ease with which it can be laid, and its attractive appearance. It is, of course, extremely serviceable. In addition to covering the shelves, enough American cloth should be provided so that it will overhang the front edge by about 1 inch. The edge should be cut in a suitable pattern, and, if necessary, may be kept in position with drawing-pins or a spot or two of seccotine; but the latter should be used very sparingly.

The Edging.

The edging may be cut in either a dog-tooth, dentil or escallop pattern. Before cutting, you could sketch the shape in pencil, or, if the shape is very elaborate, prepare a preliminary paper pattern. Shelf edgings can be made

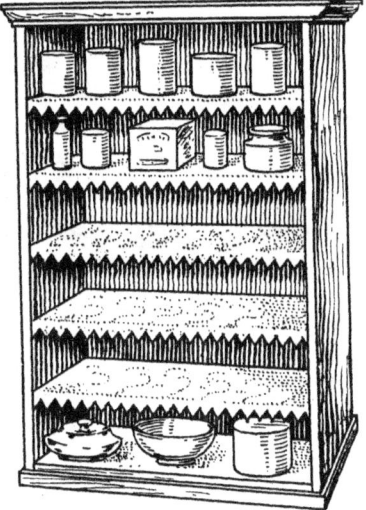

Fig. 4.—Kitchen Shelves lined and edged with American Cloth.

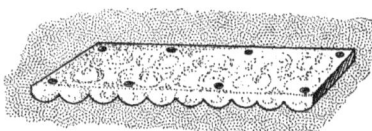

Fig. 5.—American Cloth should be fixed in Position with Drawing Pins.

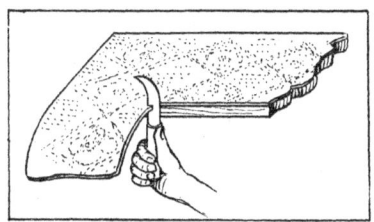

Fig. 6.—If Linoleum is used for Shelf Lining it should be trimmed Flush with the Edge of the Shelf.

in pieces separate from the linings, if preferred.

If the shelves are covered with American cloth and no ornamental edging is used, the cloth should be laid flat on the shelf and should be wide enough to fold down over the front edge and should be secured with drawing-pins on the underside of the shelf.

Edgings may also be made of chintz or taffeta, but the advantage of American cloth is that it may be left with raw edges. With chintz the edges could be bound with a contrasting colour, but this means that the edging must be left in a plain straight line or very simply scalloped. Alternatively, the edges of either chintz, casement cloth or taffeta may be left unbound if they are lightly touched with seccotine on the side which does not show.

Covering Shelves with Glass.

Another suggestion which should not be overlooked is the possibility of covering the shelves with removable slabs of plate glass. These would be obtained through any builder's merchant and should be supplied in a size to fit the shelves exactly. At cleaning time all one has to do is to clear the shelves of their contents, remove the plate glass and wash it down.

If it is a question of installing new shelves, there are shelves of plate glass with rounded corners. These should be supported on metal brackets specially designed for the purpose, which, while holding the glass with complete security, enable it to be withdrawn easily for cleaning. Shelves of this kind are excellent either for the pantry or the bathroom.

Another useful position for removable plate glass linings is on interior window-sills. The glass is a protection to painted or finely figured woodwork, or ornamental tiles, which may thus be seen and enjoyed without fear of injury.

FITTING A CLOCKWORK DOOR BELL

Electric bell installations are usually non-existent in the modern house of modest style. Some form of annunciator bell is a definite advantage and none is more effective and reliable than a good quality "clockwork electric-action door bell," to give it the full official designation.

Bells of this type (as in Fig. 1) consist of a heavy gong about 3½ inches diameter which, when turned to the right, winds up a long mainspring. This is normally restrained by a catch which, when released by a "bell press," causes a hammer to rotate within the gong and "ring" the bell in a similar way to an electric bell. If the bell is habitually given a turn every time the door is

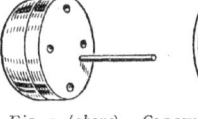

Fig. 1 (above).—Clockwork Door Bell.

The spring is wound up by turning the gong to the right. When the press is pushed in the spring is released.

Fig. 2 (right).—How the Bell should be Fitted.

The spindle connects the press with the bell.

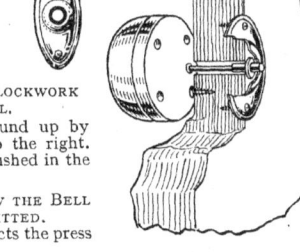

opened, there will be no risk of failure due to the spring being run down.

The release spindle projects from the back of the bell and may not be in the centre—according to the make of bell. Before fixing the bell, take note of this point and arrange the position of the bell-press accordingly. Next, drill a hole through the door twice as big as the diameter of the spindle, then unscrew the gong by turning it backwards, put the bell in place with the spindle through the hole and screw the backplate of the bell to the door.

If the spindle is too long, cut off a portion with strong cutting pliers, a hacksaw or, failing either of those tools, use a file. Then screw the press to the outside of the door, give it a push to make sure that it works properly, then replace the gong. The sketch (Fig. 2) shows the bell inside and the press outside the door and exactly how they should be arranged.

How to Make a Cold Frame

This garden frame, or light, seen in Fig. 1, will be found valuable for autumn cuttings, the rearing of seedlings, or for forcing vegetables.

The dimensions given in Fig. 2 are of general utility, but, of course, can be altered if thought fit; the slope of the top should, however, be about equal to that shown, to ensure the rainwater draining away.

Joints should be Butted and Screwed.

The joints can all be butted and well screwed together, but on the score of durability all the joint faces should be liberally coated with paint or with a waterproofing preservative stain; either of which must be applied before the joints are finally fastened together.

Materials.

As regards the materials, these may be any good sound wood 6 inches wide; deal answers very well, but oak or elm is better when available at a low price. Thickness ought not to be less than 1½ inches for deal and 1¼ inches for the hard woods.

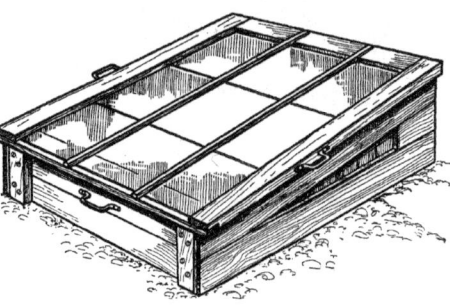

Fig. 1.—The Finished Frame.
A simple but invaluable addition to the equipment of the garden.

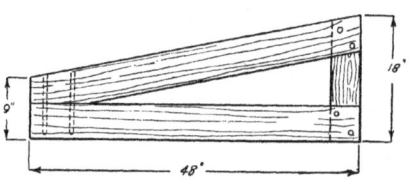

Fig. 2.—Dimensions of Side Framework.
The frame is made of 6 × 1¼ inch hardwood with mortised or halved joints.

The Light or Cover.

The light, or cover, is composed of a rectangular frame with the necessary glazing bars reaching from top to bottom. The joints at the corners of this frame can be mortised and tenoned, and should also be fox-wedged to ensure the maximum of rigidity. If the making of this joint is beyond the powers of the handyman, it will be necessary to fall back on the simple halved joint and to well screw them together; this, followed by the addition of flat "ell" irons on the underside, will result in a tolerably durable joint.

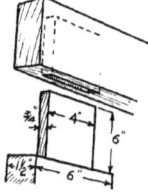

Fig. 3.—Detail of Mortise and Tenon Joint.
The alternative is a simple halved joint well screwed together.

Order of Construction.

As regards the order of construction, the first step is to acquire the timber and plane it flat and true on all faces, as a smooth surface takes the paint or preservative stain better, and the whole will be more durable.

Next proceed to make two side frames—as shown in Fig. 2—using timber about 6 inches wide and 1½ inches thick. Mortise and tenon the joints at the back, as in Fig. 3, or halve them as previously mentioned. The butt joint at the front can be secured by two long hard-wood dowels ½ inch diameter, as in Fig. 4, driven through the edges of the boards. The joint is further secured by a long screw.

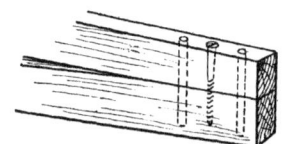

Fig. 4.—Oblique Butt Joint.
This is formed by sawing and planing the top piece, to the correct angle, and is then dowelled and screwed to the bottom member.

The gap between the framework is then closed by nailing stout matchboards vertically across it from top to bottom. The matchboard should be at least ⅝ inch thick, and can always be replaced or repaired when necessary, and the life of the frame thus increased.

Both sides are alike, but the matchboard must be fixed right and left handed, so that it comes on the inside. The front and back ends are made of solid boards 2 feet 3 inches long, with cross battens screwed firmly to each end.

Assembling Framework.

Now assemble the framework by standing the four sections upright with the sides against the end parts; fix them temporarily with a nail, and complete the job with good long screws, not forgetting to drill and countersink the outer frames so that the screws will clear, and drill a small hole for the threads to bite into. Put a little vaseline on the screws to prevent rusting.

Then add four upright square-sectioned pieces in the inner corners, as shown in Fig. 5, fixing these also with screws.

Now prepare the frame for the light, as previously mentioned. The sides and top cross rail are 4 × 1½-inch stuff, the bottom rail 1 inch thick.

Fig. 5.—Outside Corner Joints.
The parts are screwed together and strengthened with corner pieces on the inside.

Fit the glazing bars; the upper ends being fitted into slots or mortises in the top rail and the lower ends notched to fit on to the lower cross rail, as shown in Fig. 6. Paint the whole of the woodwork, and when it is dry fix the glass, which may be laid in three or more sections per length, beginning from the bottom and allowing about an inch of each of the other sheets to overlap, and thus make rain-tight joints. Bed the glass in putty and finish with an outer fillet of putty in the usual way.

A point to note while making the cover frame is to work a throating T, Fig. 6, along the overlapping edges, as shown, and to fix the retaining strips G underneath the top and sides.

Fig. 6.—Enlarged Detail of the Light.
Side frames and cross-bars are halved and screwed; fillets, F, are run under the inner edge, a groove or throating at T, and a retaining strip, G, to hold the light in place on the framework.

Provide a couple of struts to hold the light up when required.

House Name-Plates in Wood

THE making of a name-plate for his house is work which the average reader may very reasonably undertake. Such plates may be produced in several ways and with many materials, but the house-owner will naturally turn to wood as the medium which will answer his purpose best. Even when he uses this material as the base, to the exclusion of all others, there is a wide variety of styles at his command.

The first requirement in constructing a name-plate is that it should be legible and, second, that it harmonises with the particular house for which it is intended. Other considerations are that it must be durable, ornamental and pleasing.

Choosing a Suitable Wood.

When making a plate, the choice of the particular kind of wood and the size it is to be must be determined at the outset. Almost any wood will do as long as it is not resinous nor disfigured by ugly knots. If either of these is present there is no possible hope that the plate will remain in a satisfactory condition for any length of time. As a resinous board is useless, pieces of pitch pine should be rejected, but beyond them it hardly matters how ordinary the wood is as long as it is dry and seasoned.

Size.

Naturally there is a good deal of latitude in the matter of size, but the following dimensions are worth considering: 10 by 8 inches, 12 by 5 inches, and 12 by 7 inches. The thickness may be as little as $\frac{1}{4}$ inch or as much as $\frac{3}{4}$ inch. Of course, it will be understood that the size depends in a measure on the style of the house and the position which the plate is to occupy. If, for instance, it is to be fixed on the eye-level, it may reasonably be smaller than when it is required to hang from the arch of a porch.

Preparing the Surface of the Wood.

Having decided on the size and the wood being cut to shape, the next thing will be to go over the surfaces with glass-paper and render them perfectly smooth. It should be noted that, if the edges are bevelled, there is less likelihood of the corners becoming splintered or otherwise damaged in course of time. On no account should a moulding be run round the edges of the board if it is to take up an exposed position, as the raised parts will catch the rainwater and this speedily helps to rot the plate.

Painted Surface.

The next question is to determine how the plate is to be embellished. It would be hard to beat a painted sur-

Fig. 1.—A typical example of Black Lettering on a White Ground.

A suitable arrangement for the country, but not too good in a town where the white might soon get soiled.

Fig. 2.—An effective form of Lettering—White Letters on a Black Ground.

Fig. 3.—Another form of Lettering which is not difficult to imitate.

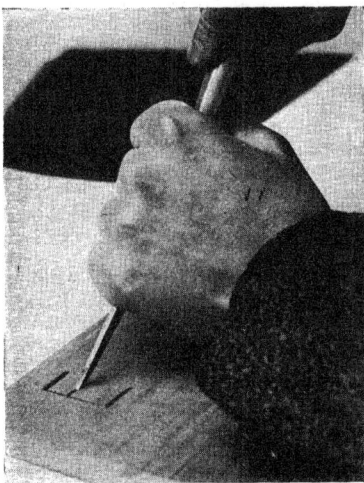

Fig. 4.—Carving Sunk Letters with the aid of a Chisel.

face on which the lettering is done in a different colour. If this scheme is adopted, the board should be given first a coat of priming and then one or two coats of a ground colour. On the score of time-saving, these coats will be done probably with a sharp, flat, quick-drying paint. The lettering may then follow within twenty-four hours. A final coat of water-white varnish will complete the job, and the plate may be put aside in a place free from dust to dry and harden slowly.

Suitable Colour Schemes.

In choosing the colours for the plate it will be found that white letters on a black ground are extremely neat and effective. If this combination is chosen the lettering must be done twice, since one coat of white will not prove sufficiently opaque. As an alternative a white ground with black letters may be suggested. The only possible drawback to this arrangement is that the expanse of white is apt to soil rather quickly, especially in towns. Where black and white are not acceptable, a brown ground with white or black letters may be considered. A green ground in certain cases is pleasing, but if the selection goes beyond these colours it will be very easy to court failure.

Style of Lettering.

In deciding on the lettering it will be advisable to follow an alphabet that permits of a slight amount of fanciful effect, though this, of course, must not be overdone. The fanciful shapes require less precision in their execution than do the more formal alphabets, and with them a line slightly misplaced or done too thickly does not damage the whole effect.

How to Paint a Letter.

For the lettering a fine sable brush is a great help. It should be dipped into the paint, rolled to a fine point on the palette, and it is then ready for use. The way a letter should be done is as follows: First the brush is placed with the tip at a corner of a letter; it is then drawn along towards an opposite corner, but when half-way it is lifted up, the whole board is turned round, the tip is placed in the opposite corner and drawn along to the place where the line left off. In other words, the brush should never finish off in a corner but always begin there. Another point to note is that, when the brush is being moved along, it should be made to form only one edge of a line and not two. The second edge is done by turning the board round and guiding the brush along the opposite sides.

It is not advisable to use paints for the lettering, which are made up in the workshop. Much the best plan is to buy the material in artist's tubes, which cost about 6d. each. Such paints are easily thinned to the required consistency with the addition of a little turpentine. Enamels are not advised when the plate is to be fixed in the open.

Letters Painted on a Natural Surface.

Although a painted board with painted letters can be made to appear very effective, there are occasions when something different is wanted. In the case of an old-world cottage, for instance, the painted board might be too formal. A much better style, then, would be produced by squaring up a piece of oak and painting the letters on the natural surface. In this instance the tube paint should be thinned with varnish rather than turpentine, as the whole surface will not be given a final coat of varnish.

Another idea, almost similar to the foregoing, is to select a piece of American whitewood, to give it a coat of any suitable oil stain and, when

Fig. 5.—Method of painting Letters on a Wooden Plate.
Note that the brush is started at a corner. The next step is to turn the plate round and begin again at the opposite corner.

thoroughly dry, to form the letters in black or white oil colours.

Letters Cut Out with a Chisel.

So far all the above suggestions have depended upon the use of paint for the lettering, but there are several other ways of providing the names. One useful plan is to take the stained board, mentioned above, to pencil the letters on it, and then to cut them out with the aid of a sharp, fine-pointed chisel. If desired, the sunk faces of the wood may be coloured with black paint, or another idea is to fill up the depressions with a composition of coloured plastic wood, black being preferable in this case.

Using Gesso Paste or Plaster of Paris.

Yet another way is to fill up the spaces with a white gesso paste, or even plaster of paris, mixed with a little gilder's size. The drawback to these two fillings is that they may fall out in time if exposed to much strong sun or a great deal of rain.

Raised Letters.

For the carpenter who can handle a fretsaw neatly there is the method of employing raised letters. The letters forming the name are individually cut out of thin fretwood and then fixed with small pins to the baseboard. They may be painted or stained, whichever is thought advisable.

DOES YOUR WIRELESS SET DISTORT?

ONE of the most frequent causes of distortion in a wireless set is due to the fact that incorrect grid bias is being applied to one of the valves. It is quite a simple matter to find out which valve is not working properly, and the only instrument required is a milliammeter, which can probably be borrowed from a friend if you do not possess one yourself.

A Word of Warning.

It must be remembered that the effective life of a power valve can be considerably shortened by failing to switch off the set when making adjustments to the grid-bias voltage, although it may seem that the operation of changing the grid bias from, say, 7·5 to 9 volts can be accomplished in such a short time that it is unnecessary to switch off the set; there is a definite reason why the set should be switched off. It is not the actual alteration in grid bias while the set is working that does the damage, but the fact that while the alteration is being made there is for a few moments no grid bias at all on the valve. This results in a large increase in the plate current, an increase that is far greater than the valve is designed to withstand, and consequently damage is done to the filament. Therefore always switch off the set before making any alteration to the grid bias.

How to Use the Milliammeter.

First open up the set so that access can be obtained to the inside. Disconnect the wire that connects to the plate terminal of the valve holder and connect it to one terminal on the milliammeter. Connect a wire from the other terminal on the milliammeter back to the plate terminal of the valve holder. Now switch on the set again and watch the needle. If everything is in order, the needle will remain steady, or, rather, should oscillate slightly above and below the mean value of anode current.

If the milliammeter needle kicks upwards, *i.e.*, gives a higher reading, this indicates that the valve is over-biassed, and consequently the plug on the grid-bias battery should be tried in the next lower position, until the needle remains steady.

If the needle kicks downwards, this indicates that the valve is under-biassed, and therefore the grid-bias voltage must be increased.

To make quite sure that the valve is working under the proper conditions, check the reading shown on the milliammeter with the maker's quoted value of anode current at the working anode voltage and working bias voltage. A table giving these values will be found on the instruction sheet issued with the valve.

If the first valve you try seems to be perfectly satisfactory, repeat the test with each valve in turn until the fault is located.

Incidentally, it should not be assumed that, because the grid-bias lead is plugged into the socket marked, say, 6 on the grid-bias battery, a bias of 6 volts is really being applied. An old grid-bias battery may give very much less than its nominal voltage, and may require renewal.

Distortion due to an Old Valve.

After a valve has been in use for a long time, it is liable to suffer from loss of emission, and this will also cause the set to distort. If this is the case, when you use the milliammeter as described above, you will find that no matter how the grid bias is adjusted, the reading of the milliammeter will be lower than the normal rated current of the valve. The only remedy is to replace the offending valve with a new one.

A comprehensive fault-tracing chart for all types of wireless receivers is given later.

Replacing a Broken Pane of Glass

A BROKEN window pane is not only unsightly but is a source of danger, and no time should be lost in effecting a repair which is quite within the scope of the home handyman.

Tools Required.
Old knife (or special hacking knife if one is obtainable).
Chisel.
Hammer.
Two or three small pins or brads.
Putty and putty knife. The putty must be fresh and moist, and not dried and crumbling. If it is only slightly hard it can be made plastic again by mixing a little linseed oil with it, which should be well worked in by kneading it thoroughly with the fingers.
Priming paint and small brush.

First remove Broken Glass.
Nearly all windows are fixed from the outside, and examination of the window will reveal a sloping fillet of putty which holds the glass in place. A downstairs window can be dealt with from the ground, but in the case of an upstairs room it may be best to take the entire window frame out, especially if the pane is a large one. If it is a sash window it may be best to remove the sash from the framing. A small pane can probably be dealt with either by sitting on the window-sill or by working from a ladder.

Remove the Old Putty.
The old putty must be removed by placing the point of an old knife in the recess in which the glass fits and tapping the back of the knife with a hammer as shown in Fig. 1, until all the old putty has been removed. Take care that the blade does not bite into the woodwork.

How to avoid Splinters of Glass.
To avoid splinters of glass flying up into the face it is advisable to strike the knife always downwards or away from you. It is a good plan, too, to wear a pair of gloves while doing this.

Measuring for the New Glass.
Having removed all the old putty and taken out the old glass, the next thing is to measure for the new glass. If two sides of the old glass are intact these can be measured, or else the wood frame should be measured. The glass must not, however, be a tight fit, and ⅛ inch should be allowed off each measurement so that it fits in easily. If this is not done the glass will almost certainly crack when the wind rattles the window or it is violently shaken.

What to do with a Window of Awkward Shape.
Don't use a tape measure to take the measurements, but if possible use a steel rule, or, failing this, a wooden ruler. If the window is of an unusual shape and cannot be easily measured, the best plan is to make a template of

Fig. 1.—The First Operation—removing the Broken Pane of Glass.

The old putty should be chipped away with an old knife or hacking knife. Tap the back of the knife with a hammer, taking care that the blade does not bite into the woodwork. When the recess has been cleared and the old glass removed, it must be given a coat of priming paint or knotting before applying the new putty.

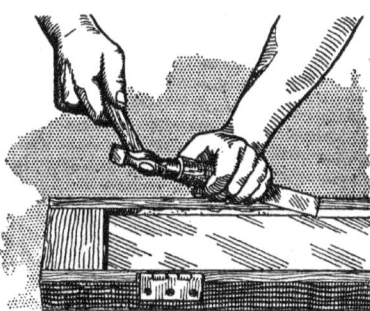

Fig. 1A.—When dealing with an Upstairs Room it may be found advisable to remove the Window from the Frame.

If you have not got an old knife handy, a chisel can be used to remove the old putty.

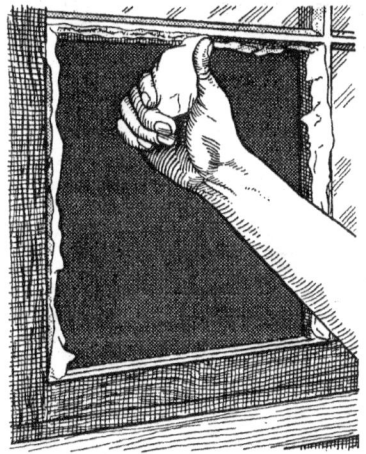

[*Fig. 2.*—Placing the Bedding Putty in the Rebate.

Hold the putty in the palm of the hand and press it in the rebate with the thumb, so as to provide a bedding for the new glass.

cardboard and take this to the glazier's and have it copied exactly.

Also, as it may be difficult to measure the exact thickness of the old pane, a piece of the broken pane should be taken when obtaining the new piece.

Now Paint the Exposed Woodwork.
The rebate into which the new pane is to fit should be coated with a priming paint, which must be allowed to dry before putting in the new glass. If this priming paint is omitted it is possible that the woodwork will absorb the oil from the putty and cause it to crumble and break away.

If a quick repair is required a patent knotting could be used instead of the priming paint. This will dry in a few minutes.

Laying in the Bedding Putty.
A small quantity of the soft putty must now be placed evenly round the rebate of the woodwork. Hold the putty in the palm of the hand and press it in with the thumb as shown in Fig. 2. This is to provide a bed for the glass to rest upon.

Fitting the New Pane in Position.
The lower edge of the pane should be pressed in first and then the whole glass pressed gently against the putty so that all surplus putty is squeezed out. Do not press on the centre of the glass but preferably at two corners as shown in Fig. 4.

Fix the Pane temporarily in place with Brads.
As soon as the glass is nicely bedded down, put a brad into any two edges of the wood so as to prevent the pane falling out. The brad must be driven in parallel with the glass as shown in Fig. 5, and not at an angle, and the hammer should lie flush against the glass when driving the brad in so that there is no danger of cracking or breaking the glass accidentally. The brads should not be applying any pressure to the glass but should be just close enough to keep it in position.

Applying the Facing Putty.
The next operation is to apply the facing putty, and this is best done with a putty knife, such as that shown in Fig. 6. Roll the putty between the thumb and finger and place it in rough strips along the rebate. Now level off with the putty knife as shown in Fig. 7.

Hold Knife Flat on Putty.
Do one side at a time and hold the knife flat on the putty, drawing it along from corner to corner. The blade should be at approximately 120 degrees from the glass so that about ⅛ inch of the bedding putty shows through the glass. The edge of

REPLACING A BROKEN PANE OF GLASS

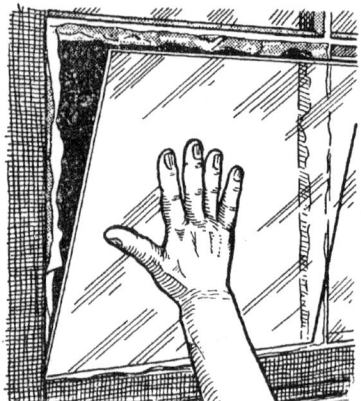

Fig. 3.—How to place the New Pane in position in the Bedding Putty.

The lower edge of the pane should be pressed in first and then the whole glass pressed gently against the putty.

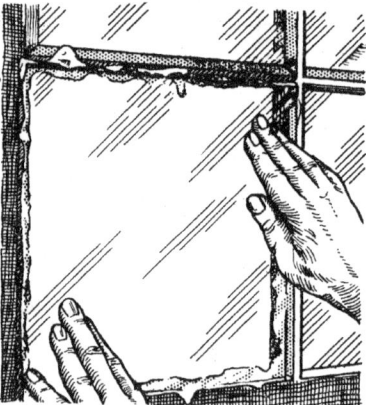

Fig. 4.—When placing the Glass against the Putty, press from the Sides and not the Centre.

Any surplus putty that is squeezed out can be removed later with a putty knife.

Fig. 5.—When the Glass is bedded down put a Brad into any two edges of the Wood, so as to prevent the Pane from falling forward.

Note how the hammer is held flat against the glass.

the facing putty should not be visible from the other side of the glass.

Remove Surplus Bedding Putty.

Any surplus bedding putty that has been squeezed out by the glass should now be removed with the knife. Leave the window for at least twenty-four hours before attempting to clean, so as to give the putty time to harden.

Special Note on Frosted or Patterned Glass.

When dealing with frosted glass, rub a piece of soap round the edge to a distance of about ½ inch so that when brought into contact with the putty there will be no danger of the oil from the putty leaving a greasy mark on the ridges.

Glass with an Embossed Surface.

Similarly, when dealing with glass that has an embossed surface, special care should be taken not to use too much putty so that it does not find its way into the relief of the pattern.

LEADED WINDOWS.

The treatment in the case of a broken pane in a leaded window is slightly different. No putty is used, the glass being kept in place by the leads, which are of an H section, one edge of one pane of glass fitting into the top half of the H and one edge of another pane fitting into the lower half of the H, and so on.

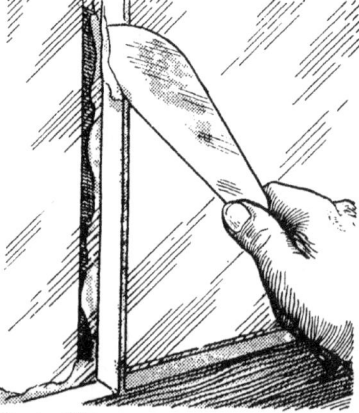

Fig. 6.—The Facing Putty should be applied with a Putty Knife.

Roll the putty between the thumb and finger and place it in rough strips along the rebate. Then smooth it off with the putty knife.

Fig. 7.—When smoothing the Surface, hold the Putty Knife at approximately 120 degrees from the Glass, as shown above.

About ⅛ inch of the bedding putty should be visible through the glass.

Fig. 8.—First Stage in dealing with a Broken Pane in a Leaded Window.

Turn up the edges of the lead with a chisel or putty knife by inserting the tool between the glass and the lead.

Removing the Broken Glass.

To remove a broken glass it is necessary to turn up the edges of the lead as shown in Fig. 8. This can quite easily be done with a putty knife or chisel, which should be inserted between the glass and the lead, and the lead raised as shown in Fig. 8. The corners are soldered and care must be taken not to loosen any adjacent leads when raising.

Having taken out the old glass, open up the rebate fully, and smooth where necessary so that the new pane will fit properly.

Lay the new pane in the recess and push back the lead again, tapping it carefully with a hammer as shown in Fig. 10.

Broken Joints should be Soldered.

If it has been found impossible to avoid breaking the joints at the corners, these must be re-soldered in the usual manner, the only precautions necessary being to see that the hot iron is not brought into contact with the glass, and that hot solder is not dropped on to the glass.

GLASS FIXED IN WITH BEADS

With some types of windows especially in the case of glass cabinet doors,

REPLACING A BROKEN PANE OF GLASS

the glass is held in position with beads instead of putty. These beads consist of thin strips of wood rounded at one edge and fixed to the framing with small nails.

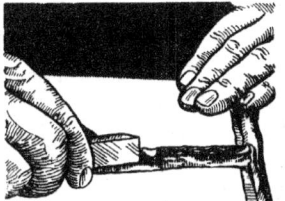

Fig. 9.—Having removed the Old Glass open the Rebate fully.

Fig. 10.—The Lead is Tapped back over the New Glass with a Hammer.

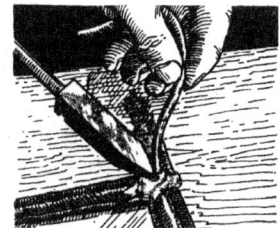

Fig. 11.—Applying Solder to a Broken Leaded Joint.

Removing the Beads.

These beads must be removed before taking out the old glass, and this can be done with a thin chisel or knife. Place the tool next to one of the nails near the centre between the bead and the framework. Give it a slight twist so as to loosen the nail. Repeat this process at each nail in turn until the centre nail can be levered right out. Then lever out the remaining nails and remove the bead. Once the first bead has been removed the others will come out quite easily.

The nails will, of course, come out with the beading, and can be removed by tapping the points with a hammer while holding the beading over the side of a bench or table.

Fix Beads back in Original Positions.

As it is advisable to fix the beads back in their original places, and to use the old nail holes, so as to avoid more holes than necessary, a slightly longer nail should be used when refitting the bead so as to ensure their gripping properly.

Now measure the frame in the same manner as already described and allow $\frac{1}{16}$ inch off each of the two dimensions when ordering the new pane from the glazier's.

Fixing the new Glass in position.

If possible, lay the framework on a bench and place the glass in its rebate. Place the beading back in its original place and drive in the nails, taking care to keep the head of the hammer flat against the glass during its stroke, sliding it back and forth as shown in Fig. 5.

What to do if Framework cannot be Removed.

If the framework cannot be removed and the glass must be inserted upright, tap a nail lightly into the top and bottom edges to keep the glass in position while the two side beads are fixed in position.

To finish off with a neat job, the nails can be punched in and the holes filled in with plastic wood or wax.

MENDING BROKEN CHAIR FRAMES

FAILURE usually occurs at the joints between the chair legs and the seat frame. It can be remedied in various ways, differing in detail according to the nature of the breakage and the design of the chair.

Provided there is no objection to their use, effective repairs can be made with some of the various fitments obtainable at an ironmonger's and costing only a penny or so each.

Chair brackets (Fig. 1) can be screwed into the angle between the leg and frame when the surfaces are flat, but on curved parts the stamped bracket (Fig. 2) is preferable and is a much more rigid type.

Fractures across any part of a chair frame can be remedied first by gluing together the parts and, when dry, recessing the wood and screwing repair plates across the joint. In some cases a tee plate (as in Fig. 4) is more useful, for example, at the junction between the frame and a central cross member.

A great many repairs can be made

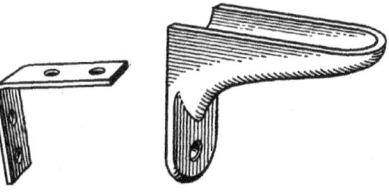

Fig. 1.—Simple Chair Bracket.   Fig. 2.—Stamped Bracket.   Fig. 3.—Stamped Steel Ell Plate.

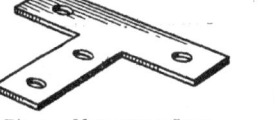

Fig. 4.—Malleable Iron Tee Plate.

Fig. 5.—Bright Iron Screw Plate. A flat plate with a screw shank, very useful for corner joints.

Fig. 6.—Application of Repair Plates.

effectively with the stamped steel "ell" plates (Fig. 3), especially at the point where the leg enters the framework.

The plate should be fitted flush into a recess chiselled out of the wood; preferably after the joint has been effected with glue. This preliminary treatment holds the parts in place, but would not be sufficient of itself to constitute a permanent repair.

In such cases the plate should be as long as possible, so that it spans the joint as indicated in Fig. 6, as this arrangement provides the maximum support.

Flat brackets are fixed under the frame in the angles between it and the leg—thus together the three plates constitute an effective, durable and inconspicuous repair.

The Screw Plate.

The screw plate (Fig. 5) is useful whenever it can be screwed into position, and the other part then placed and screwed to it; for example, the leg of a Windsor chair which fits into a hole in the seat.

TIME, LABOUR AND MONEY SAVING IDEAS

A HAMMER IMPROVEMENT.

The ordinary claw type of hammer, although useful for the purpose of withdrawing nails from timber, etc., has the disadvantage of giving insufficient leverage for extracting refractory nails. As soon as the pressure is applied to withdraw the nail, the leverage point, or fulcrum, moves along to the edge of the hammer head, as shown on the left.

To overcome this disadvantage, a

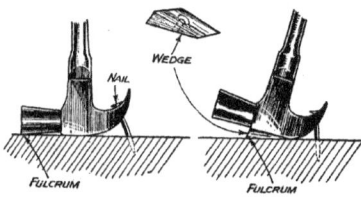

wedge of metal, such as aluminium or brass, should be screwed to the head of the hammer as shown. It will then be found that the fulcrum is right under the shaft of the hammer, so that about twice the leverage is obtained for extracting nails.

CURING WHITE POWDERY BRICKS AND TILES.

A common defect in brickwork and tiles used in house construction is that of a white powdery deposit which resembles a mould or fungus. This deposit usually appears after the house has been built for a short time. It has been identified as sulphate of magnesia and is believed to form from the magnesia present in the original clay from which the bricks were made or from the lime used in the mortar.

To effect a cure, apply dilute hydrochloric acid or ordinary vinegar, made into a solution with water, to the surface. It will generally be necessary to repeat this process a few times, after which the magnesia salt becomes neutralised and colourless.

Another alternative method suitable for brickwork is to apply a liberal coating of well-thinned-out paint to the surface.

A WOOD POLISHING TIP.

A good polish can be given to the surfaces of cabinets, boxes, panels and similar wooden articles in the following manner. First smooth down the surface as much as possible with fine sand-paper. Then take a flat piece of pumice stone and some water and pass regularly over the surface until the rising of the grain has been removed. Then take a mixture of powdered tripoli and boiled linseed oil and polish with a piece of soft cloth, until a bright surface has been obtained.

PREVENTING SCREWS FROM RUSTING.

Steel screws which are to be used in exposed places where rusting may occur, due to the timber becoming damp, should be given a smear of a mixture consisting of graphite and soft tallow. They will then remain rust-proof for many years, and when they have to be removed will present no difficulty.

Screws which have rusted in place may be removed by applying a piece of heated metal to their heads for a minute or so. Afterwards it will generally be found that the screwdriver will readily unscrew them.

REMOVABLE DRAINING BOARDS.

In small houses where every bit of space is important, it is of special advantage to be able to remove the draining board after the washing-up has been completed.

A simple form of detachable draining board is shown below. It is made from white, or Georgia pine of about 1¼ to 1½ inch thickness, and of suitable dimensions for the sink and the side space available. In order to attach it to the sink, two battens, of hard wood, A and B, are securely screwed to it as shown. These battens should be about 1 inch thick and run right across the width of the board. The batten B should be about 4 inches to 5 inches deep, whereas A need only be about 2 inches deep. The weight of the board being all on one side of the battens, a self-locking action is obtained.

In the example shown a timber support on an adjacent wall is utilised to take part of the weight, so that the two battens C and D can be made

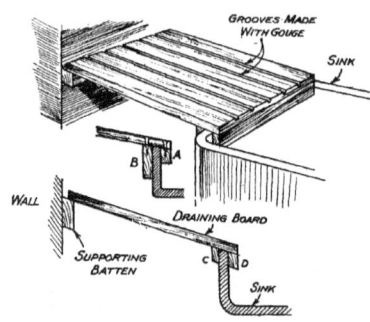

of equal depth, namely about 1½ to 2 inches. In some cases, where the width of the draining board is appreciably less than that of the sink, it may be necessary to locate the board by means of two dowel pegs in the timber support on the wall.

SHARPENING GARDEN SHEARS.

The usual method of sharpening the blades of garden shears is to remove the hinge or pivot bolt and to sharpen each blade upon a grindstone or emery wheel.

For the majority of household workers who do not possess these grinders, and who do not wish to go

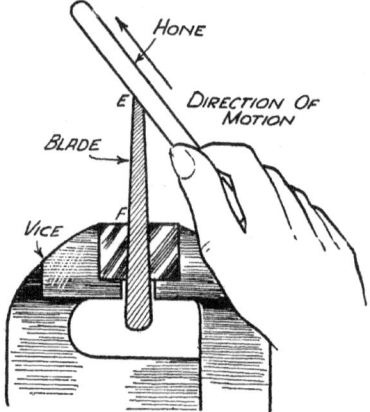

to the expense of sending their shears away to be sharpened, the following is a satisfactory method that we have used repeatedly.

First separate the two blades by removing the hinge bolt, and clean off any surplus oil or dirt. Then fix securely each blade in turn in the vice and with a flat hone work across the oblique edge of the blade, as shown in the sketch.

The hone should be of the flat type used for sharpening scythes and hand hooks, the carborundum grade being the best for this purpose.

When using the hone, apply pressure only on the forward stroke as shown by the direction of the arrow in the sketch, and employing the same action as when filing.

After removing a small amount of metal from the blade, examine the edge E for any burrs or dents, and continue honing until a thin bright edge is obtained. Then give the flat face EF of the blade a few light rubs with the hone, in order to remove any burrs.

A USEFUL TIP

When a soldered joint is made to an object which is buried in the ground, as in the case of a wireless earth connection, the chemicals in the earth may eventually cause the joint to corrode, with the result that the wire may become disconnected. This can be prevented by covering the whole of the joint with pitch, which can be obtained from an old H.T. battery.

Graining

The process known as "Graining," by which is meant the exact imitation in paint of the colours and markings of real wood, is not quite so popular as it used to be. Some people object to it on the ground that, being merely an imitation of nature, it is therefore inartistic.

The Merits of Graining.

It certainly possesses some advantages, however, over plainer treatments. A grained surface generally lasts for a long time. Once it has been properly executed it can be revarnished from time to time, which often makes it again like new. Also, if it suffers any knocks or abrasions, these can be more easily touched up, so that they do not show, than is the case with plain coloured paints, especially if the touching up be done just prior to one of the periodical revarnishings.

Real Graining.

Real graining, i.e., the exact imitation of the markings of oak, mahogany, walnut, maple or other wood, is not easy. Indeed, relatively few professional painters can do it well and, therefore, because of the high degree of skill required, it is generally carried out by specialists. But, happily, there are modifications of the process of real graining which possess all its advantages, without any pretence of being reproductions of real wood.

Broken Colour Effects.

These alternative treatments do not call for long practice or high technical skill and they do not depend for their effect on an exact imitation of the wood, but are designed to produce a suggestion or impression of it.

The variety of these alternatives is very great. Indeed, their number is only limited by the ingenuity and taste of the person engaged in carrying them out. It is our purpose to describe some of these comparatively simple processes, and the tools and methods required to carry them out.

Grounds upon Which to Work.

All the treatments to be described call for a groundwork of plain paint, and this always requires to be in the lightest colour of the real wood.

If the old paint on the surfaces is in smooth condition it will only require rubbing down with waterproof sandpaper, or a piece of smooth pumicestone, and water used as a lubricant. This is partly for the purpose of removing any trace of grease, which would prevent the paint drying, and partly to give a "key" for the new paint. When this preparatory work has been done, two coats of paint in the appropriate shade should be applied.

Colours of Grounds : Light Oak.

If a light oak effect is proposed, the ground should be made from white lead and sufficient yellow ochre to make a very light buff.

Medium Oak.

For medium oak, white lead, stained with yellow ochre and a little venetian red, is required.

Dark Oak.

For dark oak, white lead, yellow ochre, a trace of venetian red and a rather larger quantity of raw umber are needed.

Mahogany or Rosewood.

The ground for mahogany or rose-

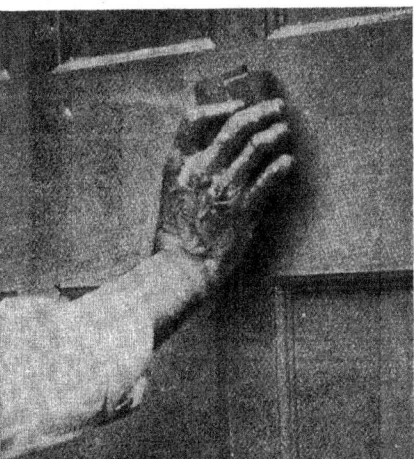

Fig. 1.—Cleaning up the Surface to be Treated.
This is done by rubbing down with waterproof sandpaper, using a small block of wood to keep the sandpaper flat against the surface.

wood is venetian red, used alone for a dark shade, and with a little white lead added for a lighter colour.

Walnut.

For walnut the ground can be made from yellow ochre, burnt sienna and umber. And so on, and so on, according to the final effect desired.

Paste or Liquid Driers.

To all these mixtures a little paste or liquid drier must be added, and they will require thinning with a mixture of linseed oil and turpentine, in the proportions of from half and half of each to three-fifths of oil to two-fifths of turpentine. Paints can be purchased mixed ready for use.

As in all other painting, ample time should be allowed (from twenty-four to forty-eight hours) for the first coat to harden before the second coat is applied, and for the second coat to harden before the finishing treatment is proceeded with.

The Graining or Scumble Colour.

Graining colours or scumbles are generally oil colours mixed from such colours and at such a consistency as to be semi-transparent. Whereas ordinary paints are made to be as opaque as possible, the materials we now require must permit the ground colour partly to show through.

Fortunately, it is not necessary to make these. Transparent graining colours or "scumbles," as they are called, are made by many of the paint firms in a large variety of colours and in tins containing from 1 lb. upward. These compounds are made ready for use except that they may need the addition of a little turpentine if they are rather darker in shade than required. Or, if they show any tendency to dry too rapidly for comfort in working, a few drops of linseed oil added will retard the setting.

There is also an additional advantage in using these ready-made scumbles in that a sample of the appropriate colour for grounding is often shown on the tins.

Tools Required.

The number and kind of tools required will depend upon the particular effect aimed at. Two brushes will certainly be required, preferably of the flat type, one about 1 inch and the other 2 or 2½ inches wide. If, as is probable, brushes of this type have been used for painting the ground, the same will do for the finishing treatment, always provided that they have been thoroughly washed free from paint in either turpentine or warm water and soap. Any admixture of ordinary paint with scumble colour will muddy the latter and prevent a clean effect being obtained.

A painter's " duster " brush costing about 1s. or 1s. 6d. will be required, both in the grounding process, for dusting off any grit before painting, and in the scumbling process now to be described.

Other tools will be needed, but, as these will vary according to the method we are adopting, we shall describe them in their proper places.

Brush Graining.

This is done by simply coating the ground colour with the appropriate scumble colour laid on very sparingly and perfectly evenly with the small brush and brushed out, all in one direction, with the larger brush. It is best to tackle such parts of the work as doors in separate sections. Thus the panels are done one by one, then the mouldings, next the upright middle stiles, followed by the crossrails and, finally, the outside upright stiles.

Some operators prefer to do all or

GRAINING

Fig. 2.—"Laying off" the Scumble with the "Duster."

part of this "laying off" of the colour with the "duster," and this is quite a good method.

The above is the simplest form of brush graining. Variety can be lent to it, either by laying on a rather thicker film of colour on certain parts, say the stiles of a door, or by repeating the original process on such parts when the first coating has thoroughly dried.

Combing.

This consists of laying on the scumble in the manner described above and then combing it while wet with grainers' combs.

These are a special form of steel comb, sold usually in sets of twelve, of varying size of tooth and in various widths. These are held at an angle of 30 to 40 degrees downward and applied to the coated work. They are steadily drawn along, removing the colour in their track, and, if the work is carefully done, the effect is of straight-grained wood.

Effect of using Different Combs.

By using different combs on different parts of the work, or by combing first with a coarse comb and then again with a fine one, considerable variety of effect will be achieved.

Another Effect.

Further variety is produced by combing with a piece of cloth tightly wrapped across the blade or even by using combs made by cutting notches in the edge of a piece of rubber.

A little practice on a separate piece of board, or even on an unimportant part of the work under treatment, will open up quite a range of possibilities in combing. The chief precaution to be observed is to wipe the comb blade after each stroke. Otherwise the colour taken up on one stroke will be partly put back on the next, with unfortunate results to the appearance of the work.

The same order of working on doors and panelled work should be followed as was described for brush graining, and the narrowest combs are the most suitable for combing the mouldings.

Softening Off.

It may be that the effect of the straight combing, just described, will appear rather too sharp and crude. If so, it can be softened while the colour

Fig. 3.—Straight Combing with a Grainers' Comb to obtain an effect of Straight-grained Wood.

The comb should be held at an angle of 30 to 40 degrees downward and applied to the wet scumble.

is still wet. For this purpose use the "duster" previously mentioned.

This brush should be held at right angles to the work and the tips of the bristles struck lightly against either the whole of the combing or only such parts as are considered to need it.

Or, alternatively, "flog" the work by holding the brush at an acute angle and patting the surface with the side of the bristles.

Broken Colour Effects.

This title can be properly applied to any coating that is not left even, but it is generally used to describe such processes other than brush graining and combing. And in many of these processes "stipplers," which are brushes consisting of a square or rectangular stock with a large number of bristles or strands of rubber fixed in at right angles and a handle attached to the back, are used.

These stipplers are used for striking the wet coating of scumble immediately after it has been applied, thus producing most interesting "broken" effects.

Obviously a large equipment of hair and rubber stipplers is rather costly, but a few experiments will prove that many other appliances can be found or made to serve similar ends. One small rubber stippler will be a good investment and, if it is well cleaned after each time of using, it will last for a long time and serve many purposes.

Stippling.

The scumble colour is brushed on, but no special pains need be taken to do this evenly as the stippler will spread it. The stippler is simply struck against the wet scumble or glaze in a succession of blows, gradually covering the whole surface. The result will be a most pleasing granulated or mosaic effect, produced by the contrast between the ground colour exposed and the scumble.

How to obtain Variety of Pattern.

Variety of pattern can be obtained in a number of ways. For instance, some parts of the work, say the panels, can be stippled with the hair duster while the rest of the work may be

Fig. 4.—If the effect of the Comb is rather too sharp, it can be softened by using the "Duster" while the Colour is still wet.

Hold the brush at right angles to the work and strike the tips of the bristles lightly against either the whole of the combing or only such parts as are considered to need it.

done with the coarser rubber stippler. Or the contrary procedure may be followed.

An Easily Made Form of Stippler.

Another form of stippler can be made by cutting a piece of rubber, say part of the inner tube of a bicycle tyre, and nailing it at intervals of about an inch to a flat board. Between the nail heads the rubber will bulge, and these bulges of rubber, when the improvised tool is struck against the scumble, will create an entirely different grain to that made by the other forms of stippler.

Rolled Effect.

This is done by means of a rag, wrung out in turpentine and made into a rough roll. Beginning at the top, the roll is turned over and over until the bottom is reached. A strip at a time is done, allowing each strip of rolling slightly to overlap that previously done.

Or a roll of crumpled paper may be used, without the soaking in turpentine, in a similar way, and this will produce quite another type of effect.

The Scope of the Method.

Further variety is possible by laying on the scumble thicker and darker in one part than another, thus producing a shaded result. Indeed, there is hardly any limit to the variety of textures and patterns possible by the exercise of the worker's taste and ingenuity in devising tools and gadgets. And the whole business will prove intensely fascinating as new discoveries are made.

Varnishing.

All surfaces treated by these methods will require varnishing, partly for the sake of appearance and partly for protection against wear and tear.

The work should be allowed to become thoroughly dry and then be very lightly smoothed with " spent " sandpaper, by which is meant the finest grade of sandpaper, two faces of which have been rubbed together to lessen its abrasive quality. Then the work should be well dusted down and a coat of varnish carefully applied.

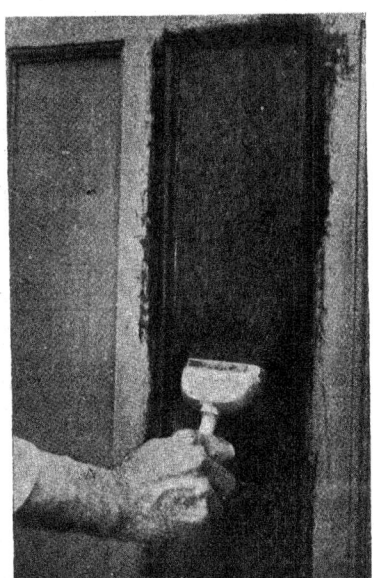

Fig. 5.—ANOTHER METHOD OF SOFTENING THE SHARP EFFECT OF THE COMB.

This consists of " flogging " the work by holding the brush at an acute angle and patting the surface with the side of the bristles.

Fig. 6.—USING A STIPPLER TO OBTAIN A BROKEN COLOUR EFFECT.

Dark Colours.

For dark colours a copal oak or inside carriage varnish will serve, but lighter colours call for the use of pale maple or pale decorative varnish.

Dull Finish.

If a dull or eggshell finish is desired a flat varnish should be used, but as this is not so durable as the gloss varnishes already mentioned, it is not suitable for use outside the house.

Even when used inside, it is best first to give a coat of one of the gloss varnishes and then, when this is dry and hard, a coat of flat varnish may be applied over it.

Burning Off Old Paint.

Sometimes all or portions of old paint on the woodwork to be treated is not fit to work upon. It may be cracked or blistered. In that case,

Fig. 7.—METHOD OF OBTAINING A ROLLED EFFECT.

This is accomplished by wringing a rag out in turpentine and making it into a rough roll. Beginning at the top, the roll is turned over and over, covering the surface in strips, each strip of rolling slightly overlapping that previously done.

it will be necessary to remove it.

Treating Knots.

When the bare wood has been revealed by the removal of old paint, it will probably be found to contain knots. These require treatment to prevent the resinous matter they contain from exuding out and showing through the finished work.

This unsightly effect will be prevented if, before any new paint is applied, the knots are coated with shellac knotting. This is a quick-drying compound, and it can be applied by means of a small brush (a 1*d.* gum brush is quite suitable), and in such a way that the knot is completely covered, and a small area of the wood surrounding it.

Clean Edges.

Reference to the illustrations will show that, in coating the panels with scumble, and in the processes of producing broken effects described, some of the colour has invaded the surrounding stiles.

If this is left on until all the panels have been completed it will become turbid.

Therefore it will make for cleanliness in working if, as each panel is finished, this surplus is cleaned off. This is best done by soaking a small piece of rag in turpentine, folding it into a wad, and using it to carefully wipe the edges clean. As the rag becomes charged with colour, it should be refolded to present a new surface.

Anti-Glare Shades for Electric Lamps

IF you appreciate a nice, soft light with no glare, on the one hand, nor any harsh shadows, on the other, then make these shades for your electric lights. They are in keeping with modern styles, and there is nothing trivial about their design.

A Box Pendant.

The first illustration shows a box pendant. It is made of a skeleton of wood, and the panels are filled in with ordinary cartridge paper. It is suitable for hanging from the centre of the ceiling of a dining-room, study, library, etc.

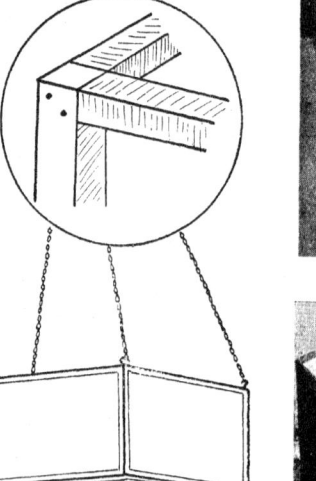

Fig. 1.—A Box Pendant.
Showing how corners are fitted. The panels are filled in with ordinary cartridge paper and are stuck down with glue.

How the Frame is Constructed.

The frame is made of strip wood, ½ inch square in section. The horizontal face is 16 × 16 inches, and the sides are 7 inches high. Thus eight strips, each 15 inches, and four strips 7 inches in length, are required. The ends are simply faced together—there is no need to halve or mortise the joints—and each is held by two panel pins, 1 inch long. If these pins are used, there is very little fear of splitting the wood.

The Sides and Bottom.

When the frame is finished, the four sides and the bottom are covered in with white cartridge paper. These panels are easily stuck down with the aid of tube glue; but care must be taken to see that no smears are made on the paper. Then the edges are bound with strips of black passe-partout paper, 1 inch wide.

At each of the four upper corners of the frame a very small cup-hook is fitted, while four more similar hooks are screwed into the wooden rose in the ceiling. Silken cords or blind cord is then used for supporting the shade, which will throw the light upwards, while the ceiling will deflect it to every portion of the room, giving a cosy, diffused effect.

A Desk Light.

Fig. 2 shows a triangular box light suitable for fitting over a desk or for a reading light above a bed-head. In this particular case, the shade is hung under a shelf. Accordingly, it is necessarily enclosed above; it is also enclosed in front and on the side that shows in the picture. But, as every shade should have at least one open face, the triangular side, not showing

Fig. 2.—A Light over a Desk.

Fig. 3.—Another view of the Desk Light, and, on the right, Skeleton Frame of Pendant shown in Fig. 4.

in the picture, was left uncovered. This can be seen from the view given in Fig. 3. The screen was made of strip-wood, ½ inch square in section, and covered with cartridge paper, as in the first case.

A Hall Light.

The right-hand model in Fig. 3 is the uncovered frame, shown in a finished state in Fig. 4. It was constructed to hang in a hall. Similar strip wood and cartridge paper was used as before; but the four sides, alone, were covered in—the top and bottom being left open. The longer strips of wood are 12 inches, and the shorter 8 inches in length. Instead of binding the edges with passe-partout paper, some light-green poster paper was obtained and cut as required. This was done so that the frame might match the colour scheme of the hall, which is light green and white.

This hall shade is hung on the lamp collar (not on the light bulb) by means of two diagonal cross wires, the ends of which are twisted around small nails—one being driven in at each upper corner of the wooden frame.

Fixing Electrical Fittings to the Frame.

Occasionally it is necessary to fix some portion of the electrical fittings to the frame itself. When this is so, stouter strip wood than that mentioned so far must be used. For such work, lengths 1 inch square in section are suitable.

Boxlight Over Doorway.

Wood of this thickness was used for the shade shown in Fig. 5. This particular shade is fixed to the wall, immediately over a door. The sides and bottom are covered in with cartridge paper, while the top is left open. A lamp collar is fitted at each end; thus, a very fine soft light illuminates the doorway. It produces a remarkably pleasing effect which is well worth copying. In this case, the ends were screwed together and black passe-partout paper was used for binding the edges.

From these short descriptions, it will be seen that attractive shades can be made quite easily, at very little cost, which give a light that is as near perfect as possible.

Fig. 4.—A Hall Light.

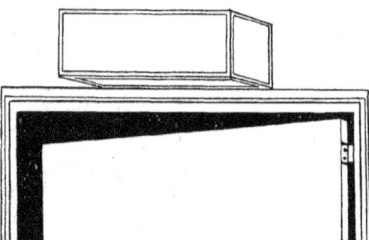

Fig. 5.—A Box Light fitted over a Doorway.

Cleaning a Gramophone Motor

THE reproduction of recorded music suffers more through the irregularity of motors than from any other cause. Much of this is easily remedied by a little careful attention. The process is quite simple if the position of all parts is observed as and when they are dismantled.

Make sure Spring is Completely Run Down.

Firstly, make sure that the springs are completely run down, giving the turntable a few extra turns in that direction to make quite sure. Otherwise, as soon as the plate screws are released there may be a tearing grind of teeth and pinions which burrs their edges and makes them run noisily ever after.

Remove Bottom Plate.

Having placed the motor-board face downwards on a cloth-covered empty box, loosen the screws and remove the bottom plate (Fig. 1). Watch for all loose parts clinging to the grease and carefully note where they came from. Place them in paraffin oil in a jam jar or saucer, to soak and clean themselves while the other parts are being attended to.

Leave the Governing Arrangements Alone.

The governing arrangements which engage by a worm drive in the fibre wheel of the axle, should be left severely alone at this stage. If necessary, adjustments can be made at the subsequent testing of the motor, but in unskilled hands the whole mechanism can be ruined in two seconds, so let well alone, cleaning with a paraffin rag and afterwards oiling with a little good lubricating oil of a light nature.

Cleaning the Holes in the Plates.

The holes in the plates are best cleaned by sharpening a few pieces of firewood. Match-ends would do, but the holes are usually somewhat larger than a match. There is no need to wriggle a corner of rag into them as is sometimes seen. Fig. 2 shows the method.

Fig. 1.—When the Motor-board has been removed it should be placed Face Downwards on a Cloth-covered Box.
The screws holding the bottom plate can then be removed.

Fig. 2.—The Holes in the Plates are best cleaned with Pieces of Sharpened Firewood.

Fig. 3.—The Teeth of the Wheels should be cleaned with a Piece of Rag, after a Thorough Soaking in Paraffin Oil.
By crooking the first finger of the right hand and stretching a piece of rag over it, a sharp double edge of rag is formed which can be stroked up and down in between the teeth of the wheels.

Best Way to Clean the Wheels.

Having soaked the wheels in a jam jar of paraffin oil for an hour or two, wipe as much of the excess dirt off as possible, using always a good quality linen rag rather than a whiskery flannel one which will cause much annoyance by clinging to all burred edges. By crooking the first finger of the right hand and stretching a piece of rag over it, a sharp double edge of rag is formed which can be stroked up and down in between the teeth of the wheels (Fig. 3). Only by individual treatment can the tightly embedded metallic and graphitic pieces be dislodged. Some people prefer to use a stiff brush, but the rag makes a cleaner job of it.

Cleaning the Springs without removing from their Barrels.

If it is considered too much trouble to remove the springs from their barrels, soak them in paraffin for twenty-four hours, but take care to swill out all traces of paraffin afterwards by a liberal application of lubricating oil. This is not economical, and the mechanically minded person will doubtless prefer to do the job properly and remove the springs (see "How to Replace a Gramophone Spring").

How to get between the Coils of the Spring.

In order to clean between the coils of the spring, hook the rag over a nail and then draw the spring backwards and forwards, proceeding inch by inch along it until every portion has been reached (Fig. 4). Near the centre less rag must be used, because the coils are stiffer and closer, but the central portion should not be neglected because of this. The bottom of the barrel should then be covered with good grease and the spring fed gradually into the barrel, using the palm of the hand to retain it step by step until the inner end snaps in suddenly.

Reassembling after Cleaning.

As soon as every part is cleaned, oil each plate hole and proceed to stand the wheels in position on the base plate. Then lay the other plate on top and juggle the various pivots into position, but use no pressure until all are ready for the plate to be lowered. The plate then snaps down and each wheel can be tried to see if it has the necessary "logger-room" in which to work freely. The worm drive may seem to have too much freedom, in which case the cam adjustment at one end may be turned a fraction. Since this component serves to reduce the power of the spring while lengthening its time of operation, it must have complete freedom, and so long as it engages the fibre wheel fairly and squarely it need not be tight.

Apply vaseline to all pinions, in small quantities rather than in huge lumps. Turn the winding handle a few times and note with satisfaction that the whole motor runs without vibration or noticeable sound.

Speed Regulation.

The adjustment of turntable speed should always be done under actual working conditions, carrying a heavily cut record, and, if the motor is a good one, a subsequent test *without* a load will show no increase of speed. The regulator lever system ends in a small felt pad which touches the revolving disc and prevents the governor weights opening the springs by centrifugal force. The very slight increase in speed which some motors show when accurately tested with a stroboscope is due to the softness

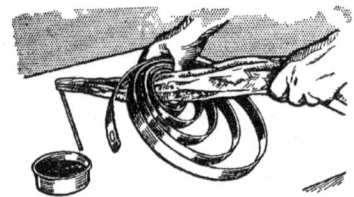

Fig. 4.—To clean the Spring, hook the Rag over a Nail and draw the Spring backwards and forwards until every Portion has been reached.

Fig. 5.—Replacing the Plate in Position.

of the felt pad, which "gives" slightly to the extra pressure.

The lever under the speed dial will seldom have to be bent after reassembly, but if there is no screw adjustment for accurate setting at 80 revolutions per minute, it is better to use small fibre washers to lower the lever until the motor gives exactly twenty revolutions in a quarter of a minute. It must be remembered that a movement of one division on the dial-plate (say $\frac{1}{8}$ inch) is reduced by the leverage system to about one-twentieth of this at the felt-pad end. Consequently the slightest looseness of any of the pivots causes an unreliable behaviour on the part of the motor, and what is accurate one day will be several revolutions wrong the next.

When the speed gradually alters during the running of a record, the fault is generally due to the looseness of the regulator thread in its brass jacket. This is easily remedied by dismantling and squeezing the brass sides closer together before returning the screw. Having seen to it that the motor gives 80 revolutions per minute when the dial reads "80," nothing more can be done to ensure accurate readings at other speeds. Fortunately the newer motors approximate very nearly to the truth when properly adjusted, but the early ones could not do so owing to the variation in the length of lever used by assemblers. In a large cabinet, the full length was used, and in a small cabinet several inches were cut off.

REPAIRING FRACTURED FURNITURE LEGS

WHILST the repair of furniture legs of thick sections presents little difficulty to the domestic craftsman, when it comes to the question of repairing fractured furniture legs of small and delicate sections he is frequently at a loss as to the best method to employ.

The principal difficulty experienced is that of making a strong joint, so that the two portions are exactly in line afterwards.

There is no doubt that the only practical method of repairing such fractures is by the use of dowels, but the amateur is seldom able to place a dowel so that the two parts joined are absolutely in a line. The following is a method which any amateur can employ with perfectly satisfactory results.

Referring to the illustration, diagram (1) shows a table leg fractured at A. Diagram (2) shows another view of a portion of the table leg. The lower fractured portion is removed and a suitable size of hole for the wooden dowel is drilled down into it—as indicated by the dotted lines. This hole should be at least 1½ inches deep, and should be drilled as centrally as possible.

Next take a fine-toothed tenon or backing saw and cut right through the fractured leg at BB, diagram (2). Before sawing right through, however, make a fine mark with a piece of glass crayon, or chalk, to show the corresponding two parts. Then, as shown in diagram (3), glue the upper end of the leg to the other part of the table leg, at A, and when the glue has set, drill the dowel hole into the upper fractured part (above A), using the hole that already exists in the lower part C, as a guide. The three holes in D, C and the upper part of the table leg will now all be in perfect alignment, so that the dowel peg can be driven into the upper portion AC, the flat faces BB glued and the lower part of the leg D then driven on to the projecting part of the dowel. The repaired table leg will then be as strong as it was originally, and the joints practically invisible. Diagram (4) shows the finished job.

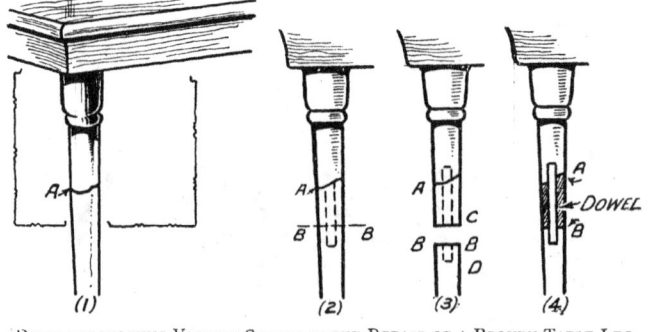

Diagrams showing Various Stages in the Repair of a Broken Table Leg.

Enamelling Whitewood Furniture

A GREAT deal of whitewood furniture is now made and sold at very low prices. If left in the rough it has no decorative value, but when carefully enamelled it may be made to appear highly attractive. Anyone who wishes to furnish a room cheaply can buy whatever pieces he requires, in whitewood, and decorate them all in the same style. He thus has a very striking suite of furniture and the cost is decidedly reasonable.

Make Sure the Articles are Sound and Well Made.

As a rule, whitewood furniture is finished off roughly and some of the pieces, when exposed for sale, reveal clumsy workmanship.

The screws of a hinge may be tightened with advantage; a thin film of wood, if shaved off the edge of a door may make all the difference between a perfect and a bad fit; a streak of plastic wood will hide an ugly joint, and a dozen other things may be done, each the work of a minute or two, which will help to make the articles perfect.

Preparing the Surface with Glass-paper.

The next step is to procure some No. 0 glass-paper and to rub over all the surfaces that show.

Dust the Surface Carefully.

After the sanding a good dusting is necessary. This step may be easily overlooked, but it is very important because, should it be omitted, the enamel will pick up the tiny particles and they will stand on the surface in the form of countless pimples.

Fig. 1.—Rubbing the Surfaces Smooth with Fine Glass-paper.

Use a Cellulose Lacquer.

We now come to the selecting and laying on of the enamel. There are various kinds of enamel that may be used but, as most amateurs are somewhat anxious to proceed with the work without being delayed, it will be advisable to choose a cellulose lacquer which has the merit of drying hard in an hour or so.

Three Coats.

Three coats are usually necessary when dealing with whitewood; but, as each will dry in about two hours, it is easily possible for an article to be put into commission the day after it arrived home, though, of course, it is advisable to allow three or four days, when possible, in order that the lacquer may have time to harden thoroughly.

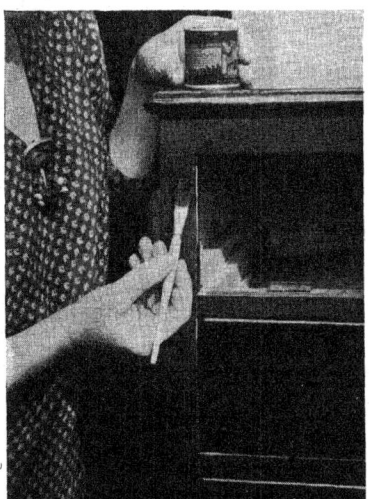

Fig. 2.—Use a Small Brush to Enamel along an Edge.

Hints on Applying the Lacquer.

A soft brush should be used and it ought not to have seen service with other paints in which white lead is the base. The lacquer needs applying fairly generously, as it cannot be stroked out a great deal. Thus, the tendency is to put it on so thickly that it runs down in tears. To prevent this it is an excellent plan, when covering a large expanse, to rest the surface that is being done horizontally. No tears are then possible and the article can be turned to present another horizontal surface a few minutes later.

Two-colour Schemes.

When an article is being ornamented in a two-colour scheme, it is always advisable to arrange for one of the colours to predominate and for the other to take a secondary position.

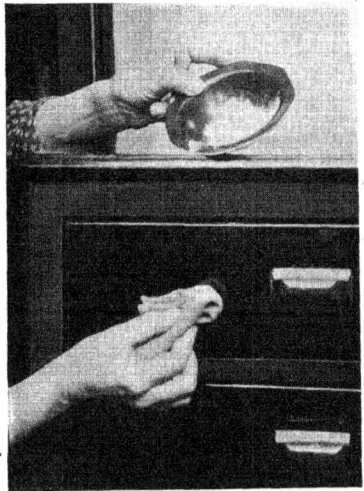

Fig. 3.—To provide a Velvet Finish rub the Surface with Pumice Powder.

Place the powder in a saucer, make up a little soapy water, soak a pad of soft felt in the water, dip it in the powder and rub the surfaces.

In other words, the whole of the surfaces should not be halved between the two colours. Naturally, some difficulty may be experienced in keeping a straight line where the two colours meet; but the work will be considerably simplified if it is planned to let them touch in places where the shape of the article forms a right-angled edge.

What to do before putting on Second and Third Coats.

Before putting on the second and third coats it will help if the surfaces are very lightly smeared with a sheet of No. 0 glass-paper which has been worn almost smooth. If no worn piece of paper is handy, tear a new piece in halves and rub the two faces together until they have lost most of their "bite."

Obtaining a Velvet Finish.

When the third coat has dried the article is ready for use; but some people prefer a velvet finish to the high gloss which all cellulose lacquers provide. This velvet finish is obtained by rubbing the surfaces evenly with pumice powder. Place the powder in a saucer, make up a little soapy water, take a pad of soft felt, soak the felt in the water, squeeze it out, dip it in the powder and rub the surfaces, taking great care not to wear through the edges of the lacquer. When all the glaze has disappeared, sponge over with some fresh soapy water and dry with a soft cloth. The article will have, now, a surface like porcelain. Note that, while this treatment is excellent for most colours, it is not quite satisfactory where black is used.

Hiding Defects in Wallpaper

A TEAR, finger-mark or grease stain in an otherwise perfect expanse of wallpaper is unsightly and irritating, and spoils the appearance of the whole room. Fortunately, there are almost certain to be some odd bits left over of the rolls that were used when the room was papered, and with these it becomes quite a simple matter to effect a repair that will be practically unnoticeable.

How To Deal with a Tear in Patterned Paper.

Let us suppose that there is a tear in the wallpaper a few inches in area caused by a sharp corner or edge of a piece of furniture. First examine the wall very carefully. If the plaster has been damaged it must be filled with Keene's cement and smoothed off level with the rest of the wall.

Now cut from the odd bit of paper a piece to correspond with the pattern of the torn piece, leaving a moderate margin all round.

How to trim up the New Piece.

With a sharp pair of scissors trim the piece along certain well-defined lines of the pattern. For instance, if the tear has occurred in the middle of a leaf or petal, cut out the new piece

Fig. 1.—Have you an Unsightly Tear like this?
The torn piece of paper is indicated by the upper arrow, while the lower arrow points to the new section of the paper which is being cut to fit. Note how the new piece is being cut along a definite line in the pattern. Note that if the plaster of the wall has been damaged when the tear was made it must be filled with Keene's cement so that the surface is quite smooth before applying the new patch.

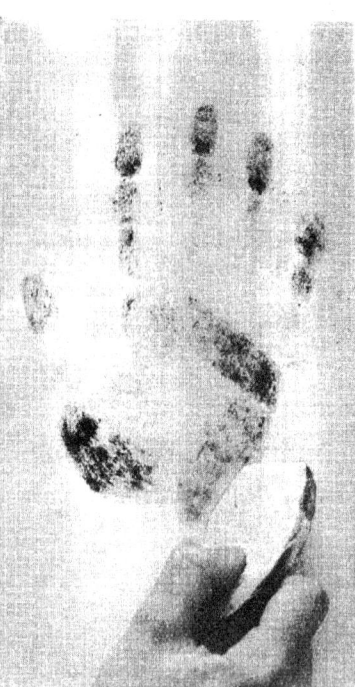

Fig. 2.—If there are Children about the House, this Mark will often be seen.
A simple method of removing finger marks is to clean them off with stale bread. Take care to break off the crumb as soon as it becomes soiled and never to rub with a grimy piece of bread.

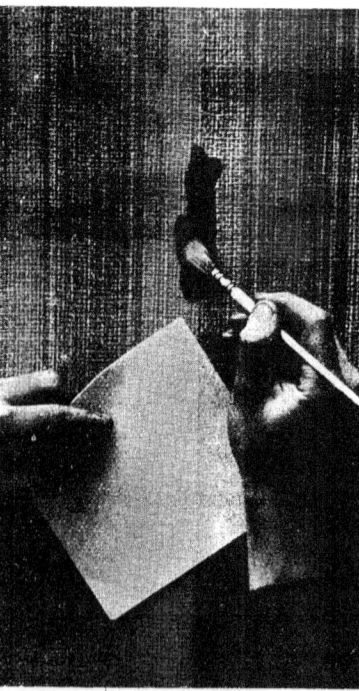

Fig. 3.—Grease Stains should be treated with Benzene.
Apply with a small brush. Note the piece of blotting paper ready to catch any drips. Allow about 10 minutes for the benzene to dry and if the grease stain is still visible repeat the treatment again.

along the outline of the leaf.

Rub the Edges of the Tear with Glasspaper.

Having prepared the new piece, now turn your attention again to the wall. Any upstanding edges of the tear must be stuck down and, when dry, rubbed over with a piece of very fine glasspaper. The object of this is to thin down the edges so that they will not show when the patch is stuck over them.

Applying the New Patch.

The next thing is to place the cut-out piece of wallpaper face down on a sheet of newspaper and paste the back lightly and evenly. The paste should be fairly stiff and not too wet; any kind of photo-mountant will serve the purpose very well. Now place it on the wall so that it exactly covers a similar part of the pattern. Dab it smooth with a duster, but do not rub, or the colours may be smeared. If the edges of the paper show white when the patch is dry, colour them to correspond with the surrounding pattern with a small artist's paint brush.

How to deal with a Tear in Plain Paper.

A tear in a plain wallpaper is not quite so easy to remedy, and greater care must be taken in preparing the new piece.

HIDING DEFECTS IN WALLPAPER

Fig. 4.—When Trimming up a New Patch, always cut along well-defined lines of the Pattern.

As there are no lines of the pattern to follow, the new piece can be any shape that is convenient, but it will be found that the most satisfactory result will be obtained if the edges are cut slightly wavy and not too regular, so that when the new piece is pasted down there are no hard angles or corners to catch the eye.

Treating the Edges of the New Patch.

Having cut out a suitable shape that will completely cover the tear, place it face down on a firm surface and rub the edges very gently with fine glasspaper. They must be made as thin and as tapering as possible, and as they will be very frail care must be taken not to damage them in any way when pasting on.

Now rub down the tear on the wall, as already described, and apply the paste to the patch sparingly and evenly, putting as little as possible on the edges.

Apply the patch over the tear and press down very gently with a duster. Any rubbing will almost certainly result in the edges tearing away.

It is impossible to obtain any idea of how the patch will look until it is dry, for the thin edging of the patch will present a very messy appearance while wet. Provided the above instructions have been correctly carried out, there is no reason to suppose that the result will not be perfectly satisfactory.

Finger-marks on Wallpaper.

Quite a common cause of disfigurement of wallpaper is a black fingermark or imprint of a hand—especially if there are children about the house.

If the mark is dry and free from grease, it will probably yield to treatment with stale bread. Cut a piece of stale bread and rub it over the dirty areas, taking care to break off the crumb as soon as it becomes soiled, and never to rub with a grimy piece of bread. After the surface grime has been dislodged, the patch can be cleaned up in a general way with a soft piece of indiarubber.

Another method of treating a fingermark is to deal with it as though it were a tear and cover it with a new patch.

What to do with Grease Spots.

Repeated applications of benzene will generally prove successful with grease spots. Use a small brush to apply the benzene and have a piece of blotting paper ready to catch any drips that start to trickle down the wall. Naturally, the longer the spots have been left without treatment, the greater will be the difficulty in removing them, and many applications may be necessary before the stain finally disappears.

When the benzene is applied it will make a wet patch that looks almost the same as the grease spot, and therefore it is impossible to tell until it has dried whether the grease has been removed or not. Start by applying the benzene for about two minutes, then blot off and wait until it dries, which will be about ten minutes. If the grease spot is still noticeable, repeat the benzene applications.

Ink Stains.

Painting fresh ink stains with a weak solution of oxalic acid will usually remove them. Apply the acid with an artist's paint brush and then dab with clean blotting paper. Repeat the process until the stain has been removed. It must, however, be remembered that the oxalic acid not only takes out the ink stain, but may also remove the colour on the wallpaper as well. Probably the colour can be matched up quite well with a few dabs of water-colours, and the result will certainly be less noticeable than the ink stain.

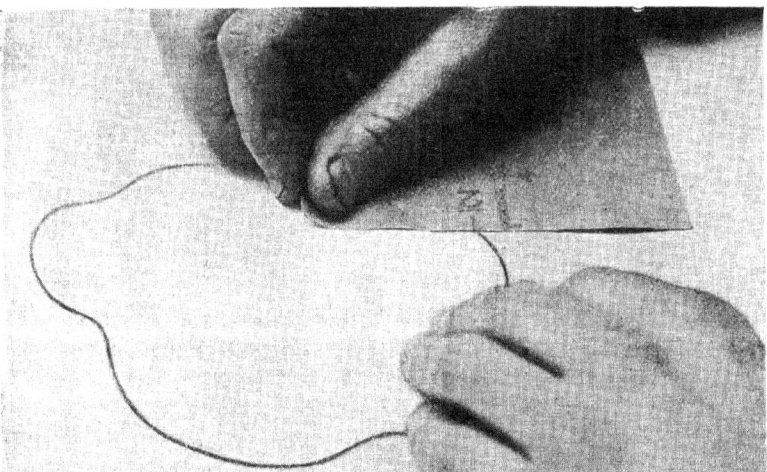

Fig. 5.—When dealing with a Tear in a Plain Wallpaper, the edges of the New Patch should be thinned on the Underside by gently rubbing with Glasspaper.
[Note also how the new patch has been cut in wavy lines.]

Extending the House Wiring

THE applications of electricity in the home have become so extended during recent times that the need of the householder for additional points for attachment of electrical apparatus is often keenly felt. In step with this advance has been the progress in the systems of electrical wiring.

Choosing the Wiring System.

For house wiring, especially in new houses, the metal-conduit system is most generally employed, the electrical contractor co-operating with the builder during the erection of the house, so that the whole of the conduit is hidden in the walls and under flooring. It is a form of wiring which does not lend itself well for amateur construction. It is not a flexible system, in that it cannot easily be altered or extended.

When to Choose Lead-covered Cable.

Lead- or copper-covered cables have the great advantage that they may be bent round to follow the contour of the building on which they are to be fastened. For all exterior work, such as wiring a porch lamp, or extensions to an outside shed or workshop, metal-covered cables will give the best protection against damp. If the extension contemplated is to supply a point for running a mains-driven radio receiver in which the aerial will run closely to the mains supply, metal-covered cable is to be preferred. The covering will prevent an external field and thus avoid the nuisance of mains hum due to direct pick-up. The disadvantage of metal-covered cables, and this applies also to steel conduit, is that precautions must be taken to earth efficiently the outside conductor in order to safeguard the system against the possible leakage of the internal conductors.

The Henley Wiring System.

This method of wiring employs a metal sheath, protecting the conductors, which is of special alloy, harder and tougher than lead yet possessing sufficient flexibility to bend where required. The difficulties of properly earthing the system have been overcome by bonding strips and clamps for use where the continuity of the covering is broken. Various fittings are obtainable to ensure the greatest adaptability of the system, which renders it quite suitable for amateur erection.

In the wiring extensions described tough rubber twin cable is used, but if required the Henley or Siemens systems can be equally well applied.

For all general indoor purposes, however, the tough rubber cable is advised. It is lighter, cheaper, easier to erect and less likely to mark the walls and ceilings. It has the further advantage that no earthing is required.

Considering the Probable Load.

The method of carrying out the wiring extension will depend mainly upon the amount of current likely to be required for the new apparatus. If the load is light, such as the addition of an extra point for a table lamp or a cellar light, the extra leads can be joined to the existing fuses without fear of overloading them.

Make a Plan of the Wiring.

In the great majority of houses an

Fig. 1.—THE FIRST THING TO DO WHEN EXTENDING THE HOUSE WIRING IS TO LOCATE THE DISTRIBUTION SWITCH-BOX.

In most houses this will be found in the hall or landing. The extension wire is taken from this point, if convenient for the wiring run.

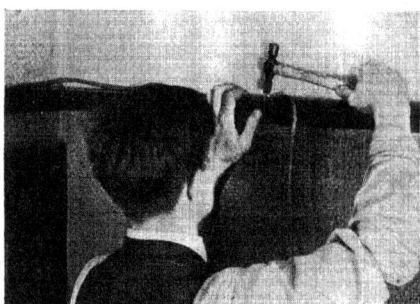

Fig. 2.—A GOOD METHOD OF CONCEALING THE WIRE IS TO TACK IT DOWN AT THE BACK OF THE PICTURE RAIL.

enclosed fuse-box will be found, similar to that shown in Fig. 1, each pair of fuses serving a particular branch of the house wiring system. This can be tested by cutting out the main switch adjacent to the meter and removing one pair of fuses. When the main switch is restored, each local switch is connected in turn to ascertain which part of the supply is cut off due to the removal of the fuses. A note should be made of this and a plan of the house wiring produced by removing each set of fuses in turn.

When this has been done, it can easily be seen which pair of fuses carries the smallest current, with the view of adding the extra extension lead to this pair. It may be of advantage, also, to consider the times when various lights are likely to be required and to add the extra load to those fuses which will not be used at the same time. For example, an additional garage or workshop light might be connected to the fuses controlling the bedrooms if they are unlikely to be used at the same time.

WIRING FOR ONE EXTRA POINT.

Supposing an additional point is required for a table lamp, an electric vacuum cleaner or other appliance, and it is decided not to connect up to the existing house fuse-box. Then fit an extra pair of fuses which will be independent of those in use.

The following table shows the size of wire required for various appliances. This is based on the wattage of the appliance, and it will be understood that if the appliance were a vacuum cleaner rated at 100 watts, the size of cable would be the same as that required for a 100-watt lamp.

Point.	Cable Size.	
	200/230 volt supply.	100/120 volt supply.
40-watt lamp	1/·044	3/·029
60 ,, ,,	1/·044	3/·029
100 ,, ,,	1/·044	3/·029
600 ,, ,,	3/·029	3/·036
1,000 ,, ,,	3/·036	7/·029
2,000 ,, ,,	3/·036	7/·036

The above sizes are ample for the work. It is better to use cable a size too large than a size too small.

Materials Required.

Quantity of flat twin rubber cable selected from table above.
1–5 amp. combination switch plug and 2 wood screws.
1 square or round switch block and 2 wood screws.
1 oblong fuse block 6″ × 3″ and 4 wood screws.

2 round type 5-amp. porcelain fuses and 4 wood screws.
Quantity of cable fixing clips and brads.
Quantity of electricians' staples and Rawlplug outfit.
Reel of insulating tape.
1 lb. Keene's cement.
Reel of 5-amp. fuse wire.

Planning the Runs.

In deciding upon the run of the additional wiring, its point of connection to the supply mains will have been settled. There are usually two places where this is possible of accomplishment without difficulty. One is at the outlet of the main switch-box, and the other is at the fuse- or distribution-box.

Before starting the work, careful attention must be given to the actual positioning of the wiring, so that the minimum amount of cutting and drilling is necessary. The appearance of the finished job must also be borne in mind, and, to this end, the wiring should be planned to obtain the greatest amount of concealment.

Tacking the Wire behind a Picture Rail.

If the cable selected is not too thick, a good method of hiding it where the run is across a room or hall is to tack it at the back of the picture rail in the manner illustrated in Fig. 2. If the cable is fixed at one end under one or two staples, it can be stretched tightly at the other end and again stapled down so that only in a few places is it necessary to hold it down intermediately. When tacking down to the picture rail, support it from underneath in order to avoid loosening it from the plaster.

Concealed Corner Wiring.

From the picture rail, the leads are brought down to the skirting-board

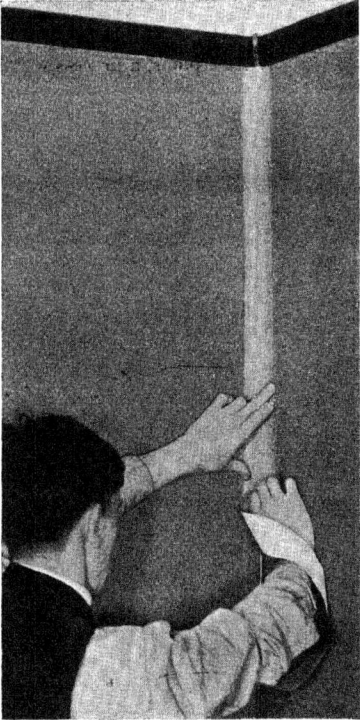

Fig. 3.—A Convenient Method of Concealing Cable in the Corner of a Room.
Cut and paste a strip of the same wallpaper over the leads to give the corner a slightly rounded effect.

or to a suitable intermediate switch position by taking advantage of the corner at adjacent walls. Stretch and staple the leads securely in the corner and then cut and paste a strip of the same wall-paper over the leads to give the corner a slightly rounded effect, as shown in Fig. 3. A slightly wider strip, pasted over the first, will give the job a more solid appearance.

Wiring under the Floor.

If the distance is only a short one, such as across the width of a door, it is not always necessary to prise up the floor-boards to conceal the wire. A channel is cut with a wood-chisel and the wire laid in the trough, which is afterwards covered with a thin strip of wood or filled in with Keene's cement. In cases where it is required to raise the floor-boards, it is often possible to take advantage of an existing gas-pipe installation. There will probably be a loose board, while the existing cuts in the joists where the gas pipe is laid will also accommodate the electrical supply.

If metal-covered cable is used, it is advisable to avoid contact with any accidental earth, such as an iron girder or gas or water pipes. With tough rubber cable these precautions are not necessary, although it is obviously as well to avoid the pipes of a hot-water system.

Concealing the Wire.

One of the most difficult problems which the amateur wireman may have to face is to conceal the wires to a lamp bracket or a switch where these occur in the middle of a flat wall. One method is to make a hole right through the wall and to allow the wires to enter from another room. If the appearance of this second room is equally important, it is obvious that no advantage is gained. It is a good plan in such a case to undertake the electrical installation immediately prior to the re-decorating of the room, when the incisions into the plaster will be completely concealed. With rea-

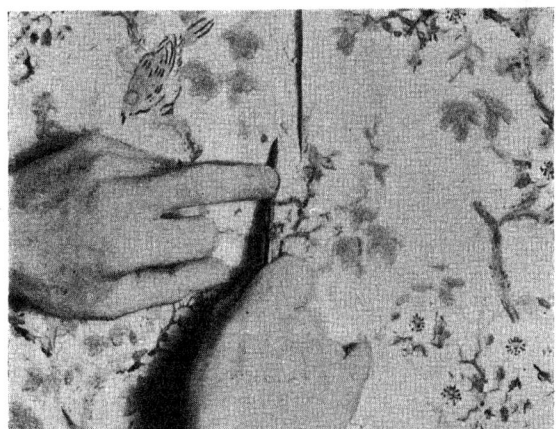

Fig. 4.—How to cut a Channel in Plaster to conceal a Cable.
First make two parallel cuts in the plaster as shown. Then prise out the plaster to a depth of about ½ inch.

Fig. 5.—After inserting the Cable in the Channel made in the Plaster, the Channel is filled with Keene's Cement.
Dip the blade of the trowel in water when smoothing over the cement.

EXTENDING THE HOUSE WIRING

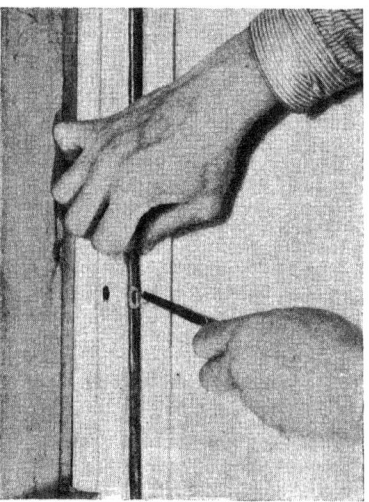

Fig. 6.—To hold the Wire securely on Wood use Clips.
The tail of the clip is threaded through the head and then bent backwards.

through the head and then bent backwards in the manner illustrated. On plaster or brick walls, the clips can be secured by Rawlplugs, a process which is described later in this article.

The Fixing of the Fittings.

The house-owner will find that the easiest method of fixing the fittings, such as power-plugs and switches, is to screw them to existing woodwork of which the skirting-board is the most useful. An example of this is shown in Fig. 7. The cable can be neatly stapled or clipped along the top edge of the skirting or along a groove if the board is moulded. A hard-wood block, of square or round pattern, is drilled as described in a later paragraph on fuses. Screw it in position with about 2 inches of the separate wires projecting. Remove the insulation from the end of each and thread the wires through the holes. This

to be removed for inspection without disturbing the electrical contacts.

Wiring up Lampholders.

If the various parts of the lampholder are laid out on the table in the order of dismantling, little difficulty will be experienced when reassembling them. Remember to thread the cord-grip and the back part of the holder over the flexible wires before attaching the latter to the contacts in the porcelain. The cord-grip must take the weight of the fitting. If necessary, wrap a strip of insulating tape round the wires where they pass through the wooden jaws of the chuck.

Finally, check that the two spring-loaded contacts are approximately at right angles to the cut-away portions forming the bayonet catch.

Switches in the Wooden Surround.

Certain makes of switches have a wooden surround which is cemented into the wall in the manner described for concealed wiring. A switch plate is then attached afterwards to come flush with the surface of the wall. This method of fixing is very firm, a feature which is highly desirable in every type of electrical fitting. It is of no use to rely upon wood screws turned directly into plaster walls. If they appear tight at the start, they will very quickly wear loose with constant use.

For the fixing of ceiling roses and porcelain connectors special long wood screws are obtainable which will reach into the wooden laths of the ceiling. Care must be taken that the screws do not merely enter the plaster between the laths.

Fixing with Rawlplugs.

In this system, suitable for brick or plaster walls, a hole of a certain size is made with a special tool similar to a star drill. A small fibrous tube, which is a push-in fit in the hole made, is set with "Durofix."

sonable care, the operation can be carried out with success without repapering the room.

How to Cut a Channel in the Plaster.

In order to cut the channel in the plaster where the leads are required to run, score two parallel cuts in the paper and plaster, about ½ inch apart, with a sharp penknife and a straight edge. When the cut in the plaster is sufficiently deep, the point of the knife is inserted between the parallel cuts and the plaster prised out to a depth of about ½ inch. The operation of deepening the cut is shown in Fig. 4. Run the cable into the channel and staple where necessary so that it lies at the bottom. A quantity of Keene's cement is mixed with water to form a fairly stiff paste.

Before applying it, the channel is thoroughly wetted with clean water applied with a brush, so that the water reaches the back of the channel. The filling-in process is shown in Fig. 5, where the cement is forced into the channel and smoothed off evenly with a small trowel. A smoother surface is obtained if the blade of the trowel is dipped in water.

Exposed Wiring.

In places it will be difficult to hide the cable, and the best that can be done is to make the job as neat as possible. The clips shown in Fig. 6 are spaced equidistantly and held by a small screw or nail. To hold the wire securely, the tail of the clip is threaded

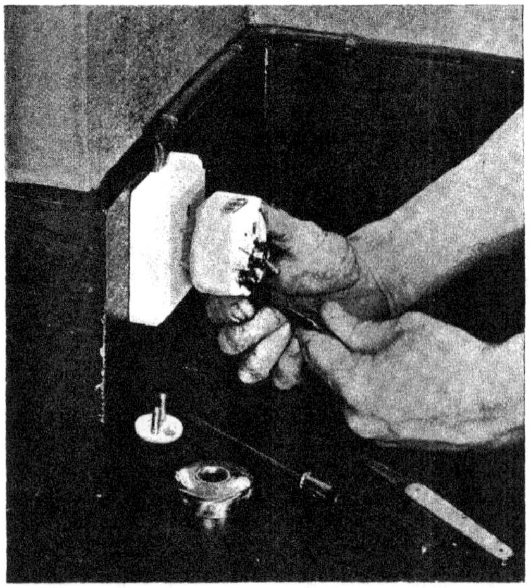

Fig. 7.—Fittings such as Power Plugs and Switches should be screwed to Existing Woodwork, such as a Skirting Board.

operation is shown in the fixing of a combination 5-ampere switch and power point, where a pair of pliers is used to bend over the ends of the wires to form a loop. By looping the wires inside the fixing hole a larger area of contact is made.

A little slack wire should always be left behind fittings in order to avoid any permanent strain. This practice also enables the fitting

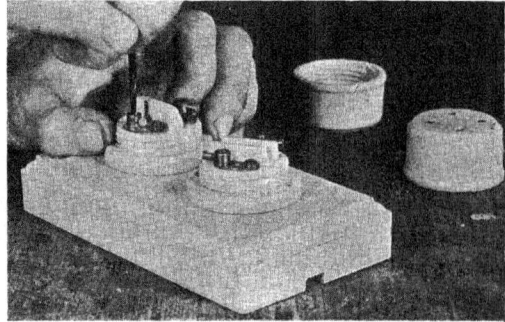

Fig. 8.—Assembling the Fuses for an Extension.

122

When the wood screw is turned home the tube expands and ensures that the screw shall be rigidly held. The method of drilling a Rawlplug hole is illustrated in Fig. 9, in which the end of the tool is sharply tapped with a hammer, taking care to turn the tool round slightly between each blow. Wait until the celluloid solution has set before attempting to turn in the screw.

Assembling the Fuses.

The fuses for the extensions can be assembled by screwing a pair of porcelain fuses to a rectangular hardwood block sold for this purpose. A slot is cut at either edge of the base to permit the entry of the leads. In marking the positions of the screw holes for fixing the fuses to the block, mark off the places where the conductors are to be pushed through the block. This can be done by unscrewing the tightening screws and holding a drill vertically through the holes where the conductors are held (see Fig. 8).

Fitting the Fuse Wire.

Before coupling up to the supply, all the extensions must be tested for short-circuit or accidental earthing. Fuse wire arranged to "blow" at 5 amperes will carry the normal load and is fitted to the fuses to complete the continuity of the wiring system. Two common types of porcelain fuses are shown, having a single and double partition. In the single type the fuse wire is clamped under its screws to form the letter "V," the apex of which is supported by a notch in the end of the partition. The wire is run between the partitions in the other type illustrated.

Testing Out.

The tests are made with the extension switches in the "on" position, but with all lamps and apparatus removed from the circuit. If a 500-volt megger tester is available, connect its two leads to the free wires from the fuses. These are shown in Fig. 10, in which the junction is being bound tightly with insulating tape to prevent the rubber covering from splitting. The insulation between conductors should give a reading approaching infinity, although a leak of 10 megohms need not be considered serious.

For the earthing test, connect the two ends of the cable together and to one megger lead. The second lead is joined to a good earth, preferably a water pipe. If lower readings than the above are obtained, repeat the test on each conductor separately. Disconnect the fittings after inspection, one by one, until the leak is found.

Failing a megger, the tests given

Fig. 9.—DRILLING THE HOLES FOR FIXING THE FUSE BOARD IN POSITION.
Rawlplugs should be used, and this photograph shows the special tool being tapped with a hammer.

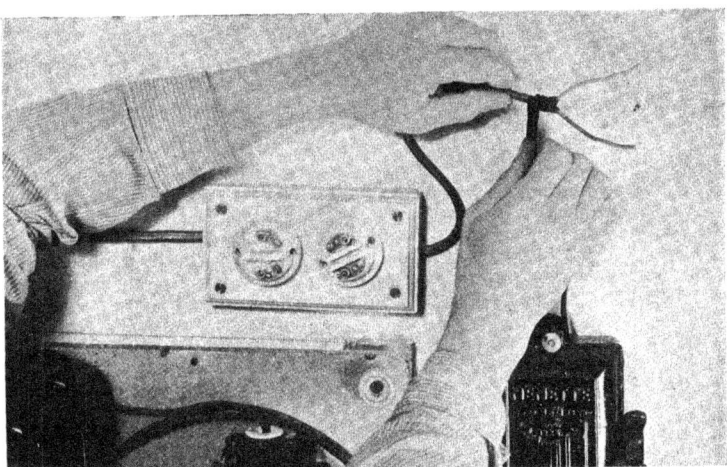

Fig. 10.—HAVING FIXED THE FUSES IN POSITION, BIND THE JUNCTION OF THE WIRE WITH INSULATING TAPE TO PREVENT THE RUBBER COVERING FROM SPLITTING.

Fig. 11.—A TYPICAL HOUSE-OWNER'S MAINS SUPPLY SYSTEM.
Showing the additional wiring connected to the combination switch and fuse box on the right.

EXTENDING THE HOUSE WIRING

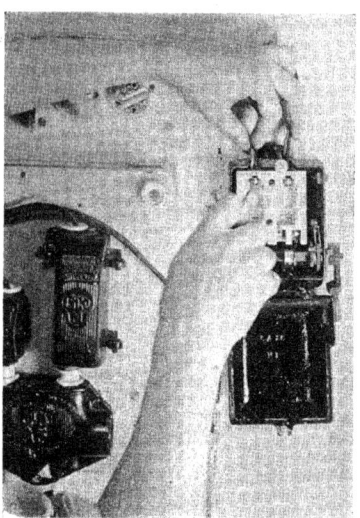

Fig. 12—Here we see how the Ends of the Extension Wires are joined to the Top End of the Main Switch.

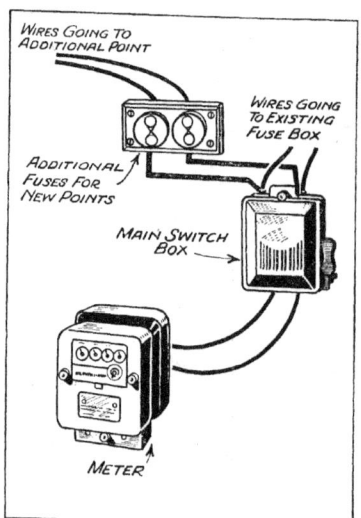
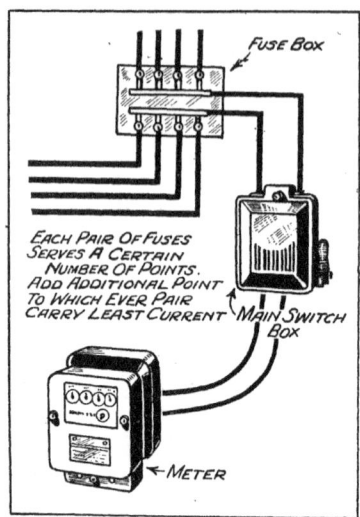

Fig. 13.—Wiring Diagram.
Left, showing method of using additional switches; Right, connecting up to existing fuse

must be carried out with a galvanometer or high-resistance voltmeter and a suitable battery wired in series with it.

Connecting to the Supply.

Adequate precautions must be taken when the completed and tested extensions are wired to the main fuses and switch. Even when this switch is in the " off " position certain parts are still alive, and accidental contact with them may cause serious personal shock or damage to the property of the supply company. There is, however, nothing to fear if the following instructions are closely followed in their proper order.

Temporary Lighting Arrangements.

Suitable temporary lighting arrangements must be made if the switch is in a cupboard or a dark corner. Remove the insulation from the ends of the wires and check that they are long enough to reach to the points of connection. Now turn the main switch " off " and check that this is correct by the failure of the house lamps to light. This action will stop any synchronous clocks wired to the supply, which point is apt to be overlooked. A pair of dry leather gloves may be worn as a precaution when removing the main fuses.

The fuses may be a separate unit, in which case the double-pole main switch need only be open-circuited and connection of the extensions made at the output or house wiring side of the fuses. This is made clear in the plan of wiring shown in Fig. 13.

In the combined switch illustrated in Fig. 11 the output leads which run direct to the local fuse- and distribution-box enter the switch-box at the top, where they connect directly to the main fuses. The two wires from the extension system enter at the same point. After removing the fuses, slacken the screws binding the existing wires and remove one of them. Twist one of the new leads to make electrical connection with it and replace the double wire. There is normally plenty of room in the hole to accommodate the extra wire.

It is important to check that all the strands have entered the hole in which they clamp. A sharp tug after the screw has been tightened will prove whether the wire is properly held. The second wire is now connected in the same way (see Fig. 12).

A Further Check against Leakage.

The voltmeter test should not be regarded as final, but simply as a precaution against a short-circuit. A further test may be made after the main fuses have been restored. Switch on the current at the mains and with all local switches " off," except those in the completed extension, check that the meter is not consuming current. It is obvious that no load is to be applied to the circuit during this test. In most electricity meters the flow of current can be detected by the rotation of the aluminium disc.

RESTORING CRACKED FRENCH POLISH

THE appearance of fine surface cracks —often in the form of a reticulated network—on French polished articles of furniture that have been in use for some time is a fairly common one.

These cracks may be caused by wood shrinkage or by swelling. In many cases where the furniture is exposed to the full effect of the sun daily these cracks will appear. In other cases they are due to the polisher using rather more oil during the polishing operation than is advisable; this oil eventually works through the surface.

Although the process of completely repolishing the surfaces affected is undoubtedly the most logical one to employ, under the circumstances this is not always a convenient method for the home handyman.

These surface cracks can, however, be removed in the following manner. First wipe the surface carefully with a soft cloth, *e.g.*, mutton or cheese cloth which has been boiled in soda water to remove any grease, soaked in hot water to which a small quantity of ordinary washing soda has been added ; a piece of soda about the size of a knob of sugar is sufficient for 1 quart of water.

Next, after wiping the surface dry, rub over with raw linseed oil. After wiping off any surplus oil apply a fresh coating of French polish, rather more dilute than usual. Each rubber charged with polish should be worked out almost dry before applying fresh polish. Allow each working to dry well before giving the next one.

Finally, after all the cracks have disappeared and a satisfactory surface has been obtained, spirit out, instead of using glaze.

Fixing Rising Butt Hinges

Have you a door that causes the carpet or floor-covering to buckle up every time it is opened? This annoying habit can be avoided by fitting a rising butt hinge as shown in Figs. 1 and 2.

Two Types.

There are two types of rising butt hinge. In one the lifting movement is obtained from a pin in the form of a square-cut spiral thread and the loose flap of the hinge, which has a similar thread formed in the inside of the joint, as shown in Fig. 3. As the door is opened, it moves upwards on the thread, so enabling it to clear the carpet.

In the other type, details of which are shown in Fig. 4, the rise is obtained by means of the flap being cut in a semi-spiral fashion at the joint. This enables the loose leaf of the hinge to ride higher as the hinge is opened, and, by reason of the weight of the door, to drop as the latter is closed. This type also tends to make the door self-closing, as the slightest impetus will cause the hinge to ride downward of its own accord.

Details for Fitting.

The two flaps of the hinge when closed are level as in C, Fig. 4, and when open the half A rises. The portion B carries a pin, and this piece must be fastened to the door-frame; the flap A which slides on to the pin is always screwed to the door.

Chisel away Recesses in the Door and Frame.

Mark out and chisel away recesses in the door and frame deep enough to sink the flaps level with the surface of the wood, 9 inches from the top and bottom of the door. Note that the slots in the door will be level with those in the frame, since, when closed, the flaps coincide. See that the cylindrical portion is quite free of the recess.

Fasten the portion A to the door, then lift it on a large wooden wedge so that, as the hinge opens, the piece B comes in position with the cavities cut in the frame. Place one screw in each hinge, remove the wedge, and see that the door closes properly. It is a good plan temporarily to fix it to the frame with a couple of 1-inch screws for testing, and finally fasten up with some 1¼ inch long screws.

Finally, oil the pins in the hinges, and the door will rise when opened and close itself when left free.

Easing a Door.

There may be many readers who have doors which have dropped slightly owing to warping of the woodwork to which the hinges are attached. It is, of course, possible to remedy this without fixing rising butt hinges.

Briefly, the method is to remove the door by taking out the screws which secure the hinges to the door post, removing the upper hinge, and cutting a deeper recess for the hinge flap in the edge of the door. Full details of this will be given in a later article. In the meantime, readers are warned not to attempt to remedy a fault of this kind by planing or chiselling the lower edge of the door. This method may be found very troublesome.

Fig. 1.—A Door before fixing a Rising Butt Hinge.
Note how the carpet is buckled up each time the door is opened.

Fig. 2.—The Same Door fixed with a Rising Butt Hinge.
The door is slightly raised as it opens, enabling it to clear the carpet.

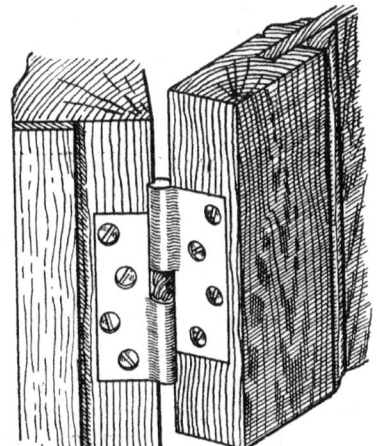

Fig. 3.—A Close-up View of the Rising Butt Hinge.
As the door is opened the spiral thread causes the door to lift.

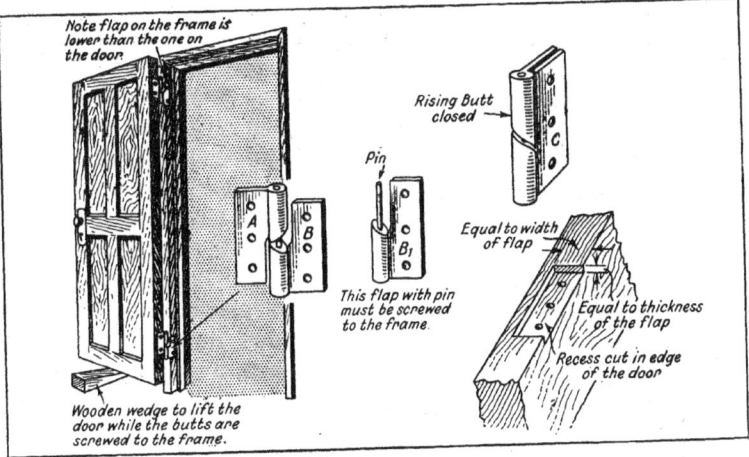

Fig. 4.—Details of Another Type of Rising Butt Hinge.
The flap is cut in a semi-spiral fashion at the joint, enabling the loose leaf of the hinge to rise higher as the door is opened.

Bricks and Their Use in the Garden

Bricks, like stone, have a useful place in the garden. The flowers may paint the picture in gaudy colours but unless the canvas is framed with paths and walls the prospective and definition is lost in a shapeless mass. Walks and terraces constructed of bricks give shape and character to our gardens while their many hues provide that touch of colour so necessary in those dark, dreary days of winter.

Materials and Quantities.

1 Hollow pillar takes 26 bricks.

1 Solid pillar takes 30 bricks.

Dwarf Walling.—100 bricks builds 19 square feet of wall (4½ inches thick) measured on one side only.

Paving.—100 bricks will cover 28 square feet of ground.

1 cwt. of cement mixed with 2 bushels of sand makes sufficient mixture to lay 400 bricks.

The Kind of Bricks to Buy.

Many people like to purchase old bricks from the housebreaker, and, provided the variety of colour is wide, this is a good plan. When buying new specimens, choose a good hard type as used by engineers for bridges, especially for paving work. Cheap "wire cuts," as used for interiors, soon disintegrate when exposed to the weather. Good "stock" or facing bricks can be bought for 10s. to 12s. per hundred in small quantities.

How to Make a Brick Path.

Roll the site perfectly level, sprinkling over the ground a layer of ashes or sand to provide drainage. Strings or

Fig. 1.—A Dwarf Wall Built to Form an Entrance to the Lawn.

Full details for a wall such as this are given in the accompanying article.

Fig. 2.—Another View of the Attractive Dwarf Wall.

wooden battens should be stretched along the sides to keep the edges regular. Fig. 17 shows three different ways in which the bricks may be laid.

Throw down on the prepared site a loose layer of ashes or sand, place the brick in position, and with a mallet tap it so that it beds down in the sand. When half a dozen have been put in place, try the surface with a spirit level. Should the corner of a brick project above the others it can easily be pulled up by pushing a trowel down the side and giving a sharp upward jerk. A little sand placed under the lower end and a portion removed where the corner is high, and the brick can be replaced and will be absolutely level.

Filling in the Joints.

When several yards have been laid, brush sand over the surface to fill the cracks; a little water sprayed on top will facilitate the process.

It is not advisable to cement the bricks in position as, should one sink, it is then difficult to remove it; further, the sand-filled crevices provide excellent drainage, and small tufts of moss or creeper growing between them adds to their charm.

The Edging.

A pleasing border to such a path can be made by fringing it with bricks placed sideways at 45 degrees and resting one upon another, as in Fig. 10.

A Brick Parapet Wall.

Fig. 1 shows a dwarf wall built to form an entrance to the lawn. The two curved sections are quadrants of a circle and the ends terminate in pillars, two of which are solid and support flower vases, while those at the entrance are hollow to take clipped shrubs or pyramid box trees.

The Foundation.

Set out the foundations as shown in the plan, Fig. 5, marking the limits with pegs and string. Excavate the top layer to a depth of 6 inches and ram the bottom of the trench hard and fill in with concrete made of a mixture 3 parts rubble and 1 of cement. This foundation need only be 3 inches thick as the first course of bricks is laid below ground level. The first layer is shown by the dotted lines in Fig. 5. Note that the pillars are one-and-a-half bricks thick, *i.e.*, 13½ inches, while the wall is 4½ inches wide except for the first foundation course, which is 9 inches, or one brick, across.

To Lay a Brick.

Having prepared a foundation, spread a layer of mortar or cement ½ inch thick, but not quite so wide as a brick. Place the brick on this and give

Fig. 3.—How to Cut a Brick.

Mark a chalk line on the brick, and then chip into this all round with a cold chisel. A sharp blow with the cutting tool will then usually split it into two pieces with a fairly clean edge.

Fig. 4.—How to Lay a Brick Path.

Throw down on the prepared site a loose layer of ashes or sand, place the brick in position, and with a mallet tap it so that it beds down in the sand.

BRICKS AND THEIR USE IN THE GARDEN

it a sharp downward tap with the handle of the trowel, when some of the mixture will squeeze out, and this should be scraped off with the trowel. Proceed the same way with the second brick, this time spreading mortar up the end of the fixed one, so that there will be a gap of $\frac{3}{8}$ inch (approx.) between the ends.

To Cut a Brick.

It is necessary to cut the bricks across for curved walls, and longitudinally for hollow pillars. The amateur can best do this by marking a line on the brick and then chipping into this *all round* with a cold chisel. A sharp blow with the cutting tool will then usually split it into two pieces with a fairly clean edge.

Building a Wall.

Walls should be built as shown in Fig. 6; the two ends are first carried up several courses and carefully plumbed to see that they are vertical. A line is then stretched on two nails or thin pegs driven into the ends of the wall. A full course can then be laid, the string making it easy to keep the row even. Now raise the cord one brick and proceed with a second course, and so

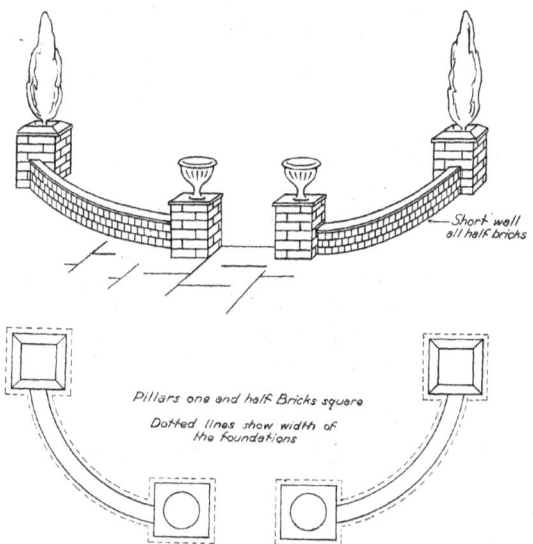

Fig. 5.—Details and Plan for the Foundations of the Dwarf Brick Wall.

on until the full height is reached.

If pillars are included in the scheme then each other course should be "bonded" into the pillar, that is, the brick immediately next to the column should lap partly into it as shown in Fig. 9.

The Pillars.

Fig. 9 shows one of the solid pillars in course of construction; it is six courses above ground, and is one-and-a-half bricks square, which leaves a 4½-inch square hole down the centre. This is filled with coke or stones to provide drainage. Fig. 11 portrays a slab of cement cast in a wooden box; this fits on to the top of the brickwork. Note the hole in the centre which coincides with a drainage vent in the base of the flower vases.

Hollow Pillars.

Fig. 11 is a hollow pillar; the first four courses are laid as in the solid type, but for the last two, the bricks are split longitudinally. This gives a large cavity approximately 10 inches square.

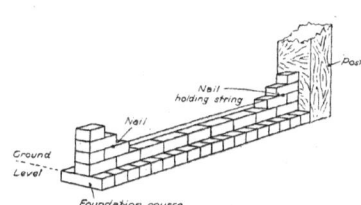

Fig. 6.—Showing the use of a String Line to keep each Course Level.

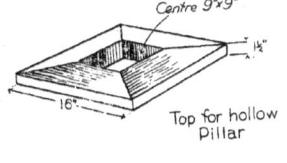

Top for hollow Pillar

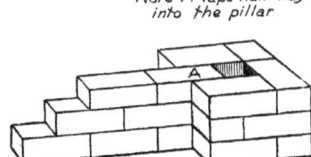

Fig. 9.—Method of Bonding the Bricks.

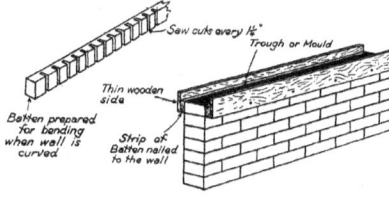

Fig. 7.—How a Cement Capping is Cast.

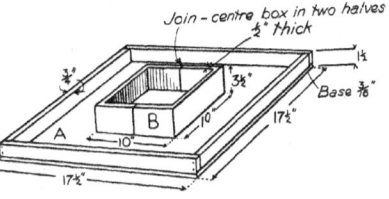

Fig. 8.—Details of a Mould for the Top of a Hollow Pillar.

The box-shaped piece B is in two halves to facilitate its removal when the cement is dry. Fill in with a 3 to 1 mixture of sand and cement, and level the surface upwards from the outer edge towards the central box. After standing for five days, remove the wooden moulds, and cement in position on top of the bricks.

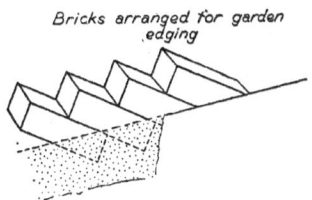

Fig. 10.—Arrangement of Bricks for Garden Edging.

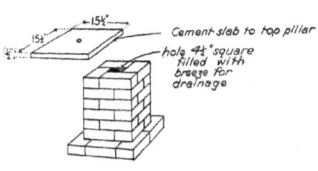

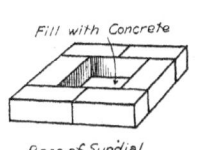

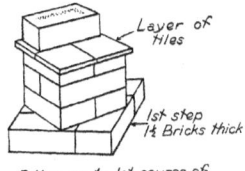

Fig. 11.—Details of Solid and Hollow Pillars.
On the left is a solid pillar suitable for use as a flower vase on the right a hollow pillar suitable for shrubs.

Fig. 12.—Some Details of the Brick Sundial shown in Fig. 13.
Showing construction of the base and pillar.

BRICKS AND THEIR USE IN THE GARDEN

The Pyramid Tops.

One of the special tops for the hollow pillars is shown in Fig. 8. It is cast in a mould, A, the box-shaped piece, B, is in two halves to facilitate its removal when the cement is dry. Fill in with a 3 to 1 mixture of sand and cement and level the surface upwards from the outer edge towards the central box.

After standing for five days remove the wooden moulds, and cement in position on top of the bricks.

To Make a Coping.

To give the wall a finished appearance a coping must be cast on the top. Look at Fig. 7; a length of batten 1 inch thick is nailed along each side of the wall, on to this foundation thin sides are nailed so as to form a trough or mould on the top of the wall. This cavity is filled with concrete mixture, the upper layer being sand and cement carefully smoothed off with a wet trowel. Allow this five days to set, when the wooden portion may be removed.

If the wall is curved the battens can be bent round by making a number of saw cuts 1 inch apart and 3 parts of the way through the wood, as shown in Fig. 7.

A Brick Sundial.

Fig. 13 shows a pleasing sundial constructed entirely of bricks and tiles. The base, see Fig. 12, is two bricks square, and set upon this is a column one brick thick. Three or four courses up a layer of roofing tiles is cemented in; these project beyond the bricks. Then another four courses are laid. Great care must be taken to use a plumb line to see that the column is perfectly vertical.

The top platform of the sundial is composed of three layers of tiles so arranged that the middle row projects further than those immediately above and below, see Fig. 15. Small holes or slots should be chipped out of those tiles towards the centre of the top platform so that wooden pegs can be driven in to take the screws which will be used to secure the dial.

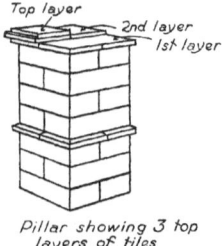

Fig. 15.—Details of the Pillar and Top Layer of Tiles for the Sundial.

The Dial.

The construction of a suitable dial is described elsewhere in this work in an article "How to make a Sundial."

Fig. 13.—An Attractive Brick-built Sundial.

Fig. 14.—How Brickwork can be used to Form a Pleasing Design in the Garden.

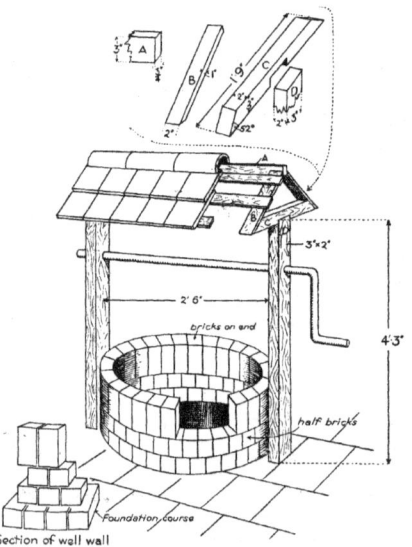

Fig. 16.—A Model Garden Well.

A Garden Well—the Brickwork.

Fig. 16 shows an ornamental well suitable as a centre of attraction in some corner of the garden. The foundation is a row of bricks laid in a circle, each one along a radius of the circle. The first two courses above ground are half-bricks, while in the top row they are stood up on end. When placing these bricks in position see that the edges on the inside practically touch while on the outside a gap of $\frac{3}{8}$ to $\frac{1}{2}$ inch will appear. This wedge shaped space is afterwards filled with cement when pointing up the work.

Making the Woodwork.

The main wooden uprights are let 15 inches into the ground. The cross-piece, C, is slotted in the middle and nailed to the post. The upper ends of the sloping members, B, are bevelled to fit flush up against the side of the ridge board A. Three roofing battens are nailed across on each side of the ridge, these should be suitably arranged to take the nail holes in the tiles. Note they project 2 inches beyond the sloping members B.

The windlass bar is a piece of iron rod bent to shape; a wooden roller and rope can be added if desired.

Tiling the Roof.

Two or three rows of tiles are needed according to the length of the specimens available; the overlap should be at least $2\frac{1}{2}$ inches. The ridge is composed of half-round ridging tiles cemented in place. One section may need cutting to length, this is best done by chipping a line round with a cold chisel and gradually making the cut deeper until the section falls in two pieces.

The Interior.

The bottom inside the circular wall should be cemented over, and may be used as a small pond.

Pointing.

When the brickwork is finished and the mortar well set, proceed to "point" with a rich mixture of cement and sand. This means pressing a filling into the crevasses between the bricks on the face side.

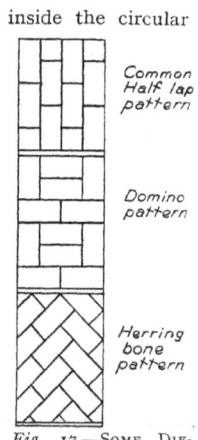

Fig. 17.—Some Different Ways in which Bricks can be Laid for a Path.

Cleaning and Repairing Clocks

The following is a description of the cleaning and repairing of a German striking-clock, and although this has been confined to one make of clock, it can easily be applied to most other types of striking movement. The photographs which accompany this article were specially staged by the well-known watch and clock specialists Messrs. Walter Davies & Sons, 148, Strand, W.C.2.

Removing the Movement from the Case.

First the movement must be removed from the case, and to do this take off the hands. These will be found to be held in position by a small pin or nut. Now turn the clock on its face, unscrew the gong, and it will then be seen that the movement is fixed by wood screws, which are passed through metal straps at each of the four corners of the front plate. When the screws are removed the clock may be withdrawn from the case and is ready for repair.

For the amateur it would be best to replace the minute hand on the movement thus rid of dial and turn same till clock is made to strike; watch the working of each part and try to memorise its position; this will probably be found most useful when you start the reassembly.

Now Unwind the Springs.

Before taking to pieces it is important to note that the springs must be completely unwound. This is done by placing the key on the winding square, then lift the click as shown in Fig. 1 and let the key turn back for half a turn. Release the click so that you may change the position of your hand, and repeat till the train is devoid of all power. This must be done with great care, for if the spring is allowed to slip it will do considerable damage to other parts of the movement.

Remove all Parts fixed on Outside.

The next step is to remove all parts that are fixed on the outside of the plates. Fig. 2 plainly shows how the striking hammer is held in position; if this should prove to be a tight fit the blades of a pair of pliers placed underneath the collet and used as a lever will remove same with comparative ease.

Then follow the pallets, pendulum rod and crutch. These are taken out by undoing two screws as shown in Fig. 3 and

Fig. 3.—THE PALLETS, PENDULUM ROD AND CRUTCH ARE TAKEN OUT BY UNDOING TWO SCREWS AS SHOWN.
They should be left together until the time comes for cleaning.

Fig. 2.—ALL PARTS THAT ARE FIXED ON THE OUTSIDE OF THE PLATES MUST BE REMOVED.
Here we see how the striking hammer is held in position. A pair of pliers placed underneath the collet and used as a lever will enable this to be removed if it is a tight fit.

are best left together, as they are removed, until the time comes for cleaning, when they can be brushed and replaced while their position is fresh in the mind.

Now Remove Parts fixed to Front Plate.

Now, turning the movement on its back, start to remove those parts which are fixed to the front plate. First take off the motion work, which consists of three wheels, held by a small split-collet, and is removed in the manner shown by Fig. 4. Follow with the rack, rack-hook and lifting lever; all of these are fixed by small but obvious pins. Next come the gathering pallet (see Fig. 5), and lastly the ratchets and covers.

Taking the Plates apart.

The plates, now stripped of repeating and winding work, may be taken apart. For simplicity it is best to remove the back plate (see Fig. 6). It will then be noticed that the wheels are divided into two trains— one for striking, the other for time-keeping—and it is best when taking out these wheels to keep them in their two respective groups. To save mixing the spring barrels which are the same size, but have different strength springs, the one belonging to the striking train should be marked with an S.

Dealing with a Broken Main Spring.

Now with respect to broken main springs; these can be replaced by the local jeweller at a very small cost and should be fitted in the following manner. The barrel cover is lifted as shown in Fig. 12 and the barrel arbour is removed. Then, holding the barrel firmly in a piece of cloth to save injury to the hand, pull out the spring centre first. Now take the new spring, which will be fixed in a wound position by a length of wire; hold this tight in a piece of cloth and cut the wire and allow the spring to open out to full size; then proceed to fix in barrel as shown in Fig. 13, outside coil first.

Moisten the Spring with Oil.

Moisten spring with a little clock or three-in-one oil and when this is done

Fig. 1.—BEFORE TAKING A CLOCK TO PIECES IT IS IMPORTANT TO SEE THAT THE SPRINGS ARE COMPLETELY UNWOUND.
Place the key on the winding square, then lift the click and let the key turn back for half a turn. Repeat until the train is devoid of all power.

CLEANING AND REPAIRING CLOCKS

Fig. 4.—How Pliers are Used to Remove the Small Split-collet which Holds the Three Wheels of the Motion Work.

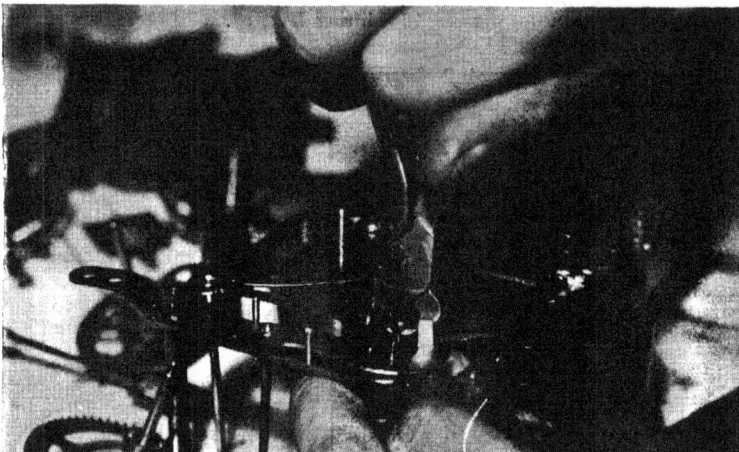

Fig. 5.—The Next Operation is to Remove the Gathering Pallet, and this can be Drawn Out in the Manner Shown.
After this, remove the ratchets and covers.

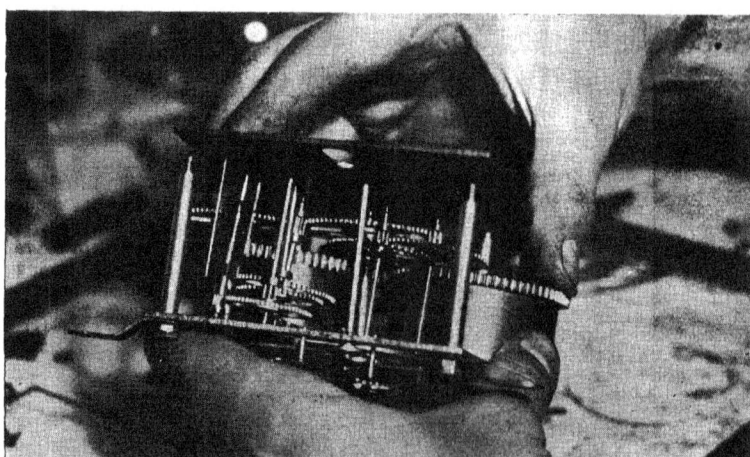

Fig. 6.—Now Remove the Back Plate.
It will be noticed that the wheels are divided into two trains, one for striking and the other for timekeeping. It is best to keep the wheels in their two respective groups.

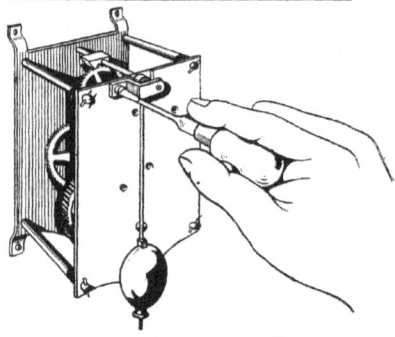

Fig. 7.—Here We See the Method of Removing a Pendulum and Pallet Cock, to Enable the Spring to be Unwound before Attempting to Dismantle.

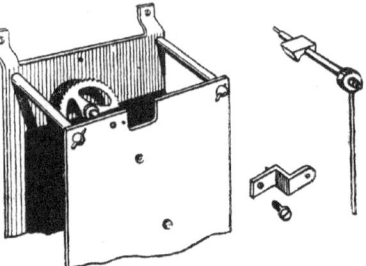

Fig. 8.—The Pendulum and Pallet Cock Removed.
This allows the wheels to be free and the spring unwinds itself.

Fig. 9.—Removing the Pins Holding the Top and Bottom Plates in Position.
Note that in some clocks nuts are used instead of pins.

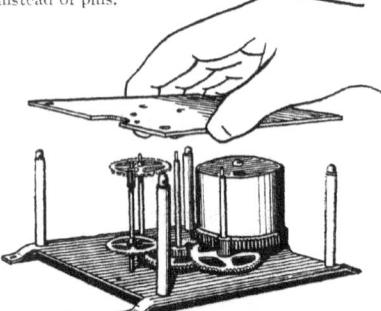

Fig. 10.—Here We See the Bottom Plate being Removed.

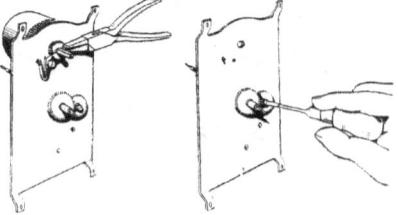

Fig. 11.—Left, Taking Out Pin for Removal of Spring Barrel; Right, Removal of Main Hand Spindle.

CLEANING AND REPAIRING CLOCKS

Fig. 12.—First Stage in Removing a Broken Main Spring.
Lift the barrel cover and remove barrel arbour. Then pull out spring after wrapping barrel firmly in a piece of cloth.

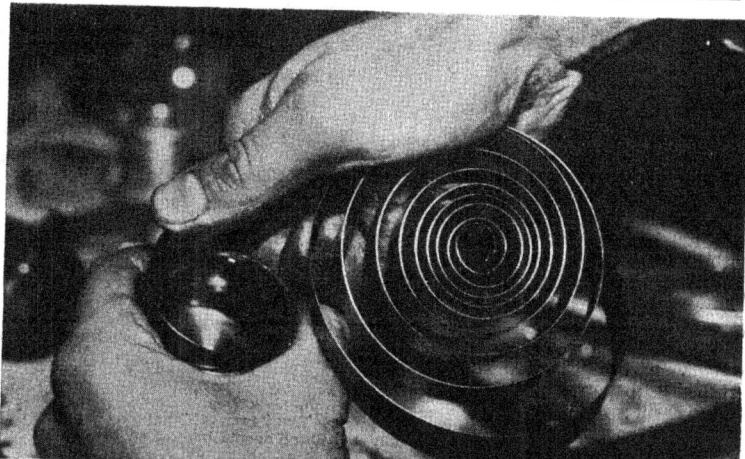

Fig. 13.—To Fit a New Main Spring, First Allow the Spring to Open Fully.
Then fix in the barrel, outside coil first. The spring will be supplied fixed in a wound position by a length of wire. Hold the spring in a piece of cloth before cutting the wire, and then allow the spring to open out to its full size.

Fig. 14.—If the Spring is only Broken on the Outside Coil, Heat it in a Gas Flame until Red Hot.
Then slowly withdraw and make a new hole as shown.

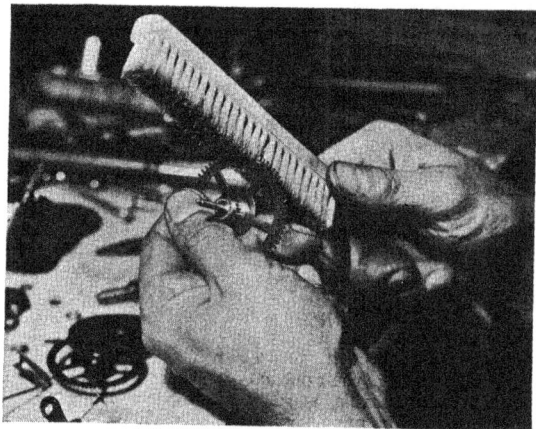

Fig. 15.—Using a Small Brush to Clean up the Parts.
After brushing with petrol, a little metal polish will be found useful in bringing up the dirtiest parts to a bright finish.

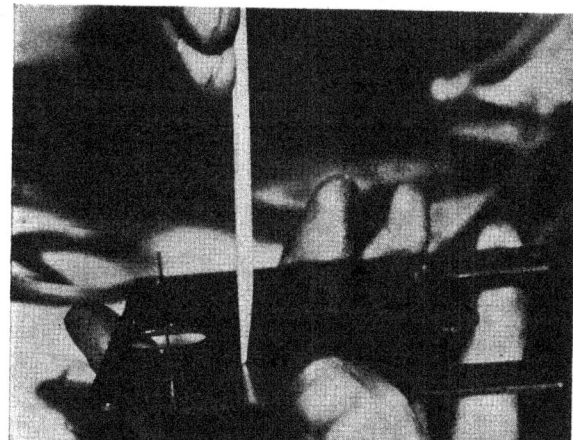

Fig. 16.—The Holes in the Plates can be Cleaned with a Piece of Pegwood which is Sharpened to a Point.

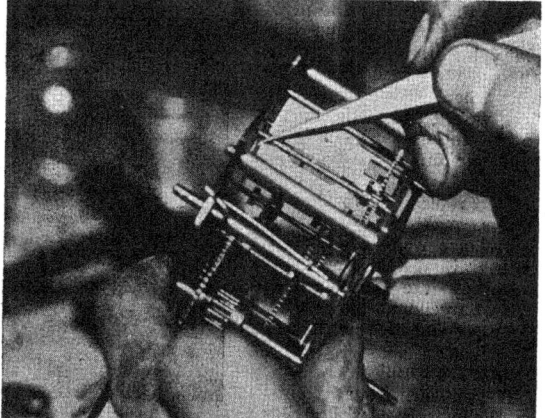

Fig. 17.—To get the Pivots Back into the Holes of the Back Plate, Screw the Two Bottom Nuts Home and then Ease each Wheel into Position, Working from Bottom to Top.

CLEANING AND REPAIRING CLOCKS

the arbour and cover may be replaced and the barrel is ready for reassembly.

What to do if Spring is only broken on Outside Coil.

In some cases when the spring is broken on the outside coil only it may be softened by holding it in a gas flame until it is red hot and then slowly withdrawing. Now drill a new hole and open as shown in Fig. 14.

Now Clean the Parts.

Each part must now be brushed with petrol until it is quite clean; a little metal polish will be found useful in bringing the dirtiest parts to a bright finish (see Fig. 15).

Giving a Final Polish with Chalk or Whitening.

To give a final polish use a small amount of chalk or whitening, but make sure no dust is left behind.

Cleaning the Holes in the Plates.

When the plates have been treated in a similar manner each of the holes must be cleaned with a piece of peg-wood, which is sharpened to a point and inserted as shown in Fig. 16.

Reassembly.

This completed, all parts are ready for reassembly. Take the front plate and begin to replace the wheels in their orginal position; when this is done the back must be put on.

A Useful Tip when Replacing the Pivots.

Some difficulty will be experienced in getting the pivots into the holes of this back plate, but if the two bottom nuts are screwed home and each wheel is eased into position, working from the bottom to the top (see Fig. 17), this will be found to be much simplified.

Next replace the ratchet and covers, making sure that all screws are well home. Wind both trains for half a turn to see they are running with perfect freedom. Now replace the lifter and rack-hook.

Fitting the Striking Train.

If you turn your attention to the wheels of the striking train you will find that the warning wheel, that which is next to the fly, has a short pin

Fig. 18.—THE CORRECT METHOD OF OILING A CLOCK.
Only a little oil should be applied to each movable part.

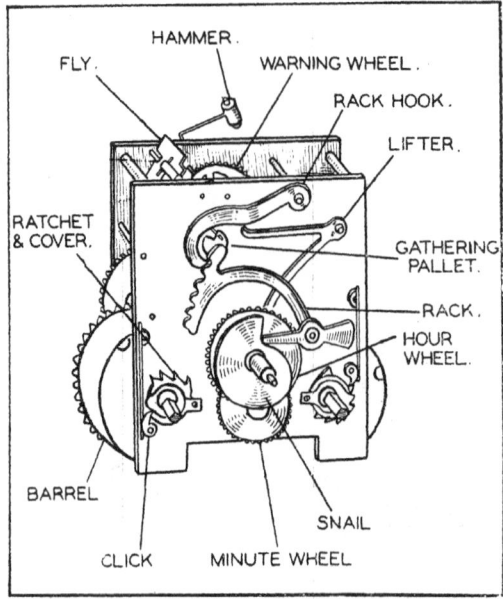
Fig. 19.—DIAGRAMMATIC VIEW OF A CLOCK SHOWING THE VARIOUS PARTS.

Fig. 20.—ADJUSTING THE CLOCK TO AN EVEN BEAT.
This is done by raising either end of the case until the tick is perfectly regular; then press the pendulum towards the side of the case, which is lifted until the clock will strike an even beat in level position.

fitted to the side nearest the plate, which as the wheel revolves will come in contact with the lifter when that part is raised. The following instruction should be noted and particular care taken to get it correct.

Take the gathering pallet and place loosely on its pivot, which will be found protruding below the warning wheel; then turn the warning wheel round with the finger till the pin is level with the top of the plate on the opposite side to the fly. Hold it in this position while you turn the gathering on the pivot till the facet caused by its irregular shape is locked on the pin of the rack-hook. Then drive it home till it is tightly fixed on its pivot. When this is done the train will be in a correct position for regular striking.

Rack and Motion Work.

We can now turn our attention to the rack and motion work. The cannon pinion and minute wheel should be placed in position. On the cannon pinion are two levers which in their turn raise the lifter till it releases the striking train; one of these levers is considerably longer than the other, and is used for releasing at the hour while the shorter acts for the single stroke at the half-hour.

Turn this pinion till it is at the point of releasing at the hour, then replace the rack and hour wheel in such a position that the pin on lower part of rack falls in the middle of the first step of the snail. This done the split-collet may be returned to the minute wheel and the pins to the rack and lifting pieces.

Now Set the Striking Side of the Movement Working.

Now place the hammer in position and partly wind up the striking side of the movement and set working. It is possible that when the last blow has been struck and the train has locked up the hammer will be raised; if this should be the case the star wheel which lifts the hammer, and is only friction-tight, may be forced round with a screwdriver till the hammer is allowed to fall in a resting position.

Replace the Pallets and Adjust to Correct Depth.

Next take the pallets and

their relationary parts and screw back to their original position (see Fig. 3). Before the final tightening of the screws the pallets must be adjusted to right depth; this can only be done by partly winding the going train and moving the pallet-cock up and down till a point is reached where the pendulum can "trip" with perfect freedom. Tighten the screws and the clock is ready for oiling and casing up. Fig. 18 shows how the oiling should be done. The clock should not be swamped with oil, only a little applied to each movable part.

Adjusting the Clock for Even Beat.

When the clock is put on test it must be adjusted to an even beat, and this is done by raising either end of the case until its tick is perfectly regular. Then press the pendulum towards the side of case, which is lifted until the clock will strike an even beat in level position.

Regulation is done by raising or lowering the pendulum bob; raise bob to make clock gain, lower to make clock lose.

Notes on the Escapement.

The escapement is one of the most important parts of a clock and it needs very careful adjustment. As there is necessarily a considerable amount of friction in the movement of the pallets they should be kept highly polished, and if there are any signs of wear such as grooves or ruts they should be smoothed out and the surface re-polished. Although the shape of the pallets fitted to different clocks varies a good deal the action is the same in all clocks.

Smoothing Down a Brass Pallet.

To smooth down a brass pallet use a fine file and follow with an emery stick, which is a specially shaped piece of wood covered with fine emery. Hardened steel pallets cannot be filed, but the surface can be trued up with an emery stick. Take great care to retain the original angle and shape as a very slight alteration of the faces of the pallets in relation to the teeth of the escape wheel may result in the movement being stopped altogether.

A Quick Method of Cleaning a Cheap Clock.

If on examining the bearings of a cheap clock it is seen that there is an excess of dust, a quick method of cleaning it is to immerse the whole movement in a bath of petrol. First take the whole of the works out of the case, then pull off the hands and remove the dial, and place the movement in the petrol. Rock the bath for a few minutes so that the petrol will wash away the dirt.

As the petrol will not only remove the dust but all the oil in the bearings, it will be necessary to oil the clock with clean oil.

HOW TO RE-SILVER A MIRROR

MIRRORS used in the household are apt to become discoloured, marked, or otherwise damaged after a few years of use; in such cases the only satisfactory procedure is that of re-silvering.

The mirror should be removed from its frame and all the old silver on the back removed.

Methods of Removing Old Silver.

This can be done by rubbing with a wetted cloth, or by means of a flat wooden scraper, taking care in the latter case not to scratch the surface of the glass; the mirror should be laid face downwards on several sheets of newspaper placed on a table, for this operation.

A much quicker method of removing the old silver is to place the mirror in a weak solution of nitric acid, made up of 5 to 10 parts of the acid to 95 to 90 parts of water. This solution acts very rapidly.

Next, rinse the mirror in warm distilled water—which can be obtained from any chemist's shop at a few pence per gallon—and clean thoroughly with a cotton-wool swab, using a mixture of powdered whiting and ammonia.

This preliminary cleaning and polishing operation should be carried out very carefully, as it has an important influence upon the final results obtained with the silvering process.

Starting the Re-silvering Operation.

The re-silvering operation can now be proceeded with, and here, whilst there is a choice of several methods, most of these are complicated and beyond the scope of the amateur. There is, however, one method—known as Drayton's—which is not at all difficult, and well within the province of the amateur. The procedure is as follows:—

Place the sheet of glass flat upon a table and then build up a wall of clay or putty around the edges, to form, with the upper surface of the glass, a trough of $\frac{1}{8}$ to $\frac{1}{4}$ inch deep; this trough is for the purpose of holding the silvering solution, the constituents of which are as follows:—

One quarter of an ounce of coarsely pulverised silver nitrate, $\frac{1}{8}$ fluid oz. of spirits of hartshorn (full strength), and $\frac{1}{2}$ fluid oz. of distilled water.

Mix these ingredients well and allow the resulting mixture to stand for at least twenty-four hours, after which it should be filtered in order to save the solid matter.

Next add to this deposit $\frac{3}{4}$ fluid oz. of spirits of wine, 60° under proof; alternatively, the same quantity of oil of naphtha can be employed. Further, add about 6 drops of oil of cassia, and allow the mixture to stand for another six hours before using.

Now pour the silvering solution upon the mirror and drop 9 to 12 drops of a mixture consisting of 1 part of oil of cloves to 3 parts of spirits of wine, in different places on the exposed face of the glass to ensure equal deposit of silver over the surface. Leave for two hours and then pour off.

The mirror should be stood on its edge to dry, and when thoroughly dry it should be lightly painted over the back (or silvered surface) with a mixture of equal parts of melted beeswax and tallow, in order to protect the silver coating. The solution poured off on completion of the silvering process will still contain silver, and it may be used again later.

When estimating the quantity of silver nitrate required to silver any given size of mirror, it is useful to remember that 18 grains of silver nitrate will cover approximately one square foot of glass.

Methods of Gluing Broken China

Undoubtedly the best thing to do when a piece of ordinary china is broken is to throw it away, but the case is different should an article that is treasured be the victim of an accident. Then the wisest course is to set about mending it.

Keep Broken Pieces Clean.

Let us suppose that a china heirloom is knocked over and smashed. The first thing is to collect up the pieces, making absolutely sure that all of them are found, to wrap them in tissue paper and put them safely away until a suitable time arrives for doing the mending. If the pieces are simply put in a drawer with other things, the jagged edges will rub against each other and make a bad fit when they are once more pieced together. Moreover, the fractured edges will pick up dirt and dust, and an edge must be quite clean if it is to stick well.

Choosing a Suitable Adhesive.

There are countless adhesives that may be used for the work—none are perfect and all appear to have at least one drawback. It is thus a question of choosing the adhesive which seems to answer one's personal requirements best. There are three outstanding cements or adhesives which are worth considering.

(*a*) *Liquid glue*, which is obtainable in tubes, has the merit of drying readily. Thus it is possible to assemble an article in a short space of time. In addition, the materials can be kept at hand, ready for any emergency. However, the joints may not withstand washing in hot water, and they will always show very clearly as a dirty line.

(*b*) *Isinglass dissolved in acetic acid* dries fairly rapidly and provides a very strong joint as long as the article is not washed. Its chief merit lies in the fact that the lines of fracture are hardly noticeable when this adhesive is used.

(*c*) *Flake white*, the material sold in tubes for the use of artists, gives a joint that is remarkably strong and one that may be washed; in addition, it is practically invisible. The only drawback is that it dries slowly, taking about a fortnight or more to become hard.

The first and the third are purchased ready for use, but the second must be prepared at home. To make this adhesive shred up a little isinglass and put it in an old cup, pour on a few drops of acetic acid and stir with a thin stick of wood. Aim at dissolving the shreds with the least possible amount of acid. Use as soon as ready and make up only sufficient for immediate needs.

Fig. 1.—A Quick Repair, but not very neat.

Showing a plate mended with liquid glue. It will be noticed that the joins are visible as a dirty line.

Fig. 2.— A Useful Tip.

Adhesive tape, passe-partout binding and similar materials are extremely useful for holding the various pieces together while the cement is drying.

Fig. 3.—How would you deal with a Jug if the Broken Piece has been Lost?

A satisfactory repair can be made with plaster of paris.

Fig. 4.—A New Piece made from Plaster of Paris has been added to this Jug.

The pattern has been matched with water-colours.

Secrets of Success.

Whichever adhesive is selected, the secrets of success lie (*a*) in having the fractured edges clean and, particularly, free from grease; (*b*) in using the minimum amount of adhesive that will do the work; (*c*) in warming the materials if the weather is cold; and (*d*) in giving the pieces the necessary support while the joints are hardening.

A Useful Tip.

In this latter connection it will be found that adhesive tape, passe-partout binding and similar materials are extremely useful for holding the various pieces together while the cement is drying.

How to Make a New Piece from Plaster of Paris.

Occasionally, when the pieces of an article are placed together, it will be found that some part is missing, or it may be that one section has been smashed into such small portions that they cannot be stuck together. The only plan then is to make a new piece to take the place of the lost or smashed area. This is not so impossible as it may appear. First assemble all the other parts and stick them; then, when the article is strong enough to permit of handling, place two or three thicknesses of passe-partout binding under the hole, or, if the damaged article is a jug, cup or vase, place the binding on the inside. If desired, a plaster of plasticine may be used instead of the binding tape. Next make up a little plaster of paris and run it into the hole, smoothing off the outer surface with the aid of a pocket knife.

Now Stick the New Portion in Place.

In a day or two the plaster of paris will be quite hard, when the work may proceed. It may be that the new area holds firmly in its space. If so, it should be left there, but usually the area is loose and can be pushed out of position. When this is the case, the newly-made portion should be stuck in its place, just as all the other pieces were.

Smoothing and Adding Pattern.

Smooth with glass-paper and add any pattern with water colour paints, apply a coat of size and finish with clear varnish.

Cleaning Household Metalwork

Among the various articles of domestic utility and also of household ornamentation, it will usually be found that quite a number of different metals are employed in their construction; among these mention may be made of tinware, aluminium utensils, brass, copper and bronze articles, steel fire-irons, cast-iron ranges, nickel and chromium-plated parts.

Unfortunately, however, with the possible exception of the last named, all of these metals (and alloys) suffer from the drawback of surface corrosion, staining and marking, so that periodically it becomes necessary to clean them. If there happened to be some universal method, or cleanser, available which was suitable for each and every metal object this would render the cleaning of household metals an easy matter. But this is not the case, so that each metal must be dealt with on its own merits, when it comes to the cleaning processes.

Strong Abrasives must not be used for Softer Metals.

It will be obvious that one cannot employ strong abrasives, such as emery papers, which are used for cleaning iron and steel articles, when dealing with the softer metals, *e.g.*, silver and silver-plate; and the alloys used for forks and spoons. Similarly, the methods used for cleaning the softer metals cannot be used effectively upon the harder ones.

Chemical or Corrosive Action.

In some cases, as with brass, silver, copper and aluminium articles, the so-called dirty surface is the result of chemical or corrosive action of the atmosphere or of the contents of the vessels used for cooking purposes. In such cases the methods of cleaning are often, although not invariably, chemical ones.

Another type of surface deposit which the householder is concerned with is that caused by oils, greases and fats, the removal of which calls for no vigorous scrubbing or abrasive action, but merely the use of a suitable solvent or soapy solution.

It is evident, therefore, that no general rules can be laid down for the satisfactory cleaning of such metals as are to be found in the home, but rather that each metal must be dealt with separately. We shall deal with these in alphabetical order, commencing with one of the most widely used domestic metals, viz., aluminium and its alloys—for pure aluminium is seldom used on account of its softness.

ALUMINIUM

Culinary vessels and utensils which have become coated with grease or oil can be cleaned effectively by first rubbing their surfaces with a piece of cloth, or waste, soaked in paraffin. If a small quantity of machine oil is added to the paraffin a much more effective cleanser will result. Next, rub off the adhering paraffin with a piece of clean cloth and then well wash the surfaces with a solution of washing soda and water.

Use Soda Cautiously.

As soda has a chemical action upon aluminium, it should be used cautiously, leaving it on the surfaces for the minimum time necessary to remove traces of the paraffin.

Vessels Discoloured with Vegetable Liquids.

Cooking vessels of aluminium which have become discoloured with vegetable liquids can readily be cleaned with hot soda solution, using a flannel or brush to get rid of hard deposits. Afterwards swill out two or three times with clean water.

Deposits Due to Burnt Fat.

In cases where hard black or brown surface deposits, due to burnt fat, have to be removed, it is generally necessary to employ a scourer consisting of metal shavings, held in a bag, to get rid of this deposit. In many cases, however, an abrasive soap powder such as Vim will remove these marks.

Pumice powder applied with a damp cloth is another effective remover of hard deposits on aluminium cooking vessels.

Do not use emery or glass-paper as this causes unsightly scratches; the fine pumice powder abrasive recommended will not do this.

Polishing Aluminium Articles.

When polishing aluminium articles such as tea-pots, canisters, thermos-flask cases and similar items, the original polished surface must not be destroyed. For this reason only the metal polishes employed for electro-plate and silverware should be used. Particulars of these are given later under the heading of "Silver."

There is one further point to mention before concluding, namely, that in cleaning greasy aluminium vessels which are not discoloured, a hot soapy solution will generally remove all grease without affecting the surface of the aluminium appreciably. The vessels should then be well rinsed in hot water and wiped dry.

BRASS

This is not a difficult metal to clean, for there are several excellent cleaning pastes and solutions on the market which will remove discolorations and polish the surface. One of the most effective of these is the liquid cleaner and polish known as "Bluebell."

Vinegar and Common Salt.

Brass and copper kettles, stewing pans, fenders, candlesticks and trays can very effectively be cleaned with a mixture of vinegar and common table salt, or alternatively, with oxalic acid solution. As soon as the articles are clean, wash well with clean water and polish with tripoli powder and sweet oil.

Corroded Brass Articles.

Badly discoloured, or corroded brass articles can readily be cleaned and at the same time restored to their original lustre by immersing them in a weak solution consisting of about 1 part of strong nitric acid to 10 parts of water. As soon as the surfaces are clean, remove the articles from the solution and rinse thoroughly in cold water, afterwards drying with a cloth.

COPPER

Use the same methods as for brass.

ELECTRO-PLATE

It is generally found that the discolorations on electro-plate are due to atmospheric action. More particularly is this the case when gas stoves or gas burners are used in the rooms in which the plate is stored.

The use of abrasives, such as metal polishing pastes and solutions is not recommended, on account of the relative thinness of the plating.

If the deposits are not very bad ones, they can often be removed with hot soapy water, using a thick piece of flannel, or a felt pad, and rubbing vigorously.

Paraffin and Powdered Whiting.

Usually, however, it will be found necessary to rub, lightly, with a piece of soft cloth which has been damped with paraffin and then dipped into powdered whiting. In this case there is very little risk of the plating being abraded, but in the cleaning process a fine polish is obtained.

Removing Tarnish.

The tarnish on electro-plate can also readily be removed by immersing the article in a solution consisting of 1 gallon of rainwater and 4 ozs. of potassium cyanide. This solution—which is poisonous—should be kept in a jar provided with a cork. After immersion, rinse with warm water and dry with fine sawdust.

Another method is to rub the discoloured areas with a piece of chamois leather dipped into some jeweller's polishing rouge. This extremely fine polishing powder will only remove the minimum amount of the plating.

LACQUERED WARE

Lacquered brass, bronze and similar parts frequently become dirty owing partly to a gradual intensifying of colour on the part of the lacquer used, and partly to deposits of dust.

In such cases an appreciable improvement in the appearance can be obtained by washing the articles in hot soapy water, afterwards washing off in clean hot water. Discoloured lacquer cannot readily be restored by the amateur; in most cases relacquering is the only effective remedy.

NICKEL

Dull nickel-plate can be restored to its original lustre by polishing with a liquid metal polish, using a soft cloth to finish off with. The use of abrasives is not, however, recommended as their frequent use will cause wear right through the plating.

Rust or Corrosive Spots.

Rust, or corrosive spots on nickel can be removed by smearing them with animal fat (lard or tallow) and then allowing the article to stand for several days. Afterwards rub the spots with a piece of cloth soaked in ammonia. If the rust is deep use a diluted solution of hydrochloric acid, taking care not to touch the unaffected nickel; afterwards rinse well in running water.

Nickel-plated articles that have become corroded, or discoloured, may be cleaned very readily by placing them in a solution of alcohol containing about 1 part in 50 of sulphuric acid. After a few seconds have elapsed remove and wash in running water. Finally, rinse in alcohol and rub dry with a linen cloth.

The articles will then be found to have a brilliant polish free from any stain or surface marks.

PEWTER

The usual method of cleaning and polishing pewterware is first to remove any grease and fingermarks with petrol, benzene, or Thawpit and then apply ordinary knife polish with a thick felt pad. Afterwards finish off by polishing with powdered whiting or one of the proprietory makes of plate powder. A piece of Selvyt or soft cloth should be used for the final polishing operation. It is not advisable to use a liquid metal polish on pewter as the black deposit usually finds its way into the creases, corners and surface indentations.

SILVER

Silver and silver-plated articles that have been tarnished by exposure to the atmosphere of rooms having coal or gas fires can be cleaned effectively by using a solution made by mixing powdered whiting with liquid ammonia.

Removing Bad Tarnish Stains.

If the tarnish stains are bad ones they can generally be removed by rubbing with a preparation made up as follows:—

Beechwood ashes . 12 parts.
Venetian soap . . ¼ ,,
Cooking salt . . 12 ,,
Rain, or distilled water . . 48 ,,

Cleaning and Polishing.

A particularly good method of cleaning silverware and at the same time polishing it to a high degree is as follows: Pour boiling water into an enamelled basin in which the silver articles to be cleaned are placed. Then throw in a handful of common washing soda for every pint of water in the basin. Allow the soda to dissolve and then throw in some aluminium scrap such as pieces of aluminium sheet cut off with the shears, filings or turnings. Within a few seconds the blackest of silver articles are converted into white polished ones of new appearance. The articles should then be taken out of the solution and, after rinsing in hot water, wiped dry with a clean cloth.

The method used is an electrochemical one, depending upon the silver and aluminium making contact in the soda solution electrolyte. The result is to remove the silver sulphide causing the tarnish.

For light tarnish stains on silver use whiting or rouge, applying this by means of a soft piece of cloth. Powdered chalk and white soap made into a paste, if rubbed on with a dry brush, will also remove light tarnish from silver.

STEEL AND IRON

There are two kinds of surface deposit, or dirt, to deal with when considering these metals, namely (1) greasy deposits containing dirt—as in the case of machine parts, and (2) rust effects.

Greasy Deposits.

Dirty machine parts, tools and similar items that have been used with lubrication can most effectively be cleaned by placing them in a bath of hot soda water. In most cases ordinary washing soda is good enough, but in stubborn cases, caustic soda should be used. In this connection, bicycle, mangle, sewing machine and similar parts can readily be deprived of all grease and dirt. Ordinary paraffin oil is another good medium for cleaning greasy iron and steel parts.

Rust.

Rusty parts if not too badly affected can be cleaned with emery cloth, a little patience being necessary in the application of the latter.

A quicker method is to use a chemical solution for getting rid of the rust. One way is to dip the rusty articles into a saturated solution of stannic (or tin) chloride. The parts should be left in this solution for twelve to twenty-four hours. After removing the parts from the solution they should be well rinsed with water and then with a solution of ammonia.

Another method of removing rust is to immerse the articles in turpentine or paraffin oil, for about twelve hours, and then rub with smooth emery cloth.

One further method that gives good results is to dip the parts in a solution consisting of 2 parts of muriatic acid to 3 parts of water. The length of the process depends upon the amount of rust to be removed, but it can be checked by examining the articles from time to time. After all traces of rust have disappeared remove from the solution and wash in hot soda water.

Cleaning Iron Articles which are not too badly Rusted.

Iron articles, which are not rusted very seriously, may be cleaned by first washing with soapy water, to which ammonia has been added, and, after drying, coated with sweet oil and powdered quicklime. Allow to stand for a day or two and then brush off, when a bright surface will be obtained.

TINWARE

Ordinary domestic tinware consists of iron or steel sheet coated with tin or a tin-alloy. The tin itself does not corrode, or oxidise, very readily, so that any surface discolorations found in practice are generally caused by deposits of burnt fats, dried vegetable matter, grease, etc. In the usual way a liberal washing with hot soda water will remove all of the grease, whilst a scouring with an abrasive powder such as pumice will get rid of any of the harder deposits. This powder should not be applied "wet," but on a slightly damp or wrung-out cloth. In some cases where an excessive deposit of dark matter is present it may be necessary to scrape this off with the back of a knife before using the abrasive powder; afterwards hot soda water should be used to get rid of any other traces of dirt.

Another Method.

Another excellent method of cleaning tinware is to powder some common washing soda and rub this on to the surface with a moistened piece of newspaper screwed up into a ball. Afterwards polish with another dry piece of newspaper and the tinware will have a new appearance.

ZINC

To clean articles of zinc, stir rye bran into a paste with boiling water and add a small quantity of silver sand and a little vitriol. Rub the article with this paste, rinse well with water and then polish with a cloth. Liquid metal polishes should not be used for cleaning zinc as they leave a black deposit.

CHROMIUM-PLATING

Contrary to the general belief, chromium-plated parts require periodical cleaning, for whilst immune from the usual corrosive effects, they experience surface deposits of dirt, grease, fingermarks, water stains, etc.

A certain amount of care is necessary when cleaning chromium-plate, for if an abrasive polishing paste, powder or liquid is used, the relatively thin coating may, in time, wear through to the base metal.

As there are no actual corrosive effects to reckon with and the surface is fairly hard, it can readily be cleaned with a damp cloth upon which a little yellow soap has been rubbed. Stains due to liquids can be removed with whiting and paraffin, whilst grease-stains are readily disposed of by rubbing with a piece of cloth damped with petrol or paraffin.

Protection against Surface Stains.

Chromium- and nickel-plate, it should be remembered, can *be protected against surface stains* by first applying a little polishing wax over the surface, using a soft cloth and then rubbing with another piece of cloth; this leaves a practically invisible surface coating which acts as a protection to the metal.

WALLPAPERS FOR PERIOD FURNITURE

For rooms with furniture of definite style, wallpaper may be desired which will represent the type known to have been in use during the period to which the furniture belongs. In the Victoria and Albert Museum there are examples of wallpapers from the sixteenth century onward, so that doubt need not exist regarding the characteristic features which wallpapers display during the varied phases of their development. Practically every type of importance is produced to-day either in hand- or machine-printed papers.

Jacobean and other Period Needlework Designs.

There are wallpaper designs based on "Jacobean" needlework which closely follow the original hangings which are still in existence and which can hardly be improved on for present usage; others represent the needlework and printed linens of the Queen Anne period, and are still amongst the most desirable wallpapers for bedrooms, sitting-rooms, breakfast-rooms, in fact, every room of homely and useful character. Probably there is no furniture more popular to-day than that based on Jacobean and Queen Anne pieces, which to some extent accounts for the numerous wallpapers which owe inspiration to the same period of artistic activity.

Papers for Chippendale Furniture.

When Chippendale and others of the same period were producing their mahogany furniture, important rooms were hung with damask and Genoese velvet or flock papers which closely imitated them. Similar papers are obtainable to-day, but the somewhat heavy colourings of the period are not so favoured as are the lighter and brighter colourings of the middle and later years of the eighteenth century when furniture by Sheraton and Hepplewhite became the vogue. In bedrooms of the same periods were chintz hangings with designs of flowers and ribbands naturalistically rendered. Such designs in wallpapers are well suited for rooms in which an old-world atmosphere is desired.

Oak, Walnut and Mahogany.

Oak furniture is historically associated with crewel work hangings, wool tapestry and leather-covered chairs. Walnut furniture with embroidered and printed linen also velvet. Mahogany with silk damask and brocade.

Each of these types has its characteristic emotional appeal. A sense of completeness is achieved when in a room the furniture and decoration both exhibit a similar standard of craftsmanship and artistic merit as well as contributing to the scheme, colour, texture and other qualities equally desirable and obviously appropriate.

FITTING A COILED DOOR SPRING

One of the simplest ways of making a door or gate self-closing is to fit a coil door spring. The ordinary type shown in Fig. 1 measures from 9 to 12 inches in length and is suitable for the normal small door or gate. The new "upright adjustable coil spring" (shown in Fig. 2) has a pleasant mild action and is very durable, and is suitable for most of the usual domestic doors and garden gates.

When fitting them the secrets of successful working are first to so place the spring that the coil tightens up when the door is opened. Secondly, the initial tension must be adjusted so that the door closes properly after it has only been partly opened.

It should be appreciated that the more the door is opened the greater is the pressure of the spring, hence it pushes the door more violently than it does when only partly opened.

One end of the spring is fixed permanently to a triangular plate, the other end is free to turn in the fixing plate and is prevented from turning by putting a stud or steel pin into holes drilled through the spring end-piece and the plate.

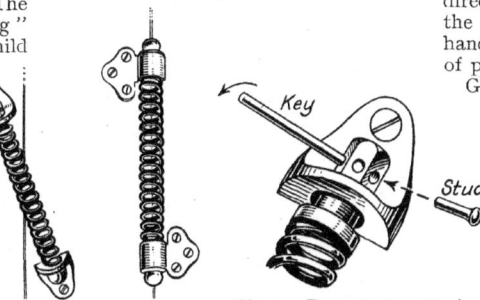

Fig. 1.—Adjustable Coil Spring. Fig. 2.—New Type Upright Spring. Fig. 3.—Details of the Adjusting Stud. The spring is turned with the key and secured by the stud.

To fit one of these springs, put it inside a door that opens inwards and outside a door that opens outwards. Set the spring slantwise across the door and frame, tap the prong on the fixing plate into the wood and fasten it with a screw to the bottom, then screw the adjuster plate to the top. Insert the key into a hole in the spring end and turn it as far as possible in a direction that winds up or tightens the spring. Hold the key with one hand and insert the stud with a pair of pliers held in the other hand.

Gently release the key and the spring will turn backwards until further movement is stopped by the stud. It is best to use pliers when putting in the stud as, should the spring be prematurely released, it will fly back and may damage the fingers. Adjustment can be made at any time by turning the key as in Fig. 3, and inserting the stud in a different hole in the spring end.

The upright pattern is fixed in the same way, but the end-plates are fixed on opposite sides of the spring which should be vertical.

Stencilling for Various Purposes

STENCILLING is a method whereby a design may be duplicated with ease and rapidity; thus it offers an unlimited array of possibilities for those who wish to repeat a piece of ornamentation a considerable number of times.

The Process Briefly Described.

In a few words, the process consists in obtaining a plate having the design cut out of it. The plate is then placed on the material to be ornamented; colour is brushed over the plate, and only where there are areas cut away can the colour reach the material. In this way, the material receives one impression of the design. By lifting the plate and arranging it elsewhere, the design may be repeated. And this process can be continued until the material has received as many impressions as are required to complete the work. No artistic skill is needed, once a suitable plate has been obtained, and it would not be impossible for thirty or forty impressions to be taken in an hour from a plate. Thus, the saving in time is, alone, a feature which makes stencilling a decorative process of enormous value.

The Uses of Stencilling.

There is no end to the uses to which stencilling may be put. For making such things as Christmas cards, book plates and other designs on paper, it offers an excellent method of executing a number of similar copies in the shortest space of time. For articles such as blotting cases and reading cases for magazines, it is extremely useful, because one small piece of design may be repeated perhaps a dozen times to make a large, elaborate design. The process can be resorted to for embellishing articles in whitewood, glass, china, leather, etc.

Fig. 1.—A Typical Stencil Design.
Note that it is not possible to give the swan a white edge.

For Interior Walls and Furniture.

In addition, it is a form of decoration which has several valuable uses where interior walls and furniture are concerned. Suppose that the walls of a room are panelled and that they have been given a coat of paint or distemper. By the judicious use of a stencil, it is possible to make the panels far more attractive than if they were left plain. Or, take the case of a suite of furniture that has been

Fig. 2.—A Stencil Brush.

painted. It is quite conceivable that the addition of a small stencilled design, applied to each of the pieces, would impart to them a touch of character that was not possessed by the plain pieces.

Making a Stencil Plate.

Stencil plates can be purchased for a few pence each in a wide range of designs. Nevertheless, it is certain that anyone who attempts the work will not be long in desiring to make designs which bear his or her personal stamp. Thus, it is useful to know how a plate may be made.

The Material to Use.

The first thing is to decide on the material to be used. Specially prepared paper, known as oil-royal, may be obtained from dealers of artists' materials. It cuts easily and withstands much rough usage; but any good grade of drawing or writing paper will serve. If only required for a few impressions, such paper demands no further treatment; but should it be needed for repeated use, it is advisable to cover it, both back and front, with a coat of shellac varnish. This should be done after the design has been cut out and not before.

The Pattern.

The next consideration is the pattern. Seeing that a stencil design is formed by the parts that are cut away, it will be appreciated that unless special precautions are taken, when creating the design, there is a possibility that whole areas may drop out. This will happen if an "island" of paper is required to be left in the plate, with a cut-out portion totally surrounding it. The remedy lies in leaving three or four narrow bridges of paper, called ties, to join the "island" to the remainder of the plate.

Cutting Out the Design.

When the design has been created, the next step is to cut it out. To do this, place the paper on some hard substance—there is nothing better than a sheet of glass—and do the cutting with the blade of a knife. There are special cutters, but they are in no way better than a pocket-knife which is repeatedly sharpened.

With the paper arranged flat on the glass, place the tip of the knife where you intend to begin the cutting, and put the index finger of the left hand in front of the blade, with the thumb behind it. As the knife proceeds along the line, the finger and thumb

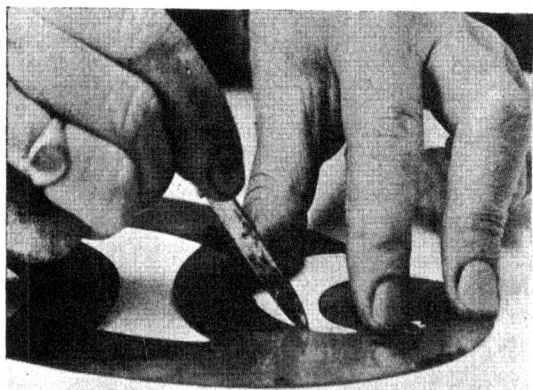

Fig. 3.—A Sharp Pocket-knife can be used to Cut out the Design.
The paper should be placed on a hard substance, such as a sheet of glass. Note how the finger and thumb precede and follow the knife.

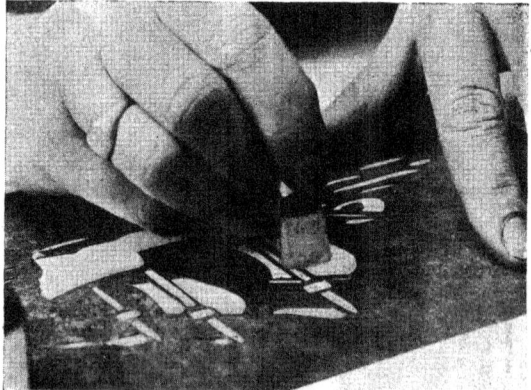

Fig. 4.—The First Stage in Applying the Colour.
The stencil should be fixed to the material with drawing pins, adhesive strips or other means. Note that the brush must be held vertically when applying colour.

are drawn along to preserve these positions. Their special work is to keep the paper flat and to prevent the knife from lifting it up into creases. Where straight lines occur, it will naturally help if a ruler is used as a guide and, in the case of curves, one of the celluloid shapes used by architects, which consists of curved outlines, will be equally handy.

Special Notes on Corners and Angles.

It is in cutting corners and angles that most skill is required. If cut too far, a streak of colour may be revealed in the finished picture and, if not cut far enough, the unwanted parts will not come away from the rest of the plate as they should. Clearly, the correct thing is to cut just enough, but not too much. The ideal is to manage so that all the unwanted parts of the plate drop out of position, of their own accord, when the plate is lifted off the glass.

Using a Stencil Plate.

Whenever possible, place the article to be stencilled on a flat, horizontal surface, such as a table. Arrange the plate in position, and it will be as well to fix it by some means or other so that it cannot move while the paint is being applied. Drawing pins, adhesive strips and rubber bands have their uses in this matter. Then, with a stencil brush, apply the paint evenly with the flat head of the brush. The bristles of the brush must come down on the plate with a vertical action, because if they are drawn horizontally along the plate some of the paint will be forced under and cause smudges.

Although most stencil designs are carried out in monochrome, it will be recognised that it is quite easy to use two or more colours if required. When this is desired, all that is needed is to reserve definite areas of the plate for the colours decided on and to apply all the colours before lifting the plate.

As soon as an impression has been made the plate must be wiped both back and front, and it is always advisable to use a different brush for each colour.

Fig. 5.—BEFORE LIFTING THE STENCIL AWAY FROM THE MATERIAL IT IS ALWAYS ADVISABLE TO RAISE ONE CORNER TO SEE HOW THE WORK HAS BEEN DONE.

The Colours.

For stencilling on paper, cardboard or similar substances, ordinary water colours, but preferably those sold in tubes, serve quite well. They should be mixed with some such medium as Florentine. Poster and show card colours are, also, suitable. The paint must be used in a fairly stiff condition.

For working on wood, oil-painted walls, glass, fabrics, leather, etc., oil colours are needed. A little of the colour is squeezed out of a tube and worked up to a creamy consistency with some medium, or a good varnish may be used if a few drops of turpentine are added.

Other Considerations.

Here, the bare outline of the process has been described, but it will be readily appreciated that stencilling permits of many attractive variations. For instance, an admirable design could be produced, in full colour, by cutting three or four stencils so conceived that each dealt with only a portion of the complete design. By using all the plates, one after the other, on the same piece of material, it would be possible to obtain a very beautiful effect, caused by the overlapping and graduating of the colours.

Another departure from the usual practice of stencilling is to cut out a shape of paper, to apply it to the material which is to receive the design, and to brush the colour around it. This gives an effect which is the reverse of the usual. The shape is plain, while the surrounding background is coloured.

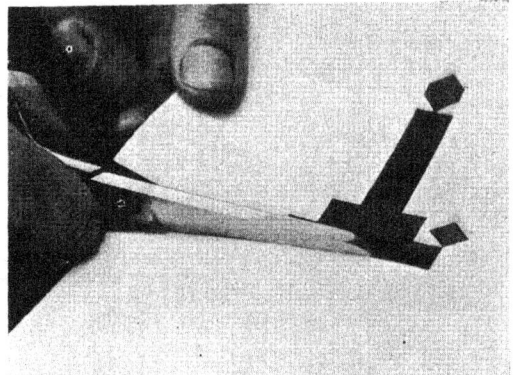

Fig. 6.—CUTTING OUT A SHAPE FOR USE AS A TEMPLATE.

RUST PREVENTERS

IRON and steel articles which are liable to rust should be protected with a coating of a suitable substance. Bright metal parts that have to be stored for long periods can be liberally coated with ordinary lanoline.

Another useful protecting mixture is made from equal parts of ordinary white wax dissolved in benzine. If this solution is applied to the warmed surface it will leave an almost invisible coating of wax on the surface.

Ordinary motor car lubricating grease, or Stauffer cup grease is also quite satisfactory for protecting bright metal parts, such as fire-irons, fenders, stoves and skates, which are to be stored.

For the outdoor protection of iron and steel there is probably nothing to equal the bituminous base paints now on the market, such as Bitumastic and Bowranite paints; these are obtainable in a range of different colours. The paints are of a "thin" constitution and therefore are economical in their use; a small quantity will cover a relatively large area.

How to Make Rust-preventing Paints.

Rust-preventing paints can be made up by the handyman; the following are some good recipes for these:—

(1) Tar oil . . . . . 1 part.
    Hydrocarbon lubricating oil . . . . 1 ,,

Any good mineral lubricating oil can be used for this purpose, the best results being obtained from the steam and petrol engine lubricating oils.

(2) Asphaltum . . . $1\frac{1}{2}$ lbs.
    Shellac . . . 4 ozs.
    Turpentine . . . 4 pints.

(3) Boiled coal-tar . . 1 gallon.
    Naphtha . . . $\frac{1}{4}$ pint.
    Boiled linseed oil . $\frac{1}{4}$,,

The coal-tar should be boiled until the watery vapour and naphtha are expelled.

Varnishing Interior Woodwork

Every householder is more or less interested in beautifying or keeping his interior woodwork in good condition. He may wish to stain and varnish the surrounds of a room, or probably he fills in his spare time making useful articles from varying classes of wood such as birch, beech, plywood, etc., but nearly in all cases a bright finish is required.

Three Classes of Varnish.

Three classes of varnish may and can be used: (*a*) oil, (*b*) spirit, (*c*) brush varnish or brush polish. Each has its own particular use, and the groundwork must be specially treated to suit the particular varnish. Each job must be carefully planned and the correct materials and methods employed.

For instance, one would not apply spirit varnish to doors which had been oak-grained and expect first-class results. Various grades of oil varnish are sold, taking from eight to twelve hours or longer to dry, such as fine oak, hard-drying inside oak, hard-drying inside copal, pale elastic inside oak, flatting, etc., with prices ranging from 8s. to 20s. per gallon. Spirit varnishes are quick drying, taking from one to six hours to dry, hence they have little or no elasticity when compared with the oil variety; the range or classes are of a limited nature, viz., brown hard varnish, naphtha varnish, white hard varnish, which in turn may be graded according to price. Brush varnish or brush polish is a mixture of spirit varnish and French polish in varying proportions, which can be mixed by the householder.

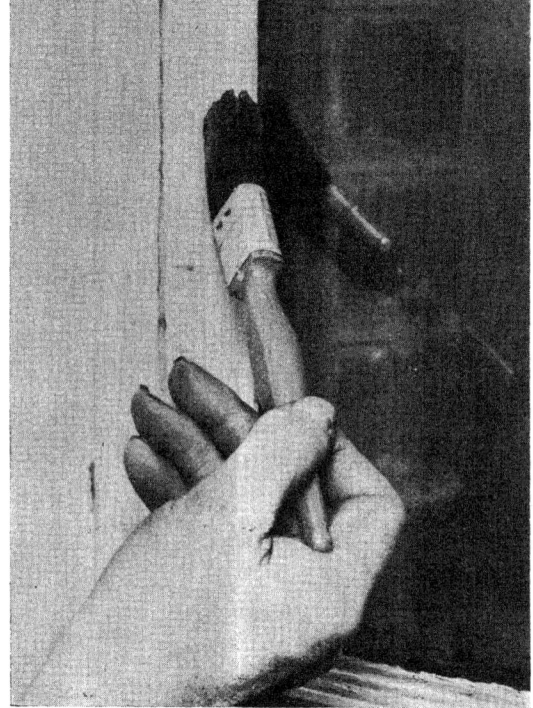

Fig. 1.—The Correct Method of holding the Brush when Varnishing Window Sashes.

Preparing a Room for Re-varnishing.

Having outlined the materials in general use, we will assume that a room has been chosen for re-varnishing. The doors, window frames, picture rails, wainscots, etc., are to be dealt with. First, well wash the work with a warm soda water solution as to remove all dirt and grease, sponge with plenty of cold water until all soda has been removed, then allow to dry; look over all woodwork and remove any tacks or nails which may be present; fill holes with putty or white lead coloured, if possible, to match the paint or stain.

Examine the panels and beadings of doors. If they have shrunk showing a white streak, do your best to cover these streaks, matching as near as possible the existing colour; finally, do your best to rectify any blemishes that may appear. Failing the means of putting right any faults, either proceed to varnish or to re-stain or re-paint to desired colour all woodwork to be treated, after which varnish.

The Varnish.

Obtain from the local stores 1 pint of a good make of oil varnish of the hard-drying type for interior work, also two flat varnish brushes, sizes 1 inch and 1½ inches, and pour out the varnish into a wide-top tin.

First the Window Frame.

Start your work by first coating the window sashes and frames. Use the 1-inch brush, and begin to varnish carefully the woodwork around the glass giving a fairly free coat, taking care to clean off all varnish from the glass before proceeding. Now coat the stiles of the sash, first along the top, then the bottom, finally the two sides; continue the operation until all sashes and frames have been treated, and leave window sashes open a little at top and bottom to allow of ventilation.

Next the Picture Rail and Doors.

Next, follow by coating picture rail, then doors. When varnishing doors start by first applying the varnish to the top panels, if any, working down the door until all panels have been

Fig. 2.—How to use the Scraper when stripping French Polished or Varnished Surface with a Solvent.
Showing the old material being lifted off after treatment.

Fig. 3.—Showing the Method by which Brush Polish is applied.
The brush polish is a mixture of spirit varnish and French polish in varying proportions.

covered, follow by coating centre stiles, finally finishing by doing the top and bottom stiles and then the sides.

Finally the Wainscot.

Complete the room by varnishing the wainscot. At least twenty-four hours or longer should elapse before using the room.

Pour any varnish that may be over back into the pint tin, and well cork for future use; the brushes are best kept in condition by suspending them in a glass jar filled with linseed oil. Bore a hole through the handles and insert a piece of wire, which should be long enough to rest on the top of the jar.

All varnishing should be performed in daylight and as early as possible during the day; never apply varnish if it is raining or the atmosphere is of a heavy nature; dampness will cause a varnish to bloom and prevent hard drying, thereby giving disappointments. Even draughts should be avoided, so do all varnish work when weather conditions permit.

Varnishing the Surrounds of a Room.

The surrounds of a room can be varnished either by using an oil or a spirit varnish each having its advantages and disadvantages. The floor boards should be clean and smooth, otherwise labour and material are wasted; smooth by using grade No. 1 glasspaper. If the colour required be oak, dark oak, or walnut, purchase some Vandyke crystals; or if mahogany—mahogany crystals; make up a stain solution as follows (1 lb. to 1 gall. water), prepare by dissolving the crystals in about half the quantity of water (boiling the mixture will help considerably). Water is now added until desired shade or colour is obtained; it is best to test the colour on a piece of spare like wood before applying to job.

Apply the stain with a piece of coarse rag, well rubbing across the grain, then allow to dry, then apply a solution of XD. or glue size with a flat varnish brush; this coating acts as a grain filling. Allow to dry, lightly paper with grade No. 0 glasspaper, wipe over with a clean piece of rag to remove all dust, and then proceed to varnish.

If an oil variety is to be used, purchase some hard-drying floor varnish and apply with 1½-inch flat varnish brush; twenty-four hours or longer should be allowed before the room is used.

If a spirit varnish is decided upon owing to its quick-drying nature, purchase a quantity of naphtha varnish and garnet polish, make a mixture of half and half and apply with 1½-inch flat varnish brush. Compared with oil varnish, spirit varnish will be found to be easily scratched and marked

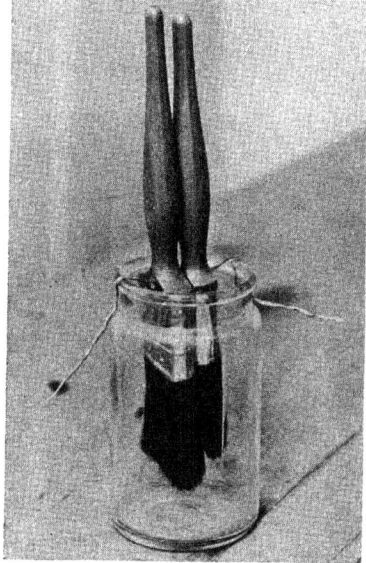

Fig. 4.—When Brushes are not in use they should be thoroughly cleaned and then suspended in a jar as shown.

showing white streaks owing to its hardness and brittleness, lacking the elasticity of oil varnishes.

To sum up, the quicker the varnish dries the less elasticity is to be expected, which means quicker deterioration of the finish. It is advisable to allow ample time and use a first-class oil floor varnish.

Spirit Varnish Stains.

There are on the market materials known as spirit varnish stains, which as the name implies are a mixture of spirit varnish coloured with an aniline dye. These mixtures, when applied, stain and dry with a gloss, but being of a spirit varnish composition are only recommended for use on articles which are not intended for hard use or wear. If such a mixture is used on floors first apply a coat of XD. or glue size; when dry follow with a coat of varnish stain, and, if necessary, lightly paper with grade No. 0 glasspaper and apply a further coat or until desired finish is obtained.

Cleaning Brushes after using Spirit Varnish.

To clean brushes after using spirit varnish well wash them in methylated spirit and allow to dry.

Fig. 5.—Showing the Effect of Dampness when applying Spirit Varnish, giving a White or Gloomy Surface.

Hardwoods.

Where hardwoods, such as birch or beech, are used, good results may be obtained, for these woods may be stained and varnished or polished (refer to article on French Polishing and follow method as outlined for oak), giving little or no trouble. Prepare work by first papering job with grade No. 1 glasspaper, then stain either with Vandyke crystals for water as previously described, or naphtha, which may be obtained at any polish or varnish manufacturer's, the shades ranging from a light golden colour to a dark fume. A range of shades can be obtained varying from a light brown to a black brown by purchasing 1 pint of Brunswick black and 1 pint of turpentine or turpentine substitute, mixing the two together in varying proportions to produce the desired shade of colour. This class of mixture is known as oil or turps stain; it has the advantage of being permanent, and like the naphtha variety will not raise the grain. To stain with either naphtha or oil apply by rubbing across the grain with a piece of coarse rag; wipe off superfluous stain and set aside for twenty-four hours to dry, then paper with grade No. 0 glasspaper, first taking off cutting edge by rubbing two faces together, and well wipe with a clean dry duster.

Finishing.

The job is now ready for finishing, which may be done by using (*a*) oil varnish, (*b*) brush polish, (*c*) wax.

For oil varnishing use the hard-drying interior variety as previously mentioned. Apply a thin even coating and set aside for forty-eight hours or until hard; if a further coating is required lightly paper with grade No. 0 glasspaper without cutting edge, well dust and apply a second light coat; continue until desired result has been obtained.

Brush polish is a spirit varnish mixture and the householder would be well advised to make or mix his own, as only a skilled worker can apply a spirit varnish to give a smooth even finish, due to the quick-setting nature of the varnish. The mixture for dark-coloured groundwork should be naphtha varnish and garnet polish; for light-coloured groundwork white hard varnish and button polish or white polish. Purchase a quantity of varnish and polish; proceed to make a mixture of half and half and apply by using a 1½-inch flat varnish brush to a spare piece of wood.

Should a dragging or sticky feel be noticeable add a little more polish to the mixture or until the brush works freely, apply a coating and set aside for twenty-four hours, paper lightly with grade No. 0 glass-paper, clean with a piece of rag and apply a further coat. Continue until finish of a desired nature is obtained.

For waxed finishes apply a brush coat of brush polish, allow twenty-four hours to dry, then apply a thin film of a hard grade of wax polish.

When using spirit varnish and French polish always work in a warm dry atmosphere, for should dampness or low temperature be worked in, these materials being made with methylated spirit quickly chill, producing over your finished surface a whitish gloomy appearance which is difficult to remove, and in most cases rotting the shellac which is present in the materials, thereby necessitating the stripping of the job.

Plywood.

Plywood, which is used so extensively by the amateur, gives more trouble to obtain a first-class finish than any other class of wood, for invariably several grades are used in the building of a job; then if staining is done of a lightish colour, no uniformity can be obtained. Never apply water stains; they should be used only for interior parts, for once having raised the grain of this class of wood hours of labour may be wasted with poor results when finished. When staining plywood use oil or turps stain as previously mentioned; little or no raising of the grain results and a darkish colour can be made and should be used. After staining, paper lightly with grade No. 0 glasspaper and proceed to varnish with either oil or brush polish as already described. Naturally, each job must have careful thought and attention, for what will suit one class of work will not suit another; experience of handling will come with practice, so if the work is disappointing never lose heart, begin

Fig. 6.—Different Effect of using Water or Naphtha Stains.

On the left-hand side can be seen the raised grain when water stains are applied to birch plywood; on the right it will be seen that the grain is little or not affected by using naphtha or oil stains.

again, strip the job and profit by your experience.

Stripping.

It may be helpful if we outline the methods of stripping work which has

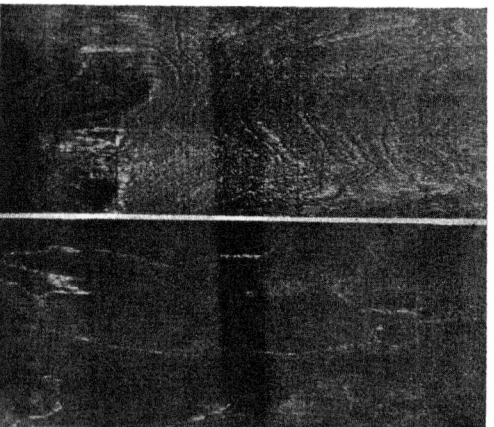

Fig. 7.—This Photograph shows the Necessity of Staining Plywood to a Dark Colour, obviating the Difficulty of having to Colour to Uniformity

been oil varnished or French polished; there are two outstanding methods which are employed, first, the use of common soda and, secondly, a liquid solvent.

Make a hot-water solution with soda, about 2 lb. to the gallon, and apply freely over the work, allow to stand for about fifteen minutes and apply a further coating; then with a flat scraper well scrape the job taking care not to scratch the work, repeat the operation until all varnish or polish has been removed, then well wash with plenty of cold water, wipe dry and paper with grade No. 1 glasspaper. The work is now ready for the preparation for the desired finish.

Liquid solvent can be purchased from any good-class oil and colourman in tin containers, varying from ½ pint to 1 gallon. Apply to the work with an old brush giving a free coat, allow to stand for a few minutes and scrape with a flat scraper, repeat until the wood surface is clean, well wash the work with methylated spirit and allow to dry, paper with grade No. 1 glasspaper and proceed to obtain the necessary finish.

Why Methylated Spirit is used for Washing the Work.

The reason for using methylated spirit to wash the work after the use of solvent is to neutralise any chemical material which may be left upon the surface of the wood.

The Two Methods Compared.

Comparing the two methods we would advise in all cases to use solvent, as this mixture will not harm the wood, especially oak; actually it tends to bleach, whereas the soda solution darkens the wood. Nearly all solvents are inflammable and should never be used near a naked flame.

By carefully choosing the most suitable class of varnish from the instructions given in this article it is possible to make a thoroughly satisfactory job of any varnish work that the householder may care to tackle.

REPAIRING A BROKEN DECK CHAIR

THERE is one weak feature about most deck chairs of the folding type, namely, the notches which are cut in the inclined members to take the adjustable struts for altering the position of the seat. The effect of these notches is greatly to reduce the strength of the members in question, with the result that cases frequently occur of fracture through the notched portions, as shown at AB in the accompanying sketch.

In such cases a neat and strong repair can readily be effected in the

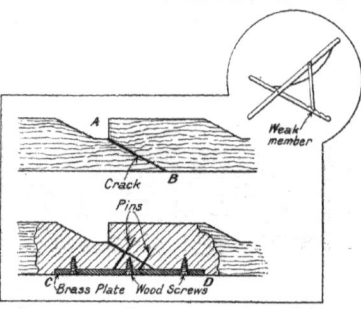

Details for Repair of a Deck Chair.

following manner. First glue the fractured surfaces of the two broken parts of AB with a strong waterproof glue such as Croid, or the cellulose base glues, e.g., Durofix. Pin the joint in two places, in order to hold it in position whilst the glue is setting.

Next cut a recess CD on the lower side of the member and let in a brass plate of about $\tfrac{1}{16}$ to $\tfrac{3}{32}$ inch thickness. Screw this plate to the wood with three wood screws of $1 \times \tfrac{3}{16}$ inch size and a very strong repair will be obtained.

TIME, LABOUR AND MONEY SAVING IDEAS

TEMPORARY REPAIR TO BURST WATER PIPE.

Lead composition and iron water pipes which burst as a result of frost action can be repaired temporarily in the following manner.

If the burst is only a small one in a lead pipe, the water should be turned off at the main and the pipe emptied by the simple process of turning on the taps in the scullery and bathroom. If there is a hot-water boiler in the house its fire should be drawn. Having wiped the surface of the pipe around the burst dry, cover the pipe with plastic wood all around the section containing the burst. Allow this to dry partially,

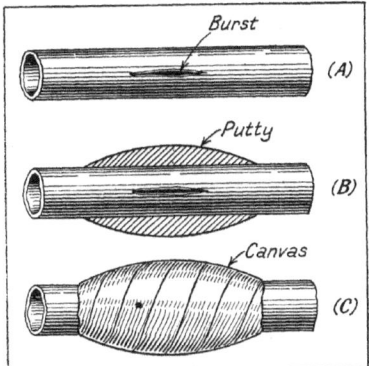

and then bind the section tightly with two layers of electrician's insulating tape. This will effect a good repair, which will last for a long time in the case of small cracks.

For larger cracks a liberal application of soft putty should be made around the crack, and this should be bound fairly tightly with a long strip of canvas or calico wound spirally, as shown. Finally, the canvas or calico binding should be strengthened by two or three layers of insulating tape, or, alternatively, with a cord binding arranged on the same principle as the binding on a cricket bat handle.

WALNUT STAIN FOR CABINETS.

Wireless and gramophone cabinets can be given an excellent walnut finish by staining with a solution made up as follows :—

Dissolve 3 oz. each of potassium permanganate and sulphate of magnesia in 1 quart of hot water. Apply the solution with a brush, repeating the operation until the desired depth of stain has been attained. The result obtained is of a permanent nature.

After rubbing down any raised grain with pumice stone the surface may be polished in the ordinary manner.

MATERIAL FOR MOULDINGS.

In cases where it is desired to build up mouldings on picture frames for small ornaments, artificial flowers and similar parts, a good cheap material can be obtained by mixing ordinary bread with glue or gelatine to which a little glycerine has been added. Ordinary gum, to which a little alum water has been added, can be used equally well. This product sets into a hard, tough substance.

CLEANING PAINT BRUSHES.

Although turpentine is usually employed for cleaning paint brushes, it is apt to prove expensive, unless it can be used again as a paint thinner ; this applies only to its use in paints of similar colour to that on the brush.

Ordinary paraffin, which is very much cheaper, will do equally well. Wash the brushes with paraffin and, after rinsing them in petrol, shake them out thoroughly. They may be dried afterwards by rubbing with a piece of clean rag.

If the brushes are to be used within a few days of cleaning them, they should be hung in a vessel of paraffin or turpentine with the bristles submerged.

If, however, the brushes are to be put away for some time, they should be washed well with soap and water and afterwards rinsed in clear water. They should then be hung, bristles downwards, to dry.

A BOOT REPAIRING HINT.

In some homes the boot repairing bill is an item of considerable proportions. When this is the case, any means whereby it may be lessened is welcomed. Here is a hint that will help to save half the cost of repairing heels.

When a rubber heel is worn down and calls for replacing, cut along the centre, from instep to outer curve, with a sharp pocket-knife, and remove the worn half, but leave the other half. This piece that is left will be almost if not quite sound, since most people walk over on either one side or the other.

Then cut a new rubber heel in halves and fit one of the pieces on the boot to take the place of the part that has been removed. Do not forget to run three or four nails along the edges of the old and new sections where they meet.

Thus, one new heel is made to serve for a pair of boots, and its fellow is available for some other occasion.

SANDPAPERING CURVED SURFACES.

The ordinary cork or wooden blocks used for sandpapering purposes are unsuitable for working on curved surfaces. In order to overcome this drawback a split wooden block similar to that shown in the sketch should be used. In this case four parallel strips of wood and two end pieces, suitably curved to enable the fingers to grip the finished block, are glued to a strip of leather or felt in such a way that there is a space of about ⅛ inch

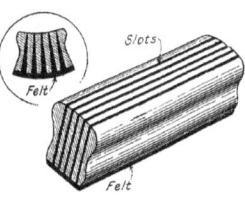

between the consecutive pieces. A piece of sandpaper is placed partially around the lower part of block. It can either be glued in position on the leather or, better still, tied in place with the string arranged in a lengthwise position —not across the sandpapering face.

For rubbing down concave faces of timber it is only necessary to press the tops of the strips together, when the bottom face will become convex.

The same device can be used for sandpapering convex surfaces, for it is then only necessary to open the strips at the top, when the bottom face will become concave (or hollow).

CURING WARPED PLYWOOD PANELS.

The usual cause of warping is that of absorption of different amounts of moisture from the air by the two sides of the panel. This results in the unequal expansion of the sides so that a curved form results. If one side of a panel is varnished or painted and the other side is left untreated, warping will occur.

It is advisable, therefore, to varnish or paint both sides of the panel, and, further, to use the same number of coats upon each side.

Untreated plywood panels that have warped during storage, or otherwise, may be flattened by exposing them to a moist atmosphere, such as the vapour from hot water, until they have become damp, and then placing them under a press, or upon a flat table under weights.

Fault Tracing Chart for All

FAULTS COMMON TO ALL TYPES

Symptom.	Possible Cause.	What to Do.
No signals.	Faulty aerial or earth connection.	Check over all connections both outside house and at set.
Ditto.	Two wires touching inside set.	Examine all wiring.
Ditto.	Wire has become detached.	Tighten up all terminals. If soldered, see contact is still good by giving a slight pull.
Ditto.	Loud speaker disconnected.	Check connections from set to loud speaker.
Ditto.	Loud speaker defective.	Disconnect leads from set and connect one lead to one terminal of an accumulator. Touch other lead on other terminal. A click should be heard.
Ditto.	Valve broken.	Test by substituting a new valve.
Ditto	Broken component.	Test the following components with phones and battery, when clicks should be heard if components are in order :—Coils and coil holder with coils in position ; choke, L.F. transformer.
Ditto.	Broken down gridleak.	Substitute new gridleak.
Signals weaker than usual.	Corroded aerial and earth connections.	Examine aerial and earth connections.
Ditto.	Valves old.	Substitute new valves.
Ditto.	Loud speaker weak.	Try new loud speaker.
Ditto.	Dirty lightning switch.	Examine and clean.
Two or more stations heard at once.	Set not sufficiently selective.	Try inserting a ·0001-mfd. condenser in series with aerial. Increase reaction.
Ditto.	Ganged condensers incorrectly trimmed.	If ganged tuning is employed, loosen screw which holds each set of moving vanes, after tuning in to weak station. Rotate each set of vanes until signal is at its loudest and tighten up screws.
Continual crackling noises, especially on long waves.	Atmospheric disturbance.	There is no cure for atmospheric disturbance.
Ditto.	Outside interference due to a nearby motor or other cause.	The only remedy for outside interference is to locate the source of the trouble and try and get the owner of the offending machine to take steps to prevent interference.
Crackling noises which continue when aerial and earth are disconnected.	Loose connection inside the set. Joint improperly soldered.	Examine all connections.
Ditto.	Dirt or moisture on terminal strip due to use of corrosive soldering fluid.	Examine surface of ebonite between terminals. If greasy or dirty, fit a new panel or terminal strip.
Crackling noises which continue after checking connections.	Valve legs not making good contact.	Remove valves from holders and open up contacts.
Crackling noises not due to any of three causes above.	Component in set broken down.	Test anode resistance, intervalve transformer, choke or condensers.
Crackling and scratching noises when tuning.	Moving vanes of variable condenser touching the fixed vanes.	Examine vanes and listen for rubbing sound while turning the knob. Bend vanes if necessary.
Ditto.	Metallic dust between two sets of vanes.	Clean between vanes with a pipe cleaner.
Ditto.	Bad connection to moving vanes.	Examine connections.
Whistling noises which vary in pitch as set is tuned.	Set oscillating.	Turn down reaction control.
Good reception on short waves ; none on long waves, and *vice versâ*.	Wave-change switch not making proper contact.	Examine contacts to make sure they are making contact and are free from dirt.
Metallic ring when set is touched or moved.	Microphonic valve.	Use springy valve holder or pack wadding round valve.

BATTERY SETS

Symptom.	Possible Cause.	What to Do.
No signals.	L.T. battery run down or H.T. battery exhausted or not connected.	Test batteries with voltmeter and replace if necessary. Check connections at wander plugs.
Signals weaker than usual.	H.T. battery exhausted.	Test with voltmeter.
Ditto.	Dirty accumulator terminals or H.T. wander plugs.	Scrape clean with knife.
Reception fades slowly.	Battery run down.	Replace.
Crackling noises in loud speaker.	H.T. battery running down.	Test with voltmeter.
Ditto.	Gas bubbles in L.T. accumulator.	Shake the cells so as to help disperse the gas and then allow battery to stand for a while before using.

TYPES OF WIRELESS RECEIVERS
BATTERY SETS—*continued*.

Symptom.	Possible Cause.	What to Do.
Low frequency valve gets hot.	Faulty grid bias battery or battery disconnected.	Test voltage and examine wander plugs.
Hum which stops when aerial or earth is removed.	Induced hum due to proximity of lead-in to mains wiring.	Alter position of lead-in.
Motor-boating.	Decoupling resistance too low or shorting. Decoupling condenser inoperative.	Check by substitution.
Continual pop-pop-pop heard when set is switched on.	Defective gridleak.	Replace gridleak.
Distortion.	Volume control too far advanced.	Turn back knob.
Ditto.	No or incorrect grid bias.	Adjust if necessary.
Ditto.	H.T. voltage too high.	Place wander plug in a lower socket.
Ditto.	Faulty gridleak.	Replace.
Ditto.	Loud speaker out of adjustment.	Adjust knob on loud speaker.
Ditto.	Dust in gap of moving coil loud speaker.	Clean out with thin strips of plasticine.
Reception is low-pitched in quality.	Too many additional loud speakers.	Try set with only one loud speaker connected.
Ditto.	Incorrect volume control across output.	Replace with volume control of different value.
Valves do not light.	Fuse broken.	Replace fuse.
Ditto.	"Pull-and-push" switch not making contact.	Examine switch and clean if necessary.

MAINS SETS

Symptom.	Possible Cause.	What to Do.
No signals.	Switch on skirting board turned off.	Switch on.
Ditto.	In A.C. set broken connection to mains transformer or mains transformer primary winding burnt out.	Test primary winding of mains transformer by inserting a lamp in series with it and the mains. If it glows, the transformer winding is O.K.
Ditto.	In D.C. set suspect resistance between the mains and filaments.	Check continuity of resistance.
No signals, but valve filaments glow, or valves get warm.	Fault in some part of high tension equipment, or loud speaker inoperative or disconnected.	Check high tension winding on transformer for continuity, also choke and anode resistance.
Reception stops suddenly.	In A.C. set mains transformer may be burnt out, or in D.C. set voltage resistance may be burnt out.	Same as for no signals.
Ditto.	Valve burnt out.	Leave set switched on for a short while, then feel all the valves. If one is cold, this should be replaced.
Crackling noise in loud speaker.	Smoothing condenser punctured.	Test by substitution.
Ditto.	Noisy H.F. valves, faulty grid bias resistances or faulty connection to resistances.	Replace H.F. valves and grid bias resistances.
Steady hum suddenly develops.	Earth disconnected.	Check to make sure that a wire has not become disconnected either inside or outside house.
Ditto.	Breakdown of smoothing condenser.	Test smoothing condenser by charging up from a D.C. supply of about 100 volts, leaving it for five minutes, then bridging the terminals with a screwdriver. If a spark is obtained the condenser is O.K.
Valves burn out almost as soon as they are replaced.	Set being used on incorrect voltage.	Make sure that your supply is the same as that from which the set is supposed to operate.
Ditto.	Mains transformer incorrectly wound.	Have the filament windings of the mains transformer tested.
Hum which is only noticeable when the gramophone attachment is used.	Pick-up leads inadequately screened.	Substitute metal-braided wire for pick-up leads.
Ditto.	Motor not earthed.	Connect a wire from some point on the motor frame to the earth terminal on the set.
Hum always present.	Mains plug in wrong way.	Reverse it.
Ditto.	Mains adjustment incorrect.	Try a lower tapping on the mains transformer.
Ditto.	Interaction between loud speaker and the set.	Move the loud speaker away from the set.

Wormholes in Furniture

THE small round holes frequently found in old furniture and oak beams are caused by the boring activities of a small grub or worm, known as the Xestobium, which is the larva of the death watch beetle, so called from the sound which it makes, resembling the ticking of a watch.

These larvæ are very destructive if allowed to proceed unchecked, and they will eventually honeycomb a piece of timber so that it has little strength or substance.

The amateur woodworker is often called upon not only to prevent the attacks of this grub upon modern furniture, but to eliminate it when it is actually at work inside the timber.

Preventative Measures.

To prevent the grub from attacking furniture is not a difficult matter, provided that the articles in question are not stored away in a dry place for any length of time. The usual method consists in regular washing down of the surfaces of the furniture with vinegar water made by mixing about 1 oz. of vinegar in a quart of water; any superfluous moisture left on the surfaces should be removed after this treatment.

Another preventative is ordinary furniture polishing wax containing also a small quantity of vinegar. If the polish be applied with a piece of cloth damped with vinegar, this will prove equally effective.

Some authorities recommend the spraying of the furniture with petrol or benzine mixtures, but we do not advocate such methods for domestic furniture on account of fire risks.

Treatment of Worm-infested Wood.

If the grubs are actually at work inside the timber, they will be found to eject from the holes a fine powdery dust; this will be observed either around the holes, near, or on the ground immediately below the holes.

In cases where the pieces of timber are fairly small, the grubs can be killed by heating the wood in an oven to the temperature of boiling water (212° F.) for an hour or so; valuable pieces of furniture that might warp or crack cannot, however, be treated in this manner.

Treatment for Short Pieces of Furniture.

Short pieces of timber may be rid of the grubs by immersing in a bath of a solution consisting of the following constituents:—

Carbon tetrachloride   1 gallon
Naphthaline   .   . 8 ozs.

Fig. 1.—A Simple Pipette for injecting the Insecticide can be made from a piece of Glass Tubing in which a Bulb is blown part-way along and a Fine Point afterwards drawn out.

Each of these materials is inexpensive, and may be obtained from any chemist's.

The soakings should be repeated two or three times after allowing the timber to dry each time.

If the timber is in long lengths, it should be brushed well with this solution, giving several applications after each has dried off.

Leroy's Paste.

An excellent substance for the destruction of worms in furniture is

Fig. 2.—The Finished Injector.
The larger open end is provided with a rubber bulb for drawing up the liquid into the glass container.

that devised by the late Professor Leroy—an eminent authority on insects—and known as Leroy's Paste. It consists of a chemical known as paradichlorobenzine, 90 per cent.; castile soap, 7 per cent.; and citronella oil, 3 per cent. This paste can be obtained from any prescribing chemist's. It has a strong smell, and is—as its name implies—a paste to be rubbed over the infected surface, so that it fills up the open ends of the worm holes.

The paste, on account of its evapora-

Fig. 3.—The Method of using the Injector.

tive properties, should be kept in a glass container with a ground glass or screw cap.

Liquid Worm Destroyers.

Perhaps the most effective agents for destroying the grubs are those having a liquid constitution, which are applied by injection into the worm holes. Although this method is apt to become somewhat tedious, it is certainly the safest and surest.

Any convenient form of injector can be used for this purpose, provided it has a fine outlet so that the liquid is injected right into the worm holes. An oil-can, hypodermic syringe or a chemist's pipette can be used for this purpose.

Making a Simple Injector.

A simple pipette for injecting the insecticide can be made from a piece of glass tubing in which a bulb is blown part-way along and a fine point afterwards drawn out, by first heating over a spirit flame as shown in Fig. 1, and then pulling out. The larger open end is provided with a rubber bulb for drawing up the liquid into the glass container, whence it is ejected by pressing the rubber bulb.

Some Suitable Solutions.

An excellent liquid for the injection method is the one previously mentioned, containing 8 ozs. of naphthaline in 1 gallon of carbon tetrachloride; the latter liquid is used in fire extinguishers and for cleaning clothes.

Another satisfactory liquid is made up by dissolving about 8 ozs. of camphor in 1 gallon of paraffin oil.

An effective insecticide can be made by diluting crude carbolic acid—otherwise known as *phenol*—with about twice its volume of water. It can, however, be used in the undiluted state, but is apt to leave a slight discoloration around the holes in the case of light furniture.

When surface treating furniture, the back-boards should be given a washing or application of one of the solutions mentioned.

The grubs causing the damage are active between May and August. The treatment should be repeated every three or four weeks during the spring and summer months for at least two years in order to ensure the complete extermination of all grubs.

Finally, to ensure freedom from this destructive grub, all furniture, beams and woodwork liable to attack should be examined annually, and, if necessary, treated by one of the methods described.

CLOTHES RENOVATIONS

One of the most satisfactory methods of removing stains or spots and giving a freshened appearance to articles of clothing is by dipping them in petrol. Provided reasonable precautions are taken, there is no danger, for although petrol is highly inflammable, if the work is done out of doors and kept well out of the way of any fire, flame or lighted cigarette, nothing untoward can happen.

Materials Required.

Two white-enamel bowls, large enough to contain sufficient petrol to cover the work.

An old soft toothbrush.

About 1 gallon of petrol, the exact quantity depending on the size and number of the garments.

An old clean sheet, which will serve as a pad on which to place the garment while cleaning.

Method of Cleaning.

First make sure that the two bowls are perfectly dry; then place them on a table or on an old mat laid on the ground.

Now pour sufficient petrol into the bowls. Place the garment in one of the bowls and gently squeeze it all over to get as much dirt out as possible. Gently rub the more soiled parts together. Pay special attention to any parts such as the collars of a dress, which will generally be found to be more soiled than most parts.

Having well squeezed the material all over, lift it out of the petrol and lay on the clean sheet and gently

Fig. 1.—When cleaning a Garment that is badly soiled it is advisable to Dip the Whole Garment in Petrol.

Two bowls are required, and after squeezing out as much dirt as possible in one bowl the garment is rinsed in the second.

scrub on the right side with the toothbrush. Now place it back in the bowl again and rinse. When all the dirt and stains seem to have been removed, rinse the article in the clean petrol in the second bowl.

The garment can now be hung up to dry, taking care to pull it into shape. Leave until thoroughly dry and free from smell, when it can be ironed.

Removing Small Spots.

When a garment is only disfigured with a few spots it may not be considered necessary to immerse the whole article in petrol, but to treat each spot individually. A pad of flannel or soft rag will be needed. In order to prevent a dark line appearing round the edge of the place where the petrol is applied, place a teaspoonful of salt in the petrol.

The garment should be laid out on an absorbent pad or piece of blotting paper. Pour some petrol into a saucer and dab the spot lightly with the pad, which should be dipped frequently in the petrol.

If the spot does not yield to this treatment, try lightly scrubbing it with a toothbrush, taking care not to spoil the surface of the material.

CLEANING WITH FULLER'S EARTH

An excellent method of cleaning dresses of crêpe-de-Chine, georgette, etc., or woollen jumpers, is to use Fuller's earth. This is a form of dry cleaning and can, of course, be done indoors, as there is danger of fire. For a dress that is not too soiled a 2d. packet of coarse Fuller's earth would probably be quite sufficient, although it is advisable to buy sufficient to enable a second application to be made if necessary.

Place a small quantity of the Fuller's earth in a saucer and mix into a fairly thick paste with clean water, the handle of a teaspoon making a very useful instrument for mixing.

Now place the article to be cleaned on a piece of white paper or sheet and rub the powder in all over. The paste which has been made up should be applied to any spots or grease marks fairly thickly. In the case of a badly soiled garment, the paste should be applied all over instead of powder.

The garment should now be wrapped and folded up in paper and left for a few days, after which the article can be removed from the paper and the Fuller's earth shaken out. Lightly rub the parts where the paste was applied with a similar action to washing.

Finally give another brushing to remove any traces of powder before

Fig. 2.—Small Stains can be treated individually and should be rubbed with a Pad dipped in Petrol.

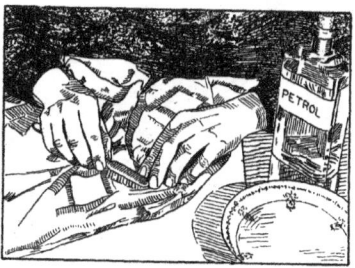

Fig. 3.—If Rubbing with a Pad does not remove the Stain, try scrubbing with a Small Brush.

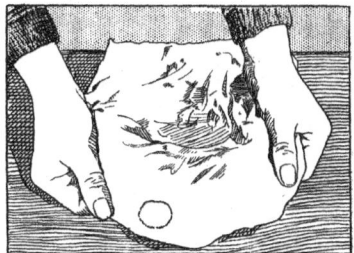

Fig. 4.—A Dark Line round the Petrol Mark can be avoided by mixing a Teaspoonful of Salt with the Petrol.

Fig. 5.—How to mix Fuller's Earth into a Paste.

Place a little powder in a saucer and mix into a thick paste with water.

Fig. 6.—The Fuller's Earth Paste is dabbed on to the Material with a Pad.

For a general clean, paste should be applied all over the garment.

Fig. 7.—Rub the Paste in with a Small Brush if there are Bad Stains.

Lay the material aside for a few days and then lightly brush out the powder.

CLOTHES RENOVATIONS

Fig. 8.—Obstinate Spots on Washable Garments such as Cotton and Artificial Silk will be helped by Shaking a Few Soap Flakes on them when Washing.

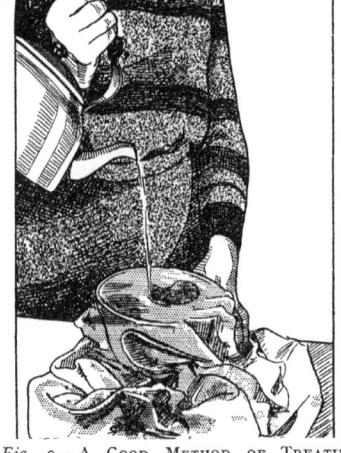

Fig. 9.—A Good Method of Treating Fruit Stains.
Place the stain over a bowl and then pour boiling water on it from a height.

Fig. 10.—Spots from Cloth can often be removed with Hot Soapy Water.

Fig. 11.—Rub Obstinate Spots with the Thumbnail and then Brush again with the Soap Solution.

Fig. 12.—The Juice of a Lemon, and Salt are very useful for Removing Stains such as Ink and Iron Rust.

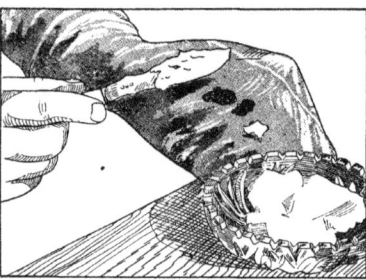

Fig. 13.—Tar on Stockings can be Removed by First Softening with Butter or Lard and then Washing as Usual.

Fig. 14.—To Treat Tar Stains on Delicate Fabric rub with Lard and then rub in some Fuller's Earth, Brushing it Off after a Few Days.

Fig. 15.—Sea-water Stains should be Treated with Fuller's Earth made into a Paste and Brushed Off when Dry.

pressing out the creases with a warm iron.

A second application may be necessary in the case of a very soiled garment.

Spots and Stains on Suits.

Another effective method of dealing with spots and stains is to scrub them with a stiff nail-brush dipped in warm soapy water to which a little liquid ammonia has been added. While scrubbing, scratch away any surface dirt with the finger-nail or a blunt knife.

The soapy solution must be removed by scrubbing with several applications of clean water.

PERSPIRATION STAINS

Slight stains caused by perspiration will generally yield to washing with a borax soap or in borax water. Alternatively rub with lemon juice and then wash.

If neither of these remedies proves effective, try bleaching by immersing in a weak solution of hypo-sulphite of soda, which is the fixing solution used by photographers.

GRASS STAINS ON FLANNELS

Rub some glycerine on the stain and leave for about an hour. Then wash with warm soap and water in the form of a lather, when both the stain and the glycerine will be removed.

TAR STAINS

The essential treatment for tar stains is first to soften the tar and then remove it with some suitable solvent. First rub the spot with lard, butter or olive oil until it softens or spreads. Then apply turpentine or benzene to remove the stain.

In the case of silk stockings or other washable garments, the tar should be softened as before and the article then washed in the ordinary way.

With delicate fabrics, the treatment is slightly different. First soften the tar with lard and then rub dry Fuller's earth in very thoroughly so as to cover the stains and a little past the edge. Leave for a few days, then lightly brush and rub off. Give a second application if necessary.

PAINT STAINS

A paint stain (other than cellulose paint) on clothing, if dealt with promptly, can generally be removed by rubbing with turpentine, turpentine substitute or benzene. Cellulose paint will require the particular solvent supplied by the makers, or if this is not available use amyl-acetate.

If the paint has been left for some while a preliminary application of oil, lard, butter or paraffin should be given before applying turpentine, to which a few drops of ammonia has been added. The material should then

Fig. 16.—Press the Waistcoat First, as this is the Simplest Garment.

The sleeve-board is used and the pressing begun at the buttonhole side.

Fig. 17.—First Stage in Pressing the Coat.

The sleeves (but not the cuffs) should be pressed first, working on the uncovered half of the sleeve-board.

be washed with soapy water afterwards, or if the garment does not lend itself to washing, wipe away the turpentine with vinegar and water.

FRUIT STAINS

As with paint stains, the treatment for marks caused by fruit juice depends on the length of time the stains have been allowed to remain.

If they can be treated at once, the material should be spread over a large basin and boiling-hot water poured on the stain from a height. If the stain persists, dip in a weak solution of ammonia. For a stain on a coloured fabric use methylated spirit with a little ammonia solution or a few drops of strong ammonia added.

Stains from stewed fruit containing sugar are more difficult to remove than fresh fruit stains. First dissolve the sugar with hot water and then apply ammonia to neutralise the acid.

In the case of old fruit stains apply glycerine or pure lard and leave for a few hours. Follow with hot water.

SEA-WATER STAINS

Flannel trousers or canvas shoes which have been damaged by sea-water should be treated with Fuller's earth made up into a paste, and brushed off when dry.

HOW TO PRESS A SUIT

The best method of reviving the colour and the surface of a suit of clothes is to press it with an iron and a damp cloth. This is not quite so easy as it sounds, and requires a certain amount of care and practice, and the beginner would be well advised to work on a spare piece of material at first until some idea of the correct heat for the iron and the pressure required has been obtained.

Apparatus and Accessories Required.

Iron about 10 lb. or slightly lighter,

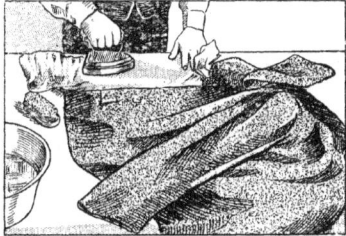

Fig. 18.—When Pressing the Forepart of the Coat Start with the Buttonhole Edge.

Note how the pressed sleeve has been turned back so as to avoid creasing it.

together with iron stand and two iron-holders.

Piece of calico or similar strong

Fig. 19.—Do not Forget to Pull Out the Pocket when Pressing the Skirt of the Coat.

If this is not done the edges will be seen on the outside of the coat in the form of shining ridges.

material suitable for the "damp cloth."

A sleeve-board.

Clothes brush.

Basin of clean cold water.

How to Make a Suitable Sleeve-board.

If you do not already possess a sleeve-board, one can quite easily be constructed from two pieces of fairly stout board joined together by a thick block of wood placed in the middle. The arrangement is shown in Fig. 16. Round off the edges, making one end slightly pointed and cover one-half of the board with cloth, the edges of which are fastened on the underside of the board.

It is not advisable to use a table with a French polished surface when ironing, as the polish may be spoilt by the iron. Preferably use a wooden kitchen table.

Clean the Suit First.

Pressing a suit with an iron and damp cloth will not remove dirt. Therefore the suit must be thoroughly brushed before pressing. Don't forget the "turn-ups" of the trousers or the insides of pockets. These should be turned out and all dust brushed off. Spots of grease should be removed with a small piece of rag dipped in petrol, or with soapy water as already described.

General Notes on Using the Iron and Damp Cloth.

Whether satisfactory results will be obtained depends on the correct combination of two things: the heat of the iron and the length of time the iron is applied to the damp cloth.

Judging the Correct Heat for the Iron.

The iron must be used very hot, but not too hot to scorch, and to test this it is advisable to keep a few white rags or white paper handy on which to test the iron before applying it to

Fig. 20.—The Shoulders are Pressed on the Sleeve-board, starting from the Buttonhole Side.

Lay the coat out as smoothly as possible, and work round the shoulders in overlapping stages, so as not to spoil the work already done.

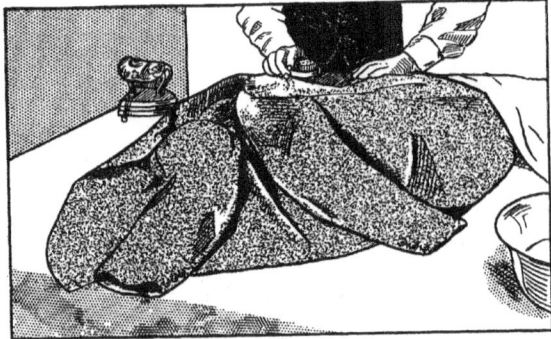

Fig. 21.—The Shoulders are completed by Turning the Coat Round on the Board.

The back of a clothes brush will be found useful for smoothing down any wrinkles or bumps in the cloth while it is still damp.

the clothing. If, however, the work seems to hang fire and takes too long, it is a sign that the iron is not hot enough.

How long should the Iron be applied?

If the iron is not kept on the damp cloth long enough it will be noticed that when the cloth is removed from the garment it has a puckered appearance, which is due to the expansion of the woollen material caused by the hot steam. If, however, the work is continued with the hot iron, the steam evaporates, the puckers disappear and the cloth is correctly pressed. Should the iron be used for too long on the now dry portion of the damp cloth, the result will be that the garment will begin to get hard and shiny. This, of course, is just what should be avoided. It is only by experimenting on a spare piece of cloth that you can judge the correct moment to remove the iron.

First deal with the Waistcoat.

The waistcoat should be pressed first, so that it can be hung on a coat-hanger or back of a chair while the remainder of the suit is being dealt with.

Use the sleeve-board with the cloth-covered portion uppermost and lie the buttonhole side flat on it. Now dip the cloth in water, wring it out as dry as possible with the hands, and place it smoothly on top of the waistcoat. Apply the hot iron with reasonably firm pressure up and down the front edge as far back as the pockets.

When this is judged to be correctly pressed, draw the waistcoat towards you so that portions from the pockets to the back now lie upon the board. Naturally that part of the damp cloth which was used first will now be dry, so a fresh part should be used, otherwise there will be no moisture to produce the necessary steam. The iron must never be applied to a dry portion of the cloth, or the garment will become shiny.

The Next Stage.

The next part to receive attention is the upper part of the cloth upon the shoulder. Then, in turn, the other shoulder, the back half of the button side, and the button edge. When dealing with the latter, move the point of the iron between the buttons as well as along the farthest edge.

While the damp cloth is lying over the buttons rest the iron lightly upon them for a moment and pass a stiff brush over them when the cloth is removed. This will often result in quite a surprising amount of dust coming away and will give the buttons a much improved appearance.

Both the sides and shoulders of the waistcoat have now been dealt with, so that when the centre of the back is being pressed the two finished halves will be lying out on either side of the sleeve-board, free from creases.

As soon as the centre of the back has been finished place the waistcoat on the coat-hanger.

Next Press the Coat—the Sleeves.

The sleeves of the coat should be tackled first, and the uncovered side of the sleeve-board should be used for the purpose.

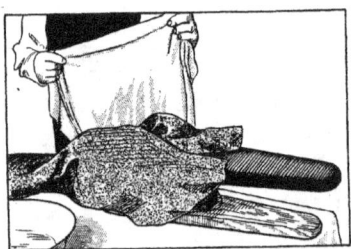

Fig. 22.—The Top Part of the Trousers should be attended to First.

After pressing the upper part draw the trousers farther upon the sleeve-board and press the fork.

For the preliminary pressing no crease or fold should be allowed, and the cuffs and shoulders are not touched for the time being. Three distinct strokes with the iron should be made. First lay the sleeve with the portion that, when worn, is nearest the body, on top. Run the iron down the centre only. The second stroke is down the centre of the outside of the sleeve; the third stroke with the back seam uppermost, which will make the wrinkles and gloss on the elbows disappear.

Now treat the other sleeve in exactly the same manner.

The Facings and Front.

Leave the sleeves for the moment, and now deal with the "facings," *i.e.*, the pieces of cloth inside the fronts of the coat. The sleeve-board will not be needed for this portion, the coat being laid out as flat as possible on the table. The facings are treated in the same manner as the waistcoat. Next press the fore-part, which is the outside of the breast, corresponding to the facings which have now been finished. As the sleeves will still be damp from their treatment, take care not to crease or spoil them.

The Skirt of the Coat.

When pressing the skirt of the coat, don't forget to pull out the pockets so as to prevent ridges being formed. The flaps of pockets and such-like are given an extra firm pressure.

The Back.

The back of the coat is now pressed, still using the table. The two halves of the back should be done separately so that each portion can lay perfectly flat for pressing in its own turn.

The Armpits.

The next stage is the armpits and for these the sleeve-board will be required again. As there will probably be numerous wrinkles at this spot, it is necessary to use plenty of heat and pressure. The coat should be drawn neck first over the big end of the board and the sleeves turned up over the collar so that they are resting on the board.

Now the Shoulders.

The shoulders should now be dealt with. Keep a clothes brush handy and use the back of it to flatten any slight wrinkles or bumps while still hot.

Use the big end of the sleeve-board and start pressing from the button-hole side of the coat and work round, right across the shoulders to the button side, keeping the coat as flat as possible.

The idea to keep in mind is to work n overlapping stages without spoiling the finish of the part of coat already treated.

Now Press the Cuffs.

The next stage consists of finishing off the sleeves. It will be remembered that the cuffs were not pressed, so each cuff must be slipped over the points of the sleeve-board and the edges pressed. Give the cuff a quarter turn at each pressure so that the edge is finished in four turns.

The Final Stages.

The only parts still to be pressed are the points where the sleeve joins the shoulder, called the sleeve-head, the lapels and the collar. The large rounded edge of the board will be found useful for dealing with the sleeve-head, as this part of the coat can be fitted against it.

To press the collar, lay the coat on the table and raise the collar to bring it over the broad end of the board. The lapels are treated in a similar manner unless a "rolled" effect is required, in which case they should be drawn clear upon the sleeve-board and pressed independently.

This completes the coat, and it can now be hung up upon the coat-hanger.

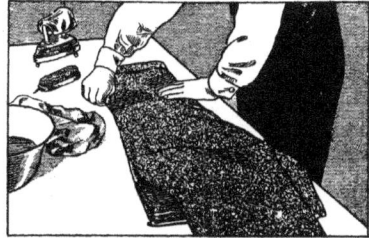

Fig. 23.—How to Make a Satisfactory Crease.

Lay the trousers out flat in approximately the position of the original crease and then run the iron first down the back crease and then the front. Now stretch the back crease along its length and then stretch the leg sideways above and below the knee.

How to Press the Trousers.

First roll the pockets up out of the way and then draw the tops of the trousers with the buttonhole side uppermost on to the sleeve-board. Press this part of the cloth and then move the trousers in successive stages over and under the board until the buttons finally come on to the top of the board.

Having dealt with the top part, the next operation is to get the fork of the trousers open upon the board. This is done by drawing the garment a bit farther upon the sleeve-board and lifting one leg over and laying it right along. This will enable the creases in the fork to be pressed out.

Now the Legs.

We now come to one of the most important stages, *i.e.*, the crease down the legs. Lay the trousers out flat upon the table with the right leg underneath so that they are as near as possible in the original creases. Pull the pockets away from the body portion and then lift the left leg right up over the seat out of the way.

How to Remove Bagginess.

Place the damp cloth over the right leg and run the iron first down the back crease and then down the front crease. Now stretch the back crease while still hot and damp along its length. Next grasp the two creases and stretch the leg sideways, pulling first below and then above the knee. Follow this by running the iron over the creases once more. The creases to the tops of the trousers are completed in a second stage.

Finish the outside of the right leg by turning the trousers over, and then press the bottom with a firm pressure on either side of the seam, but a softer pressure at the seam itself.

Repeat the above operations on the left leg, first drawing the left leg down on top of the right one, turning the trousers over sideways and lifting the finished right leg by the bottom and laying it clear.

Before turning the trousers to deal with the outside of the left leg, bring the right leg back over the left one so that it need not be creased when reversing the position of the trousers for the final touches.

DRILLING SOFT WOODS WITHOUT SPLINTERING

ONE of the most difficult jobs in amateur carpentry work is that of boring holes in soft woods, such as deal or pine, without leaving an ugly splintered edge on the side where the drill, or bit, comes through.

If an ordinary carpenter's brace and bit is used to bore a hole of, say, ¾-inch diameter in a piece of deal, it will invariably be found that the wood breaks away all around the hole on the lower side; this is true of both flat and spiral bits.

Fortunately, for the woodworker, there are satisfactory means of overcoming this difficulty, and we shall now describe two excellent methods.

One of these is first to drill a pilot hole through the wood, using a drill of about ⅛ to 3/16 inch. This hole must, of course, be bored quite square with the face of the timber. Next, using the brace and bit, bore the hole of the required diameter about two-thirds the way through the timber, using the pilot hole as a guide.

Then turn the timber over and complete the drilling of the last one-third, from the opposite side to that commenced with. The resulting hole will be found to be quite clean and free from splinters at the edges.

The second method is to clamp, securely, to the lower face of the timber to be drilled, another piece of flat timber, preferably of the same kind of wood.

Drilling with the brace and bit is then proceeded with in the ordinary way, but the hole is drilled partly through the second piece of timber. In this way, as the two pieces act as a solid one, no splintering will occur at the junction of the two, that is to say, at the lower face of the upper piece of timber.

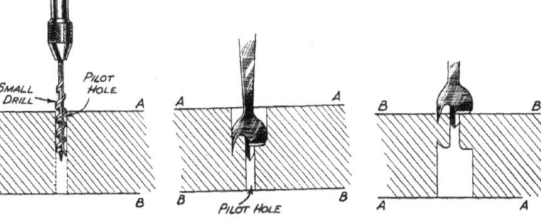

Diagrams illustrating the method of Drilling Soft Woods without Splintering.

How to Make a Wagon Tea-table

THIS original design gives the reader a useful wagon on rubber-tyred castors, which can be easily wheeled through a doorway, and then by releasing a catch quickly converted into an afternoon tea-table. The trays are held vertically one above the other on pivoted levers, the lower one being held firmly by a ball catch and stop carried in a cross member of the framing. On releasing the catch the upper tray swings downwards and the lower one moves upwards like a see-saw to meet it; when they are on the same level a ball catch in the side of the upper one springs home and secures them together while a turn-button underneath completely locks the table, preventing the slightest movement.

As the surface of the two trays remains horizontal throughout, this swinging movement enables the wagon to be converted into a table without moving or endangering any of the articles placed on them.

Material Required.

9′ × 1⅞″ × 1⅞″ machined oak.
17′ × 1¼″ × ⅞″   ,,   ,,
12′ × 2″ × ½″ tray moulding.
2′ 9″ × 2′ 6″ × ¼″ oak-faced ply.
4 oak buttons 1¼″ diameter.
Set of 4 rubber-tyred castors 4″ diameter.
3 ball catches.
6′ × 1¼″ × ⅛″ brass strip.
6′ × ¼″ brass rod.
1 doz. metal washers.
18 assorted screws.

Making the Legs.

Fig. 3 shows one of the four legs, the lower inch and a half of which is chamfered off so that it just takes the head of the castor socket (see Fig. 6). Note that three mortices are required in each leg, two in one face and the third in the adjacent one. The measurements given should be carefully adhered to as it is important that the lower tray as it is swinging downwards should engage with the catch carried on the cross member. Any variation in the distance between the side and pivot rails will mean altering the size of the swing levers.

It should be noted that the mortices are so arranged that all the rails fit flush with the inside of the leg (see B, Fig. 2); C in the same picture shows the ornamental button glued to the top of each leg.

The Rails.

Fig. 4 shows the size and shape of the three types of rail; the side and end members have tenons which fit into the legs; the tie piece, however, is held in a groove, cut on the inside of each end rail (see A, Fig. 2).

Gluing up the Frame.

First of all glue together the two ends of the structure, taking care to measure the diagonals of the resulting rectangle to ensure that it is square. When the ends are well set, fit in the two side rails and the tie bar, the latter must be pinned as well as glued; the cross member which carries the stop and catches is fastened in position last.

Fitting the Wheels.

It will be seen that each castor (see Fig. 6) is composed of a tubular socket which is driven into the leg and a wheel carried on a fork to which a stem is fitted.

Invert the complete framework so that the feet of the legs are uppermost. Now bore a hole in the centre of each that will just take the socket when driven; the hole should be at least 1 inch deeper than the length of the socket to accommodate the ball head at the end of the stem on the wheel fork. With a bradawl make four small holes into which the claws (see Fig. 6) can fit, then finally drive home. Before fitting in the wheel stem, smear it well with grease; a strong downward push is necessary to force the ball on the stem through the split end, F, of the tube. Once in place the ball prevents it from dropping out when the table is lifted.

Making the Trays.

Fig. 5 shows one of the trays; it is composed of a stout ply base with a rebated moulding fitted round three sides; the corners are mitred, glued, and pinned.

See P, Fig. 5, and observe that the open side of the tray is not square. The edge of the upper one slopes forwards at 100°, while the lower tray slopes backwards at 80°; the edge of the ply is bevelled in the same way as the moulding. This sloping edge enables the trays to come together without fouling one another.

Note that the open side of the upper tray is opposite to that of the lower one; thus, when the two are joined, there is an unbroken surface.

The Swing Levers.

The shape and size of the four levers can be seen in Fig. 7. Two of them are similar to the sketch J while the other pair are like K and have a slot filed out of one arm; this accommodates the distance washer fitted to the end of J. There are three holes in each bar—these are countersunk to take the heads of the fixing screws; observe that the centre

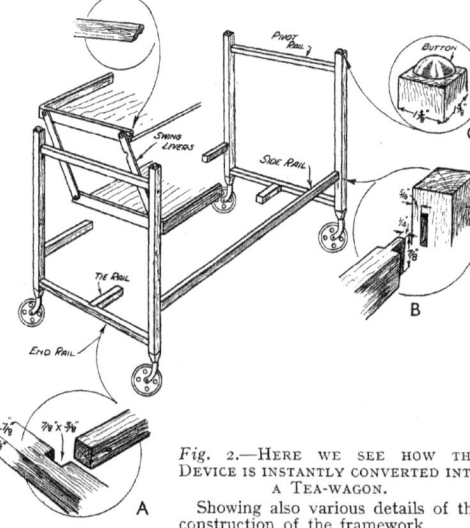

Fig. 2.—Here we see how the device is instantly converted into a tea-wagon.
Showing also various details of the construction of the framework.

HOW TO MAKE A WAGON TEA-TABLE

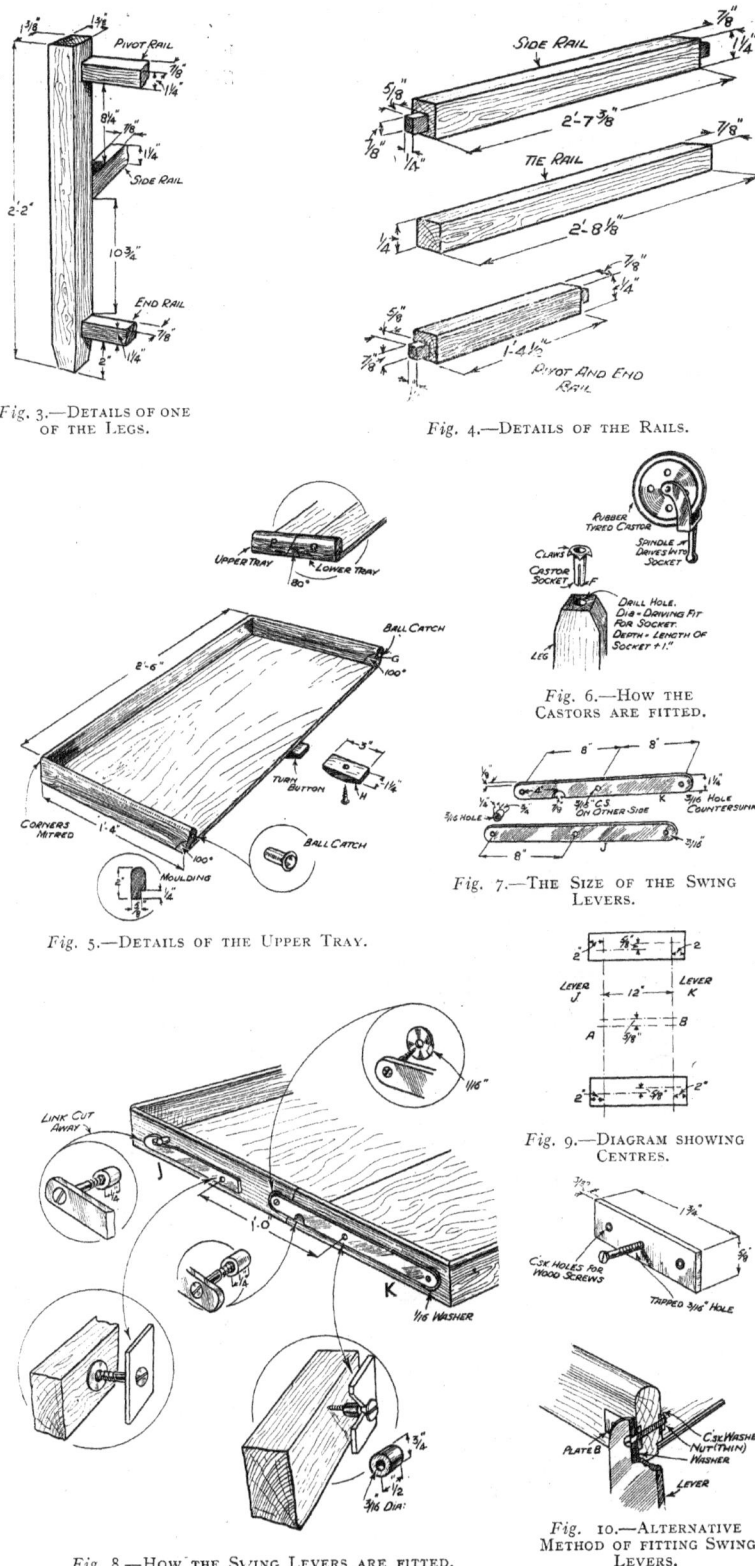

Fig. 3.—DETAILS OF ONE OF THE LEGS.

Fig. 4.—DETAILS OF THE RAILS.

Fig. 5.—DETAILS OF THE UPPER TRAY.

Fig. 6.—HOW THE CASTORS ARE FITTED.

Fig. 7.—THE SIZE OF THE SWING LEVERS.

Fig. 8.—HOW THE SWING LEVERS ARE FITTED.

Fig. 9.—DIAGRAM SHOWING CENTRES.

Fig. 10.—ALTERNATIVE METHOD OF FITTING SWING LEVERS.

hole is countersunk on the opposite side to that of the end holes.

Two pairs of distance pieces are required, a couple for each set of levers. These keep the member J (Fig. 8) ¼ inch away from the ends of the tray, so that when the leaves are closed, that is in the horizontal position, the near one (Fig. 8) fits in behind the outer one, J. Note that the end of J nearer the centre of the trays slips into the slot L.

Fitting the Levers.

The ends of the levers screw on to the trays 2 inches from the ends, but the centres of the screws for the inside bar, K, are ⅝ inch above those of the lower one, J. Fig. 9 gives in diagrammatic form the position of the various centres. A and B on which the levers are pivoted are not in line, B is ⅝ inch above A; similarly, the ends of the levers which fasten on to the trays are not level, but one is ⅝ in. above the other.

The best way to proceed is to place the trays side by side with the ball joint engaged as in Fig. 8; mark the centres and screw on the bar K. Then similarly fasten on the bar J with its centres ⅝ inch below those of the lever K. When fixing the second lever J use ¼-inch distance pieces instead of washers, and see that they fit snugly into the slots.

Alternative Method of Fitting Levers.

Screws will be found quite satisfactory to fix the levers provided well-seasoned oak is used for the framing. If any difficulty is experienced in getting the work rigid, or a soft wood is used, then Fig. 10 shows an alternative method which will ensure the pivots keeping firm. The plate is sunk into the tray moulding and the bolt screws into a hole tapped 2 B.A. The sectional sketch shows how the bolt passes through the tray moulding and is fastened with a thin locking nut on the inside of the tray.

Fixing to the Frame.

Now if the levers are correctly fitted one tray can be swung above the other; while in this position temporarily fix rigid with several thin pieces of batten so that they cannot move. The tray assembly should now, when lifted, slide freely into place in the main frame between the two pivot rails. Having carefully marked the position of the centres on these rails, screw the swing bars in place. On removing the temporary fixing battens the trays should swing freely up and down like a see-saw and the ball joints should snap home when in the horizontal position.

When fixing the levers to the pivot rails look at Fig. 11, and note that J requires a washer at its centre while K requires a ½-inch distance piece, as shown.

The Stop and Button.

Fig. 12 shows a stop and button on the cross member; these hold the trays firm in the vertical position and should be fitted after the swing levers are finally in position.

Bring the bottom tray down to its lowest point, when it should miss the cross member by approximately ¼ inch. Plane up a piece A (Fig. 12) the correct thickness so that the tray just clears. Glue and screw A in position, after which a ball catch can be sunk into the rail; a small hole and eyelet in the base of the tray must also be fitted. With the catch sprung home, fasten a small fixed stop as shown in Fig. 12, and at the other end of the cross rail screw in position a small wooden turn-button. The latter must be thin, so as to miss the edge of the tray in its upward path.

The ball catch will be found to hold the trays firmly in position, but the turn-buttons shown make it absolutely rigid.

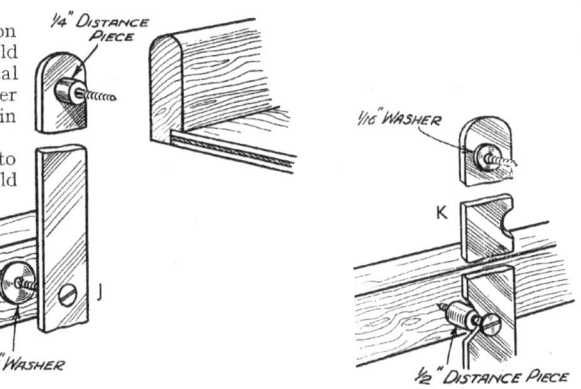

Fig. 11.—Details for fixing the Levers.

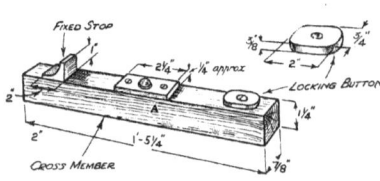

Fig. 12.—The Stop and Button on the Cross Member.

The Finish.

The woodwork should be scraped and given a good coat of water stain with a soft brush. Fill the grain with a coating of wet plaster of Paris well rubbed in and scraped off before it dries hard. Then brush on three coats of French polish, and when dry finish with a rubber of cotton wool covered with a piece of fine linen.

The brass levers and fittings can be cleaned with metal polish, buffed with rouge and a chamois leather and finally lacquered. They can, if preferred, be sent to the platers to be electro-plated at a small cost.

It is important when fixing the arms to make sure that the screws grip firmly in the wood without the slightest shake. This is quite easy when using oak or hard wood, but when soft material is used it is advisable to use the alternative method of fixing shown in Fig. 10.

AN EASILY MADE PLYWOOD FIRESCREEN

A FIREPLACE can be a very ugly spot in an otherwise attractive room, especially if the fire is laid and not lighted. At all times, when there is no fire, the best plan is to hide the grate by means of a screen.

The screen described and illustrated in this article is easily made, the cost is very little, and it has a most dignified appearance.

The Wood.

A sheet of plywood, 36 by 26 inches and ⅜ inch thick, is carefully trimmed up, particular attention being taken to see that the corners are properly squared. This sheet is placed flat on the workroom floor and strips of wood, ¾ inch thick and 1¾ inches wide, are nailed with light pins around the four edges. Then strips, 2 inches wide and ¼ or ½ inch thick, are nailed across and around the inner edge of the plywood to form the six panels shown in the illustration.

The exact dimensions of the strips of wood are unimportant as long as they approximate those suggested here, and as long as the final effect is a set of panels formed by raised strips, the whole being edged with a frame still more raised. While speaking of the dimensions, it may be well to point out that the screen described here serves to hide a rather large fire-grate. If required for a fairly small grate, the best plan is to make it with four panels, and thus leave out the two upper ones.

Fig. 1.—The Completed Firescreen.

Fig. 2.—How the Feet are constructed.

How to keep Plywood from Twisting or Warping.

When this face has been made, a strip of wood is nailed on the back, from one corner to the opposite corner, but not coming close to the edges. Any narrow piece of wood will serve the purpose, as it is merely required to keep the plywood from twisting or warping.

Constructing the Feet.

The feet are the next items to consider. These are constructed from wood 3 by 2 inches in section. Fig. 2 shows how they are planned. The bottom strip of each foot is 12 inches long, while the upper strip is about half this length. The latter is cut in two equal pieces and one is placed each side of the frame. Each piece is nailed both to the under strip and to the frame. Thus the screen and the feet are joined together, and the completed article will be found to stand firmly.

Colouring the Wood.

The final operation is that of colouring the wood. If the screen is required for a room furnished with oak, mahogany or walnut, the easiest plan will be to purchase a small quantity of whichever stain is appropriate and apply two coats. Then to finish off with a wax polish or an egg-shell varnish. Of course, the screen will present a handsome appearance if decorated in cellulose lacquer of two suitable colours.

RE-UPHOLSTERING A DINING-ROOM CHAIR

FIG. 1 shows a chair typical of a type made forty or more years ago. Such chairs, although now somewhat old-fashioned, were well made, and still have many years of wear in them if repaired. The type is known as the "stuff over," by which is meant that the upholstery is taken right over the seat rails.

As shown, the upholstery is in a bad way, the webbing below having given way, allowing the springs to drop, and the cover is hopelessly beyond repair. The only thing to do is to remove completely the upholstery and re-cover it. Had the webbing only broken, the cover still being good, it might have been possible to carry out a repair from beneath by removing the old webbing and fixing new. The method of doing this is dealt with elsewhere.

Removing the Old Upholstery.

Fig. 2 shows how the old upholstery is removed. An old screwdriver and a hammer are required. The point of the former is placed beneath the tack head, and a sharp blow struck with the hammer. This forces out the tack. It is advisable to point the screwdriver in the direction of the grain where practicable. The old stuffing can be used again provided it is not unclean. If ticks are suspected it should be burnt and new provided. Remove *all* the tacks, whether they are still holding the covering or not.

When free from all material, any repairs that may be necessary to the woodwork should be carried out. For details of repairs of this kind see another article on this subject. It is as well also to brighten up the polish. The whole thing should be washed down with *weak* soda water—one

*Fig. 1.—*HAVE YOU A CHAIR LIKE THIS?
It will be seen that the upholstery is badly torn and the springs need repairing. This article tells you what to do to the chair to enable you to obtain many more years' service from it.

lump of soda in a basin of water—and swilled down with clear water. A rubber of polish can then be given (see another article).

Fixing the Webbing.

Webbing is obtainable in rolls. Double over one end about 1 inch and fix it to the underside of one seat rail with five large tacks. Special large tacks for the purpose can be obtained. To avoid splitting the wood the tacks should be staggered as far as possible so that they are not in a line with the grain. Fig. 3 shows the doubled end of the webbing being tacked down.

Using a Webbing Strainer.

It is obviously desirable to stretch the webbing as tight as possible, and to do this a special webbing strainer is used. There are various types available, all similar in principle. One simple form is shown in Fig. 4. It is of stout wire with a movable bar on the parallel lower ends. The webbing passes from the fixed end above the movable bar, and through again beneath it. Thus, when the strainer is levered backwards it bears tightly on the free end of the webbing, which necessarily falls between it and the seat rail. The more the tool is strained backwards the more it bears against the webbing.

The strainer being forced backwards, two tacks are driven in, as shown in Fig. 4. The webbing can then be cut off about 1 inch beyond the tacks, and doubled over, when the remaining three tacks can be knocked in. Do not remove the strainer from the webbing, because it is now threaded in position for the next strand. It is merely a matter of pulling the webbing through.

The Cross Strands.

Keep the new strands of webbing in the same positions as the old. Finish all those running in one direction first, and then complete the cross strands. Note that these interlace alternately, as shown in Fig. 5.

Covering the Webbing with Canvas.

To give a neat finish, a piece of canvas is fitted below the webbing (Fig. 5). It is cut approximately to

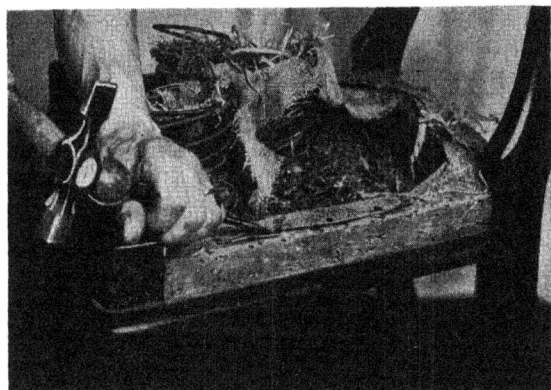

*Fig. 2.—*THE FIRST THING TO DO IS TO REMOVE THE OLD UPHOLSTERY.
A screwdriver and a hammer should be used, the screwdriver being placed under each tack head and given a sharp blow.

*Fig. 3.—*WHEN ALL THE OLD UPHOLSTERY HAS BEEN REMOVED, THE NEW WEBBING CAN BE FIXED IN POSITION.
Note how the webbing is doubled over before being tacked down.

RE-UPHOLSTERING A DINING-ROOM CHAIR

Fig. 4.—THE WEBBING SHOULD NOW BE STRETCHED AS TIGHT AS POSSIBLE.
A special webbing strainer should be used if one is available. When the webbing is tight two tacks should be driven in and the webbing cut about 1 inch beyond the tacks and doubled over.

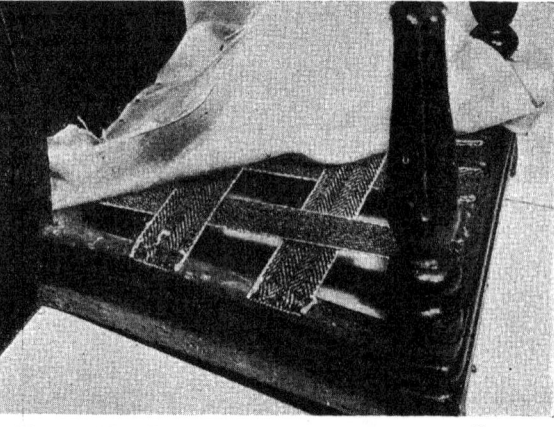

Fig. 5.—A NEAT FINISH IS OBTAINED BY FITTING A PIECE OF CANVAS BELOW THE WEBBING.
Start fixing the canvas at the back, double over the edges and drive in tacks at intervals of about 1½ inches.

size (the exact shape does not matter) with an allowance all round for a turnover. Begin at the back, doubling the edge and driving in tacks at intervals of 1½ inches or so. Small tacks are used for this. Pull the canvas over to the front, double this edge and tack down. The sides are dealt with in the same way. It will be seen that as the edge is doubled over in every case the exact shape is unimportant as the free edges project inside where they are not seen. The corners are fixed last. They are turned and folded neatly, the corners being nicked where necessary.

Tying the Springs.

The chair can now be stood on its feet. For convenience in working it is as well to raise it upon some low trestles. There are four springs, and to prevent them from moving about they are stitched to the webbing. Correctly, the end of each coil should be fixed down with a piece of wire. In new springs this is done, but the wire is sometimes detached in an old one. In Fig. 6 the spring to the right has its end free. This should be fixed down to the coil immediately beneath it with a piece of wire bent round with pliers. The front spring to the left is fixed down in this way. This, of course, is done before the springs are stitched down.

Use proper upholstery twine for the stitching. It is threaded through a needle, and the latter passed right through the webbing. Make each stitch self-locking by passing the needle through the loop. Otherwise, if the twine should break, the whole would work loose. There is no need to cut

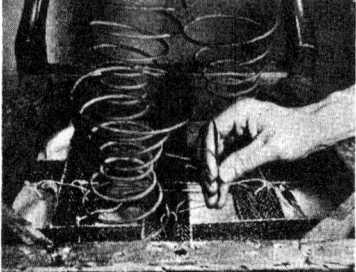

Fig. 6.—THE NEXT OPERATION IS TO STITCH THE SPRINGS IN POSITION.

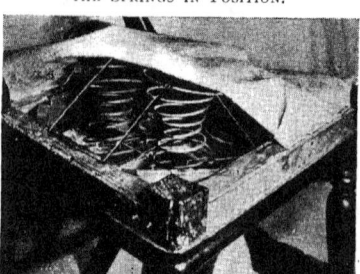

Fig. 7.—NOW COVER THE TOP WITH CANVAS.

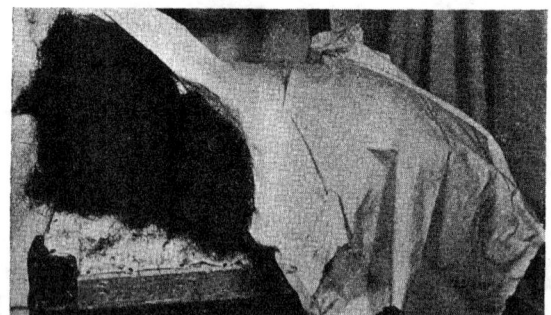

Fig. 8.—THE CHAIR IS NOW READY FOR THE STUFFING TO BE INSERTED.
Here we see the first stuffing with the canvas cover pulled back at one corner to expose the hair. The cover is tacked to the back rail, the hair placed in position and the cover fixed down with tacks.

the twine after each stitch. It can be taken from one to the other. Three stitches to each spring are enough.

How to Keep the Tops of the Springs in Position.

To keep the tops of the springs in position they are looped to the seat rails with twine and to each other. Fig. 7 shows the twine holding them. To fix the twine to the rails, a tack is driven half in, the twine taken a couple of turns round it, and then driven home.

Fixing the Canvas Cover.

A canvas cover is now laid over the whole. As before, the approximate shape is cut with an allowance for doubling all round to the edges. Fix the back first, driving the tacks into the top edge of the rails. Stretch the canvas forwards and put in a single tack at the front. Work towards the sides, driving in the tacks every 1½ inches or so. The edge is doubled as at the back. Do the same thing at the sides. It will be found that the tops of the legs project upwards, as in Fig. 7. The canvas is taken up to these, and a tack driven in right in the angle. The corner is folded and tacked on top of the leg as seen to the left in Fig. 7. At the back the corners can be nicked to fit around the legs.

The First Stuffing.

If the old stuffing is clean it can be used again if thoroughly teased out. Horsehair, which is the best stuffing, especially requires to be pulled out so that lumpiness is avoided. The

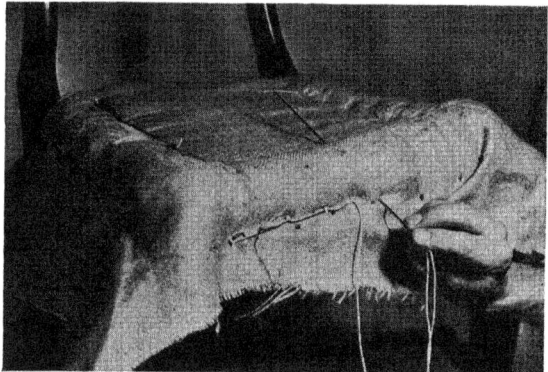

Fig. 9.—After the first Stuffing has been inserted, the Seat must be Shaped.
This is done by stitching with a double-ended upholsterer's needle. Begin at one side at the back and work towards the front.

Fig. 10.—When the Seat has been Shaped, the second Stuffing is added.
Flock stuffing can be used, and, as before, a canvas cover should first be tacked at the back edge.

best way of doing this is to spread two sheets of paper on the table and put the stuffing on the one. A small bunch is then taken, and pulled well apart with the fingers, and dropped into the other sheet. It is a process which takes a fairly long time when done thoroughly, but it is essential.

Before placing it on the chair, cut out another canvas cover and tack it to the back rail, driving the tacks this time into the back edge. The edge is doubled as before. This cover is pulled back, and the hair placed on the seat beneath. The important point is to keep plenty of hair around the edges. There will probably appear to be far too much hair, but when the cover is pulled over it will all pack away. About 1 lb. of hair is needed.

Pull the cover forward and drive a tack into the front edge of the front rail, and work towards the corners. Fig. 8 shows the cover pulled back at one corner to expose the hair. The sides having been tacked also and the corners neatly turned, the hair is worked finally into position. Professional upholsterers use what is known as a regulator, an instrument about 9 inches long, pointed at one end and with the other end rounded. It is passed right through the canvas cover and the hair forced along wherever necessary. If one is not available a tool such as a thin screwdriver can be used. Remember that the edges must be well packed with hair.

How to Make Edges Firm.

As the seat is now it is springy, but

Fig. 11.—Before the final Cover is fixed, a Sheet of Cotton Wool should be laid over the whole Seat.
The new cover is then placed in position ready for tacking.

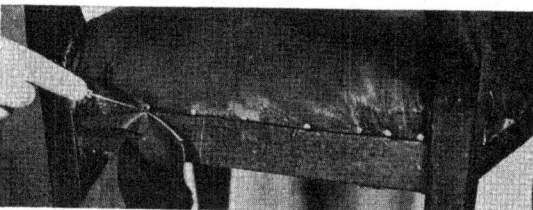

Fig. 12.—The Final Stages.

the edges are rounded. To make firm edges with a well-defined shape stitching is necessary. This stage is shown in Fig. 9. Begin at one side at the back and work towards the front. A double-ended upholsterer's needle is used. Thread the twine through the eye. Pass in the point near the edge of the seat rail at the side, bringing it out diagonally at the top as in Fig. 9. Pull the needle right out and reinsert it about 1 inch along, bringing it out near the seat rail again. When the point has emerged about 2 inches take the hanging loop of twine a couple of turns round it and pull tight. This will hold it firmly.

Proceed along so that a firm roll is formed as in Fig. 9. The surplus canvas can then be cut away.

The Second Stuffing.

The effect of the roll is to form an indentation in the centre, and a second stuffing is laid over this, as in Fig. 10. Flock stuffing can be used. As before, another canvas cover can first be tacked at the back edge. Work the stuffing evenly and draw over the cover, tacking it to the sides of the seat rail. The surplus canvas is trimmed away with a knife.

Before the final cover is fixed, a sheet of cotton wool can be laid over the whole, as in Fig. 11. If the original cover is in reasonably good condition, it can be used as a pattern when cutting out the new. This is a great advantage, as it indicates where it can be cut and how the corners are folded.

Begin at the back, driving in all the tacks. Pull it forwards and drive in a centre tack. Pull the sides tight and put in centre tacks here also. Then work towards the corners, carefully smoothing out all creases. It may prove necessary to remove some of the original tacks as the work proceeds. Consequently it is a good plan not to drive the tacks right home at the start. A double fold is made at the corners.

Fig. 12 shows how the cover is trimmed finally with a keen knife. Finally the tacks are hidden and a neat finish given by the addition of gimp fixed with gimp pins driven in at regular intervals.

Plywood for Floors

AN INEXPENSIVE AND ATTRACTIVE TREATMENT

Fig. 1.—A Floor surfaced with Plywood Squares.

Fig. 2.—Nailing down the Plywood Squares.
If this method is adopted instead of gluing, the heads must be sunk below the surface and levelled with plastic wood.

HAVE you counted the cost of a parquet floor and come to the conclusion that the expense is too great? If so, cover the floor yourself with plywood. There is nothing difficult about the job, and once it is finished, it should look attractive and last for ever. Moreover, the initial cost will be no more than that of a fair grade of lino.

We will take first the floor of a bedroom. The first thing is to see that the boards are in good condition; that they are level and there are no cracks, due to shrinkage, between them. If there are any perceptible gaps, they will have to be plugged with newspaper boiled to a pulp in a little water, and mixed with hot glue.

Measuring the Surface of the Floor.

The surface of the floor is now measured up and then sufficient plywood, ⅜ inch thick, bought for the purpose. There are dozens of kinds of plywood, some good and some poor. The writer selected sheets faced with birch, but oak and ash are equally serviceable. What should be avoided are the very cheap woods that are spongy in texture and which have no attractive grain or markings.

The idea for this particular floor was to cover it with small squares or rectangles of plywood, each piece being about 12 to 18 inches in dimensions. Naturally, the exact measurements of the pieces must depend on the size of the large sheets, seeing that they ought not to be cut to leave any waste.

Have the Pieces Cut at the Wood-yard.

As the cutting of the pieces is likely to prove a very laborious task it is advisable to get it cut at the woodyard, where it can quickly be done with a circular saw. For about an extra 2d. for each large sheet, all the pieces can be cut, with corners dead true, no jagged edges, and every square exact to size.

Stain Half the Squares a Darkish Brown.

As soon as the pile of squares is delivered, half of them must be stained a darkish brown and the remainder left in the natural colour.

Laying the Squares.

The work of laying can now be begun. Three ways of doing this suggest themselves. The best way is to heat up some Scotch glue and to stick each square to the surface of the floor. Another method is to nail each piece, and the third to use small screws.

When nails or screws are employed it is necessary to sink the heads below the surface and to level over them with plastic wood, coloured to match. All this adds to the labour and makes gluing a quicker process.

Lay all the Pieces on the Floor before Fixing.

It is not a bad plan to lay all the pieces on the floor before any are fixed. A slight shifting of position may help to give a better effect and as it provides a more attractive finish if the squares or rectangles do not go right up to the skirting boards, but are edged around with a frame of strip plywood, this preliminary setting out is helpful in deciding just how much edging is necessary.

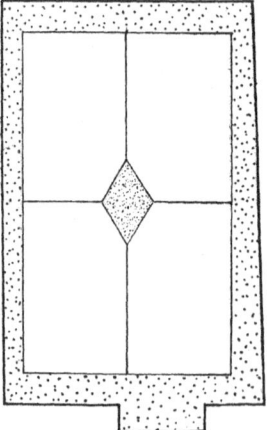

Fig. 3.—Diagram showing how the Plywood Surround fills up the Unequal Dimensions of the Floor.

Finish Off the Surface by Wax-polishing.

When the whole floor has been covered and the pieces fixed down, finish off the surface by giving it a thorough wax-polishing. The wax should be rubbed well in, so that it fills up all the grain of the wood and the joins between the pieces. Then the whole of the floor presents one level surface which gives an appearance which approximates that of parquet.

Dealing with a Rectangular Hall.

When dealing with a surface such as a rectangular hall, the treatment is slightly different. Four squares of oak three-ply should be laid together in the form of a large square, and an edging of the same material fitted around them, so as to fill the remainder of the surface. The squares are not cut up into small pieces, as in the first case, but the grain laid in alternate directions, and this supplies all the pattern that is necessary. No staining is done, the wood being left in the natural colour. After it has been in wear for more than a year it begins to mellow and appears even better than it did when first laid. It should be wax-polished, as in the other instance.

Another Method.

Another suggestion for laying a floor on these lines is to cut the corners of the four sheets where they meet, and insert a small diamond-shaped piece to form a centre.

How to Cure Draughts under Doors

ALTHOUGH, in the case of the well-built house, little difficulty is experienced in connection with draughts coming past closed doors and windows, it is a fact that in many houses, owing to ill-fitting of these parts, a good deal of discomfort may be caused through direct draughts.

Doors may shrink, or may have to be re-hung in order to swing freely, so that there is a space between the bottom of the door and the floor. In other cases, notably with old houses, there may also be sources of much draught past the sides of the door.

In regard to windows it is usually a simple matter to exclude draughts by means of curtains, so that we shall confine our attention in this article to the methods of excluding draughts from doors only.

OUTSIDE DOORS

Outside doors are undoubtedly the worst offenders in the matter of draughts, for they are directly exposed to the external elements, viz., winds and rain, whereas in the case of doors inside the house it is only the internal air which is concerned.

How Draughts are Caused.

In passing, it should be noted that draughts are caused by air rushing from places of higher pressure to those of lower pressure, or of lower to higher temperatures. Thus, in a room where there is a fireplace with a fire going, the air required for combustion of the gas or coal must come into the room from outside. We cannot—and indeed should not attempt to—exclude this air, but should prevent it from entering the room in such a manner as to cause discomfort.

Using Triangular Section Weatherboard.

In the case of outside doors, bottom draughts can to some extent be prevented by means of a triangular section weatherboard fixed near to the bottom of the door; this will exclude some of the draught and all of the rain, as it provides a longer and narrower path for the air to pass through (Fig. 1).

Another Method.

A very effective method of dealing with doors which have no protection against draughts is that shown in Fig. 2. The object of this device is to lift the draught-excluding board B clear of the floor when the door is opened, but to force it downwards against the step or floor when the door is closed.

How the Device is Constructed.

From Fig. 2 it will be seen that there is a strip of wood B hinged, by means of countersunk wood-screws at each end

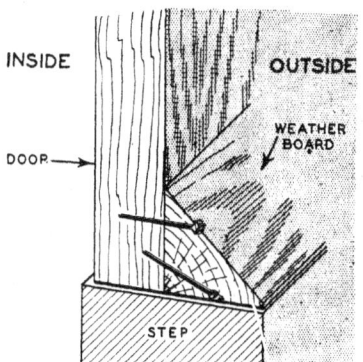

Fig. 1.—A Triangular Weatherboard Fitted to an Outside Door will help to Minimise Draughts and will also Prevent Rain from Blowing Under the Door.

to a brass plate at each side of the door near the ground. A weatherboard

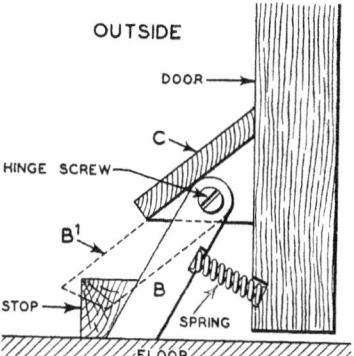

Fig. 2.—An Effective Method of Dealing with an Outside Door which has no Protection against Draughts.

The object of this device is to lift the draught-excluding board B clear of the floor when the door is opened, but to force it downwards against the step or floor when the door is closed.

C acts not only as a weather protection to the upper part of B, but also as a stop when the door is opened.

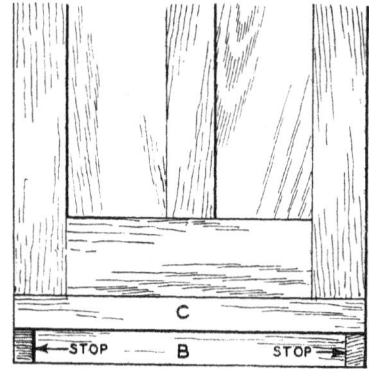

Fig. 3.—How the Draught Excluder shown in Fig. 2 is Fitted to the Door.

The springs shown force B upwards, as given by the dotted position B¹. In order to keep the lower end of the hinged strip B down against the floor when the door is closed, a pair of stops is fitted, one at each side of the door frame, as shown in Fig. 3.

An advantage of this draught-excluder is that there is no wear on the lower end of B, for it does not slide along the ground, being lifted clear when the door is opened; it can thus be made to clear any mat or carpet inside. The board B should be about 3 inches wide by ½ inch thick, and of oak, whilst C should be about 2½ inches by ¾ inch, and of deal.

INSIDE DOORS

There are several alternative methods of draught prevention in the case of inside doors, the particular method employed depending upon considerations of effectiveness and neatness of appearance.

Using Rubber-piping Material.

Where the draughts to be excluded are not of a very serious nature, the simplest and most effective method is, no doubt, that of nailing strips of rubber piping material along the edges of the door, as shown in Fig. 4. In order to obtain the best results from this material it is best to tack it—by means of brads or tin-tacks—to the outside of the door (assuming the door opens inwardly); in this way the rubber is forced between the bottom of the door and the floor *when the door is closed*.

Fixing.

The material in question can be purchased at any hardware stores, or house furnishers, and is fixed by means of tacks arranged at intervals of about 1 inch.

Wooden Roller covered with Baize.

Another method which has been in use for some appreciable period of time is that shown in Fig. 5. It depends upon the use of a wooden roller covered with a thick material such as baize. This roller is arranged to rotate in brass plate slotted bearings provided at each end. It can, therefore, not only roll over the floor or carpet when the door is opened, but can also move up and down in its slotted end-plates, in order to take into account any irregularities in the floor, thickness of mats or carpet.

From these particulars it will be obvious that such a device is not difficult to construct and is most effective in use. If necessary, however, the material covered rollers can be purchased, together with the end-plate fittings, at any hardware shop.

HOW TO CURE DRAUGHTS UNDER DOORS

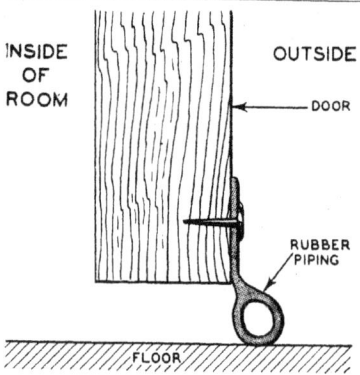

Fig. 4.—How Rubber-Piping Material is used to Prevent Draughts Under an Inside Door.

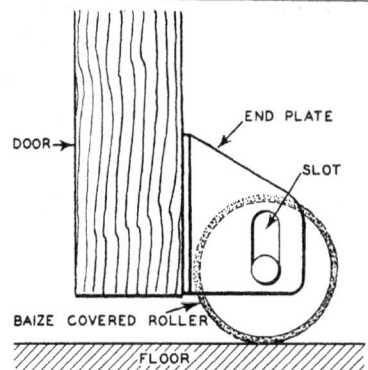

Fig. 5.—The Baize-covered Roller Method of Excluding Draughts.

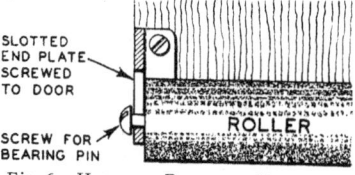

Fig. 6.—How the Roller is Mounted in the Slotted End-plate Bearings.

Fig. 7.—The Sliding Rubber-insert Strip Board Draught-Excluder.

Fixing the Roller.

In regard to the wooden roller, ordinary wood-screws are used for the end bearing pins, so that there is no possibility of these pins coming out of the plates (Fig. 6).

The roller should be about 1½ inches diameter, made of pine or beech, whilst the end-plates should be made from ⅛-inch brass, and have 3/16-inch wide slots for the end bearing pins or screws. The plates should each be attached, by means of two wood-screws, to the door.

In this case it is immaterial upon which side of the door the roller is mounted, as in either case its weight keeps it in contact with the ground; it must, of course, touch the side of the door all the time.

Sliding-board Type.

As a final example of a draught-excluder we shall refer to the sliding-board type (Fig. 7). This consists of a piece of board, of about 2 inches to 2½ inches width by ⅜ inch in thickness, provided at its lower end with an inserted strip of rubber or felt. Ordinary rubber piping material may, however, be used as an alternative.

The board is provided with three or more slots, and it is fastened to the bottom of the door by means of 3/16-inch round-headed wood-screws; one of the latter for each slot. The screw shanks should be a free fit in the slots.

It will be seen that as the door swings open or shut the board can slide vertically so as to slide over any irregularities in height on the floor. The slots are often made inclined in order to clear the door posts when the door is fully opened. The weight of the strip keeps it on the floor all the time.

REPAIRING GARDEN TOOL HANDLES

THE pine or ash handles of brooms, rakes, forks and spades are sometimes broken, either accidentally or by too much pressure when in use, in the manner indicated in Fig. 1. It is not necessary, however, to scrap the handle, as a very strong repair can be made in the following manner.

First, take each of the broken portions and apply to the fractured surfaces a coating of a good strong waterproof glue, such as Croid or Durofix. Allow this to dry a little before pressing the two broken portions together, so that the corresponding portions of the fracture fit. Place the handle under pressure so that the two parts are held together with a certain amount of force whilst the glue is setting.

Scrape away the surplus glue after the joint has set, and proceed to splice the joint in the manner shown in Fig. 2.

Fig. 1.—The Fractured Handle.

Strong cord of about 1/16 inch diameter should be used for this purpose and the total length of the splice should be about three times the diameter of the handle.

The method of commencing and finishing the splice so that the loose ends of the cord are securely locked in position will be clear from an examination of the two end portions, A and B, in Fig. 2. At the starting end a short length of the cord should be held by the thumb along the length of the handle, and the cord should be wound around the handle over this short length for three or four turns, as shown. Then these few turns should be pulled tightly together and the loose, or surplus, end cut off with a knife.

Next give the outside of the handle about the glued joint a coating of glue, and whilst the glue is still wet proceed to wind the cord tightly along the handle so that consecutive cords touch, as indicated by the black portion in Fig. 2.

The handle can be turned to do this splicing, as this will usually be found more convenient than winding the cord around the fixed handle.

The splice is finished off securely by placing the end of the cord under the last three or four loops, as at the start, and working the loose end and the loops until the latter are quite tight, when the free end of the cord can be cut off. To enable the end of the cord to be passed through the last four turns, the latter should be wound over a match stick, nail or piece of wire of about the same thickness as the cord used, when the end may readily be pulled through the loops thus formed, after which the stick, nail or wire can be withdrawn.

Finally, give the finished splice two coats of varnish or waterproof glue in order to hold the cords together and to protect the splice.

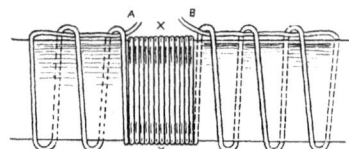

Fig. 2.—Details for Splicing the Joint.

Fig. 3.—The Finished Repair.

THE PERIODICAL EXAMINATION OF A HOUSE
WHERE TO LOOK FOR EXTERIOR AND INTERIOR DEFECTS

HUMAN nature being what it is, the hardest task to do is the simple one that may be done at any odd time. A piece of work urgently required is finished off, no matter how busy we may be, but the job we promise ourselves we will do next when we have half an hour on hand is the one that will be found still undone a month or two hence. The best way to overcome this human weakness is to fix a limit of time for such a task, provided of course it is worth the doing, and treat it as a matter of urgency to get it done within that time, no matter how pressing other things may be or how disinclined we may feel to undertake it.

Of all such jobs, probably the easiest to postpone are the little odds and ends that need attention in the home. The screw working loose, the rusty piece of metal which needs repainting, the tile calling out to be refixed, the tap constantly telling us by its drip that a new washer is required, these are the little tasks that the ordinary man puts off doing until they have grown big ones.

If these things, seen every day, are neglected, what of those unobserved defects, the decayed wood, the damp patch, the broken slate, the cracked pipe. Only when the storm has come and the effect has become serious do we notice them at all unless we have formed that admirable habit of examining the house periodically, with the object, not exactly of looking for trouble, but of looking for likely causes of trouble.

Importance of Discovering and Remedying Defects in their Early Stages.

It will be generally agreed that money and inconvenience will be saved by discovering and remedying defects in their early stages, but the difficulty for the person without much technical knowledge of buildings is what to look for and how to recognise a defect when seen. The object of this article is to show the owner who takes a pride and interest in his house how to examine it from time to time with a view to spotting defects before they assume large proportions.

THE EXTERIOR

Slates, Tiles and Chimney Stacks.

Let us begin with the exterior, for this is the part that has to resist the full force of wind and weather, and is therefore most likely to show parts dislodged or decayed and also most likely to cause damage if left in disrepair.

Commence at the top, for a peck of troubles can lie here unheeded (Fig. 1). The slates or tiles—are any cracked, broken, slipped out of place or missing altogether? Does the ridge want pointing? And the chimney stacks, do they show any cracks, or are there any open brickwork joints to be pointed? The easiest place for wet to get in is at the junction of two kinds of material, where, for instance, the roof tiles join the chimney stacks. Such joints are generally covered with lead or zinc, the edges of the metal being tucked into joints of the brickwork and the other edges lying on or under the tiles. See if the lead or zinc has drawn out of the mortar joint, if so, water will assuredly trickle down inside. Also see if the leadwork needs dressing down flat on the tiling.

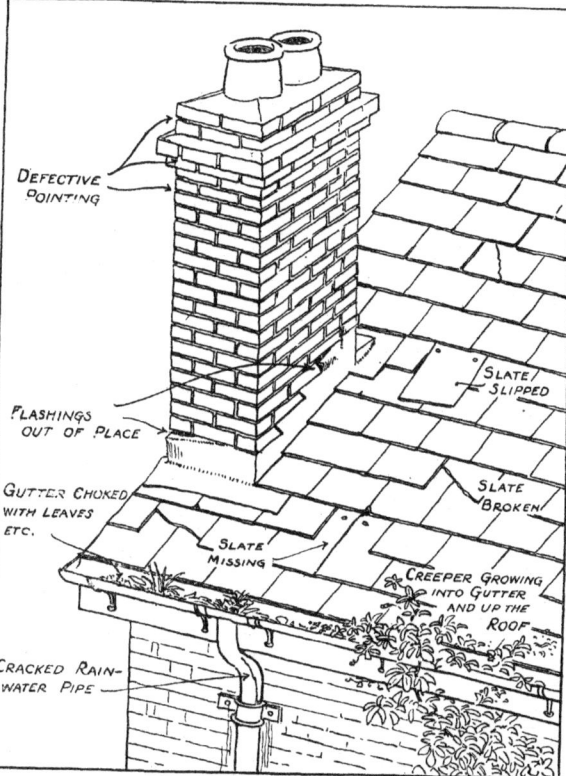

Fig. 1.—THE FIRST PLACE TO EXAMINE IS THE OUTSIDE OF THE ROOF. This diagram shows clearly the various points which may need attention.

Are the Gutters Choked?

Next examine the gutters—the roof is planned for water to flow into them, so if they are choked with leaves or an accumulation of dirt, or if creepers have grown over and into them, they will not function, and instead of passing on the water into the drains they will probably let it run down the walls and soak them as no driving storm would do. Birds take a delight in nesting at the top of a rainwater pipe (the vertical pipe leading from gutter to drain) and a nest will completely choke a pipe.

Some lengths of the eaves gutters may have dropped, and if so, the rainwater will flow away from and not towards the outlets.

Cracked Gutters or Rainwater Pipes.

It is worth while to see if any sections of the gutters or rainwater pipes are cracked. Such cracks will probably be on the side towards the house, not only because of the natural perversity of things, but because the casting of the pipe is weakest on the rough part which the builder sets against the wall, also pipes do not get so well painted at the back.

How to Tell whether a Pipe is Whole.

A tap on the pipe with a penknife or anything else handy will tell by the ring or the dull sound if the pipe is whole. Do not forget to look at the shoe (Fig. 2) which discharges over the gulley: is it choked and is there a collection of leaves blocking the gulley? The nails holding the pipe to the wall sometimes get drawn away, and then in time the pipe will drop.

Look at the Walls for Cracks or Bulging.

Now give an eye to the walls and watch particularly for cracks, joints of brickwork to be pointed, any bulging parts and signs of dampness. Slight cracks may not be serious, all buildings settle down, and initial cracks are hard to avoid, but if the cracks are extensive, and particularly if they are near the corners of the building, the opinion of an expert is desirable. Brickwork should not get out of upright or develop bulges; if they are noticed, the advice of a person who thoroughly understands building con-

THE PERIODICAL EXAMINATION OF A HOUSE

struction should be sought, for if the defect has not gone far, it is often possible to effect a small repair and secure the wall from further movement.

Dampness.

Dampness or damp stains should be looked for. Wet rooms are most unhealthy, also dampness in building materials hastens their decay, wood rots, brick and stone crumble, and iron rusts. Apart from defective gutters and rainwater pipes previously mentioned, frequent causes of damp walls are :

(1) Earth banked up for garden beds too high, reaching above the damp-proof course (a course of material such as slates or bitumen impervious to water) intended to keep the moisture from the earth rising in the substance of a wall (Fig. 2). In brick-faced walls the position is shown by a wider joint than the others.

(2) Shrubs too close to a wall, especially around rainwater pipes.

(3) Open joints in pavings against walls letting water run in without an opportunity of escaping.

(4) Cement plinths or skirtings intended to keep the bottom of the walls dry, but because they have worked away from the face of the wall, water trickles down behind, and then the walls will be more damp than if there were no cement work at all (Fig. 2). Such skirtings should always finish at a brick joint and be " tucked " into the joint at least ¾-inch.

Blocked Gratings.

Gratings or airbricks are usually to be found near the ground. They serve

Fig. 4.—A LITTLE ATTENTION MAY SAVE A FENCE FROM FALLING DOWN.

Here we see the lower part of a fence with the following faults : beginning to lean over—post rotting—earth banked up too high—palings split and loose rail coming out of place.

Fig. 2.—DON'T FORGET TO LOOK AT THE SHOE WHICH DISCHARGES OVER THE GULLEY.

Showing (left to right) earth banked above damp-proof course and blocking up ventilating grating—rainwater pipe cracked—pipe nail loose—shoe partly blocked—gulley covered with leaves—cement plinth drawn away from the wall allowing water to trickle behind—paving cracked by the wall allowing water to flow into the foundations.

the useful purpose of admitting a current of air to the space under the lowest floor. If there were no ventilation, dry rot would probably appear in the floor timbers. The gratings readily

Fig. 3.—A LIKELY PLACE TO LOOK FOR DECAYED WOOD.

Bottom of a door and frame, showing by dark lines where rot is most likely to occur first.

become blocked ; they should be kept clear of all obstruction.

Painting.

The painting of woodwork and ironwork, looked upon by many chiefly for its decorative value—giving the house a well-cared-for look—or the reverse, has the very practical use of preserving the material to which it is applied. If this purpose is considered, attention will be given to the parts which do not show equally with those which all may see. If paint is much worn, or the material has perished, its protective value will have been impaired, and decay or rust will follow as a certainty.

Where to Look for Decayed Wood.

The points at which decayed wood is more likely to be found are at the bottom of door frames (Fig. 3), sills of windows, and the bottom rails of sashes and doors. The woodwork of half-timbered buildings of the " Tudor " type is often badly protected from the weather and readily decays.

Outbuildings and Fences.

The outbuildings, fences and gates should be examined even more frequently than the house, as perishable material enters more largely into their construction. An extra coat of creosote, or an application of paint applied as soon as wanted, will save expensive repair and renewal later.

The falling down of fences may cause much annoyance and bad feeling between neighbours. This could be avoided if a little attention is given earlier on when the first signs of decay appear in the posts or the fence begins to lean over (Figs. 4 and 5).

THE INTERIOR

The condition of the decorations and the repair of fittings in regular use will not need a special examination, as they will force themselves upon the attention of the householder who takes a pride in his house, and so they will be passed by here. What can be overlooked, and therefore is in need of some effort of will to examine, are the hidden things and the automatic appliances which ordinarily look after themselves, and only now and again require some little attention.

Don't Forget to go up into the Loft.

The roof loft—what a glory hole this usually is ! There will probably be a trap door, and perchance some high steps are handy, but it is a dark and dirty job to get up there, and yet that is where the cistern is almost sure to be (Figs. 6 and 7). Frequently innocent of any cover at all, or a makeshift

Fig. 5.—HOW THE FENCE SHOWN IN FIG. 4 SHOULD BE PUT IN ORDER.

The following details have been attended to : made upright—secured by a spur—rotted timber cut out and replaced with new—high earth removed—palings made good and secured.

THE PERIODICAL EXAMINATION OF A HOUSE

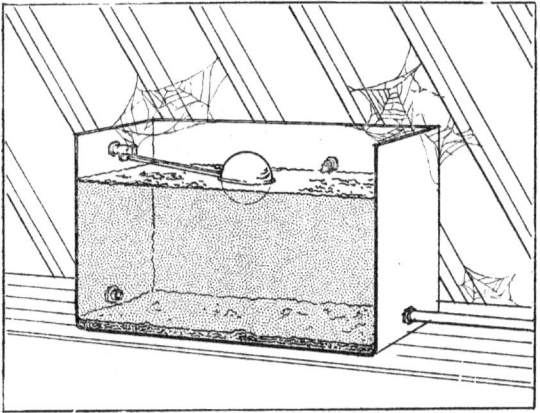

Fig. 6.—Is your Cistern like this?
The faults shown here are: uncovered and dirty cistern—scum on the surface—overflow pipe choked—sediment collected on the bottom—pipes exposed to frost.

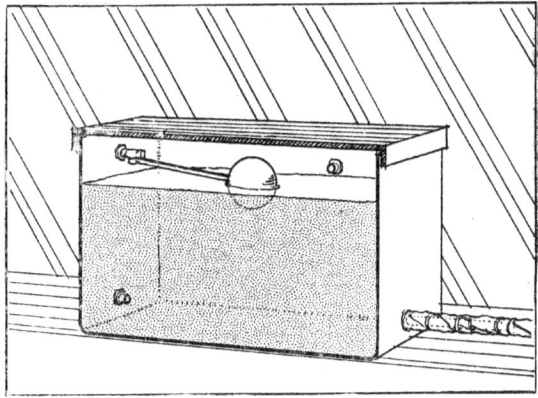

Fig. 7.—Or like this?
Showing a covered and clean cistern—all scum and sediment removed—overflow pipe clear—pipes covered with felt.

one at best, the dust and dirt can get into the domestic water supply.

Clean out the Cistern Once a Year.

A certain amount of deposit from the main water supply is also inevitable, consequently, if the water drawn off for household use is to be pure, the cistern should be cleaned out periodically once a year; at any rate it should be looked to regularly. In cleaning out a cistern it is important not to stir up the sediment before running away the water through the pipes, else hard sharp pieces of rust or grit will get into the pipes and will be most difficult to clear, and, in addition, it may be found necessary to re-washer taps, etc. On no account should water be drawn from any of the hot water taps while the cistern is empty, or air may be drawn into the pipes and cause bother when the system is refilled.

Examine the Ball Valve.

An overflow pipe is fitted to a cistern in case the ball valve does not act; it is rarely called into service, but it should be examined from time to time to see if it is clear for eventualities.

Cover Water Pipes with Felt.

The water pipes in the roof are subject to attack by frost and should therefore be covered with felt. Various gas pipes, electric conduits, etc., run through the roof space and may get rusty.

Faults to Look for in Rooms.

Within the rooms the chief things to look for are damp stains, signs of dry rot—decay of materials and settlement cracks. Damp stains are principally due to external defects which may have been noticed when the house was examined outside.

Window Sills.

Look under the windows, because faulty construction of window sills is all too common. Rain gets in between the wood sill and the stone or tile sill unless a proper water bar of metal has been inserted between the two sills, and, not being seen, it is often omitted and the pointing is depended on to keep out the rain. This may be sufficient when all is new, but when the sun has shrunk the wood and the pointing works loose, the water easily finds an entry.

Damp Stains along Lower Parts of the Walls.

If damp stains are noticed along the lower parts of the walls (see illustration on page 24) suspicion should be cast upon the efficiency of the damp-proof course, or it may be the earth is too high on the outside, as mentioned already in the external examination of the house.

Dampness in Cupboards.

Mildew or dampness are not neces-

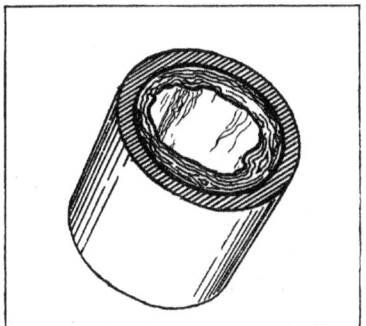

Fig. 8.—Section of a Hot Water Supply Pipe "Furred" Up.
Note reduced water way, choking flow of water and assisting further and more rapid deposits.

sarily due to a defective structure. Very often dampness in cupboards or other closed places arises from a lack of ventilation. If the joinery is well made and tight-fitting the circulation of air is less than with ill-fitted cupboard doors. Fortunately, lack of ventilation in such cases can soon be corrected by the boring of two or three small holes to give a through current of air.

Dry Rot.

Dry rot is a fungoid growth which attacks and saps the virtue from woodwork. The conditions that favour its growth are stagnant air and moisture, and so the space under the ground floor is where it is most frequently found. Before laying linoleum right over a floor the provision for ventilation under the floor should be examined. There should be a sufficient number of air bricks so arranged that a current of air will pass under every part. If any dry rot is discovered the wood must be cut away and burnt, otherwise the infection will spread rapidly and a large area will become involved.

Damage Caused by Wood Beetle.

Another destructive agent is the wood beetle. The death watch beetle, of which we have read so much in our newspapers lately, confines its attention to hard woods such as oak. The beetle that does most damage in ordinary houses is the furniture beetle. It has a particular taste for sapwood, and is more rarely found in the heartwood which alone should be used in building. If any wood is found to be badly affected by the beetle—its presence can be detected by numerous small holes in the surface and a very fine powder in the wood—it should be cut out and burnt. If the wood is only slightly attacked the best plan is to creosote it thoroughly—provided, of

THE PERIODICAL EXAMINATION OF A HOUSE

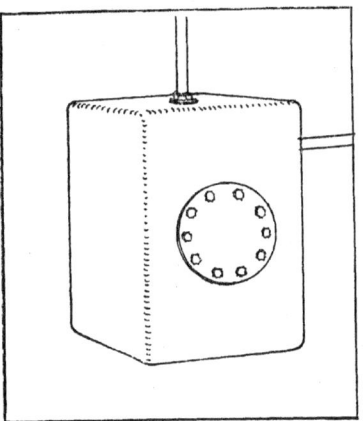

Fig. 9.—The Hot Water Tank should be Cleaned Occasionally.

The bolted circular plate can be removed for cleaning out the tank.

allowed to go on undisturbed, and yet much trouble may be gradually—very gradually—accumulating.

It has been noted in the case of the cold water cistern that sediment is deposited from the water. Similarly in the hot water system this sediment held in suspension in the water supply will gradually fall, and, more important still, the lime in solution in the water will be deposited by the constant heating of the water and form a crust or "fur" in the boiler tanks and pipes (Fig. 8) just as furring takes place in a kettle. Hard water contains a high percentage of lime, and consequently the furring is more rapid with hard than soft water. It will be seen that boilers and tanks are provided with removable covers to openings, called mudholes or manholes (Fig. 9), and thus the sediment that has been deposited can be removed.

DRAINAGE

It speaks volumes for the modern method of drain construction, how very seldom manhole covers are lifted and drains inspected. It is no uncommon thing to find such covers rusted in, or even with fences and other things built over them. It is, however, unwise, even with the best laid drains, to allow them to pass unexamined for indefinite periods.

Where to Look for Faults.

The points to be looked at in a drainage system will be briefly alluded to. First, there are the gulleys receiving waste water from sinks, baths and lavatory basins; soap and grease constantly passing into or over the gulleys is sure to collect, and if allowed to remain too long it will eventually choke the gratings and block up the traps. The gulleys should be cleared of sediment and the gratings and pipes swilled out either with a hose or a bucket of water.

Lift Manhole Covers to see that Water is running clear.

The manhole covers should be lifted occasionally to see that water is running clear, that no material has got into the drain to choke or partially choke it, and that the cement work of the manhole has not cracked or fallen.

Fig. 10.—When attending to the Drainage System examine the Fresh-air Inlets and their Valves of Mica.

In the diagram above they are partly choked up and the mica flap cannot close to check the outlet of foul air from the drains.

When examining drains it is a good plan to allow water to flow through from a bath or sink to see if it is clear and free flowing.

The fresh air inlets (Fig. 10), with their valves of mica, should also be examined. If broken or stopped with leaves, air from the drains can get out freely, and usually in places close to windows or to pavements.

Periods of Examination.

Each owner should make his own schedule of times for examining his house according to the quality of the building, and his own circumstances. The following are merely suggestions:

Exterior—twice yearly, spring and early autumn.

Interior—roof, once a year; rooms, twice yearly, spring and early autumn.

Drainage—gulleys, once a month; manholes, yearly.

It may sound rather frightening to read of all the defects to which a house is liable, almost as fearsome as reading a list of symptoms of diseases; fortunately, in both cases one rarely experiences more than one or two at a time, and that at wide intervals. The worst danger for both body and building is neglect, timely examination and speedy repair soon put the defects right.

course, creosoting is in keeping with the decorative treatment, if the woodwork is exposed. Another useful preventive is a coating of beeswax and turpentine.

Cracks in Walls and Ceilings.

Cracks in walls and ceilings are the cause of much fear and even alarm for householders and house occupiers. They may be due to movements in the structure, in which case they may be serious, or they might be due to slight shrinkages in materials, such as timber, which is unavoidable, and these cracks may be of no more importance than their unsightliness. As mentioned before, when considering the exterior of the house, in case of doubt it is best to consult someone who thoroughly understands building.

Hot Water Boiler and System.

Of all the parts of a house and its fittings, the one that will almost assuredly be left last for examination is the hot water boiler and system, the reason being that it is beyond the powers of the ordinary handy owner to empty the system, undo bolts and make them thoroughly watertight once again. Provided hot water can be drawn from the taps the system is

SOME GOOD FURNITURE POLISHES

(1) A good furniture polish which is frequently used in furniture factories and shops is made up as follows:—

Rubbing oil	7½ parts.
White vinegar	1 part.
Alcohol	2 parts.
Oil of citronella	½ part.
Butter of antimony	½ ,,
Water	1½ parts.

This mixture should be stirred well.

(2) Beeswax mixed with turpentine to a pasty consistency gives an excellent furniture polish.

(3) A good red furniture polishing paste can be made up as follows:—

Turpentine	3 pints.
Water	3 ,,
Beeswax	1½ lbs.
White wax	1 oz.
White soap	9 ozs.
Red lead	6 ,,

The soap should first be cut up and dissolved in warm water, the solution then being heated until the water has evaporated down to 3 lbs. Next melt the two waxes by heating, and then add the turpentine and red lead. Finally, pour in the soap solution and stir the mixture as it cools. The colour of the paste may be lightened or darkened by using less or more of the red lead constituent.

Simple Methods of Rejuvenating Carpets

THE average carpet is subjected to a good deal of harsh usage; accordingly, it is not surprising that a time quickly arrives when something must be done if it is not to prove an eyesore in the room. Fortunately, there are many ways of remedying defects in carpets and prolonging their life of usefulness, as the following paragraphs show.

Shampooing a Carpet.

When a carpet becomes dirty in patches, put some soap flakes in a bowl of hot water and add a tablespoonful of liquid ammonia. Dip a clean scrubbing brush in this and go lightly over the carpet. Do a patch at a time, and then finish off by having another bowl of clear warm water, wringing out a rag in it and sponging over the scrubbed surface. Always finish off by stroking the carpet the way of the pile.

Bad Spots.

Have a cake of soap at hand and, if a spot needs special attention, rub the part well with the soap and then scrub it.

Aim at wetting the carpet as little as possible and, if done in the winter time, light a fire in the room. Should much water be used and there is no heat to dry the carpet, mildew may appear in course of time.

Ridge Marks in Carpets.

When the floor boards are not perfectly level—and very few are—or when the under-felts overlap in places, ridge marks soon become apparent on the surface of the carpet. If these are allowed to remain for any length of time, the pile will wear and the marks become permanent. In order to prevent this, it is an excellent plan to lift a carpet every three months if the room is in daily use, or at least once a year in other rooms, and to rearrange the felts underneath. There is no need

Fig. 1.—To Clean a Carpet that has Become Dirty in Patches, put some Soap Flakes in a Bowl of Hot Water and add a Tablespoonful of Liquid Ammonia, and scrub the Carpet with this Solution.

Do a patch at a time, and then finish off by having another bowl of clear warm water, wringing out a rag in it and sponging over the scrubbed surface.

to take up the carpet entirely. A portion can be laid back and attended to; then another part can be similarly treated.

Using Old Newspapers to Remedy a Raised Floorboard.

In the case of a floor board that is

Fig. 2.—An Exaggerated Example of an Upstanding Floorboard.

Showing how old newspapers can be arranged on either side to deaden the sharp edges of the board and save the carpet. Alternatively plane the board down level with the rest of the floor.

perceptibly higher than the one on either side of it, it is a good plan to put several sheets of newspaper flush with the raised edge of the board and to tear the sheets so that each is a different width. Thus, the thickness of the papers will gradually lessen as they recede from the upstanding board, and no sharp raised edge will occur on the floor to make its impression on the carpet.

Painting a Worn Part of the Design.

Certain parts of a floor are subjected to more wear than others, with the consequence that a carpet may be practically perfect except in one spot, and that is, perhaps, almost threadbare. If the pile is short, it is comparatively easy to colour the threadbare patch to match the rest and, thus, to make the carpet appear new once more.

Obtain some bottles of ink of the colours possessed by the carpet. If black is included, do not use ordinary black ink, but buy some indian ink. Then, with a small paint brush, fill in the design. In a short while it will be possible to obliterate all the area showing a string-like surface and merge it into the rest of the carpet.

Ridding a Carpet of Moths.

Moths are liable to attack the carpet of a room that is only used occasionally. When this pest is suspected, place a tablespoonful of liquid ammonia in a bowl of hot water, wring out a cloth in it, fold the cloth into two or four, put it flat on the carpet, then go over the cloth with a hot iron until it is quite dry. Not only will the live moths be killed by this method, but the grubs will be too.

It is not a bad plan to put sheets of newspaper under a carpet that has been attacked by moths. These creatures detest the smell of printers' ink.

Crushed naphthaline is often sprinkled over the floor for the same purpose. It has a most offensive smell, does little or nothing to destroy the unhatched moths and, therefore, cannot be recommended.

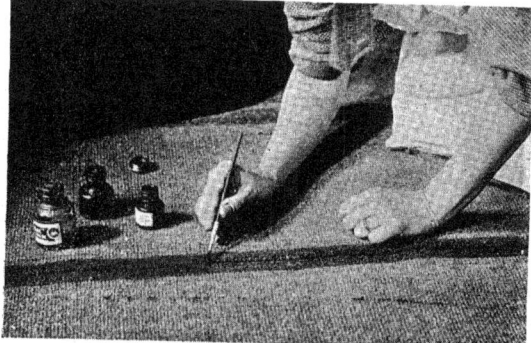

Fig. 3.—Painting the Threadbare Portion of a Hair Carpet to make it Match the Rest.

Obtain some bottles of ink of the colours possessed by the carpet, and fill in the design with a small paint brush.

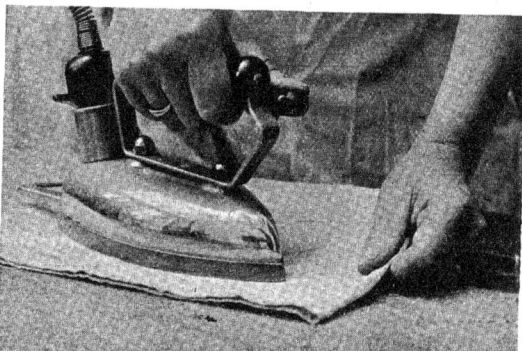

Fig. 4.—A Practical Method of Destroying Moth in a Carpet

Wring out a cloth in a bowl of hot water to which a tablespoonful of liquid ammonia has been added. Place it flat on the carpet and go over the cloth with a hot iron until dry.

SIMPLE METHODS OF REJUVENATING CARPETS

Spots and Stains.

All sorts of things, from ink to fruit-juice and tar are liable to be spilt on carpets. In all cases the secret of success lies in dealing with them without any loss of time. Here are some useful suggestions.

Ink.—When ink is spilt, soak up as much as possible with clean blotting paper; then flood with milk and rub with a clean flannel.

Tar.—While still soft, rub the tar with lard, then lift up as much of it as possible with the blade of a knife. Apply more lard and continue until all the tar has disappeared. Then wash the place with hot water and soap flakes.

Tea and Coffee Stains.—Wash the part with warm water in which a little borax is dissolved.

Grease Spots.—Without loss of time, soak up as much of the grease as possible with clean blotting paper. Then, follow with blotting paper on which a hot iron is pressed. Lastly, rub the area with a piece of cloth dipped in spirits of turpentine.

Fruit Stains.—These are troublesome, yielding erratically to treatment. However, the best plan is to rub them with spirits of wine containing a few drops of ammonia.

Soot.—Avoid anything which forces the soot to cling to the carpet; therefore, do not rub it. Merely sprinkle salt over the soot and flick the mixture of soot and salt into a dustpan. If any marks are left, wash them with hot water and soap flakes.

Mending Carpets.

Carpets often require sewing. No special difficulty is presented by this work, except that a carpet is an awkward thing to handle. To overcome this trouble, place the bulk of the carpet on a table and draw the remainder so that it hangs over the back of a chair which is placed about two feet away from the table. Arrange the part that needs mending so that it comes between the table and the chair. In this way, it is a simple matter to pass the stitches from the upper to the under surface.

Suppose that a piece of red-hot coal has fallen out of the fire and burnt a small hole in the carpet. Obtain some 4- or 5-ply wool of the requisite colour, arrange the carpet over the table and chair, as suggested, then fill in the damaged part with French knots. Or suppose that strips in the weave of a chenille Axminster have broken away and left a rib of string. Again, arrange the carpet as described and sew the strips of chenille in their original positions. Whatever it is that needs sewing can be readily performed while the carpet is arranged in this manner.

FITTING A NEW RUBBER TYRE TO A PRAM WHEEL

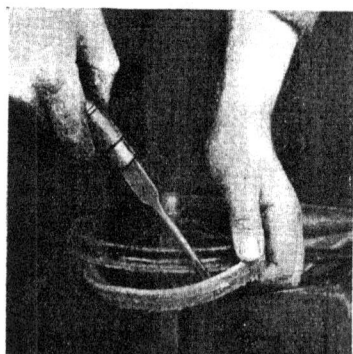

Fig. 1.—First remove the old Tyre, using a screwdriver if necessary to lever the Tyre off.

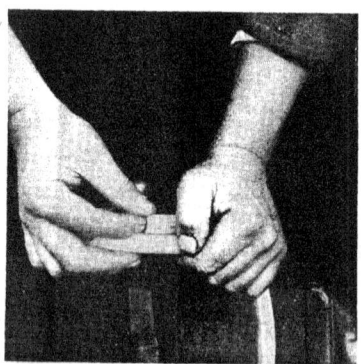

Fig. 2.—Then measure the new length of Tyre round the Wheel, leaving about 1½ inch overlap.

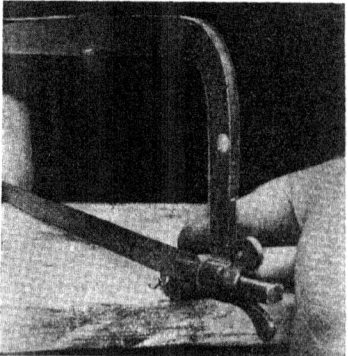

Fig. 3.—The Rubber is now sawn off from the overlapping pieces, revealing the Spiral Wire.

WHEN the rubber tyre on a pram wheel has become badly worn and keeps on coming off, it should be replaced by a new tyre. As wheels vary a good deal in size, the most convenient method is to buy a length of the special tubing sold for pram tyres, which has a spiral wire in the centre.

First remove the old tyre, using a screwdriver if necessary, then measure round the wheel with a length of new tyre, allowing about 1½ inch overlap each side. The next thing is to saw the rubber off from the overlapping pieces, which will reveal the spiral wire.

Screwing the Ends Together.

The ends are now screwed together,

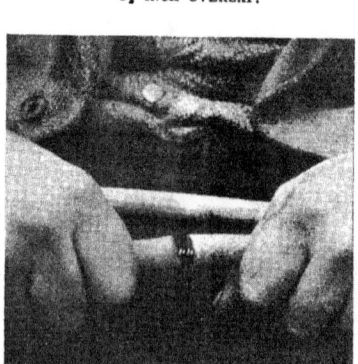

Fig. 4.—Before screwing the two ends together give the Rubber several twists in the opposite direction of the thread

thus forming the tyre. One thing must be remembered, namely, that as screwing the tyre causes the rubber to coil itself up, it will naturally uncoil itself again as soon as it is let go. To avoid this, screw up the rubber in the opposite direction of the thread before starting the screwing operation. The rubber will then unscrew itself as the two wires are screwed into each other.

If a vice is available it will be found convenient to fix one end in the vice and then screw the other end on it.

When the tyre is completed it will be found quite easy to force it on to the wheel.

Painting Ironwork

It is not so widely realised as it should be how great is the annual loss caused by the corrosion of metals used in building. One authority has estimated it at over £500,000,000.

Scientists tell us that absolutely pure air does not attack iron or steel at all, but this knowledge is of small interest because the atmosphere about us is never quite pure. It always contains various agents which act detrimentally, causing rust and corrosion.

Therefore it is imperative that all iron and steel used in the construction of buildings, and exposed to these harmful influences, should be kept properly protected by means of paint.

General Principles.

It is equally necessary that the paint should be of the right kind, that it should be properly applied, and that it should be renewed from time to time. And the time that will elapse before repainting is necessary will largely depend upon the manner in which the previous painting has been done.

Corrosion proceeds rapidly. Nor is it very easy to stop it when once it has begun. Consequently, it is in the interest of every householder or owner of property to see that it does not begin, for this is easier and more economical than checking it.

This is illustrated by the fact that, if rust be painted over, it by no means follows that further rusting is prevented. Indeed, it may be accelerated, for it is quite possible, and it often happens, that paint is applied (sometimes in an inefficient manner) and then, within a comparatively short time, the paint and rust fall away in flakes.

From all this it follows that, if corrosion has unfortunately been allowed to begin, all traces of that corrosion must be completely removed before painting is proceeded with.

The exposed external ironwork of a house generally consists of rain-water pipes, gutters and, often, metal gates, railings, ventilating grids and the like. Sometimes there are exposed steel beams or a corrugated-iron building, such as a garage or tool shed.

The New House.

In the case of a new house being erected, it is in the owner's interest to insist that structural ironwork be painted at least one coat before delivery to the site. This, while being by no means sufficient for permanent protection, will prevent deterioration for the time being. But further coats should be added as soon as may be practicable.

The Occupied House.

But what is most likely to concern us is the ironwork of the house wherein we live, and this will, from time to time, require repainting. And we will suppose that the time for such a renovation has arrived. How should we proceed?

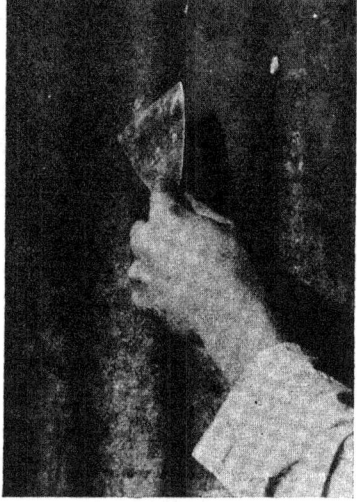

Fig. 1.—ALL LOOSE RUST MUST FIRST BE SCRAPED OFF THE METAL SURFACE.
A painter's scraper will be found useful for this purpose.

The first thing to do is to ascertain whether any replacements are required. There may be a cracked length of rain-water pipe or gutter, or a new length of iron railing may be needed.

The new articles or section may come to us unpainted or, if painted, it may have been with a mere wash of paint of poor quality. The first thing to be done, therefore, is to prepare it for painting.

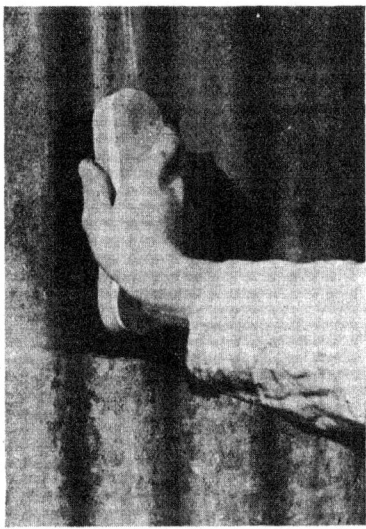

Fig. 2.—RUSTY IRON SHEETING CAN BE CLEANED BY MEANS OF A WIRE BRUSH.

Preparation.

A vigorous rubbing with a coarse-grade sandpaper may be sufficient to remove a slight film of rust or any loose paint.

But, if the article has been in store for some time, and the rusting is considerable, it will be necessary to use a wire brush which, as its name implies, is a brush containing wire, instead of hair, strands. In the case of railings, a strong knife or chisel will be required for getting well into the interstices or more intricate parts.

Similar preparation will be required by the older ironwork already part of the structure of the house, the amount and kind of such preparation depending upon its condition. Should any portion have been so neglected that corrosion is far advanced, it may be necessary to use a hammer or file to remove the scale.

Whatever the amount of rust present, it must be completely removed, down to the bare metal. Otherwise, painting will be practically a waste of time and money.

The Priming.

Next, all loose dust must be brushed from the work and the first coat of paint applied. This first coat is called the "priming" and, in all kinds of painting, the priming coat is important, but never so much so as in the case of metal.

It has to serve three purposes. It has to play its part in the protection of the surface from further attacks from the atmosphere, it has to provide a firm foundation or anchorage for later coats and, finally and most important of all, it should possess a positive power to prevent rust.

Much research has been devoted to devising paints having this last-mentioned quality, and there are several for which it is claimed that they are effective. But some of them are still in the experimental stage, and there is a consensus of opinion that, for priming ironwork, there is nothing superior to, if as good as, a red-lead paint.

Red Lead.

Red lead certainly does possess the quality of preventing rust. It dries extremely hard, and it also needs less assistance, in the form of added driers, to make it dry. Indeed, a mixture of red lead, either dry or in thick paste form, with boiled linseed oil, needs no added drier at all. But, if raw linseed oil alone is used to thin the paint, a small quantity of drier will require to be added.

The writer personally prefers to use a mixture of raw and boiled linseed oil as a thinner for red-lead priming when used on structural metal, and recommends the following proportions:—

Genuine red-lead paste . 14 lbs.
Genuine raw linseed oil . 1 pint.
Genuine boiled linseed oil . 1 pint.

With such a mixture no driers will be necessary. And the quantity mentioned will cover about 350 square feet of surface one coat.

Any paint merchant will make up such a paint, but, as red-lead paints are comparatively quick setting, they should be kept well stirred and should be used as soon as conveniently possible after they are mixed.

How to Apply Red-lead Priming.

Red-lead priming should not be applied too thinly, and care should be taken to brush it well into all hollows or irregularities of surface, particularly at joints or around bolt heads and rivets.

Applying the Paint.

Any kind of brush, being of convenient size and having moderately stiff bristles, is suitable for applying the paint. The important thing is to see that the surface is completely covered, and the best assurance of this is thorough brushing, so as to avoid pinholes or missed parts.

Following Coats.

When the priming coat is completely dry and hard, other coats may be applied. If an interval of, say, twenty-four hours can be allowed for this hardening, all the better.

On new or previously unpainted ironwork, a total of three coats is desirable. One of these, the "priming," has just been described.

In the case of existing ironwork which has been previously painted, perhaps several times, all parts where the old paint has decayed, or which show the slightest sign of rust, should be prepared and coated with the red-lead priming, as described above. If, however, the old paint film is in good condition and no signs of rust are anywhere visible, the red-lead priming can be omitted, and two coats of paint will be sufficient.

What these coats, or in the case of primed work, the second and third coats, of paint shall be made from will depend, to some extent, upon the choice of a finishing colour.

Alternative Materials.

What are called "bitumastic" paints, containing a certain proportion of bitumen in their composition, are sometimes used on metalwork, and they often possess considerable protective quality. But the range of shades obtainable is comparatively limited, and they have the disadvantage that they may affect the colour of other kinds of paint subsequently applied.

Aluminium paint is also suitable for coating iron and steel, and is sometimes used for street lamps and railings.

Fig. 3.—IF ANY PARTS OF THE METAL HAVE BEEN AFFECTED BY CORROSION, THEY MUST BE TREATED WITH RED-LEAD PRIMING.

But, here again, we are even more limited in choice, practically to the natural shade of the aluminium from which they are made.

For general painting purposes, the best course to adopt is to purchase the appropriate quantity of a genuine ready-mixed tinted white lead paint in the shade required, making sure that it is labelled as being made according to the British Standard Specification for this type of paint.

This saves all the trouble of mixing, the cost is no greater than if we compounded the material ourselves, and we may be assured of getting a paint possessing the maximum possible of enduring quality.

Fig. 4.—APPLYING THE FIRST COAT OF PAINT. Painting should always be done when the weather is dry.

Quantities Required.

The amount required to cover a given area of surface will depend, to some small extent, upon the colour selected, for pigments vary somewhat in weight and spreading quality, but, in any case, it will go rather further than the comparatively heavy red-lead priming. A 14-lb. tin of Ready Mixed Tinted White Lead Paint will probably be sufficient to cover about 460 square feet of surface one coat.

Galvanised Iron.

This kind of metal, which is generally in the form of sheets, requires a rather special treatment. When new the surface is so extremely smooth that it does not give a satisfactory "key" to paint.

If, however, it can be left unpainted for, say, the first six months of its life, a natural weathering process takes place, resulting in a slight roughness which provides the necessary "key."

Should it be necessary to paint quite new galvanised iron the surface can be artificially weathered. This is done by giving it a coat of a solution made by dissolving chloride or acetate of copper in the proportion of 8 ozs. to the gallon, in water.

A coat of this solution is applied, allowed to remain for, say, two days, and is then swilled off with clean water. The iron is then allowed to become thoroughly dry, after which painting can proceed as previously described.

Old galvanised iron which has been left unpainted too long will probably have developed patches of rust. In such a case, thorough cleaning and the treatment of the exposed areas by the means already described will be called for. And the priming of such parts with red-lead paint is a necessary part of the process of renovation and protection.

Additional Hints.

In the painting of ironwork it is care rather than skill that is called for. As already pointed out, thorough cleaning before painting is imperative if good results are to be obtained.

Should any grease be present it must be removed or the paint will not dry. This removal can be effected with any cheap solvent, such as naphtha, turpentine or paraffin.

Painting should always be done when the weather is dry. No paint will adhere properly to a moist surface.

In priming galvanised iron, the red-lead paint may be used slightly thinner than on other types of ironwork so as to make sure that there is a complete penetration of even the smallest irregularity of surface. This is assisted by thoroughly brushing the paint in every direction.

RUSTIC WORK IN THE GARDEN

THERE is probably no method of decorating a garden which is so successful as the introduction of rustic work, since it retains the natural elements and creates that old-world touch which is so admired. Furthermore, the cost is quite within the pocket of the amateur, and one can start in a small way and gradually add to the rustic work.

Purchasing and Cost.

The price naturally varies in different parts of the country, but lengths can generally be bought for $1\frac{1}{2}d.—2d.$ per foot. In selecting the poles, good stout ones should in every case be chosen. It is mistaken economy to buy light thin ones, even though they may be very much cheaper. This is proved by the large amount of rustic work which one sees, that has fallen down or at an angle, or otherwise looks a disgrace, solely because very thin poles were used. Rustic work carefully erected and made from stout poles will easily last for many years. Poles should be chosen which look "healthy," and ones to which the bark is firmly adhering.

The Secret of Successful Rustic Work.

There is one fundamental point on which the successful erection of all rustic work is based, and that is that under no circumstances must the fancy work introduced be used as a means of stabilising or steadying the structure. The main essential pieces should stand up on their own. Every upright should stand firmly by itself and should not rely for support on its neighbour through the intermediary of fancy cross pieces. Thus in Fig. 1 a man should be able to swing from cross-bar A without undue strain being put on the uprights, so that when the structure is complete, as in Fig. 2, a really stable arch results.

UPRIGHTS
Depth to be Buried.

These should be buried in the ground to a depth equal to a quarter of the total height of the pole. Thus a pole which is to stand 6 feet out of the ground should be buried to a depth of 2 feet.

Preliminary Treatment.

The pole before burying must first be treated to a depth equal to 6 inches above that to which it will be buried; thus the pole in the preceding paragraph must be treated for 2 feet 6 inches. The usual method is to paint with tar, which can be obtained through the local ironmonger. The tar must be warmed before use in order to make it flow sufficiently easily to be brushed. It is of the utmost importance to ensure that the tar is worked well into the crevices of the bark and the pores of the wood, not forgetting the bottom of the pole. After this has been completed there should be a continuous film of tar about $\frac{1}{16}$ inch thick over the whole of the treated portion of the pole.

Three Methods of using Bitumen.

Slightly more expensive, but far more effective, since, unlike tar, it does not deteriorate in course of time, is to paint the poles for the required depth, as above, with bitumen. For this there are three methods available, namely :—

(1) Use solid bitumen, after it has been melted, by heating—one coat about $\frac{1}{16}$ inch thick is sufficient;

(2) Apply two or three coats of a bituminous emulsion, allowing each coat to dry before the next is applied; and

(3) Give two or three coats of a bituminous paint as in (2).

Creosote should not be used, unless it can be impregnated as described in the article on page 88.

Pre-treatment of Poles.

Owing to the fact that after several years rustic work tends to shed its bark, a few people prefer to strip off all the bark before erection, and to give the wood underneath a coat of varnish. Unless one is constructing some high-class garden furniture, such as seats, etc., this is not recommended, since not only does it entail much extra labour, but also most of the "rustic" effect is lost; furthermore, after a period of years, one

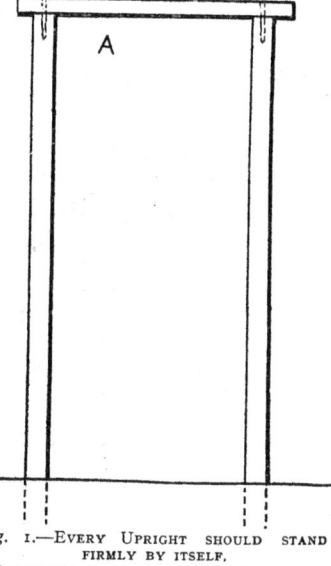

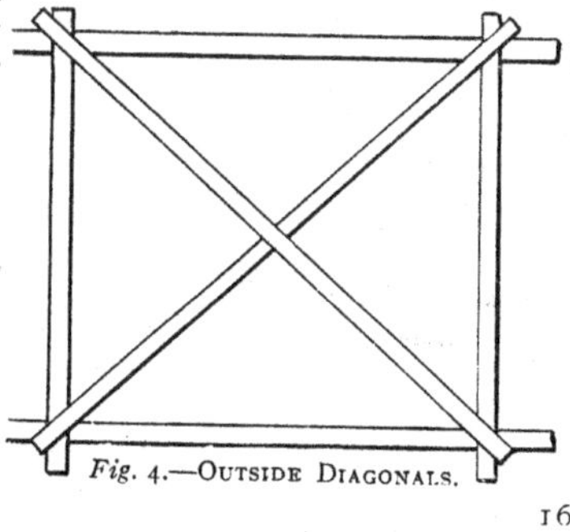

Fig. 1.—EVERY UPRIGHT SHOULD STAND FIRMLY BY ITSELF.

A man should be able to swing from crossbar A without putting undue strain on the uprights.

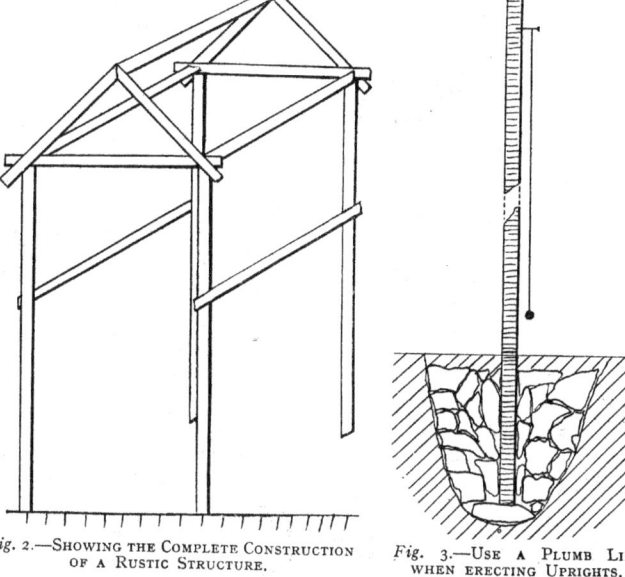

Fig. 2.—SHOWING THE COMPLETE CONSTRUCTION OF A RUSTIC STRUCTURE.

Fig. 3.—USE A PLUMB LINE WHEN ERECTING UPRIGHTS.

Fig. 4.—OUTSIDE DIAGONALS.

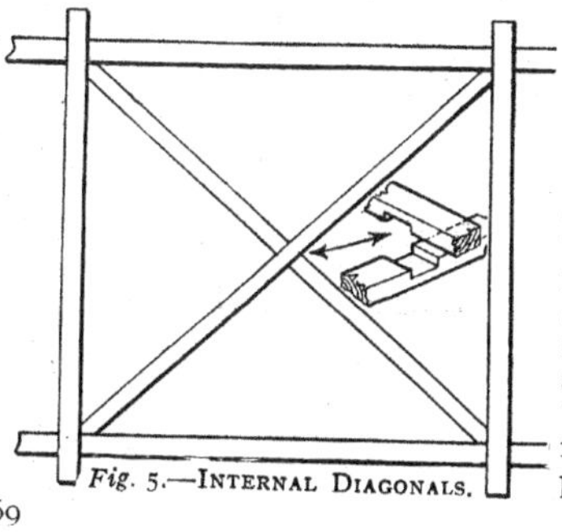

Fig. 5.—INTERNAL DIAGONALS.

Fig. 5A.—(Left) THE SIMPLEST TYPE OF GARDEN BENCH SEAT.

This consists of a flat top and either four or two legs; the latter if a couple of logs of sufficiently large diameter are available; four if such diameters cannot run to more than 3 or 4 inches, and forked if such branching pieces can be spared. Note that the top of the seat should be about 16 inches from the ground.

Fig. 5B.—(Right) DESIGN FOR A GARDEN SEAT WITH ARM RESTS.

In this design fairly small timber is used. The top of the seat is made from two planks and the method of assembly is clearly shown in the two views.

Fig. 5C.—(Left) DESIGN FOR AN ARTISTIC RUSTIC TABLE FOR THE GARDEN.

For tables the tops are formed from planks sawn from tree trunks. When two planks are used, one of the natural edges on each plank must be sawn away to form a straight joint between the two. Battens will be needed which can be made from small branch wood, sawn longitudinally.

RUSTIC WORK IN THE GARDEN

Fig. 6.—ONE OF THE MANY ATTRACTIVE USES FOR RUSTIC WORK. Used as a dividing line or boundary to a path.

Fig. 7.—ANOTHER ARRANGEMENT OF RUSTIC WORK FOR MAKING A BOUNDARY TO A PATH OR MARKING A DIVIDING LINE.

could, if one wished for a change, strip the bark from the work *in situ*, and then varnish. A fairly slow drying varnish should be used. The bark is stripped by making one longitudinal cut with a sharp knife, to the depth of the bark, down the length of the pole and then several cuts at intervals round the circumference of the pole. The bark can then be eased off.

Erection.

First dig a hole to a depth of 3 inches more than that to which the pole is to be buried. Place in the bottom of the hole one large stone, 3 inches thick, or, alternatively, a 3-inch layer of stones, well rammed tight. Now place the pole resting on the stone in the bottom of the hole and get an assistant to hold it upright. Carefully pack stones in the hole around the pole. As each layer is put in the larger stones should be put around the outside and the

Fig. 8.—RUSTIC WORK USED AS AN ATTRACTIVE SURROUND FOR A LARGE SHRUB.

smaller ones used as wedges to tighten the pole (see Fig. 3). Preferably small stones should be used for filling in between the larger ones, or, if these are not available, then the loam which has been removed when digging the hole can be used.

The main essential around the buried portion of the pole is good drainage, in order to stop the rainwater from hanging around the base of the pole and, in time, rotting it. This latter is possible, since when ramming the stones in the hole it is practically impossible to avoid scraping off small pieces of the protective paint.

Use a Plumb Line.

A plumb line should always be used to ensure that the uprights are not sloping at an angle. One can easily be constructed by attaching a weight to a piece of string, this should be attached to the pole by means of a long nail driven in just sufficiently to hold it (see Fig. 3).

Fig. 9.—SOME RUSTIC ORNAMENTATION THAT WILL BE WELL WORTH CONSTRUCTING.

Showing a garden seat about 5 feet long and 1½ feet high. The end pieces are first cuts of a large tree.

Fig. 10.—SOME RUSTIC ORNAMENTATION THAT WILL BE WELL WORTH CONSTRUCTING.

A tea-table made from a section cut from the trunk of a tree. See Fig. 13 for details of construction.

Fig. 11.—SOME RUSTIC ORNAMENTATION THAT WILL BE WELL WORTH CONSTRUCTING.

A bird haven which might be constructed on rather similar lines to the tea-table.

RUSTIC WORK IN THE GARDEN

Fig. 11A.—Another Garden Seat Built for Comfort.

Fig 11B.—Another Design for a Rustic Table.
The rails are notched into the legs as shown and secured with round-headed bolts.

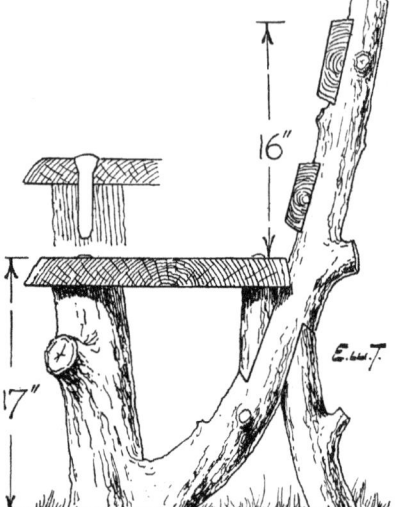

Fig. 11C.—Another Seat with Back but without Arms Rests.
Note the oak-nail joint.

Fig. 11E.—Rustic Framework for a Movable Sun Shelter.
Such a shelter would be made up of very light material with the exception of the half-round rails which rest upon the ground. The blind material of the usual green or striped kind will be provided with rings to slip over hooks screwed into the top front horizontal rail and hang down over the back rail.

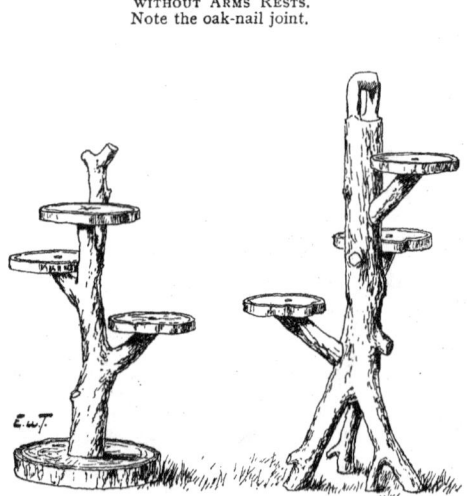

Fig. 11D.—Two suggested Designs for Cake Stands.

USES

Rustic work can be classed under the following headings:—
(1) Arches.
(2) Screens and supports for climbing or rambling plants.
(3) Fences—Boundary.
(4) Specialistic work—garden furniture, etc.

Arches.

Whatever fancy work is included afterwards, the principle of arch construction is shown in Fig. 1. The uprights for this should be not less than 2¾ inches diameter at the base and not less than 2¼ inches diameter at the top. They should be 6 feet 6 inches above ground (say 8 feet 6 inches in all). If the arch is placed on a step, then care must be taken to add the height of the step to that of the uprights, or one will not be able to walk up the step without bending down.

Keep to Bold Long Lengths.

When deciding on the decorative part of the rustic work, the amateur is in all cases strongly advised against putting in a lot of small pieces; unless these latter are extremely well done and infinite care has been taken in their cutting and fitting, a poor-looking job will result, whereas if the fancy work is kept to bold long lengths an imposing-looking structure will result.

Outside Diagonals.

When the fancy work consists of the diagonals of a rectangle or square, it is much easier for the amateur, and in fact equally correct, to nail them both to the outside (see Fig. 4). If the length of the diagonals is sufficiently long, then they can usually be sprung sufficiently to allow for this, but otherwise lengths can always be found having a slight twist which will allow for such a construction.

Internal Diagonals.

Internal diagonals, as in Fig. 5, rarely look so well, but, if used, should be jointed at the centre, as in the illustration.

Nails used in all rustic work should be sufficiently long to go through the first piece and two-thirds through the second. In a case such as nailing A in Fig. 1 to the uprights, the nail should be of a length at least twice the diameter of A.

Screen and Supports for Climbing or Rambling Plants.

Rustic work used as a support for climbing or rambling plants is a useful means of dividing one part of a garden from another. A useful height is 5 feet 6 inches above the ground, and a suggested design is given in Fig. 12.

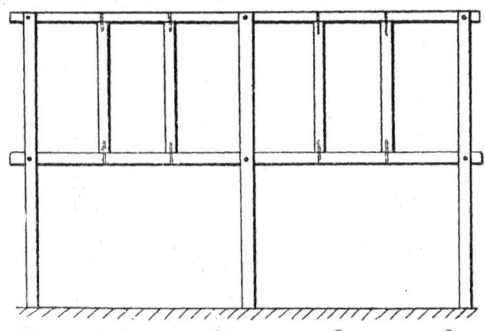

Fig. 12.—A Suggested Design for a Screen and Support for Climbing and Rambling Plants.

Fences—Boundaries.

Here we have rustic work used purely for decorative purposes. Its function is simply as a dividing line, as clearly indicated in Figs. 6, 7, 8. In Figs. 6 and 7 we have it as a boundary for a path, while in Fig. 8 it makes a peculiarly attractive surround for a large shrub.

Specialistic Work—Garden Furniture, etc.

There is ample scope for the design by the amateur of rustic garden furniture. A few examples are shown in Figs. 9, 10, 11.

A Garden Seat.

Fig. 9 shows a garden seat constructed as follows:—

The end pieces are first cuts (from a sawmills) of a large tree. They consist of the bark attached to a minimum of wood. The seat is a plank cut from a smaller tree with the bark still adhering to the edges. The seat in the photograph is about 5 feet long and 1 foot 6 inches high.

Attractive Tea-table.

Fig. 5 is a tea-table made from a section cut from the trunk of a tree; it is supported on a length cut from an ordinary rustic work pole. Details of construction are shown in Fig. 13.

Fig. 11 shows a simply constructed bird haven.

While the actual design of the bird haven can well be left to the ingenuity of the amateur, it should always consist of a base or floor board firmly attached to the top of a pole. The easiest and most rustic looking construction for the former is a transverse section about 1½ inches thick, cut from the trunk of a tree, as previously suggested for the top of the rustic table, while the latter should be a rustic pole of a minimum diameter of 3 inches. Suggestions for the actual walls of the haven are (a) longitudinal first cuts from the tree trunk, (b) short lengths of rustic pole nailed together side by side.

GENERAL NOTES

The following will help the amateur in the erection of his rustic work:—

(1) The best time to erect rustic work is when the ground is wet and soft, since it is then much easier to dig the holes for the foundation of upright poles.

(2) When nailing the rustic work, do not use the hammer direct on the head of the nail right up to the finish of driving it in, since by doing so it is definite that the bark would be seriously injured. It is better to drive in the last ½ inch of the nail by means of a nail punch, which should be held securely against the head of the nail whilst it itself is being hit.

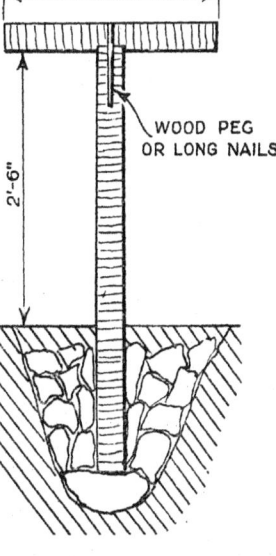

Fig. 13.—Details for the Construction of a Simple Tea-table made from Rustic Work.

(3) To estimate the quantity of rustic poles required sketch on paper the actual rustic work which it is proposed to erect. Then mark against each of the poles in the sketch its length. Next, find out from the local supplier the length of the poles which he has available; then count up the number of uprights and see what lengths will be over, after they have been cut off, e.g., if eight uprights are required 8 feet long, and the average length of the poles which can be obtained is 12 feet, then there will be to spare eight 4-feet lengths. These can be used for the fancy work.

Now count up the total length of the main horizontal pieces in the structure. These lengths must be purchased in addition to the poles already ordered for the uprights. The amount of extra timber to be purchased for fancy work over and above the pieces which will be over from the uprights, depends entirely upon the type of structure being erected and the amount of fancy work which is being put in.

Repairing and Sharpening Scissors

MANY people who make a regular practice of keeping their knives sharp would never think of extending the same treatment to their scissors. Yet the latter require just as much attention if they are to do their work efficiently.

When a pair of scissors fails to cut properly, the cause usually lies in one of two directions. Either the edges are blunt or the pivot is loose.

A Loose Pivot.

Let us consider the case of a loose pivot first, as it provides the most frequent reason why a pair of scissors will not cut satisfactorily. Grip the scissors in both hands and open the blades wide. If there is more than a slight amount of "play" on the pivot, it is definite proof that the rivet is loose. If the rivet is loose, it will not hold the two blades together. There will be, in fact, a certain amount of space between them. Into this space will fold any material that is brought to the scissors, and the folding will prevent a cut being made. Thus, however sharp the blades may be, the scissors will not cut properly if the pivot is loose.

To tighten the pivot is a very simple

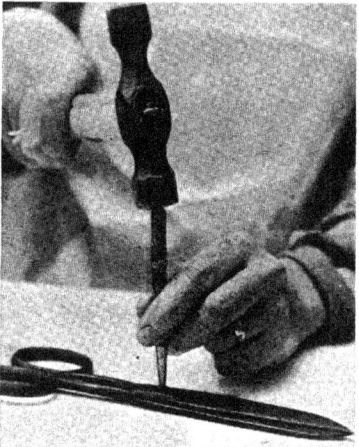

Fig. 1.—Scissors will not cut properly if the Pivot is Loose.

To tighten the pivot use a hammer and a punch.

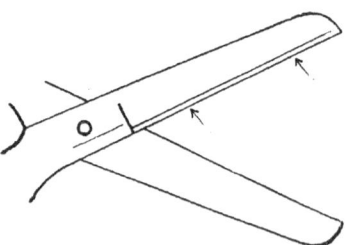

Fig. 2.—The Bevelled Edge that requires Sharpening is shown by the Arrows.

business. If the pivot is screw-headed, *i.e.*, if it has a groove across the head to take a screw-driver, give it a slight turn first. Then turn the head over, place it on a flat piece of iron, with blades closed, and tap gently with a hammer on the other end of the rivet. Tap so that the soft metal is spread out. The spreading of the metal will shorten the length of the rivet and thus tighten up the blades of the scissors. A very little adjustment will make a considerable differ-

ence to the scissors, and one tap too many may tighten the blades so that they will not open or close. Therefore, test the opening and shutting after every two or three taps.

When Sharpening is needed.

If a pair of scissors be examined, it will be noted that each blade has a flat side, and that the other side is separated from it by a bevelled edge. It is this bevelled edge that is faulty when the scissors become blunt. To give any attention to this bevelled edge is almost impossible while the two blades are hinged together. Therefore, the first thing is to separate them by taking out the pivot.

To take out the pivot, open the blades, turn them so that the tail of the pivot is uppermost, and then file round the tail and so remove the burred edge. When this is done, the pivot will drop out and the blades become separated.

It may be easier to file away all the upstanding part of the tail of the pivot, instead of merely filing round it, as we suggest; but, if this is done, the pivot is made so short that it cannot be used again, and a new one must be found to replace it. By our method, the same pivot can be used over and over again.

Using an Oilstone.

If the scissors are merely dull and not exceedingly blunt, place a few drops of oil on the oilstone, hold one of the blades by the tip and the heel, so that the bevelled edge lies flat on the stone, then draw it from end to end along the stone. Have the stone so that one of the short ends is close to you, the other short end farthest from you; begin the stroke at the further end and complete it at nearer end. Then lift the blade, place it again on the further end, and make a second stroke. Continue in this way until the bevel has been perfected. Follow by treating the other blade in the same way.

The important thing to remember is that the only part to touch the oilstone is the bevel and that the flat side must not be ground at all. If anything is done to this side the proper closing of the scissors may be ruined.

Using a Grindstone.

When scissors have been badly treated or used excessively, the bevel may be in such a state that

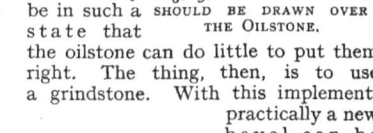

Fig. 3.—How the Blade should be drawn over the Oilstone.

the oilstone can do little to put them right. The thing, then, is to use a grindstone. With this implement, practically a new bevel can be formed, but it is important to see that the new one bears exactly the same angle to the flat side as did the old one. Turn the grindstone slowly, and be careful not to overheat the metal. If the metal becomes warm, put the blade on one side for a few moments and attend to the other blade.

Fig. 4.—The Correct Method of holding the Blade on the Oilstone.

Fig. 5.—Repairing the Bevel of the Blade by means of the Grindstone.

When the grindstone has provided the new bevels, finish them off on the oilstone, as already described.

Setting the Blades.

Although it is usually sufficient to renew the edge of the blades, as here described, to make a pair of scissors cut properly, it must be admitted that, for the finest precision, some attention should be given to their setting.

To understand what the setting actually is puzzles many people; but it may be explained in this way. Take a pair of scissors that are known to do their work efficiently—new ones, for preference. Hold them up to the eye level and look towards the light. It will be noticed, when the blades are completely closed, that the edges do not touch all the way along. They do touch, however, at the tips and at the pivot; but there is a very narrow bowed space between these limits. The space is widest half-way along the blades, and it gradually tapers down to nothing as the above limits are reached. Such scissors are properly set.

Now turn to the scissors that are under repair. If they show the same features, there is obviously no need to alter their setting; but if they show a very wide gap or no gap at all, something must be done to them. Naturally, it is necessary to make this test before the pivot is knocked out and the blades separated.

A moment's thought will show that when the gap is too wide, each blade must be flattened a fractional amount, and when there is too little gap, they must be arched. Either of these conditions may be performed by putting the blade on an anvil or vice and tapping gently with a hammer. It must be observed that a very little adjustment is all that is needed in even the worst cases.

Reassembling the Scissors.

It may be that, while filing away the burr of the tail of the pivot, the face of the blade was considerably scored. If so, the first thing is to file the surface smooth. That done, the two blades are put together, the rivet is slipped into the pivot holes, and the scissors are rested on a flat piece of metal, the cap of the rivet being underneath. Then, with a hammer and a punch, the tail of the rivet is burred over so that it grips the two blades together. While doing this, follow the instructions, given above, regarding the method of tightening the pivot.

Should the rivet be mislaid or, for any reason, a new one is necessary, cut down a large French nail to the requisite length. It will serve the purpose quite well.

NOTES ON GARDEN SHEARS

These are merely scissors on a larger scale, for, as far as the cutting action is concerned, they are exactly the same. To sharpen them, therefore, the blades must be separated; but as a rule there is no rivet. With them, the blades are held together by means of a nut and spring washer, acting on a bolt.

A professional will renew the cutting edge by using a large grindstone. As few amateurs will possess a stone large enough for the purpose, some other means must be resorted to. A good plan is to fix the blade in the jaws of a vice and to use a fairly coarse file for providing the necessary edge. Naturally, the blade will be moved along in the vice as the filing of the edge proceeds from tip to shoulder. As with ordinary scissors, the flat face of the blades must not be ground or filed. That is why the practice of using a hone first on the top and then on the underneath of the blades is wrong; yet many people resort to this method. All that may be done is to renew the bevel, exactly as has been already explained for ordinary scissors.

Reassembling the Blades.

In reassembling the blades, the bolt goes through the two holes first; then the spring washer is fitted to the tail-end of the bolt, and the nut is twisted on to the washer, so as to compress it. Usually, when a pair of shears cause annoyance by working loose, it will be found that the spring washer has not been fitted. The remedy is, of course, to fit one, when, as often as not, the trouble entirely disappears. Occasionally, the thread on the bolt or in the nut has worn to such an extent that it will not hold. In such cases, it is a simple matter to fit a new nut and bolt. The old spring washer can, generally, be used indefinitely.

Fixing a loose Wooden Handle.

When a pair of garden shears have seen much service, it sometimes happens that one of the wooden handles develops the knack of dropping off. A temporary method of curing the fault is to wind a piece of paper round the metal stub and to force it into the wooden handle. This serves for a while, but not for long. A much better method is to mix plenty of sawdust with hot glue and to fill the cavity in the handle with it; then to ram the metal stub into the cavity. This plan usually answers indefinitely.

Rust.

Probably shears become blunt more because they are allowed to become rusty than through constant cutting. They are used on wet grass and similar vegetation and are then put away without any attention. It should be made a regular habit every time a pair of shears are put away to wipe the blades and then to run a streak of lubricating oil along the bevels. There is no need to see that every part is covered, as the oil has remarkable powers of creeping.

LEATHER REVIVER AND ITS USE

LEATHER reviver is a shellac solution into which analine dyes are dissolved to produce varying shades of colour such as blue, green, crimson, yellow, brown, black, etc. The use of this material is limited, and, as the name implies, can only be used on leather, and articles where leather is used, such as leather-covered suites, attaché cases, handbags, and the interior linings of motor cars, etc.

The material is mostly used by the skilled craftsman, who will produce results equal to new, although the amateur may with care and practice obtain quite good results.

Leather revivers are little used by the novice, perhaps because they either have never heard of such a material or that they think it is waste of time to try to renovate old leather articles, but a good many of these can be made to look like new, thereby saving expense. It may be of interest if we give a rough outline as to how the work is done by the craftsman on new work, followed by how the amateur should proceed to use the reviver for renovation.

First, the craftsman stains the leather to the desired colour, using a stain or dye of a special nature; when dry, this is followed with a coating of a leather varnish which dries from a semi to a bright finish according to the number of coats applied, the coating of varnish being more or less of a thin film which together with the particular ingredients of the varnish give to a large extent considerable elasticity.

For renovating, first remove all dirt and grease from the leather by washing with warm water and soap (no soda). When *perfectly dry* apply the reviver very thinly (not paint it on) with a brush or sponge. Always apply in a warm, dry atmosphere if possible. If necessary a second thin coating may be applied two or three hours after the first. If a brush is used purchase a camel hair mop size about No. 8; the best results, however, are obtained by using a small Turkey sponge, and the sponge should be charged with reviver, and then well squeezed so as just to allow dampness only. Then with light even pressure pass over the work, repeating the operation until the whole of the job has been treated, the repeated application of a too heavy coat may result in cracking. To clean brushes or sponges after use well wash in methylated spirit.

AN ATTRACTIVE EXPANDING

FULL CONSTRUCTIONAL DETAILS ARE GIVEN IN THIS ARTICLE FOR MAKING THIS SPLENDID BOOKCASE. IT IS SIMPLE TO MAKE, YET ITS BEAUTY WOULD ENHANCE ANY ROOM.

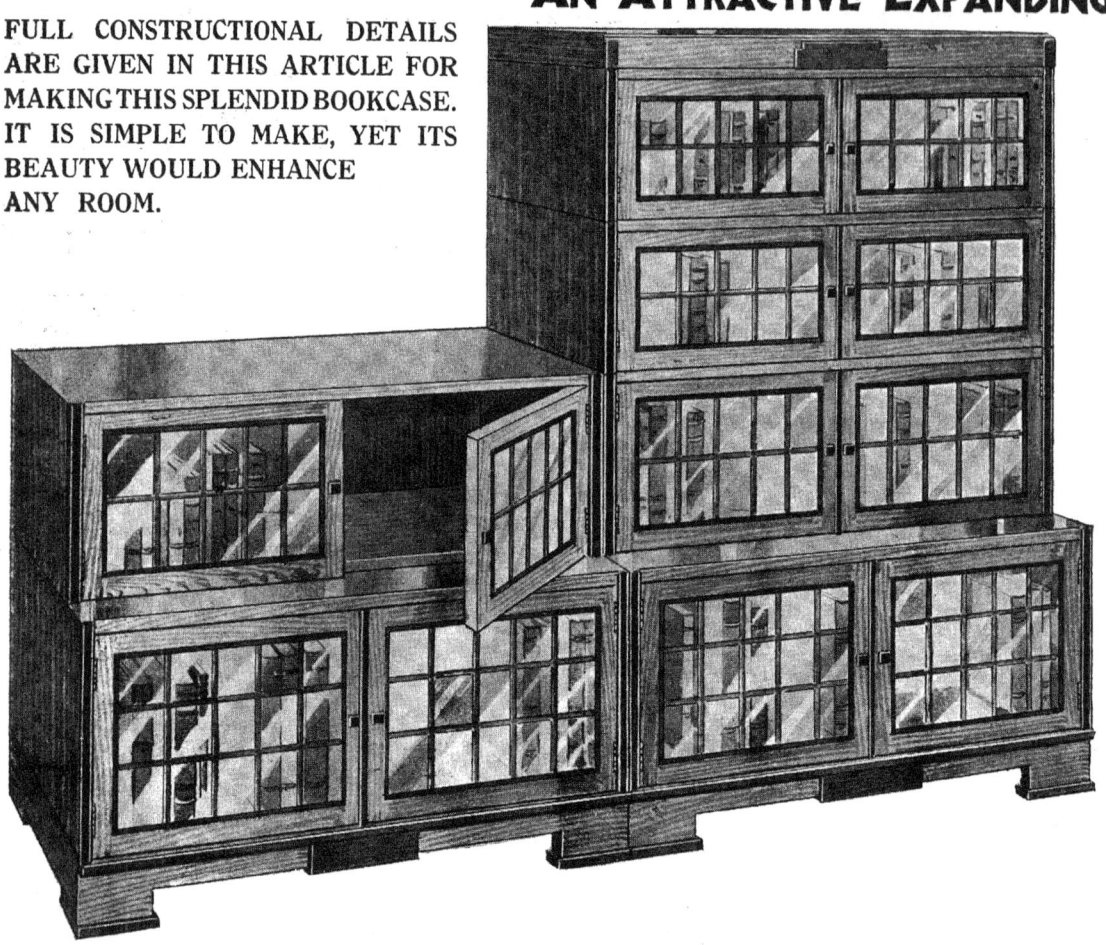

Fig. 1.—The great advantage of the Expanding Bookcase is that it can be added to at any time.

The advantages of the expanding bookcase are fairly obvious. It can be added to at any time without upsetting the general arrangement; there is little or no waste space; its cost is comparatively low since standardisation enables the labour involved to be cut down to a minimum; it is practically dustproof, so keeping the books in good condition; it is of attractive appearance; and it is suitable for every room, from a drawing-room to an office.

In the design in Figs. 1 and 2 we have kept simplicity of construction steadily in view. Any man handy with tools could undertake the work successfully. At the same time, readers who prefer to call in the local handy man will find that the job could be made economically.

Choice of Size.

In the accompanying diagrams we give details of three different sizes of bookcase; a small one for average handbooks; a medium size, which will accommodate both the average size and the rather larger book; and the large which holds the largest books likely to be in the possession of the average man.

It is a case in which the reader should use his discretion, choosing that which will best suit his library. The scheme we recommend is that shown in Fig. 1, in which all three sizes are used. However, if the reader has no really large books he may feel that the small and medium sizes will cover his requirements. It really makes no difference, except that in this case the plinth, which is made separately, must not be so deep. It will be noted from Figs. 1 and 3 that the largest size is deeper as well as higher. It is merely a matter of making the plinth $9\frac{7}{8}$ inches deep instead of $11\frac{7}{8}$ inches as given.

The Wood.

Oak is suggested as the most suitable wood to use, at any rate, for all the show parts. A soft wood could be used for bottoms and sides. Mahogany also would be in order. Certain of the parts, such as the upright mouldings, door mouldings, and the little panels in frieze and plinth would look well stained a darker colour. For a finish, French polish is recommended as being the most durable finish. As an alternative, wax polish could be used for an oak job.

Leaded Light Effect to Doors.

The doors are given a leaded light effect by the use of lead strips laid over the glass. Special strips of lead with a cement can be obtained from Messrs. Perma-Led, 4 Tulip Place, S.E.16, or from Messrs. Handicrafts Ltd., Weedington Road, Kentish Town, N.W.5.

Decide how many Units you will want.

Although the bookcase can be enlarged at any time, it is an advantage for the reader to decide at the outset how many units he will require,

OR SECTIONAL BOOKCASE

Fig. 2.—ONE OF THE COMPLETE SECTIONS.
The leaded light effect is produced by strips of lead laid over the glass.

because it is more economical to make a quantity at a time. He can cut all similar parts to length at the same time, cut all joints, and so on. He should also come to a decision as to the method of construction he intends to adopt for the doors.

Three different methods are given in Fig. 10. The dowelled joint at A has the advantage of simplicity in that the rails have merely to be cut square to length and holes for the dowels bored. For a really good job the mortise and tenon joint is best, as it gives maximum strength. C, in which the whole framework is made up of two thicknesses, is intended for those who wish to avoid cutting any special joints. It is not the best method, and it costs the most, but is reliable if carefully done. Note that the butt joints run in opposite directions in the two thicknesses.

Cutting List.

The following are *finished* sizes. Extra should be added to length and width for cutting out. In the door parts it is assumed that dowelled joints are being used. Extra should be allowed if the mortise and tenon joints are used.

Frieze.

Front and back, 2 pieces	2′ 11½″ × 2″ × ¾″.
Sides, 2 pieces	9⅞″ × 2″ × ¾″.
Top, 1 piece	3′ 0″ × 9⅜″ × ⅜″
Panel, 1 piece	7″ × 1¾″ × ⅛″.
Ornaments, 2 pieces	1¾″ × ¾″ × ⅛″

Small Bookcase.

Top, 1 piece	2′ 11½″ × 9⅞″ × ¾″.
Bottom, 1 piece	2′ 11½″ × 9″ × ¾″
Sides, 2 pieces	10½″ × 9⅞″ × ¾″.
Back, 1 piece	2′ 11½″ × 10″ × 3/16″. [ply.
Door Stiles, 4 pieces	9¾″ × 1¼″ × ⅞″.
Door Rails, 4 pieces	1′ 2¾″ × 1¼″ × ⅞″.
Moulding, 2 pieces	10½″ × ¾″ × ¼″.
Moulding, 1 piece	9¾″ × ⅜″ × 3/16″.
Moulding (door), 4 pieces	1′ 2¾″ × ¼″ × ¼″.
Moulding (door), 4 pieces	7¼″ × ¼″ × ¼″.

Medium Bookcase.

Top, 1 piece	2′ 11½″ × 9⅞″ × ¾″.
Bottom, 1 piece	2′ 11½″ × 9″ × ¾″.
Sides, 2 pieces	1′ 0½″ × 9⅞″ × ¾″.
Back, 1 piece	2′ 11½″ × 1′ 0″ × 3/16″ [ply.
Door Stiles, 4 pieces	11¾″ × 1¼″ × ⅞″.
Door Rails, 4 pieces	1′ 2¾″ × 1¼″ × ⅞″.
Moulding, 2 pieces	1′ 0½″ × ¾″ × ¼″.
Moulding, 1 piece	11¾″ × ⅜″ × 3/16″.
Moulding (door), 4 pieces	1′ 2¾″ × ¼″ × ¼″.
Moulding (door), 4 pieces	9¼″ × ¼″ × ¼″.

Large Bookcase.

Top, 1 piece	2′ 11½″ × 11⅞″ × ¾″.
Bottom 1 piece	2′ 11½″ × 11″ × ¾″.
Sides, 2 pieces	1′ 2½″ × 11⅞″ × ¾″.
Back, 1 piece	2′ 11½″ × 1′ 2″ × 3/16″ [ply.
Door Stiles, 4 pieces	1′ 1¾″ × 1¼″ × ⅞″.
Door Rails, 4 pieces	1′ 2¾″ × 1¼″ × ⅞″.
Moulding, 2 pieces	1′ 2½″ × ¾″ × ¼″.
Moulding, 1 piece	1′ 1¾″ × ⅜″ × 3/16″.
Moulding (door), 4 pieces	1′ 2¾″ × ¼″ × ¼″.
Moulding (door), 4 pieces	11¼″ × ¼″ × ¼″.

Plinth.

Front and Back, 2 pieces	3′ 0″ × 3¼″ × ¾″.
Sides, 2 pieces	11⅜″ × 3¾″ × ¾″.
Top length, 2 pieces	3′ 0″ × 2″ × ¾″.
Top sides, 2 pieces	7⅞″ × 2″ × ¾″.
Feet, 4 pieces	4¾″ × 2½″ × ½″.
Panel, 1 piece	7″ × 2″ × ⅛″.
Moulding, 1 piece	3′ 0″ × ¾″ × ¼″.

Dowels, corner blocks, and other small parts are not included. In addition, two pairs of 1½ or 1¾-inch hinges are required for each bookcase, and two knobs. Also perma-led and glass.

CONSTRUCTION

As the construction of the bookcases are the same in every case, we will take one of them only. It should be remembered, however, that when making sets, materials should all be marked out at the same time, so ensuring their being alike.

Details of the bookcase construction are given in Fig. 4. The sides are rebated as shown in the inset sketch, leaving a lap of ¼ inch. The top and bottom fit in these rebates, being glued and nailed. As the doors fit *beneath* the top and *in front of* the bottom, the latter is narrower than the top by the thickness of the doors (⅞ inch). To simplify the construction the rebates run right through, and little blocks are glued in at the front as shown in Fig. 4. These are hidden later by the applied moulding.

Marking Out.

To ensure the corresponding parts being the same size a sort of key should be made. This is shown in Fig. 5. The front edge and one end of, say, the top are planed square. A strip of wood is then prepared, and a block of wood glued and nailed to one end. The distance between the inner edge of the block and the opposite end of the strip should equal the correct length of the top.

AN ATTRACTIVE EXPANDING OR SECTIONAL BOOKCASE

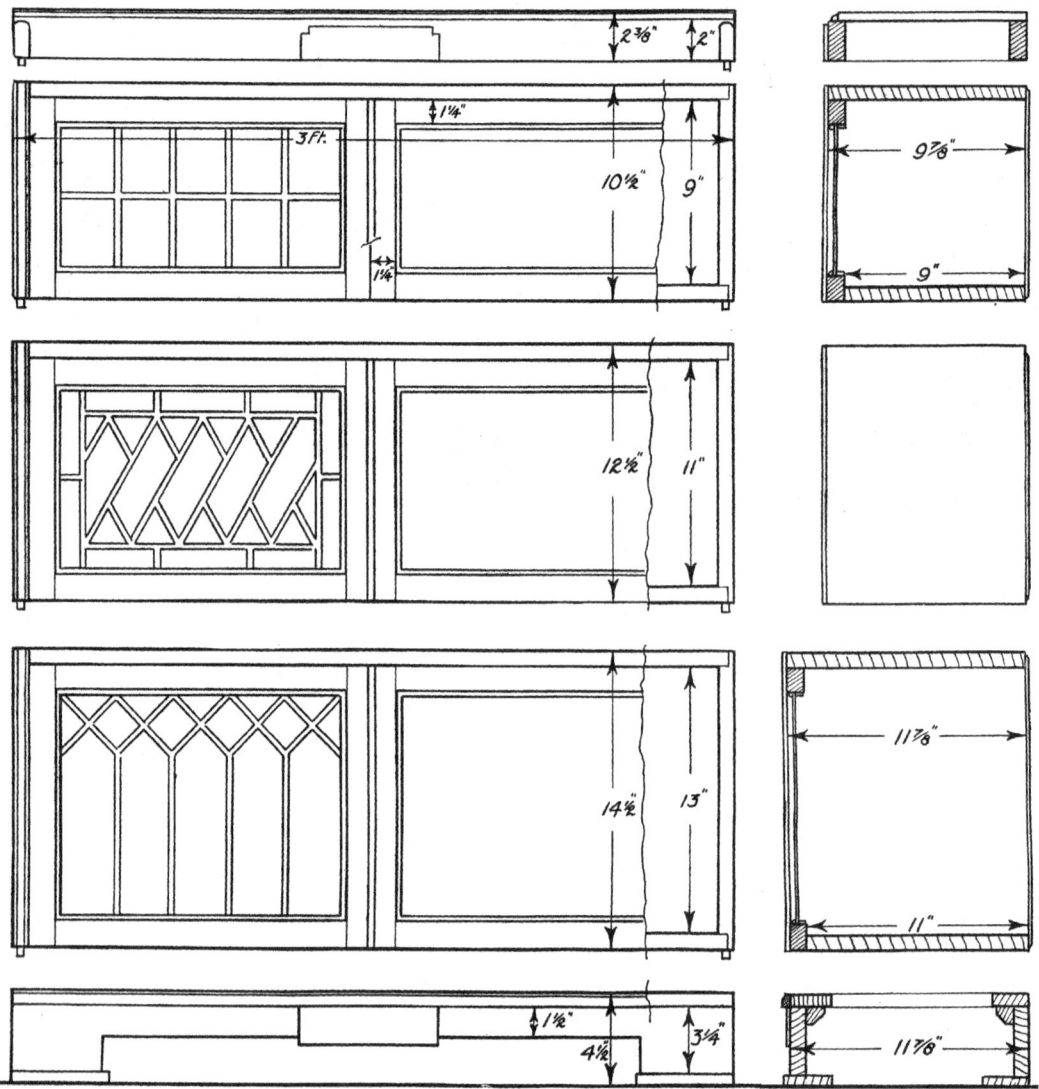

Fig. 3.—Main Sizes of the various parts.
Note that alternative designs for the leaded doors are given.

This strip is placed with the block against the squared end of the top, and a mark with a knife or chisel made at the other end as in Fig. 5. This mark is squared round. All the tops can be marked out in the same way. A second key could be prepared to give the correct width. A similar idea could be adopted for most other parts.

The Joints.

The sides having also been marked out and finished to size, the joints can be cut. Set a gauge to ¼ inch (the lap thickness) and gauge the top and bottom edges, holding the fence of the gauge always from the outer surfaces. Re-set the gauge to the thickness of the top and bottom (¾ inch), and mark the inner surfaces, working the fence along top and bottom edges.

As the saw has to cut across the grain it is a good plan to cut a little sloping groove against the gauge cut on the *waste* side as shown in Fig. 6. This provides a channel in which the saw can run, so ensuring accurate cutting.

Having cut down across the grain as far as the gauge line, the waste is chopped away with the chisel, as in Fig. 7. Hold the chisel just above the gauge line at the first cut, and then finish off cleanly up to the line.

Assembling.

The main carcase can now be put together. Glue the rebate and place the top in position. When driving in the nails make them slope in alternate directions so that they have a "dovetail" grip. The bottom is flush with the back. Test carefully with a square to see that the whole is true and set aside for the glue to harden. The little blocks at the bottom can also be glued in.

When set, clean up the joints and add the moulding to the front edges of the sides. It should be of a wide flat section as shown. The back is stained first and then nailed on. The various units all have dowels at the bottom,

AN ATTRACTIVE EXPANDING OR SECTIONAL BOOKCASE

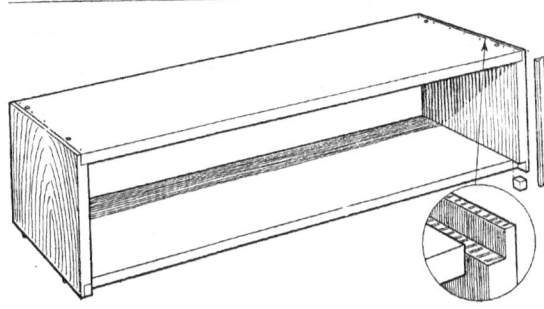

Fig. 4.—How the Bookcase Unit is Made.

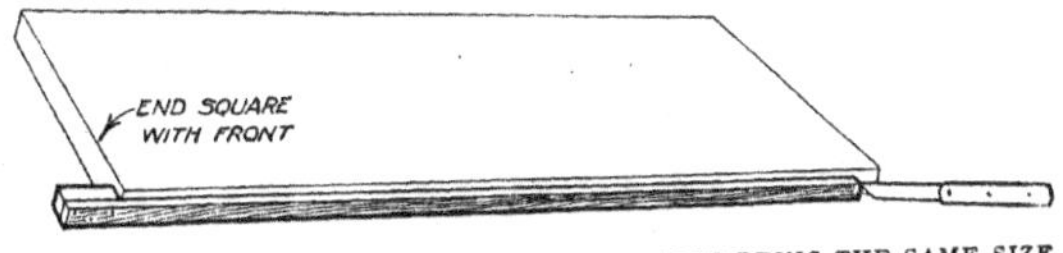

Fig. 5.—To ensure the corresponding parts being the same size, a sort of Key should be made.

The front edge and one end of, say, the top are planed square. Then a strip of wood is prepared and a block of wood glued and nailed to one end. The distance between the inner edge of the block and the opposite end of the strip should equal the correct length of the top. This key is then used as shown above.

holes being bored in the tops in corresponding positions. In every case these dowelled holes should be marked with the gauge, the latter being used from the same corresponding surfaces in every case.

Making the Doors.

A section through a door is given in Fig. 8. Here is the plain framework joined at the corners by one of the methods given in Fig. 10. A quarter round moulding is mitred round the inner edges to form a rebate for the glass, the latter being secured by a bead at the back.

When marking out the stiles (or uprights) and rails (horizontals) in sets, fix a cramp across them and square the marks across all as in Fig. 9. If all cannot be dealt with in one operation, complete one set, and use one of them as a guide for marking the remainder, cramping it in with them. It will be found an advantage to use a chisel or knife for marking rather than a pencil for the rails so that a small channel can be formed on the waste side (similarly to that in Fig. 6) to act as a guide for the saw.

In the dowelled joints the marks are squared round and the waste sawn away half from one side and half from the other. Remember, in the case of a mortise and tenon joint to allow sufficient length for the tenons. A gauge is used to mark both dowels and tenons.

The use of a cramp is advisable when gluing up. Test for squareness, and see that the frames are not in winding by holding them on a level with the eye. The front and back rails should appear parallel.

Mitre the moulding, using a mitre block, and fix it with glue and nails (Fig. 8). The glass and bead are not added until after staining and polishing. Very little fitting should be needed. The joints, however, will require levelling. The hinges should be let in flush in the edges of the doors. The addition of the closing moulding to the right hand door completes the main woodwork.

The Frieze.

Fig. 11 shows how this is made.

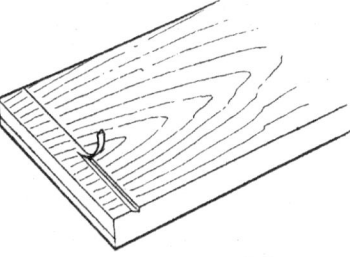

Fig. 6.—Showing small Groove cut against Gauge Line to provide a Channel in which the Saw can run.

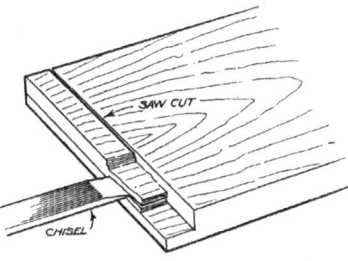

Fig. 7.—Chopping away Waste with a Chisel after Sawing across the Grain.

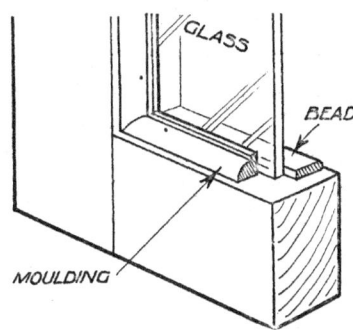

Fig. 8.—Section through a Door.
Showing how glass is held in position by beads.

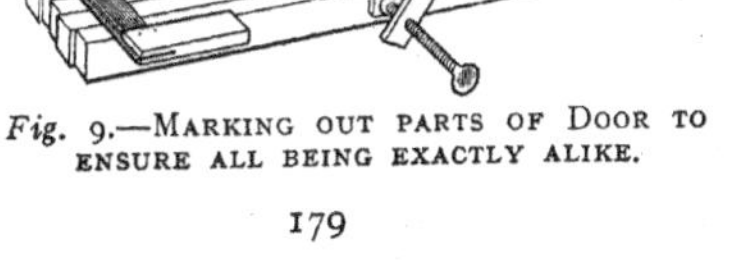

Fig. 9.—Marking out parts of Door to ensure all being exactly alike.

The corners are put together with a rebated joint in the same way as those of the bookcase, except that they are upright. The general marking out and assembling is the same. As there is a tendency for ordinary solid wood to shrink, it is a good idea to use thick plywood for the top. The thicknesses are hidden at the front by the applied moulding. Glue blocks can be added at the corners to strengthen the whole.

The front decorative panel is fixed with glue and fine nails; also the decorative end pieces. The last-named serve to hide the joints. Dowels are let into the underside so that the whole rests securely in position on the bookcase beneath.

The Plinth.

Details of the construction of this are given in Fig. 12. It is similar to that of the frieze, except that top pieces are fitted on, and feet fixed to the lower edges. Note the use of glue blocks to make the whole thoroughly rigid.

Finishing the Bookcase.

The suggestion in Fig. 1 for making certain parts darker than others certainly adds to the appearance, but we recommend that even the light portions should be stained as well as the others. Apart from the fact that French polish over unstained oak does not give a particularly nice shade, the stain has the advantage of toning the whole to an even shade. It often happens that different kinds of oak are used in the same job, and these will probably vary in tone.

Practically any of the proprietary stains can be used, though for the light parts the stain will probably have to be thinned down. The makers publish the most suitable medium to use for thinning. A fine effect for oak is obtained with walnut stain. It can be used unadulterated for the dark parts, and be thinned for the remainder. For mahogany we suggest a mahogany stain mixed with walnut stain. The latter takes off the redness, giving more of the sombre tone of a Chippendale cabinet. However, this is a matter the reader can better decide for himself.

Certain parts, such as the door heads, should be prepared in long lengths and be stained and polished

AN ATTRACTIVE EXPANDING OR SECTIONAL BOOKCASE

separately. They can be cut up on the mitre block and fixed afterwards, any little unevenness being corrected with glasspaper. If desired, the upright mouldings fixed to the cabinet sides could also be dealt with in the same way. The advantage of this is that the staining is simplified in that there is no danger of the dark stain overrunning the surrounding light parts.

Allow the stain to dry out thoroughly before beginning to polish. It will probably be necessary to rub down the surface with fine glasspaper, as there is a tendency with even the best of stains for the grain to be raised. Water stains are the worst offenders in this connection. Spirit stains, being volatile, dry out quickly and are not so liable to cause roughness. As against this they naturally cost more.

The article on French polishing, elsewhere in this work, gives full directions on this branch of the finishing. This particular job gives the worker a good chance, since he can go from one part to another, allowing each plenty of time to harden before giving another rub. If (in the case of oak) it is decided to use wax polish, it is a good plan to give a bodying up with French polish first, as this fixes the stain, as it were, and gives a slight shine which the wax soon builds up. To quicken the process a little resin can be added to the wax polish whilst still molten.

Fixing the Lead Strips.

A few alternative designs for the leaded work are given in Fig. 3. There are many other patterns, simpler or more elaborate, that the reader can use. One good plan is to select a certain pile which is going to be in, say, the centre, and give this a special treatment. For instance, a crest, shield or some other simple device could be incorporated in the design.

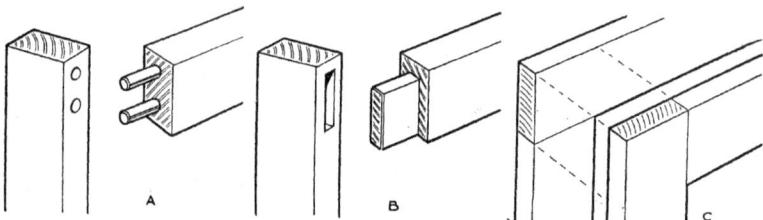

Fig. 10.—THREE DIFFERENT METHODS OF CONSTRUCTING THE DOOR.
A, dowelled joint; B, mortise and tenon; C, butted joint with two thicknesses glued together.

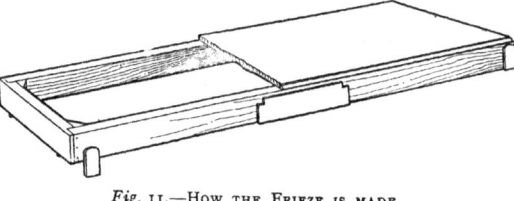

Fig. 11.—HOW THE FRIEZE IS MADE.

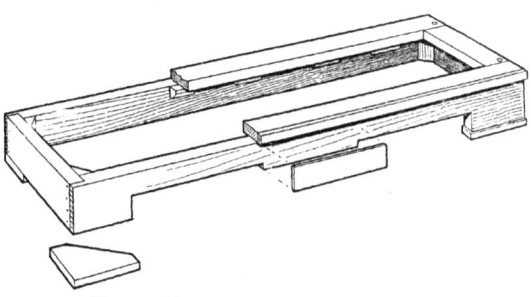

Fig. 12.—METHOD OF MAKING THE PLINTH.

Parts of this could be stained with the special glass stains made for the purpose.

As a guide for laying the lead strips a design of the pattern should be drawn. Cut a sheet of plywood to fit in the rebate of the door, and plot out the positions of diamonds or squares, or whatever design is being used, drawing lines to represent both edges of each strip of lead. The glass, of course, is already beaded in.

The lead is obtained in rolls, and is easily cut with scissors. Lay the strip on the glass over the corresponding mark on the plywood beneath, and mark the length. Cut all the strips and place them on a board ready for cementing. The cement is put up in tins, and is of the consistency of a thick paste. Apply it to the back edges of all the strips, using a brush with stiff bristles. It should be stirred up thoroughly first.

Make sure that every part of the lead is covered, but avoid a surplus. A thin, even coat is all that is required.

Allow about a quarter of an hour for the cement to become tacky. Otherwise it will not adhere properly. Begin with all the strips running in one direction, placing each in turn in position above the lines on the pattern below, and rubbing down with a rag wrapped around the fingers. Do not bear too heavily on the centre of the glass.

The strips running in the opposite direction follow. Lay them straight across the others, and press well down at the edges of each intersection. If any of the cement oozes out on to the surrounding glass it can be cleaned away with turpentine or petrol. Do not attempt to clean the whole glass until the cement has had plenty of time to harden.

It should be noted that designs involving shapes can be formed with the ordinary lead. It bends easily. The best plan is to cut a template of the shape in thick cardboard, and mould the lead around this. Two kinds of lead can be obtained; the flat strips, and a ribbed type. The latter is the more suitable for bending, as the ribs can be separated. The flat strips are for plain leaded work.

When the glass stains are used it is an advantage to apply it whilst the door is lying flat, as there is then no tendency for it to run. It requires a considerable time to dry, and, owing to its tacky nature, it should be left in a room free from dust, as this adheres readily to it.

Although the lead adheres firmly to the glass, care should be exercised when cleaning. Do not let the leather catch at the ends of the lead, as this may cause it to be pulled off.

WATERPROOF PAINT

The following is a well-tried recipe for a paint suitable for waterproofing outside walls:—

Rosin . . . . 2 lbs.
Litharge . . . 1½ lbs.
Clear linseed oil . . 1 gallon.

The two former ingredients should be boiled in the linseed oil and stirred until the solution becomes brown.

Ordinary paraffin wax dissolved in heavy coal-tar oil is also very satisfactory for treating damp walls. Apply hot in dry weather.

TIME, LABOUR AND MONEY-SAVING IDEAS

EASY METHOD OF DIVIDING WOOD INTO STRIPS

When one has a piece of wood, card, or material to divide into strips of equal width, this is not always a very easy matter. The division one has to make may involve fractions of inches, but here is a simple way of getting

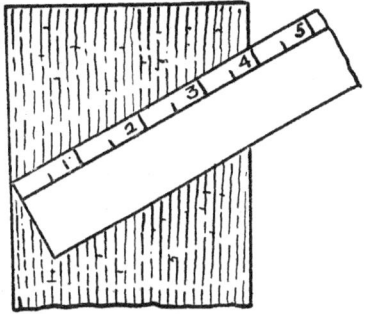

over the business. As an illustration, suppose one had to divide a piece of wood 3½ inches wide into four strips of equal width. This is easily done by holding the rule in slanting fashion at the 4-inch mark. The other inches indicate where the marks for the dividing lines should be made.

MARKING INK

The usual chemical marking inks contain several ingredients and require great care in their making, so that they cannot be recommended to the ordinary householder. Thus, the silver marking ink contains no less than nine ingredients and its making-up involves six separate processes.

A satisfactory marking ink can, however, be made with the aid of a stick of Chinese black ink. This should only be of a high grade. The ink is rubbed down with water until the usual black liquid is obtained. Use this ink to write with on the linen to be marked, and soon after the writing has been done, apply a hot flat-iron to the surface. The writing will then be made permanent, being proof against acids, hot soapy water, bleaching powder, etc.

A HINT ABOUT GARDEN FENCES

One of the weak spots in every garden fence is the flat top to the upright posts. The upper part of the

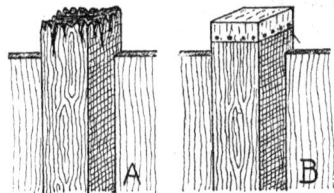

posts is liable to decay. When this happens and a post presents the condition shown at A, it is an excellent idea to fit a metal cap, as at B. Any piece of sheet metal will serve the purpose, but sheet lead is the best. It should be shaped to cover the top surface and to extend over the sides sufficiently to enclose all the decayed parts and a little of the sound wood. It is fixed with the aid of a few short nails.

If the process of rotting has become advanced it will help if some thin cement is run into the crevices formed by the decay. This should be done before the metal cap is fitted.

METAL POLISH

(1) *Liquid.*—The following is a recipe for a good liquid metal polish which can be made up very cheaply:—

Finely powdered silica	1 lb.
Paraffin oil	½ gallon.
Oleic acid	2 pints.
Stearic acid	¼ lb.

(2) *Paste.*

Finely powdered pumice	4 lbs.
Oleic acid	1 pint.
Japan wax	2 ozs.

GLUING THIN EDGES

It is by no means an easy matter to apply a uniform thin coating of glue

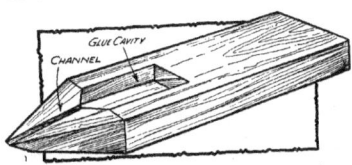

to the edges of panels and similar boards of thin section.

The device illustrated will readily overcome this difficulty by allowing the glue to flow evenly on thin-edge work such as that met with in box making. It will be observed that the device shown is a kind of a spoon (known as a "glue spoon"), and is simply a stick of wood pointed at one end, the tip being connected by means of a saw-cut to a rectangular cavity cut into the wood for the purpose of containing the glue. With this spoon, gluing of edges can be done much quicker and more cleanly than with a brush.

SAFETY-RAZOR BLADE PRESERVING SOLUTIONS

Safety-razor blades after use will preserve their sharp edges for a long period if they are stored in a solution consisting of 1 oz. of soft soap to 20 ozs. of methylated spirits to which a few drops of castor oil have been added.

Another satisfactory liquid for storing blades is ordinary medicinal paraffin oil.

INEXPENSIVE FOLDING WALL TABLE

Useful folding wall tables can be made for cost of a couple of shillings or so if a pair of "stamped steel table flap hinges" are used in conjunction with a few pieces of planed board. For example, the useful table shown may measure 30 inches long, 15 inches wide and be composed of three pieces of 1-inch tongued and grooved floorboard, 5 inches wide and 30 inches long. There will also be required one piece of planed batten 30 inches long, 1½ inches wide and 1 inch thick, also two pieces each 6 inches long, ½ inch thick, 2 inches wide and two pieces

14 inches long, 2 inches wide, ¼ inch thick.

Take the three pieces of floor-board and slip the tongues into the grooves and force them lightly together, then screw the 2 × ¾-inch battens to the ends of them. Round off the outer corners and plane off the projecting tongue from one edge and the groove part from the other.

Next take the 30-inch length of 1½ × 1-inch wood and screw it to the wall with 2½-inch screws, fixed with Rawl plugs. Hinge the table to this batten, then place the table flap hinges so that when swung outwards they come alongside the edges of the end battens, as shown above, and mark the places where the hinged ends come against the wall. Fasten the two thin pieces of wood to the wall with screws and Rawl plugs, then screw the table-flap hinges to them, driving the screws right through the wood into Rawl plugs.

STOPPING A CHIMNEY FIRE

A fire in a chimney can invariably be extinguished by placing a small quantity, viz., about an eggcupful of powdered sulphur on a shovel and holding the latter over the fire, in order to allow the fumes to escape up the chimney.

Renovating Pictures and Picture-Frames

IT pays to take care of the framed pictures that hang on our walls, yet many people give them no attention at all beyond an occasional dusting or wiping. The result is that valuable examples are often seen which are rapidly decaying, though a little care bestowed in the early stages would save them from ruin.

What to do with Oil Paintings.

Oil paintings suffer from neglect more than any other kind of picture; accordingly, we will begin by describing how they should be treated.

At least every two or three years an oil canvas should be taken from its frame and examined. Probably it is dusty and it is certainly dirty on the surface. Therefore, take a soft duster—one that cannot cause any scratches—lightly wipe over the painted surface, and then deal with the back, especially in the corners and the folds, in a little more vigorous manner.

Washing a Canvas.

All the surface dirt being removed, take a bowl of warm water and, with another clean and soft rag, lightly sponge the surface. Do not use any appreciable amount of pressure and work with as little water as possible. When the surface is clean, wipe it gently, put the canvas where it can dry slowly, and leave it for at least a day.

Do not Use a Raw Potato.

For this sponging no soap of any kind should be used; moreover, it is dangerous to follow most of the hints that are current with regard to cleaning pictures. A favourite is the one that advises the use of a raw potato. The juice of the potato certainly has the effect of brightening the colours for a little while, but only for a little while. Against its use lies the fact that to introduce vegetable matter of this kind to the surface of the picture is to provide a very attractive breeding-ground for many kinds of bacteria, and, once they are present, there is no limit to the damage they may do.

Fig. 1.—Tapping in the Wedges at the Back of a Canvas will cure any Sagging.

Tightening a Loose Canvas.

When the canvas has been allowed sufficient time to dry, tap in the wedges at the back. This will have the effect of tightening the canvas, and it should cure any sagging which is often apparent when pictures are becoming venerable.

Re-varnishing.

The next step is to examine the surface critically. If the old varnish has merely lost its shine, this is easily restored. Procure some very good mastic varnish and paint it evenly over the surface. Do not work the brush about vigorously or you may cause the varnish to froth. Merely paint it on in gentle strokes, and, if it tends to drag or stick, put a spot or two of turpentine with the varnish.

How to Remove Old Varnish.

But the varnished surface of the picture may be more than dull, it may be cracked and perished. The latter can be recognised by the little grains of golden powder that had to be dislodged from the folds of the canvas and which are reposing in the corners of the frame. The thing to do in this case is to remove all the old varnish. The work is not difficult; merely warm the fingers of one hand and rub, in a circular manner, all over the old surface. This action will cause a fine powder to be formed which should be shaken off every few minutes, since it must not be driven into the colours.

When no more powder forms, dust the surface and give it a coat of varnish, as already described. As soon as it is dry the picture is ready to be returned to its frame.

Filling in Holes and Cracks.

There are some defects which the painting may possess that only an expert should try to remedy, but there is one thing more that may fall to the lot of the average handyman. Suppose that, while washing or rubbing the canvas, some part of the solid

Fig. 2.—If the old Varnish on an Oil Painting has lost its Shine, it should be revarnished with a good Mastic Varnish, applied evenly over the Surface.

Do not work the brush about too vigorously or it may cause the varnish to froth.

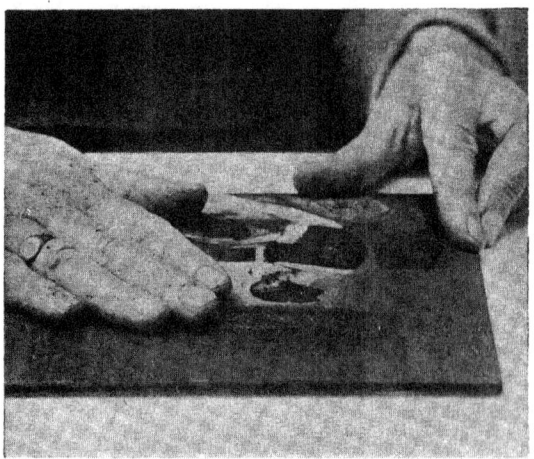

Fig. 3.—Perished Varnish can be removed from an Oil Painting by Rubbing with the Flat of the Hand.

Warm the fingers and rub in a circular manner all over the old surface.

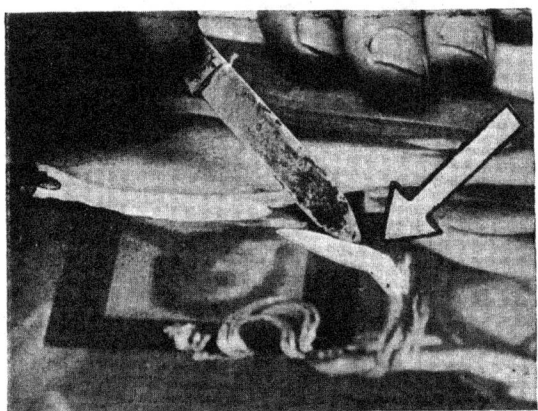

Fig. 4.—Deep Cracks in a Canvas should be filled in with a Putty made by mixing a spoonful of Finely Powdered Whitening with a little Hot Size.

Apply the putty and level with a knife. When hard, colour to match the rest of the picture.

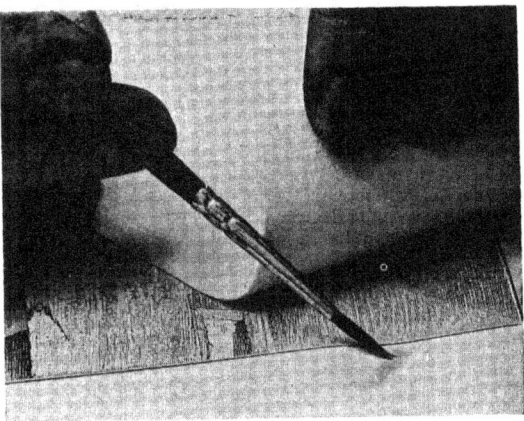

Fig. 5.—Benzine can be used to remove a Grease Stain from the Edging of a Print.

Dab the spot with a brush and mop off the surface moisture with clean blotting-paper.

paint cracked away from its backing and became loose. What can be done? Mix up a spoonful of finely powdered whitening with a very little hot size, so as to form a putty. Next paint the gap where the hard paint fell out with a little of the size, and, while it is still wet, put the putty in position; then level the surface with the tip of a pocket-knife. In a very little while you will have a hard white patch which can be coloured with oil paints to match the rest of the picture. Naturally any deep cracks which may mar the canvas can be dealt with in exactly the same way.

Cleaning Prints.

Now let us consider the prints that hang around our walls. Although they are invariably exhibited under glass, they become dusty in course of time. To freshen them there is no better way than to place them in a tray of cold water and to leave them out in the sun all day. The tray, it must be added, should be large enough to accommodate the print without it being creased or folded.

After twelve hours lift out the print and place it between two sheets of clean blotting-paper, then leave it to dry slowly, not close to a fire. While the print is still wet do not handle it more than necessary, and be very careful not to rub any parts of it.

This sun-bathing process is only possible with black and brown prints, and must not be attempted where multi-coloured prints are concerned. In their case nothing more drastic than gentle friction with a handful of bran is permitted.

Grease Marks on Prints.

When grease marks disfigure a print, a certain method of removing them is to apply a solution of pyridine by means of a wire brush. It is not easy for everybody to obtain this chemical, however, and a more popular way is to dab the spot with a small ordinary brush dipped in benzine, and to mop off the surface moisture with clean blotting-paper, repeating the operation a number of times. It is hardly necessary to say that benzine must not be used near a fire nor any naked lights.

Fox Marks on Prints.

These are rusty-coloured marks, ranging in size from pin-points to long streaks, which disfigure prints that have been attacked by damp. There was practically no way of removing them successfully until the British Museum Laboratory discovered that they would yield to the following treatment: In one dish dissolve 2 oz. of bleaching powder in a pint of cold water, in another dish pour ½ oz. of hydrochloric acid and a pint of cold water. Arrange the print flat in the latter dish and leave for twenty minutes, then take it out and put it for a similar period in the first solution. Follow by putting the print back again in the acid bath for twenty minutes, and finally soak in cold water for three hours. At the end of that time the print should be placed between clean blotting-paper and then allowed to dry.

Water-colour Drawings.

It is very dangerous to experiment with water-colour drawings, as the colours may easily run, but this is how they are dealt with by experts if the pigments have blackened, due to the action of the air on the compounds of lead and other substances incorporated in the paints. An aqueous solution of hydrogen peroxide is shaken up with an equal quantity of sulphuric ether. These substances are not difficult to obtain from a good chemist. When the mixture has been allowed to stand for a few minutes an ethereal layer will float on the surface. A camel-hair brush is dipped into this upper layer—it must not be allowed to reach the lower layer—and the liquid is painted on to the blackened patches of colour. Instantly, the colours are restored and all that remains is to dry the picture.

Gilt Frames.

Before the pictures are returned to their frames it will be advisable to give an eye to the frames themselves. In the case of gilt frames with a florid moulding, the first thing is to go into all the recesses with a dry and clean paint brush and to remove every particle of dust. Then sponge all the gilt with warm onion-water, made by boiling a large onion in sufficient liquor to cover it. Mop the surfaces dry and do not rub them, as the gilt can be easily wiped off.

Should any part of the relief pattern be missing it can be replaced by making a putty of whitening and glue, and pressing it into the position of the lost portion. Paint the surface to which it is required to adhere with a little of the hot glue. When hard, the new part should be touched over with some liquid glue.

Wood Frames.

Other frames may be revived by washing them in ordinary warm water and polishing with furniture polish. If a stained wood frame appears shabby after being washed, give it a coat of suitable stain before the polish is applied.

Reassembling.

Place all the articles in front of a fire before they are put together, use a stiff paste and not a wet one to fix the backing paper, and do not hang the frame on a damp wall. In all cases a frame should hang so that it is tilted.

Fitting and Repairing Roller Blinds

A ROLLER blind should roll up freely, the ends keeping perfectly even and the lower edge absolutely horizontal when in the *up* position. The two essentials to secure this are, firstly, to tack the blind with its side square with the roller; secondly, when mounted on its brackets, the spindle must be perfectly horizontal.

Fitting the Ends.

Slightly chamfer off the ends of the wooden roller so that they just fit tightly into the sockets of the brass end-pieces, then secure with a ¾-inch No. 6 screw.

Fastening on the Fabric.

Fig. 1 shows the best method of fastening on the material. The roller is supported on three small wedge blocks, one at each end, and the third is moved along immediately beneath the spot where a tack is being driven in. The top edge of the fabric is "turned in" to give double thickness.

The stiffening bar at the bottom slides through a hem in the material.

Fixing the Brackets.

First of all screw up the left-hand bracket 2 inches above the window. With the blind hanging down, engage the end in the bracket hole, then, holding up the other end, see that the material hangs down vertically, and that the roller is level. Now mark the position of the slotted bracket and screw up in place.

There should be practically no end-play on the roller when resting in the brackets.

Fitting the Cord.

Take a length of good linen cord and thread the end through the eyelet as in Fig. 2, and knot the end; this should be done while the blind is completely rolled up, remembering that the material winds up on the window side of the roller in an anti-clockwise direction.

What to do before placing Roller in Brackets.

Before placing the roller in its place in the brackets, wind the cord round the reel *three* times in the opposite direction to that taken by the fabric. Now, as the blind descends, the cord should wind up on the reel enough times to cause the blind to ascend when the cord is pulled.

The Stops.

Fig. 3 shows a small hollow wooden knob secured in place by a knot; threaded on the cord above the stop is a screw eye. Fix the eyelet first, then lead the cord through and knot the knob in position so that it stops the blind when down; but see that there is still at least one complete turn of material left on the roller; this prevents the fabric tearing away from the tacks.

When the blind is down, cut off the cord to length so that it reaches to the bottom of the fabric. Now fit an acorn as shown in Fig. 3, the cord is knotted into the upper part of the fitting and the lower half is then screwed into position.

How Spring Blinds Work.

It will be seen from Fig. 4 that the spring roller is in two pieces; the outer cylinder revolves about the inner rod, at the end of which is fitted a rachet wheel. Two paws attached to the outer shell engage with the rachet. These paws are so arranged that a quick jerk dislodges them and permits the revolving of the outer roller, but when movement ceases the paws engage with one of the teeth on the rachet, stopping the blind at the desired height.

How to Fit Spring Blinds.

The two brackets (see Fig. 14) are exactly alike; the left-hand one has a hole which takes the round spindle of the roller, while the right-hand one has a slot which takes the square-ended spindle.

Fix on the fabric and screw up the brackets as previously described for plain roller blinds. With the material wound on evenly and tightly, introduce the round spindle into the hole in the left-hand bracket; now twist the squared end round four times to put tension on the spiral spring before slipping this end into the slotted bracket.

Faults in Spring Blinds.

After a time the paws in the rachet mechanism become clogged with dust and dirt; they then fail to engage with the toothed wheel and so stop the blind. In such cases clean away the obstruction with a brush dipped in paraffin, then add a drop of thin machine oil to the paws, when the blind should work as well as formerly.

In the unusual event of a broken spring, do not attempt to mend it—a good job is never accomplished; always fit a new roller.

Removing the Fabric.

When it is necessary to remove the fabric to fit a new roller, take a small screwdriver with a sharp blade, force

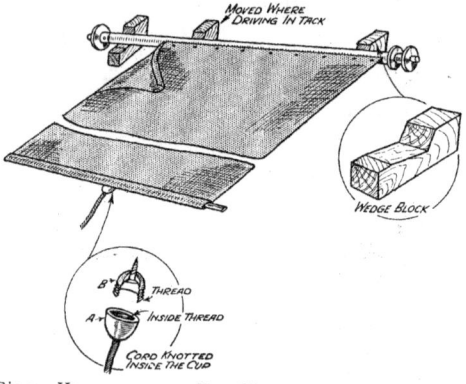

Fig. 1.—Here we see the Best Method of fastening on the Material.

Support the roller on three wedge blocks, one at each end, and a third which is moved along immediately beneath the spot where a tack is being driven in.

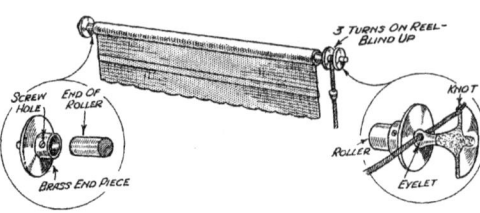

Fig. 2.—How to fit the Cord.

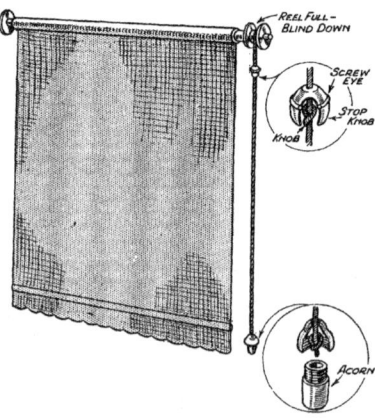

Fig. 3.—Details of the Method of fitting the Stops.

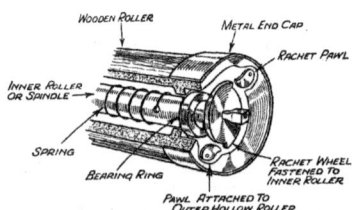

Fig. 4.—Diagram showing how the Spring Blind Works.

FITTING AND REPAIRING ROLLER BLINDS

Fig. 5.—Working a Metal Barrel Spring Roller Blind.
Releasing the trigger of a cap and rack spring, and holding the centre cord to prevent the blind running up too quickly.

Fig. 6.—Wood Spring Roller fixed.
Note that no side cord is required. To pull up the blind, the centre cord is jerked. This releases the pawls and allows the spring to revolve the roller. See also Fig. 11.

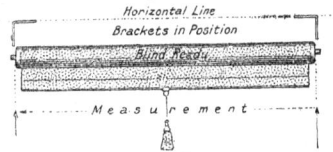

Fig. 7.—Accuracy in Fitting essential.
This indicates the importance of fitting the fixing brackets of the blinds spirit-level true. Otherwise the blind will not roll up properly.

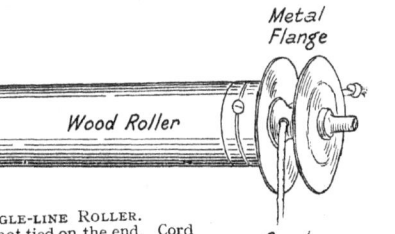

Fig. 8.—How Cord is attached to Single-line Roller.
Cord is inserted through hole in flange and a knot tied on the end. Cord is wound round flange as shown in Fig. 12A.

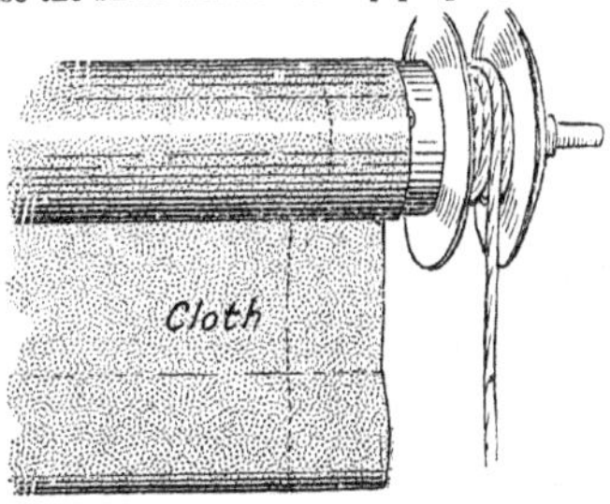

Fig. 9.—A Single-line Roller.
Showing the way the cord is wound on the flange.

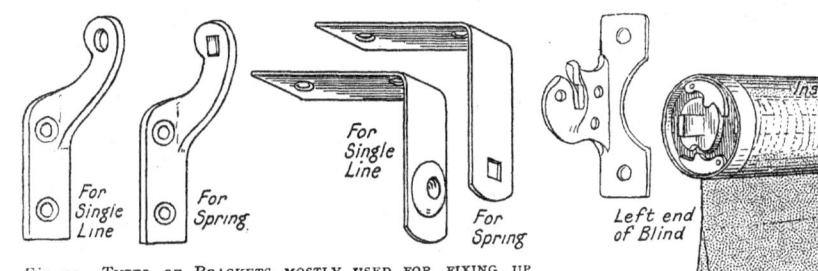

Fig. 10.—Types of Brackets mostly used for Fixing up Roller Blinds.
Those with the square hole are for spring rollers and those with the round hole are for wood rollers.

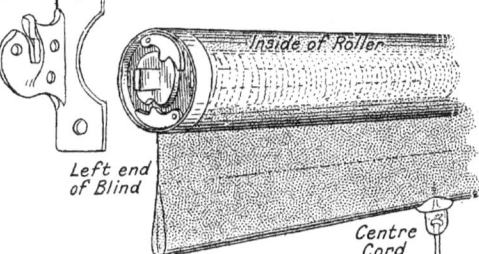

Fig. 11.—Details of Wood Spring Roller Blind.
This type of roller obviates the necessity of having any side cords. The cloth of the blind rolls up with a jerk.

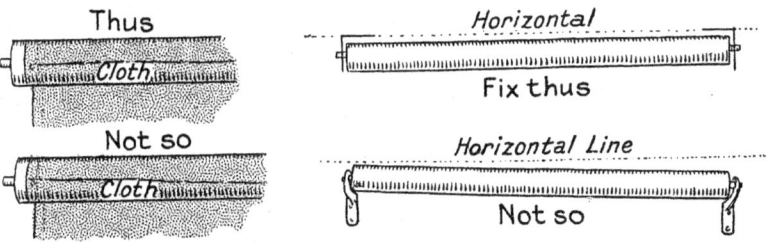

Fig. 12.—Faults in fixing Roller Blinds.
If the blind does not roll up correctly, the fixer should look to see that the cloth is sewn on to the roller truly. Also test whether the roller is dead horizontal.

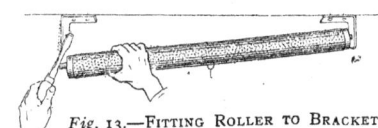

Fig. 13.—Fitting Roller to Brackets.
Method of levering back bracket to insert pin.

FITTING AND REPAIRING ROLLER BLINDS

it carefully under the head of the tack and lever up with a prizing movement. When refixing, fold in the material an extra inch, and re-tack, making fresh holes.

Fitting the Pull Cord.

Fig. 1 shows a neat fitting for attaching the cord by which the blind is pulled down; it is much neater than the usual screw eye. The cup-shaped base B is screwed to the wooden slat running through the end of the blind. The cord is knotted into the cup A, which then screws on to the cup B, forming a neat yet obscure fitment.

SOME NOTES ON TYPES OF ROLLER BLINDS.

Altogether there are four main types of roller blinds in use, namely:

1. Wood single cord flange.
2. Wood spring.
3. Metal barrel spring.
4. Single cord action.

Wood Roller Blind.

The wood roller blind has a double metal flange at one end through which the cord passes. Flax cord is the strongest. The desired length of cord should be cut off, one end threaded through the hole in the flange, and twisted round the box of the flange about six turns in the opposite direction from the roll of the cloth.

Wood Spring Rollers.

Wood spring rollers are made by boring an auger hole down the middle of a round wood roller into which is inserted a spiral spring. This type of roller is generally used in the smaller design of house. No side cord is required, as shown in Fig. 6.

Metal Barrel Spring Roller.

This has a ratchet action and there is a side cord attached to the ratchet action which is threaded through the metal lever (see Fig. 5).

The two types of brackets generally used for fixing roller blinds are shown in Fig. 10. These are the metal angle bracket and the swan neck bracket. The former is mostly used for fixing blinds to the head of the window and the latter for fixing to the face of the window.

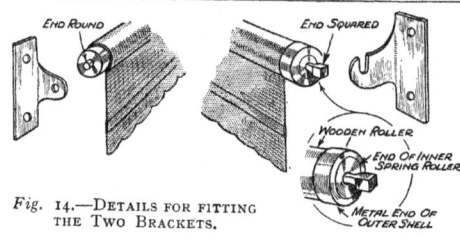

Fig. 14.—DETAILS FOR FITTING THE TWO BRACKETS.

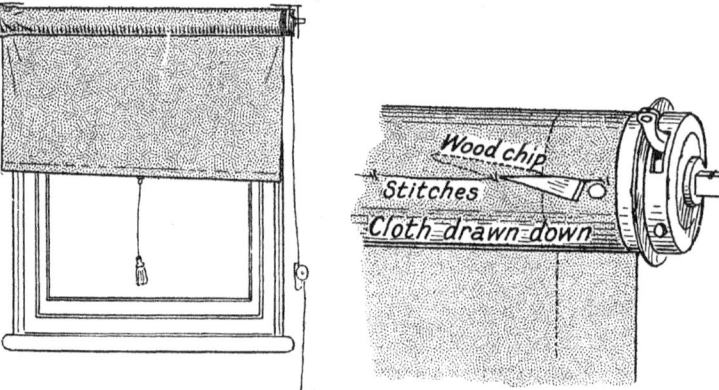

Fig. 15.—A SIMPLE REMEDY FOR FAULTY BLINDS.
A chip placed in the cloth where it is sewn on to the roller will make that side of the roller larger than the other and cause the blind to roll up that way.

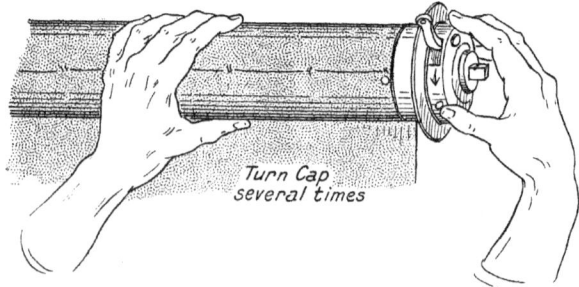

Fig. 16.—CHARGING METAL BARREL SPRING ROLLER.
The fixer is here charging the spring roller before attempting to put it in position between the brackets. The method of doing this is to turn the cap action round six to ten times. The blind is then fitted between brackets and tested for correct operation.

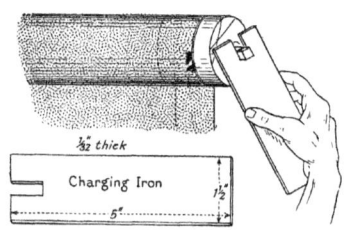

Fig. 17.—CHARGING IRON IN USE ON SELF-ACTING SPRING ROLLERS.
Note the two cross cuts on the wood block at the end of the roller. This indicates the "cap end" or "right-hand end" of the spring, and allows the fixer to recognise which way the spindle turns.

Charging a Metal Barrel Spring Roller.

There is a cap and rack ratchet action at one end of this type of roller. Before putting the blind into its position, the spiral spring requires what is known as "charging." Take hold of the cap action and turn it about six to ten complete revolutions. When this is done place the blind between the brackets and pull down the blind by the centre cord and raise it by the cord attached to the lever. If the blind should not work properly either because it is too powerful or not sufficiently powerful, take the blind out of the brackets and add or decrease the number of revolutions already given to the cap and rack action (Fig. 16).

How to "Charge" Self-acting Spring Rollers.

It will be found that there are two cross-cuts on the wood block at one end of the roller. This is called by professional blind fitters "the cap end" of the spring or "the right-hand end" (see Fig. 17). The reason for these two cross-cuts is to indicate which way the spindle is to be turned. The charging iron is used for these blinds.

How to Make a Blind Roll up Truly.

First see that the cloth of the blind is mounted squarely and truly on the roller. Assuming that this is in order, make sure that the roller has been fixed perfectly horizontally. If this does not cure the trouble, or the blind still rolls up incorrectly, take a chip of wood or cardboard and insert it at the top of the cloth on the opposite side to that which does not roll up correctly (see Figs. 12 and 15).

Blinds over Skylights.

Blinds for this class of work always have metal barrel spring rollers. The roller has no cap and rack action, but is self-acting.

The method of fixing the brackets is similar to that for ordinary vertical windows, but the fixing of the roller is somewhat different.

Laying Crazy Paving

PATHS and areas paved with random pieces of flat stone have a durability and charm unequalled by any other paving material.

Unfortunately, the cost of the work when done by a contractor is a very considerable item, but when undertaken by the house owner the cost is comparatively small.

It will be found that the cost of a path will work out from 2s. 6d. to 4s. per square yard, depending on the quality of the materials used and the amount of preparation required by the site on which the path is to be laid.

There is nothing particularly arduous about the work, nor is it difficult if done in an orderly and progressive manner.

THE MATERIALS REQUIRED

To estimate the quantity of material for a given job, it is first necessary to ascertain the area in square yards of the path—or yard—or whatever surface is to be paved.

For example, a path 30 feet long and 3 feet wide is $30 \times 3 = 90$ square feet. Divide by 9 to bring this to square yards, and we have 10 square yards in area. Similarly, a rectangular court 25 feet long and 12 feet wide measures 25×12, equals 300 square feet, and dividing by 9 gives 34 square yards, reckoning to the nearest number of yards.

Suppose for the sake of clarity that a path and small courtyard are to be paved, having an area in total of 36 square yards, and that around the court is to be a low stone wall, totalling 24 feet in length.

Prices of Paving Stones.

The next procedure is to obtain particulars and prices of various kinds of broken paving stone; "crazy" paving stone and the like. The price will be "per ton" and should include free delivery to the door. When comparing prices, take note of the condition and style of the stone, its thickness and covering power, also that the price includes delivery. An apparently low price quoted "f.o.r." that is, free on rail, may prove very expensive after paying the rail and transport charges.

The next thing to do is to select the best stone, choice must be governed by personal fancy; for example, some people prefer a reddish sandstone, others a "Yorkshire," and so forth, while in many districts there are local stone quarries from which supplies can be drawn quite cheaply. It is also possible to obtain random marble—which makes a durable and attractive paving.

Next take note of the thickness—which is purely a nominal figure—the stone is never of uniform thickness nor smooth, unless so stated, or described

Fig. 1.—Pleasing Treatment at Entrance Gate.
Note that a path should always widen out at the gate.

Fig. 2.—Preliminary Drainage.
When necessary transverse trenches should be dug across the line of path as here shown.

Fig. 3.—A Bush Drain.
The trench is filled in with faggots or brushwood.

Fig. 4.—Lining Out the Path.
The site is defined with pegs and lines spaced the correct width apart.

Fig. 5.—Excavating the Site.
The next proceeding is to dig out the soil to a depth of at least 6 inches.

as "dressed one side" or some similar description.

Hard or Thin Stones.

Financial considerations will probably limit the choice, but, roughly speaking, the harder the stone the thinner it may be, in fact, a hard "facing" stone about $\frac{3}{4}$ to 1 inch thick is ample; but the softer stones should be bought rather thicker, as they wear much more rapidly. Any stone to be set in sand and not "grouted" or pointed with cement ought to be from $1\frac{1}{2}$ to 2 inches thick.

How Much Stone is Required?

Although stone is sold by the ton, it must be borne in mind that some stones are much harder and heavier than others, consequently the covering power is governed partly by weight as well as by thickness. The correct procedure is to make sure how many square yards the selected stone will cover; for example, a thin hard facing stone may cover 22 yards to the ton, whereas a thick soft stone may only cover say 12 yards.

For the chosen example, sufficient stone will be needed to cover 36 square yards, and on the average this will take about $2\frac{1}{2}$ tons of paving stone, and for the low wall about $\frac{1}{2}$ ton of "walling" stone. Walling stone is simply fairly thick paving stone roughly hewn to a nominal width of about 4 to 6 inches.

It is economical to build a low wall when laying paving, as it forms a convenient way of using up odd small pieces of stone that cannot well be employed for paving, but a certain amount of walling stone is necessary in addition to bond the whole and make a neat finish.

Other Materials Required.

The only other materials required are "hard core," sand, and a small quantity of Portland cement. Hard core is any hard clean material such as broken brick, gravel ballast, clinker, boiler ash, or even "burnt ballast," that is, clean clay burnt hard.

Hard core is essential when the base consists of material only recently tipped. Ordinary ground after excavation is sometimes hard enough on which to put the paving, especially if an inch or so of clinker is put in first.

Sand should be the soft or river sand with a tendency to bind together when squeezed in the hand. The exact amount of hard core needed for a reasonable foundation depends on the nature of the soil, a very hard ground will need less, a very soft or sandy soil will need more, but an average is one "yard" of hard core to every 6 square yards of surface.

In addition, half the quantity of sand will be needed, thus for 12 square yards

LAYING CRAZY PAVING

of paving allow 2 yards of hard core and 1 yard of sand.

If the stones are to be grouted, allow 1 cwt. of Portland cement for about every 12 square yards of paving. Note that a "yard" of sand or hard core is a nominal amount equivalent to 1 cubic yard or enough to fill a box 1 yard square and 1 yard deep.

In some places material is sold by the ton and not by the cubic yard. It should be remembered, therefore, that 1 cubic yard of hard core weighs approximately 24 cwt., and 1 cubic yard of sand 27 to 28 cwt.

Summary for Estimating and Ordering Materials.

To summarise the procedure for estimating and ordering the materials, first ascertain the number of square yards of surface to be paved, next select the stone and ascertain the number of square yards that can be covered by 1 ton, then order requisite number of tons. Order also 1 yard of hard core and $\frac{1}{2}$ yard sand for every 6 square yards of paving.

As a guide, the following table will be helpful in judging the requisite quantities for any given job.

Table of Quantities.

Width in Feet.	Length in Feet.	Area in Square Yards.	Hard Core 6 ins. deep Cubic Yards.
1' 6"	10'	1 and $\frac{2}{3}$	$\frac{1}{3}$
2' 0"	15'	3 and $\frac{1}{3}$	$\frac{3}{4}$
2' 6"	20'	5$\frac{1}{2}$	1
3' 0"	20'	7	1$\frac{1}{4}$
3' 6"	25'	10	1$\frac{3}{4}$
4' 0"	50'	22	4

PREPARATION OF SITE

If any part of the site for the path or paved area is known to be waterlogged, or if the surface water flows across it during very wet weather, it will be necessary to drain the site at those places, but this is seldom necessary except on some sloping sites or those with a slight hollow.

Draining.

When such drainage is necessary begin by digging trenches about 9 inches wide and at least twice as long as the pathway is wide across the site for the path—as sketched in Fig. 2—and about 15 inches deep.

Fill in the bottom of these trenches with faggots or bundles of brushwood, or if they are not available then use large pieces of broken brick or clinker, or lumps of coke.

This should be loosely filled to a depth of 9 inches—as in Fig. 3—and note that the ends of the trench should be an inch or so lower than the middle part.

Fig. 6.—Removing Soil with Barrow.

Avoid damage to lawns by laying boards where necessary over which to wheel the barrow, or use one with a pneumatic tyre.

Fig. 6A.—Consolidating the Trench.

Ram the earth at the bottom of the trench to make a good firm foundation or give it a thorough rolling.

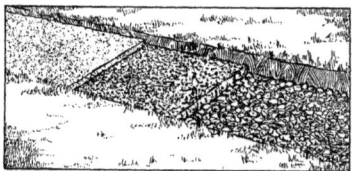

Fig. 7.—Preparing the Sand Bed.

Cover the hard core with an inch layer of fine stuff, roll and water it, then spread an inch layer of sand on top and rake it over to make it level. These stages are here shown progressively.

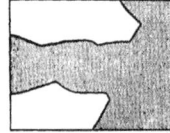

Fig. 8.—Bedding a Stone.

Place the stone in position on the sand and work a trowel under it around all available edges to ensure that the stone beds down "dead" and does not rock, otherwise it will be found that the path will always give trouble.

Fig. 9.—Arranging the Stones.

Begin at one end, lay a stone at each side, choosing those with straight edges to set against the side of the path, as here shown in plan.

Fig. 10.—Laying Main Stones.

Continue by laying several large pieces of stone, placing them where the tread is most likely to come in the centre of the path.

Fig. 11.—Completing a Section.

Fill in the gaps with smaller stones, fitting them closely but not pressing against one another.

Now Mark the Position of the Path.

Next drive pegs into the ground at the beginning and end of a straight path or area, and at any positions where the path changes direction if it is otherwise than straight.

Space the pegs an inch wider each side than the outer edges for the path, then stretch a string very tightly between them on each side of the intended pathway, as shown in Fig. 4, then dig out the space between them as in Fig. 5, using the lines as a guide to keep the edges straight. Take care that the edges of the ground which form the "shoulders" of the path are kept firm and clean—if the soil is very loose, fix wooden strips temporarily along the sides to prevent the soil falling inwards. If these wooden edgings are used, leave them in place for a week after the path is finished, then pull them out and press the soil firmly against the path foundation.

Removing the Soil.

Now remove soil to a depth of at least 6 inches, and deposit it on the garden beds or elsewhere.

It is important to make sure that there are no roots of weeds left in the site of the path. All roots should be carefully removed, and it is even preferable to coat with weed-killer, so as to prevent trouble with weeds coming up through the path after it has been completed.

When assistance is available and a wheelbarrow is not to hand, a very strong wooden box about 30 inches long, 18 inches wide and 15 inches deep, or any other reasonable size, should have two long handles of 2 by 1$\frac{1}{2}$-inch batten—about 7 feet long is a convenient length—screwed to the sides, and it can then be carried bodily, by two persons.

The next step is to consolidate the ground by ramming the bottom of the trench, as in Fig. 6A, or by a thorough rolling.

Follow this by spreading the hard core over the trench to a depth of 4 inches, rake it to make it level and even in thickness, then spread over it a layer of "fine stuff"—that is, small pieces of hard core mixed with sand. Do not use garden soil or friable material or the path will speedily sink.

BEDDING AND SETTING THE STONES

The stones are bedded on a layer of sand only—at least 1 inch thick, spread over the fine stuff, as shown in

LAYING CRAZY PAVING

Fig. 12.—Cutting a Stone.
Lay the stone on a thick bed of dry sand, then chip across the stone with a cold chisel and hammer until the stone parts asunder.

Fig. 7, and raked loosely to a level surface. Do not spread more than a yard or so at a time, and do not consolidate it, but endeavour to keep the sand "free," so that it can settle under the weight of the stone.

Bed the stone by laying it flat on the sand, then slip the trowel under it—as in Fig. 8—and move it about to loosen the sand, and thus allow the stone to settle gently but solidly into position.

When properly set, the stone must be "dead," that is, it must be quite inert and not rock about in the slightest, otherwise the path will always give trouble.

Stones cannot be held in place by cement—contrary to general belief—they only keep properly in place when bedded firmly on to sand. Note particularly that the sand must be free from lumps or pebbles, otherwise the stone will bear on the lump and speedily develop a movement.

The whole secret of a good crazy path is correct bedding, so pay attention to this matter and do not leave a stone until it is secure.

The stones should not be trodden upon until a considerable section has been bedded and finished, otherwise the setting will be disturbed.

How to Lay the Stones.

Begin at one end, set the corner stones first, as in Fig. 9, with the straightest and longest edges parallel with the path edge, then place and bed a few large stones, as in Fig. 10, and fill in the gaps with smaller pieces. Avoid long unbroken joints, stagger the stones, as in Fig. 11, so that a lengthways joint is crossed by a solid piece of stone; this tends to check motion and early breaking of the joints.

A Useful Tip.

A great deal of time and trouble can often be saved by taking a large stone, say one about 2 feet square, laying it carefully, and then giving it a light but sharp tap with a fairly heavy hammer. It will then split up into four or five pieces, and these jump far enough apart to allow the joints to be pointed afterwards. Thus four or five stones are laid and fitted in one operation.

Cutting a Stone.

If the stock of stone is graded on delivery—that is—the stones are stacked in heaps—large pieces with a straight edge in one heap, small pieces in another and so on, the time is well spent, because the selection of suitable stones is facilitated when laying them.

A stone can be cut by a mason with remarkable accuracy and skill, but the novice will find it breaks anywhere but where it is wanted. The best way is to bed the stone on a heap of dry sand, then chip across the stone, as in Fig. 12, with a sharp cold chisel and a hammer. Give sharp ringing blows more in the

Fig. 14.—A Paved Area.
Arrange the stones in groups or lines to form a simple but irregular pattern.

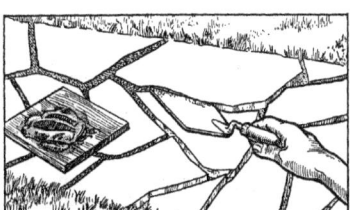

Fig. 15.—Cement Pointing.
Sand between the stones is raked and brushed out, then wetted, and the space filled in with cement mortar.

Fig. 16.—Building a low Edging Wall.
Sectioned view showing arrangement of stones and capping, all being bedded in cement mortar.

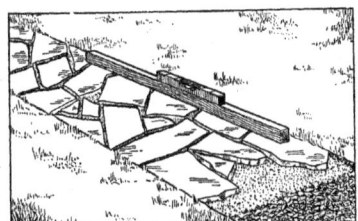

Fig. 13.—Levelling the Surface.
Test the level with a batten and spirit-level and adjust the stones by adding or removing sand until the stones are nice and level, especially from side to side of the path.

nature of a tap and endeavour to chip a narrow groove across the stone first. Repeat this on the under side, then give a few heavy "dead" blows with the hammer and chisel about the centre of the chipped line—the stone should then crack along the line.

Levelling.

After a few yards have been laid, test the surface level, as shown in Fig. 13, with a long straight batten and a spirit-level. The path may have a "fall" or slope—which will have to be maintained—but the "bubble" in the spirit-level will show this.

The most important test is across the line of path, as this ought always to be level—or very slightly raised or "cambered" in the centre.

At an entrance gate the path ought to widen out beyond the gate-posts to allow room for visitors to pass the gate when it is swung open. A pleasing idea is sketched in Fig. 1, which makes this point clear.

Paved Areas.

Paved areas are treated in the same way as paths. The larger stones can be arranged, as in Fig. 14, to form a simple pattern. Varied coloured stones can be used in moderation.

After a few yards of path or area have been paved, the sand should be raked out from between the stones and spaces filled in with cement mortar, gauged 1 part of cement to 5 or 6 parts of sand. Press the mortar well down into place, as shown in Fig. 15, and always have a wide board to kneel on while doing so—to avoid any chance of shifting the stones.

Finishing Off.

Finish off by "grouting," when all the paving is finished.

Grout is simply diluted Portland cement poured on to the path and brushed into the cracks.

Leave it for an hour or so, then brush off the surplus with a hard broom and plenty of clean water. A path laid in this way should stand for several years without attention—if any cracks develop—"grout" them in again as before described.

Rock Plants amongst Crazy Paving.

An attractive type of crazy paving is one where rock plants are planted amongst the paving stones. In this case the stones can either be laid "dry," i.e., direct on the mould, or else on mortar which is cut away at the junctions where it is proposed to plant.

The Wall.

Pleasing edges can be built—as shown in Fig. 16—with small pieces of paving stone bedded in cement mortar, gauged 1 of cement to 5 or 6 of shard sand. Use a line as a guide when building this wall. Finish off with walling stone of uniform thickness and width.

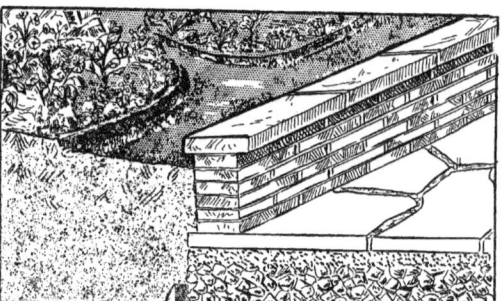

Fig. 17.—Stone Edging against Raised Bed.
The stonework against a garden bed should be "battered," that is, should slope backwards towards the bed.

When the wall abuts a garden bed—as in Fig. 17—the wall should have a "batter" or inwards slope towards the bed—a fall back of about 1½ inches in 1 foot of height is suitable. Set the best edges of the stones to the face; there is no need to bother much about the other side, as they will take a firm hold on the soil. When building a low stone wall in dry weather, always wet the stones thoroughly to delay the premature setting of the mortar and ensure a good solid job.

Crazy paving stone can be closely imitated by using concrete and cement mixtures, and full instructions are given in a later article.

LAYING A COLOURED CONCRETE FLOOR

THE laying of a concrete floor in colour does not present much difficulty to those who are familiar with ordinary concrete making.

One method is to mix the appropriate colouring material with the aggregate and cement before moistening these materials. This is a somewhat wasteful method, however, for floors, as it is only the surface layer that requires to be coloured to a depth of ½ inch or so.

The better method is to lay an ordinary concrete floor, using the usual proportions of sand, cement and aggregate, and to roughly level this floor to within about ½ to 1 inch of the required finished level.

The final coloured cement mixture is then laid on top of this foundation, and is smoothed off before setting. The operation of laying a red coloured concrete floor is as follows :—

First mix together ordinary concrete in the proportions of 1 part cement, 2 parts sand, and 4 to 5 parts of aggregate, e.g., stones, broken brick rubble or crushed whin of about 1 inch mesh. Lay this to a depth of 2 inches, tamping the wet mixture well and levelling off with a striking board.

Allow this to set for at least twenty-four hours.

The coloured surface mixture for a depth of 1 inch, say, should then be mixed and laid.

It is advisable to use a waterproofing ingredient, such as Pudlo, which must be added to the dry cement in the proportions of about 3 per cent. of Pudlo; this works out to about 3 lbs. of Pudlo to each bucketful of cement.

Next mix some ¼-inch granite chippings containing a fair proportion of granite sand in the proportion of 2½ parts to 1 part of the Pudlo-cement mixture previously referred to.

Finally add 2 lbs. of red oxide (per bucketful of Pudlo-cement mixture), and mix the ingredients thoroughly in the dry condition, before wetting to the pasty state. Then apply this mixture to the floor, to a depth of 1 inch, and carefully smooth over before it sets, by means of planks laid across and moved up and down the floor. A smooth finish of the desired colour is obtained.

Other Colour Effects.

Various colours may be obtained for concrete floors by employing suitable pigments. The latter should be mixed with the dry cement before it is added to the coarser material. Unless the mixing process is thoroughly carried out, the resulting surface will tend to become streaky.

The following colouring materials are recommended as suitable for use with Portland cement :—

Blue :   Parts.
  Portland cement . . . 86
  Azure Blue, or Ultramarine . 14
Green :
  Portland cement . . . 90
  Oxide of Chromium . . 10
Yellow :
  Portland cement . . . 88
  Yellow Ochre . . . 12
Brown (Chocolate) :
  Portland cement . . . 88
  Black Oxide of Manganese . 6
  Red Oxide of Iron . . 4
  Black Oxide of Iron, or Copper 2
Black :
  Portland cement . . . 90
  Carbon Black, or Black Oxide of Manganese . . . 10

In each of the above cases the Portland cement should be of the finely ground grade.

WATERPROOF CEMENT

The following recipe is for a waterproof cement suitable for making joints in stoneware, china, porcelain, marble and metal :—

  Powdered whiting . . 2 lbs.
  Ordinary sand . . . 1 lb.
  Litharge . . . 1 "
  Plaster of Paris . . . 1 "
  Resin . . . . ½ "

Mix together dry, and when thoroughly compounded make into a paste with copal varnish.

PAINT FOR ROOFS

Leaky slates, guttering or tiles may effectively be waterproofed by treating with a paint made up as follows :—

  Pulverised slate . . . 70 parts.
  Pulverised mica slate . . 60 "
  Powdered rosin . . . 70 "
  Pure coal tar . . . 100 "

The mixture should be boiled in order to mix thoroughly the ingredients.

STRAW HAT CLEANER

A readily made cleaner giving excellent results is made up of the following items :—

  Sodium bisulphite . . 5 parts.
  Tartaric acid . . . 1 part.
  Borax . . . . 5 parts.

Moisten the powder and apply with a toothbrush; afterwards wipe off with a damp cloth. A solution of "salts of lemon" (citric acid) and water is also employed for the same purpose.

REPAIRS TO KNIVES, FORKS AND SPOONS

It is an excellent plan for the handyman to spend an evening, every now and then, in going through the household store of table knives, forks and spoons, and in effecting any little repairs that the individual articles may require. As a rule, the repairs needed are easy to perform, while their usefulness is considerable. To dine, for instance, with a blunt knife or a twisted spoon is sufficient to spoil the meal, yet the work of putting them right is a very simple matter.

Sharpening Knives.

Probably the first thing that you will do if you spend an evening in this way will be to test the edges of the knives. In most households these implements are used for a multitude of purposes other than those for which they are intended, with the consequence that the blunt specimens will be much in evidence.

A certain amount of edge may be put on a blunt knife by running it a few times across a steel, in the manner adopted by butchers; but more lasting good will be effected by using an oilstone.

To sharpen a knife on an oilstone, first put a few drops of lubricating oil on the face of the stone and smear it fairly equally over the surface. Place the stone on the table, the short ends parallel to your body. Grip the handle of the knife in your right hand and put the blade close to the further short end of the stone. Arrange the fingers of your left hand on the blade and press them down firmly. See that the blade lies flat and that the cutting edge points away from you. Now draw the knife towards your body and, as you do so, take a diagonal course along the stone. This is done because the blade is wider than the stone, and

Fig. 1.—The best method of Treating a Blunt Knife is to Sharpen it on an Oilstone.

First smear a few drops of lubricating oil on the stone. Draw the knife towards your body and take a diagonal course along the stone. The blade is pressed down on the stone with the fingers of the left hand.

every part of it must come in contact with the stone.

When you have drawn the knife to the nearer edge of the stone, lift it up and carry it back to the starting position at the further edge. Then draw it once more along the stone as before. Repeat this about a dozen times, then reverse the process by turning the blade towards you and draw it along the stone away from you. The knife should now possess a keen edge.

Stainless Steel Knives.

Stainless steel knives have the reputation of being permanently blunt. This is certainly true of those made when the process was first introduced, but the later kinds can be treated in exactly the same way as ordinary steel knives, though it slightly spoils their appearance. Perhaps the best way with stainless steel knives is to run them up and down a leather razor strop.

Straightening a Blade.

After a good deal of hard use a knife is often found to be possessed of a blade with a wavy edge; in extreme cases there may even be a small piece broken out of the cutting edge, or perhaps there is a slight crack. The thing to do when any of these defects are present is to place the long sides of the oil stone parallel to your body, and, having put a few drops of oil on the stone, to stand the knife on it so that the cutting edge is alone touching. Then draw the knife up and down and across the stone. Keep moving it to different parts in order that the smooth face of the stone may not be damaged by grooves. In a very short while the blade will be provided with a straight edge, and then it must be subjected to the sharpening process already described.

Trimming the Tip of a Knife.

It is not unusual to find a knife that has a damaged tip; it may be that the rounded end has been broken off or that it has worn so much that the shape is no longer as it should be. A new tip is easily provided if a pair of metal shears or snips are possessed. Hold the knife firmly and cut the end of the blade into a half circle, being careful to remove as much of the steel as has worn as thin as paper.

In doing this you may bend the tip

Fig. 2.—If you have a Knife with a Wavy Blade caused by continual wear, it can be remedied by Drawing the Cutting Edge up and down the Stone.

Keep moving it to different parts of the stone so that the smooth surface of the stone does not become grooved.

Fig. 3.—A fault that is often found in Knives is a Damaged Tip.

A new tip can be easily provided with a pair of metal shears or snips. Cut the end of the blade into a half circle. If you accidentally bend the tip, place it on a stone and tap with a hammer.

REPAIRS TO KNIVES, FORKS AND SPOONS

slightly. If you do, place the new end on a piece of stone or metal and tap it flat with a light hammer. Then true up the edge that has been cut by rubbing it with a file, and finally sharpen the whole blade on the stone. In this way you will have a knife that is once more as efficient as it was when new, even though it may be half an inch shorter than it was originally.

Fixing a Loose Knife Handle.

Knives with loose handles are frequently found. This is because those who wash up in the scullery allow them to stand in hot water. If any specimens need your attention on this account, examine the handles and search for a metal pin, running through the ivory or celluloid.

If, as is usual, no pin can be found, and the blade is separated from the handle, clean out the cavity in the handle with a piece of wire. Then fill up the space with powdered resin, mixed with a little silver sand, or use four parts of powdered resin, one part of beeswax and one of plaster of paris. When the cavity is well charged, hold the knife blade with a pair of pliers and put the tang in a gas flame until it is red hot, then push it into the hole in the handle. The heat melts the resin and allows the tang to force its way in as far as necessary. In a short while the cement will cool down and harden, and then the handle should hold tightly.

Using Plastic Wood.

Another method is to fill the cavity with plastic wood, and then to lose no time in inserting the tang of the blade. Push in without rocking the blade, and do not use the knife for a day or two.

In cases where the blade is loose, but not entirely separated from the handle, place the knife in boiling water. In a few minutes the two parts should be so loose that they can be readily pulled asunder.

Dealing with Handles that are Pinned.

So far we have only dealt with handles that are not pinned. Should a pin be noticed, it does not necessarily follow that the tang and the blade are held together by means of a piece of metal wire. Sometimes a false pin is inserted merely for the sake of appearance. In such cases it has no effective use at all and the handle can be refixed in exactly the same way as when no pin is apparent.

But when a real pin is present, the treatment is a little fidgety. Fix the handle in the jaw of a vice and drill out the pin with brace and bit, then the two loose portions will come apart, on pulling them. Refixing the tang is done on the lines already explained, with the additional operation of repinning.

How to Insert a New Pin.

To insert a new pin, first be quite sure that the tang is forced home to its fullest extent, then heat a piece of fine wire and push it through the handle and the tang. If the pin goes from side to side, the wire will have to penetrate through the handle, then through the tang, and finally out through the opposite side of the handle; but in some instances the pin only goes from the base of the handle into the tang. Whichever case is present must be followed by the red hot wire in order that the resin may be cleared away. When this is done, the hole is plugged with a short length of brass or German silver wire, the ends are snipped off and filed flat.

Spoons.

Spoons will call for very few repairs. Some will be found to have the stems bent or twisted and others may have a rough lip, due to excessive wear. To straighten the stem, wrap a piece of rag around the twisted part and press it straight, using a pair of pliers for the purpose. For roughened lips rub the edge very lightly with a piece of the finest glasspaper.

What to do if the Bowl of the Spoon is dented.

If the bowl of a spoon happens to be dented, place it on a curved piece of wood, such as the end of a broom handle, wrap a cloth around the wood, fit the bowl over the curve and tap lightly with a hammer.

Pad the head of the hammer by covering it with a piece of smooth cloth so as not to damage the surface of the spoon.

Forks.

With these the usual trouble is that the prongs may be bent inwards. To straighten them, wrap a piece of rag around the stem of a screwdriver, place this between the bent prongs and lever the prongs back to the normal position. It will be found quite easy to get the fork back in its original shape.

Lastly, if the tips of the prongs happen to be rough, touch them with a piece of very fine glasspaper or a smooth file.

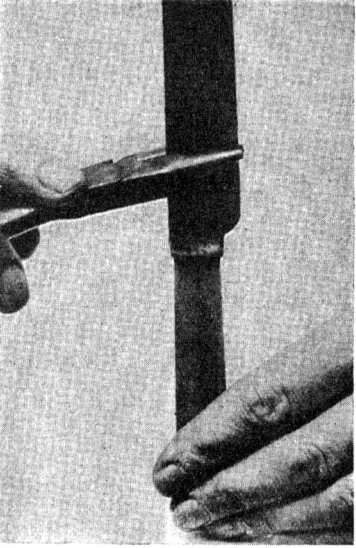

Fig. 4.—Have you any Knives with Loose Handles?
Separate the blade from the handle and fill up the hole with powdered resin mixed with a little silver sand. Then hold the blade with a pair of pliers and heat the tang until red hot, when it is pushed into the hole in the handle.

Fig. 5.—To Straighten the Stem of a Spoon that has become Twisted, wrap a piece of Rag round the twisted part and bend straight with a pair of Pliers.

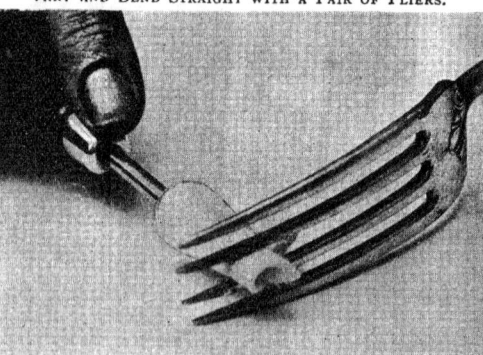

Fig. 6.—If the Prongs of a Fork require straightening, wrap a piece of Rag round a Screwdriver, place this between the Bent Prongs and lever back into the correct position.

Practical Notes on Yale and Mortise Locks

Keys for Tumbler Locks.

FIRST obtain from the ironmonger a "key blank" corresponding in form to the original key, then remove the lock and take off the back plate, thus exposing the mechanism. The number and position of the wards and tumblers, or levers, will then be revealed, and it is easy to file away the blank to clear the ward and to lift the lever or tumbler.

This done, a further movement of the key will bring it into a slot in the bolt. Shoot it along and allow the levers to drop and hold the bolt in position. Next turn the key backwards to make sure it will unlock the bolt, then replace the back plate and refix the lock. The actual cutting of the key is done with very thin "warding" files, and the best procedure is first to reduce the blank to such a size that it will pass through the keyhole and bear against the back plate or against the shoulder on the shank of the key, according to the type of lock.

Keep the sides, top and all edges of the blank square and flat at this stage. See that the hole in the lock, or the pin on which the key turns—as the case may be—does not stop the key from entering fully, if so, enlarge the hole in the blank or reduce the diameter of the shank on the blank by filing, or by turning if a lathe is available.

Smear Ends of Wards with Black Paint.

Next, try the key in place, lift the levers or tumbler and turn the key; if the blank is correct it will tend to push the "follower," or piece that moves the bolt forwards and backwards. The wards in the lock prevent full movement of the key—so the next step is to smear the ends of the wards with black paint and turn the blank against them. The marks impressed on the blank will then be a guide to the shape of the slots which have to be filed out of the blank, as indicated progressively in Fig. 15. Grasp the blank in a vice and work carefully, tak-

Fig. 1.—Simplest Method of Duplicating a Key for a Yale Pattern Lock.
The key that is to be used as a template, and the key blank are placed side by side in a vice and the new key cut to pattern with a three-cornered file.

ing especial care to keep the slots on the small size and their edges square and true.

The action of the blank can be tested in the lock if the levers are lifted or removed. When the slots in the blank are correct the key can be turned and will shoot the bolt in and out.

The final stage is to file the top of the key sufficiently to enable it to lift each lever in turn. If there is more than one lever, as in Fig. 17, first find out which is the master lever, usually it is the one with the slot nearest the lower edge of the lever.

File the blank at the spot exactly opposite this lever until the blank when turned will raise the lever the required amount and bring the locking pin into the long slot in the lever. Remove

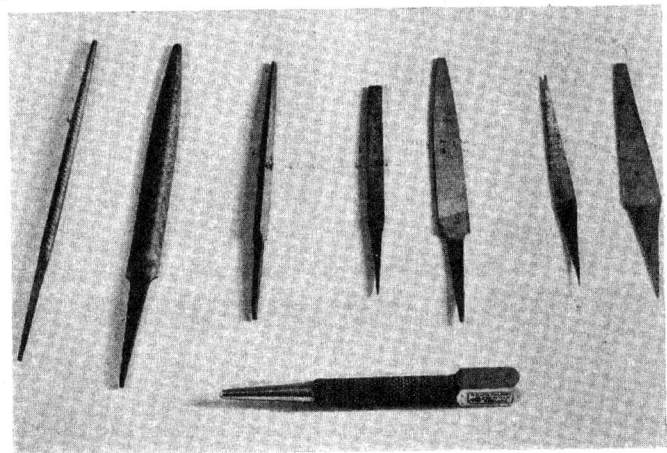

Fig. 2.—A Set of Warding Files and Centre Punch used for Key Cutting.

the other levers while fitting to the first, then deal in the same way with the others.

Duplicating a Key.

When the lock cannot be taken to pieces, the shapes for the blank can be found by coating them lightly with wax and pressing the key firmly in the lock and filing to the impressions in the wax.

When the lock is not available and a duplicate has to be made of an existing key—the whole of the work must be done by measuring with calipers or by making an impression in hard wax, or by pressing the original key into a piece of sheet lead.

In key duplicating always work from the "shoulder," as in Fig. 16, or that part of the key which bears against the lock case. First reduce the blank to size and thickness, then file out all the various slots, but keep all parts of the blank on the full side. Finally, go over all the slots with a fine file, carefully checking the shape by comparison with the original key and by measuring from the shoulder or from a part that is known to be accurate.

Do not measure from slot to slot, but always measure from one fixed place, as by so doing the chances of error are greatly reduced.

KEYS FOR CYLINDER LOCKS

Keys of the pattern colloquially known as a "Yale," although the name should be reserved for products of the Yale and Towne Company, have to be cut in rather a different way.

First obtain a fluted blank that will slide into the shaped slot in the cylinder. If the new key is to duplicate one already available, file the blank to match exactly, measuring from the shoulder along the blank, and from the bottom or flat edge upwards.

Removing the Cylinder.

When a key is not available, the cylinder must be removed from the lock shell, taking the greatest care that none of the little pins

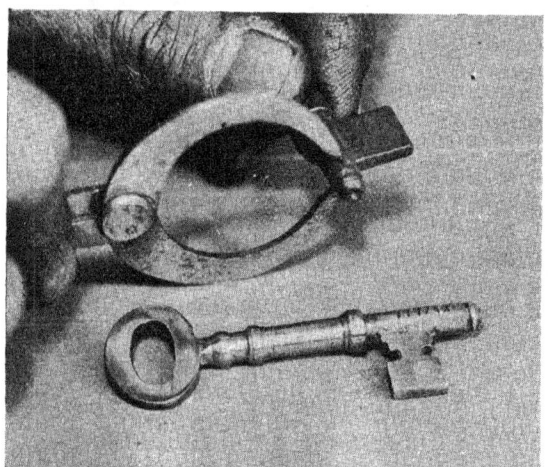

Fig. 3.—THE FIRST STEP IN CUTTING A KEY FOR A MORTISE LOCK.
Gauging pin key with calipers.

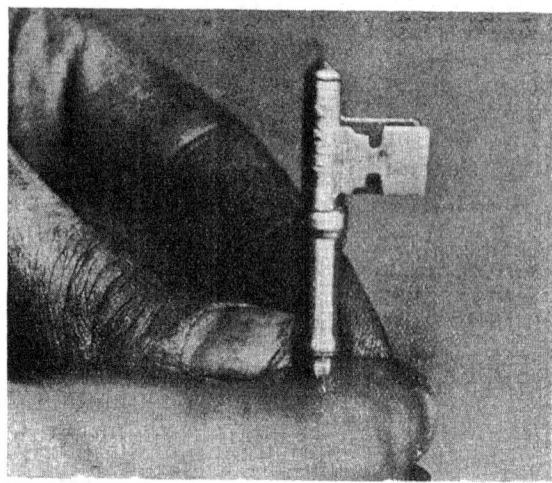

Fig. 4.—HERE WE SEE THE KEY BLANK FOR A MORTISE LOCK BEING COMPARED WITH THE KEY WHICH IS TO FORM THE PATTERN, TO MAKE SURE IT IS FULLY TO SIZE.

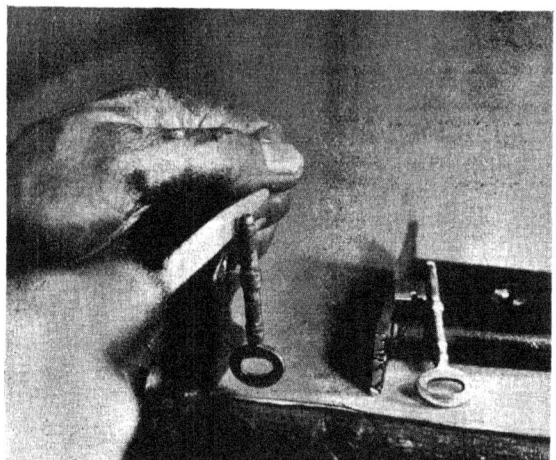

Fig. 5.—MAKING THE FIRST CUT WITH THE WARDING FILE
Note how the key is held in the vice. The sides should be packed to prevent marking by the vice.

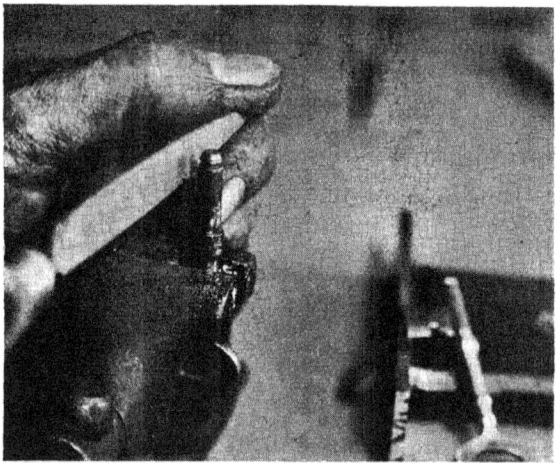

Fig. 6.—MAKING THE SECOND CUT.
Showing the incorrect method of holding the key in the vice.

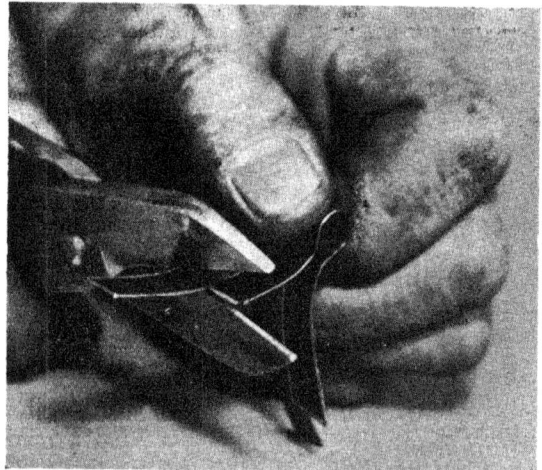

Fig. 7.—FITTING A NEW SPRING TO A MORTISE LOCK.
Cut the spring to size with shears. Make sure the eye of the spring is not too large for pin of lock.

Fig. 8.—FITTING A NEW SPRING TO A MORTISE LOCK.
Showing spring being put over pin.

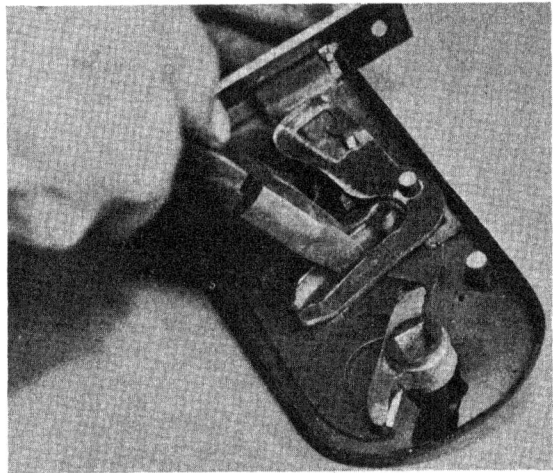

Fig. 9.—Fitting a New Spring to a Mortise Lock.
Showing the spring being pressed into place with pliers. Place finger on ward to prevent riding up.

Fig. 10.—The New Spring finally Fixed in Position.
Make sure the spring is the correct width.

Fig. 11.—The Lock Spring and Pin of a Rim Lock.

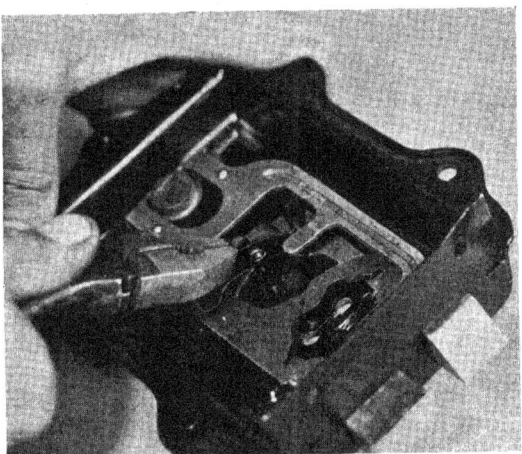

Fig. 12.—Inserting the Spring of a Rim Lock in place with Pliers.

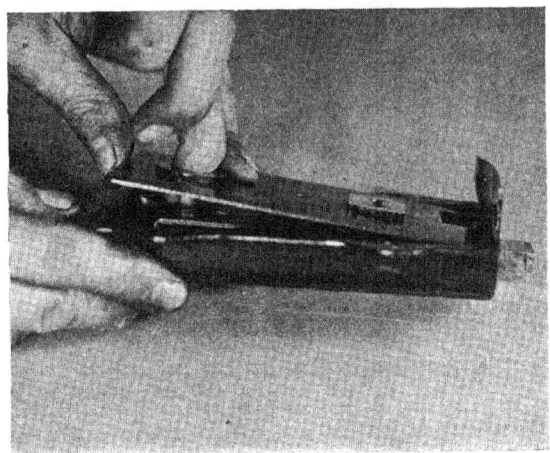

Fig. 13.—When replacing the Back Plate of a Rim Lock, take care to keep the Finger on the Follower.

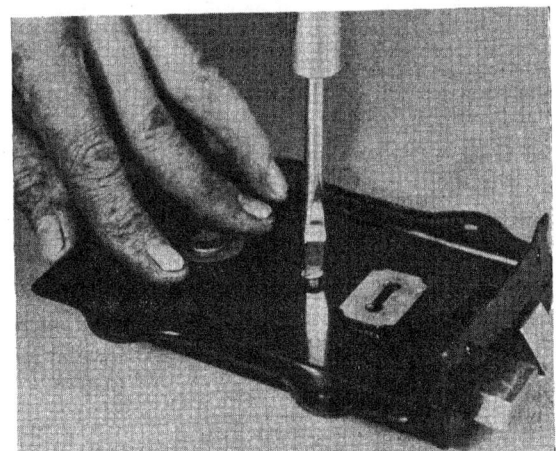

Fig. 14.—Holding down the Back Plate while screwing home the Fixing Screw.

fall out of their holes. Generally the cylinder can be removed by undoing a screw at the back and sliding out the cylinder towards the front.

There are two sets of pins, one set is in the cylinder and they move up and down as the key is inserted. The second set of pins are located in the shell and need not here be considered, as they play no part in the cutting of the key. Set the shell aside with the pins in their proper holes.

Precautions Necessary when Withdrawing Cylinder.

The most important item when withdrawing the cylinder is to do it slowly and carefully—as it is drawn out—a small pin will appear, as in Fig. 18, which should be lifted out and put on one side and designated Number 1.

Gradually pull out the cylinder, removing each pin in turn and noting its position as before. If the order of the pins is lost or they are put in the wrong holes it may take hours to discover their correct placing, and until this has been done the lock cannot be used.

Now Fit the Key Blank to the Slot.

Next, fit the key blank to the slot, should this be necessary to make it slide easily—but without shaking into and out of the slot. Next put pin Number 1 into the first hole while the key blank is in its place in the slot. Measure the amount the pin projects above the surface, remove the pin, insert a sharp scriber through the hole and mark on the blank the exact whereabouts of the pin. Withdraw the key, then carefully file across it and make a slot just deep enough to allow the pin to drop flush with the cylinder.

Importance of Accuracy.

This is vitally important, because if the pin projects even slightly it will engage the hole in the sleeve, and if the pin drops too far into the hole in the cylinder it will allow the sleeve pin to drop: in each case the result is the same, the pin will lock the cylinder and prevent it being turned by the key.

Fit each pin the same way, but work carefully and get all the pins about right first, then touch up the blank with a fine file until all the pins are perfectly flush with the cylinder.

Bevel the Sides of the Slots Slightly.

The sides of the slots in the blank should be bevelled slightly to cause the pins to slide up and down as the blank is moved along. This is a feature of pin tumbler locks—one or more pins always lock the cylinder until the key is pushed home, in which position, as shown in Fig. 19, all the pins will be flush.

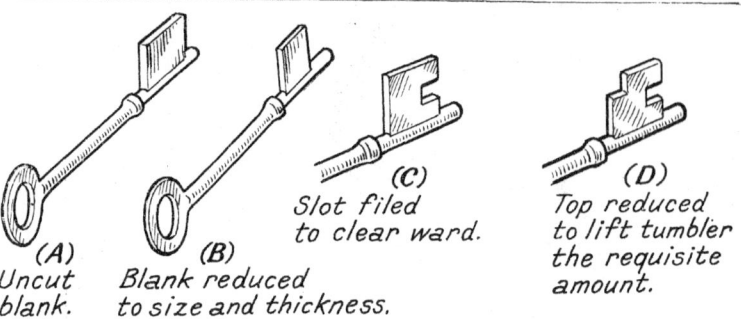

Fig. 15.—Diagrams showing Progressive Shaping of a Blank for a Tumbler Lock.

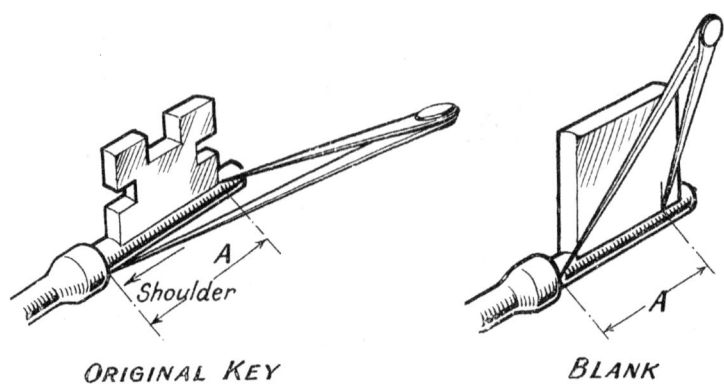

Fig. 16.—Duplicating a Key by Measurement with Calipers.

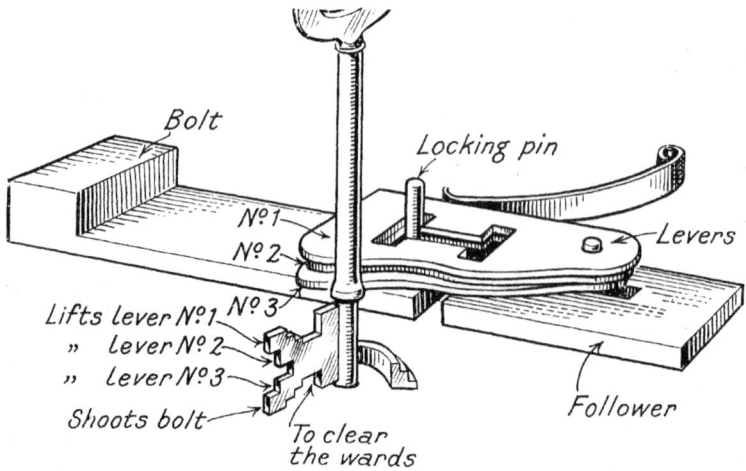

Fig. 17.—Arrangement of Levers and Wards of a Tumbler Lock.

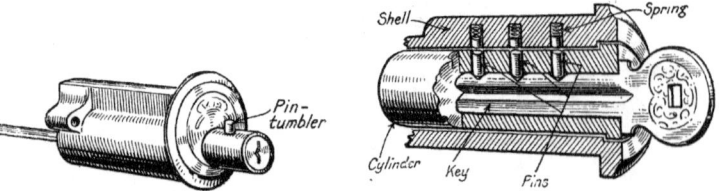

Fig. 18.—Removing Cylinder from a Pin-Tumbler Lock.

Fig. 19.—Fitting a Fluted Key for a Yale-pattern Lock.

PRACTICAL NOTES ON YALE AND MORTISE LOCKS

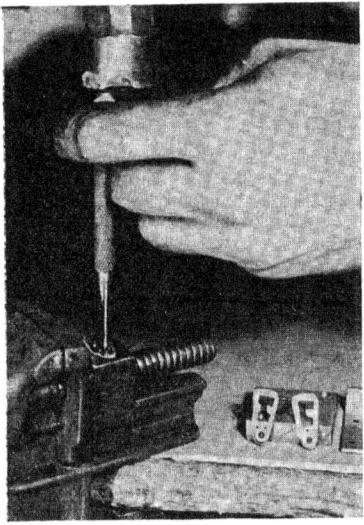

Fig. 20.—MARKING LEVERS OF A TILL LOCK AS THEY ARE REMOVED.

This is done by placing the lever on a metal surface and marking with a punch. It will be seen that the levers on the bench have been marked one and two.

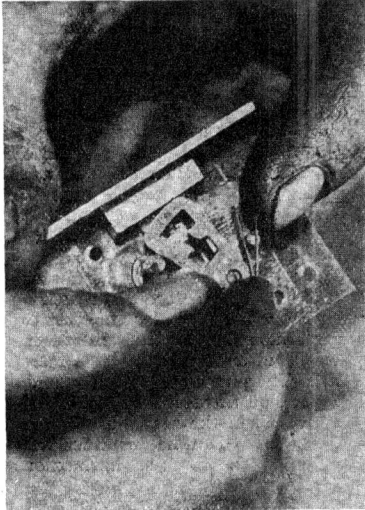

Fig. 21.—PLACING ONE OF THE LEVERS OF A TILL LOCK IN POSITION.

The key is then cut until it raises the lever sufficiently to clear the locking pin.

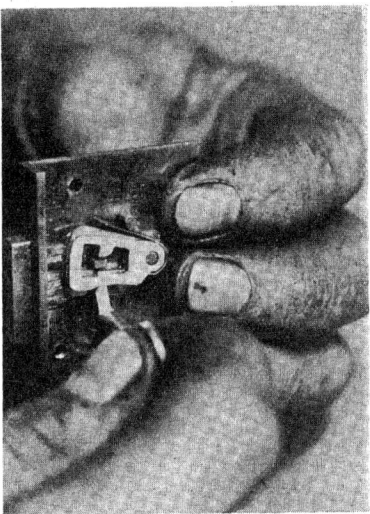

Fig. 22.—TESTING THE LEVER ACTION OF A TILL LOCK.

All the levers are now back in position.

Altering the Locking Sequence.

It may be pointed out that, if the new key is to be used in conjunction with existing keys, the order of the pins must on no account be altered; but if a complete new set of keys is wanted—or is desirable—as in the case of a new tenant of a building wishing to have the assurance that the door cannot be unlocked with existing keys, it is only necessary to deliberately alter the sequence of the pins in the cylinder and cut a new set of keys as described above. None of the original keys will then unlock the door and the expense of a new lock will have been saved.

When a complete set of new keys have to be cut, there is no necessity to be careful with the height of the pins—if they are practically flush and only project a trifle when the key is in place any surplus can be filed off the pins

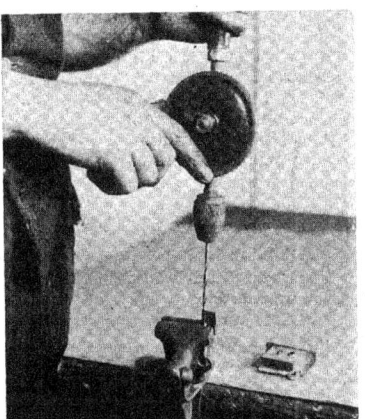

Fig. 23.—HOW TO DRILL THE BARREL OF A TILL LOCK KEY TO FIT THE PIN.

to make them flush with the cylinder. Any burrs or roughness around the end of the pin should be filed off and the ends left perfectly smooth.

The second and subsequent keys should be cut by measurement of the first, or master key,

TILL LOCKS

When cutting a key for a till lock and no pattern is available the cover of the lock and the spring must be removed. Then remove the levers, marking each one with a centre punch as in Fig. 20. If the key is of the rim type file away sufficient from bottom of key to clear the rim. Now place back the first lever and file the key blank sufficient to raise the lever into position to clear the locking pin. Replace the second and third levers in turn and repeat the process.

FIXING DRAWER KNOBS

THE knobs of drawers, used in ordinary households, have a habit of working loose; in some cases they cannot be tightened up securely owing to worn threads or loose screws. There are two common kinds of drawer knob in use to-day, namely: (1) the china knob, and (2) the wooden knob.

The china knob is generally provided with a metal screw *S* (see diagram) for attaching it to the drawer. This screw is held into the china part by means of a lead plug made by running molten lead into the hole around

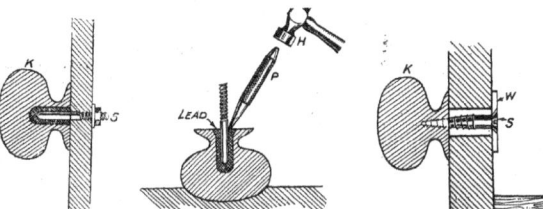

DETAILS FOR FIXING CHINA AND WOODEN KNOBS.

the screw end; the latter is flattened so as to allow the lead to grip it.

After a time the shank of the screw works loose, so that it turns in the lead, so that it is impossible to tighten the nut *S*. In such cases, if the knob is removed, placed upon a soft wood block, and the lead caulked with a flat-ended punch, *e.g.*, a nail punch *P*, using a hammer, *H*, it can be expanded so as to grip the shank securely.

How to Plan the Redecoration of a House

Sooner or later every room needs redecorating, and when that time comes the question arises, shall the old style and the old colours be followed or could a change and an improvement be made?

During the last few years great progress has been made in decorative materials. Older types of materials have been improved in quality and in the range and purity of the colours and several new materials have been introduced, so that the choice of treatment has been much widened. The taste for colour has changed, too, the drab tints so prevalent a short while ago are giving place to brightness and gaiety. Elaborate patternings have gone out of favour and simplicity and restfulness are now considered to be the keynote of decoration. If at times the simplicity borders on severity and bareness, this trend of popular taste is in the right direction; beauty and harmony are not dependent on elaboration.

Colour Combinations.

Most of us have preferences for certain colours or combination of colours, and in choosing a new colour scheme we consciously or unconsciously incline towards those tints that please us best, but in so choosing we should not overlook the circumstances of the room to be decorated, such as its aspect, the amount of light it receives, and its size and proportion.

Have you a Room with a Northern Aspect?

A room with a northern aspect and indifferently lighted can be made cheerful and appear full of sunshine if certain tones of yellow and orange are used, whereas green or particularly blue would be cold and cheerless.

Or a Southern Aspect?

A strongly lighted southern room could stand a rich blue and produce a sense of airiness combined with a quiet restfulness.

Red Makes a Room Look Smaller.

Red is a very insistent colour; it forces itself on the attention and makes any surface to which it is applied appear to come forward. Consequently, red reduces the apparent size of a room.

Green for Restfulness.

Green is the most restful of colours, but care must be taken to avoid a green-tinted light; it gives a sickly pallor to the complexion.

Use Browns and Buffs if Rest of Room is Brightly Coloured.

Browns and buffs are also quiet colours, very useful for decoration of rooms where the hangings and furnishings are to be of bright colour.

Don't choose a Pronounced Colour for Fireplace Tiles.

Unless a decision is made beforehand as to the colour of the hangings, it is important to use a "safe" colour scheme for the general decoration. When a strong decided colour such as red or blue is chosen for a wall, everything in the room must be selected to harmonise with and be subordinate to it. For this reason it is a very great mistake to choose a pronounced colour for parts of a room which cannot be redecorated, such as tiling for a fireplace, for the possible colour schemes are henceforth so very limited, and changes cannot be introduced. The purchaser of a new house will often be attracted by the bright fireplaces when the rooms are empty, only to find when he furnishes how difficult it is to get harmonious effects.

Effects obtained by Different Textures.

While colour undoubtedly plays the greatest part in a scheme of decoration, texture is also important. An entirely different effect is obtained by glossy or matt surfaces in paintwork, or by smooth or rough textures in wall finishings. In highly patterned designs texture is of little consequence, but in large and unbroken surfaces it counts for a great deal.

The wallpaper manufacturers have given much attention to this of recent years, and a wide selection of textures is obtainable.

Pay Attention to Proportion.

The proportion between the several parts of the decorative scheme is all important, and yet it receives little attention. For instance, how often do we see a dining-room with both a dado and a deep frieze dividing the wall up into three strips of so nearly equal a height that not one of them predominates. If the dado is desired, the frieze should be dispensed with, and the picture-rail should be fixed close to the cornice.

If you have a large Number of Pictures.

It is a common practice nowadays to divide up the wall surfaces into panels, either by wood strips or by paper borders. Happy results can be obtained by this means if pictures are not to be hung on the walls. If, however, the owner is the proud possessor of a collection of pictures which he loves to see, it is necessary to keep the wall surfaces as plain as possible. From what has been said, it is clear that to obtain a pleasing effect in a room it is essential to decide what is to be the dominating feature—the furnishings—the pictures—the fireplace—or the decoration itself.

Some Practical Considerations in the Selection of Materials.

In the selection of the materials to be used and also to some extent in the choice of colour, practical considerations should be given due weight. Parts that are liable to become dirty in use, such as doors, lower parts of staircases and passages, should not be finished in a light material that will not stand frequent washing. Walls subject to steam and as bathrooms and kitchens should not be decorated with materials which will peel off when damp. This is so obvious that it seems unnecessary to mention it, were it not for the very frequent overlooking of the point.

Notes on the Choice of Decorative Material.

There is a wide choice of decorative material on the market suitable for all purposes, and giving an extensive range of colour and texture combinations at a price within the limits of the ordinary purse. The chief of them will now be referred to with notes of their advantages and disadvantages.

Washable Distemper or Water Paint.

Washable distemper or water paint is the easiest material to apply. The way to prepare and apply it is described fully in another article. Some very delightful colours are obtainable from the best makers, and incidentally it is a false economy to buy secondrate distemper or paint, for the cost of the material is small in comparison with the labour involved in applying it. Distemper gives a broad restful effect, it stands well on new walls, and is so reasonable in price that it can be renewed at frequent intervals.

Preparing the Plaster Surface for Distemper.

It is, however, difficult to keep clean in spite of its name "washable." It can certainly be washed down without coming off the wall, but stains and grease marks are not easily removed as in the case of oil paint. Distemper requires a good plaster as a base, for it has not the protective quality of wallpaper. The hard plasters now in general use are excellent for receiving distemper. They should, however, be sandpapered before the first coat is applied, as the surface is so smooth that the distemper cannot otherwise get a proper hold or "key" to the plaster. A rougher sanded surface gives a delightful texture for a distempered wall, and also prevents condensation of moisture from collecting and running down the walls in streaks.

Distempering Ceilings.

Distempering of ceilings need not be done in white; light colours such as buffs or blues are a welcome relief. Before deciding on ceiling colours and the depth of the tint one should notice how near the windows reach to the ceiling. If the top of the window is low, the ceiling will be in shadow, and only a very light colour will be suitable. Remember also that the colour of the walls will be reflected on to the ceiling, and impart a tinge of its own colour.

Wallpaper.

The wallpapers of twenty or thirty years ago were so often of atrocious colour and pattern that there has been a revolution of taste towards the self-coloured and very simple patterning of the majority of present-day papers. When more ornamentation is desired, borders, panels and cut-out ornaments give ample scope to the fancy.

Papers with graded colours from a darker shade at the bottom to a lighter one above can also be obtained.

Embossed papers are little used now in private houses, but there may be places where they are of value.

Painting in Oil Colours.

This ancient method of decoration is still in the forefront to-day. The variety of colour and treatment obtainable, its lasting and preservative qualities, and its cleanliness commend painting as one of the best amongst decorative materials. Painted plaster walls with gloss finish are too much associated in the mind with offices and institutions to be wholly satisfying in sitting-rooms. If, however, a matt surface is given to the paint with a broken graded tint, the effect can be quite soft and pleasing. In bathrooms and kitchens there is no better finish for plastering than painting in oil colours. Plaster to receive paint must be smoothly and truly finished, even the slightest bulge or depression will show up when painted, particularly with a glossy finish, because the light reflected will vary with every change of surface.

Painting need not be of a plain even colour over the whole area treated, gradations of the same tint from darker to lighter shades or a gradual change from one colour to another can be produced, but naturally such work requires considerable skill and practice on the part of the painter.

Another type of variation from plain painting is stippling, in which the last coat of paint is partially removed by a brush of bristle or rubber or even by a rag used in all sorts of intriguing ways. The amateur should be warned not to overdo these effects; they are much more telling if confined to panels or similar parts of the scheme set off by plain painting for the remainder.

Plastic Paint.

A material of fairly recent introduction, plastic paint is much used for large wall surfaces in theatres, cinemas and other public buildings, but if handled with care, it is also suitable for house decoration.

It is supplied as a powder to be mixed with water, and can be applied to any clean surface with a brush, or, if used thickly, with a trowel. Before it has set it is worked over to give the requisite degree of ruggedness and surface modelling desired. The effects are attained by a variety of methods. Stippling with a brush of bristle or rubber, or with crumpled paper or a rag, lined with a painter's comb, worked with a palette knife or by other ways that suggest themselves to the decorator. Modelling in low relief of figures, landscape or ornaments of various kinds is possible.

When set it can be painted either with ordinary oil paint or with metallic paint. Two-colour treatment is very suitable, the whole being painted one colour, and allowed to dry, the second is applied and then wiped off from the high lights whilst still wet. It will be readily understood that only the less rugged textures are suitable for a house where, above all, restfulness of treatment is so desirable.

Spray Painting.

The application of paint by spraying machines is making rapid progress. Where the work is extensive it is an economical method and has much to commend it, but for the ordinary repainting in the house it cannot as yet be regarded as a serious rival to the brush.

Staining.

The staining of woodwork does not, perhaps, come under the heading of redecoration, for when wood is painted it cannot afterwards be stained. Staining is only used on new woodwork, its value lies in the showing of the grain of the wood and its ease of application. If the wood has been carefully chosen for its figure some highly decorative effects can be obtained. Staining is easily renewed, and when wax polished is charming, but the joinery must be well done. Carelessly prepared wood showing saw marks, unevenness and large knots looks bad indeed. These defects cannot be covered up as they can be with paint.

Panelling.

Most people would like to have some of their rooms panelled, but cost has often proved prohibitive. The small size of wood panels to prevent shrinkage showing has been another disadvantage, there are so many ledges to keep clean. But with the introduction of plywood and laminated woods, the expense has been reduced. These sheets do not shrink, and consequently large panels are obtainable. It is important that sufficient timber backing strips are fixed to the walls or the panels will bulge. The size of the panels should be governed by the sizes of the sheets obtainable, for all joints should be covered by the woodwork of the framing.

Wall-boards.

For many purposes fibre wall-boards have taken the place of plaster for ceilings and walls. The main problem in their use is the joint between the sheets. To make a satisfactory finish these must be covered by a strip of some material such as wood, thus producing a panelled effect. It needs some ingenuity to make a pleasing arrangement of panels when on the ground of economy one is limited by the widths of the boards for the size of the panels.

DRILLING HOLES IN GLASS

SMALL holes can be drilled through glass with a plain piece of very hard cast steel, worked like a drill in a small hand drilling machine (as shown in Fig. 1). The glass is lubricated with turpentine, and carborundum powder used as a grinding compound.

Larger holes can be drilled (as shown in Fig. 2) with a piece of brass tube of diameter equal to the desired hole. A guide for the drill must be rigged up on the lines shown in the sketch to keep the drill in place. Make a few slots in the cutting end of the drill which can be rotated by a hand drill or brace. If the tube is too large for the brace, rig up a handle on the top of the tube and rotate the tube with a cord coiled several times around the tube and kept taut by a weight or long spring. Charge the drill with coarse emery or carborundum powder and lubricate with water or turpentine.

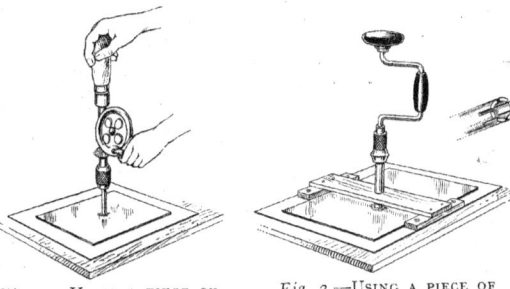

Fig. 1.—Using a piece of Hard Cast Steel.

Fig. 2.—Using a piece of Brass Tube.

Heating Apparatus for a Glass House

This apparatus comprises a boiler and two pairs of hot water pipes through which approximately 3 gallons of water continually circulate; in addition it has a hot air flue through which all fumes are conducted and cooled, finally being discharged into the atmosphere. The source of heat is a double burner Beatrice stove, the total radiating surface is about 12 square feet. The plant has been tried out through a severe winter and can be relied upon to defy frost, and in a small house 8 × 6 × 10 feet will maintain a minimum temperature of 45° F. on a really cold night, while a day reading of 55° F. can be ensured in mid-winter. Little or no attention is needed except the daily filling of the lamp; special cowls prevent all down draught, which may put the lamp out or cause smoking, while the external chimney eliminates fumes in the house.

Materials Required.

8 square feet block tin sheet, gauge 20–22.
3 6′ lengths of galvanised stack pipe, 2″ dia.
2 6′ ″ ″ ″ ″ 3″ ″
1½′ × 1½′ sheet iron.
1½′ × 1½′ × ¼′ plywood.
12 to 18 bricks.
6″ × ⅜″ copper pipe.
12″ × ¾″ × ⅛″ iron strip.
6 ½″ No. 8 iron screws.
Solder.
Asbestos string.
4′ quartering 3″ × 3″.
Liquid flux, *i.e.*, killed spirits or Baker's solution.

The Boiler Shell.

The sides of the boiler are in two pieces. Fig. 8 shows how each half is set out, the flanges are bent up at right angles along the chain lines, while a bend through 180° is made along the dotted lines. It is best to cut out the holes to admit the water pipes before

Fig. 1.—A Close-up View of the Heating Apparatus Installed in a Glass House.

The source of heat is a double-burner Beatrice stove, which heats a boiler to which are connected two pairs of hot-water pipes.

any bending is attempted. These large holes are easily cut with a metal work fretsaw blade, *i.e.*, a specially tempered blade for cutting metal (see Fig. 2).

Note that on one half of the boiler the 180° bend is made inwards, while on the other it is outwards. The two halves are then fitted together as in Fig. 8 with the edges interlocking as in the small sketch. A block of wood is now placed inside the boiler and the seam hammered down tight; it is then ready for soldering, which should be done on both sides of the joint.

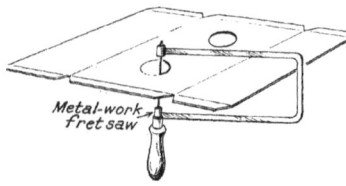

Fig. 2.—The Large Holes in the Metal can best be Cut with a Fretsaw Blade.

A specially tempered blade can be obtained for cutting metal.

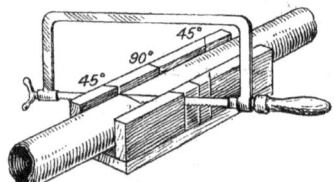

Fig. 3.—To Cut the Four Pipes to the Required Shape Rig up a Wooden Template as shown.

Fitting the Horizontal Pipes.

Cut the four pipes off to length and shape one end of each as in Fig. 5, so that it fits round an upright length of pipe. This can be done by first marking a line and then cutting away wedge-shaped pieces and finally cleaning up with a file.

Turn the boiler on its side and introduce the plain end of a length of pipe so that it projects ¾ inch inside, wedge it up firmly in position at right angles to the side of the boiler and wrap some cotton waste round the pipe inside the tank to prevent solder running through. A clean joint can then be made on the exterior of the boiler, remembering to have a generous flow of metal; hold the pipe vertically when soldering. Repeat the operation for the other pipes.

The Central Boiler Flue.

The boiler tube should be 13 inches long, so that it projects into the lamphouse and also above the top of the water chamber. Fig. 9 shows this tube soldered into the boiler top plate. Be very careful to see that the tube is square with the cover and remember to wrap rag or cotton waste round the pipe immediately below the plate; this prevents the liquid metal running through.

Fixing the Boiler Top.

Having soldered in the small copper expansion pipe (see Fig. 4), which provides an outlet for steam or excess water through expansion, fit the top in place and solder round the edge. The ½-inch flange along the edge of the boiler facilitates the operation.

Making the Base of the Boiler.

As will be seen by Figs. 6 and 11A,

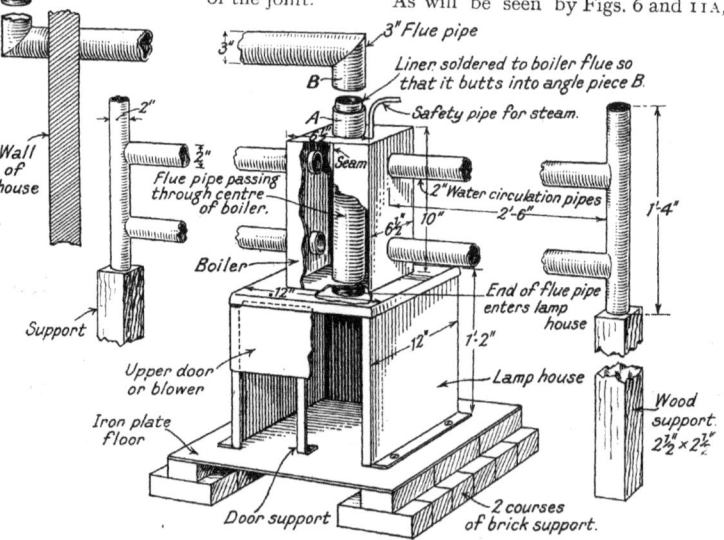

Fig. 4.—Main Layout of the Hot-water Apparatus.

HEATING APPARATUS FOR A GLASS HOUSE

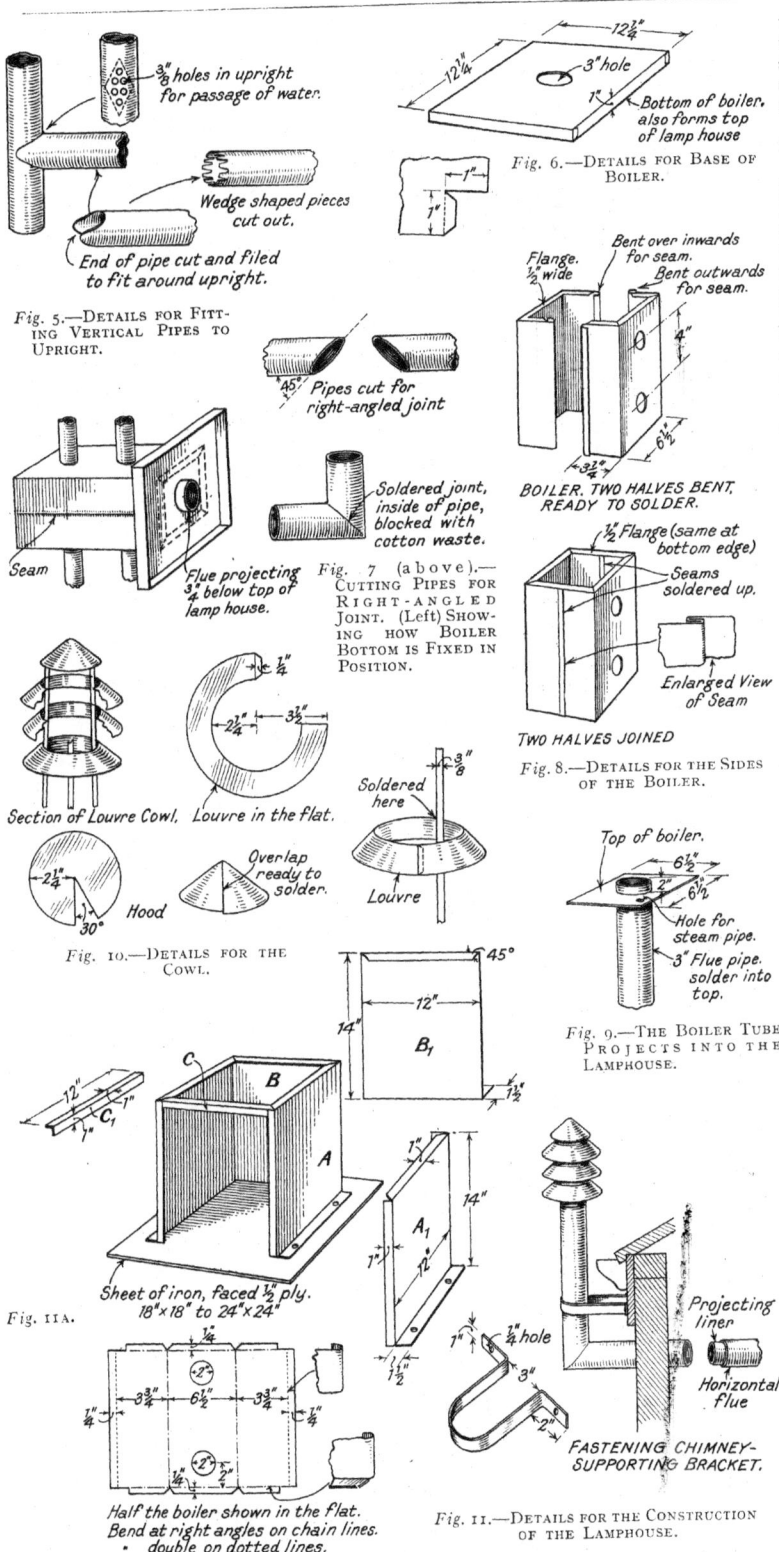

Fig. 5.—Details for Fitting Vertical Pipes to Upright.

Fig. 6.—Details for Base of Boiler.

Fig. 7 (above).—Cutting Pipes for Right-Angled Joint. (Left) Showing how Boiler Bottom is Fixed in Position.

Fig. 8.—Details for the Sides of the Boiler.

Fig. 9.—The Boiler Tube Projects into the Lamphouse.

Fig. 10.—Details for the Cowl.

Fig. 11A.

Fig. 11.—Details for the Construction of the Lamphouse.

the base of the boiler also forms the top of the lamphouse; for the size and shape of it, see Fig. 6; note the small sketch which shows how the metal is folded at the corner.

Fixing the Base.

The boiler is now complete except for the bottom. This is introduced into position as in Fig. 7, with the central tube projecting through. Stand the assembly so that the boiler is upright, apply downward pressure to make the bottom flange of the tank bed down on the top of the lamphouse and then float in a generous supply of solder, slightly tilting the work to ensure the metal running well under the flanges.

The Vertical Water Pipes—Testing.

Cut the upright pipes off to length and with the boiler standing on a flat surface fit each in turn into place and mark on the vertical tube the area covered by the shaped end of the four horizontal members, when the two are butted together. Before marking see that the lower ends of the upright are level with the base of the boiler. The marked area will be roughly diamond shape; in the middle of this drill six to eight ¼-inch holes, keeping well away from the edge of the line. The uprights can now be soldered in position, the lower ends sealed with circular tin plates and the job is ready for testing with water.

Pour water in through one of the open uprights until the boiler is full and the water level is 2 to 3 inches below the top edge of the vertical tubes. Mark any spots which may weep, and then resolder after the apparatus has been drained.

The Lamphouse.

Fig. 11A shows the lamphouse; it is composed of two sides similar to A and a back B, which are soldered together. C is an angle-shaped bar which ties the two sides together along the top of the front. The finished lamphouse is thus open at the front and top, and the whole is screwed down to a metal floor plate. A square of ½-inch ply faced with sheet iron is quite satisfactory for this.

The boiler assembly can then be placed in position on the top of the lamphouse; it is well to bed it down on white lead and gold size, and so prevent the escape of fumes at the joint.

The door only covers the upper half of the front; it fits under the top flange of the house and is held up by means of a strip iron support.

The External Flue.

The length of this varies with the size of the house and the position of the chimney. Cut the horizontal flue so that it reaches from the top of the boiler tube to within 3 inches of the inside wall of the structure. A right-angled bend, as in Fig. 11, must be made. A liner is soldered into the top of the boiler tube and this fits inside the short arm of the external flue pipe. This joint can be made gastight by introducing a couple of turns of asbestos string into the space between the pipe and the liner.

The Chimney.

Fig. 11 shows the chimney, the lower end of which is jointed to pass through the wall of the house and connect up with the flue pipe; note the liner which projects at the end of the horizontal smoke pipe and joins up with the chimney.

A small iron bracket (see Fig. 11) is required to support the vertical portion of the chimney; it is bent out of a piece of strip iron and loops round the pipe to which it is soldered.

The Cowl.

This is a very important part of the apparatus, as without it a high wind will cause the lamp to smoke and possibly blow out. A cowl, as shown in Fig. 10, will absolutely eliminate any down draught. Three or four ring sections are cut out as shown, and soldered up to form a dished ring (see Fig. 10). Three vertical strips of tin are then soldered equidistant apart to the first ring. The next ring is then fitted in place ¾ inch above the first and held in position with three blobs of solder; repeat this for the other rings.

A small conical cap (Fig. 10) is fastened over the top to prevent rain entering the chimney. The three uprights continue 3 inches below the base of the cowl and secure it in the chimney and yet permit its withdrawal for cleaning.

The Extra Flue.

An extra flue pipe can be fitted to the side of the lamphouse, rising in a sloping direction, and connected to a second chimney, if the main flue is short.

The Final Finish.

The whole apparatus should be given two coats of heat-resisting aluminium paint.

A small drain tap can, if desired, be fitted in the side of the boiler.

Erecting the Plant.

The finished apparatus should be erected underneath the staging at one end or along one side of the house; two courses of brickwork make a good foundation to support the lamphouse and boiler. The extreme ends of the water pipes can be propped with stout wood quartering or supported on a column of bricks. If the flue pipe is long it should be steadied with a bracket screwed to the plant staging.

Fig. 12.—A Stage in the Erection of the Hot-water Apparatus.
Testing the vertical pipes to see that they do not leak. Pour water in through one of the open uprights until the boiler is full and the water level is 2 to 3 inches below the top edge of the vertical tubes. Mark any spots which may weep, and resolder after the apparatus has been drained.

Fig. 13.—Fitting the Cowl to the Chimney.
This is fixed in place by three uprights which continue 3 inches below the base of the cowl.

Fig. 14.—The Completed Apparatus in Use.

REPAIRS TO ATTACHÉ CASES

Fig. 1.—Making a Permanent Repair to the Link that joins the Handle Grip to the Handle Plate.
The ends of the link should be pressed close together and then soldered.

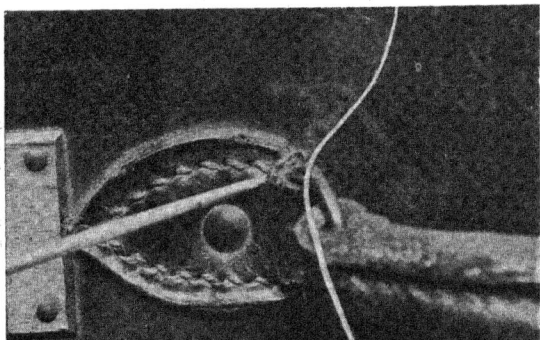

Fig. 2.—Stitching a Loose Handle Plate.
The awl is seen on the left and is making the last hole. The thread is on the right ready to follow the awl when it is withdrawn.

ATTACHÉ cases are made of a variety of materials. The better-class ones are fashioned out of cowhide; those of second quality are built on a foundation of cardboard and covered with a thin composition of leather; whilst the cheapest kinds of all are made of compressed fibre, glazed cardboard, or similar material. All are liable to need repairing, sooner or later, but it is only in the case of the better types that extensive repairs are worth undertaking.

Repairs to Handles.

Handles constitute one of the most vulnerable points, and it is here that repairs are frequently needed. It is not unusual for the metal link to open out and allow the leather grip to part company from the handle plate, fixed to the top of the case. On examination, it will be usually found that the link is made of a piece of circular metal rod that is merely bent to the necessary shape. The weight of the case has pulled the link out of shape and the two ends no longer touch. As a consequence, the gap between them allows the link to slip out of position and release the handle grip.

A Permanent Repair.

It is quite an easy matter to rethread the link through the loop in the handle and the loop in the plate, and then to force the two ends together by the aid of a pair of pliers. The repair is finished, but the link may open out again at any moment, and constant annoyance is likely. The best plan is to deal with the link once and for all. To do this, thread it through the two loops and bring the ends of the rod to the side where they can be seen. Press them together with the pliers and then put a touch of solder on them.

Fig. 3.—How to deal with a Riveted Handle that has worn loose.
It will generally be found that the hole has worn too large to take the new rivet, and it will be necessary to cut a circle of thin tin-plate about the size of a halfpenny on which the ends of the rivet can be turned back.

Fig. 4.—Removing an Old Lock which has broken, so as to substitute a New One.
The interior covering of the case will have to be lifted up, the four pins which are normally doubled over, straightened, and the lock lifted out of position with a screwdriver.

They are now joined together permanently. All that remains is to force the link round so that the soldered joint is seated within the loop of the handle plate.

Stitching on Handle Plate.

Not infrequently the handle plate comes away from the top face of the case. The repair, in this instance, depends on how the plate was originally fixed. Usually, it is stitched on; sometimes it is held by a rivet, and, in the best cases, there are both stitches and a rivet.

To restitch the handle plate, first pick out the old and broken stitches; then obtain some stout thread, usually yellow or buff is required. Cut a length of about 18 inches and fix to both ends a hair taken from a paint brush. They should be fairly tough hairs, each about 2 inches long, and the fixing is done by rolling around the join a very slight amount of sealing-wax. A cobbler's wax-end is made in the same way and would serve this purpose, but it is a little too thick and clumsy.

The leather handle plate is now placed in exactly the original position and a fine awl is pressed through the existing stitch-holes in the plate, but these holes are extended so that they come out on the inside of the case. When three or four of these holes are made the thread is passed through them and knotted on the inside. The bristle tips, it should be said, allow the thread to work its way through the leather without catching. As soon as the first three or four holes have been stitched, a few more are made with the awl, and work proceeds in this way until the entire edge of the leather plate has been dealt with. The sewing may be done with a needle, but it is not advisable since the chances are that the needle will break.

How to Deal with a Riveted Handle Plate.

When the plate is held on by a rivet, release the old one, if it is still clinging to a part of the leather, and then obtain a new one to take its place. Arrange the handle plate in its original position and force the new rivet through the hole so that the tips come out on the inside of the attaché case. In all probability the leather has been torn here and the hole is far too big for the legs of the rivet to hold when they are turned over. To make a good job of the repair, cut out a circle of thin tin-plate, about the size of a halfpenny, and punch a hole through the centre. The rivet is now passed through the handle plate, then through the body of the case and, lastly, through the circle of tin. The tips are beaten over flat and then the plate will be fixed strongly. It will be just as well to stick a small patch of suitable material on the inside of the case to hide the stitches, the circle of tin and the tips of the rivet.

Sometimes the handle grip becomes unsewn and falls to pieces. It is not much use to try to mend it and a better plan is to buy a new handle for sixpence. This should be provided with the metal links to replace the old ones or, better still, with snap catches to hook into the existing links.

Damaged Locks.

When a lock fails to act properly it usually points to the fact that some part has broken or become considerably worn. To mend it is often a long job and, as a new lock may be bought for a few pence, it is hardly worth the trouble to try to put it right. The old lock is usually held by four pins and the catch by two. If the interior covering of the case be prized up, the points of the pins can be reached; then it is a simple matter to draw them out and lift off the old fittings.

The new lock should be set in much the same position as the old one, and long pins used for holding both it and the catch. Unless there is plenty of length to turn over on the inside, the pins will drag out and the lock becomes loose. If in removing the old lock the interior of the case is much torn or otherwise damaged, it is advisable to fit on the inside a rectangle of tin, slightly larger than the lock and perforated with holes to correspond with those of the lock. The pins can then go through the leather wall of the case and, also, through the tin, where they may be flattened over tightly.

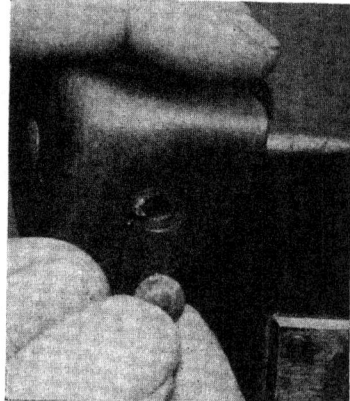

Fig. 5.—FITTING A CORNER CAP OVER THE CORNER OF AN ATTACHÉ CASE WHICH HAS SPLIT.

The corner is held by rivets, and a hole is shown in readiness to take the rivet which can be seen in the lower hand.

Indented or Broken Corners.

The corners provide one of the weak spots in most attaché cases, for it is here that they are most liable to be indented or broken. Not infrequently a corner of the lid splits open as far as the side panel and, then, small articles can easily fall out of the case. When any of these defects arise, it is usually possible to bring the edges together again by sewing them with a bristle-

Fig. 6.—GIVING AN ATTACHÉ CASE A COAT OF LEATHER VARNISH AFTER IT HAS BEEN THOROUGHLY WASHED AND DRIED.

tipped thread, as suggested above; but a stronger repair can be made by fitting a corner cap and fixing it with three rivets, one through the middle of each face of the cap.

These caps are made of a very tough composition of fibre and will take a surprising amount of rough usage. They can be bought in sets for a few pence, or it is often possible to use caps that have done duty on an old case that has been discarded.

Although one corner only of a case may need reinforcing, it is not advisable to fit a single cap, since the other corners would appear odd. The best plan is, if any caps are to be fitted, to put four of them on at least. This method preserves the trim appearance of the case.

Cleaning the Leather.

Brown leather cases that have become shabby in appearance may be cleaned and made to look fresh by scrubbing them with warm water and soap. Following that, they should be sponged with clear warm water and then gone over with a pennyworth of oxalic acid, dissolved in about a quarter of a pint of water. The success of this treatment depends on the leather being thoroughly damp before the acid is applied and on the acid being put on uniformly. Note that oxalic acid is a poison.

When the leather is perfectly dry it should be given a generous coat of any wax polish (floor polish or brown boot polish will answer the purpose) and then rubbed until a good shine is obtained. Another plan is to brush on a coat of leather varnish.

To take an ink stain out of a brown leather case, use some oxalic acid, as above, but make it up in a more concentrated form. Avoid rubbing beyond the stain as much as possible.

Perished Leather.

After several years of use, the leather of a case often shows signs of perishing. It then becomes dry and powdery. If taken in time a complete cure may be effected by painting the surfaces with a generous coating of salad or olive oil and, after a few days, giving a good rubbing with a wax polish.

Renovating a Fibre or Cardboard Case.

Wash lightly with warm water and soap, taking care not to wet the case much, and, when perfectly dry, give an even coat of leather varnish.

Renewing the Initials.

If it is desired to renew the initials on a case, be very careful to preserve the outline of the existing letters while washing and especially while using the oxalic acid. Paint in the fresh initials with a small camel-hair brush and some black enamel. Keep to the outline of the old letters and form every right-angled corner with the tip of the brush. Thus, if the letter "I" is to be painted, put the tip of the brush in the top corner and come half-way down. Then turn the case round, put the brush in the bottom corner and draw it up to the point where the first stroke ended. All the lettering should be done before any wax polish is applied.

Uses of a Small Power Transformer in the Home

APART from those wireless enthusiasts who build their own radio mains receivers, there is quite an ignorance in the mind of the average householder concerning the uses in the home of a small power transformer. To the layman the word " transformer " conjures up the large electricity supply stations, and it comes probably as a surprise to know that for about a pound can be purchased an efficient and reliable small transformer, adaptable to various uses in the home. This article cannot deal with every one of those uses because some are not generally applicable to the average house. We do deal, however, with several ways of utilising the small transformer which should prove both interesting and educative.

Only suitable for Alternating Current.

A transformer can only be used on A.C. (alternating current). If it is used on D.C. (direct current), it will be destroyed. As the name indicates, a transformer " transforms " or changes electrical voltage. With the small transformer used on the house supply, the A.C. voltage is stepped either up or down to suit the needs of the individual requirement. These different voltages are obtained by using so many turns of copper wire of various gauges. On the thickness of the wire depends, also, the amount of current which the transformer can carry. This explanation is probably a crude one, but it is hoped it will suffice as a simple one for the layman.

How the Transformer is connected to the Home Supply.

The small power transformer used in the home will give anything from 5 to 20 volts at from 1 to 5 amperes, according to the model bought. On the primary or input side of the transformer must be made the connection to the house supply. You will have two leads, one of which should be taken to the common " 0 " terminal and the other to the terminal marked with the voltage of your house supply. Most transformers have a tapped primary of 0–200–230–250 volts. If you are on 230 volts, you should, of course, connect to the 0 and 230 volt terminals. If the house supply is 220 or 240 volts, then connect to the next highest terminal, i.e., the 230 or 250-volt one as the case may be.

Some Precautions to Remember.

Always take care when connecting your transformer to the mains, and remember the maxim that should apply to all electrical apparatus : " Never make a connection or an alteration unless you have first switched off the mains supply." If you do not connect one of the wires to the common " 0 " terminal but take it to one of the terminals with the house voltage marked on it—that is to say, you have both wires on two terminals showing different voltages—you will burn the transformer out. For instance, never connect to the 200- and 250-volt terminals or the 230- and 250-volt terminals. Be careful, also, that loose strands of wire do not bridge across two terminals or you will damage the transformer. This rule also applies to any part of an electrical apparatus you are wiring up. The neater you make the connections the safer and better is the finished job. A power transformer made by a reputable firm is a perfectly safe component to handle if you observe the points just given ; it is only the foolish and careless who get an occasional " shock."

CHARGING THE RADIO ACCUMULATOR

The building of a charger for the radio accumulator is one of the most popular ways of using the small power transformer. There are many advantages in charging your own accumulator. The running costs of the charger are negligible, and the small initial outlay for the parts is soon repaid by the saving in service station charges. Regular and constant charging at home ensures long life to the accumulator, and there is no possibility of its being run down when some interesting item is being broadcast. Further, the trouble and delay in sending the accumulator to the service station in all kinds of weather, and at inconvenient times, ceases when you charge at home.

The Three Essential Components.

The construction of a small charger is extremely simple. Only three essential parts are required—the transformer, a metal rectifier, and a suitable resistance. These parts can be mounted on a wooden baseboard with a panel at one end at right angles to it. This panel carries the positive and negative output terminals of the charger. Very little wiring is necessary and the complete charger can be constructed in half an hour.

A Suitable Type of Charger.

There are several types of chargers which can be built, but a very satisfactory one which will meet the needs of the average accumulator used in a radio set is that capable of charging 2, 4 or 6 volts at a current of 1 ampere. The price of a good transformer will be under £1, the metal rectifier (Westinghouse Type L.T. 4) is sold at 13s., and the resistance should be obtained for about 2s. All three parts, and the necessary terminals, should be easily obtainable from the local radio dealer.

The Transformer Outputs.

The transformer should be suitable for the mains voltage of your house and have secondary outputs of 7·5 volts, 9 volts and 11 volts. These three different outputs are required so that the charger will be suitable for 2-, 4- and 6-volt accumulators. You must remember that the voltage drops as it passes through the metal rectifier. The regulating resistance should be of the pre-set type, having a value of 2 ohms.

Connecting up on the Baseboard.

When mounted on the baseboard the parts should be wired as shown in Fig. 1. The two leads from the transformer connect to the two terminals marked A.C. on the rectifier. At the other end of the rectifier are two more terminals marked + and −, and from these go the positive and negative leads to the appropriate terminals on the panel. The negative lead, however, goes via the regulating resistance, the slider arm of which is adjusted to approximately 1·75 ohms. There will thus be about seven-eighths of the resistance in circuit. This resistance should be left at this value irrespective of the voltage of the accumulator which is being charged.

The Transformer Connections.

To construct a charger suitable for dealing with 2-volt accumulators, the " 0 " and 7·5 terminals of the transformer should be wired to the A.C. terminals on the rectifier. With a 4-volt accumulator use the 0- and 9-volt transformer terminals, and when a 6-volt accumulator is to be charged, make the connections to the 0- and 11-volt terminals.

Use Red and Black Terminals.

It is as well to have the two terminals on the panel of different colours, such as red and black. The red terminal can be used for the positive output, and the black terminal for the negative output. Make absolutely certain that the accumulator is connected up correctly to the charger ; that is, the positive terminal of the charger to the positive terminal of the accumulator and the negative terminals each to each. If connected up the wrong way the apparatus will more than likely be damaged. When charging unscrew the cap on the accumulator and put this aside until charging is finished.

USES OF A SMALL POWER TRANSFORMER IN THE HOME

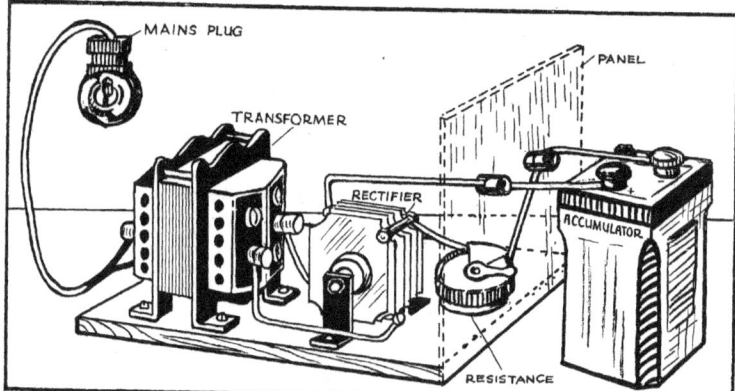

Fig. 1.—Diagram showing the simple manner in which A.C. can be used to Charge an Accumulator.

Only three essential components are required, namely, the transformer, the rectifier and the resistance. These parts can be mounted on a wooden baseboard with a panel at one end of it. This panel carries the positive and negative output terminals of the charger. This diagram, and the two below, show the apparatus in its simplest form, and it is assumed that precautions will be taken to see that any terminals are suitably insulated.

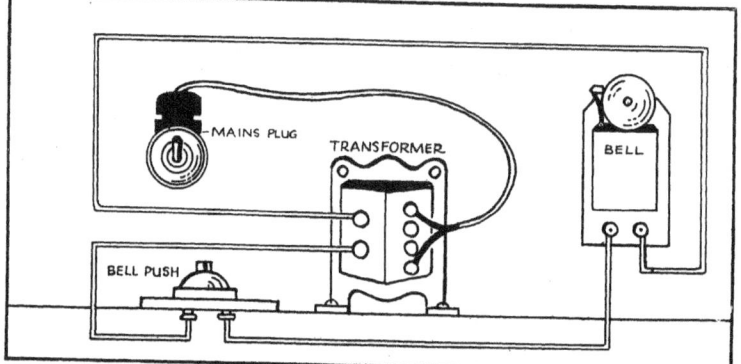

Fig. 2.—One of the simplest methods of using a Small Transformer for working the Bells of a House.

It will be seen that there are four terminals on the side of the transformer which is connected to the mains plug. One of these terminals is the common terminal marked "0" to which one wire must be connected. The other terminals will probably be marked 200-230-250 volts respectively, and the other wire from the mains plug is connected to whichever voltage corresponds to the voltage of the house supply.

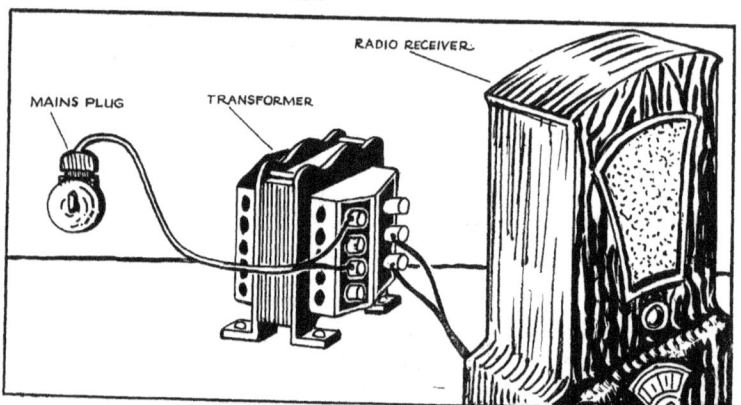

Fig. 3.—Stepping the Mains Up or Down.

Many people think that if they move to a new district where the electricity supply is at either a higher or lower voltage, any existing electrical apparatus they may possess is useless. This is not so, and the apparatus can be used by connecting a separate transformer known as a voltage converter between the apparatus and the mains. The above diagram shows how this is applied to a wireless set.

Make Sure You are using the Correct Output Terminals.

Always be sure that you are using the correct output terminals on the transformer, as explained above, *i.e.*, the 0 and 7.5 for charging 2-volt accumulators, the 0 and 9 for 4-volt accumulators, and the 0 and 11 for 6-volt accumulators. Never attempt, for instance, to charge a 6-volt accumulator when your charger is wired up suitable for a 2-volt accumulator or for a 4-volt accumulator.

How the Charger Works.

You will no doubt be interested to know how your charger really works. The voltage coming from the secondary side of the transformer is raw alternating current, but in its passage through the metal rectifier it is changed or rectified to direct current. The regulating resistance is inserted as a controlling safeguard. You will note that in its passage through the metal rectifier and resistance the voltage has dropped 5 volts, and this makes it suitable for the particular accumulator which it is desired to charge.

Time required to Charge an Accumulator.

The time required to charge the accumulator fully will depend upon its condition when first connected. Naturally, if the accumulator is well run down, it will take longer to charge than if it is only half down. With a home charger there is no excuse for allowing the accumulator to become entirely exhausted, as the charger is always at hand and can be used for a short time every day when the radio set is not in use.

OPERATING AN ELECTRIC BELL

The operation of an electric bell is another way in which a small power transformer can be used in the home. The ringing of the bell is only intermittent, and therefore only a cheap transformer is required. Some are available for as low a cost as 5s., but always make sure that well-insulated terminals are provided. The transformer takes the place of the usual dry battery which is often used. The simplicity of the connections is clearly shown in Fig. 2. The method shown would be specially suitable for use when fitting a new bell, and when there is a convenient plug point which is not in use for any other purpose. The practical method of converting an existing battery-operated bell installation to mains working is described in another article. Make sure all the connections are well insulated, as once the transformer is installed it will probably be looked at only at very rare intervals.

RUNNING AN ELECTRIC TRAIN

For the boy who is interested in electricity, one of the most interesting introductions to this fascinating subject is the running from the mains of his electric model railway system. The power transformer is the key to successful operation, and it is very essential that a transformer made by a well-known and reputable firm is chosen. Although the transformer can replace the battery it must be definitely understood that the output of the transformer is raw A.C., and it is therefore unsuitable for model engine motors which are designed for D.C. only. Make sure, therefore, that the motor is the universal or A.C. and D.C. type.

Details are nearly always given with the model train concerning the type of motor, but if in any doubt ask a competent electrician or radio stores.

STEPPING THE MAINS UP OR DOWN

With the varying mains voltages in different parts of the country, the householder is often faced with the problem of apparatus designed for a certain voltage being unsuitable for his particular supply. For instance, he has lived in a town where the mains are 200 volts, and his all-electric radio set has been purchased to work on this pressure. He is transferred to a new district where he finds the mains supply is 110 volts. The first thought that probably comes to him is that his receiver is useless, or will need to be pulled down, and a new transformer fitted. The simplest method, however, is to install a separate transformer known popularly as a Voltage Converter, outside the set. This transformer steps the mains up or down. A typical model is made suitable for mains 200–230–250 volts, and 100–110 volts. A person who has moved to a new district merely connects his house mains of 110 volts to the appropriate terminals on the transformer, and his radio receiver to the 200-volt terminal, and the common 0 on the secondary side.

These transformers are sold in different sizes according to the wattage consumption of the apparatus with which they are to be used. The average radio set takes under 50 watts, but always allow 10 per cent. margin for the efficiency of the apparatus. Never use these transformers for heavy wattage apparatus such as vacuum cleaners or washing machines unless the transformer has been specially designed for them. If you do, the transformer will instantly burn out. Fig. 3 shows the simplicity of installing one of these transformers between the mains and your radio receiver.

A BATH SPONGE RACK

THIS all wooden sponge rack forms a useful accessory to the bath. It lays across the sides, and being made of birch, does not scratch the enamel and is large enough to accommodate a sponge, soap and all the necessary requisites associated with the bath.

Material Required.

Piece of oak or other hard wood, 1′ 6″ × 3″ × 5/8″.
Birch wood rod, 3/8″ diameter, 12′.
Birch wood rod, 1/2″ diameter, 5′.
4 brass nails, 1″ long.

Making the End Pieces.

The two hard-wood end pieces are cut out to size with a bow saw and shaped up with a spokeshave. When truing up the corners, it is a good plan to clamp the two pieces face to face and thus ensure an exact pair.

The Holes.

Scribe a line round each end piece 7/16 inch from the edge and then set out the centres for the holes, which are 1 1/8 inch apart. It is important that the holes in the two pieces of wood should exactly coincide, and to make sure place one end on the other and prick through the centres with a fine bradawl.

Care must be taken to select a bit which will bore a hole into which the

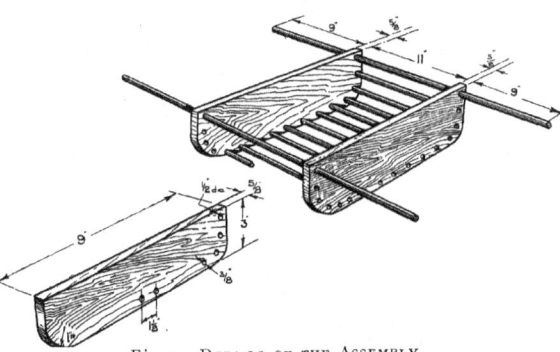

Fig. 1.—Details of the Assembly.

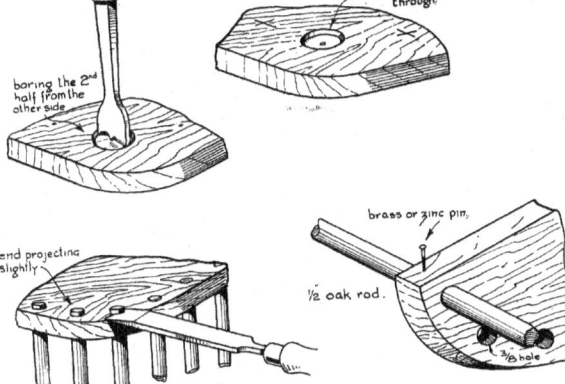

Fig. 2.—Details for the construction of the End Plates.

rails fit so tightly that they need driving home with a mallet. Drill each half-way through until the point of the centre bit just pierces the opposite side, then turn over the wood and bore away the remaining waste material; this method leaves a clean sharp edge to the hole.

Note that the two extreme holes which take the bearer rails are larger than the others, being 1/2 inch in diameter.

Assembling the Rails.

Having cut the rods to length, tap one end of each into their respective holes, then fit each in turn into the holes in the second end piece and drive well home with a mallet. The bearer rods are fitted last, the tray being clamped in the vice while they are forced through into place by tapping. These two rails are secured with four brass nails.

However carefully the rods are cut, some ends will protrude a little; these are trimmed up with a chisel, as shown in Fig. 2.

The Finish.

The wood is cleaned up with fine glasspaper, but no stain or polish is applied. The moisture which will find its way into the wood will cause it to swell and thus keep all the joints tight, it is therefore not necessary to use glue when fixing the rods. It is essential to use beech or birch for the rails, as these woods have a very close grain.

Painting a Kitchen

ONE evidence of the increasing interest taken in home decoration is the greater importance now attaching to the more domestic parts of the house.

No longer is the kitchen regarded as a mere place of domestic drudgery, entirely practical in purpose and without any claim to beauty. On the contrary we are now realising that because it must be useful, there is no reason why it should not also be good to look upon, possessing its own distinctive charm as a place wherein much time has to be spent.

This is equally true whether the lady of the house or a domestic help is the principal user, for it is now generally recognised that domestic work is all the better done if those who have to do it have the benefit of a pleasant environment.

Supposing, then, that it has been decided to renovate our kitchen, how shall we go about it?

Much will depend, of course, upon the condition in which it now is and our own personal preference. But the fact that it is a place where cooking and other domestic work has to be done will largely govern our choice. Obviously, many of the materials and treatments suitable for an entertaining room would be quite out of place here.

Alternative Treatments.

There are, however, three alternative types of treatment which, in varying degree, would be practicable for the ceiling and walls.

The first is to treat them with a washable distemper or water paint in appropriate colours. And, if the house is a new one and the plaster surfaces are in good condition and have never been covered with anything before, such a scheme would be quite suitable.

The second is to use wallpapers of suitable design and texture and of a type which is impervious to steam and wear and tear.

"Sanitary" papers (by which is meant wallpapers which are printed in oil colours) are fairly durable and can be made more so by varnishing, either during manufacture or after they have been hung.

The third, and in the opinion of experts the best, method is to use paint, for a properly painted surface is not only extremely durable, but is easily washable and, therefore, particularly hygienic.

Fig. 1.—The Correct Preparation of the Surface is important. Plaster of Paris made into a thick paste with water should be used to fill any cracks or abrasions.

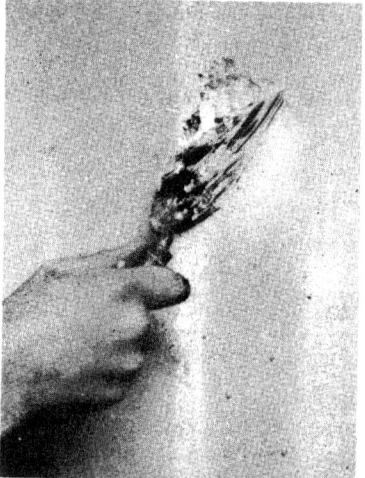

Fig. 2.—The Plaster is applied to the Wall with a Small Trowel.

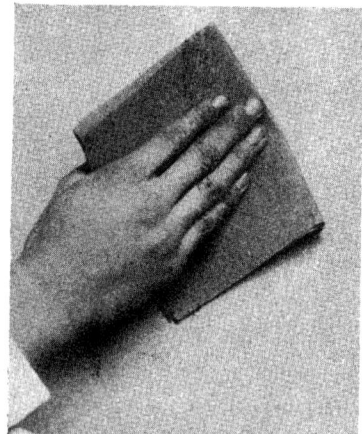

Fig 3.—The whole Surface should be thoroughly sandpapered to remove all Loose Grit.

Preparation of the Surface.

In all kinds of painting the preparatory processes are important. Upon the manner in which they are carried out depends much of the success of the final result. And this is particularly true of interior surfaces, such as walls, which are under a constant and close inspection.

Bare plaster, provided that it is dry and that, if new, it has been left long enough for the lime content to become dormant, is the easiest kind of surface to prepare.

Any cracks or any abrasions of any kind that there may be should be filled up with plaster of Paris made into a thick paste with water.

As this sets rapidly, it should be mixed in small quantities and used immediately. The crack to be filled should be thoroughly wetted, the plaster mixture put in with a knife or trowel and, before it has time to set, it should be carefully smoothed level with the bare tool, which itself should be kept wetted.

A thorough sandpapering of the whole surface so as to remove all loose grit and a careful dusting down is all the further preparation required before proceeding to paint.

But our plaster work is more likely not to be new, but to be covered with old distemper, wallpaper or paint.

Removing Old Distemper.

If old-fashioned whiting distemper is present, it must be washed off by scrubbing with a stiff brush and the use of water, preferably hot. This is rather a messy process unless it is carried out in the right way.

Taking one fair-sized section at a time, it should be well soaked so as to loosen the distemper. Then the softened material should be removed by means of a sweeping motion of the brush (an old whitewash brush is best) and the brush is then scraped out on the edge of a bucket. This process is repeated until the wall is bare down to the plaster.

If a really washable distemper or true water paint has been previously used it will be sufficient to remove merely the loose portions, and the rest may be left on.

When this has been done, the wall should be allowed to become thoroughly dry. Sandpapering and dusting are next done, and then painting can proceed.

Removing Old Wallpaper.

If, however, the surface has previously been papered, the old paper will require removal. This is done by thoroughly soaking with water, after which the paper can be easily removed by means of a painter's scraper.

After the whole of the paper has been cleared away, the surface should be washed down with warm water, so as to dissolve and remove all traces of old paste. Then, when the plaster is dry, follows the sandpapering and dusting previously described.

We may, however, have to deal with a surface previously covered with a varnished paper. In that case, removal would be an exceedingly difficult and tedious proceeding. And, if the paper is in fair condition and fast to the wall, removal is not necessary. All that is needed is to give the surface a very thorough sandpapering with a coarse grit grade of paper.

The object of this is to remove or "kill" the gloss of the varnish, and particular attention should be paid to the joints of the paper, which will probably protrude a little above the adjoining surface and should therefore be rubbed level. When this sandpapering has been done, the whole of the surfaces should be washed down with warm water in which a very small amount of washing soda, say 1 oz. to a gallon of water, has been dissolved.

This is to kill any dirt or grease remaining, and, after washing, swilling down with clean water is advised. Then the work should be given ample time to dry.

Preparing Previously Painted Surfaces.

But our ceiling and (or) walls may have been previously painted. In that case the preparation will consist of the washing with weak soda water, the clean swilling, the making good of cracks with plaster, a thorough sandpapering, and a final dusting down.

Having described the various preparatory processes that may be necessary, we are now ready to proceed with the actual painting.

On a previously painted or varnished surface which is in fairly good condition, and provided no great change of colour is desired, two coats of paint may be sufficient. On bare plaster three, or preferably four, coats will be needed.

Mixing the First or Primary Coat.

On bare plaster, the first or priming coat should be mixed as follows :—

(A) Genuine white lead paste   56 lbs.
    Genuine boiled linseed oil 14 ,,
    Genuine turpentine   . 2 ,,
    Patent paste driers   . 2 ,,

This will yield 74 lbs. or about $2\frac{3}{4}$ gallons of paint, and cover about 2,400 square feet, one coat.

After this has been applied and allowed from twenty-four to forty-eight hours to harden, the surface should be looked over and, if there are any irregularities, these should be made good with linseed oil putty to which a little stiff paste white lead and dry whiting have been added.

This should be applied with a pointed putty knife, pressing the putty well in and smoothing it off with the blade of the knife. The whole surface should then be lightly sandpapered down with a fine-grade paper, and dusted off.

Mixing the Second Coat.

Next apply the second coat, which should be composed in the following proportions :—

(B) Genuine white lead paste   28 lbs.
    Genuine raw linseed oil $2\frac{1}{2}$,,
    Genuine turpentine   . $2\frac{1}{2}$,,
    Patent paste driers   . 1 lb.

This will make 34 lbs. or about $1\frac{1}{4}$ gallons of paint and cover approximately 1,200 square feet, one coat.

After again allowing full time for drying, sandpaper and dust again.

The composition of the third and final coat will depend upon whether a glossy, an egg-shell or a dull finish is required.

How to obtain Various Finishes.

For a dull finish, the following formula will be suitable :—

(C) Genuine white lead paste   28 lbs.
    Genuine turpentine   . 4 ,,
    Copal varnish   . $\frac{1}{4}$ lb.
    Patent paste driers   . $\frac{3}{4}$,,

Here we get a total of 33 lbs. or about $1\frac{1}{4}$ gallons of paint, to cover about 1,250 square feet of surface.

For an egg-shell or half-gloss finish the quantity of varnish should be increased to 1 lb. and the turpentine should be decreased to $3\frac{1}{4}$ lbs.

If a full gloss is required the same formula should be modified by reducing the turpentine to $\frac{1}{2}$ lb., omitting the varnish and substituting $3\frac{1}{2}$ lbs. raw linseed oil, and increasing the driers to $1\frac{1}{4}$ lbs.

It may be mentioned here that if liquid driers are used instead of the patent paste type, only one-quarter the above quantities will be required, as they are much more powerful in action.

It will be observed that all the above formulas are for white paints. If, as is most likely, coloured paints are required, the only alteration to the formulas required is that for the second and final coatings there will require to be added a sufficient quantity of paste colour or colours to produce the required tint. The correct method of mixing is as follows.

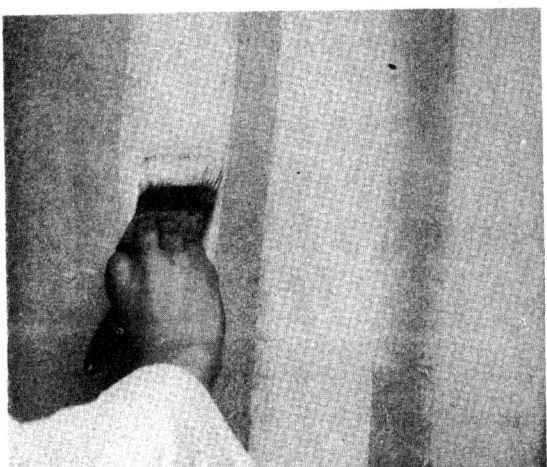

Fig. 4.—The Correct Method of applying the Paint. First Stage.
It should first be laid on in perpendicular bands.

Fig. 5.—The Correct Method of applying the Paint. Second Stage.
The perpendicular strips should be crossed in a horizontal direction.

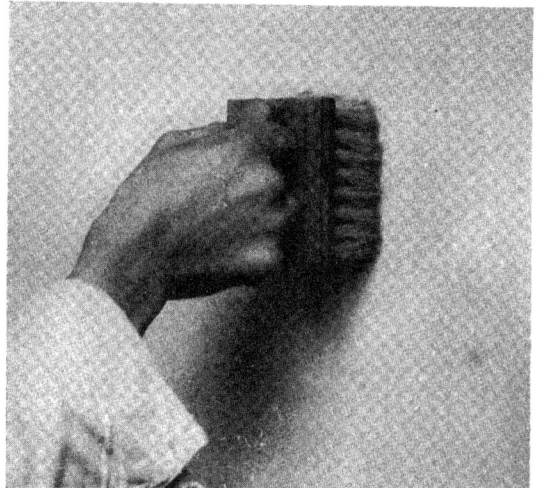

Fig. 6.—For an extra good and even Finish the Final Coat should be stippled while still Wet with a Special Stippling Brush.

Fig. 7.—A Final Reminder—Clean your Brushes after using. Showing the stippler being washed out in soap and water.

How to Mix your Paint.

Place the white lead paste and driers in a sufficiently large vessel. Gradually add small quantities of the oil and turpentine, constantly stirring until a uniform soft paste is obtained. Then add the rest of the oil and turpentine. Mix each of the tinting paste colours, in separate receptacles, with linseed oil and (or) turpentine to the same consistency as the white paint and add small quantities at a time until the right shade is obtained, constantly stirring and amalgamating each addition before the next is made. Finally, strain the complete mixture through a metal strainer or a fine cloth tied over the mouth of another vessel.

Correct Method of Painting.

In applying the paint to the surface, two brushes will be required; one such as a No. 4 tool or a 1-inch flat brush for cutting in edges, and a larger (and the larger, within reason, the better) for the broad parts. Any brush of the oval pound type or the flat form up to 4 inches wide is suitable.

The paint is first laid on in perpendicular bands, then crossed in the horizontal direction and finally " laid off " very lightly with the tips of the brush in upward and downward strokes.

For an extra good and even finish, it is desirable to stipple the final coat, while it is still wet, with a special stippling brush. Such brushes, being rather costly, are not always available. But if one is obtainable, its use eradicates all traces of brush marks.

A Four-coat Job.

If a four-coat job is required, the third coat may be similar in composition to the second, described above.

All the above refers to work where we begin with a bare plaster surface. On surfaces which have been previously painted or varnished, the number of coats required will be one less.

But the processes required will be as those already given, omitting only formula A and its application.

A Varnish Finish.

If it is desired to add a varnish finish to the work or any part of it, the last coat of paint should be mixed according to the directions given for a flat finish, as varnish should always be applied over a dull undercoating.

Also, when varnish is to be applied, there should not be any stippling of the finishing coat of paint, but it should be laid off as smoothly as possible with the brush.

In applying varnish, the most scrupulous cleanliness must be observed. If the same brushes that have been used for painting are to be used for varnish, they must be first thoroughly washed in turpentine, then in soap and warm water, then swilled out in clean water, and allowed to become perfectly dry before being put into the varnish.

A spotlessly clean vessel (a large jam jar is quite suitable) must be used, and care taken to avoid any dust in the room, both during application and for at least twelve hours after.

The type of varnish used will depend on the colour of the paint to be covered. If the colour is dark, a copal carriage varnish will suffice. But, if the colours are pale, such a varnish would darken them. In such cases, an extra pale decorative or white oil varnish is called for.

The varnish is applied much as is described for painting, except that excessive brushing must be avoided. Once the surface is covered with the right thickness it should be left. And the theory of sound workmanship is that, whereas coats of paint should be well brushed out into a thin film, varnish should be as generously applied as may be without it running.

HOW TO PREVENT SILVER FROM TARNISHING

To prevent silver articles from tarnishing in a room in which there are gas burners or gas coal or coke fires, they must be coated with a suitable transparent coating, which must be thin enough not to have any noticeable effect on the appearance of the silver.

A suitable solution can be made by dissolving ordinary gelatine in hot water until a syrup-like consistency is obtained. Then add sufficient potassium bichromate to give the solution a light lemon colour.

This solution should be applied warm with a camel-hair brush. Make sure that all corners, niches, etc., are coated, as discoloration is most likely to start at these places. Small objects can often best be dealt with by immersing them in the solution and allowing them to drain whilst suspended over the dipping vessel. It will be found that the action of ordinary daylight upon gelatine having potassium bichromate is to convert it into a tough colourless film which will be quite permanent.

Soft Soldering

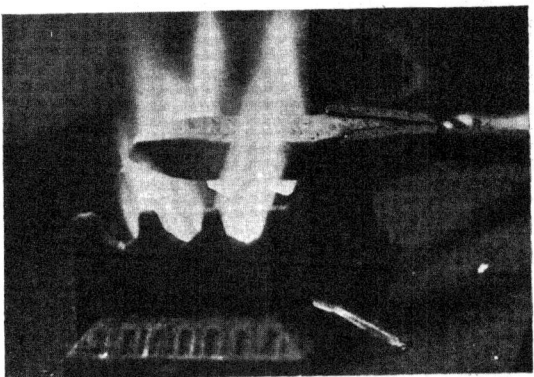

Fig. 1.—The Iron should be heated in the Flame of a Gas Ring or Bunsen Burner.

The flame should be applied just above the point of the bit, and the iron is correctly heated when the flame of the burner turns a brilliant green.

Fig. 2.—It is important to keep the Four Sides of the Bit properly Tinned.

Obtain an old tin lid and place a dab of fluxite on it. Then heat and clean the iron and rub it on the surface of the tin lid, applying solder at the point of contact.

Soft soldering is a method of uniting metals, by means of an alloy composed of tin and lead. The process is suitable only when the joint area is large, or where a joint of low mechanical strength is sufficient.

Metals which can be Soldered.

It is not possible to join all metals with soft solder. The following metals are readily united, with ordinary tinmans' solder:—

Copper.
Brass.
Gunmetal.
Bronze.
Nickel-silver.
Lead.
Zinc.
Tin-plate.
Wrought Iron.
Mild steel.

Pewter Solder.

By the use of special low melting-point solders, bismuth, tin and pewter can be soldered. Bismuth and pewter melt at a lower temperature than ordinary solder, so that a special solder, containing bismuth, is used for uniting these metals. Tin can be soldered with a solder containing 60 per cent. lead and 40 per cent. tin, but great care is necessary because the melting points are very close. However, the soldering of pure tin is of rare occurrence. In this connection, tin should not be confused with the familiar tinned sheet mild steel, which is readily joined with ordinary tinmans' solder.

Metals not to be Soft Soldered.

Cast iron is the principal common metal which cannot be soft soldered with any degree of success. Although gold and silver articles can be soft soldered, by the same methods used for brass, special hard solders should always be used. The subject of hard soldering is dealt with in a separate article on pages 13 and 14.

Soldering Aluminium.

It is possible, by the use of one of the several patent solders, to join aluminium with a soldering bit. With solders in which the chief metals are tin or lead, stearin is used as a flux. The soldering of aluminium cannot be regarded as a satisfactory process where the finished article is to be used for boiling water.

Cleaning the Work.

The first essential in soft soldering

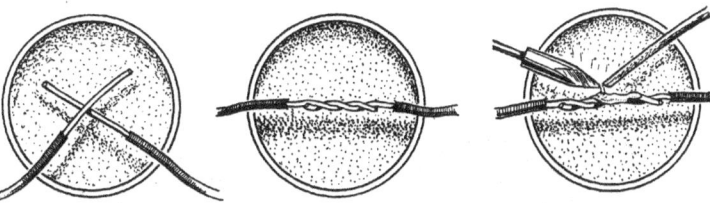

Fig. 3.—How to Solder Two Pieces of Wire together.
First bare the wires, then twist them together and apply solder.

is to clean properly the surfaces of the joint. It is not only necessary to remove dirt and grease, but also to obtain a chemically clean surface. Certain patent fluxes and solders, such as Soldo, obviate the cleaning prior to soldering, because they contain powerful solvents, which dissolve the dirt and oxide from the metal, under the action of the heat of the soldering iron. For the usual job, where ordinary solder and fluxes are used, the metal is first cleaned up bright with emery cloth, and in badly rusted material, with a file or scraper. In this respect iron or mild steel is more difficult to prepare than brass or copper, because the surface of the corroded iron is pitted with the rusting. A wire brush is used for cleaning rusty steel articles.

Fluxes.

The object of using a flux is not only to assist the flowing of the solder, but to prevent the surface of the clean metal from oxidising when it is heated by the soldering bit. There are three fluxes which cover the requirements of most soldering jobs. They are zinc chloride, resin and tallow.

Killed Spirits.

Zinc chloride is commonly known as "killed spirits." It is prepared by dissolving strips of zinc in spirits of salts, until the solution ceases to effervesce. Another way is to purchase the solid zinc chloride and make a strong solution of it in water. A small amount of spirits of salts may be added to provide a cleaning agent in the flux. Zinc chloride is the best

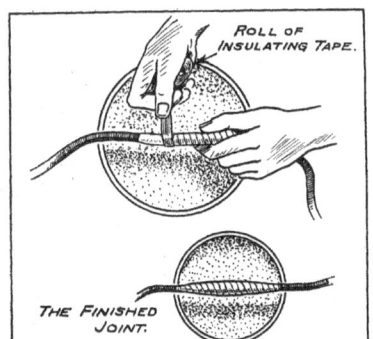

Fig. 4.—After the Solder has been applied the Joint should be covered with Insulating Tape.

SOFT SOLDERING

flux to use for soldering tinned steel, brass and copper, where it is possible to wash the joint properly after soldering. This flux is corrosive in its action and it is essential to remove all traces of it after doing a job or the surrounding metal will corrode and the joint fail. Fluxite and similar preparations are good substitutes for killed spirits. After using Fluxite the work can be readily cleaned with methylated spirits.

Resin.

Resin is the only flux which should be used for making electrical connections. It is not quite so easy to solder copper with resin as a flux, but no trouble will be experienced if the surfaces are freshly scraped before the flux is applied. In order to make the resin easy to apply, it is dissolved in methylated spirits; 2 oz. in half a pint of solvent is a good proportion.

Tallow.

The best flux to use for soldering lead pipes or sheet is tallow. The lead must be scraped bright before the tallow is applied, because this flux has no cleaning action on the lead.

The Soldering Bit.

The copper bit must weigh at least half a pound for general work. A smaller bit will not hold the heat long enough to make more than one or two very small joints. For running long seams or for soldering thick articles, especially those of copper and brass, at least a 1 lb. bit is necessary. It is always easier to solder, even a small job, with a large bit, than with a small one. The large bit retains sufficient heat longer without having to overheat it.

Gas and Electric Solderers.

The soldering bit with a self-contained gas

Fig. 5.—One of the many uses of Solder in the Home—Repairing an Ordinary Baking Tin.
First clean the part to be soldered, and rub on some fluxite. Pick up a blob of solder on the heated iron and apply with a backward and forward movement until the solder runs on to the now heated joint. As soon as the solder has run, remove the iron and when cool wipe away all traces of flux.

burner is invaluable for soldering tanks and other kinds of work with long seams. It enables a long smooth joint to be made without removing the bit from the metal. An electrically heated bit has the advantage that it cannot overheat, provided that it is connected to the correct supply voltage. The suitability of an electric solderer is judged by its rating in watts, and not by the weight of the bit. The 75-watt size is used for small work and wiring, while the 150-watt size for heavier work.

Heating the Bit.

A gas ring or bunsen burner is the best means of heating the soldering iron. The flame is applied just above the point of the bit, so that the tinned surface is not readily burned. The copper bit should never be put into a smoky fire. If no means other than a fire is available for heating the bit, place the bit in a clear red part, or make up a fire of coke or coalite. Particular care must always be taken not to overheat the bit. When over-heated, the tinned end becomes eroded, because the solder eats into the surface of the copper.

Judging the Temperature.

The next essential is to heat the copper to the correct temperature. This can only be judged by some practice. The bit is heated until it will just melt the solder, then, after a few more minutes' heating, it is held near the cheek. The temperature of the bit can be judged in this way after a little practice. Another way is to heat the bit until the tinned surface of the bit colours rapidly after wiping it with a rag. When using a small bit for a large job, it is necessary to overheat it in order to be able to transfer sufficient heat to the job. This rapidly corrodes the tinned surface of the bit and makes soldering difficult.

Tinning a New Bit.

One of the most important points in soldering is to keep all four sides of the bit properly

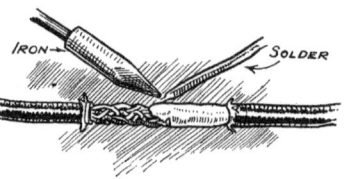

(A) First bare the cables.

(B) Then remove the centre core.

(C) Now twist the strands together.

(D) Apply solder over the twisted strands.

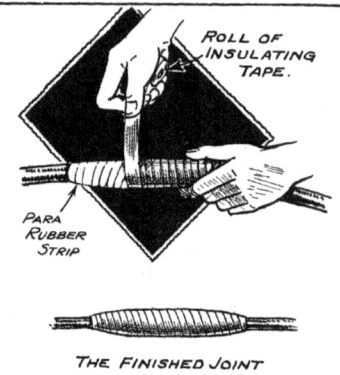

(E) Finally cover with insulating tape.

Fig. 6.—How to solder two 7-Stranded Cables together.

covered with solder. There are two methods of tinning a new bit or re-tinning an old one. The first is to heat the bit for a few moments in a gas flame, then plunge it quickly in and out of killed spirits. It is then further heated until it just melts the solder. The bit is again fluxed with killed spirits if necessary, and tinned on the four faces. Wipe the flux from the bit while it is still hot. The second method is to heat the bit until it will readily melt the solder and then rub it on a block of sal-ammoniac along with some beads of solder. The sal-ammoniac removes the oxide from the copper and the solder takes to the bit.

Applying the Solder.

When the job has been cleaned and flux applied to the surfaces to be joined, it is ready to solder. For a small job, the copper bit will hold sufficient solder to make the joint. The solder is taken from a stick on to the tinned surface of the bit. The bit is then brought into contact with the joint and held there for a moment to allow it to heat up. The solder runs from the bit to the joint if it is clean and properly fluxed.

Running a Seam.

For soldering a long seam, the work must be arranged so that both hands are free to manipulate the bit and a stick of solder. The bit is well heated and brought into contact with one end of the joint and held there until the solder runs from it. The stick of solder is now placed lightly in contact with the uppermost face of the bit and both drawn slowly along the seam. As the bit is moved it is kept flat on the work so as to heat the seam in advance of the bit. Towards the end of the seam, when the tip is cooling off, it is moved more slowly to give it sufficient time to heat the job. The bit should not be lifted from the work while running a seam, or an untidy job will result.

When the Solder does not Take.

The principal reason for an unsuccessful attempt at soldering is insufficient heat. The bit must not only be hot enough, but it must also be given sufficient time to heat the job. Although the solder may flow, it will not adhere if the work is not hot enough. This difficulty is more likely to be encountered when joining two plates of different thicknesses. The thin material takes the solder while the thick plate, which heats up more slowly, is, relatively, more troublesome. When the solder does not adhere although there is sufficient heat, the bit may be dirty and the work not properly fluxed. Clean the work and the bit with a rag while hot and apply more flux.

Sweating.

Sweating is soft soldering without a bit. For jointing large pieces, the clean parts are fluxed and wired or screwed together, then heated. The solder is then fed into the joint. For this purpose the solder should be in thin sticks. When joints of large area have to be sweated it is essential to tin each surface first. The pieces are then held together and closed up while the tinned faces are molten.

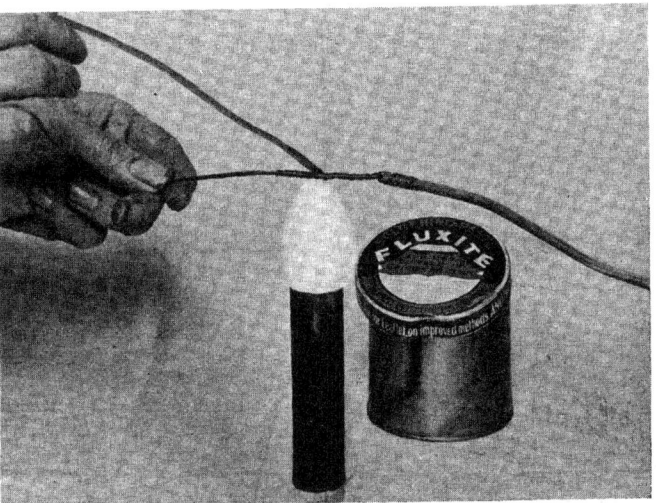

Fig. 7.—A Simple Spirit Lamp which can be used when soldering out of doors, or when it is not convenient to use a Gas Flame to heat the Iron.

Resin-cored Solder.

Cored solder is the best material to use for wiring. The wire ends must first be perfectly clean. The solder is melted above the job and the resin allowed to run on to the wire and the terminal. The solder is then transferred from the bit to the joint.

SOLDERING OUT OF DOORS

It sometimes happens that a soldering job is required to be done out of doors, or in a place where access to a gas ring cannot easily be obtained. For this class of work a spirit lamp will be required, and one can quite easily be constructed in the following manner : Obtain a piece of metal tube about ¾ inch in diameter, one end of which is capped. Fill the tube with wadding soaked in methylated spirit. This will form a very satisfactory lamp.

To use the lamp, clean the wire or material to be soldered and apply a flux, such as Fluxite, and then make the wire hot by holding it in the flame, as shown in Fig. 7. When hot apply a little blowpipe solder, and, if the flux has been properly applied, the solder will run and join the wire successfully.

If it is inconvenient to hold the part requiring soldering in the flame, it will be found that the lamp will heat a small soldering iron quite successfully.

CELLULOID CEMENTS

Broken celluloid or cellulose-base articles can readily be repaired with a suitable celluloid cement. Celluloid sheets can be joined and parts built up by cementing them together. The same cements will be found extremely useful *for repairing broken glass and china articles*, such as domestic drinking vessels, vases and similar ornaments. Not only do these cements give strong joints, but the latter are waterproof and will withstand the action of boiling water.

The method of repairing a broken article with celluloid cement is as follows : First apply a thin coating of the cement to each of the two fractured surfaces and allow to dry thoroughly ; this process will only take a few minutes, as a rule, with the more volatile celluloid cements. Next apply a second thin coating to each of the surfaces and after allowing a minute or so for the cement to become " tacky," press the two broken parts together and allow the cement to dry for a few hours. It is best to place the parts under light pressure whilst the cement is drying. The following is a recommended recipe for making celluloid cement :—

Celluloid scrapings or parings 1 part (weight).
Amyl acetate . 10 parts ,,

This cement can be made of a more syrupy consistency by increasing the proportion of celluloid.

TIME, LABOUR AND MONEY SAVING IDEAS

REPAIRING CRACKED GLASS VESSELS

Cracked glass vessels such as jars, garden cloche, etc., may be well repaired with the help of the liquid water-glass (sodium silicate) which is sold for egg preserving. Put a lighted candle end in the centre of a dish, fixing this in place with hot wax. Then, on to the dish, pour a thin layer of water. Invert the glass vessel as shown in the photograph. Then smear water-glass along the crack on the outside of the jar.

The candle flame soon dies out but not before its warmth has caused the expansion of the air in the vessel. The air outside the jar is of course at normal pressure, and this forces the water-glass into the crack, completely sealing it up. As time passes the water-glass hardens into a flint-like substance so that a good repair is the result. In the case of a bottle heat this in front of a fire or by standing in hot water with the cork out. The cork is then replaced and the water-glass smeared along the crack outside. Again the air pressure inside the vessel is less than that outside and so the water-glass is forced into the crack.

STEAM FROM GEYSERS

Much of the steam which condenses and makes everything damp in a room in which a geyser is being used can be quite easily avoided by fitting an extension pipe to the spout of the geyser. As a rule with geysers the spout is quite an appreciable distance above the top of the bath, and it is while the water is pouring from the spout into the bath that much of the steam is given off.

The remedy is to fit a long piece of rubber tubing over the spout and carry it right down into the bath, so that when the bottom of the pipe is covered with water there is no further escape of steam into the atmosphere except off the water in the bath. Incidentally this method also helps to conserve the heat.

Suitable tubing can be bought from most ironmongers, and the size required can be obtained by measuring the outer diameter of the spout.

A GOOD VARNISH REMOVER

Mix together 2 oz. of caustic soda, 6 oz. of fresh powdered lime and 8 oz. of ordinary whiting. Then add sufficient water so as to form a paste of creamy consistency.

One pound of this paste added to a gallon of water makes a good cleanser for varnished surfaces, but if it is required to remove the varnish altogether apply the paste to the surface. After about half an hour it can be wiped off and with it will come the varnish.

OIL STONE LUBRICANTS

It is a mistake to use the first grade of lubricating oil on which you can lay your hands when using an oil stone. There are certain kinds of lubricants which you should use for certain purposes, and it should be remembered that ordinary lubricating oils soon thicken and become useless, due to the fine particles abraded from the metal of the tool and from the stone.

For tools that have a not too keen edge, such as wood chisels, gravers, etc., a fairly heavy-bodied lubricant is necessary, a suitable grade for the purpose being one composed of ordinary glycerine to which a few drops of methylated spirits have been added to each ounce of glycerine.

For fine-edged tools, such as razors, scalpers and cutting knives, a thinner lubricant is required, such as paraffin or turpentine. Many experts use a mixture consisting of 3 parts of glycerine to 1 of alcohol when dealing with razor sharpening.

Motor-car engine lubricating oil should only be used for drills and lathe tools, or other tools of fairly blunt angle.

FITTING A BOARD

At times one has to fit a board to an irregular surface. On such occasions the following is a very good method of procedure. Suppose that the uneven surface happens to be a floor. Arrange

the board horizontally in contact and then run along it a pencil marked A kept parallel to the uneven surface by a notched guide. If one then cuts along the line made by the pencil the board will fit into the ups and downs of the floor.

A HINGELESS BOX

A box that has no hinges, and yet can be securely locked, can be made on the lines shown in the sketch. Any well-fitting box may be used and the lid should be cut longways, about in half. Nail one half of the lid down on to the box and treat the other part in

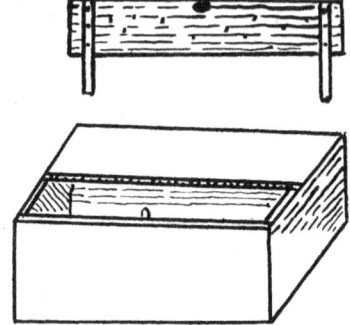

this way. Screw or nail cross bars on the other side of the lid, making these long enough to go well under the fixed portion. Drive a staple into the front board of the box and a hole to correspond in the free section of the lid. When the lid is slipped over the staple the padlock may be applied.

FLEXIBLE PAINT FOR CANVAS

A good flexible paint for treating canvas articles contains the following ingredients:—

Yellow soap	.	.	$2\frac{1}{2}$ lb.
Water	.	.	$1\frac{1}{2}$ gallons.
Oil paint	.	.	$3\frac{1}{2}$,,

The soap should be dissolved in the boiling water and the oil paint—which should be of a good quality—mixed thoroughly with this soapy solution.

USING UP SMALL COAL OR SLACK

If you should find yourself faced with an accumulation of small coal or slack in the coal cellar, the following is a good way of using it. Mix the coal dust with Portland cement in the proportion of seven of the former to one of the latter, and then add water till the mixture is thoroughly wet and about the consistency of stiff porridge. Then pour the mixture into flower-pots, and turn out the moulded blocks as soon as they are stiff enough to hold their shape. Leave them in the coal store, on several thicknesses of newspaper, for at least two days. They will then be ready for use and can be broken with a poker like ordinary coal. The fire should not be actually lighted with them, but once alight the fire can be kept in for many hours.

Repolishing Old Furniture

Whether a piece of furniture has been neglected, or whether it has been kept in condition with continued applications of revivers, there generally comes a time when repolishing becomes necessary. In the former case dirt has probably accumulated and corners have been knocked off, and the surface become scratched and bruised. When it has been carefully tended, an accumulation of grease is inevitable, and many revivers have the effect of gradually reducing the french polish over which it is applied. The exception to this is in the case of wax-polished furniture, which steadily improves with continual waxing.

The time for repolishing usually coincides with general woodwork repairs. Possibly a leg has broken, a strip of moulding become detached, or whatever it may be. In every case all such repairs should be carried out first. The article which begins on page 69 deals with general repairs, so that we may assume that the whole job has been made structurally sound and any patching completed. The job then is in a generally dull condition with several patches of new wood where repairs have been made.

Washing Down.

It is useless to attempt to polish over a dirty surface. The grease alone would prevent a satisfactory polish, and the dirt would show through badly. To clean it, take out all drawers and remove metalwork wherever possible. For instance, drawer handles should be taken off (this applies equally to wooden knobs); also any metal decorations. Take a pail of warm water and drop in one or two lumps of ordinary household soda. On no account use strong soda water.

Fig. 1.—The first thing to do before Repolishing is to Wash the whole Job down with *Weak* Soda Water.

This is really important, because the effect of this would be to strip off the existing polish, probably in patches, which would mean that the whole polish would have to be scraped off. All that is needed is to remove the dirt and grease, and weak soda water does this quite well. Dip a swab in the soda water and go thoroughly over the whole thing, as shown in Fig. 1. Deal with each separate surface at a time.

For instance, if it is a chest of drawers being dealt with, go over one side and immediately swill down with clean, cold water and dry. It is important that the soda water is not allowed to dry on the surface.

Cleaning Antique Furniture.

In antique furniture it is a mistake to attempt to remove the black accumulation which takes place in corners and in the recesses of mouldings, and so on. This enhances the appearance, giving relief to the high lights. What is mainly needed is a clear surface, over which the new polish can be applied. Do not neglect the interior. The swab can be used fairly dry, so that the dirt is removed without danger of swelling the wood. In fact, in any case it is advisable not to use a great deal of water anywhere, as this may penetrate and possibly cause any veneer to work up.

Now Stain any New Patches of Wood.

The job being dry, any new patches of wood should be stained to match the surrounding surface. A number of proprietary stains are available, and these can usually be mixed to obtain any special shade, providing that the stains chosen are of the same make. Water stains have the advantage of being cheaper. They can be obtained in powder form, requiring only to be mixed. A disadvantage is that they are somewhat liable to raise the grain. As, however, only small patches have usually to be coloured, this does not matter a great deal. The surface can be rubbed down, after it has dried, with fine glasspaper.

Try out the Stain on a Spare Piece of Wood.

Always try the stain on a spare piece of the same kind of wood first. This is specially important in the case of mahogany, as most "mahogany" stains are too red. A little walnut stain mixed with it usually produces the right shade. Walnut stain is also useful in the case of oak. Often this alone will match up well.

Using Chemicals.

An alternative to using proprietary stains is the use of certain chemicals. For instance, bichromate of potash is useful for both mahogany and walnut. It is obtained in the form of orange crystals. Several lumps are put into a jar of water, and after a while the water assumes a rich orange colour. This colour bears no resemblance to the shade it causes the wood to assume, as the action is a purely chemical one, causing the wood to darken.

Its particular use is in the case of old

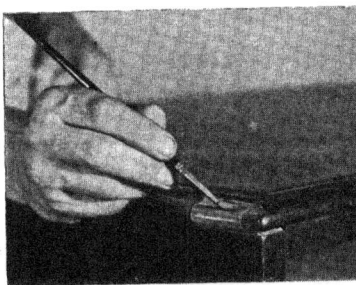

Fig. 2.—Small New Patches can be Stained with a suitable Stain applied with a Small Brush.

Fig. 3.—All New Patches must be filled in with Plaster of Paris after being Stained.

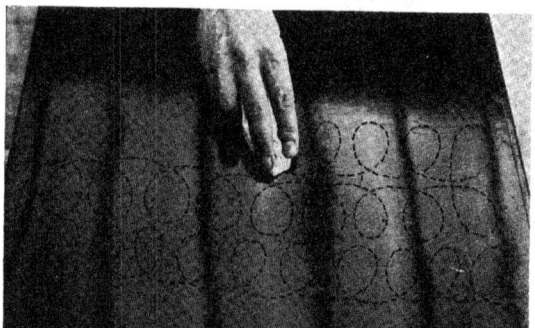

Fig. 4.—When Bodying-up, the Polish is applied with a Circular Motion.

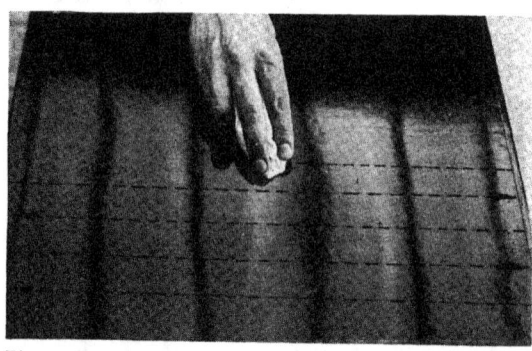

Fig. 5.—The Finishing-off Strokes are *with* the Grain of the Wood.

mahogany, which, although of a warm shade, is not red. It may be that when dry the colour will be too cold, but this does not matter, as the polish to be applied can be coloured to correct it. A yellowish powder may be left on the dry surface. This should be brushed off. For oak, bichromate of potash can also be used, or ammonia. Use ·880 ammonia and apply it with a brush. It is liable to burn the fingers if used with a rag. Avoid bending over the bottle when opening it, as the fumes are strong. Neither of these chemicals can be used for deal, as they have no darkening effect on soft woods.

Applying the Stain.

The new patches being small, it is convenient to use a small brush for the stain. Fig. 2 shows a new piece of moulding being stained. It does not matter if the stain runs a trifle over the polished surface, as it will not penetrate. One point to bear in mind is that end grain usually soaks up the stain quickly, and is liable to become extra dark. A little diluted stain can be used for such parts.

Filling in the Grain.

Mahogany is invariably french polished, and this necessitates filling in the grain. Before this is done, however, it is advisable to give one coat of french polish to seal the stain. With a piece of fine glasspaper rub the new parts smooth (after they are dry). Make up a polishing rubber with cotton-wool and a fluffless cover (this is described in the article on french polishing), and, having charged it with polish, go over all the new patches.

Allow time for the polish to harden, and once again rub down smooth with glasspaper. The filler is made with plaster of paris mixed with water or a little of the stain used to colour the wood. Shake the plaster on to a piece of paper and dip a damp rag into it. Apply it to all the patches, rubbing it across the grain, as shown in Fig. 3. Avoid leaving a surplus on the surface. It is only the grain that has to be filled. When it has dried thoroughly, rub down smooth with glasspaper again. Any large holes or indentations can be filled with plastic wood or wax to which a suitable powder colour has been added when in a molten state.

When water has been mixed with the plaster of paris it will dry out, leaving white flecks in the grain. (It is to avoid this that stain is preferable to water.) These flecks are toned down by rubbing all the parts with linseed oil. Use it sparingly, and allow as much time afterwards as possible for it to dry out. Otherwise it is liable to ooze out later after the polishing has been completed.

Polishing the New Parts.

It will be realised that the old surface has already a coat of polish, whilst the new parts are bare. Consequently, the last named must be given a bodying up of polish before the whole is polished. The rubber can be charged fairly generously at first, because the grain soaks up the polish quickly. Go from one patch to another, allowing as much time as possible between the applications.

When they have assumed a fair shine, it may be found that the colour does not quite match. This can be corrected by adding a little colour to the polish. Dragon's blood is a bright red, and a little added to the polish soon brightens up the shade. It is useful for mahogany. Umber is used to darken the polish in the case of oak. It can be applied with a fine camel-hair brush in a similar way to that shown in Fig. 2.

Repolishing.

As a preliminary, go over all surfaces with a duster so that they are clean. Avoid working in a place in which dust is liable to be blown about, as this will settle on the tacky polish and spoil the finish. Also avoid draughts. These may cause the polish to assume a milky shade. Ideal conditions are a fairly warm room out of all draughts.

The process is similar to that of ordinary french polishing described elsewhere in this work. The cotton-wool is charged with polish, and the cover wrapped around it free from all creases. It will be found that a better result is obtained by using a somewhat thin polish. A little methylated spirit is added to it. Go over the whole surface with a circular sweeping movement, covering every part, and working first from right to left, and then back and forth. To enable the rubber to work freely, the merest trace of linseed oil can be added to the rubber. Just dip the point of the finger in the oil and place it on the rubber. It has later to be worked out.

Using the Rubber.

Fig. 4 shows the movement of the rubber. Deal with each surface at a time, and go from one to the other, so that one has a chance to harden whilst the others are being dealt with. For instance, in the chest in Fig. 1 the top could be bodied up, followed by the sides, the front, and the drawer fronts. When the whole sequence has been gone through, repeat the process. Rub down with the finest worn glasspaper between each application.

When a fair polish has been attained, the movement can be changed for long straight strokes, as in Fig. 5. The rubber is taken right through off the end and on again an inch or two farther along. Eventually a high polish will result, though not quite free from smears. The last named are due to oil, and these are removed in the final spiriting-off process.

Care must be taken in this. The great thing to avoid is using too much spirit. The whole idea of spiriting-off is to burnish the surface, not to soak it with spirit. Take a fresh rubber, and work the merest trace of spirit into the cotton-wool, pressing it well with the fingers so that the spirit does not remain in one part. Wrap the rubber around it and try it on a spare piece of wood. It should *not* leave a damp smear. Pass it lightly over the work in straight strokes, gradually increasing the pressure as the spirit evaporates. This will remove all smears and give a fine, clear polish.

An Electric Fire-screen Radiator

This appliance performs a dual function; it acts as an ornamental fire screen during the summer months, yet it can be transformed immediately into an efficient electric radiator by removing the detachable centre boss and switching on the current.

The centre panel is made of sheet copper, the framing is of brass or copper according to taste, strengthened with an internal liner. The ornament shown is of a repoussé nature, but the reader can, if he cares, supply his own artistic touches.

Material Required.

Sheet copper, 2' 0" × 1' 9", gauge 24.
        "   2' 4" × 1' 2"   " 22.
Angle brass or copper, 8' × ⅝" × ⅛"—3/32" thick.
Sheet brass 14" × 4", gauge 18.
Strip brass, 6' × ⅝" × ⅛".
   "   3" × ⅝" × ⅜".
Strip iron, 8' × ½" × 3/32".
Piece of iron, 6" × ⅝" × ⅝".
1–750 Watt element of suitable voltage.
2 yards 5 amp. flex and plug.
Sheet tin, 8" × 8", gauge 22.
Strip of fibre, 4" × 4" × 1/16".
Brass rod, 3" × 7/16".
1 dozen 2BA nuts and bolts.

Making the Flare or Reflector.

The reflector takes the form of a hollow truncated hexagonal pyramid shaped from a sheet of copper. Fig. 2 gives the size and shape of one sector of this flare; a paper pattern should be made and set out six times on the metal so that it appears as in Fig. 2. Now bend sharply along the dotted lines and solder the seam A as in Fig. 2. A small hexagon with two holes to admit the contact sockets is then soldered to the small end of the pyramid to form the back of the flare.

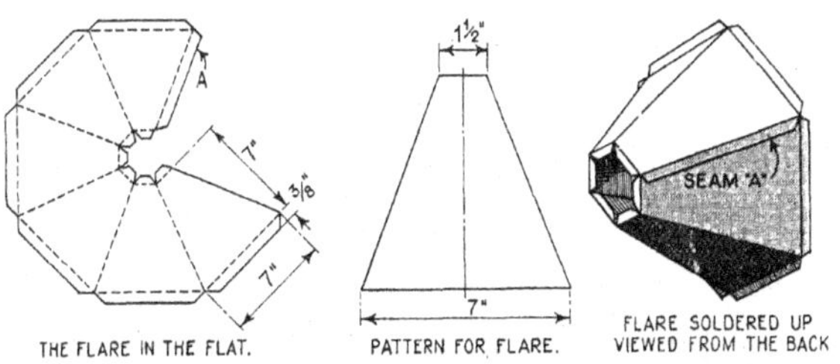

The Flare Assembly.

Fig. 3 shows the complete assembly at the back of the flare which carries the heating element. The two studs C and D are threaded through the back A, and their heads soldered to the copper back. The hexagonal fibre strip which carries the contact sockets fits on to the studs C and D, and is held securely clamped between two pairs of nuts in such a position that the two sockets pro-

Fig. 1.—The Finished Fire-screen.

This serves the dual purpose of acting as an ornamental fire-screen during the summer months, yet it can be transformed immediately into an efficient electric radiator by removing the detachable centre boss and switching on the current.

trude ⅜ inch into the inside of the reflector. The bared ends of the flex are secured under the two nuts at the end of the hollow sockets.

Fig. 4 shows the safety-box H which fits on to the studs C and D in Fig. 3, and shuts down tightly on to the back plate A; it is held in place by two nuts on the projecting studs. Thus the electrical connections are safely covered and all danger of shocks prevented.

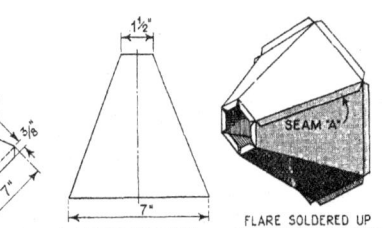

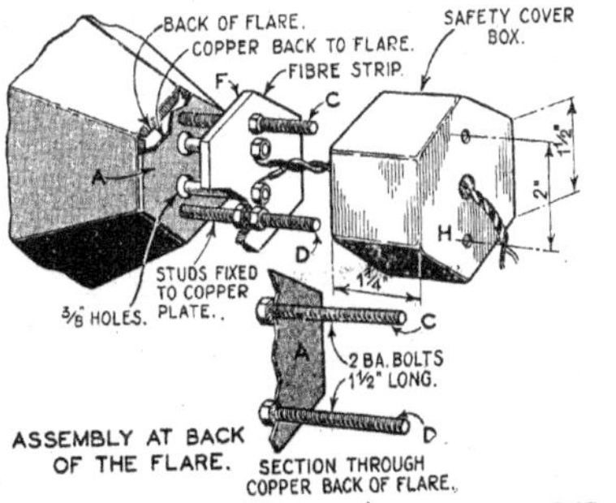

Fig. 2.—Details for the Construction of the Flare.

The Contact Sockets.

The two sockets (see Fig. 4) can easily be made from a piece of brass rod; a 7/16-inch hole is bored in one end of each to a depth of ¾ inch to accommodate the legs on the base of the element, while the other ends are turned or filed down and threaded (2BA). Special care must be taken when assembling the contacts to see that the sockets pass freely through the back plate A (Fig. 3) without touching; as an extra safeguard they can be covered with fine asbestos or fibre to prevent contact with the reflector.

Making the Copper Panel.

The main panel of the screen should be cut to size and the edges bent at right angles as in Fig. 5, then place the reflector centrally upon it and mark round the edge. Before cutting out the hexagon with a metal fretsaw remember that the opening in the screen is ⅜ inch smaller all round than the flare.

Note the two round-headed screws which project 3/32 inch beyond the surface of the screen. These support the boss which covers the opening when the radiator is not in use. The small section (Fig. 5) shows how they are fitted; a nut is soldered to the back of the screen and the screw threads in. A locknut can be fitted if desired.

The reflector is fastened to the screen by soldering the flange on the flare to the back edge of the opening in the panel.

The Framing.

The framing consists of two iron angle supports A (see Fig. 5), which are fastened to the flange of the copper screen, and four L section brass strips like C which complete the frame.

Figs. 5 and 6 should make the assembling quite clear — the two iron pieces fit round the flange of the panel and the brass strips which are right-angled in section cover this joint. The various members are held secure with bolts which go through all three thicknesses of metal; several of the bolts perform a dual function in

Fig. 3.—The Complete Assembly at the Back of the Flare.

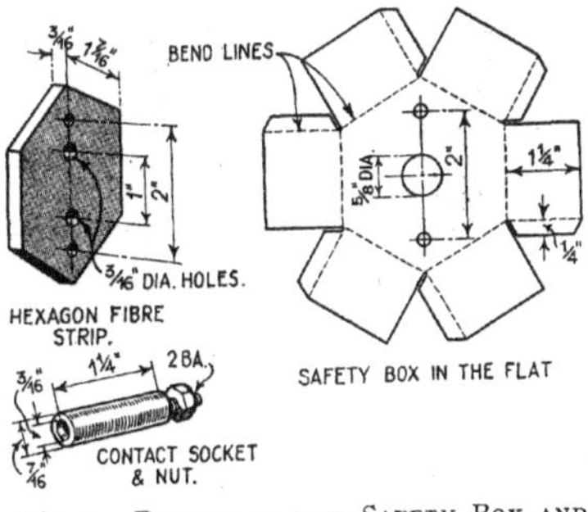

Fig. 4.—Details of the Safety Box and Contact Sockets.

AN ELECTRIC FIRE-SCREEN RADIATOR

holding the corner pyramids and feet in place.

Making the Feet.
Fig. 7 shows how the feet are made from strip brass. A wooden mandrel is used as a kind of anvil to bend the curves, while the sketch A indicates a method of securing uniformity in the contours of the feet. The metal should be well annealed before attempting to bend it.

Fitting the Feet.
These are attached by bolts through the frame of the screen just above the bottom rail. Fig. 6 shows how this is done; note the small piece of iron packing which is used to make the lower corner of the frame solid; this ensures the rear foot being firm.

Making the Boss.
Fig. 9 gives details of the hexagonal boss. Note that on two opposite parallel sides a slot is cut in each to engage with the projecting screws on the surface of the panel.

The Top or Handle.
The upright piece K in Fig. 8 is cut out of sheet brass, the five oval openings being sawn away with a metal fretsaw, and the upper and lower edges turned over to form a narrow flange. The square bar M which forms the top is soldered to the upper flange of the sheet K, while the complete handle is similarly attached to the upper framing N.

The Corner Pyramids.
These are fitted as shown in Fig. 6. They are filed up to shape from ⅝ inch square brass, a ³⁄₁₆-inch hole is bored into the base and this is then tapped out (2BA) and a stud screwed in. As can be seen in Fig. 6 this forms the bolt which holds together the frame and panel in addition to securing the ornamental pyramids.

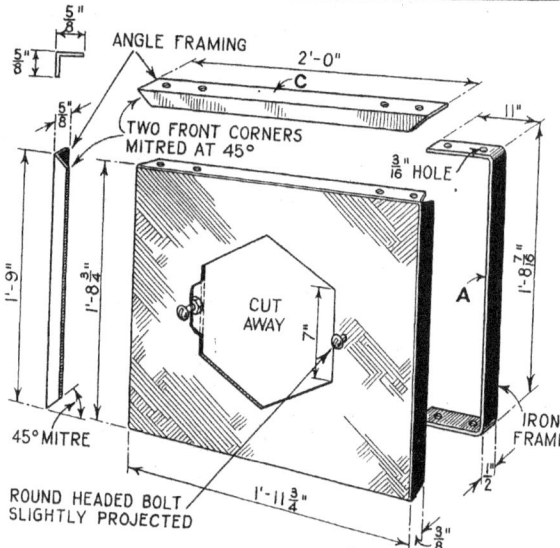

Fig. 5.—Showing the Construction of the Main Panel of the Screen and the Framing.

Note the two round-headed screws which project ³⁄₃₂-inch beyond the surface of the screen. These support the boss which covers the opening when the radiator is not in use.

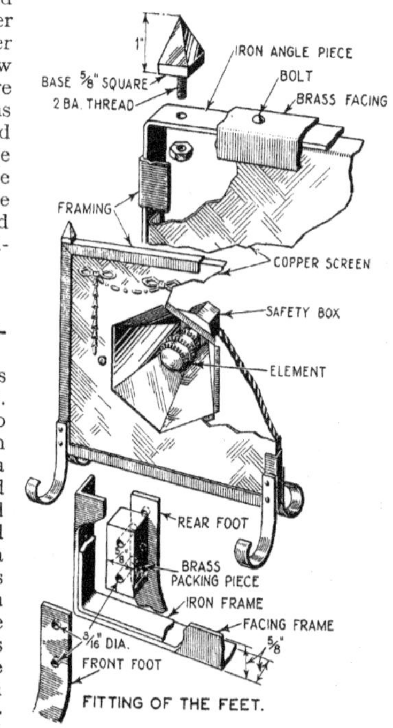

The Repoussé Ornament.
The design shown on the panel and the boss is of a repoussé type, but the reader can vary this to suit his taste; he may choose to solder on ready-made cast ornaments which can be purchased.

Fig. 10 shows the corner of the panel

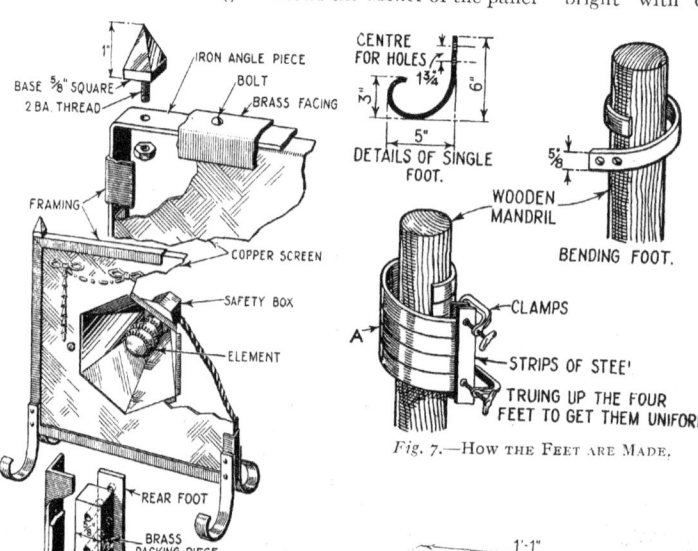

Fig. 6.—Details showing the Assembly of the Framing.

Fig. 7.—How the Feet are Made.

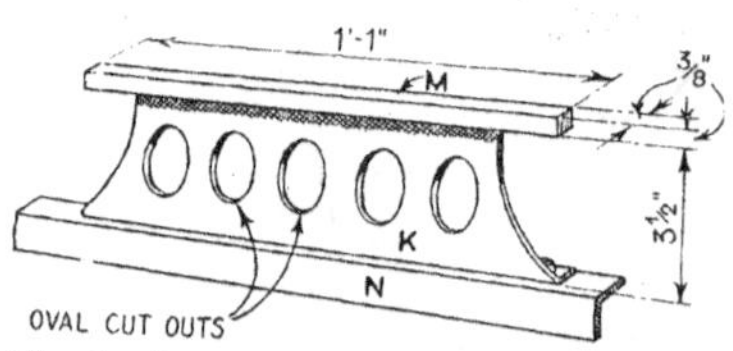

Fig. 8.—Details of the Ornamental Top which also forms the Handle.

placed on a pitch block ready to beat out the raised pattern which has been previously marked out on the back of the metal. The pitch in the wooden box is heated on the surface with a gas flame to soften it; the metal is raised into relief by hammering it with blunt punches of suitable size. If the relief is not made too high a sheet of thick felt or crêpe rubber may be substituted for the pitch block.

Fig. 11 portrays how the small dents or hammer marks associated with a beaten metal surface are obtained.

The Heating Element.
This can be purchased ready wound; choose a ball-shaped one in preference to the tall pillar types—one of 500–750 watts will be suitable. Be sure that the voltage is the same as that of the supply.

Burnishing and Lacquering.
Some readers may prefer to have the finished job oxydised and lacquered at a professional plater's, but a really good durable surface can be obtained at home.

The reflector should be cleaned up bright with ordinary metal polish, then burnished by rubbing vigorously with a chamois leather pad coated with rouge and moistened with methylated spirits. When a high polish has been obtained warm the copper over the gas, taking care to leave no finger marks on the surface. As soon as the metal is warm to the touch quickly brush over a coating of pale gold lacquer, using a soft camel mop. If brush marks are visible clean off the lacquer with methylated spirits and relacquer.

When cleaning up the panel and boss make the high points as bright as possible, while the portions in lower relief should be left less highly polished. This gives a pleasing appearance.

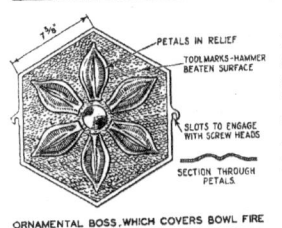

Fig. 9.—The Ornamental Boss which covers the Bowl Fire.

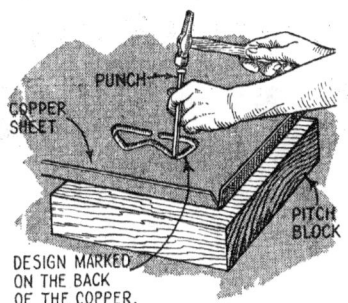

Fig. 10.—Beating out the Raised Panel.

Fig. 11.—How the Small Hammer Marks are Obtained.

The framing strips should be buffed up with the leather and rouge, making all the rubbing strokes lengthwise, as this gets rid of all scratches.

Choice of a Lacquer and Final Notes.

The best type of lacquer to use is a pale, almost colourless spirit solution shellac, and not the new cellulose types now being offered.

The electric fire can be used as a toasting rack by bending up a simple wire frame to hold the slices of bread and attaching the cage to the two small screws which normally carry the boss or cover plate.

The radiator can readily be carried from room to room, and should prove a useful appliance in any room.

HOW TO MAKE AN EFFICIENT SPRAYER

THERE are so many domestic uses for a hand-sprayer of the type illustrated, that every household should certainly possess one. Not only is it very cheap to construct, but it will give a very fine spray of liquid when the plunger is pushed inwards by means of the handle P.

Such a sprayer will be found very efficient for spraying paint—in place of brushing methods—and for use with insecticides. Flies and other winged pests in the house can be exterminated merely by closing the doors of each room and spraying the air with one of the advertised insecticides, *e.g.*, Flit.

Green-fly on roses, black-fly on broad beans, and white-fly on the tomato plants can all quickly be destroyed with the aid of the sprayer illustrated.

One particular advantage of the device in question is that it is very economical in use, as it gives an extremely fine "mist" effect.

The Two Main Parts.

The sprayer consists of two parts, namely, the pump unit and the liquid reservoir. At one end of the pump barrel a small hole A, about $\frac{1}{8}$ inch diameter is made. Level with the centre of this hole the end B of a tube of about $\frac{3}{32}$ inch internal diameter, is arranged. The other end of this tube goes nearly to the bottom of the liquid reservoir.

When the pump plunger is forced inwards (towards the hole A) a high velocity air stream is caused to rush across the top of the tube B. The effect of this air stream is to cause a reduction of pressure, or a suction effect, in the tube B, so that the liquid is drawn up it from the reservoir. This liquid, meeting the high velocity air stream, is atomised into an extremely fine spray and projected with some force into the region ahead.

Construction.

The actual construction is very simple. An old motor car pump can be used for the pump unit—although this does not give a very big capacity. It is better to employ a piece of thin metal tubing of about 2 inches diameter, and from 15 to 18 inches in length.

A piece of $\frac{1}{4}$-inch brass or steel rod, provided with a cup-shaped leather, held between two nuts and two washers, forms the plunger, whilst a wooden cap held by screws to the tubing forms a satisfactory guide and bearing for the plunger.

The liquid container is soldered at right angles to the plunger tube. This container can be adapted from any convenient size of tin—such as a cocoa-tin, but it should have an opening, at or near the top, which can be closed with a screw-cap or a cork; a small air vent must, however, be provided in the cap or cork.

The only important item in this sprayer is the positioning of the sprayer tube B and the hole A; details of this are shown in the lower illustration.

Lubricate the Plunger Barrel.

Before using lubricate the plunger barrel, lightly with ordinary lubricating or engine oil; this enables the leathers of the plunger to work efficiently.

Details showing the Construction of the Sprayer.

FURNITURE REVIVERS AND THEIR USES

FURNITURE reviver, as the name implies, has for its functions varying ingredients with which a polished surface is restored and a bright finish obtained, always bearing in mind that the material is not a French polish, and can be only used on a polish treated surface.

What a Reviver does.

Therefore, the action of a reviver is the reverse to the operation of French polishing. The object in view is to produce a mixture which will soften the shellac surface, allowing the operator to regain a brilliant surface by friction. We would point out that the repeated use of a polish reviver will ultimately ruin the polished surface, when it will be found essential to strip and re-French polish the job.

The following recipe may be safely mixed and used:—

$\frac{1}{2}$ oz. butter of antimony.
3 ozs. raw linseed oil.
4 ozs. acetic acid or vinegar.
$\frac{1}{2}$ pint methylated spirit into which is dissolved
1 oz. lump camphor.

Remember to give the bottle or jar a good shaking; then use by partially saturating a cotton-wool pad, and then apply first in straight strokes with the grain, finally finishing in a circular movement; then polish briskly with a clean soft duster.

Practical Notes on the Construction of Garden Paths

The type of construction used for garden paths depends on the purpose for which the path is to be used, and what local materials are available, but in all cases a good foundation is necessary, not only to prevent any subsequent sinkage but also to stop any clay or loam from working up through the path.

Preparation.

The width of the path must necessarily depend on the purpose for which it is required, but useful widths are 18 inches for a narrow path, up to 3 feet for a wider one. Having decided on the width and site, one should carefully mark it out with a string line down either side—this can be pegged at intervals in the case of a curved path.

Edging.

One has the choice of wood boards or rock stones. The former should first be given a coat of tar or creosote: 7 × 1 inch boards are most useful for this purpose, and should be pegged down at each end by a pointed 2 × 2-inch peg, nailed vertically to the plank. The boards should be laid so that $1\frac{1}{2}$ inches show above the final surface of the path and in such a manner that there will be a fall from one end of the path to the other of 1 inch in 50 feet. This will ensure that all rain water will run away. Rock stones should be of about the same size and should be buried to two-thirds of their depth, and so that the most flat face is on the inside of the path.

Excavation.

The existing mould, etc., should now be excavated for a depth of from 3 to 5 inches, according to the type of path which is to be laid.

Weeds.

It is extremely important at this stage to remove the roots of all weeds and grass, or else they will certainly push their way up through the path later on. If there are many of them it will even pay to give the site a dressing of weed killer.

Clinker Base.

As a means of preventing the subsoil from working up through the path a layer of clinker should now be laid. This is of most importance where the base is clay, when clinker should be laid to give a thickness after consolidation of 3 inches. In other cases 2-inch consolidated thickness will suffice.

Fig. 1.—Checking the Surface for Pot-holes by means of a Straight-edge.

The low portion indicated by the shadow under the straight edge is being marked out by chalk. The patching material will then be put in the hole so that it just extends over the chalk line, and will then be well punned, as shown in Fig. 2.

Fig. 2.—Consolidating the Material by means of a Punner.

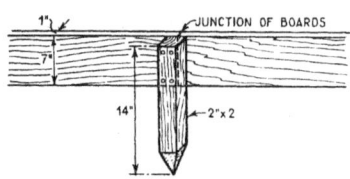

Fig. 3.—The Method of Pegging Down Edging Boards.

One peg is nailed to two boards at their junction.

TYPES OF PATHS

The path proper can be of many types, as detailed below, all of which, with the exception of the first, can be satisfactorily laid by the amateur.
(1) Mastic Asphalt.
(2) Single-coat Tar or Bitumen Macadam.
(3) Two-coat Tar or Bitumen Macadam.
(4) Pre-coated $\frac{1}{8}$-inch dust Limestone, Slag, etc.
(5) Grouting.
(6) Waterbinding.
(7) Using Local Mould, Sand, etc.

1. MASTIC ASPHALT

This is an expert's job, and, if desired, one should get in touch with one of the asphalt firms. It will give a smooth surface which should last without further attention for ten years. The base, however, has to be very solid, and the finished cost, if the mastic asphalt is laid 1 inch thick, would be in the region of 6s. per yard super, excluding cost of the preparation of the base.

2. SINGLE-COAT TAR OR BITUMEN MACADAM

The method is to lay the macadam on the top of the clinker and consolidate same to a thickness of from $1\frac{1}{4}$ to 2 inches, varying with the amount of traffic on the path. The macadam can be obtained from a local quarry. Graded material of from 1 inch down in the case of a $1\frac{1}{4}$-inch coat (e.g., 60 per cent. 1-inch, 20 per cent. $\frac{1}{2}$-inch, and 20 per cent. $\frac{1}{4}$-inch), or from $1\frac{1}{2}$-inch down in the case of a 2-inch coat (e.g., 60 per cent. 1 to $1\frac{1}{2}$-inch, 20 per cent. $\frac{1}{2}$-inch and 20 per cent. $\frac{1}{4}$-inch), should be obtained and the price will be approximately 12s. 6d. per ton, and 12s. respectively ex-quarry. A ton will cover approximately 12 square yards for 2-inch coat.

Consolidation.

The heaviest possible hand-roller should always be used. If, owing to width, it is impossible to use a roller, then the macadam must be punned in with a punner. This can probably be obtained on hire from the local highway authority.

Spreading.

The macadam can be spread with a garden fork or shovel, allowing $\frac{1}{2}$-inch for consolidation. Care should be taken to see that it is taken evenly, i.e., not large stones one time and fine the next. It should be spread a little thicker on the crown or centre of the

PRACTICAL NOTES ON THE CONSTRUCTION OF GARDEN PATHS

Fig. 4.—Surface Dressing a Tarmacadam Drive with a Bituminous Emulsion which is applied with a Brush. Note that the part near to the gate has already been covered with the screened chippings.

Fig. 5.—A Close-up of a Section of a Bitumen Macadam Path. Showing clinker in the base, followed by 1¼-inch graded macadam, then topping of ¼-inch or ⅛-inch macadam. The top surface of this latter is also shown.

path in order that rain water will run to the sides. After initial consolidation the surface should be tested longitudinally with a straight-edge in order to detect any high or low spots. The straight-edge should touch the surface of the path at all points—if there is a high spot then some of the material must be taken away—if a low one then it must be filled up. The amateur will get the best results with a long straight-edge, i.e., 12 to 15 feet. The surface of the path made by this method will consist of large stones, surrounded by smaller ones.

3 TWO-COAT TAR OR BITUMEN MACADAM

The method adopted is exactly as in the case of (2) except that the macadam is laid in two layers : (a) a base coat of, say, 1¼-inch macadam, and (b) a topping coat of ¼ or ⅛ inch. The surface obtained is much closer than in the case of (2) because it consists of only ¼ or ⅛-inch coated stones. The ⅛-inch is preferable but is not always obtainable at quarries. The 1¼-inch macadam is first spread and properly consolidated to a thickness within ¼ inch of the final path surface. It will give approximately 23 square yards per ton for a 1¼-inch coat, and will cost approximately 11s. 6d. per ton ex-quarry.

The toppings, which will cost approximately 14s. 6d. per ton ex-quarry, will cover 80 square yards per ton. They are spread evenly over the base coat just to cover same, and are then consolidated as above. Care must be taken to ensure that the proper crossfall is obtained and the surface must be tested periodically with the straight-edge.

4 PRE-COATED ⅛-INCH DUST LIMESTONE, SLAG, ETC.

Where one has in their locality a quarry that makes a pre-mixed bitumen material of their ⅛ inch dust stone, this forms an admirable surface for paths. It will give a fine smooth asphalt finish. It should be laid to a consolidated thickness of ¾ to 1 inch.

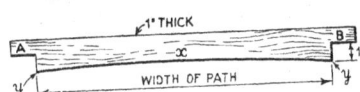

Fig. 6.—Camber Board in Section.

If, after spreading the material, a board as above is drawn longitudinally along the path it will ensure that the material is spread evenly and to correct shape. A and B rest on the edging boards or must be high enough to clear the rock stones. The fall from x to y prevents the rain from hanging on the path.

If, however, the base is soft it should first be strengthened by rolling in clean 1½-inch stones to a thickness of 2 inches. These latter will cost approximately 6s. per ton ex-quarry, and will cover 15 square yards per ton.

More care is necessary with spreading this type than in the case of (2) and (3), since these latter are not absolutely watertight, and therefore the rain will tend to percolate through them, but in the case of this material it is impervious to water, and therefore the surface must be true in all directions so that rain water will run off.

5 GROUTING

This is a means of using up all the stones, etc., found in the garden. Break all the stones down so that there is nothing larger than 1¼ inches and spread them on the clinker for 1½-inch thickness. Use the larger stones first, and after rolling these, fill in the voids between them with the smaller ones, packing them in tight until a level surface is obtained.

Use a Bituminous Emulsion.

For grouting use a bituminous emulsion which can be obtained from any reliable firm (if in difficulty your local Council Surveyor will give you the address of a firm). It is in liquid form and is applied cold by means of an ordinary watering-can, either fitted with a rose having ⅛-inch diameter holes, or, better still, having a piece of tin fitted (as in Fig 10) to the mouthpiece. It should be applied evenly to the surface of the stone at the rate of one half-gallon per square yard. Then spread evenly on the top clean small ¼-inch stones at the rate of about 120 square yards per ton and well roll. Repeat the rolling daily and at the end of three days sweep up all surplus fine stones which are on the surface. The bitumen emulsion will cost approximately from 10d. to 1s. per gallon, according to the quantity required.

Alternatively to using garden stone, one can purchase clean stone from a local quarry. If there is not a sufficient quantity of clean ¼-inch stones in the garden, then a supply of clean ¼-inch chippings can be obtained from the local quarry for covering the grout, as above.

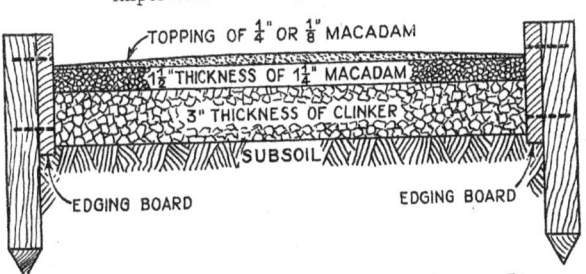

Fig. 7.—Diagram Section showing Bitumen Macadam Path.

PRACTICAL NOTES ON THE CONSTRUCTION OF GARDEN PATHS

Fig. 8.—Spreading Pre-coated ⅛-inch Dust Limestone by means of a Rake.

6 WATERBINDING

This method, although cheap, will only give a surface which can be kicked up and which will be washed about by heavy rain. Furthermore, it will always be dusty in dry weather.

The stone from the garden, broken to a maximum 1¼ inches, is spread on the clinker. All voids are packed tightly with small stones and finally with ⅛-inch to dust stone. It is then well watered and rolled tight.

The filling with dust, watering and rolling treatment can be repeated from time to time.

Alternatively, the necessary stone, or part of it, can be obtained from the local quarry.

7 USING LOCAL MOULD, SAND, ETC.

Bituminous emulsions can be obtained which are mixed with local fine materials, and the resulting product is spread 1 inch (say) thick on a prepared base. This is then thoroughly rolled, forming a bituminous carpet. Detailed instructions can be obtained from the various firms who supply such emulsions.

GARAGE DRIVES

These can be constructed by any of the methods given above, but (2) or (3) will probably be found most easy to lay by the amateur. The cross fall, *i.e.*, from the centre of the drive to the edge, should be 4 inches in 10 to 12 feet, and the longitudinal fall 1 inch in 50 feet.

It is of very much greater importance in the case of garage drives to ensure that the base is really solid before applying the surfacing material. The best results will be obtained if the latter is laid to 2 inches thickness and consolidated by a 30-cwt. petrol roller, which can be hired quite cheaply.

MAINTENANCE

It is an easy matter for the amateur to treat an existing path or garage drive so as to give it (say) four or five years further life, or, alternatively, to alter the colour of the surface. For this work one can either use a hot tar, or bitumen compound, or what is much more easy to handle, since no heating is required, a bituminous emulsion such as referred to under "Grouting." The following notes apply equally well to a grouted, waterbound, tar or bitumen macadam path.

Re-shaping.

The first step is to ensure that the general shape is correct, paying attention to cross falls, etc. All high spots must be cut off and depressions filled in as under "Pot-holing."

Pot-holing.

Liberally paint the emulsion in the pot-hole and then cover with ¼-inch chippings and pun them in. If the pot-hole is deep it is better first to paint the pot-hole with the emulsion and then fill in with ¾-inch (say, according to the depth of it) chippings, which have been previously mixed with the emulsion at the rate of approximately

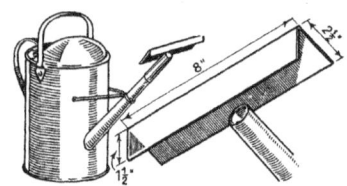

Fig. 10.—Details of a Tin Fitment for Pouring Emulsion from a Watering Can.

Fig. 9.—Applying a Bituminous Emulsion by means of a Grouting Can.

two-thirds of a gallon to 1 cwt. Then well consolidate by punning, or rolling in the case of a big one.

Another method of filling pot-holes is to do so with ¼-inch tar or bitumen macadam. The pot-holes are filled with this material and then well punned or rolled.

Surface Dressing.

When satisfied that the surface is in a fit condition to receive the surface dressing coat, apply the emulsion at the rate of from 3½ to 6 square yards per gallon. The covering capacity depends on the surface to which the emulsion is applied. On an open tar macadam surface, or a waterbound one, it will require the emulsion at 3½ square yards per gallon, while a previously dressed surface will require only 6 square yards per gallon. Immediately cover with either clean limestone or granite chippings, gravel or sand; ¼-inch gravel or chippings is the best size for the amateur to use. The chippings should be spread on thick so that they just touch and should then be well rolled.

The colour of the surface can be easily altered by choosing the right kind of aggregate for covering the emulsion.

HOW TO COLOUR ELECTRIC LIGHT BULBS

Occasions often arise for the colouring of electric light bulbs, either high or low voltage, for decorative purposes. The method employed is of such an easy nature that excellent results can always be obtained, saving expense. One ½ pint of electric lamp lacquer will colour quite a large number of bulbs. The lacquer is a shellac mixture coloured with aniline dye to produce all shades of colour, giving a moderate amount of permanency; naturally, the higher the voltage, the more brilliant is the light, which in turn causes quicker fading of colour.

Having obtained the required colour or colours, first well clean the bulb with a piece of soft rag damped with methylated spirit, so as to remove all grease and smears, then polish with a dry rag; refix bulbs to holders and light; pour out lacquer into a wide-topped tin or some suitable container large enough to allow the bulb to enter. While the bulb is alight, immerse into the lacquer by holding the container underneath; when all glass has been covered, lower container and hold beneath so as to catch any drips and until lacquer is dry. The heat evolved quickly hardens the lacquer, which can be handled in a few minutes. To remove the lacquer from the bulbs immerse in methylated spirit, then wipe with a clean piece of rag.

Making a Useful Ironing Cabinet

The folding ironing table, shown in Fig. 1, opens and locks with a single movement, is perfectly simple to make and is invaluable in the average kitchenette, where space is very limited.

To close the table the front is lifted, the leg pushed backwards and the whole simply pushed into the cabinet fixed on the wall. When the door is closed—as in Fig. 2—the space occupied is negligible, and the cabinet can if desired be fixed to a cupboard or in any place where it will be most convenient.

Special Features.

The folding ironing table is self-supporting and does not bring any strains on the wall—or whatever it may be fixed to—there are no catches or fasteners to manipulate, nothing to get in the way of the ironing; moreover, it is quite rigid and entirely free from annoying whip or spring.

Action of Table.

The table top or ironing board is pivoted to a pair of runners while the leg folds in between them—being hinged to the underside of the ironing board.

To erect the table, as in Fig. 4, simply open the door and pull the ironing board forwards. When this is being done the runners drop in their guides until they reach the bottom, meanwhile the leg falls outwards under the board and is pushed automatically into position by a simple spring.

Materials Required.

The following comprises all the parts needed for the ironing board and cabinet.

Sides.—Two pieces plywood, ½ inch thick, 2¾ inches wide, 47¾ inches long.

Door.—One piece plywood, ½ inch thick, 12 inches wide, 45 inches long.

Back.—One piece plywood, ⅛ inch thick, 12 inches wide, 48 inches long.

Ironing Board.—One piece deal, 1 inch thick, 8¾ inches wide, 45 inches long.

Leg.—One piece deal, 1 inch thick, 7 inches wide, 31 inches long.

Rails.—Two pieces hard wood, 1⅜ × 1 × 12 inches long.

Cross Bars.—Two pieces hard wood 1⅜ × 1 × 8¾ inches long.

Runners.—Two pieces 1⅜ × 1 × 30½ inches long.

Guides.—Two pieces 1⅜ × 1 × 47¾ inches long.

Top and Bottom.—Two pieces plywood, ⅛ inch thick, 3¼ inches wide, 12 inches long.

All the above are finished sizes.

Sundries.—One piece white cloth, 12 × 46 inches; 3 yards tape, ¾ inch wide; a few brass-headed nails; one strong hinge, 4 inches long; three brass hinges, ½ inch wide and about 1½ inches long; two pieces asbestos card 9 × 6 inches; two stout wood screws, 2½ inches long.

In addition, a few screws for the hinges, a dozen screws, 1½ inches long, a few small nails and some paint and enamel for the finishing. One small knob, one spring ball catch.

Commencing the Work.

Begin operations by preparing all the parts to the shapes and sizes shown in Fig. 6, taking care to have all corners square and everything exact to size.

Next prepare the two cross rails shown in Fig. 7 by cutting notches, ½ inch wide and ½ inch deep, at each end. These can be fashioned with a tenon saw by cutting very carefully to lines marked on the wood, but if the worker is not

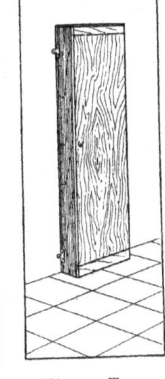

Fig. 1.—The Ironing Cabinet opened ready for use.   *Fig. 2.—The Cabinet closed.*

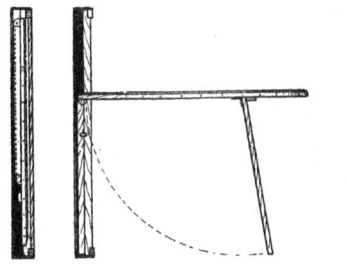
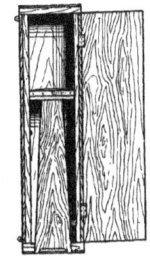

Figs. 3 and 4.—Side View, showing Cabinet closed and open.   *Fig. 5.—Front View of Cabinet open.*

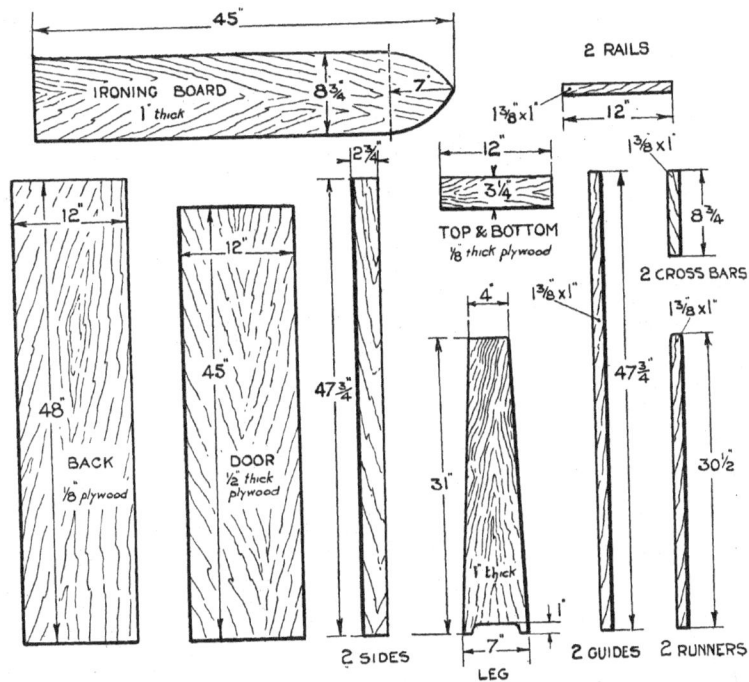

Fig. 6.—Shapes and Dimensions of all the Wooden Parts required for the Cabinet and Ironing Board.

MAKING A USEFUL IRONING CABINET

expert with the saw the wood should be cut on the waste side of the lines and then shaped with a chisel.

Shape each end of the two guides in a similar way, but follow the dimensions given in Fig. 8.

The relationship of these simple joints is shown clearly in Fig. 9. The rails project beyond the sides at the front and the guides finish flush with the front edges of the sides and the back stands ⅛ inch above the ends of these pieces at top and bottom.

Assembling the Cabinet.

Put the cabinet together in the following order: First, glue the guides to the sides, then glue and screw the rails into place—as shown in Fig. 10—and see that everything is square and free from winding. Next fix the top and bottom pieces to the sides and front.

Screw the back temporarily in place; then hinge the door, as shown in Fig. 11, so that it closes on to the sides and fits neatly between the top and bottom rails. Three hinges are used, each being recessed equally into the back of the door and the side pieces. A spring ball catch should be fitted to the top to hold it shut.

Wall plates are screwed to the sides to hold the cabinet to a wall.

The Ironing Board.

Prepare the underside of the board by screwing cross pieces to it, as shown in Fig. 13, then tack a piece of asbestos card to the square end on the top surface, as in Fig. 14, this being used as a resting place for the hot iron. Nail a second piece of asbestos to the inside of the cabinet.

The two runners are plain straight pieces and should move freely up and down in the space between the fixed guides and the back. The top ends should be slightly rounded, as shown in Fig. 16.

Drill small holes for the screws to "start" in into the end of the back cross piece on the ironing board, also shown in Fig. 16, then screw the runners to the board leaving them just slack enough to allow the runners to turn easily.

Hinge the leg to the underside of the board, as shown in Fig. 15, then coil up a piece of spring wire, as shown in Fig. 17, and fix as shown.

Inserting the Runners.

Remove the back from the cabinet, put the runners and the board into place, then refix the back.

To prevent the runners moving sideways, fix a thin metal steady piece to each side, as shown in Fig. 18.

The top of the board should be padded with a few strips of old linen laid lengthways, as sketched in Fig. 19, and covered with white cloth secured to the sides with tape and brass nails. Finish the woodwork with enamel.

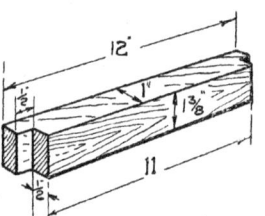

Fig. 7.—First Stage of Construction.
Cut the notches at the ends of the rails to the sizes shown in the above diagram.

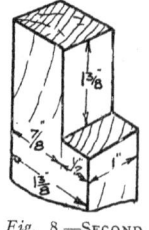

Fig. 8.—Second Stage of Construction.
Notching ends of guide pieces.

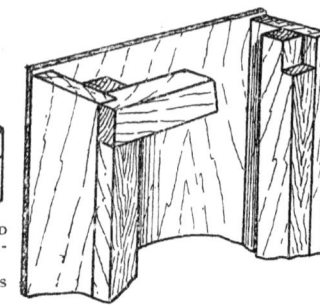

Fig. 9.—How the Guides, Rails, Side Pieces and Back are assembled.

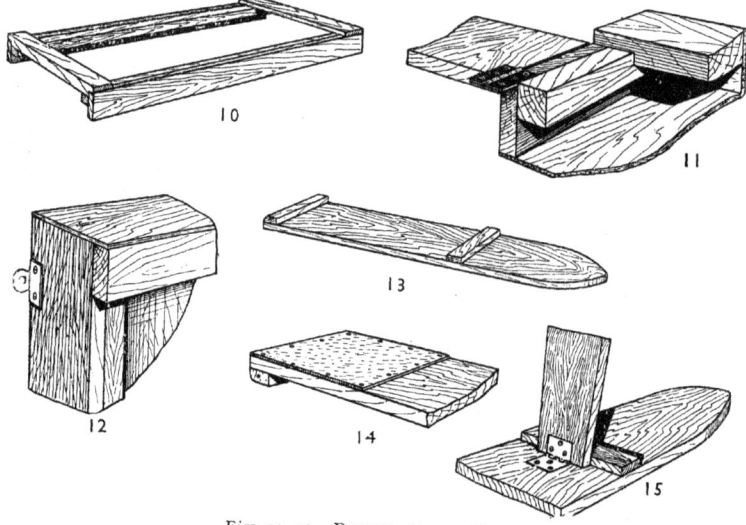

Figs. 10–15.—Details of the Board.
(10) Assembling the cabinet by gluing the guides and side pieces, then fixing the rails. (11) How the door-hinges are fixed. (12) Details of the fixing plates. (13) The cross pieces fixed to underside of ironing board. (14) Fix a piece of asbestos card at upper inner end. (15) Detail of pivot.

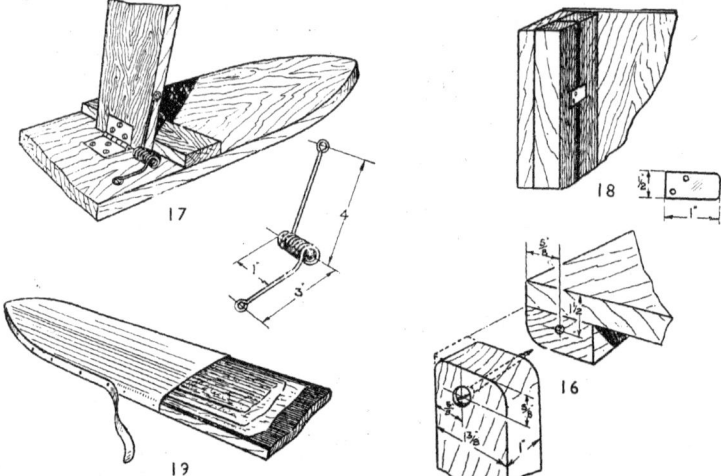

Figs. 16–19.—Details of Method of fixing Leg and padding the Top.
(16) How the leg is hinged. (17) The spring is bent to shape from spring wire and secured with two screws. (18) Fixing the steady pieces to keep the runners in place. (19) The top is padded with linen and cloth and nailed to the edges with tape.

Simple Rules for Colour Harmony

No matter how small one's home nor how simply it may be furnished, the skilful use of colour in the decorations and soft furnishings can create an impression of charm and tastefulness. Some people know instinctively whether a certain colour combination is going to look right or wrong, but there are many others who are without this fortunate gift. These people, too, may be sure of getting good colour schemes in their homes if they will give a little brief study to the nature of colour and then follow one or two simple rules.

The first point to realise is the fact that, from a psychological point of view, there are only four colours: Red, yellow, blue and green. All other colours are variations, more or less easily recognisable, from these four.

The Three Primary Colours.

But from a physical point of view there are only three colours: red, blue, and yellow. These are known as the three primary colours. It is from combination and mixture of these three colours in varying proportions that the countless graduations of hue are obtained.

If any two of the three primary colours are taken and mixed together in equal quantities, the result is a pure secondary colour. Thus red and yellow produce orange, blue and yellow produce green, red and blue produce violet. The three secondary colours, therefore, are orange, green and violet.

The Fundamental Facts of Colour Harmony.

If the three pure primary colours, red, blue and yellow, are used side by side in equal amounts the result is not so much discordant as lacking in subtlety and interest. It will be loud and crude. This is, however, the most elementary way of using colour.

Better harmonies are obtainable with the aid of secondary colours, each of which is the natural complement of a primary. Inasmuch as it is obtained by mixture of red and yellow, orange is complementary to blue, while green (blue and yellow) is complementary to red, and violet (red and blue) complementary to yellow.

If, therefore, a room is decorated in one primary colour and its complement, a simple but perfectly safe and correct scheme should result provided that both colours are diluted by admixture with white. The room will seem restful and complete, because the three primaries are all there, but not in an obvious and crude form. In other words, the safest and most satisfactory simple colour schemes are those based on a primary colour and its complement: orange and blue, green and red, violet and yellow. Yellow and green, and blue and green, may also be relied on to go together well.

Colour Discords to beware of.

Discord in the use of colour is far more liable to result from the use of two similar but slightly different tones of the same hue than from actual contrasts. The contrasts may seem startling but they are more likely to produce a chord, and they can generally be harmonised by introducing an intermediate complementary colour.

Fig. 1.—IN DECORATING AN INTERIOR, THE WALLS SHOULD BE LIGHTEST IN TONE AND GENERALLY WITH A FLAT FINISH.
The woodwork represented by skirting, picture rail, door and window architrave, and door should be darker and may be in glossy or semi-glossy paint. Any panels on the door may be a shade lighter than the other woodwork.

Just as in music the worst discords result from the sounding of tone or semi-tone intervals, so in the use of colour the most distasteful clashes result from slight divergencies; for example, a yellowy green and a pale olive green used side by side, or a greenish yellow with an orange yellow. These are the real discords, to be avoided at all costs.

The Subtler Uses of Colour.

So far we have dealt with pure primary and secondary tones, but this, of course, is only colour in its simplest and most elementary form.

Another point which it now becomes necessary to appreciate is the fact that all colours have three qualities: hue, value and brightness. Hue is the actual tint, as red or yellow; value is the strength of the colour, pale or deep, and is affected by the amount of white mixed with the pure primary, and brightness, on the contrary, is affected by the degree to which the colour tends to absorb light, in other words, whether it contains black. As an example of this, we often remark that the colour of a red rose is either bright or dark.

In addition, there are white and black—the latter sometimes defined as absence of colour and the former as all colours together. Mixture of white and black produces grey, and mixture of black and red, or red, blue and yellow, produces brown.

So we have black, white and grey; the three primary colours, red, blue and yellow; and the three complementary secondaries, violet, green and orange. Moreover, we have these six colours in countless lighter, subtle tones (technically, less "pure") obtained by mixing with white, also countless darker tones obtained by admixture of black or by admixture of green and red.

Use of Colour for Interior Decoration and Furnishing.

The application of the foregoing principles and knowledge to the decoration of one's home is comparatively easy as soon as one or two simple rules are clearly understood.

(1) Use primary colours sparingly, and seldom in their pure state. Dilute them with white.

(2) When a secondary colour is used with a primary the former may be slightly brighter in value than the latter.

(3) Use greyed or light-tone secondary colours for painting or distempering walls and ceilings. As a general rule the lighter the better.

(4) Another secondary or a primary colour may be used for the woodwork, but it should be light in tone—as a general rule not more than a shade darker than the walls. It is not often practicable to use pure primary colours except, perhaps, for picking out mouldings.

(5) The brightest accents of colour should generally be concentrated in the curtains and upholsteries.

With regard to the floor covering, for very bright and arresting schemes there are many beautifully coloured carpets. Some are "self" coloured, and others are patterned and have the dominant colour in the background.

SIMPLE RULES FOR COLOUR HARMONY

A coloured carpet may be salmon, burnt orange, royal blue, or green, but *a plain patternless carpet in a neutral shade of beige or fawn will harmonise perfectly with almost any colour scheme.*

Some Practical Schemes.

Taking as a guide the rules which we have laid down, it should now be quite easy for anyone to build up their own practical colour schemes. Below, however, are one or two detailed suggestions which may help in showing you the kind of effect it is desirable to obtain :—

Entrance Hall.

Walls and ceiling ; Pale pink-beige water paint.
Woodwork : Medium green semi-glossy paint.
Curtains : Cretonne with pattern in pink, green, blue and orange on a cream ground.
Lampshades : Similar to curtains.
Carpet : Fawn.

Lounge.

Walls and ceiling : Parchment yellow flat oil paint or water paint.
Woodwork : Jade green glossy paint.
Curtains : Shot or striped casement material in brown, beige and buff.
Upholstered furniture : Tweed or damask in green, brown and grey.
Lampshades : Parchment yellow.
Carpet : Fawn.

Dining Room.

Walls and ceiling : Cream, slightly tinged with pink.
Woodwork : Shell pink.
Curtains : Shot artificial silk in light and dark blue.
Furniture : Limed oak.
Lampshades : White opalescent glass.
Carpet : Blue.

Principal Bedroom.

Walls : Pale green waterpaint, or a modern wallpaper in light yellow, green, putty colour and mauve.
Ceiling : Cream.
Woodwork : Pale apricot or pale pinkish orange.
Curtains and bedspread : Green and golden yellow artificial silk.
Furniture : Jade green cellulose lacquer.
Lampshades : Cream.
Carpet : Deep green.

Second Bedroom.

Walls and ceiling : The shade of light grey-blue water paint known as Grey Lavender.
Woodwork : Scumbled light sky blue over a white ground.
Bedspread and curtains : Light and dark blue, beige and yellow.
Lampshades : White opalescent glass.
Carpet : Royal blue.

When deciding on colour schemes one should consider not only the purpose for which the room is to be used, but also whether it is large or small, high or low, light or dark, and whether it gets much or little sunshine, or possibly none at all.

Schemes for Small Rooms.

In a small room darker colours can sometimes be used without creating such an overpowering effect as results in a larger interior. But the small room must be also light. Warm browns and orange, especially, can be used in a den or study for an effect of cosiness.

In a small room which is also dark, the colours used must reflect as much light as possible. Black, brown, purple, dark green and dark blue absorb light and are unsuitable for a dark room ; but white, cream and pale tones in general reflect the light and make a dark room seem lighter.

If the ceiling is low it should be distempered lighter than the walls. If too high, it should be a tone darker than the walls. Tall narrow panels increase the effect of height ; panels with greater breadth than height reduce the apparent loftiness of the room.

Also, perpendicular lines on the walls increase the effect of height, while horizontal lines make a room seem lower.

Schemes for Large Rooms.

In a large light room you may safely use dark tones of brown and orange or any of the light colours such as cream, peach, pale green or pale blue. Do not use undiluted primary or secondary colours for extensive areas, whether the room be large or small.

Cool Colours for a Room facing South.

If the room has a south aspect very light apple green or pale blue should be conspicuous in the colour scheme, for these have a cool effect where there is much sunshine.

Warm Colours for a Room facing North.

For the room with a north aspect, use sunshine yellow, orange, crimson and shades of tawny brown. These are all warm colours.

Some Colours are Stimulating, others Depressing

Some colours are stimulating in their effect, and others depressing. Bright red, orange and yellow are all stimulating ; light green and light blue, though less stimulating, are cheerful ; olive green, dark blue, tan, terra-cotta and brown are definitely reposeful, while black, mauve and purple can be unmistakably depressing. The effect of any of these colours, however, will be modified by the various other hues with which they are combined, but it is safe to say that the room in which the *dominant* colour is bright red or orange will be stimulating in its effect ; while if the dominant colour is light blue, the room will be cheerful, and so on.

Although the rules which we have given will be found reliable in practice, the actual weight and proportionate quantity of any given colour in a particular colour scheme must always make a difference to the effect, and on this point something has generally to be left to the discretion of the individual. To a certain extent everyone has to exercise his or her personal taste, combined with ordinary common sense. If reasonable care is taken, however, it should be possible to achieve a tasteful and artistic colour scheme without risk of failure.

CURING TIGHT DRAWERS

THE most common cause of drawers sticking in their slides is swelling due to dampness. The remedy is to dry out the drawer, when it will generally be found that it has contracted sufficiently to enable it to be moved backwards and forwards freely. When the wood has become dry it is obvious that steps must be taken to prevent the trouble taking place again. A good plan is to rub the wood with paraffin wax or heavy motor grease. It is advisable to sandpaper the runners before applying the lubricant, in order to remove any surface irregularities and to give as smooth a sliding surface as possible. A good temporary remedy for a drawer that is tight is to rub a piece of candle grease on the sliding members.

In the case of a very stubborn drawer which will not yield to the above method, pull the drawer out as far as possible without using excessive force and rub the exposed drawer runners down with a coarse grade of sandpaper. Then apply grease to these runners, and, if they are accessible, to the runners at the back of the drawer.

By moving the drawer backwards and forwards and making several applications of sandpaper and grease to the exposed runners it will be found that the drawer will gradually work out far enough to be removed.

A few shavings should now be planed off the runners, followed by sandpapering and greasing.

Another useful material for protecting and lubricating the exposed wood of drawers is raw linseed oil. It should be well rubbed in and the wood allowed to dry before replacing the drawers.

Venetian Blinds

PRACTICAL NOTES ON OVERHAULING, REPAIRING AND FIXING

After a long period of use these blinds and their fittings generally require attention, and in some cases repairs. If there is nothing radically wrong with the working of the blind, it should be examined for frayed ladder tapes and cords, as these may, subsequently, cause trouble. If, however, these are found to be in good order, give the slats a good dusting and repaint if necessary. The pulleys should be examined for excessive wear and broken flanges; if found satisfactory, they will require nothing more but a little oil on their bearings.

Common Troubles Experienced.

The common troubles met with are as follows:—

(1) Frayed or broken ladder tapes (shown at B in Fig. 2).

(2) Broken cords (at E and D).

(3) Broken laths.

If a cord breaks, or becomes frayed, it should be replaced with a new cord; *no attempt should ever be made to join or otherwise repair an old cord.* Moreover, the new cord should be of the same type and diameter as the old cord; suitable cords can usually be obtained at the local hardware stores.

To Put in a New Cord.

To put in a new cord, first remove the tacks from the bottom lath and cut off the knots holding the cords in place. The cord (shown at D, in Fig. 2) can then be drawn out.

Having done this, it is advisable next to take out all of the laths in order to reduce the weight to be handled. It will then be necessary to remove the top lath from the window framing and take off the reversing cord (shown at E), and the ladder tapes (shown at B), from the second lath.

It will be necessary to lower the blind completely for these operations. An examination of the blind will show how the tapes are fixed, so that their removal will readily be understood; this is generally quite an easy matter.

Renewing Cross Tapes.

It is important to remember, when renewing cross-tapes, that they are fixed at standard distances apart; this distance is about 2¼ inches. If the new tapes are fitted at different distances, it will be found that the blind, when let down to its full extent, is either too long or too short; if too long it will not close properly.

It is important also to check the lengths of the new tapes. For this reason the old tapes should always be measured before taking them away from the blind. The new tapes should be fixed in place with tacks of a similar type to those previously removed from the laths.

Incidentally, the tapes can be removed in the manner we have described, for cleaning purposes.

Fitting New Cords.

When fitting new cords, these should be passed **over** the pulleys before the **top** board is screwed up into its place again. The top board having been secured, the tape will then be left hanging down. The laths (which should have been cleaned or repainted) should then be replaced. The bottom lath should be put back first, in order to keep the tapes tight; this will then greatly facilitate the replacement of the other laths.

Having put the latter back, the hanging cords should then be threaded through the laths, commencing at the top. After threading through the lowest lath, a knot should be tied in each cord in order to secure it.

One important point to remember when threading the cord through the tapes is that this cord must pass alternately on the left- and right-hand sides of consecutive tapes.

The Cord Pulleys.

It is always advisable to inspect the cord pulleys and to see that these run quite freely. If they are found to be rather on the tight side, apply a little paraffin oil to the pins and pulley holes forming the bearings, and work the pulleys backwards and forwards until they are quite free.

Afterwards, lubricate with ordinary motor engine oil. See that the edges, or flanges, of the pulleys are not broken in places, as this defect will often cause the cords to run off and jamb in the space between the pulley and the wooden slot. In order to prevent this, a piece of plywood should be nailed on either side of the pulley, as shown in Fig. 3.

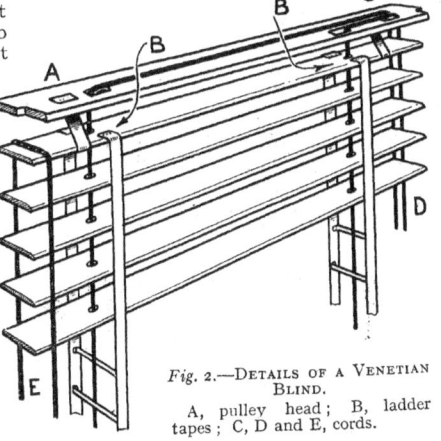

Fig. 1.—Fixing a Venetian Blind in position to the Head Lining of the Sash Frame.
Note how the blind rests on the left knee, thus leaving both hands free to raise the pulley head to the top of the window.

Fig. 2.—Details of a Venetian Blind.
A, pulley head; B, ladder tapes; C, D and E, cords.

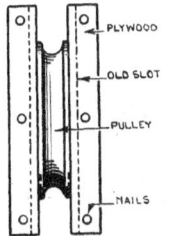

Fig. 3.—Method of Preventing Cord from Slipping off Pulley.

VENETIAN BLINDS

Finally, test the pulley and blind fixing screws for tightness.

HOW TO FIX A VENETIAN BLIND IN POSITION

There are three positions in which a venetian blind can be fixed, namely,—

(1) Fixing to the face of the sash frame.

(2) Fixing blind between the stop beads.

(3) Fixing to the splayed linings.

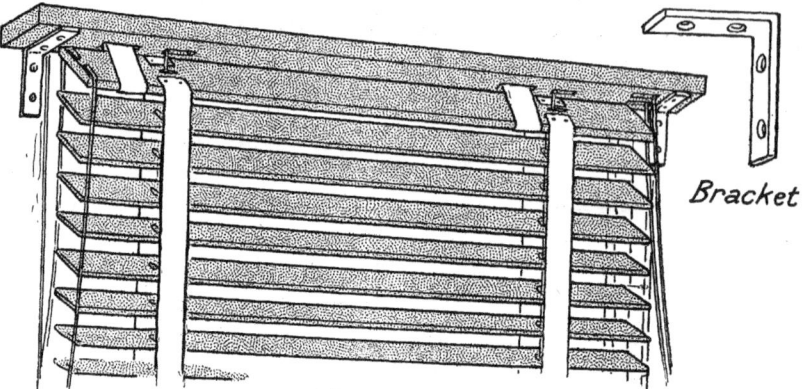

Fig. 4.—ONE OF THE BEST METHODS OF FIXING A VENETIAN BLIND.
In this case the blind is supported on small shelf brackets which are attached to the face of the lining. This method has the advantage that there is little likelihood of the blind bumping half-way down on the top of the lower sash.

Fixing to the Face of the Sash Frame.

This is one of the best methods of fixing a venetian blind. It is fixed between the mouldings of the window frame and is supported by a pair of shelf brackets 2 × 3 inches. These brackets are fixed to the face of the lining about 2 inches from the bottom edge of the top moulding and the pulley head is placed on these brackets. To keep the blind in position, stout screws about ¾ inch should be inserted through the shelf brackets into the pulley. No other fixing is required, and the blind will pull up and down free of the sash.

Fixing Blind between Stop Beads.

This method is not so good as that previously described, for it has the disadvantage that blinds fixed between stop beads are liable to bump half-way down on the top of the lower sash. When a blind is fixed in this manner it will be necessary to obtain two stout screws about 2½ × 12 inches. Holes should be bored in the pulley head of the blind about 6 inches from each end and 1 inch back from the front edge. The exact width between the stop beads should now be measured and the pulley head cut to fit that width. The blind is then ready for fixing.

As the screws are inserted 1 inch back from the front of the pulley head, it will enable them just to free the stop bead, and the points of the screws will enter into the lining of the sash frame. As most of the strain will be on the right-hand side, *i.e.*, where the draw-up cords are, special care should be taken to see that this screw is up tight. The screw on the left-hand side will not get so much strain.

Fixing Blind to Splay Linings.

When it is intended to fit the blind to splay linings, the blind will be obtained with the pulley head considerably longer than the thin laths of the blind.

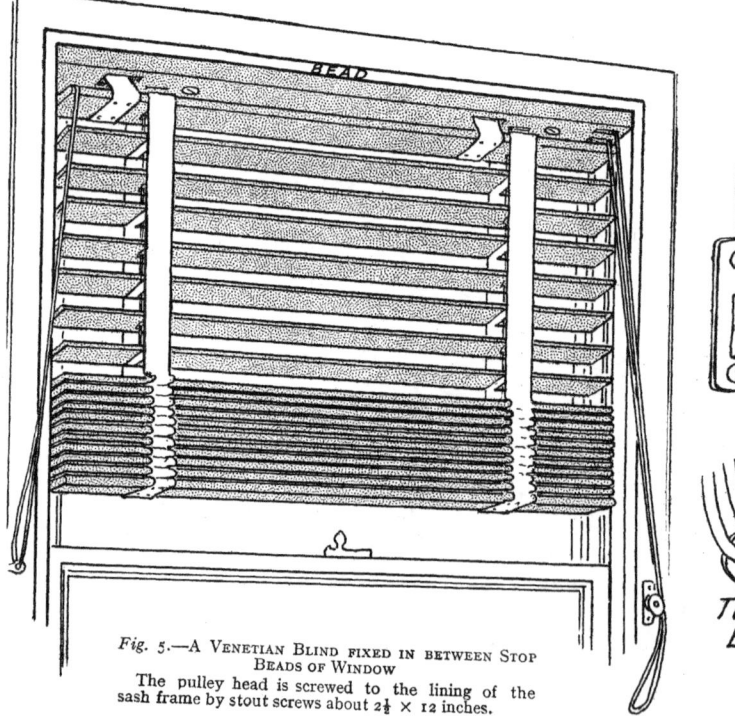

Fig. 5.—A VENETIAN BLIND FIXED IN BETWEEN STOP BEADS OF WINDOW.
The pulley head is screwed to the lining of the sash frame by stout screws about 2½ × 12 inches.

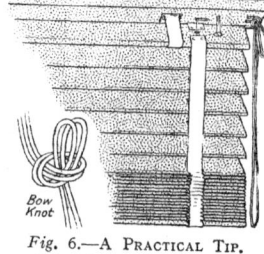

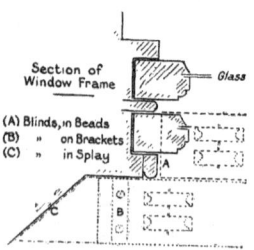

Fig. 6.—A PRACTICAL TIP.
When fixing a Venetian blind release about six or eight laths and then tie a bow knot in the cord. This takes the weight of the remainder of the blind and prevents it falling down the window.

Fig. 7.—SECTION OF A WINDOW FRAME SHOWING THE THREE METHODS OF FIXING VENETIAN BLINDS.

The first thing to do is to make a template of the splay of the window lining and then cut the pulley head to fit this bevel. The method of fixing is similar to that for stop beads, *i.e.*, two stout screws about 2½ × 12 inches and holes must be bored in the pulley head to take the screws. The blind is then ready for fixing.

SOME PRACTICAL NOTES ON FIXING

A pair of steps will be required, and these should be placed in front of the window. Now untie the cords of the blind and leave them loose. Release the pulley head and about six or eight laths, thus undoing the top portion of the blind. Then tie a loose bow knot in the cords, as shown in Fig. 6.

Now mount the steps with the blind, not forgetting to take the screws and a screwdriver. In order to have both hands free when screwing the pulley head to the top of the window, the blind should be rested on the left knee, as shown in Fig. 1. Now insert the screws and screw up tight. The bow knot that was temporarily tied in the cord can now be undone and the blind allowed to fall down in position.

Now make sure that the thin laths are perfectly free of the cross tapes of the ladder-web. The fact that the laths have probably only recently been painted may make them likely to adhere to the cross tapes and so prevent the blind from properly shading. Each lath should be raised separately from the cross tape and examined.

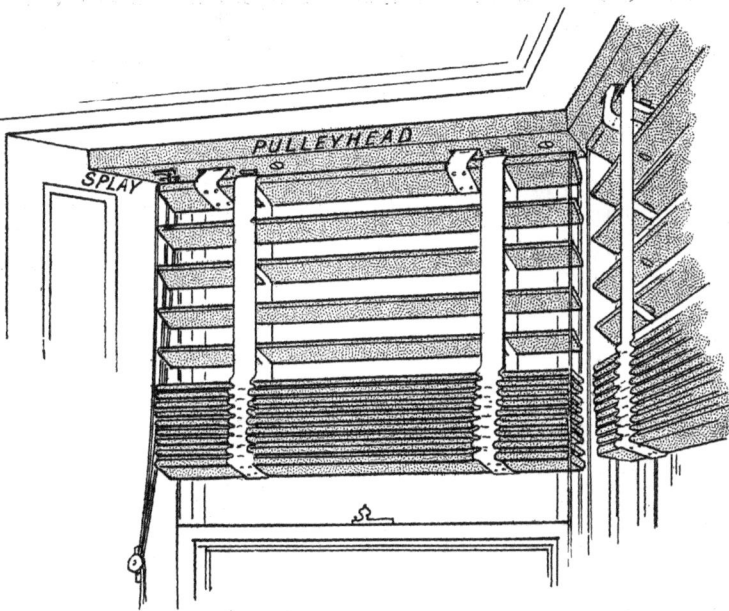

Fig. 8.—Method of fitting a Venetian Blind to Splay Linings. The pulley head of the blind is shown cut to the splay of the window lining at one end. The other end is mitred to the pulley head of adjoining window.

Lastly, fit the Turning Cord.

All that remains now is to fit the turning cord which opens and shuts the blind. It will be seen that there is a brass eye threaded on this cord (see Fig. 5). This eye should be driven into the woodwork of the window in a convenient position. Do not pull this cord down too tightly; it is best left rather on the loose side, so as not to prevent the blind from turning freely. Finally, fix the fastening cleat on the other side of the blind.

What to do if Blind is too Long.

If it is found that the drop of blind is too long, the only way to shorten it is to take out one of the laths and retie the cords at the bottom. It will be realised that as each of the thin laths are spaced 2 inches apart, as each lath is removed the blind will be 2 inches shorter.

If the Blind is too Short.

Should the blind be too short, it will only be possible to lengthen it about ½ inch, and this can be done by slightly lengthening the swing tapes at the top.

KEEPING A GAS COOKER CLEAN

BY giving a gas cooker regular attention a great deal of trouble can be saved. A dirty gas stove is not only unsightly, but will give off objectionable fumes every time it is lit. A simple but practical tip is to wipe off any grease or spilt liquid, immediately after cooking, with old newspapers rolled up into a ball.

Once a week, at least, the stove should be thoroughly cleaned with strong soap suds or soap powder in order to keep the enamelled surfaces clean and bright. Provided all grease has been carefully removed with newspaper, as described above, it will not be necessary to use soda.

Removing Grit and Rust.

If grit and rust are present on the bars or burners, it is a good plan to dip a rag in paraffin and wipe over the parts. Do not forget the burners inside the oven. Soda could be used if paraffin is not available, but the latter is preferable as it forms a protection from rust and corrosion. It is hardly necessary to add that none of the burners should be alight while cleansing operations are in progress.

Cleaning Burners.

To clean burners that have been neglected, use a stiff brush with some turpentine. Should any of the holes be actually stopped up, they should be cleaned out with a carefully pointed wooden skewer or an orange stick. Before starting operations it is a good plan to test each burner in turn, making a note of any in which some of the holes are stopped up.

Small Orifice in the Tap.

Another point that should be given attention is the small orifice in the tap. If there is dirt or grit in the hole, clear it with the point of a wooden toothpick, or, failing this, a needle.

How to Keep the Surfaces of the Top Surround Bright.

To keep the surfaces of the top surround bright, rub with fine emery cloth, or a soft rag on which a little knife polish has been sprinkled. The dull iron portions, such as the door, with its handle, hinges and sides, should be wiped over with an old piece of soft flannel that has been dampened with turpentine.

Practical Uses for Old Safety Razor Blades

A PROBLEM confronting most users of safety razors is that of the disposal of the worn blades. These usually accumulate and, in time, become regarded as waste material.

Many uses can, however, be found for these disused blades, for, although they may not be sufficiently sharp for shaving purposes, they are quite satisfactory for numerous other cutting operations.

There are two principal types of safety-razor blade in popular use, namely, the Gillette double-edged type, and the Valet, single-edge variety. Whilst the latter can be used for many of the purposes referred to in this article, unless it is of the perforated pattern, it is by no means so convenient as the double-edged type.

The latter is provided with two holes, or in the slotted flexible type, with a variable contour recess which can be regarded, for all practical purposes, as the two holes. These holes, or their equivalents, are very useful for attaching the blades to other objects forming supports or guides for them.

The blades in themselves, on account of their thin sections, are unsuitable for the majority of purposes, so that they require some kind of attachment or support to relieve the blade of any other duty than that of cutting.

Methods of Supporting the Blades.

Three alternative methods of attaching and supporting the double-edged type of blade are shown in Diagrams A, B and C, Fig. 1.

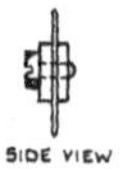

The simplest way is to screw the blade to a metal support, using two screws, one in each of the holes of the blade, as shown at A, Fig. 1. A stronger support is obtained by clamping it between two strips of metal, e.g., brass or aluminium, using screws and nuts, as shown at B, Fig. 1.

When the blade has to be attached to a wooden support, ordinary round-headed wood-screws and washers can

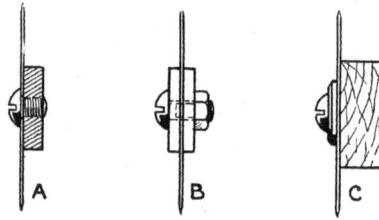

Fig. 1.—Showing Methods of supporting Double-edged Blades.

be used for this purpose, as shown at C, Fig. 1.

The single-edged type of blade usually has a semi-circular depression at each end, as shown at X, Fig. 2.

These depressions are useful as a means of attaching the blade to a

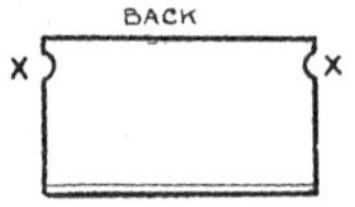

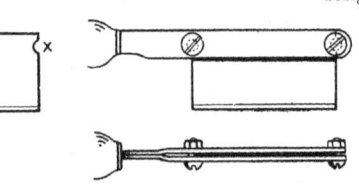

Fig. 2.—Single-edged Blade. The depressions X form a useful method of support.

Fig. 3.—Method of supporting Blade, using the Depressions X.

holder, in the manner indicated in Fig. 3.

In this case the screws just bear against the sides of the depressions X, and thus prevent endwise movement; at the same time the blade is clamped securely to the support.

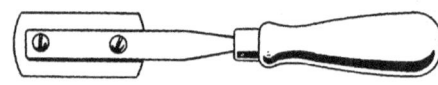

Fig. 4.—Print Trimmer and Paper Cutter.

SOME USEFUL APPLICATIONS
Print and Paper Cutter.

Either type of blade can be mounted on a strip of metal and used for trimming prints or cutting paper, cardboard and similar soft material sheeting. Fig. 4 shows how a double-edged blade is mounted for the purposes in question. A piece of strip brass of ¾ × ⅛ inch section will do quite well for the support; by tapering one end like a file tang it can be fitted into a wooden handle, as shown.

The advantage of this cutting device is that as soon as the edges become blunt or broken a new blade can be inserted, as it is hardly worth while to attempt to resharpen them.

The cutter shown in Fig. 4 is also very useful as an erasing knife for artists, draughtsmen and photographic retouchers.

String Cutters.

There are many alternative forms of string, cord and wool cutters, utilising safety-razor blades as cutters. In designing such cutters it is important to arrange the blade so that its edges are guarded, in order to obviate the possibility of cutting one's fingers when using it.

Fig. 5 shows a bench or counter type cutter having a Vee-depression for guiding the string to be cut. It can readily be made from a piece of brass strip or brass angle; the other flange of the latter is used for screwing the cutter to the bench or counter.

Fig. 6 illustrates a portable string cutter consisting of two brass plates, made first to circular shape and then filed in the manner indicated in order to expose a small portion of the edge of blade. The blade is shown held by a central screw and two register pins, but it may also be clamped by two screws in the manner previously described and illustrated, at B in Fig. 1.

When it is necessary to change the blade, the two screws are taken out, so that the two sides are free and the blade drops out.

Multiple Paper Cutter.

A simple but convenient cutter for making strips of paper for packing material and similar purposes is made by clamping a number of blades and distance pieces together, utilising the

Fig. 5.—A Counter, or Bench Type String Cutter.

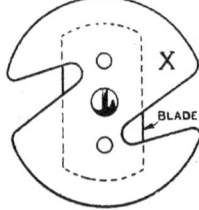

Fig. 6.—A Portable String Cutter.

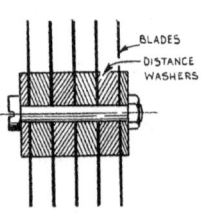

Fig. 7.—Multiple Paper Cutter for Strip Material.

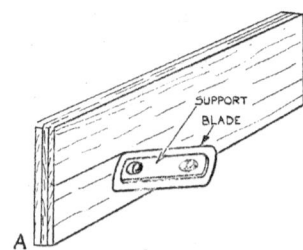

Fig. 8.—Plywood and Millboard Cutter or Recesser.

PRACTICAL USES FOR OLD SAFETY RAZOR BLADES

existing holes in the blades, as shown in Fig. 7. The packing pieces may be in the form of brass or aluminium washers. The two end pieces are extended and, after clearing the backs of the blades, are bent together and fastened to a suitable wooden holder; in effect, therefore, the blades and washers are held in a forked member mounted in a wooden handle.

Pencil Sharpener.

A simple but efficient sharpener for pencils and similar objects is shown in Fig. 9. It consists of a blade attached to a strip of ebonite, hardwood or plywood, by means of two screws and nuts. The edge of the blade should be about $\frac{1}{16}$ inch below the edge of the other material, as a protectory measure. The handle should be from 4 to 6 inches in length.

Cutter for Thicker Materials.

Where it becomes necessary to cut through, or to recess materials such as three-ply, cardboard, millboard, rubber, canvas and similar materials, the device shown in Fig. 8 will be found suitable.

It consists of a block of beech or oak, of appropriate dimensions to suit the user, to which a safety razor blade is attached in the manner shown. The blade, it is seen, is slanting and projects below the base of the block, by an amount equal to the thickness of the material to be cut. It is an advantage to have a metal support—in the form of a metal strip to hold the blade firmly to the wooden block, as shown.

In use, the lower edge, A, of the block is held against a straight-edge, whilst the block is drawn along the material to be cut.

Incidentally, old razor blades used in a similar manner will be found very useful for cutting, trimming and squaring up the ends of plywood.

Fig. 9.—Pencil Sharpener.

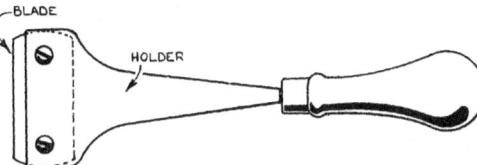

Fig. 10.—Scraper for Removing Paper from Glass Windows.

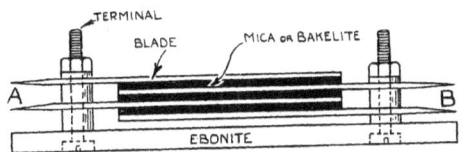

Fig. 11.—An Electrical Condenser.

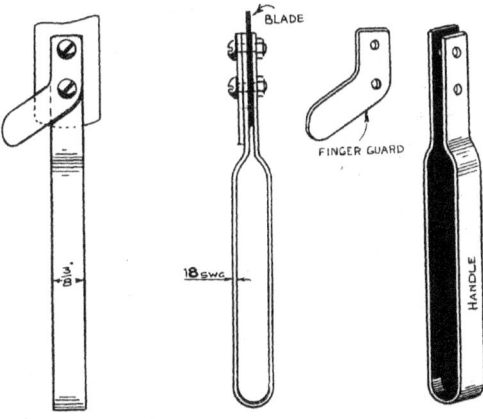

Fig. 12.—A Handy Device for Cutting Card, Paper, Plywood and Veneer.

Paper Scraping Tool.

For removing paper labels, notices and similar items from glass windows, the tool shown in Fig. 10 will be found particularly effective. In this case the whole edge of the blade is arranged at right angles to the axis of the blade handle. The support should be of $\frac{1}{8}$-inch mild steel, with a steel or brass plate as a clamping piece. The screws can be of $\frac{3}{16}$-inch steel, working in holes tapped in the metal holder.

The device illustrated in Fig. 10 may be used, also, as a paint and varnish scraper.

An Electrical Condenser.

A novel use to which old razor blades can be put is shown in Fig. 11. In this case a number of blades are mounted with mica or bakelite insulation upon a piece of ebonite to form an electrical condenser for wireless and similar purposes. Being thin, the blades take up very little room. It is necessary, of course, to ensure that the two sets of blades A and B are well insulated from each other, otherwise any possibility of a short-circuit may be attended by serious consequences; this condition applies of course to all fixed condensers.

Using two blades only, one on each side with mica insulation between, a series aerial condenser can be made. Further, by arranging to vary the area in contact with the mica, by swivelling the blades sideways, the capacity can be varied also.

Fixed condensers of any desired value may be built up by using different numbers of blades.

It is an advantage to grind the cutting edges down a little before assembling the blades, in order to avoid cutting one's fingers when adjusting the condenser.

HOW TO REMOVE A STUBBORN NUT

WHEN a nut has become so firmly fixed to its bolt or stud that it is impossible to loosen it with a spanner in the ordinary way, it is a good plan to heat the end of the spanner before it is placed on the nut. The object of this is to cause the nut to expand slightly and so enable it to be unscrewed.

If this treatment fails to move the nut, paraffin or turpentine should be applied liberally to the exposed threaded parts. Wipe off any surplus liquid and play the flame of a blow-lamp around the nut.

Place a set spanner that is a good fit over the nut while it is still hot and hit the free end of the spanner with a hammer. In most cases this jarring will loosen the nut.

If, however, the nut and bolt have become badly rusted together it will be necessary to cut them partly through with a chisel or hacksaw and then force them off with a spanner. Note that the cut should be made parallel with the axis of the screw.

How to Gild with Gold Leaf

Gilding with gold leaf is well within the scope of the amateur. It can be put to many uses, such as gilding picture frames, lead lights, name boards, wicker work, designs on silk shades, and the ornament on book covers. Leaf gilding must not be confused with so-called "gold" paints, which tarnish in time; the sheets are pure gold beaten out extremely thin, and since the royal metal is unaffected by exposure they keep their lustre and colour for many years.

Tools Required.

The necessary equipment is quite simple and inexpensive; the only special tools needed are a gilder's tip (the square brush in Fig. 1), a gilding mop, and a supply of small brushes for applying the size and isinglass. In addition to these an artist's palette and some cotton wool will complete the outfit.

How to Buy Gold Leaf.

The gold is sold in books containing 25 sheets of leaf each 3 inches square; the thin paper leaves of the book are coated with rouge to prevent the metal sticking to the paper. It can also be purchased as transferred gold; that is, the leaf is stuck to waxed paper. It is more expensive to buy this way, and as it is quite easy to transfer it as required it is better done at home.

How to Transfer Gold Leaf.

Cut some squares of clean tissue paper 4 × 5 inches, then, holding one corner, rub (in one direction only) the surface with a block of white beeswax; half a dozen strokes will be sufficient to coat the paper. Now insert the tissue paper between the leaves of gold with the waxed side towards the metal and then lay the book on a flat surface. Holding it down firmly at one corner with the left hand, stroke the cover two or three times with the right hand, applying considerable pressure. The gold will now be found evenly attached to the waxed surface of the tissue paper.

Sometimes

Fig. 3.—How the Mop is used to Punch on a Leaf when Gilding a Picture Frame.

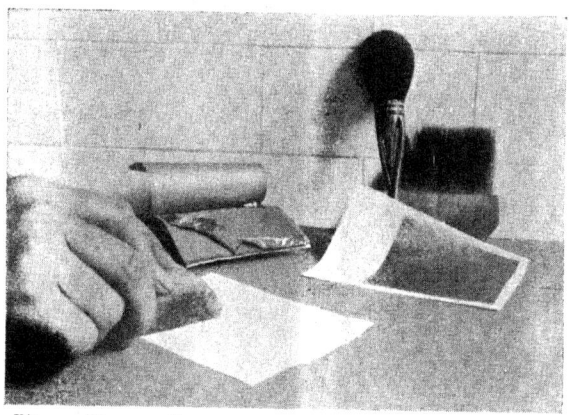

Fig. 2.—How to Transfer the Gold Leaf to the Waxed Paper.

Cut some squares of clean tissue paper, then, holding one corner, rub the surface in one direction only with a block of white beeswax. Then insert the waxed paper between the leaves of gold with the waxed side towards the metal and lay the book on a flat surface. Apply pressure over the book with the hand.

when opening the book to insert the waxed tissue the metallic leaves will be found slightly crumpled. On no account must you attempt to smooth it out with the fingers, but by gently blowing the crinkled leaf can be coaxed to lay quite flat on the rouged surface of the book.

Transferred gold is the best form to use when gilding a flat wood or metal surface, but loose leaf must be used when working on glass or on a picture frame which is in high relief.

How to Gild Lead Lights.

Carefully rub over the lead work with a rag moistened with turpentine to remove all traces of grease. With a small writer's pencil (brush) evenly coat the lead strips with "gold size" purchased from the colour shop. Leave the size to dry partially until it becomes "tacky." The time required before this state of things happens will vary from half an hour to three hours, according to the dryness of the atmosphere.

Now proceed to gild by laying a piece of transferred gold face down on to the tacky size; rub the back of the tissue with a wad of cotton wool, applying pressure, then pull the tissue away and the gold will be found adhering to the lead. Continue in a similar manner until all the lead is coated with gold. Take care to overlap the joints in the leaf slightly.

Gilded lights are best covered on the weather side, or outside with a sheet of plain glass, although the gold will stand up to sun and rain for years without changing colour.

Gilding Picture Frames.

Clean the frame thoroughly with soap and water ready for sizing. Into a small quantity of gold size put a little chrome yellow to colour it slightly. This serves a double purpose in showing up any points missed with the brush and hiding small holes left when gilding.

When the size is "tacky," take a book of untransferred gold and pick up a leaf on the gilder's "tip." To do this lightly drag the "tip" across the head to pick up a minute film of grease, then apply the brush to the edge of the

Fig. 1.—The Equipment required for Gilding.
The only special tools needed are a gilder's tip, a gilding mop and a supply of small brushes for applying the size and isinglass.

HOW TO GILD WITH GOLD LEAF

Fig. 4.—Before applying the Gold Leaf to a Name Board the Letters should first be painted with Gold Size.
When tacky, place the tissue face downwards on the size, rub the back with a wad of cotton wool and then tear off.

leaf and it will stick to the "tip" like a magnet holds a nail. Throw the leaf on to the tacky size and punch it in gently with the gilding mop; if the frame has high relief it will be necessary to cast on a second leaf over the first. This double gilding ensures that all the little crevices and corners are all covered.

Later the spare broken gold can be dusted away with the mop and all flat surfaces should be lightly rubbed with a wad of cotton wool to produce a burnished appearance.

Gilding a Name Board.

When writing a name in gold on a piece of wood carefully prepare the surface and stain it the desired colour, finally giving it a thin coat of French polish to prevent too much suction, and then mark out the letters in chalk. Readers who find difficulty in making good-shaped letters can trace the letters from some printed matter on to a piece of paper, then prick small pin-holes round the outline and so produce a "pounce." Lay this on the wood and dust the surface of the "pounce" with a whitening bag; the fine powder will penetrate the holes in the paper, leaving a clear outline on the wood.

Now paint in the letter with gold size, and when "tacky" proceed to gild with transferred gold, placing the tissue face downwards on the sticky size, rubbing the back of the paper with a wad of cotton wool and then tearing off the tissue, leaving the gold in position stuck to the size.

Finally wash off with a soft sponge and give a flowing coat of varnish.

Glass Gilding—First Steps.

When gilding on glass the first step is to set out the work on the face side of the glass, preparatory to gilding on the back of the glass. Supposing it is required to write a name on glass, cut out the required letters in paper (suitable ones can often be found in papers and magazines) and stick them in place on the face side of the glass, taking care to space them evenly.

Fig. 5.—Gilding Lead Lights with Transferred Gold.
All traces of grease must be removed by rubbing the lead work with a rag moistened with turpentine. Apply gold size, and then proceed to gild by laying a piece of transferred gold face down on the tacky size and rubbing with a wad of cotton wool.

While the paper letters are drying prepare a solution of isinglass by dissolving a half-spoonful of the flakes in a cupful of warm water, and finally straining off the clear liquid through fine linen.

How to Stick the Leaf.

Float a flowing coat of the isinglass solution on to the *back* of the glass, spreading it generously to cover the area occupied by the lettering. Allow it partially to dry; this may take several hours in damp weather. Then pick out the leaves of gold one at a time on the gilding "tip" and cast each in place on the glass until the whole area is covered with leaf gold. Take care to keep the gold from crumpling, and if it tears, leaving small holes, cut a small piece of leaf and throw it on to the glass to cover the spot. The gold can be cut in the following way: partly open the book, bending back the pages and displaying a portion of the leaf, then lightly mark across the metal with a knife. The small piece can then be picked up on the "tip."

Backing Up the Gold.

When the leaf has stuck to the back of the glass place it in a position so that the light shines through. The shape of the paper letters on the face of the glass will then show plainly on the gold. Now take a small brush and with ordinary black paint outline the letters on the gold itself. The shape of the letters can easily be traced as the paper pattern letters can be seen through the gold.

When the paint is dry take a sponge and warm water and wash off all the gold which has not been "backed up." The paint will prevent the leaf being washed away where it is required. When viewed from the front the letters will now appear in burnished gold, while seen from the back they appear black.

Pencil Varnishing.

Whenever possible the gold should be left unvarnished, but sometimes, for example, when gilding the mouldings on a front

Fig. 6.—Gilding on Glass—the First Steps.
Casting on the leaf with a tip on the back of the glass after applying a coat of isinglass solution to the glass. Note the paper letters stuck on the front.

Fig. 7.—Gilding on Glass—Final Stages.
By placing the glass in a position so that the light shines through, the shape of the paper letters will show through the glass. The outline of the letters is then filled in with black paint on the gold, after which any unwanted gold is washed off.

Fig. 8.—Gilding the Letters on a Book.
The letters are first punched out with a lettering tool, cleaned with methylated spirit and sized with a water size made with isinglass. A little leaf is then punched in with a stencil brush.

door, the gold may be pencil-varnished.

This means a coating of varnish may be floated over the gold with a writer's pencil (brush). This will slightly change the colour of the gold, but will prevent it from being rubbed off.

Gilding on Books and Leather.

Some readers who bind their own books may wish to gild the titles on the covers. With a lettering tool punch out the letters so that they appear counter-sunk into the cover, clean the surface of the characters with a methylated rag brought to a point on a steel knitting needle and size them in with water size made with isinglass. When this is "tacky" punch in a little leaf with a stencil brush.

Gilding and its Uses.

In addition to the uses outlined above gold-leaf gilding will be found useful in a number of ways. Many marble clocks have ornamental lines in gilt. These can easily be renewed, making the timepiece look like new. Tarnished brass fittings on Louis furniture can be renovated by gilding them, while artistic effects can be obtained on chairs enamelled in soft art shades, then "picked out" or bespangled with touches of gold.

Silk lighting shades can be brightened up and made to look like new by gilding in selected portions of the faded design. When gilding on silk always use the water size described above.

HOW TO MAKE AND USE ALUMINIUM AND GOLD PAINTS

THE average householder can find plenty of opportunities for the use of these classes of paints, the outstanding disadvantage being that they so quickly tarnish, but if the following methods are followed, the disadvantage may be greatly overcome. Naturally, gold paints can never be made properly to resemble English gold leaf or to keep its colour for the same period.

Gold bronze may be had in three grades, namely, pale, middle, and deep, with each in turn having varying qualities; the cheaper the bronze the greater is the adulteration, which means quicker deterioration. Always purchase good quality bronze powders. The method employed to produce the finished paints is to mix the bronze into a selected medium by well stirring, after which the mixture is ready for use.

Past experience has shown that when making gold paints only sufficient mixture should be made to complete the work on hand, for if stored for future use it will be found that through chemical action, that is to say, between the bronze and the medium, decomposition takes place, thereby rendering the paint useless. This reaction is seldom seen in aluminium paints, which therefore may be kept for future use.

Mediums in General Use.

The mediums in general use are as follows: (*a*) A mixture of pale gold size and turpentine in the proportions of half and half. (*b*) A mixture of pale hard carriage varnish and turpentine in the proportions of half and half. (*c*) Celluloid lacquer or varnish. The mediums described all give quite good results and may be used with confidence. (*a*) and (*b*) will be of a slow drying and hardening character, with (*c*) as quick drying. The following data will assist householders who may wish to make their own paints:

- ½ pint turpentine.
- ½ pint pale gold size or pale hard carriage varnish.
- 2 ozs. gold bronze or aluminium powder.

Or again,

- 1 pint celluloid lacquer or varnish.
- 2 ozs. gold bronze or aluminium powder.

Dealing with Old Work.

For coating old work, first well wash with weak warm soda water to remove all dirt and grease, then with cold water, so as to neutralise any soda present; allow to dry. Now apply paint with an ordinary paint brush, giving a free coating; when all work has been covered, set aside for about twenty-four hours. Now apply a thin coat of the medium used; this acts as a protective film and adds lustre.

Dealing with New Work.

For new work it is best to give the woodwork, etc., a thin coating of a flatting paint to act as a backing. For bronze colour paints a stone colour should be applied, and for aluminium a light grey colour. In both cases the paint must dry flat and hard; when dry apply the bronze as previously described. To clean brushes where mediums (*a*) and (*b*) have been used, well wash in turpentine; if medium (*c*) has been used, purchase a small quantity of cellulose thinners in which brushes are easily cleaned. Should thinners be found necessary to thin the paints, use turpentine for (*a*) and (*b*) and cellulose thinners for (*c*).

An Easily Made Fireguard

FIREGUARDS are of various patterns. Some are easy to make, whilst others present many difficulties. Those composed of a cast-iron framework, into which several upright metal rods are fitted, belong to the latter class, and may be considered as being beyond the skill of the average homeworker.

However, if the frame is built of wood and ordinary wire-netting is used as the filling, the work becomes simple. There need be no fear of the wood catching alight with the design described here, as the guard stands well away from the fire. The cost in this case is no more than two or three shillings; thus it is possible to furnish several fireplaces with a guard each at no considerable outlay, if desired.

Measuring-up for the Guard

The first thing is to decide on the measurements. These will be determined partly by the individual fireplace and partly by the materials at hand. Place the fender in its usual position and measure up so that the guard will eventually stand just outside and so that it fits against the outer edge of the two upright mantle breasts. This will give all the dimensions necessary, except the height. The height should be about 3 feet, but it may be an inch or two more or less, according to the wire-netting that can be bought.

The Frame.

The frame consists of two wooden shapes, as shown in Fig. 2, the first for the base, the second for the top rail. These are made of strips of wood, 2 × 1 inches or, if preferred, 3 × 1 inches in section. It will be best to join the corners by means of the halving joint (see Fig. 3), and as children have to be considered, it will be advisable to round slightly the extreme corners with the aid of a chisel and spokeshave. It should be carefully noted that, as the halving joint shortens the effective length of the wood, due allowance must be made when cutting the sections.

These two shapes are held one above the other by means of a number of upright posts which are cut from strip wood, 1 × 1 inch in section. The exact number of these uprights depends on the size of the fireguard, but usually it will be sufficient if one is placed, each at A, B, C and D (Fig. 1), and three more between B and C, making seven in all. It will be advisable to arrange the corner posts, B and C, not quite on the angles, seeing that they are to be rounded off. If planned to come about an inch nearer to A or D, they will be simpler to fix and not so likely to cause harm should a child happen to fall against them. Fig. 4 gives an idea as

Fig. 1.—The easily made Fireguard described in this Article.

Fig. 2.—Two Wooden Shapes such as that shown above are required, one for the Top Rail and the other for the Base.

Dimensions are not given because they depend mainly on the size of the fireplace. The height should be about 3 feet, and 2 × 1 or 3 × 1 wood should be used.

to where these corner posts may conveniently come, and it also shows the space which must be cut out of the base or top rail, as the case may be, to take a vertical post.

Fixing the Wire.

When the wooden body of the

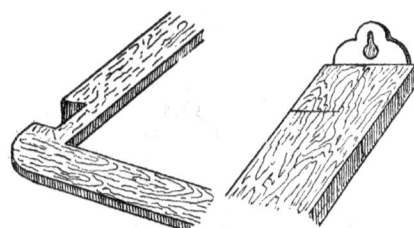

Fig. 3.—A simple Halving Joint should be used at the Corners.

Fig. 4.—The Corners should be Rounded and a Recess cut for the Uprights.

Fig. 5.—A Brass Hook should be fixed to the two Flying Ends of the Top Rail.

guard has been put together, the next step is to fit the wire. For this a coil of wire can be obtained and the strands woven backwards and forwards until the entire space has been filled in with a diamond-shaped mesh. This plan is not advised, however, as it is much simpler to buy about a yard and a half of close-meshed wire-netting and to fit it in one piece. The netting should go round the guard on the outside of the upright posts. If it is put on the inside, it may appear a little neater, but there is a chance, only a slight one, it is true, that should a child happen to lean on the netting, it might give way and the child would be precipitated into the grate.

In fixing the netting, it must be attached by U-pins in four or five places to each upright. The edge should be turned over and pinned to the under-side of the base, also to the upper side of the top rail. This will give a rough edge, in both cases, but by nailing a smooth lath over these edges, a neat finish is provided.

Finishing the Guard.

There is no reason why the fireguard should not be painted in some bright colour, or several colours, to please the child's fancies, but if it is thought that the heat may damage the paint, the wire can be given two coats of stove black and the woodwork darkened with an appropriate stain.

A Fixing Hook.

By way of precaution, it is advisable to fix a hook, as shown in Fig. 5, to each of the two flying ends of the guard. Then if two nails are driven into the wall to correspond with the hooks, the fireguard will stand absolutely firm, no matter how it is pushed or otherwise treated.

By using the hook shown, the fireguard can, of course, be moved from room to room as required and can be hooked firmly in position in each room. It should be remembered, however, that the small cost of making the fireguard makes it possible to have a separate fireguard in each room if desired. Each fireguard could then be painted to tone with the general colour scheme of the room.

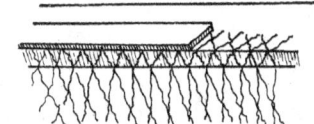

Fig. 6.—How the Wire Netting is fixed to the Top Rail.

It will be noticed that a thin lath is nailed over the rough tips of the wire.

The Law Regarding Fireguards.

By the Children Act of 1908, it is laid down that every open fire must be protected by a fireguard, if a child under the age of seven is in the room, and failure to comply with this regulation renders the person in charge of the child liable to a fine of £10.

Painting a Greenhouse

Quite a considerable proportion of the horticulture of this country is done under glass. Not only are there the extensive greenhouses and forcing frames of the professional fruit and flower growers, but even the small householder often finds the possession of a greenhouse to be a necessary adjunct to his gardening equipment.

A considerable proportion of every such building necessarily consists of wood framework, and while glass is impervious to weather conditions, even the best timber is not, unless it is kept well protected by means of periodical painting.

Exceptional Conditions.

In no other kind of building is the neglect of painting more wasteful or even as wasteful as it is in the case of such erections as the framework of a glasshouse, for the conditions to which it is subject are exceptionally severe.

The roofs of such buildings are nearly always of wood framing, and this is fixed at such a low pitch that moisture falling on it does not run off so speedily as from a perpendicular surface.

The glass is fixed in place by means of putty, which, if unprotected, lasts only for a time, and then disintegrates and falls away, with a consequent leakage at the edges of the glass.

And, lastly, the interior is subjected to a combination of deleterious influences arising from heat, excessive humidity and the various emanations thrown off by plants.

Precautions.

The owner or erector (they are often the same person) will therefore, if he is wise, take care that, right from the beginning, his greenhouse is properly painted with the right kind of paint, which should be renewed from time to time. And he will do this mainly because proper painting is a great deal cheaper than the drastic repairs which soon become necessary if the painting is neglected or improperly done.

The New Greenhouse.

Let us first consider the case of a new greenhouse in course of erection. The timber from which it is made will vary according to the purse of the owner, but it should be thoroughly dry and well seasoned. And nothing is more important than that, before the various sections leave the dry atmosphere of the place where they are made and become exposed to the weather, they should receive one or, better still, two coats of paint.

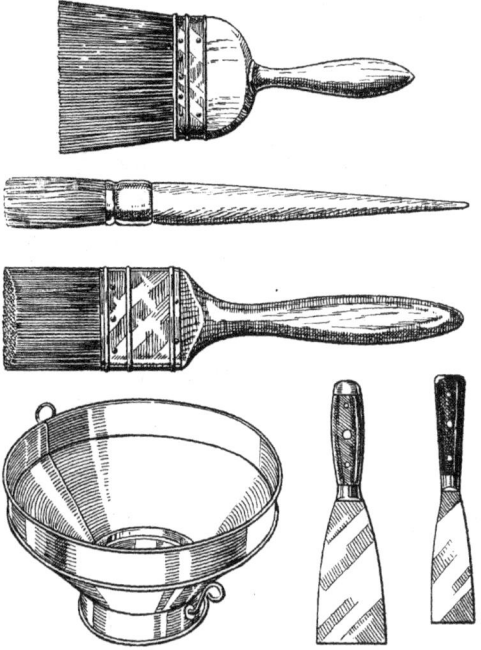

Fig. 1.—Some of the Tools required for Interior and Exterior Painting.

At the top is what is called a " duster," and it is used in practically all painting processes to clean the surface. Next is the round or " tool " type brush made in many sizes, but for all practical purposes the No. 4 (small) and No. 12 (large) will be sufficient. Then there is the flat type of brush, of which the 1-inch and 4-inch serve most purposes. The strainer should be about 7 inches across or have a 40 mesh. Next to the strainer is the scraper, which is used for repairing the surface, while lastly is the glazier's putty knife, which will only be needed when dealing with exterior window frames. With a set of tools such as those shown above practically any painting job could be tackled with confidence.

Fig. 2.—Straining the Paint before using serves two Purposes.

It removes all lumps and makes the paint easier to use, and it also ensures complete amalgamation of the various ingredients.

Knotting.

The first thing to be done is to treat the knots so as to prevent the resinous sap they contain from exuding out and lifting off or badly staining the paint to be, later, applied over them.

A small quantity of knotting varnish, which is a mixture of shellac and methylated spirit, is obtained, and a coat, or better still two thin coats, of this is applied, by means of a small brush, so as to cover each knot and extend slightly beyond it. When this knotting is dry, which will be in a very short time, priming may proceed.

Now, whatever opinions there may be as to the relative virtues of various types of paint, there can be little doubt that for this kind of work a lead paint is best.

Red and white lead paints possess those qualities necessary for greenhouse painting in a greater degree than any other class of paint pigment, and therefore they should always be used if durability is the chief requirement.

Priming.

While a white lead priming is good, a mixture of white and red lead is even better, and is here recommended. Cheap priming paints, often stained pink to imitate the colour produced by red lead, but of very small protective value, because they contain little or no lead, should always be avoided.

A good formula for a first-class priming for this purpose would be :—

(A) Genuine white lead paste . . . 56 lbs.
Genuine red lead paste . . . 7 ,,
Genuine raw linseed oil . . . 8 ,,
Genuine turpentine . . . 3 ,,
Patent paste driers 2 ,,

If the liquid form of driers were used instead of the paste, ½ lb. would be a sufficient quantity.

Amount Required.

The amount of paint needed to cover a given surface will vary according to the absorption

Fig. 3.—All Loose Putty must be scraped off the Frame before Painting if the Greenhouse is to be Watertight.
This can be done either with the scraper as shown or with the glazier's putty knife.

of the wood, and it is also not easy to calculate the superficial area of such work as frame bars. But the total quantity of paint in the above-mentioned mixture is 76 lbs. by weight, or about 2¾ gallons by measure, and on a plain solid surface this quantity would cover, approximately, 2,500 square feet.

It may be mentioned here that the turpentine part of the paint has no protective value. It is included to make the paint easier to apply, and to assist it to penetrate into the pores of the wood. When these functions have been performed, it simply evaporates away.

Application of Priming.

In putting on the priming coat, the brush should be vigorously plied so as to help the paint to penetrate. And every care must be taken to see that paint is forced into all nail holes, joints and other crevices in the timber. Any parts that will be inaccessible after erection should have one or two extra coats of the priming.

When these operations are completed and the priming coat is thoroughly dry and hard, the various sections of woodwork can be assembled on the site and the erection of the building completed.

Glazing Putty.

Glazing does not come within the strict purview of this article, but one hint relative to it may be given.

Glass is always bedded in, and often bevel pointed, with putty. The best commercial putty is merely a mechanical mixture of whiting and linseed oil, but its adhesive and hardening qualities can be greatly improved by the addition of a proportion of stiff white lead paste. This will probably make the putty too thin and sticky for convenient use, but it can be stiffened again by a further addition of dry whiting.

All nail holes, cracks, open joints, and indeed every irregularity in the woodwork, should next be "stopped" (which means filled up) with putty of the composition just described, after which one day, at least, should elapse before proceeding further.

The greenhouse is now primed, erected, glazed and stopped, and is ready for the second coat of paint.

Second Coating.

This time a "straight" white lead paint is required for both the inside and the outside woodwork. A suitable formula would be:—

(B) Genuine white lead paste 56 lbs.
    Genuine raw linseed oil . 5 ,,
    Genuine turpentine . 5 ,,
    Patent paste driers . 2 ,,

If liquid driers were used, ½ lb. would be sufficient. The above mixture totals 68 lbs. in weight, or about 2½ gallons by measure, and will cover about 2,500 square feet, one coat.

When the second coat has been applied, the work should be allowed to stand for at least two days for hardening.

Finishing Coats.

In the writer's opinion, four coats of paint is the minimum for the complete protection of a new greenhouse, and the third coat should be of the same composition as that of the second.

The fourth and final coat might be made up as follows:—

(C) Genuine white lead paste 56 lbs.
    Genuine raw linseed oil . 7 ,,
    Genuine turpentine . 1½ ,,
    Patent paste driers . 2½ ,,

If liquid driers were used, ¾ lb. would be ample.

This batch of paint would weigh a total of 67 lbs., would also measure about 2½ gallons, and would cover about 2,800 square feet, one coat.

It will be noted that in this finishing paint the linseed oil content is larger and the turpentine content is smaller than those of the earlier coats. The reason for this is that it is desirable that the paint should dry with a gloss. This gloss improves the appearance of the final coat and makes it more impervious to the weather. These qualities would be further increased if, say, 1 lb. of a good copal varnish were substituted for a similar weight of the oil.

Mixing the Paint.

The correct method of mixing the various ingredients is as follows:—

Place the white lead paste in some kind of vessel which would hold three times as much. Gradually add small quantities of the linseed oil, constantly stirring until a uniform soft paste is obtained.

Next add the driers, and thoroughly incorporate it by stirring. Then add the rest of the oil and mix. Finally, add the turpentine and mix.

The success of proper mixing entirely depends upon vigorous stirring or

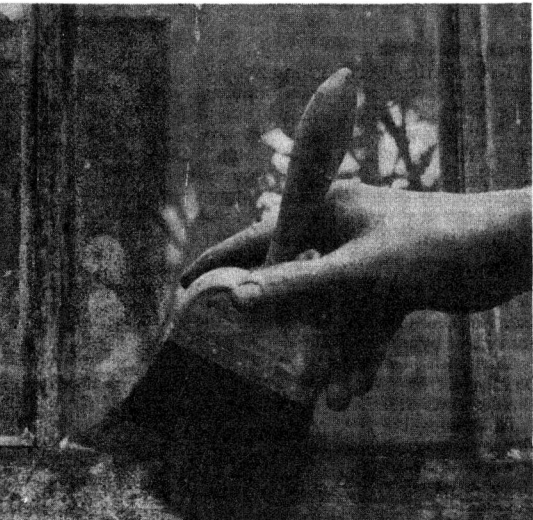

Fig. 4.—All Dirt and Decayed Paint should be completely removed with the Duster to ensure proper Adhesion by the New Paint.

Fig. 5.—Whenever Old Putty has been removed, a Preliminary Coat of Paint should be applied to the Surface of the Wood before placing New Putty in position.

Fig. 6.—New Putty must be applied to all Bevels from which the Old Putty has been removed. Smooth off with Glazier's Knife.

breaking up of the pigment and the very gradual addition of the oil in small quantities at a time. The result should be a smooth paint of the consistency of very thick cream, containing no appreciable lumps and with the whole of the various component materials thoroughly amalgamated.

Straining.

But whether the mixture is apparently quite smooth or not, it will almost certainly contain some small variations in consistency. It may even contain small particles of paint skin or foreign matter. Therefore, it should be strained, before use, through a fairly fine-meshed strainer (see Fig. 1), costing about 1s. 6d., or through fine cloth.

The straining is done, a small quantity at a time, into another vessel. The paint is then ready for use.

Brushes and Tools.

The painting brushes required for greenhouse work are two in number; a large " tool," No. 12, and a small " tool," No. 4 ; or, alternatively, two of the flat type, one 1 inch wide and the other 2 inches wide. And a putty knife and " duster " brush will be useful at every stage.

The paint should be laid on smoothly and evenly, avoiding thick or " fatty " edges of paint. And, before each section of the work is painted, the surface should be cleared from dust by means of the " duster."

The paint in the can in use should be stirred from time to time to keep the contents of uniform consistency.

In coating the bars next to glass, the edges of the paint should be kept straight and should only just cover the edge of the putty and $\frac{1}{16}$ inch of the glass.

Repainting an Old Greenhouse.

If all the old paint work on the woodwork of a greenhouse is intact, repainting will be simply a matter of well washing down the surface, allowing it to become thoroughly dry, and then giving it two coats of white lead paint made according to formulas (B) and (C).

But if, as is far more likely, some parts of the old paint have disintegrated, more thorough preparation will be required. All paint that is flaking or cracking must be thoroughly scraped or burnt off down to the bare wood.

If any moisture has percolated into any part of the woodwork, that moisture must be allowed or encouraged to dry out. To apply new paint over dampness is a quite useless proceeding.

All places which are bare, or are made so by the scraping and cleaning,

Fig. 7.—When painting the Bars, use a 1-inch Flat Brush or a No. 4 Tool.

will require a preliminary priming coat, and this should be made up according to formula (A). And all holes, cracks and open joints should also be soaked well with priming, and this allowed to dry before a very thorough stopping with putty is undertaken.

Killing Stains.

The interior surfaces of such buildings, owing to the influence of moisture and the emanations from plants, often develop most unsightly stains, which are actually produced by a very minute fungoid growth.

The best way to kill these stains and to prevent their recurrence on the new paint is to treat them with a solution of corrosive sublimate. Great care is called for in the use of this substance. It can be purchased in the form of small tablets, two of which should be dissolved in half a teacupful of hot water. By means of a piece of stick with a pad of cloth or sponge on its end, the affected parts should be touched with the solution. When dry, the parts so treated should be given a coat of the knotting varnish previously mentioned.

Another preventative of this trouble is to add a few drops of carbolic acid to the first coat of paint.

And a third alternative treatment is to wash down the whole of the interior woodwork before painting with coal-tar naphtha.

General Observations.

No painting should be done during damp or foggy weather. What is to be sought for is a condition of absolute dryness in the work under treatment.

A Final Caution.

A large part of the secret of successful painting consists in not putting one coat of paint on the top of another that is not thoroughly dry and hard. Forty-eight hours is not too long an interval between each coat.

TIME, LABOUR AND MONEY SAVING IDEAS

A STAND FOR A CHRISTMAS TREE

A very firm stand for a Christmas tree can be made on the lines shown in the sketch. For a good-sized tree two stout pieces of wood about 2½ feet long and 4 or 5 inches wide are required. In the centre of these cut away half the

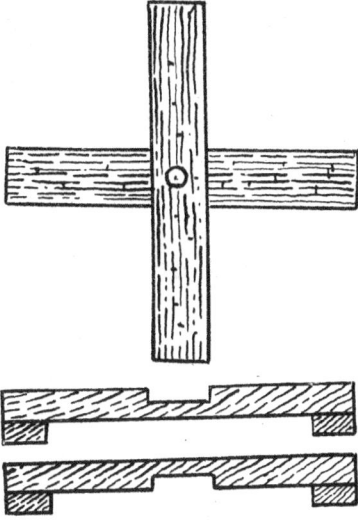

wood to a distance of about 4 inches. The cuts should be made so that the strips can be set one into the other in the form of a cross as indicated. Blocks of wood to form feet are then nailed to the ends of the strips. Also fix securely where the strips cross and make a hole here to receive the stump of the Christmas tree. If the fit is not very tight a few nails may be driven through the stump into the stand.

A USEFUL STRING HOLDER

A useful string holder can be made from a tin funnel. Make holes in the top through which strong twine or, better still, wire can be threaded so that the funnel may be suspended. The ball of string is put into the funnel and the free end is carried out at the bottom. By sharpening the tin a little at the narrow end of the funnel with a file a cutting edge may be secured.

MAKING YOUR OWN FIRE-LIGHTERS

If you live near pinewoods it is worth while collecting the pine cones and using them for fire-lighters. Take 1 lb. of resin and 2 ozs. tallow and melt them together. When hot, put in sawdust to thicken. Then spread the mixture on boards which have previously been well sprinkled with saw-dust to prevent the mixture sticking. Then spread the pine cones in a layer on top. When cold, the compound can be broken into small pieces ready for use. The resulting fuel is very inflammable and is best kept in an outhouse.

TO RENOVATE BLACK ENAMEL

A black-enamelled bedstead or fire-grate has a way of easily looking shabby, but it can be renovated remarkably by rubbing well over with a cloth dipped lightly in paraffin. Polish with a dry rag, rubbing thoroughly, or an odour may be left by the oil for some time afterward.

WHEN PACKING BOTTLES

Corks and stoppers of bottles are very apt to work loose when these have

to be packed. A very good way of preventing this is on the following lines. Cut the finger of an old leather glove and pull it down over the cork. Then tie securely as shown in the photograph. The stopper cannot then work loose, and, if there are no holes in the glove finger, a little leakage will not do any harm to other things in the packing-case.

A USE FOR CHALK

It is not generally known that if large balls of chalk are placed on a fire which has burnt up, the chalk will become as red and glowing as coal. It will give out a very good heat and last a considerable time, thereby saving a quantity of coal.

HOW TO PREVENT A WOOD SCREW FROM WORKING LOOSE

It is often found that when a wood screw is used for holding parts that are subject to vibration it tends to become loose after it has been in use some time and cause rattle and slackness. This is specially so in the case of motor-car bodywork, machinery, domestic plant and so on.

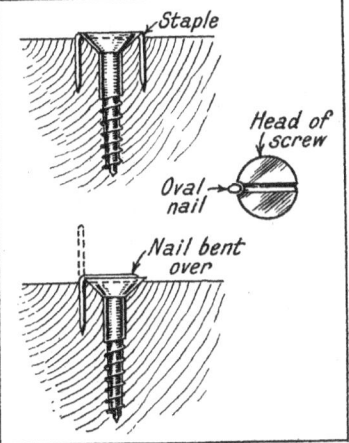

To obviate the necessity of continually having to go round with a screwdriver tightening up screws, steps should be taken to hold the screw in position.

One method is to obtain a staple of the same width as the nail and drive it into the wood over the screw so that the top of the staple fits into the slot of the screw.

Another method is to bend over a brad or oval nail so that the bent-over portion lies in the slot of the screw. A third method is to make a niche with a file on one side of the screw-head and then hammer in an oval nail.

Any one of these methods should prove quite satisfactory for preventing a screw from working loose.

A HANDY TIE HOLDER

What to do with ties so that they do not get creased, as they are liable to do when left in a drawer, is a problem that worries many people. A simple and effective holder can, however, quickly be fitted to the inside of a wardrobe or clothes cupboard door by stretching a piece of tape about 2 feet long across the door and nailing it at each end. The ties are then hung over the tape and are kept quite free from creases.

Another method is to screw in two small hooks about a foot or so apart and stretch an india-rubber band between them. The ties are then hung over the front of the band and are kept in position by the back of the band.

Easy Methods of Wiring a [Dolls' House]

Fig. 1.—An "Amersham" Doll[s']

ELECTRICITY adds greatly to the charm of the modern dolls' house. It can be used to provide illumination, ring a bell, and to represent cosy fires in open grates as well as miniature electric heaters.

Power Supply.

Electricity supplied to the dolls' house must be so arranged that it will be safe for use by children—free from risk of shocks or other preventable accidents.

Practical sources of power are primary batteries, dry cells, accumulators and low-voltage supplies obtained through a transformer from A.C. mains.

Primary batteries are objectionable because of the free acid and renewal trouble; dry batteries do not enjoy a long life and are expensive. Accumulators afford a longer life and can be re-charged, but there is a definite risk of damage should the acid be spilled, unless the jelly acid type is used.

Undoubtedly the best source of power when an A.C. electricity supply is available, is to use a small transformer such as the "Ferranti" Bell-ringer Transformer. These cost less than an accumulator, are perfectly safe, and work directly off the house supply. The relative bulk of a pocket flash-lamp battery to illuminate one lamp only, an "Exide" accumulator that will light a dozen or more bulbs, and a "Bellringer" transformer that will perform a like duty, are shown in Fig. 4, and emphasise the compactness of the transformer.

Mains Transformer.

Those who are not familiar with A.C. electric practice may care to know that a transformer is a device that changes the high voltage of the supply mains to a low voltage; moreover, when properly designed and made, it is so arranged that no matter what happens,

not more than a certain amount of electricity can get past the transformer. In the case of the "Bellringer," the output is limited to what is known as 3 volt-amperes. This is sufficient to light eight or ten miniature lamps, but is not enough to cause any damage or shock. The "Ferranti" "Bellringer" transformer is therefore an ideal source of power, it complies with the regulations of the I.E.E., and is suitable for use on any A.C. mains of 200 to 250 volts, 40 to 60 cycles.

This matter has been dealt with at length so that anyone fitting up an all-electric dolls' house can be assured that danger is negligible if a reputable make of transformer is used—it is merely necessary to connect it with ordinary twin lighting flex to any convenient lamp-holder or plug point, and switch on whenever the dolls' house lighting is wanted.

Independent switches are used in the dolls' house as required, and are manipulated in the ordinary way; in no case can the voltage on the dolls' house wiring exceed 8 volts.

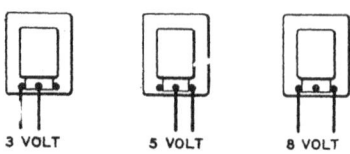

Fig. 5.—Transformer Output Connections.
Choice of output voltage is provided by varying the connections to lower three tappings.

Fitting and Connecting the Transformer.

The transformer can be fixed in any convenient place in or about the dolls' house; generally the space beneath will be found the most convenient, as the transformer can then be screwed directly to the underside of the baseboard—as in Fig. 7—showing how a British-made "Amersham" dolls' house was electrified.

Having screwed the transformer in place, unscrew the two nuts that hold the metal cover, and remove it, thus revealing a porcelain insulating block with two contact screws in it. Bare the ends of the flexible mains wire, twist the strands together, double them over, insert one wire into one contact, and fasten it with the screw. Insert the other wire in the second contact, and fasten it by tightening the screw.

See that the insulation and braiding on the flex goes into the holes in the porcelain block — then bind together the two wires with a few turns of cotton. Make sure that the wires are securely gripped by the screws. The other end of the flex is connected to a plug in the usual way.

Replace the cover and tighten up the fixing nuts; there is no further need to remove the cover. A second porcelain block will be seen opposite the first, but it has three contacts — all accessible without removing the cover.

These are the output terminals, and when looking at the transformer and the mains wires, are at the top, as shown in the diagram, Fig. 5; the output voltages can be varied by making connections to the terminals in various ways. The voltages from left to right are 3-5-8 volts consequently; if 2½-volt lamps are used connect to the left-hand pair of terminals and leave the right-hand terminal blank.

When 4-volt lamps are used, connect to the right-hand terminals, and leave the left-hand terminal blank, but for 6 to 8-volt lamps —connect to the outer terminals, and leave the

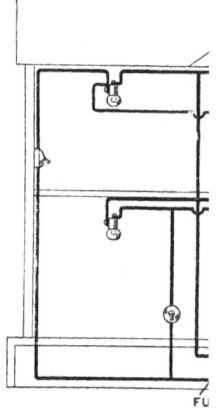

Fig. 2.—Circuit F[or]

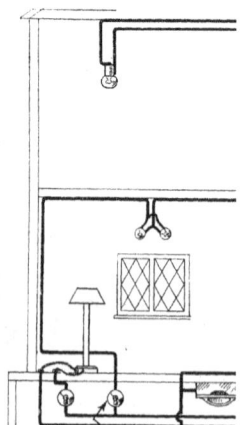

Fig. 3.—Circuit for

Fig. 4.—Comparative Sources of Power.
Showing from left to right a pocket flash lamp battery, a transformer and an accumulator.

S' HOUSE FOR ELECTRIC LIGHT

ONVERTED FOR ELECTRIC LIGHT.

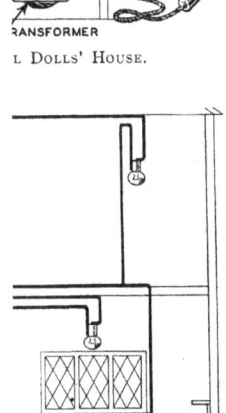

L DOLLS' HOUSE.

OMED DOLLS' HOUSE.

centre terminal blank.

A small nickel-plated terminal nut will be noted to the right of the porcelain block; this is not an output terminal, but is merely an "earth" terminal, and can be connected directly by an insulated wire to the earth or to the metal casing or "conduit" of the electric light supply. It must not be connected to any live wires. If the transformer is inaccessible—for example, in the hollow base—it need not be earthed.

What the Transformer Does.

A peculiarity of a transformer is that although it is connected to the mains supply and current to it is switched on, nothing happens until a lamp or some other device is connected to the output terminals. Directly this is done, a certain amount of current flows automatically, and as more lamps are introduced so the flow of electricity increases up to the maximum capability of the transformer, but if too many lamps are connected, the voltage cannot increase, and the lamps burn dimly —which is a practical indication that the maximum output has been reached, and no more lamps should be switched on.

As the output is "raw" A.C., it is useless attempting to measure the voltage with an ordinary voltmeter, such as could be used with a battery. There is no need to try; the brightness of the lamps is the best practical guide.

Materials Required.

Owing to the great variation in size, style, number of rooms and constructional details of dolls' houses, it is obviously impracticable to give exact quantities of material needed, but the following tables give details of requirements for three average dolls' houses, while the remainder of this article is devoted to various practical ways of wiring up the house and making a number of accessories.

Small Dolls' House, Two Floors.

Transformer.—1 "Bellringer." "Ferranti Ltd."

Mains Plug.—1 bayonet or prong-type to suit house supply.

Lighting Flex.—4 yards twin lighting flex. "Lewcos."

Fuse and Holder.—1 S.P. "Safety" type, with ½ ampere fuse. "Belling-Lee."

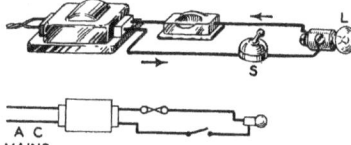

Fig. 6.—ELEMENTARY CIRCUIT.

The transformer output is taken on the flow side to a switch, S, thence to the lamp, L, and back by the "return" wire to a second terminal on the transformer. The lower diagram shows the conventional way of indicating the same circuit.

Internal Connections.—1 oz. No. 22 gauge D.S.C. wire. "Lewcos."

Lamps.—4 "M.E.S." 2½-volt (or 4-volt) bulbs. "Competa."

Lamp Holders.—4 "M.E.S." batten type. "Grafton Electric."

Switches.—2 miniature tumbler. "Grafton Electric."

The above will provide four lights, controlled by two switches.

Medium Dolls' House, Four Rooms.

Transformer, mains plug, flex and fuse as above.

Internal Connections.—2 coils red, 2 coils black, No. 20 gauge "Glazite" wiring. Miniature twin lighting flex, 2 yards. "Lewcos."

Lamp and Holders.—6 as above, 2 "Pea" lamps.

Switches.—2 miniature tumbler. "Grafton Electric." 4 "Q.M.B." S.P. "Bulgin."

Sundries.—1 piece ebonite tube, ⅜-inch diameter, 3 inches long. "Becol." 1 sheet 4-ply "Ivory" card; 1 2-foot length "Glazite" insulating sleeving.

The above provides six lights, controlled by four switches, also a miniature standard lamp and an electric fire controlled by separate switches.

Large Dolls' House, Twelve or more Lights.

Transformer.—2 "Bellringer." "Ferranti, Ltd."

Mains plug and flex as above.

Fuse Holder.—2 S.P. "Safety" type, with 1 ampere fuses. "Belling-Lee."

Internal Connections.—1 oz. No. 20 D.S.C. wire; 6 coils "Glazite"; 3 yards miniature lighting flex. "Lewcos." 1 sheet "Konductite" metallised paper. "C.A.C. Ltd."

Lamps.—10 "M.E.S."; 6 "Pea" lamps.

Lamp Holders.—8 "M.E.S." batten type. "Grafton Electric." 2 "M.E.S." pendant type. "Grafton Electric."

Switches.—6 "Q.M.B." S.P. "Bulgin." 3 miniature tumbler. "Grafton Electric." 4 small terminal bolts and nuts. "Grafton Electric."

Sundries.—As above.

The above provides for eleven lights controlled from five switches, four electric fires controlled by four switches, and one electric standard lamp.

Making the Connections.

First fix the transformer and fit up the mains flexible as already described, then screw the fuse-holder to the baseboard, near to the transformer—it shows clearly in Fig. 7—and connect one terminal of the fuse-holder to one of the output terminals on the trans-

Fig. 7.—THE WIRING BENEATH THE "AMERSHAM" DOLLS' HOUSE. Showing the transformer with flexible connection and socket for attachment to mains.

EASY METHODS OF WIRING A DOLLS' HOUSE FOR ELECTRIC LIGHT

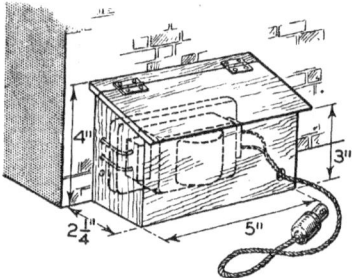

Fig. 8.—DISGUISING THE TRANSFORMER.
When the transformer cannot be put under the baseboard, it can be placed outside the building in a miniature coal shed.

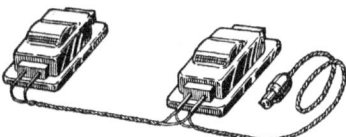

Fig. 9.—INPUT CONNECTIONS TO TWO TRANSFORMERS.
The flexible wires from the mains are taken first to one transformer and then on to the second.

former, according to the required voltage, as already explained. This completes the "mains" supply; all the rest of the connections come on the low-voltage or "output" side.

When two transformers are used, they can be placed as shown in Fig. 9, and connected to the mains by bringing the flex to one transformer, as already described, and connecting the second transformer by a short length of

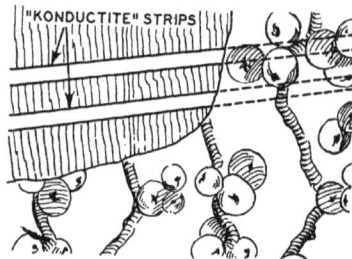

Fig. 13.—METALLISED PAPER CONNECTIONS.
A special paper called "Konductite" cut into strips and pasted on the wall and subsequently covered with wallpaper makes an invisible "wiring."

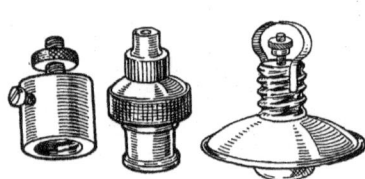

Fig. 15.—THREE TYPES OF FITTING.
Pendant M.E.S. fitting; holder with reflector and loop; holder with cord grip.

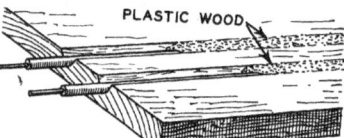

Fig. 10.—WIRES LAID IN GROOVES.

Fig. 11.—CUTTING GROOVES WITH A CUTTING GAUGE.

similar flex. The output from each transformer must be kept separate: one could supply the top floor lights, the other the ground floor lights; generally one transformer is sufficient.

Housing the Transformer.

If the transformer cannot be placed under the base, a good plan is to make a small model conservatory or a coal shed—as in Fig. 8—and use it as a

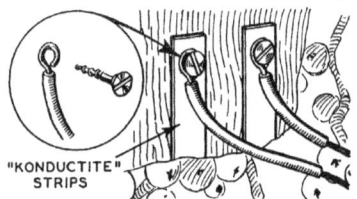

Fig. 14.—CONNECTIONS TO "KONDUCTITE."
Connections are best made with small brass screws which firmly clamp the bared end of the wire to the metallised surface.

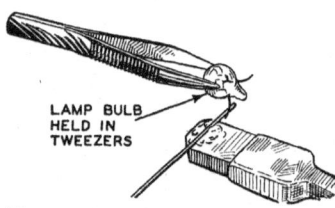

Fig. 16.—MAKING SOLDERED CONNECTION.
Hold the connecting wire on the soldering iron and allow the solder to run; do not touch the lamp bulb with the soldering iron. The lamp can be held in tweezers.

cover to hide the transformer; all connections are the same as before mentioned.

The internal connections or "wiring" must follow a definite plan. The main point to grasp is that the current must flow from one terminal on the transformer to a switch, thence to a lamp, as in Fig. 6, back by a "return" wire to the fuse, and so on to the transformer.

No part of the "flow" side must be connected directly to the "return" side of the circuit, otherwise there would be a short circuit, and the fuse would blow.

The resistance of the lamp is so arranged that when connected on one side to the "flow" wire and on the other side to the "return" wire, it takes just enough current to cause it to light up. Switches should be in the "flow" wire only, but any number of lamps can be connected to one common return wire; there is no need for a separate "return" wire from each lamp.

The wiring on all circuit diagrams is represented by straight lines, and is separated as much as possible to make the drawing clear. When studying such a diagram, begin with the "flow" wire from the transformer and follow the connections from point to point, back to the transformer *via* the "return" wire;

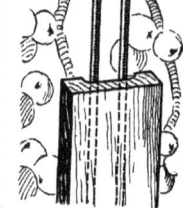

Fig. 12.—MINIATURE CAPPING.
Narrow "stripwood" grooved on the underside is glued over the wires, and thus encases them.

but when actually wiring up the dolls' house, take the wires in the shortest and most convenient method from point to point. The "flow" wire should, preferably, be a distinctive colour, say, red—the return wire, say, black; this reduces confusion while fixing the wires.

Fixing the Wires.

There are various ways of fixing the wires. On an existing dolls' house, the best plan, as a general rule, is to take the wires under the base, then up the walls, over the first floor and down through it for pendant lights. The top floor lights can be supplied from wires over the ceiling, access to the roof being obtained by carefully removing one of the roof sections.

The best way to dispose of the wires is to cut shallow grooves in the woodwork—as in Fig. 10—lay the wires in them, and cover them with plastic wood.

The grooves can be cut with a chisel when the wall surfaces are sufficiently accessible. Another plan, shown in

EASY METHODS OF WIRING A DOLLS' HOUSE FOR ELECTRIC LIGHT

Fig. 11, is to use a "cutting gauge" to incise the grooves.

Another method is to use miniature "capping," as in Fig. 12, the capping consisting of a strip of wood about $\frac{3}{8}$-inch wide and $\frac{1}{8}$-inch thick, with a groove cut along the inside; it is laid over the wire and fixed with seccotine.

When building a new dolls' house, or re-conditioning an old one, it is desirable to use double walls or sections of walls, and do all the wiring with twin flexible wires brought down between the walls or floors, as the case may be. The lining walls can then be modelled as desired, and the lamps fitted—as shown in Fig. 17—before the walls are finally fixed.

Metallised Paper.

A special kind of metallised paper, known as "Konductite," and obtainable through radio dealers, is excellent for surface wiring a dolls' house. The paper is cut into strips about $\frac{1}{4}$ inch wide and pasted directly to the walls, as sketched in Fig. 13, the "flow" and "return" strips being separated by at least $\frac{1}{4}$ inch of space. The metallised face is set outwards and connections are made from it to lamps, switches, or the like, by short lengths of wire—as in Fig. 14—fastened with small screws. When all connections are completed and the lights have been tested, the entire wall surface is papered, whereupon the "Konductite" strips become invisible.

Switch Connections.

All switches are connected in the same way; one "flow" wire is connected to one terminal of the switch; another wire is connected to the second terminal and thence taken to the lamp,

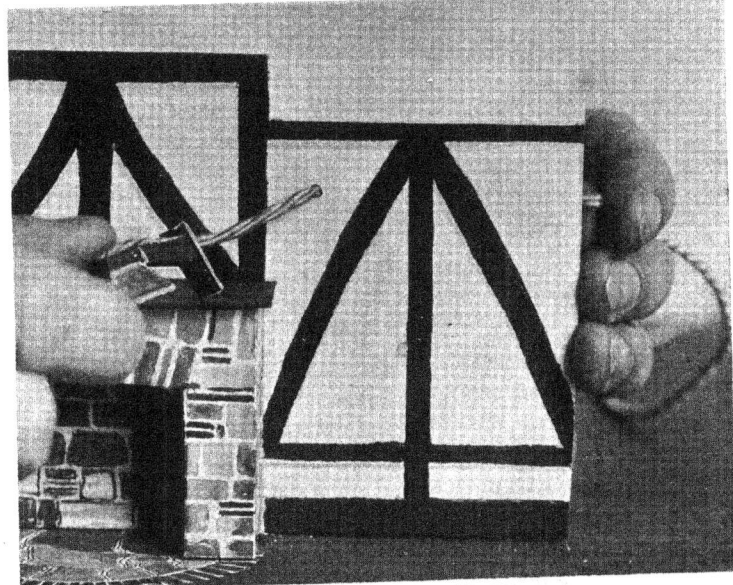

Fig. 17.—BEHIND THE WALL WIRING.
When the walls are double, or facing walls are used, the wiring can be done behind the walls with flexible wires and brought to the front at the light points.

where it should be considered as the "flow" wire.

Tumbler switches — Fig. 18 — are screwed to the wall; the connections pass through the wall via two separate holes, or the switch can be mounted on a thin wooden back plate. The smallest stock size miniature tumbler switch is rather clumsy looking, a much neater effect is obtained by using the regular "Q.M.B." "snap" switch—as shown in Fig. 19—and fixing it so that only the knob and ring is visible in the room. This is done by drilling a hole through the wall and clamping the switch to it with the nuts provided; the switch body and the connecting wires then come behind the wall, which would look bad, but in practice it is generally possible to provide a cupboard or some other piece of fixed furniture to cover the switch.

Grouping the Switches on the Baseboard.

Alternatively the switches can be arranged in a row on the baseboard or, possibly, within the garage.

Fig. 18.—How a TUMBLER SWITCH IS FITTED.
Showing wires leading through the wood to the switch.

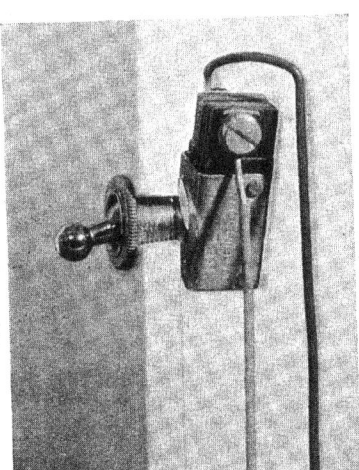

Fig. 19.—How a Q.M.B. SWITCH IS FITTED.
Showing how switch is fixed from back of wall.

Fig. 20.—A HOME-MADE BRACKET WITH PEA LAMP.
Note wires in groove and partly covered with plastic wood.

EASY METHODS OF WIRING A DOLLS' HOUSE FOR ELECTRIC LIGHT

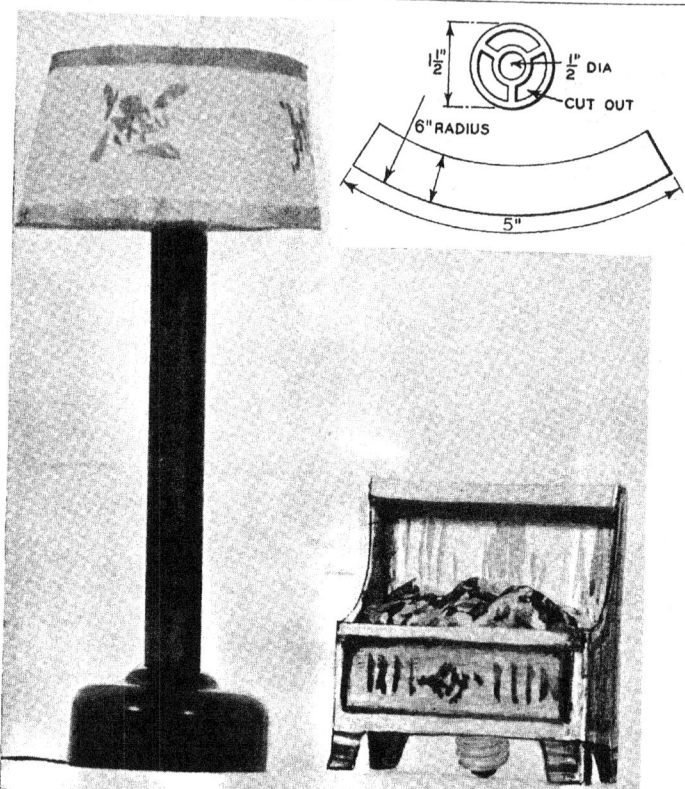

Fig. 21.—THE STANDARD LAMP AND ELECTRIC FIRE.
A full-size photograph showing these two fittings. Inset, shape of parts for lamp shade.

Avoiding Use of Switches.

When ordinary "M.E.S." or "flash-lamp" bulbs are used, switches can be omitted if desired, because by giving the lamp bulb a quarter turn it can be "switched" on or off at will.

Switches should be used or not according to personal inclination—or perhaps a combination of baseboard and wall switches with a few "lamp bulb" switches will prove the best.

Choice and Use of Bulbs.

Bulbs suitable for dolls' houses, together with a standard holder, are the "M.E.S." (miniature Edison Screw), more familiarly called "flash-lamp," bulbs, which will do for general lighting. The smallest type is the "Pea" lamp, measuring about 3/8 inch long and a little over 1/8 inch diameter. Lastly, the glass bulb can be removed from an "M.E.S." cap and used independently.

Connections from "M.E.S." bulbs are made to the centre contact and to the screwed cap; those to the "pea" lamp are made by soldering the thin wires directly to the conducting wires. Bulbs removed from "M.E.S." caps should have short wires soldered to the ends of the wires protruding from the glass.

Soldered Connections.

When soldering the connections to pea or bulb lamps, always "tin" the connecting wires first, then scrape the lamp wires clean, apply a spot of soldering flux, or use "self-fluxing" resin cored solder. Heat the conducting wire by holding it on the soldering iron—as in Fig. 16; do not touch the bulb or the lamp wire with the iron, or damage may be caused. Remove the soldering iron the instant the solder has run, to avoid burning the wire or lamp.

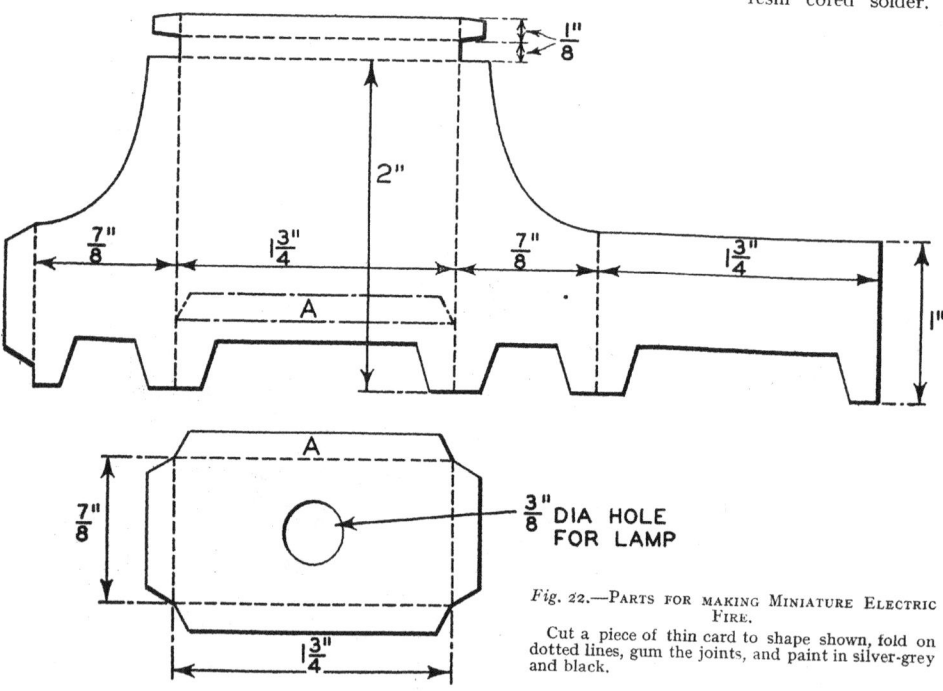

Fig. 22.—PARTS FOR MAKING MINIATURE ELECTRIC FIRE.
Cut a piece of thin card to shape shown, fold on dotted lines, gum the joints, and paint in silver-grey and black.

Miniature Fittings.

Sundry small fittings are on the market, the most useful are batten

EASY METHODS OF WIRING A DOLLS' HOUSE FOR ELECTRIC LIGHT

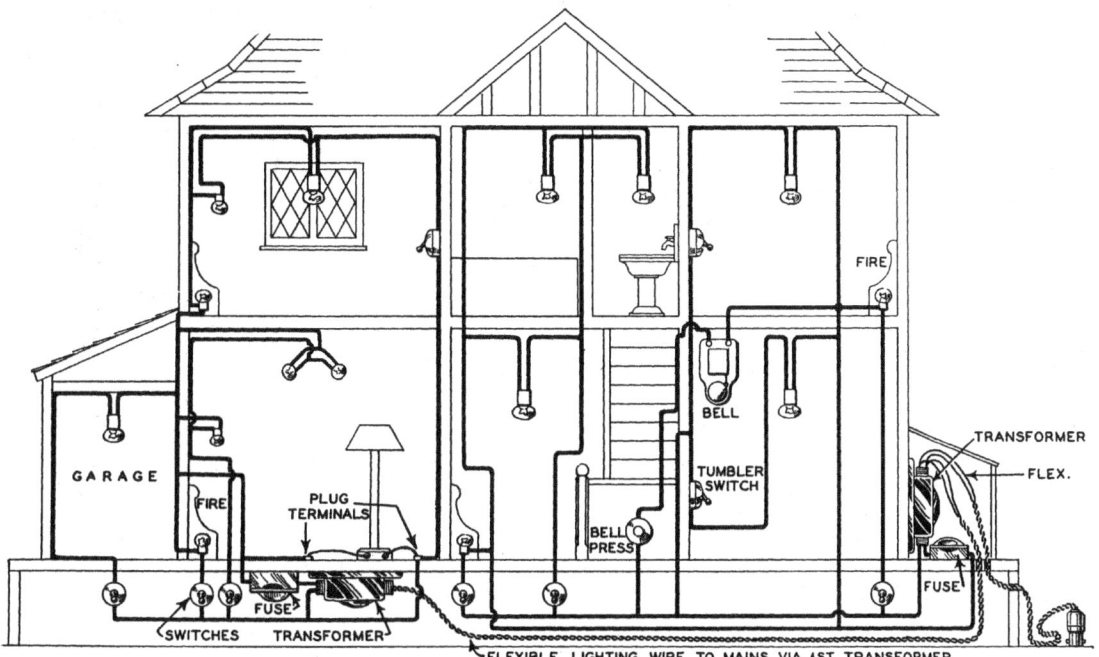

Fig. 23.—CIRCUIT FOR A LARGE DOLLS' HOUSE.
Two transformers are used and an electric bell is included.

holders—the pendant type—Fig. 15; the "reflector with loop," Fig. 15; and the shade carrier holder with cord grip, Fig. 15; which is in effect the same as an ordinary house lighting holder.

Fittings for "pea" lamps are not as a rule available, but have to be made specially; a few of the "buttonhole" miniature electric flowers and electric scarf pins with "pea" lamps can sometimes be used for miniature lighting, and "pea" lamps ready connected to a length of miniature flex are also available; they are admirable for pendant lights in the dolls' bedroom.

How to make Miniature Fittings.

There is no difficulty in making all kinds of miniature lighting fittings—a few are here described and illustrated as a guide to the method.

These were made for "Amersham," the British-made dolls' house, also shown in Figs. 1 and 7, and in Fig. 20, where a bracket light can be seen between the upper windows and a pendant light in the lower room.

The back of the bracket is a piece of leather ½ inch long, 5/16 inch wide, with a 1-inch length of "Glazite" insulating tubing, fastened into a hole with seccotine. A pea lamp supplies the light—the wires to it are separated, covered with plastic wood and passed through the tube; the wood acts as an insulator and holds the lamp in a vertical position. Part of the wiring in grooves in the wall is left visible to show the method; it is covered afterwards with plastic wood. The shade is a circle of coloured paper ¾ inch diameter, cut radially to the centre, twisted up to form a cone and fixed with seccotine.

The pendant is an "M.E.S." bulb with wires soldered directly to the holder, the shade is a disc of paper, slipped over the screwed part of the lamp, and the whole completed with a conical cap of paper.

Standard Lamp.

The standard lamp, Fig. 21, uses a bakelite cap from a miniature tumbler switch for the base—a length of ebonite tube is pushed into the hole

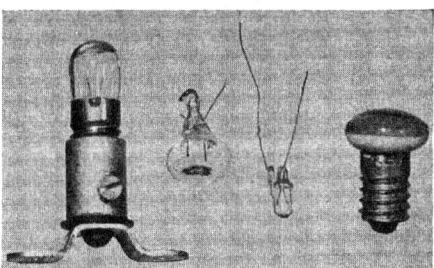

Fig. 24.—FOUR TYPES OF MINIATURE LAMPS.
Showing from left to right a miniature Edison screw bulb in batten holder, bulb removed from cap, pea lamp, and flash-lamp bulb.

therein, and fastened with plastic wood. An "M.E.S." bulb connected as before is embedded in plastic wood on the top of the tube; the wires pass down inside the tube and are taken to a light point. The shade is made of paper, shaped as in Fig. 21, gummed together and hand painted; it rests on top of the bulb.

Imitation Electric Fire.

The electric stove, Fig. 21, is made by cutting and folding a piece of 4-ply ivory card shaped as in Fig. 22, and painted silver-grey and black. A lamp is fitted through the lower part and is connected in circuit in the usual way. The "coals" and "fire" is simply a crumpled piece of tissue paper previously dabbed with small blotches of black, red and yellow paint.

Typical Circuits.

Adoption of any of the foregoing methods will certainly result in satisfaction; the best ways of wiring the three styles of dolls' house already referred to can be seen by reference to Fig. 22, showing connections for a small house with four lights; Fig. 3 a medium size house; and Fig. 23 a really splendid example of an all-electric dolls' house complete with miniature electric door bell.

Do Your Doors Shut Properly?

Doors that will not shut properly are a source of continual annoyance. Fortunately, by expending a certain amount of thought in tracing the cause of the trouble, it is generally quite a simple matter to remedy it.

There are five main reasons why a door is failing to shut properly and the following table is designed to enable you to locate quickly the most likely cause of the trouble.

the hinge plate. If they do not do so they may prevent the door from closing properly. It may be necessary to use a smaller screw, in which case the screw hole will have to be plugged as described below.

An Extreme Case.

It may be found that it is impossible to get a larger screw through the hole in the hinge plate. In such a case it will be necessary to plug the hole.

Symptom.	Probable Cause.
Door drags on floor, probably all the time it is being opened or shut.	Hinge loose or needs recessing due to the frame having swollen.
Door will not shut at top of lock edge.	Hinge loose or needs recessing due to the frame having swollen.
Door catches against frame and obstruction can be felt either at top, centre or bottom.	Tenon projecting
Lock or bolt will not catch and keep door shut, although lock is in order.	Door shrunk.
Door bangs against frame for entire length.	Door swollen.
Door catches at bottom either at hinge end or lock end.	Stile or side member swollen.

Dealing with a Loose Hinge.

Examination of the door when open will reveal that it is hung on two hinges. Either or both of the hinges may be the cause of the trouble, but it is most likely to be the top one, especially if there are children about the house who may have been amusing themselves by hanging on the handle on each side of the door and swinging to and fro.

Look at the screws and see if one has worked loose and is projecting. If so, tighten it up and the door should function properly again.

If, however, the screw refuses to hold and merely turns round and round due to the fact that the screw hole has worn too large, replace it with a larger screw.

Make sure, too, that the screws bed right down in the countersunk holes in

First open the door wide and place a wedge under it, as shown in Fig. 1, so

Fig. 2.—Two Frequent Causes of Doors not Shutting Properly.

as to take the weight of the door. Now take out the remaining screws that hold the hinge in place on the frame and turn back the leaf so that the screw holes are revealed. Measure the size of the screw holes in the wood and cut short lengths of dowel rod to the same size. Trim them up to make a tight fit in the holes and hammer flush with the surface.

Push back the leaf of the hinge, insert the screws, which will now grip tightly. Remove the wedge and the door will be found in order.

Top Hinge needs Recessing.

If the door frame has swollen at the top, the effect will be to throw the door forward so that it continually drags on the floor. To deal with this trouble, the top hinge must be removed from the frame and the recess for the hinge flap cut deeper with a chisel. Thus when the hinge is screwed in

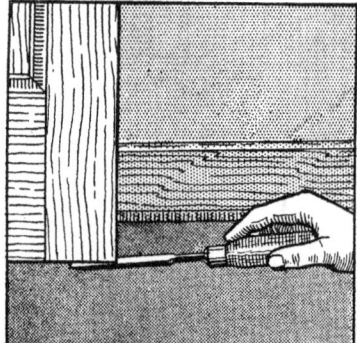

Fig. 1.—When tightening up the Hinges of a Door, the Door should be wedged up by placing a Chisel under the Bottom so as to take the Weight of the Door.

Fig. 3.—Are the Hinges of your Door Loose?

Here we see in an exaggerated manner what happens when the screws holding top hinge of a door become loose. The whole door is thrown forward, with the result that it continually drags on the floor.

position again, the door will be lifted up off the ground. Another method of remedying a door where the frame has become swollen is to fit rising butt hinges, as described on p. 125.

Tenon Projecting.

If on shutting the door an obstruction can be felt, probably specially noticeable either at the top, centre or bottom of the door, it is unlikely that a hinge is at fault. It is more likely that one of the tenons is projecting. Examination of the door will reveal that each horizontal piece of the wooden frame is slotted into the upright pieces by a mortise and tenon joint. The tenons can be seen by looking at either the lock or hinge edge of the door, and it sometimes happens that one of these tenons projects due to the wood having swollen or the stiles shrinking.

It will be necessary to remove the projecting part with a sharp chisel.

Door Shrunk.

In the case of a door that has shrunk, not only will the lock fail to hold it shut, but the decrease from edge to edge will probably result in the room being very draughty.

The remedy is first to wedge up the

DO YOUR DOORS SHUT PROPERLY?

Fig. 4.—THE FIRST STEP IN DEALING WITH A DOOR THAT HAS SWOLLEN.

The amount that has to be trimmed off has been marked on the outside edge and the door is being removed for planing. Note how the door should be steadied by holding the handle or placing the foot against the hinge edge.

sufficient planed off until the door is a good fit.

When the door is replaced on the hinges the screws will, of course, pass right through the lath and into the door so that there is no actual strain on the nails which have been used to fix the lath in position.

Swollen Door.

In the case of a swollen door it will be found that the door has a tendency not to shut along the whole of the length of the lock edge, and the only thing to do is to plane off sufficient wood from the hinge edge until the door will close.

To determine how much to plane off will require the help of an assistant. Get someone to close the door as much as possible by pushing on the inside while you make a pencil mark on the outside where the door is swollen.

The door must then be taken off its hinges and the surplus wood planed away. Although, of course, the excess

door as described above, and then unscrew the hinge leaves from the edge of the door, so that when the door is lifted away the hinges are left intact on the upright.

Now obtain a thin lath the same length and width as the edge of the door, and nail this to the hinged edge after turning the door on its locking edge. The object of the lath is to add sufficient width to the door to make it a good fit. If it is found that the lath makes the door too wide so that it hits the frame, the nails must be punched below the surface of the lath and

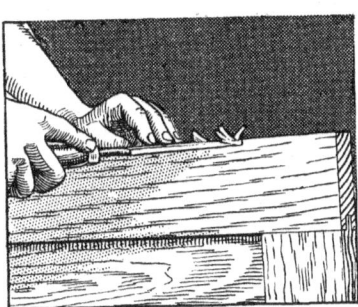

Fig. 6.—THE FINAL STAGES IN DEALING WITH A DOOR THAT HAS SWOLLEN.

Sinking the hinge recess by the same amount as planed off, prior to refixing hinges and placing door in position again.

Fig. 5.—THE NEXT STEP IN DEALING WITH A DOOR THAT HAS SWOLLEN.

The hinges have been removed and the hinge edge of the door is planed for a corresponding amount to that previously marked on the locking edge.

of width can only be marked on the locking edge of the door, the wood is actually planed away from the hinge edge. After planing do not forget to sink the butt where the hinge fits deeper by the same amount as has been planed off. This can be done with a chisel.

Stile Swollen.

If the stile only is swollen, it will be made evident by the fact that the door can be felt sticking either at the hinge end or the lock end and not along the whole length of the door. The remedy is to remove the door and plane the end of the stile level with the rail.

SIMPLE METHOD OF PATCHING A HOLE IN A TANK

It sometimes happens that it is necessary to patch or cover up a hole in a closed water tank, the inside of which cannot be reached, so that the repair has to be carried out from the outside.

This is not so difficult as it sounds. First file the hole which is to be patched until it is oval in shape. Then take an ordinary hexagon or carriage bolt of a suitable size and file the head oval until it is of the same shape, but slightly smaller than the hole in the tank. Now make a file mark at the screw end of the bolt, parallel with long side of the head so that the posi-

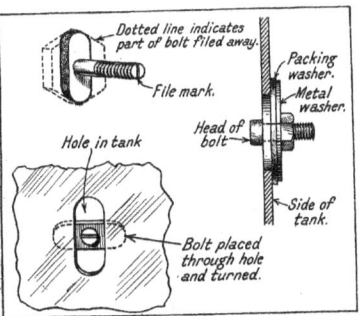

DETAILS FOR PATCHING A HOLE IN A TANK.

tion of the bolt when it is placed inside the tank can be easily located.

The next thing is to place the head of the bolt through the hole and give it a half turn so that the file mark is now horizontal. Place a suitable packing washer of asbestos cloth, Hallite fibre or leather over the bolt so as to cover the slot completely and overlap some little distance all round. Cover the packing washer with a metal washer of the same diameter, place the nut on the bolt and screw up tightly. Take care that when the nut is absolutely tight, the file mark is still horizontal.

CONVERTING A BATTERY-OPERATED BELL INSTALLATION TO "MAINS" WORKING

THE majority of public electricity supply companies now give a supply of alternating current at a pressure of 200 to 230 volts to their consumers. This type of supply can be converted with a bell transformer to give a low-pressure current suitable for operating a bell installation, and will give a much more satisfactory and efficient service than a supply of current from a battery.

Cost of Installing a Transformer.

The initial cost of the transformer and the materials necessary to install it, to replace a battery, will be about 10s. for an average type of domestic bell installation.

Cost of the Electrical Energy to Operate the Installation.

The power taken by a good bell transformer when ringing a bell is about 5 watts, and almost negligible when the bell circuit is open. With energy costing 3½d. per unit on the

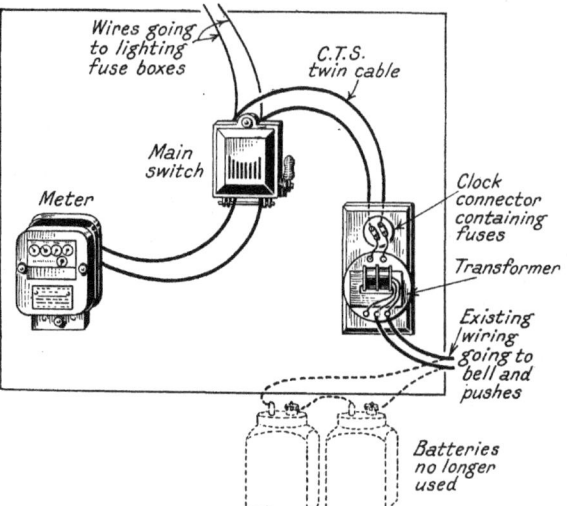

Fig. 1.—Diagram showing Simple Method of converting Battery-operated Bell to Mains Working.

The bell wires that were connected to the batteries are simply joined to the secondary terminals of a bell transformer, which is in turn connected to the main switch via suitable fuses.

flat rate, the cost of operating the installation will be less than 1d. per week.

The Materials Required.

Bell transformer with primary windings suitable for the declared mains pressure.

A Wylex clock fuse connector, or a pair of single-pole 3-ampere fuse bases.

A short length of lighting flexible.

Suitable length of 1/·044-inch twin C.T.S. cable and twin bell wire of good quality.

One 6½ × 3½-inch polished wooden pateras.

Two wooden battens, supply of screws and cable clips.

Mounting the Transformer and Clock Fuse Connector on the Pateras.

Remove the covers from the transformer and the fuse connector. The bases are now placed in position on the pateras, the clock fuse connector uppermost, and the exposed primary terminals of the transformer adjacent to the connector. The positions of the cable holes to be drilled in the pateras for the entry of the supply cables to the connector and the bell circuit cables to the transformer are marked off. A small bradawl will be convenient to do this. The marked positions on the pateras are now drilled, ¼-inch holes for the connector cables and a 3/16-inch hole for the bell wires. Remove all burrs caused by the drilling with a rose bit.

The transformer and connector bases

are now placed in the correct positions on the pateras and screwed to it with countersunk head wood screws, 1 inch × 6s.

A hole is drilled at each of the four corners of the pateras large enough to accommodate a 1½-inch × 7s countersunk head wood screw.

The Transformer Position.

The best position for the transformer will be near the main switch of the installation. The fixing of the pateras here will generally be convenient, and only a short length of C.T.S. cable will be required to connect the transformer to the supply.

Fixing the Pateras Battens.

Two pieces of dry pine, 6½ inches long, ½ inch wide and 1 inch deep, will serve as battens, to which the pateras will be fixed. These are drilled at positions 1 inch from each end; the holes should be large enough to accommodate 2-inch × 8s counter-

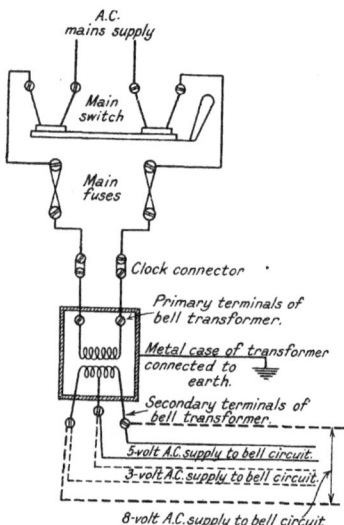

Fig. 2.—Diagrammatic Connections of the Circuit for converting the A.C. Mains Supply to the Low Voltage A.C. Supply for the Bells.

The old batteries which work the bell are discarded and the wires which were connected to the batteries are connected to the secondary terminals of the transformer. It is advisable to fix the transformer fairly near the main switch of the installation. If the existing batteries for the bell are situated some distance away from the main switch, it will be necessary to extend the bell wiring to reach to the transformer.

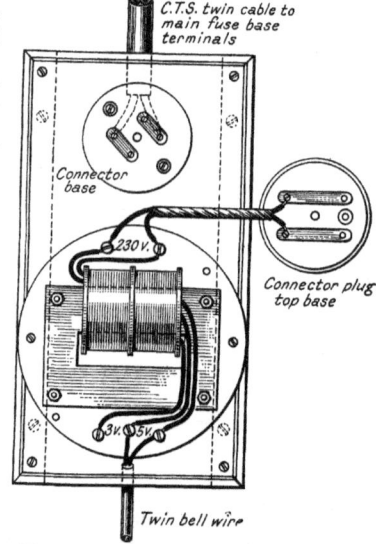

Fig. 3.—The Connections to the Transformer are quite simple.

Here we see the layout of the transformer and clock connector base with their covers removed. These are fitted on to a wooden baseboard called a pateras, which is 6½ × 3½ inches. This pateras is in turn fixed on to battens screwed to the wall near the main switch. The primary terminals marked 230 volts are connected to the terminal bars of the clock connector plug top base with a short length of twin lighting flexible.

CONVERTING A BATTERY-OPERATED BELL INSTALLATION TO "MAINS" WORKING

sunk head wood screws. If a rawlplug outfit is available, then the holes should accommodate the rawlplug screws.

The battens are laid in position on the wall near the main switch, preferably just below it, and the plug positions marked off on the wall. The plug holes are now drilled and fitted with tight-fitting wooden plugs or with rawlplugs. The battens may be now fixed to the wall with 2-inch × 8s screws or with the rawlplug screws.

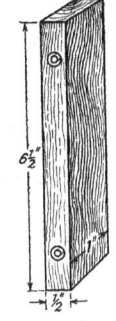

Fig. 4.—DETAILS FOR CONSTRUCTING THE BATTENS ON WHICH THE PATERAS IS FIXED.

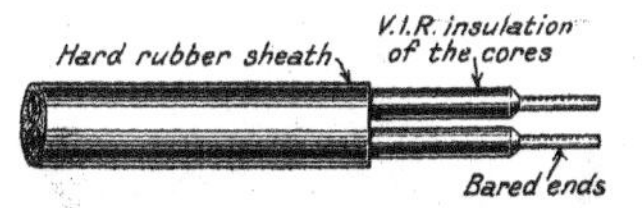

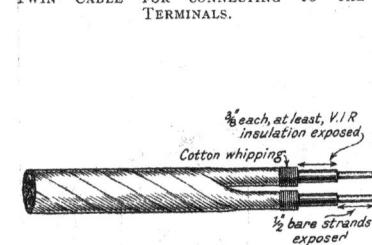

Fig. 5.—PREPARING THE ENDS OF THE C.T.S. TWIN CABLE FOR CONNECTING TO THE TERMINALS.

Fig. 6.—PREPARING THE ENDS OF THE TWIN LIGHTING FLEXIBLE FOR TERMINAL CONNECTIONS.

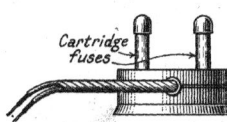

Fig. 7.—THE PLUG TOP WITH SHORT PIECE OF TWIN LIGHTING FLEXIBLE CONNECTED TO IT.

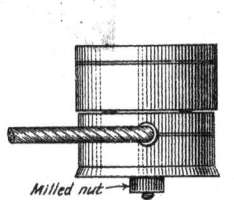

Fig. 8.—THE PLUG TOP IS HELD SECURELY IN THE BASE OF THE CONNECTOR WITH A MILLED NUT.

Connecting the Transformer to the Supply.

Turn off the MAIN SWITCH, remove the main fuse covers, and withdraw the fuse holders. Two inches of the rubber sheathing is carefully removed from one end of the twin C.T.S. cable, and the insulation removed from the ends of each of the wires for ½ inch.

The screws of the fuse base terminals, to which the cables from the distributing board are connected, are slackened, and into each of the terminals one of the bared ends of the C.T.S. is placed. These ends are pushed into the terminals from the back of the fuse base. Make sure that no bare wires protrude from the back of the fuse bases, and that the ends are pushed far enough into the terminals to allow the terminal screws to have a firm hold of them when screwed up. The terminal screws are now tightened up.

Fix the Pateras in Position.

Fix the pateras in position on the wall with the two lower screws, which should not be driven completely in. This is to allow of pushing the other prepared ends of the C.T.S. cable into the clock connector terminals. These ends are prepared in the same manner as the ends which are connected to the fuse base terminals, except that only 1 inch of the rubber sheathing should be removed.

The clock connector base terminal screws are slackened off, and into each of the terminals one of the bared ends of the C.T.S. cable is connected, making sure that the terminal screws when tightened up will grip the bared ends. The C.T.S. cable is previously cut to the correct length so as to avoid undue slack between the fuse bases and the pateras. The pateras is now finally screwed up on the wall with four 2-inch × 8s countersunk head wood screws.

The four ends of a short length of lighting flexible wire are bared and prepared for connecting the clock fuse connector plug top to the primary terminals of the transformer. When making the connections make sure that the strands of copper wire of each bared end are twisted together and that no bare wire will project from any of the terminals of the plug top and the transformer. The plug top is now plugged into the base of the connector and secured with the milled nut, to ensure that a good contact is made between the fuses and the terminal plates.

Connecting the Bell Circuit Wiring to the Secondary Terminals of the Transformer.

The ends of the bell wiring are removed from the battery terminals. The insulation is removed from each of the two ends for a distance of 1 inch and the bared wires thoroughly cleaned. Two ends of the twin bell wire are similarly prepared.

Twisted end-to-end joints are now made between each end of the bell wiring, and each end of the twin bell wire.

These joints are soldered, and when cold, insulated with pure rubber and black tape. Resin or non-acid flux should be used for the soldering process.

The twin bell wire is now run to the bell transformer position; securing it to the fixing surface at frequent intervals with insulated staples. The ends of the twin wire are cut to the correct length at the transformer position, and prepared for connection to the secondary terminals of the transformer.

A trial of the operation of the bell should be made to decide to which pair of terminals the ends will be connected, and the ends finally screwed tightly under the chosen pair of terminal screws.

Earthing the Transformer Cover.

Most of the bell transformers which are now on the market have a bakelite base and cover. Should the base and cover or either, be made of metal, it will have to be earthed.

A piece of bare copper wire should be connected between the case or cover, and the metal case of the installation main switch, which should be already earthed. If this is not the case, fix an earthing clip on the nearest water main and connect the wire to the earthing clip.

A good connection of the earth wire to the case or cover is made by bending the end of the wire round the shank of the base or cover fixing screw, placing a metal washer between the wire and the head of the screw and tightening up the screw.

CLEANING GREASY BOTTLES

IT is often difficult to clean bottles that have been used for keeping oily liquids.

One good method is to pour about half a teacupful of fine dry sawdust or bran into the bottle (assuming it to be a bottle of from 1 to 2 pints in size) and shake well until all the particles cover the whole of the inside of the bottle.

Leave for a few minutes and then pour into the bottle about a gill of cold water and shake well.

This will cause the oil-soaked sawdust to leave the sides of the bottle and float on the water.

This method will remove practically all the oil or grease, but it is best to wash out the bottle afterwards with a hot solution of washing soda in water.

SIMPLE FIRST AID FOR THE HOME

THE handyman, who is continually at work on his hobbies in the garden or workshop, is always prone to accidents in the handling of his tools, etc. These various accidents, although not serious at the time, may easily become a source of danger (particularly in the case of cuts from rusty tools) and a little knowledge of the essential rules of first aid is a useful asset, for this knowledge, properly applied, may save a good deal of trouble and expense.

What to Keep in the Medicine Chest.

A medicine chest should be a permanent fixture in every home, and should be placed in some easily accessible spot, but out of the way of children. It is not wise to keep it locked, as in an emergency there is always the danger that the key may have been mislaid. The following is a list of the most necessary articles it should contain:—

Bandages and safety pins.
White and pink (boracic) lint.
White gauze.
Strips of clean white linen.
Boracic ointment.
Zinc ointment.
Olive oil.
Vaseline.
Boracic powder.
Brandy.
Tincture of iodine.
Smelling salts.
Pair forceps.
Pair scissors.
Jaconet and oiled silk.
Ammonia.
Blue bag.
Lysol.
Adhesive tape.
Cotton wool.
Clinical thermometer.
2 oz. baking soda.
Small bottle vinegar.

HOT FOMENTATIONS (BORACIC)

How to Prepare.

Fold a linen or huckaback towel in half lengthways and place over a bowl. Cut sufficient boracic lint (three or four thicknesses) to well cover the wound or affected part, and place in the centre of the towel. Have ready a kettle of boiling water, a piece of jaconet (larger than the boracic lint), cotton wool and a bandage.

How to Apply.

Bare the wound. Pour the boiling water on the lint, well saturating it. Take the ends of the towel and turn in opposite directions, and wring till *all the water* has been squeezed out of the lint. Open out towel and shake

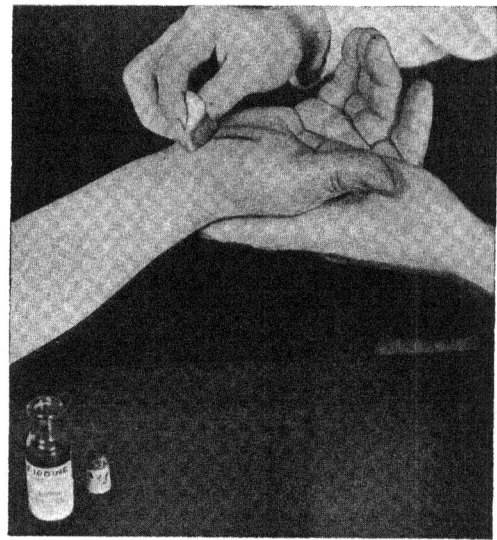

Fig. 1.—Dealing with a Cut.
Apply an antiseptic such as iodine to the cut and cover the part over.

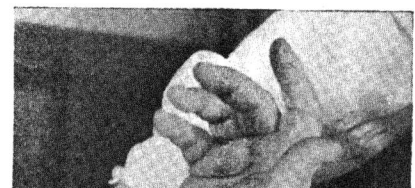

Fig. 2.—To Stop Bleeding from a Deep Cut.
A tightly bound handkerchief above the cut will suffice to check it, especially if the arm is raised at the same time.

out the lint and apply it to the affected part immediately. Cover with jaconet, then cotton wool, and then bandage tightly.

COLD COMPRESS

Saturate a piece of white lint in cold water (ice-cold if possible), squeeze out most of the water and apply to affected part. Cover with jaconet, cotton wool, and then finish off with a bandage.

N.B.—When preparing a cold compress for bruises, it is advisable to add methylated spirit to the water. Proportion: 1 part spirit to 5 of water.

SEVERE CUT WITH CHISEL OR KNIFE

Materials: Bandage, gauze, cotton wool and iodine.

First wash the wound with warm water, continuing until all particles of dirt or rust are removed (always bathe outwards from the seat of the wound). Next apply tincture of iodine and cover with a piece of white gauze, and bandage in usual manner. (See also notes on Bleeding on p. 254.)

BLACK EYE

Materials: White lint, oil silk, cotton wool and 2" bandage.

The sooner a black eye is treated, the sooner is the bruising likely to disappear.

Firstly examine eye to see that no further damage has occurred, and then place a cold water compress right over the part and bandage firmly.

BRUISES

Materials: White lint, oil silk, cotton wool and bandage.

The treatment for bruises is identical in all cases except when there is a fracture or wound, and merely consists of a cold compress.

ELECTRIC SHOCK

Electric shock is caused by a person coming into direct contact with an electric cable, wire, or rail. Insensibility usually occurs, and often the affected person cannot extricate himself from the point of contact with the current.

Treatment.

Send for a doctor.

The first thing is to remove the patient from the point of contact, but precautions must be taken to ensure that the person rendering the assistance does not also get a shock through contact with the patient. As it is not always possible to

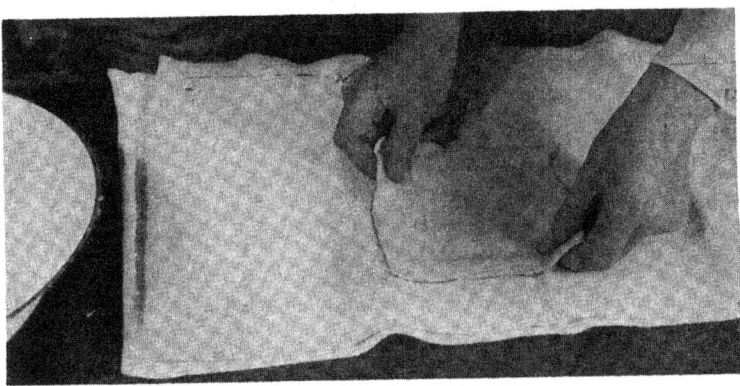

Fig. 3.—Preparing a Hot Fomentation.
Take two or three pieces of boracic lint of a size sufficient to cover the inflamed area and lay them on a face towel.

switch off the current, the first-aid assistant must first insulate himself from the earth—and this is done by standing on any rubber article, linoleum, dry cloth, wood or straw, and covering the hands with any dry but thick piece of clothing such as a cap—or even a dry newspaper—or an ordinary walking stick may be used to drag the sufferer away. In any case, avoid touching any naked part of the patient whilst he is in contact with the current.

Apply Artificial Respiration.

Having removed patient, artificial respiration must be applied at once, for it is almost certain that breathing has ceased. (The sufferer may even appear to be dead, but many persons apparently dead have been revived by prompt and persistent artificial respiration.) The method known as *Schäfer's* is the method to apply, and proceeds as follows:—

(a) Turn the patient on his stomach and lay him out straight, and turn the head to one side, resting it on his crooked arm to keep his mouth from contact with the ground.

(b) Kneel across the patient, facing his head, and place the palms of your hands on his lowest ribs, one at each side, and the thumbs parallel to each other on the small of the back. Keep your arms perfectly straight and lean your body forward, and slowly apply firm pressure downwards upon the patient's back and lower part of the chest. This drives the air out of the patient's lungs, producing expiration. Next draw back your body fairly rapidly, relaxing the pressure, but not removing your hands. The sudden relaxing of pressure on patient's chest causes the air to enter his lungs, producing inspiration.

N.B.—The forward movement should take about three seconds and

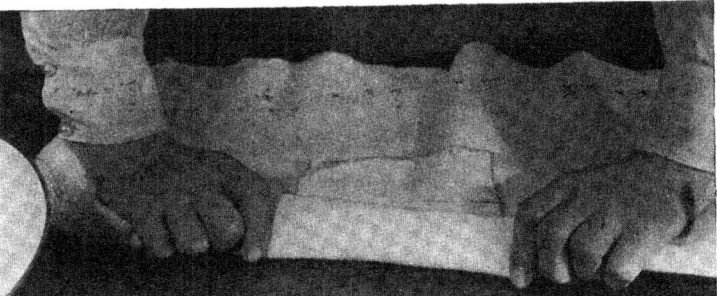

Fig. 4.—Preparing a Hot Fomentation.
Then roll up the lint in the towel.

the backward two.

(c) Continue these movements, swaying backwards and forwards, doing from twelve to fifteen a minute, and continue until breathing is restored to the patient, or a doctor pronounces life to be extinct.

As this method may have to be kept up for two to three hours, it is necessary to have assistance in the form of relays, but when changing from one assistant to another, do so without interrupting the continuity of the movements. Burns, if any, should be treated in the usual way.

BLOW ON THUMB-NAIL FROM HAMMER

Materials: Bandage, gauze, oil silk, cotton wool.

This is a common and very painful injury and is accompanied by immediate swelling and discoloration, and often means the loss of the nail.

To alleviate the pain and lessen the extent of the discoloration, hold the thumb in *ice*-cold water for several minutes. Then apply cold water compress, changing frequently.

SPLINTER IN THE HAND OR LEG

Materials: Boric lint, oil silk, cotton wool, bandage.

If the splinter cannot be removed in the usual way, viz., with forceps or clean needle, apply hot boracic foments which will soften the surrounding skin and draw the splinter nearer to the surface, making its removal an easy matter. Should this not be successful, it is advisable to see a doctor without delay, as a deeply embedded splinter can be very dangerous if neglected.

BURNS AND SCALDS

Materials: Bicarbonate of soda, strips of white lint or linen, boracic ointment and olive oil, oil silk, cotton wool, bandage.

It must at first be remembered that burns and scalds are very different, a burn being caused by *dry heat*, such as fire, friction, hot metals or electric current, etc., and a scald by *moist heat*,

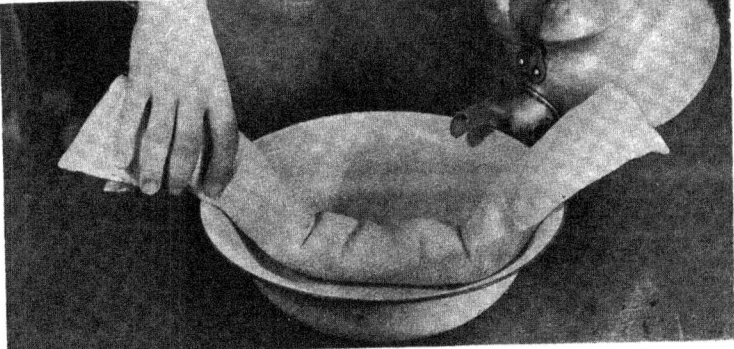

Fig. 5.—Preparing a Hot Fomentation.
Immerse the part where the lint is in boiling water.

SIMPLE FIRST AID FOR THE HOME

such as boiling water or any other liquid. The effect may be mere inflammation of the skin, blisters, or the underlying tissues may be severely involved.

General Lines of Treatment.

The general lines of treatment are as follows:—

First remove any clothing around the injured part. Should any part of the clothing adhere, do not attempt to remove, but cut around it. If possible, the injured part should be bathed in warm water (about 90°–100°) to which carbonate of soda has been added. Four tablespoons of carbonate of soda to a gallon of water make a good solution. This helps to remove anything which may be adhering, and is also soothing. It is imperative to exclude air from the injured part, and the following dressing should be applied immediately the bathing ceases. Take several strips of white lint or clean rag and cover with boracic ointment or any vegetable oil (olive, etc.), and place these on the part. (Strips are used so that the dressing may be renewed frequently without exposing the entire injured surface to the air at once.) Cover with piece of cotton wool and bandage lightly.

Should a blister have occurred, do NOT break.

Corrosive acid (spirits of salts, etc.) burns should be bathed with a weak alkaline solution such as washing or baking soda and warm water, before the above dressing is applied.

Corrosive alkali (ammonia and caustic soda) burns should be bathed with a weak acid solution such as vinegar or lemon juice and water in equal parts.

In all cases of burns and scalds, shock invariably is present (see p. 254 for treatment).

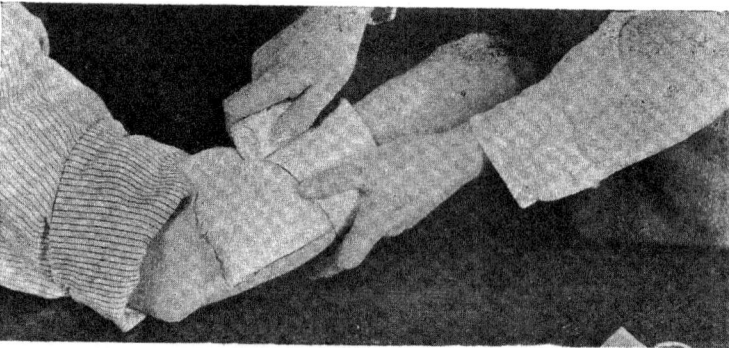

Fig. 8.—Bandaging on a Hot Fomentation.

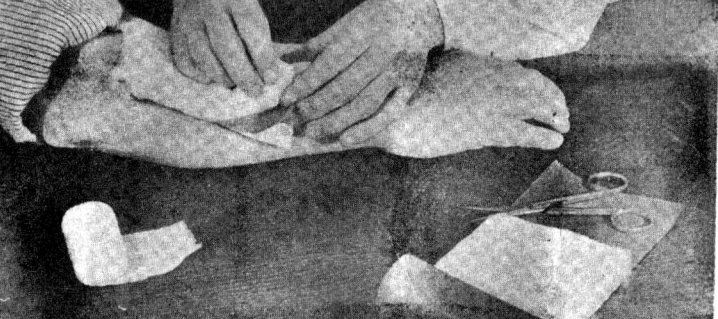

Fig. 7.—Applying a Hot Fomentation.
Gently place the heated pieces of lint on the affected part, cover the lint with a piece of oil silk, and over that place a thick piece of cotton wool.

STINGS—INSECTS AND PLANTS

Materials: Ammonia, vaseline, gauze and bandage.

Although these are only rarely dangerous, they are liable to become so, and it is always advisable to treat them promptly.

If a sting has been left in the part, remove it with forceps.

Bathe the affected part with a solution of ammonia and water. The application of the old-fashioned blue-bag remedy is as effective as anything for easing the pain. Finally apply vaseline, gauze and bandage.

FOREIGN BODY IN THE EYE

No matter how bad the irritation or pain, do not rub the eye (the old doctors' maxim "Never rub the eye except with the elbow," is very sound advice).

If the foreign body is under the upper lid, lift the lid forward and gently press the lower lid up and beneath it. The lower eyelashes brush the inside of the upper lid, and if this is done repeatedly, the foreign body will almost certainly be removed.

Should this not be successful, stand behind the patient, hold a match about ½ an inch above the edge of the lid, pressing it backwards. Take the eyelashes and pull upwards and over the match, thus exposing the inner surface of the lid. It is then a simple matter to remove the foreign body with the aid of the corner of a handkerchief.

If the foreign body is a piece of grit or a particle of metal, it is likely to become embedded in the eyeball. Should this occur, do not attempt to remove it, but pull down the lower lid, drop a little olive or salad oil on to the eyeball, close the eye, and apply a soft pad and bandage, and take patient to doctor.

SPRAINED ANKLE

Materials: White lint, oil silk,

Fig. 6.—Preparing a Hot Fomentation.
Wring the towel and lint as dry as you can.

SIMPLE FIRST AID FOR THE HOME

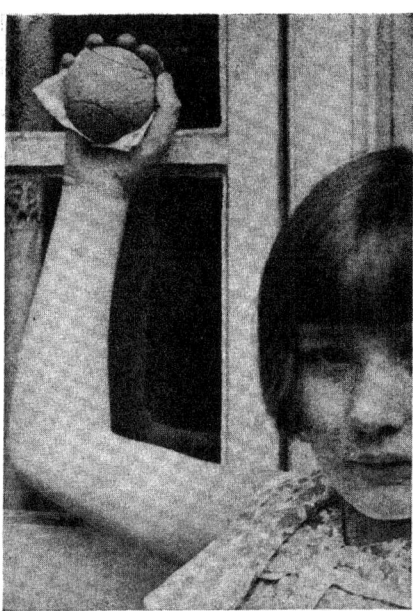

Fig. 9.—Another Simple Remedy to Stop Bleeding.

An accidental cut on the palm of the hand can very quickly be stopped from bleeding by tightly grasping a tennis-ball, with sterilised dressings, while keeping the hand elevated.

cotton wool and 3″ bandage

This is a very common form of injury, and may incapacitate one for two or three weeks.

A sprain is the result of a sudden wrench, and the tendons around the joint are stretched and sometimes torn. It is accompanied by severe pain, and inability to use the joint.

Swelling occurs immediately, and bad discoloration follows quickly. If the accident occurs in or about the house, the following treatment should be prescribed at once.

Place the patient in a comfortable position on a couch or settee, keeping the affected limb raised well above the level of the body. Remove boot and sock (cutting off if necessary) and apply a well-saturated wet dressing, use ice-cold water where possible, oil silk, cotton wool and bandage tightly. Should cold dressings fail to relieve the pain, apply hot water fomentations instead.

Remember, always, that a sprain must be treated as a suspected fracture, and every care should be taken to ensure that the limb is handled very carefully.

DISLOCATIONS

Materials: White lint, oil silk, cotton wool.

A dislocation—displacement of a bone or bones—most frequently occurs at the following joints: the thumb, elbow, finger or shoulder, and is caused by a wrench or a blow. It is always accompanied by these signs and symptoms:—

(1) Intense pain at the affected joint, and loss of power in the limb.

(2) Swelling and discoloration around the joint, and numbness of the lower part of the limb.

(3) The joint becomes fixed and cannot be moved at all, and the limb is deformed and assumes an unnatural position.

Treatment.

On no account should any unqualified person attempt to reduce a dislocation (it must be left to a doctor), but the following treatment must be applied immediately.

(1) Remove clothing from the limb, and make patient comfortable on a couch or bed.

(2) Apply ice-cold dressing to the seat of injury, and support the limb (where possible) on cushions or pillows, thus relieving the tension on the torn ligaments around the joint.

(3) If the cold dressings do not relieve the pain, apply hot ones in their stead.

(4) As patient will probably

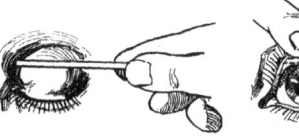

Fig. 10.—How to Remove a Foreign Body in the Eye.

Place a match-stick over the eyelid, then roll back the lid over the match. It will then be possible to remove the irritant with the corner of a handkerchief.

be suffering from shock, treat for same as instructed later.

CONCUSSION OF THE BRAIN

Concussion may be caused by a fall or a severe blow on the head, or by a heavy fall on the feet or lower part of the backbone from a height. This is a serious condition and a doctor must be sent for at once.

The symptoms vary according to the severity of the accident: unconsciousness and relaxed muscles are the main features, the skin becomes cold and clammy, and respiration and the heart-beats are slow. The patient may quickly regain consciousness, or sink into a deep coma. Should he regain his senses, keep him *very* quiet and do not allow him to talk or attempt to get up, as this state is not necessarily a sign of recovery, and a relapse into a deeper and more serious form of unconsciousness may ensue, due to injury to the brain or structure inside the cranium.

Treatment.

Having sent for the doctor, put patient to bed or on a couch, using no pillow, but keeping his head low. Keep him warm, and apply hot-water bottles at his feet (protect the hot-water bottles well with a small blanket, as the patient (being senseless), could not move should the bare bottle come into contact with his skin, and would be severely burnt).

Do not give stimulants even during any periods of consciousness, in case a hæmorrhage is occurring inside the cranium.

SHOCK

Send for doctor.

Shock may result from several causes, chiefly: (1) severe injuries, (2) emotional disturbance (such as fright or the receipt of sudden bad news, (3) loss of blood, and (4) pain.

The sufferer retains consciousness, but becomes very pale, has a low pulse and temperature, is listless and languid, but as this condition is liable to pass into coma and perhaps death, it must not be regarded as trivial.

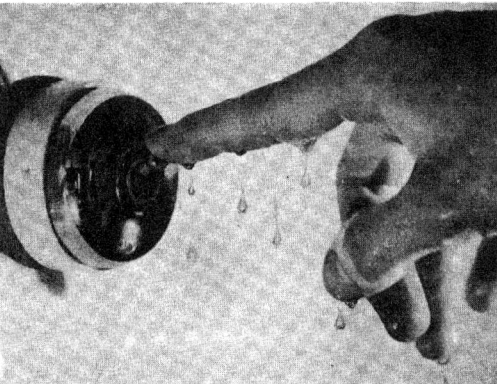

Fig. 11.—Prevention is Better than Cure.

It's better to avoid the risk of electric shock than to court it at any time by switching on the light while the hand is wet. Such an action may cause a short-circuit on the switch, which would give rise to a shock then or subsequently. With a short-circuit of this nature, and a person holding a wet object, such as a wash basin, with the other hand, there is serious risk. To do this while in a bath has caused death. Never touch electrical gear while wet!

Treatment.

Attend to injuries, if any. Put patient to bed or on a couch, and loosen ALL clothing. Apply well-protected hot-water bottles to feet and at the pit of the abdomen. Unless there is hæmorrhage (or suspected hæmorrhage) present, give patient hot drinks (tea or coffee) or a teaspoonful of brandy in half a tumbler of water may be given in sips. Elevate the foot of the bed.

FAINTING

This condition is similar to shock, but is of less severe a character.

It is due to deficient circulation of blood in the brain, and may be brought about by bad news, injuries or pain.

Treatment.

Lay patient on his back, with the head lower than the level of the body. Raise the feet and loosen all tight clothing. Give plenty of air, and give a mild stimulant such as tea or coffee on recovery.

FRACTURES (BROKEN BONES)— GENERAL RULES FOR TREATMENT

There are several types of fractures (simple, compound, complicated and compressed being the more common forms) and the chief object of first-aid treatment of them is to guard against further damage, and particularly to prevent a minor fracture from becoming a major one. Therefore, it is essential to give immediate treatment, and what is more important, to do it *without* first removing the patient from the spot where the accident happened. No matter where the patient is lying (even if in the centre of a main street) he must be treated before any attempt at removal is made.

General Lines for First-aid Treatment.

(1) If hæmorrhage is present, attend to it first, and apply clean dressing to the wound.

(2) Cover the patient with a rug or coats, and steady the limb to prevent any movement.

(3) Prepare splints from the best materials available (any rigid article such as a board, walking-stick, umbrella or broom handle will do), padding them, if possible, and ensure that they are long enough to keep the joints above and below the fracture at complete rest.

(4) Using every care (but no force), place the limb in as natural a position as can be obtained. Look for shortening of the limb, and (except in the case of a compound fracture, when the bone protrudes) if shortening is present, gently but firmly pull upon lowest part of the limb until it regains its approximate normal length. Do not let go of limb, and get bystanders to apply the splints (over the clothing) and bandages. The bandages must

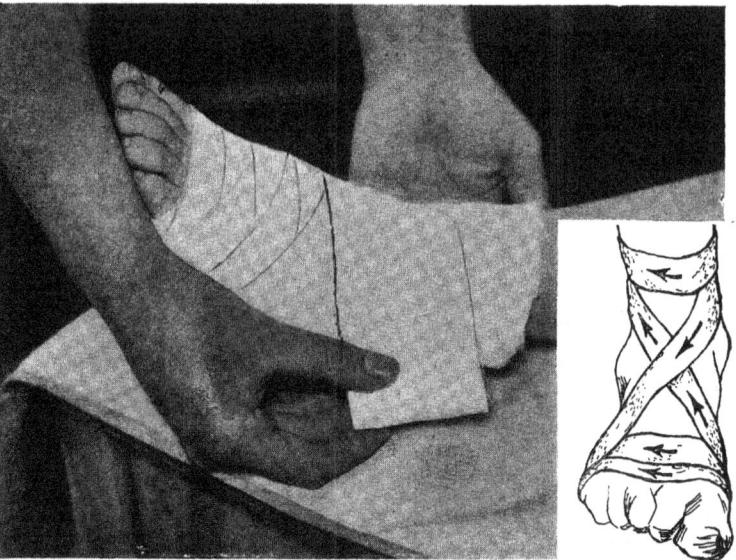

Fig. 12.—TREATING A SPRAINED ANKLE
The ankle should be bandaged by a figure-of-eight bandage. The picture shows this being done—the bandage is crossing the foot and is being passed under the leg. The course of the bandage is shown in the inset.

be applied firmly, so long as they do not constrict the blood circulation.

In applying splints to the arm, use a narrow bandage, passing it twice round the limb and tie the ends over the outer splint.

In the case of a thigh or leg, use a medium bandage, double it in centre, pass loop under the limb, bring it over the top and secure it with the two ends, tying the knot over the splint.

When applying the bandages nearest to the fracture, secure the upper one first.

BLEEDING (HÆMORRHAGE)

There are three kinds of hæmorrhage, namely :—

(1) Arterial—from an artery.
(2) Venous—from a vein.
(3) Capillary—from the capillaries. (Capillaries are the very minute blood-

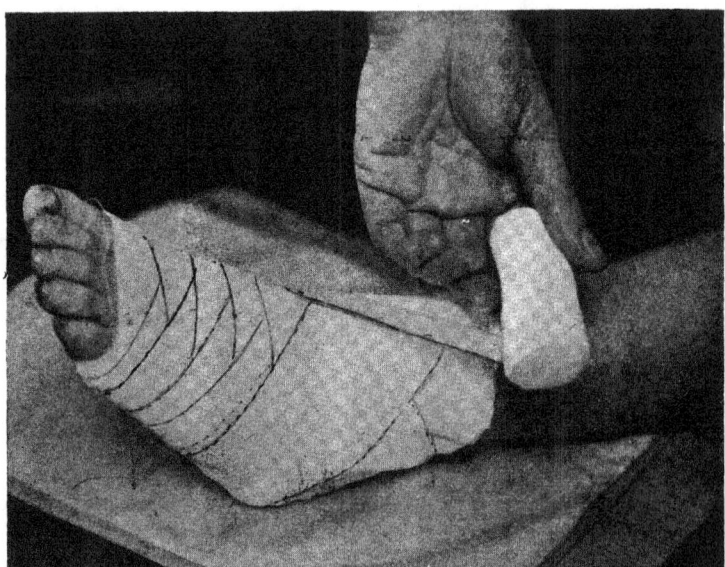

Fig. 13.—COMPLETING A FIGURE-OF-EIGHT ANKLE BANDAGE.
The bandage passing over the foot. See text for further treatment required for a sprained ankle.

vessels which form a meshwork all over the body and are the connecting link between the arteries and the veins.)

Arterial Hæmorrhage.

Arterial hæmorrhage is of a very bright red colour, and the blood comes out in jets, corresponding to the beats of the heart. This type of bleeding is very serious indeed, for if a large artery is affected, death may ensue in forty-five seconds. Therefore, immediate treatment is essential, and consists of the following (after sending for doctor).

Treatment.

Expose the wound and apply firm pressure with the ball of the thumb or the fingers. (This cannot be done if the wound is large, or contains a foreign body or is the result of a fractured bone.) With the other hand press on the artery with the thumb above the wound or nearest side to the heart. Maintain this pressure until the wound has been bathed and iodine-dressed by an assistant, the dressing to consist of pad and bandage. The pad is made by putting a small but hard article (such as a pebble) in a piece of gauze. Place the pad directly on the wound and bandage tightly.

If the wound is large and contains a foreign body or is at the seat of a fractured bone, immediately apply pressure on the artery (on the heart side of the wound) and get an assistant to prepare a tourniquet as here :—

(1) Apply a firm pad on a pressure point near to your thumb.

(2) Encircle the limb with a bandage or strap, with its centre over the pad, and tie ends at opposite side, using a half-knot. Place a short stick, pencil or spoon over the half-knot, and over it tie a reef knot. Twist the stick or pencil, thus tightening the bandage and pad, and stopping the flow of blood. Finally, lock the stick by tying a further bandage or handkerchief round it and the limb.

WARNING.—Only fix tourniquet sufficiently tightly to stop flow of blood. If after applying the tourniquet, the part of the limb below it becomes congested and swollen, loosen the tourniquet slightly.

Venous Hæmorrhage.

This is of a dark red (almost bluish) colour. The blood wells up from the wound, and the bleeding is not jerky but continuous (except in the case of a varicose vein); the blood comes from side of the wound furthest from the heart.

Treatment.

Apply thumb pressure on the wound (except over fracture or foreign body) and loosen all constrictions such as garters, etc., on the side nearest to the heart.

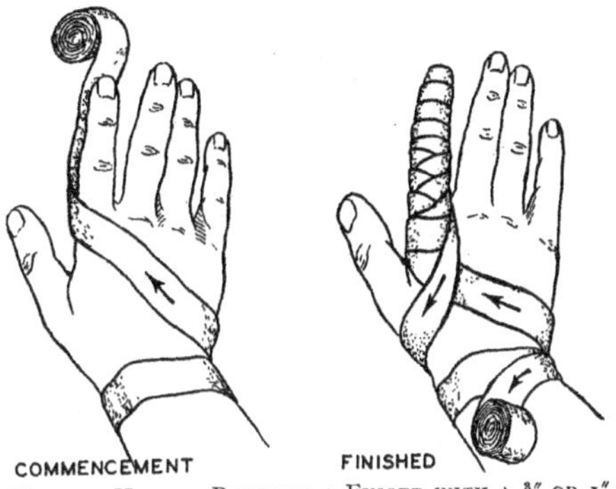

Apply a firm bandage close to the wound on the side away from the heart (this will stop the bleeding), and then dress the wound. If very dirty, bathe lightly. Apply iodine on and around the wound and dress with gauze, cotton wool and bandage.

Capillary Hæmorrhage.

This is red in colour. The bleeding is steady and continuous, and merely oozes from the wound.

Treatment.

Bathe the wound and surrounding parts, paint with iodine and apply gauze and cotton wool, and bandage firmly. This will be sufficient to stop the bleeding.

NOSE BLEEDING

In a case of nose bleeding, sit patient on a chair and get him to throw his head backwards as far as possible, and raise his arms above the head. Loosen tight clothing about the neck and chest and apply any cold substance to the back of the neck. Get patient to breathe hard in through his nose and out through the mouth. If the bleeding persists, send for doctor.

SUNSTROKE—OR HEATSTROKE

Sunstroke is caused by direct exposure to the rays of the sun and is a very troublesome ailment. The person afflicted suffers from sickness, giddiness, fainting and great thirst, and there is sometimes a difficulty in breathing. The face becomes very flushed, the pulse is rapid, and the skin is dry and burning. The temperature is high, the patient may snore heavily with every breath, and insensibility may follow.

Treatment.

As the whole of the nervous system is affected, the area to be treated is extensive. Remove the patient to a cool and shady room, and remove all clothes down to the waist. Lay him down in a comfortable position, with his head and shoulders well raised. Fan him vigorously, using a newspaper or a large piece of cardboard. Finally, apply ice-bags or cold water frequently to the head, neck and spine and continue until patient's condition improves. Keep him quiet and shut out as much noise as possible.

CHOKING

Choking is caused by an obstruction such as a piece of food becoming lodged in the throat. The person affected fights for breath, and his face becomes very congested.

Treatment.

If possible, turn patient upside down and give him some good hard thumps between the shoulder-blades. If this does not succeed, open his mouth (using force if necessary), slide two fingers along the tongue right to the back of the throat, and try to remove the foreign body. If this cannot be done, gently push it back further into the gullet. This should induce vomiting, which will almost certainly result in the foreign body being ejected. Should this fail, get immediate medical assistance.

SUFFOCATION BY GAS OR SMOKE
To Remove Gassed Person from a Gas-affected Building.

Before entering a room or building where smoke or gas fumes are known to be present, tie a wet handkerchief over the nose and mouth. Some gases are lighter than air and rise, whilst others are heavier than air and remain near to the floor.

N.B.—Coal-gas and smoke are lighter than air, and petrol fumes are heavier. Before entering the room try and ascertain as to which type of gas is present, and then follow these natural precautions. If the fumes are of the heavier-than-air type, move in an upright position; if of the lighter-than-air type, crawl in on the hands and knees. Remove the patient as speedily as possible to the open air, and loosen all clothing about the neck

Fig. 14.—How to Bandage a Finger with a ¾" or 1" Bandage.

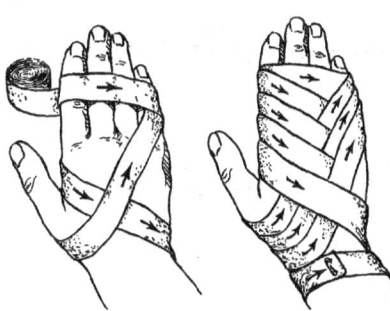

Fig. 15.—How to Bandage the Palm of the Hand using a 2" or 2½" Bandage.

SIMPLE FIRST AID FOR THE HOME

and chest. Send for a doctor, as oxygen may be necessary to revive the patient if he is badly affected. Artificial respiration must be applied in the meanwhile if necessary.

BANDAGING

A few general hints on how to apply bandages are necessary, for a badly applied one very soon becomes loose.

(1) The bandage must be tightly rolled before use.

(2) Apply outer side of the free end.

(3) Bandage from below upwards, and each layer of the bandage should overlap the preceding one by two-thirds.

(4) Apply the bandage firmly but not tightly, and finish off by securing with a safety-pin.

Finger Bandage.

Use a ¾" or 1" bandage (see Fig. 14).

Start on the inner side of back of wrist, leaving an end long enough to tie with other end on completion. Make fast with two turns around the wrist, and then run bandage over back of hand up to tip of finger. Bandage tip and work downwards and carry end of bandage over back of hand towards opposite side of wrist from which run up was made, and

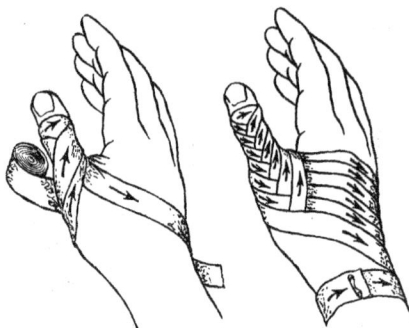

Fig. 16.—How to Bandage the Ball of the Thumb, using a 1" Bandage.

fasten off. Should several fingers require bandaging, the one nearest the little finger should be done first.

Bandage for the Hand.

Use a 2" or 2½" bandage (see Fig. 15).

Course.—Start between thumb and finger, down across back of hand and round front of wrist. Then up across back of hand to little finger nail, once round all fingers and down across back of hand again. Repeat until hand is covered and fasten off with safety-pin at back of hand.

Spica Bandage for Ball of Thumb.

Use a 1" bandage (see Fig. 16).

Course of the bandage is across front of wrist (from little finger side), up between first finger and thumb, one turn around thumb, then down across back of hand to wrist (little finger side), a turn round the wrist, and continue until ball of thumb is covered. Finish off round the wrist and secure with the two ends.

Knee Bandage.

Use a 3" bandage (see Fig. 17).

Course.—Round knee and then alternately above and below, working in outward direction from front of limb.

Bandage for Ankle and Foot (Spica).

Use a 2½" or 3" bandage (see Fig. 12).

Course.—Once round ankle and down over foot to small toe. Two or three turns around foot, and then up over foot to outside of ankle, once round ankle, and then continue till foot and ankle are covered. Fasten with pin on outside of ankle.

The above instructions relate to the most likely bandages that will be required in the home.

Fig. 17.—Bandaging a Knee with a 3" Bandage.

A SHELF IDEA FOR FLAT DWELLERS

Occupiers of part houses or unfurnished or furnished rooms will probably be interested in a method of fitting up shelves in their apartments without damage to walls or any part of their landlord's property. Shelves amply capable of bearing the weight of kitchen utensils or other moderately heavy objects may be erected in the undermentioned fashion, which is, however, dependent upon the rooms being already furnished with picture rails.

The shelves are fixed to two or more vertical battens with any suitable angle brackets, and should be cut to fit neatly round the battens at the points of contact, leaving the latter projecting about ⅛ inch from the rear edge of the shelf. Care must be taken that the backs of the battens are finished perfectly smooth, as also must be the rear edges of the shelves, to avoid damage to the wallpaper by rubbing, the ⅛-inch clearance being left to accommodate any possible slight unevenness in the wall surface. The rear shelf edges and backs of the battens may, as an additional precaution, be covered with strips of baize or felt if desired. If so, the material should be stuck to the wood with some suitable adhesive.

The vertical battens must be sufficiently long to extend from the lower extremities of the shelf brackets right up to the under edge of the picture rail. Stout wire loops or screw eyes with rings are then screwed to the front surfaces of these upper ends, the loops being hung over the lower ends of ordinary picture-rail hooks.

Two or more vertical battens may be employed according to the weight which the shelf is required to support, and, of course, more than one shelf may be fitted to the battens.

An additional advantage of this easy and quick way of putting up shelves is that the latter remain tenant's property, and may be taken away on leaving the premises.

The Shelf in Position.

How to Make Loose Covers
For Chairs of All Sizes

Making loose covers at home is a very worthwhile job, interesting in itself and effecting substantial economies. It is a good plan to start with a chair, proceeding to a larger item like a Chesterfield or couch when a little preliminary experience has been gained.

Choose a simple chair for the first attempt, one which is not too large or too elaborately stuffed, for naturally the work goes more slowly when it is new to you, and a smaller piece is therefore more quickly finished and gives confidence for something more ambitious next time. In fact, an ideal plan is to make your first loose cover for a child's upholstered chair, if you have one, of the type shown in the accompanying photographs (Figs. 1–9).

Any woman who can do ordinary household sewing can successfully undertake a loose cover. All the operations are simple ones, requiring care and patience rather than any specialised skill.

The first step is to measure the chair or other item of furniture in order to find out how much stuff will be required. Have two reliable tape measures for doing this.

HOW TO ESTIMATE THE AMOUNT OF MATERIAL REQUIRED
The First Measurement.

To estimate material for an armchair, first measure upwards from the floor at the front of the seat, continuing across the seat from front to back, up the inside back, over its top and down the outside back to the floor again. Write down the measurement so obtained. It is shown being taken on a couch, which is measured in the same way, in Figs. 17 (front) and 18 (back).

Now Measure the Arm.

Next measure the arm in the same way, from the floor upwards over the arm and down on the inside to the seat, or *vice versa*. If the chair is one with a deeply rolled-over arm, be careful to get the measure entirely round the roll, as in Fig. 19, and not merely straight down from the top of the arm to the floor. As there are two arms and you have only measured one, double this measurement before writing it down.

What to Allow for Tuck-away.

Add to each of the two measurements, the one over the back and the one over the arm, 6 inches for tuckaway where the back and arm respectively join the seat. Other turnings are allowed for by taking measurements to the floor, but if the cover is to be finished with frills, like the one shown, or there are any loose cushions to be covered, these must be measured for separately.

Measuring the Cushion.

Measure for a cushion across both depth (Fig. 20) and breadth. If the breadth will come out of half the width of the material, the length of the cushion, plus turnings, will give the amount required for the cushion, as the boxing or thickness strip, like other narrow pieces in the cover, will come out of stuff left over in cutting the larger portions. But if, as is more probable, the cushion breadth will cut into a whole width of stuff, double its length for the amount of material required, adding 2 or 3 inches for turnings.

Measuring for a Frill.

For a frill, take the depth from the bottom of the chair frame to the floor. To get the depth the frill must be cut, you need add only 1 inch turnings to this measurement, as the frill will finish, for cleanliness' sake, 1 inch above the floor, and this inch provides part of the turnings. Now measure entirely round the bottom frame of the chair; this measurement gives you the length the frill will have to be when gathered or pleated.

Gathered and Box-pleated Frills.

For a gathered frill allow half as much again for fullness, for a box-pleated frill two and a half times. Reckon the number of full widths of

Fig. 1.—The Finished Loose Cover in Flowered Cretonne.

To ascertain the amount of material required for the above chair the following measurements must be taken: Over seat and back, plus 6 inches; over arm, plus 6 inches (total doubled for second arm); estimate for frill. For the actual method of measuring, see the examples in Figs. 17 to 21, which show measurements being taken on a large couch.

Fig. 2.—Before starting to cut the Material make a Chalk Line down the vertical centre of th outside Back of the Chair.

HOW TO MAKE LOOSE COVERS

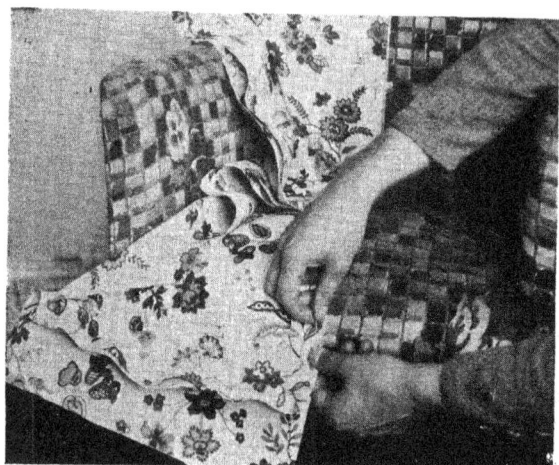

Fig. 3.—The next step is to place the fold of each doubled piece to the chalk line where it is pinned at intervals.

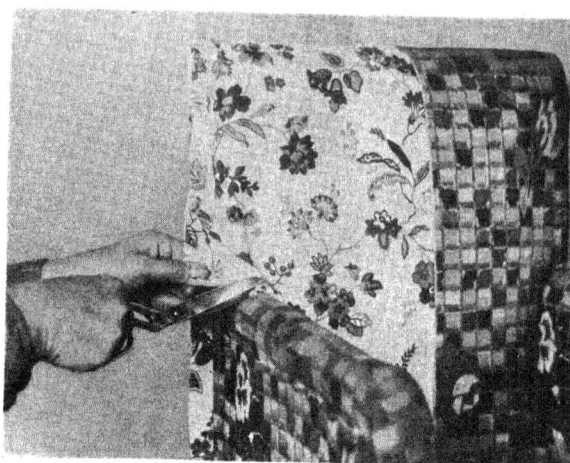

Fig. 4.—The inside back pieces where the arm joins the back should be shaped by making little slashes into the edge of the stuff until it gradually lies flat.

the material this will cut into and allow extra for the frill accordingly.

An Example.

As an example, if the frill is to finish 6 inches deep, it will need to be cut 7 inches deep. Let us suppose that the measurement round the bottom frame of the chair is 80 inches and allow one and a half times that for a gathered frill, that is, 120 inches. On material 30 inches wide, it will be necessary to cut the frill four times across the complete width. That is, a depth of four times 7 inches of stuff will be required.

So we reckon ¾ yard extra for the frill. This is 1 inch short, but such a trifling amount can be spared elsewhere on the measurements.

Piping.

The chair illustrated is piped with a contrasting cotton bias binding, and this plan is recommended, as the contrast is decorative and the use of bias binding saves the cutting and joining of bias strips to cover the cord. However, piping with self material works out a little cheaper, and if you decide on this allow ½ yard extra for pipings for a moderate-sized easy chair and more in proportion for a couch or settee.

Summary of Chair Measuring.

To sum up chair measuring, and taking the chair illustrated as an example, the following measurements added together will give (in inches) the total length of material required:—

(1) Measurement over seat and back, plus 6 inches tuck-away.

(2) Measurement over arm, plus 6 inches tuck-away (total doubled for the second arm).

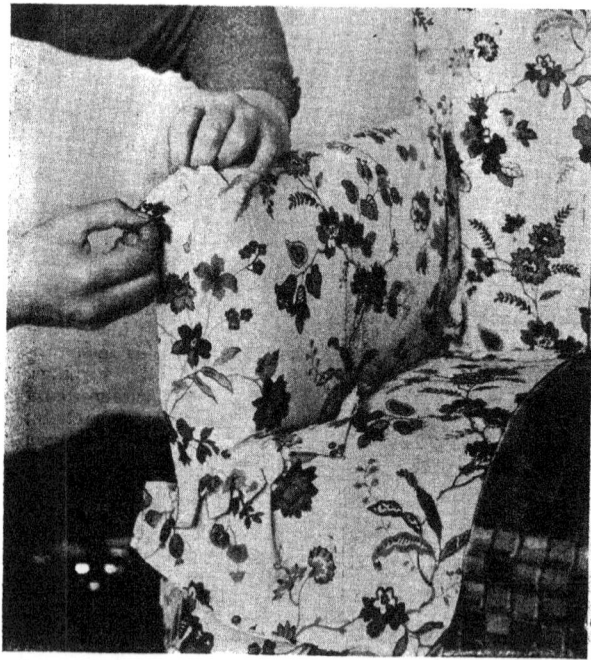

Fig. 5.—To shape the stuff neatly to the thickness of the front arm use a dart.

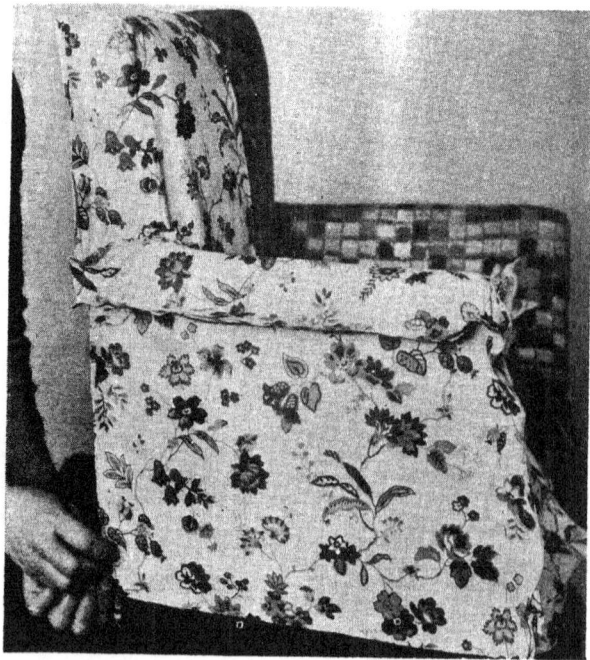

Fig. 6.—The outside of the arm should now be fitted.

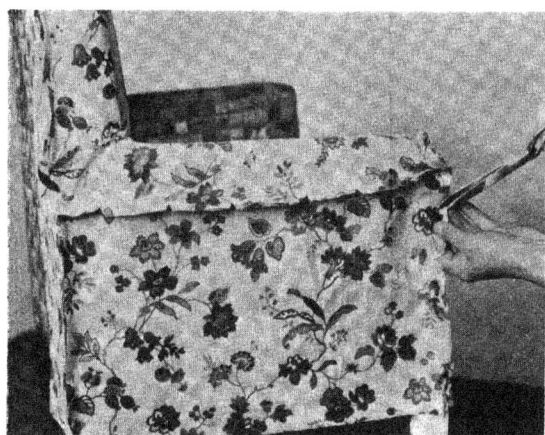

Fig. 7.—Notch the Seam Turnings through all Thicknesses by Cutting Little V's at Intervals.

Fig. 8.—By Making a Paper Pattern after Fitting a Chair, subsequent Cover Cutting will be easy.

(3) Estimate for frill, as already explained.

Additional Measurement for Couch or Settee.

A couch or settee is too wide for its cover breadthwise to come out of the width of the material. Therefore, when estimating the quantity of stuff for it, an additional measurement must be taken right along the top of the back to give the overall width (Fig. 21). From this you will be able to judge if it will cut into two or even three widths of stuff, and you will then double or treble the over-the-back measurement accordingly.

Additional Measurements for a very Large Couch.

For a very large couch such as that shown in Fig. 21, with three loose cushions, it is also advisable to allow extra for the minor pieces of the cover, as it is improbable all of these can be got out of left-overs. Therefore measure the depth of the front border or collar (the thickness of the upholstery between the edge of the seat and the bottom of the frame) and the depth of the boxing strip on the loose cushions. Make a supplementary allowance for these, bearing in mind that each will take only a portion of the width and also that the pattern must be suitably placed in each case.

THE QUESTION OF PATTERN

Mention of pattern is a reminder that your first loose cover should preferably be made of material which is plain—faintly or narrowly striped or with an all-over flowered or geometrical design which is not too large. Such materials cut up economically and present no problems of pattern matching and arranging. The cover illustrated is a good instance of the kind of design which, while very decorative when made, is easy to handle.

Large Pattern requires more Material.

If a large pattern or one arranged in definite detached motifs is chosen, you will need to increase quite considerably the amount of material

Fig. 9.—The Complete Cover Pinned up and put on Wrong Side out to Test the Fit.

bought. This is because the large motifs must be carefully centred on the inside back, outside back and seat (as shown in Fig. 16 on an armless easy chair), and also on the outside arms, where these are present. It is likewise necessary to match the part of the pattern used on the inside arms with that on the lower part of the inside back, at the same level. All this centring and matching means definite wastage between the motifs and also, as the photograph shows, narrow pieces are cut away at each side which cannot always be used elsewhere to advantage.

It is advisable for a beginner not to have to consider these pattern problems, which should be left till more experience has been gained.

Chose a 30-inch Material.

In nearly all cases 30-inch material cuts most economically, even for large couches, and should be chosen. In the case of a child's chair, however, such as the one shown here, the smaller size of the pieces enables them to be cut out of half the width of 46-inch material, which was accordingly used. This chair, suitable for a child up to eight or nine years of age, took 2¼ yards of 46-inch cretonne, 1 hank of piping cord and one 6-yard card of cotton bias binding.

A Rough Guide to Amount of Material required.

As will be seen from the foregoing remarks about measuring, the quantity of material required for full-size covers varies very greatly. But as a rough guide, it may be said that an ordinary

HOW TO MAKE LOOSE COVERS

Fig. 10.—Always Boil Piping Cord before Using.
The object of this is to shrink it, otherwise it will shrink at the first laundering and pucker the seams of the cover.

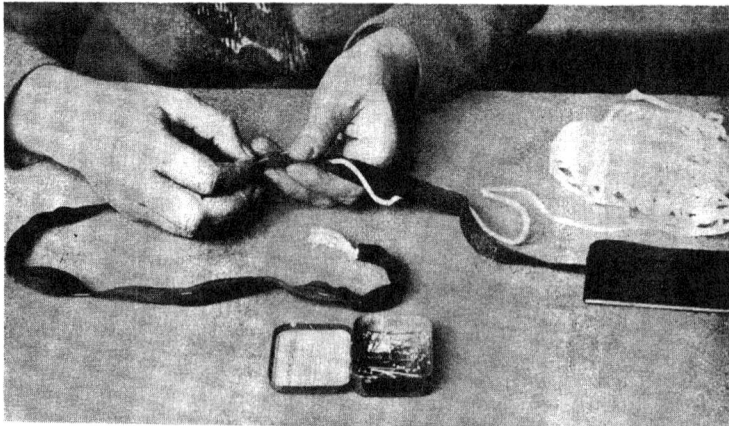

Fig. 11.—Pinning the Doubled Bias Binding over the Piping Cord.

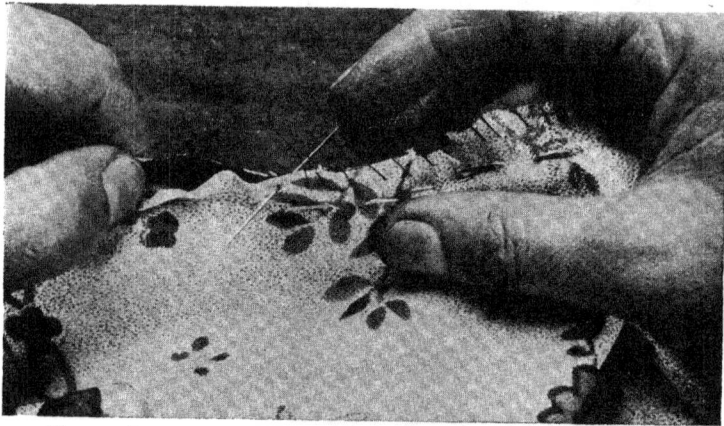

Fig. 12.—Overcasting together the Piped and Unpiped Edges of a Seam.
The piping is shown dark.

easy chair, without frills or a loose cushion, requires from 7½ to 9½ yards, plus 1½ to 2 yards extra for a loose cushion. A Chesterfield sofa requires 12 to 14 yards, and a modern two- or three-cushion settee, of the type shown in Figs. 17 to 21, from 15 to 25 yards. All these estimates are for a 30-inch wide material.

Choosing a Suitable Fabric.

There is a very varied choice of suitable fabrics for loose covers at all sorts of prices. Too-cheap material should be avoided, as it is not worth putting the work of making into stuff which will not wear and look well for a long time. Loose covers get heavy wear and must also stand laundering well, so it is really necessary that they should be closely woven and of good quality.

For plain covers a good jaspé or satin-stripe repp is hard to beat. Cretonne of reliable make is deservedly popular among flowered and geometrical patterns, and the artistic rougher-surfaced fabrics known as village or cottage weaves are an excellent modern vogue. Glazed chintz has the advantage of keeping clean a very long time, but it cannot be washed at home and is rather more difficult for amateurs to make up than the other fabrics named. Printed linen wears and looks exceedingly well, but has the disadvantage of creasing easily.

CUTTING OUT THE CHAIR COVER

Having bought the material, assemble, for cutting out, a piece of tailor's chalk, a sharp pair of cutting-out scissors (shears), a tape measure and plenty of pins.

What to do first.

Cutting out is done directly on the chair. Begin by marking a chalk line down the exact middle of the inside back, seat and front depth and also down the outside back, as in Fig. 2. If the chair upholstery might be harmed by chalk markings, a line of pins may be used instead, or a length of piping cord stretched and pinned in the correct position.

This halfway line is necessary because loose covers, like dresses, are cut half only on doubled material.

Three Measurements to be noted.

Take and note down three measurements: (1) length of inside back, going well down into the crevices of the chair; (2) length of seat, including the front thickness (also going well down into the crevice between seat and back); (3) length of outside back to the bottom of the frame.

Now cut out and pin.

To No. 1 (inside back) measurement and No. 2 (seat) measurement add 6 inches each, and cut out these lengths, the full width of the stuff, from your material. To No. 3 (outside back) add 3 inches and cut this off in the same way. Double each of the three pieces in half lengthwise, wrong side out, and pin the two selvedges together every few inches.

The Inside Back and Seat Pieces.

Pin together one end each of the inside back and seat pieces, and also pin the other end of the inside back to one end of the outside back, leaving at least ½-inch turnings outside the pins. Now place the doubled edges to the chalk line on the chair, each piece coming in its correct position on the chair, and pin the fold at intervals to the chalk line (Fig. 3).

Tuck the pinned seam of the inside back and seat right down into the crevices of the chair, so that the seat piece will take its proper position. Along the front edge of the seat pin up a fold 1½ inches deep and cut this open, as there will have to be a seam joining the seat to the collar (front thickness) in order later to insert a piping here.

Smooth the Pieces towards Outside of Chair.

Smooth all pieces nicely over towards the outside of the chair and pin together the inside and outside back pieces from the top nearly down to the top of the arm. Make this join on the edge of the outside back, including the thickness in the inside back portion, and trim off surplus material about 1 inch outside the pinned line. You see this already done in Fig. 4, which also shows how the inside back piece is cut and shaped over the junction with the arm. Use a dart to shape the top corners of the inside back.

How to get the Cover to set smoothly round the Arm.

To get the cover to set smoothly round this curve it is necessary to keep making little slashes into the edge of the stuff, until it gradually lies flat and takes the correct curve. Take time over this and slash only a little at once, constantly standing back to judge the effect, as slashes once wrongly made cannot be rectified. Do not slash quite as deep as where the seam will come, as there must be a firm turning.

Cut away any Surplus Width of Stuff.

As you continue down the inside corner where arm and inside back join, in addition to slashing, cut away any surplus width of stuff, allowing, however, ample for tucking into the crevice and for turnings. If the thickness of the upholstery swells out near the base of the inside back, to fit the hollow of the back, it may be necessary to insert a triangular gusset cut from an oddment of stuff.

Just pin it in, putting the broad base

Fig. 13.—Overcast and Machine-stitched Seam seen from the Wrong Side.

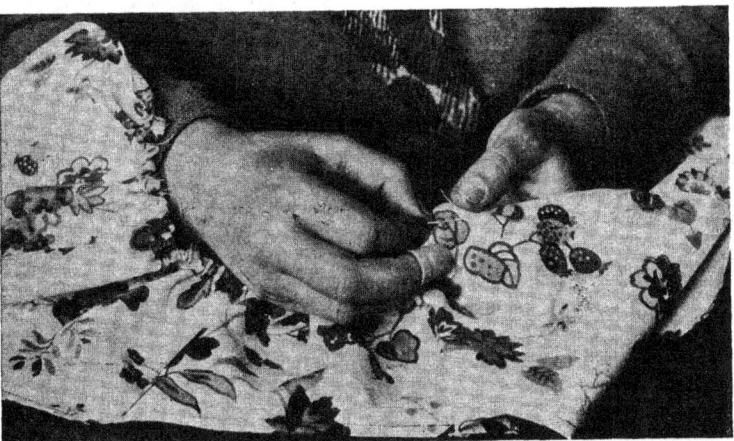

Fig. 14.—Gathering the Hemmed Frill.

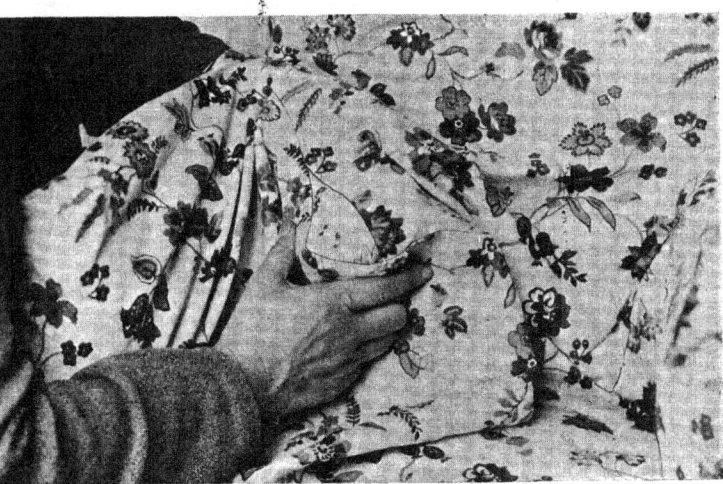

Fig. 15.—Note the Gusset inserted in the Back Corner to give more play.

HOW TO MAKE LOOSE COVERS

of the triangle to the bottom. Such a gusset is shown, after stitching, in Fig. 15.

Now cut and fit the Side of the Seat.

Roughly cut and fit along the side of the seat next. Then measure the inside and outside arms, just as you did the inside and outside back, and cut straight strips of stuff for these, allowing very good turnings on the outside piece and 6 inches of tuck-away also on the inside arm piece. Be sure the under thickness has the pattern the right way up. A join on the top of the arm would be both ugly and uncomfortable, so carry the front piece over far enough to pin the join well on the outside of the arm. (Its position is clearly seen in Figs. 6 and 7 and also in the finished cover, Fig. 1.) The front thickness of the arm is covered by the inside piece in the same way, and a dart (shown being pinned up in Fig. 5) fits up the top front edge neatly.

A Point to watch.

When cutting the top of the inside arm, by the way, be careful that you extend it outside along the top far enough back to join the outside back piece, a point often overlooked by the novice (refer to Figs. 7 and 1).

A similar point applies when shaping

Fig. 16.—A Large Design must be Centred on the Back Seat and other Important Parts of a Chair.

the front depth of the seat piece, which must likewise be extended to join the front edge of the outside arm piece for the front inch or two of its depth (see Fig. 1).

Fitting the Remaining Parts of the Outside Arm

The fitting of the remaining parts of the outside arm are clearly shown in Figs. 6 and 7. When cutting and fitting is complete and the cover sets smoothly everywhere, trim off all turnings to an even $\frac{1}{2}$ inch outside the pins. Then go all round the chair notching little V's of stuff at intervals out of all turnings, all thicknesses at once, as in Fig. 7. Do not cut the V's deep enough to come anywhere near the pins.

The cover is at present pinned up double over only half the chair. It must be taken apart in order that it may be re-pinned single, and the object of the notching is to make re-pinning easy by matching the V's on the corresponding pieces.

Make a Paper Pattern for Future Use.

Completely unpin the cut-out cover. If you are wise, you will take this opportunity of laying out one of each portion of the cover on newspaper and taking a pattern from it, carefully marking on the paper where it must be laid to a fold and other identifying marks. Lay the pattern carefully aside to be used, saving all the work of fitting on the chair, next time you make a loose cover for that particular chair. Fig. 8 shows how simple it is

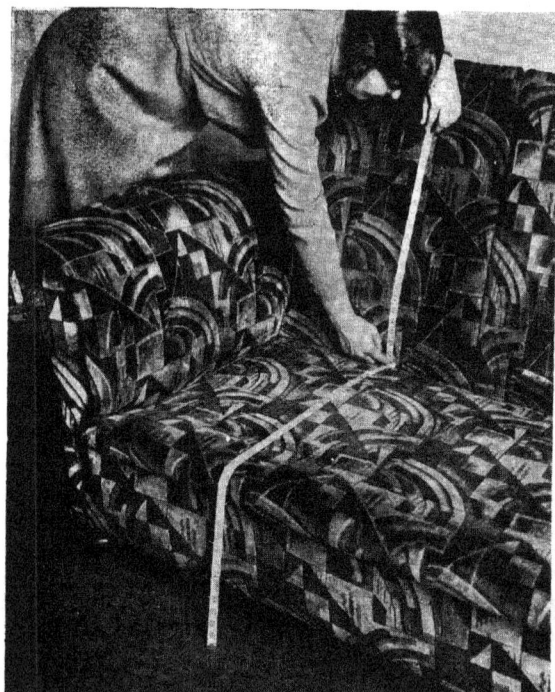

Fig. 17.—The First Stage in Measuring for a Loose Cover.

Measuring up from the ground over the seat and up the back, pushing measure well in between seat and back.

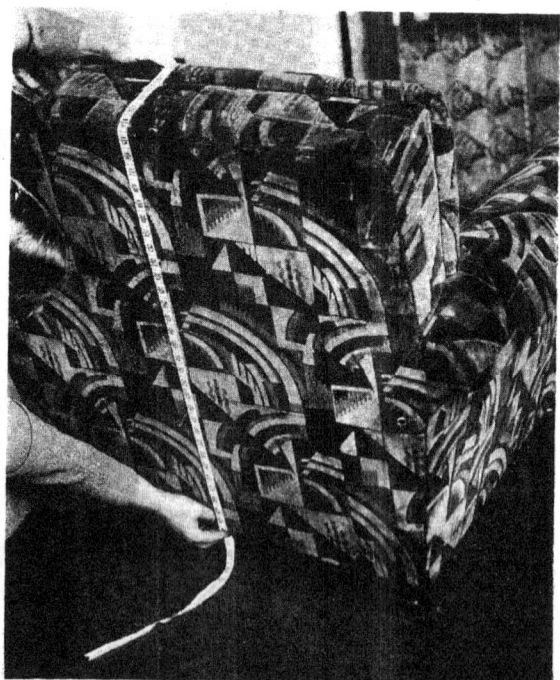

Fig. 18.—The Second Stage in Measuring for a Loose Cover.

Continue measuring up the back over the top and down the back to the ground.

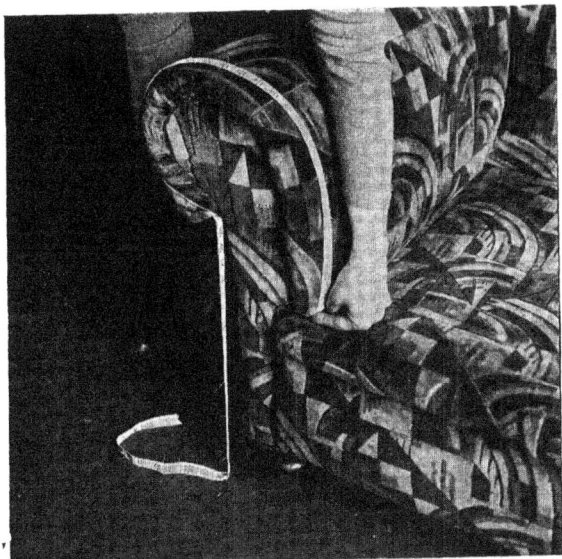

Fig. 19.—Now Measure from Seat Level over the Arm to the Ground, following the Shape carefully.

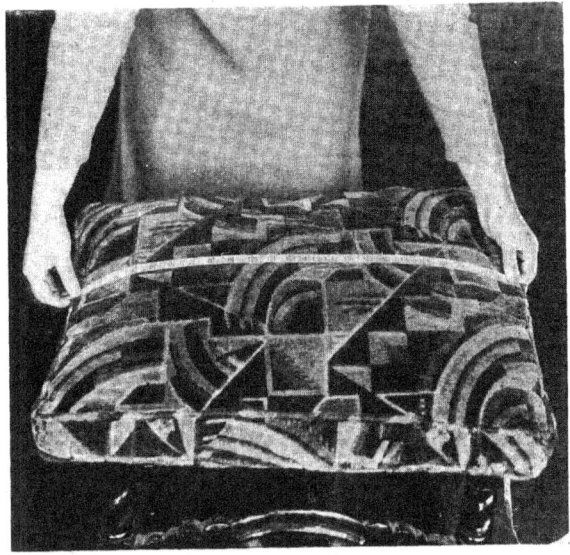

Fig. 20.—Measuring for a Loose Cushion.
This must be taken across both depth and breadth.

to cut out a cover from such a paper pattern.

This is the only way in which paper patterns can be used in loose cover making, as furniture varies so much that no standardised pattern would fit a particular chair; and covers stretch out of shape with long wear, so that it is useless to employ an old cover as a pattern for a new one.

Now re-pin the Cover in Single Thickness.

Re-pin the complete cover in single thickness, carefully matching the notches to assemble the pieces correctly. Place it on the chair wrong side out to verify fit and appearance (Fig. 9).

PIPING AND STITCHING

For an average-sized armchair you will need about 7 yards each of cotton bias binding and medium white piping cord. Shrink the cord before using it, otherwise it will shrink at the first laundering and pucker the seams of the cover. To shrink, boil the cord for a few minutes (Fig. 10), then dry it thoroughly.

Iron the ready-made creases out of the bias binding, or if you are using a self-piping, cut for it 1¼-inch wide strips of material on the true cross, joining them on the straight. Fold bias or strips lengthwise over the piping cord, and first pin (Fig. 11), and then tack the cord in position.

Seams which should be Piped.

The seams which tuck in all round the seat and the darts are not piped. The seams to be piped are the join of seat and collar, all round the bottom of the cover where the frill joins it, along the top and front edges of the arms and round the outside back.

Where to begin the Piping.

Begin by piping the front edge of the seat. Un-pin this seam and lay the prepared piping, edges outwards over the edges of the stuff, along the right side of the seat. Tack the piping down to the stuff. Lay the other half of the seam (the top edge of the collar) back in position over the piping, right sides of the two layers of stuff touching, and overcast them together, the piping inside, overcasting through the edges of the piping cover as well (Fig. 12). The piped edge tends to contract a little, so should be well stretched in the hand while overcasting.

Afterwards machine-stitch the seam stitching as close as possible to the piping cord. It will then appear on the wrong side, as in Fig. 13.

The Join of Inside and Outside arms.

Pipe and seam next the join of inside and outside arms, taking the piping continuously down the front join. Where it turns the right-angle at the front edge of the arm, nick the bias binding almost to the cord so that it will bend round neatly.

Fig. 21.—In the case of a Couch or Settee an Additional Measurement will be required, namely right along the top of the Back, to give the overall width

Is a Placket Necessary?

First tack and then stitch the unpiped seams and darts, in the case of the latter tapering off the dart imperceptibly at the narrow end. Decide if the cover can be got on and off without an opening, or whether a placket will be necessary. This entirely depends on the way the chair is stuffed. The one illustrated does not require any opening, and in this case the back and all round the bottom are piped next.

The Frill.

Cut out the various strips required for the frill, join them with plain seams pressed out flat and stitch a good ½-inch deep hem along the bottom edge (shown in Fig. 14). With pins divide the whole bottom of the cover into quarters and the frill top edge into similar quarters. Gather each quarter of the frill on a separate thread (Fig. 14), and draw up to fit the corresponding quarter of the cover. Overcast and machine-stitch the frill in place.

If a placket is required, place this down the right (when viewed from the back on the right side) outside back seam. Pipe the back piece up the left side, along the top and an inch or two down the right side. Then transfer the piping unbroken to the inside back and outside-arm edges for the rest of the way.

Now finish with a special loose cover placket, by adding a facing to the piped side of the opening and a wide wrap to the unpiped side. Fasten at close intervals with hooks and bar eyes.

To finish off the work finally, overcast the darts and unpiped seams and give the whole cover a good pressing.

Hints for more Elaborate Chair.

If the chair or couch being loose covered is more elaborately upholstered, with the very definite shaped thicknesses known as scrolls (see Fig. 19), these thicknesses, occurring at the front of the arm and at the ends of the back, should have separate pieces shaped and cut for them, instead of being included in the inside arm and inside back pieces respectively. These scroll pieces, of course, must be piped all round.

Making a Cover for a Loose Cushion.

To make a cover for a loose cushion (not possessed by the chair illustrated), cut two pieces the shape and measurements of the cushion surface, plus ½-inch turnings all round, and a long strip, long enough to go right round the cushion, the width of its thickness plus turnings. Insert the strip between the two surface pieces, piping all seams and leaving one end open. Insert the cushion and slip-stitch the unpiped edge of the opening, turned in singly, down to the piped edge, just under the cord.

LUMINOUS PAINTS

THERE are two kinds of luminous paint, namely, the *self-luminous* variety and the *phosphorescent* type. The former class are always luminous and require no preliminary excitation, but are expensive, as they contain radium salts, or some radio-active materials. The making of such paints is beyond the capability of the amateur, so that the paints are best purchased ready made. The latter class of luminous paints will glow in the dark provided they have previously been " excited " by exposure to daylight or some artificial source of light. Thus, if an object such as an electric light switch has been coated with this paint, it will remain luminous for a long time after the electric light has been switched off.

The substances used for the phosphorescent paints include phosphorescent mixtures obtained by heating strontium barium or thiosulphate with small quantities of the nitrates of thorium, or uranium.

The following are about the best recipes for well-known luminous paints:—

1. Balmains Paint.

Take 20 parts, by weight, of calcium oxide (otherwise known as burnt lime); 6 parts of sulphur; 2 parts of starch; 1 part of a 0·5 per cent. solution of bismuth nitrate; 0·15 part of potassium chloride, and 0·15 part of sodium chloride (common salt). These ingredients must be thoroughly mixed and then heated in a crucible to about 1,300° C. The luminosity obtained is of a *violet hue*. The powdered product can be mixed with amber varnish and used as a paint.

2. Lennord's Paint.

The following constituents are heated for at least half an hour to a temperature of about 1,300° C.

Strontium carbonate, 100 parts (by weight).
Sulphur, 100 parts.
Potassium chloride, 0·5 part.
Sodium chloride, 0·4 part.
Manganese chloride, 0·4 part.
The product in question gives a *violet light*.

(3) To obtain a *phosphorescent yellow light* the following chemicals should be employed:—

Strontium carbonate, 100 parts (by weight).
Sulphur, 30 parts.
Sodium carbonate, 2 parts.
Sodium chloride, 0·5 part.
Manganese sulphate, 0·2 part.
As in the preceding cases these should be fused by heating to 1,300° C.

Any good grade of varnish, such as amber varnish or white varnish, can be used to protect luminous paints.

TO MAKE OLD FUR AS GOOD AS NEW

SUITABLE materials for cleaning fur are: warm oatmeal, warm bran, and stiff hot bran mash. Powdered magnesia is also well recognised as a splendid means of restoring the whiteness to white fur. It may be employed for small things, such as baby's coats, bonnets, and gloves. The method is to rub well into the fur, roll up the object in a clean white towel, and leave at least twenty-four hours. Then take out into the open and shake and brush until the garment is clean.

A rather more professional method of home cleaning is to spread the soiled fur on a table, or on a floor over which clean newspaper has been spread, and rub lightly with wadding soaked in benzine, observing, of course, the usual precautions against naked lights of any shape or form.

Afterwards dust on plaster of Paris, and when all is quite dry, beat out all dust with a bunch of feathers.

The dyeing of fur is not a job that can be satisfactorily accomplished at home.

Storing Gramophone Records

IT is just as easy to store records as it is books; in fact, the two may be housed in practically the same way. This leads to the suggestion that a suitable bookshelf should be cleared of its volumes and the space adapted for records. Naturally, it is not every shelf that will answer the purpose. To serve for records, the shelf must be deep enough and high enough to take 10 or 12-inch discs, with a slight margin to spare.

It may be that no suitable shelf is available. In such a case it is a very simple matter to construct a box shelf of plywood, making it to whatever dimensions are desired. This box shelf can be polished or stained and stood somewhere near to the gramophone cabinet, where it will be both useful and ornamental.

How Corrugated Paper Helps.

However, we will suppose that a shelf in the bookcase has been decided on, and that all the books have been cleared out. The first thing, then, is to obtain some corrugated paper and to cut two strips, one to fit the bottom of the shelf and the other the top. That done, the paper is stuck to the wood by means of hot Scotch glue.

A good deal, of course, depends on how the corrugated paper is handled and fitted. All the edges must be neatly cut; the upstanding ribs must not be bruised or indented; and, if the bottom piece begins with a sunk ridge, the upper piece should not commence with a raised ridge.

Shellac Varnish for Preserving the Corrugated Paper.

Ordinary corrugated paper answers our present purpose quite well; but it is apt to become ragged along the outer edge, after much use. Therefore, it is advisable, though not absolutely necessary, to give it a coat of shellac varnish, such as is used for many purposes in wireless practice. This will make the paper vary hard and able to withstand rough usage. Naturally, the varnishing is done before the paper is glued to the shelf, but after it has been trimmed to shape.

When the corrugated paper has been fitted, both top and bottom, the records are slipped in tough paper or cardboard envelopes, and these are slid into the grooves of the corrugated paper. Thus they stand firmly and upright, and a hundred or more can be packed into a surprisingly compact space. The method described is shown in Figs. 1 and 2.

Fig. 1.—How a Bookshelf can be adapted for taking Records

Note the piece of corrugated paper on the shelf; a similar piece is fixed to the roof.

Fig. 2.—A Close-up View showing how the Envelopes Slide in and out of the Grooves of the Corrugated Paper.

The Need for Making the Envelopes Fit.

From this brief explanation of the scheme, it will be recognised that it is essential, if an envelope containing a record is to stand vertically, that it must exactly fit between the upper and lower strips of corrugated paper. Naturally, if the space is not high enough, there is no way of making it serve; but should it be too high, there are several methods of overcoming the difficulty. For instance, a strip of three-ply may be glued to the shelf under the corrugated paper, or the envelopes can be made a trifle on the large side, so that they catch into the grooves.

From what has been said, it is clear that the envelopes must all be of a standard size. If a habit is made of always patronising the same dealer of records, and if the dealer supplies the records in a stiff uniform case, then there is no reason why the bookshelf should not be adapted to take these cases. But it is more likely that records are purchased here and there, and the cases supplied with them are of odd dimensions. Then it is necessary to make a supply of cases all alike in pattern and size.

How to Construct the Envelopes.

There are various ways of constructing the cases, but after a certain amount of experience, the following method can be advised. Obtain some pliable cardboard, not too thick and not of the kind that easily cracks. Cut it into pieces wide enough to take a record, and long enough to stand in the corrugated grooves, without being too tight a fit. Then cut pieces of brown paper about ⅛ inch larger both ways than the cardboard. Place a sheet of the paper on one of the cards and slip a record between them; then bind up the top, bottom and one side with adhesive paper, such as can be bought in coils, 1 inch wide. As soon as the binding is done, carefully take out the record, cut a half-circle in the unbound edge for a thumb hole, and do not use the envelope until the binding has had time to dry and harden.

Fig. 3.—A Home-made Envelope.
Note the tab which permits the easy withdrawal of the envelope.

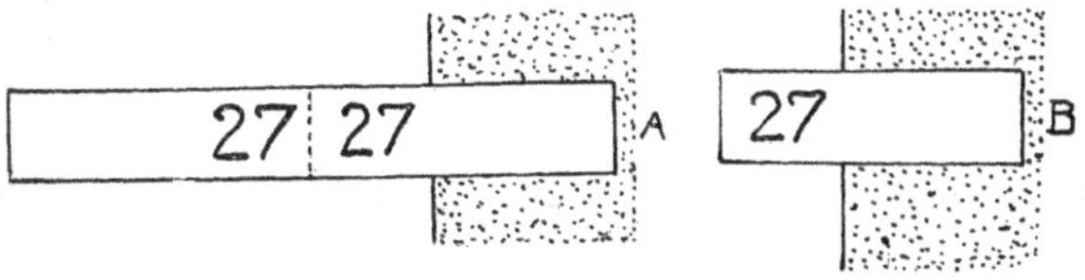

Fig. 4.—How the Tab is Stuck on the Envelope.
A strip of gummed paper is fixed as shown in A, and then doubled back as in B.

It should be, perhaps, explained that the object in binding the two materials together with a record between them is to prevent the card and the paper being joined up too tightly. If they are stuck together without anything between them, it is quite possible that a record will refuse to enter the envelope when it is finished.

Practical Notes on Book Repairs

It is not a bad plan to spend an evening, now and again, in going through one's store of books and doing any little repairs that may be needed. Usually, the work will be found quite interesting, and it will often be the means of giving many volumes a new lease of life.

Torn Pages.

The first thing will be to deal with any cases of torn pages. It often happens, when the leaves of a book are turned over hurriedly, that the corner of a page is torn completely off, or it may be that a page is ripped for a considerable part of its length. In either case, the repair is a simple one. Place a sheet of paper close to the edge of the work table, hold the book so that the damaged page lies flat on the sheet of paper and so that all the other pages are held out of the way. Then refit the torn part and stick a strip of adhesive transparent paper across the tear. Press down the strip and cut it at the ends to correspond with the edges of the page.

Loose Pages.

Often the binding stitches of a book give way and one or more pages become loose. Here the remedy depends on the condition of the binding and the number of leaves that are affected. If the cloth back is loose and an even number of consecutive leaves have become unattached, place each pair of leaves flat on the worktable and stick a strip of adhesive paper down the creased middle. When dry, refold the leaves and stitch them into the book, carrying the stitches out through the back and passing them again to the front.

If only a Single Leaf is Loose.

If only a single leaf is loose, stick a strip of adhesive paper along the inner edge of the leaf so that only a half of its width is attached and the other half is not. Then stitch the sheet into position, as before, and finish off by sticking the free half of the strip to the adjoining page.

Fig. 3.—A Loose Back can be fixed with Pieces of Linen Tape.
Note how each piece is split so that it may be stuck half on the cover and half on the stack of pages.

What to do if Stitching is not Possible.

When a page is loose and the cloth back is in good condition, it will not be possible to do any stitching. Then the best method is to place the page in position, to fold a strip of adhesive paper lengthwise, and to stick it so that one part of the fold grips the loose page and the other part is attached to the adjoining page. When this plan is followed it is usually necessary to trim a very narrow strip off the side edge of the page, as it is almost impossible to tuck it quite far enough into the book.

Loose Covers.

It often happens, especially in the case of old volumes, that the cover comes away from the rest of the book. Many people effect a repair of this nature by sticking the cloth back quite flat on the stitched edge of the leaves. This should not be done, as it prevents the book opening properly.

The Correct Treatment.

The correct way is to cut three or four strips of linen tape, each twice the width of the back of the book, and to stick them at regular intervals horizontally across the stitched back. The tapes should be arranged so that they overhang the back equally on both sides. When they have become quite firm, each projecting end is cut along the middle, lengthwise, the cover is arranged in its correct position, and the strips are stuck with one flap on the cover and the other flap on the first or last leaf of the book.

When these hinges have had time to dry and harden, the cover will be quite firm and the book opens as well as it did when new. All that remains is to paste a strip of paper along the hinged edge of both covers, so as to hide the flaps and, also, to give them strength.

If a cover is becoming loose, but has not yet parted company from the rest of the book, it will often be sufficient to stick a length of adhesive tape along the hinged edge in such a way that half the width of the tape holds the inside of the cover and the other half holds the nearest page. Naturally, this should be done to both the front and the back cover.

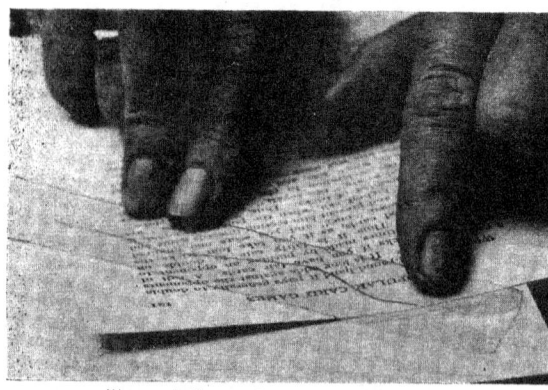

Fig. 2.—When One or More Pages become Loose due to the Binding Stitches giving way, the Pages should be fixed in by means of a Strip of Adhesive Paper.

Fig. 1.—A Simple Repair for a Torn Page.
Refit the torn part and stick a strip of adhesive transparent paper across the tear. Press down the strip and cut it at the ends to correspond with the edges of the pages.

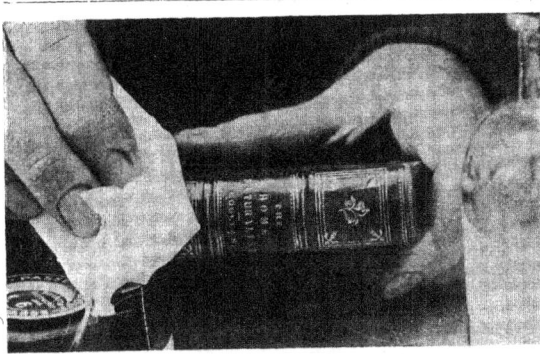

Fig. 4.—To Clean and Refresh a Leather Cover, mix up a little Milk with White of Egg in equal quantities and rub on with a Clean Rag.

When all the surfaces have been treated polish with a piece of silk.

Providing New "End Papers."

In cases where much sticking has been done on the inner faces of the cover, it is advisable to provide fresh end papers, as these will serve to hide the repairs. To fit an end paper, select a piece of paper which accords with the style of the book—it may be white, coloured or patterned. Fold it down the middle and cut one side exactly equal in dimensions to the old end paper that is pasted on the cover, and at this point leave the other side untrimmed. Stick the trimmed piece on the cover and see that the fold comes accurately in the hinge of the book. Then shut the book, turn it over, and pencil three lines on the untrimmed leaf, which should be projecting on three sides. The pencil marks must be guided by the stack of pages forming the book. That done, open the book and cut neatly along the pencilled lines.

It may be thought that a much easier way would be to cut both the leaves of the end paper before any sticking is attempted. If this is done, the flying leaf will never exactly cover the first leaf of the book, seeing that it is impossible to tell how much of it will be taken up by the hinge of the book.

Cleaning Cloth Covers.

When a volume has been kept for several years, the spine or back is likely to be dulled by grime. If the cover is faced with cloth, linen or buckram, it can often be made to look new and fresh by giving it a rub with a rag dipped in petrol. When it is dangerous to use petrol, because there is a fire in the room or because people are smoking, it is advisable to resort to one of the proprietary substitutes, which are non-inflammable, but equally serviceable.

If much rubbing is needed to remove the grime, it is possible that some of the colour may be taken off by the rag. When this occurs, it is, usually, advisable to recolour the whole of the outside of the cover. For this take one of the dyes sold for dying fabrics, and make up a small quantity in a concentrated form; then go over the surfaces with water, blot

Fig. 5.—Old Leather-bound Books are apt to Perish.

Smear with a trace of vaseline or dab with salad oil. If necessary fit a new patch of leather to the corners. Ordinary paste with a little alum added can be used to stick the patch down.

off the moisture, and paint on the dye with a wide brush. Apply it in long sweeps and do not stop until the whole is covered.

Cleaning Leather Covers.

The best substance for cleaning and refreshing a leather cover is benzine, which is almost as inflammable as petrol. If it is dangerous to use this spirit in the workroom, it is usually possible to do the cleansing in some passage, far away from any naked flame, seeing that it will only take a minute or two. The benzine should be rubbed on with a wad of cotton wool, the wad being reformed each time the face becomes soiled.

Another Method.

Another plan, which can be recommended, is to mix up a little milk with white of egg, in equal quantities, and to rub this on with a clean rag. When all the surfaces have been treated, polish with a piece of silk. This will provide a very attractive finish.

Recolouring a Leather Binding.

Should it be necessary to recolour the leather covering, first clean the surfaces with benzine, so that all traces of grease may be removed, and then use one of the spirit stains sold by leathercraft merchants for the purpose. It is advisable to apply the colour in light washes, repeating the operation two or three times, or until the exact shade is reached. This method provides a more even colouring than is likely to be obtained by one heavy wash of the stain.

Reinforcing the Backs of Paper-covered Books.

All sorts of books, magazines, pieces of sheet music, and other publications with paper covers soon fall to pieces if handled at all roughly. Once a back splits, the stitches become loose and the pages fall out. If the book, piece of music or whatever it happens to be is worth keeping, run a strip of adhesive tape down the back, so that it wraps over on to the sides. It is only the work of a moment, but it will save the publication from ruin.

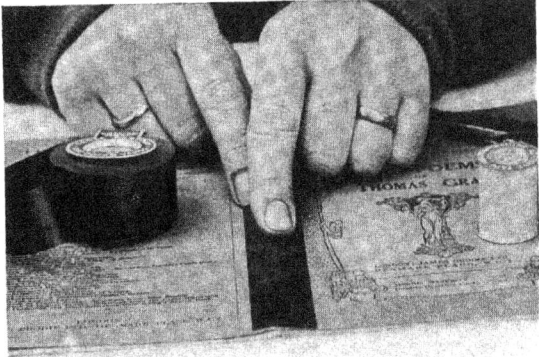

Fig. 6.—Paper-covered Books should be Strengthened by Sticking a Strip of Adhesive Tape down the Back to prevent the Cover breaking in Two.

Note how the tape wraps over on to the sides.

How to Make a Child's Scooter

Few toys give greater pleasure to children than a scooter on which they can career about the garden.

The child's pleasure is enhanced when the scooter (Fig. 1) is the handiwork of father or uncle.

The cost of material is trivial, and the technical skill required is of a very modest order.

Materials Required.

Footboard.—1 piece deal, 18¾ × 4 × ⅞ inches.

Steering Post.—1 piece oak or hardwood, 1⅜ inches square, 26 inches long.

Handle.—1 piece oak or hardwood, 9 inches long, 1¼ inches wide, ⅞ inch thick.

Wheels.—Two. 4 inches diameter, complete with spindles and rubber tyres.

Bearing Plates.—4 pieces iron, 1 inch wide, 3/32 inch thick, 6 inches long.

Steering Head.—Iron, 1 piece 1 inch wide, 3/32 inch thick, 20 inches long; 1 piece 6 inches long.

One steel bolt and nut 5/16 inch diameter, 4 inches long.

First Make the Footboard.

Begin by making the footboard, which should be sawn to the shape and dimensions given in Fig. 3, and made smooth with sandpaper.

Next the Steering Post.

Next prepare the steering post by working a chamfer on all four corners,

Fig. 1.—The Scooter in Use.
This simply-made toy will provide endless enjoyment for a youngster.

but " stopping " the chamfer about 3 inches from each end. This can be done with a chisel—cutting diagonally downwards across the grain as in Fig. 4, and finishing off by planing the corner.

Now the Handle.

The handle has to be very securely fixed to the steering post, for which purpose a form of halving joint is used. First, however, shape the handle as shown in Fig. 5, carving it to as neat a curved form as possible, and finishing by sandpapering. Hold the sandpaper in one hand, grip the wood with it, and rotate the wood briskly with the other hand.

Joining Handle to Steering Post.

Next cut a groove across the front centre of the handle, as in Fig. 6, and cut a corresponding groove across the back face of the steering post. Make this joint fit nicely, but do not fasten it at this stage.

Give the woodwork a coat of varnish and leave it to dry; meanwhile, prepare the various iron fittings.

THE IRONWORK

Two iron plates shaped and drilled as shown in Fig. 7 are needed for the front forks, they are quite easy to make; a centre line is first drawn along the metal, then the centres for the three holes are measured off and " centre popped "—that is, a conical-pointed punch is used to make a slight indentation in the metal exactly at the centre of the hole. The holes can be drilled with an ordinary carpenter's brace, and a " metal drill bit," or a small hand drill, can be used. Both plates should be drilled at the same

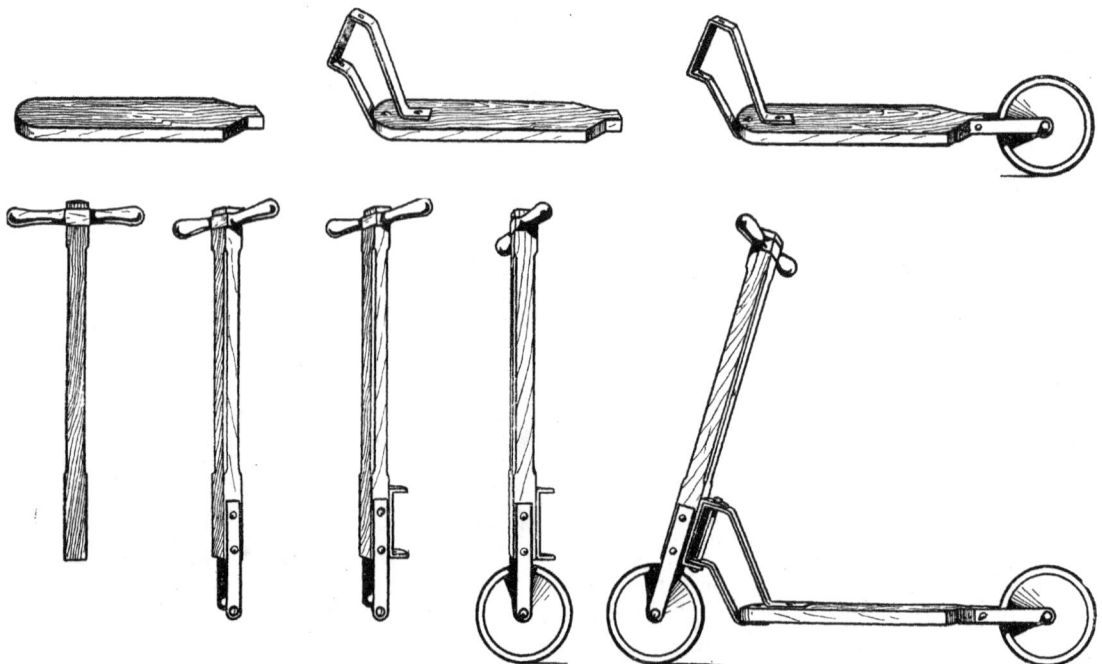

Fig. 2.—Diagram showing the Various Stages in Construction and Assembly.
Details and sizes of the various parts are given in the drawings on the facing page.

HOW TO MAKE A CHILD'S SCOOTER

time, or the second can be drilled while using the first as a guide.

Back Bearing Plates.

The two back bearing plates are similarly made, but after drilling the holes the metal has to be bent, as shown in Fig. 8, which is easily done by gripping the metal in the vice exactly at the place where it is to be bent, and then hammering the metal to bend it the required amount.

Fastening the Bearing Plates.

Fasten the bearing plates to the footboard and steering post respectively with 3/16-inch diameter steel bolts and nuts, passed through holes drilled in the wood for that purpose.

Making the Steering Head.

Work on the steering head is similar in nature to that employed when making the bearing plates.

The fork—shown in Fig. 9—should

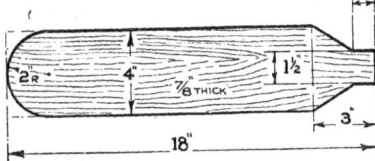

Fig. 3.—Dimensions of the Footboard.

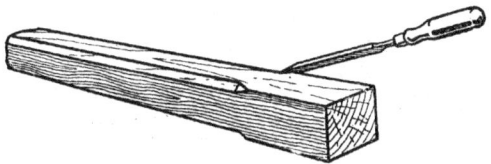

Fig. 4.—Preparing the Steering Post.
This is stop champfered as shown. A bevel is planed on each edge and is finished a few inches from the top end by chiselling.

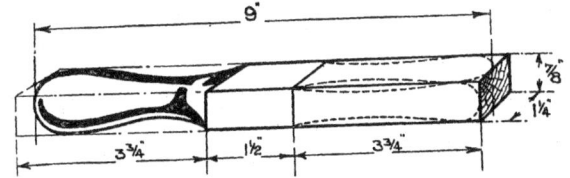

Fig. 5.—Detail of the Handle which is shaped with a Chisel and Sandpaper.

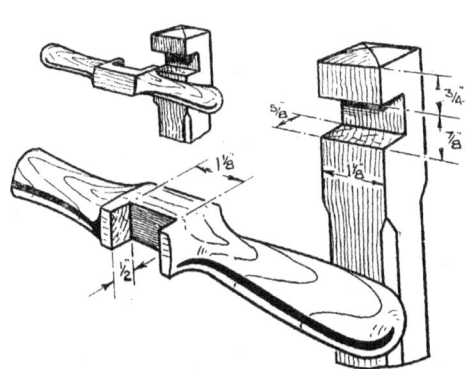

Fig. 6.—The Top Joint.
The handle is fixed to the steering post with a halved joint.

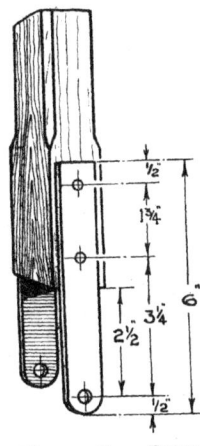

Fig. 7.—The Front Bearing Plate.

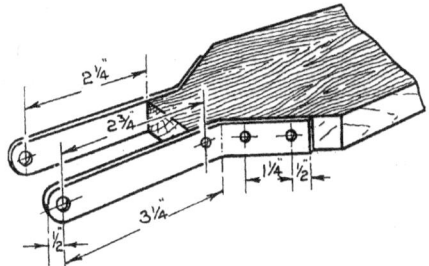

Fig. 8.—The Back Bearing Plate.

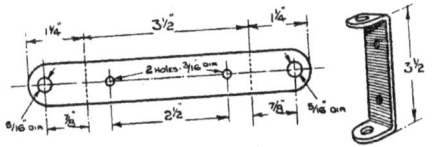

Fig. 9.—The Steering Fork.

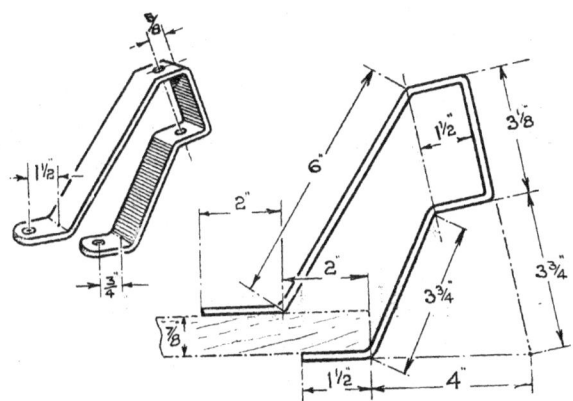

Fig. 10.—The Steering Head.
This should be bent to shape first and then drilled.

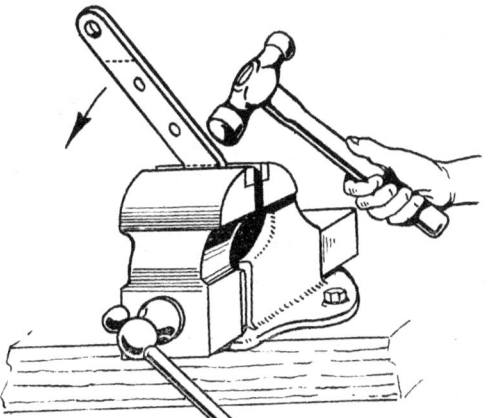

Fig. 11.—Bending the Metal.

be drilled before bending to shape, but the head—shown in Fig. 10—should first be bent to shape.

How to Ensure Accuracy.

To ensure accuracy, the strip of metal should be marked out with chalk, a line being drawn across the metal at the places where bends are to be made. The metal is then gripped in the vice—as shown in Fig. 11—and bent over as far as possible by hand, and then trued up by hammering. A good plan is to make a full-size outline drawing of the shape to which the metal has to be bent and lay the metal on it from time to time.

Mark out the positions for the holes, centre pop and drill them as before, then give all the metal parts a coat of black enamel. When dry, assemble them as shown in Fig. 12,

Fig. 12.—The Steering Head Assembled.

and make sure all the nuts are tightened up.

Fixing the Wheels.

Put the wheels between the forks formed by the bearing plates, and put the axles through the holes therein. If necessary, ease the holes with a round file. Do not forget to lubricate the axles and wheel hubs. Paint the wheels a bright red or other colour; fasten the handle to the steering post with glue and a fine screw, and finish the job with a coat of copal or hard oak varnish.

Slight Variations of Dimensions are Permissible.

Note that the dimensions given in this article suit the average stock wheels, but any slight variations can easily be made to suit any other width or diameter of wheel.

STENCILLING WITH BRONZE POWDERS

STENCILLING is one of the most interesting forms of home decoration, and is certainly one of the simplest and quickest ways of ornamenting materials that has ever been invented. The most usual form of stencilling is that in which oil colours are used, and this method is described in detail on page 138.

There is, however, a less well-known but very decorative way of doing the work, namely, with bronze powders, on silk, crêpe-de-Chine, satin and other fabrics. These powders are known by various names, sometimes as metal powders or Florescan colours—but if you ask for bronze powders you will get what you want.

Work done with these powders has a metallic iridescent effect, which is most attractive, especially if stencilled on black crêpe-de-Chine, satin or Jap silk.

After a certain amount of practice it can be made to look like embroidery worked in metallic threads, and can make a bridge or evening coat, dresses, scarves, cushions and so on look extremely handsome.

Materials Required.

Unlike ordinary stencilling, which is worked with a stiff bristle brush, soft brushes are required for bronze stencilling. A brush called a Japanese stencil brush is the one to use, but care must be taken to watch for loose hairs, as these brushes are bound in a square shape, which makes it almost impossible not to have a few unattached hairs. If, however, before using the brush it is tapped sharply on the side of the hand, the loose hairs will usually work out, and can be picked off. A separate brush is required for each colour.

You will also need the little glass bottles of bronze powders of the shades you are requiring for your scheme of colour, and a bottle of bronze medium or Florescan medium.

Do Not Use Stale Colours.

Put your powders separately in one saucer and your medium in another. Do not put out more than you will require for your immediate needs, as it is false economy to use stale colours and medium. Any material not used one day will be no use the next. It is better to start afresh each time.

How the Work is Done.

Choose a simple design to start with until you get used to the working.

Put some sheets of blotting paper on a drawing-board, and pin the material to be stencilled down firmly on to it. Next pin the stencil plate on to the material, leaving one corner free, so that, if necessary, you can lift it to see how you are getting on.

Picking up the Powder.

Now dip your brush lightly into the medium, so that just a little is picked up on the tips of the hairs, and then rub into the powder until the surface of the brush is covered with colour.

Have an odd piece of blotting-paper by you, so that you can now rub this brush of colour very gently over it, the object being to prevent any tiny lumps of powder which may collect on the brush from being transferred to the silk.

This done, proceed to stencil in the usual way, although sometimes with these powders it will be found best to work with a circular action instead of the more usual "dabbing" one. It will, however, depend largely on the surface of the fabric.

Don't Pile on the Colour.

Great care must be taken to avoid piling on the colour, or this will make your work look coarse and lose its daintiness. It will be found better to put on two thin coats of one colour than one thick coat.

When Working on Black.

When working on a black material make your first colour either silver or pale gold as a background for the other colours, and then shade your other colours on to either or both of these. For example, if you were stencilling a butterfly, you could do it first in silver all over, then a little way down the wing stencil in pale blue and then purple.

If warmer colouring is preferred, use silver, then gold, next a deeper gold and, finally, red. These are, of course, only suggestions.

Working on a Light Material.

If you are doing this form of decoration on a light material, it is, of course, desirable to make it washable. Therefore, use washable Florescan medium which, if used properly, really does wash well.

To give a really hard wear it is sometimes advisable, after it is dry, to spray it with Florescan fixative as further security from rubbing off.

Care of the Brushes.

The brushes should be well washed in turpentine each time you finish your work, and periodically after this wash them in warm, soapy water to keep them soft.

TIME, LABOUR AND MONEY SAVING IDEAS

A HINT WHEN MOVING

Most people, when moving into a new house, feel the need for hot water, either for scrubbing floors before the lino or carpets go down, and in any case for the ever-welcome cup of tea. Many are the makeshifts resorted to on such occasions. The gas-cooker is usually the very last thing to be installed in the new home, for usually a plumber has to be requisitioned for the installation. By far the best plan

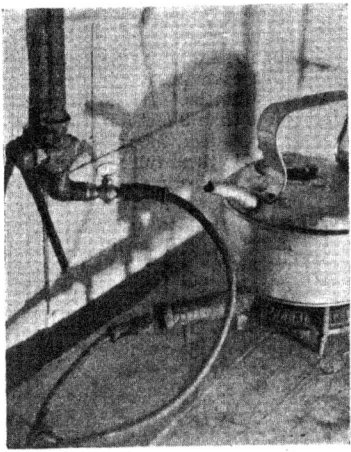

is to notify the gas company supplying the new home some time beforehand that a supply, and the necessary meter, will be required. At the same time, for a very nominal charge, they will fit a "tube-cock" to take flexible gas tubing, to a convenient point, such as that from which the gas-cooker supply is subsequently to be taken. The handyman used to such elementary jobs will find the latter a very simple matter to perform for himself. Then a plentiful supply of hot water is assured, even before removal from the old house has commenced.

CLEAN WATER

Rain water is so useful in the house that steps should be taken to catch as much as possible. The trouble is that, in its passage over roofs, the water collects a lot of smuts and it is not by any means clean. A good way of ensuring that the water is clean is on the following lines. From strong linen, or similar material, make a good-sized bag, which is tied over the mouth of the pipe. The bag is first filled with small, clean pebbles. As the water drains through the pebbles it is cleared of all smuts, etc., and comes out crystal clear. The pebbles should be taken out now and then and thoroughly washed to keep them in an efficient state.

AQUARIUM CEMENTS

There is a number of different types of cements employed for cementing the glass panels of aquaria to the corner angles and base.

One of the simplest is Chatterton's compound—a black pitchy substance sold at most hardware stores and electrical shops. This is melted by using a warmed knife or iron and run into the corners. The glass panels are then pressed into position.

Another good cement is composed of the following ingredients:—

Pitch	6 ozs.
Shellac	4 "
Rubber	2 "

These are melted together by heating over a gas-burner. Some other satisfactory recipes for aquarium cements are as follows:—

(1) Red lead . . . 3 ozs.
    Litharge. . . . 1 oz.
    Raw linseed oil Sufficient to make to a paste.

(2) Finely powdered
    litharge . . . 3 parts.
    Fine silver sand . . 3 "
    Plaster of Paris . . 3 "
    Resin . . . . 1 part.

Mix these well and add linseed oil to which a little drier has been added. This gives an exceedingly strong cement which will withstand both fresh and salt water action.

A NAIL IN A PLASTER WALL

It is often very difficult to get a nail to hold in a plaster wall. Here is a good hint for such times. File

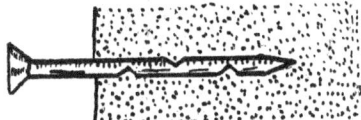

notches in the side of the nail as shown in the sketch. Then dip the nail in hot liquid glue and drive it into the plaster. Such a nail will hold well for an indefinite period.

A USE FOR AN OLD UMBRELLA

If you have an old umbrella which is no longer worth re-covering, strip the covering from the framework and use the latter as a clothes' drier for articles such as collars and handkerchiefs on wet days. A hook should be fixed in the ceiling, in the kitchen or scullery, so that the umbrella may hang near the range. To improve its appearance, the frame may be given a coat of enamel paint, and when not in use it can be closed and put away.

A SCREW DRIVING HINT

A handy little tool for the driving of very small screws can be made on the lines shown in the photograph. Get two short pieces from a spring and then push the ends into a wooden

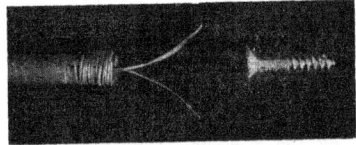

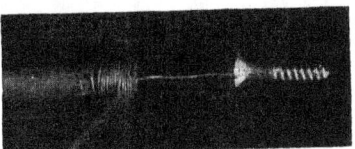

holder, finally binding securely with wire. The pieces of spring should be arranged so that they open away from one another. When dealing with a screw the springs are brought together in the groove, as indicated, and there is practically no risk of slipping at all. Screws in awkward places can also be easily handled with this tool.

TO CLEAN THE CHIMNEY

Place 2 ozs. of fine flowers of sulphur on the fire when it is bright red and glowing. This will be found to remove accumulations of soot from the flues and will enable you to postpone the visit of the sweep.

A BONFIRE HINT

When it is wished to burn up a lot of rubbish, like garden material which may not be very dry, there is often a difficulty in getting a brisk fire. A very good way of ensuring that the mass burns well is to arrange things in the following manner. Get a tin can, and with the tin-opener make holes in the bottom and round the sides.

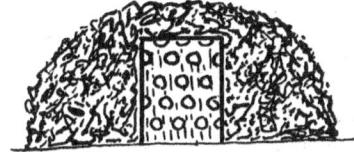

Stand the can, in an inverted position, on the ground where it is wished to have the fire. Then pile the stuff to be burned lightly over the can. Make an opening along the ground to the can and, into this, push paper or any dry kindling. Set alight and soon there will be a fine fire. The perforated can in the mass ensures that there shall be a good supply of air at the heart of the fire, and this encourages a free burning.

Paper Hanging
ON WALLS AND CEILINGS

DESPITE all the competing forms of decoration, paperhangings still maintain their popularity for the adornment of the walls and, to a lesser extent, the ceilings of the modern home.

There are good reasons for this continued vogue. In the first place, a surface is much more quickly decorated with paper than with, say, paint: and the householder likes to have a room out of use for as short a time as possible.

Secondly, not all walls are perfect, and a wallpaper hides a multitude of small defects. And, thirdly, wallpaper has a kind of durability and usefulness all its own. Small knocks and abrasions do not show readily, and the absorbent nature of the paper prevents the moisture caused by condensation from detrimentally affecting it and, therefore, avoids those rather unsightly "runs" sometimes seen on a painted or varnished surface.

A further, and often decisive, consideration is that the hanging of wallpapers, while calling for care, does not demand a very high degree of technical skill, always provided that the right methods are adopted.

Classification.

The general principles governing selection of suitable patterns have been described in the article on p. 53 of this work, and we need not dwell on that aspect of the matter here. But a few additional notes respecting the different classes of wallpapers may be useful at this point.

The cheapest class of papers are the "pulps." These are goods where the natural colour of the paper forms the ground, upon which a pattern, in one or more other shades, is printed.

"Grounds" are a rather better quality, in which one colour is laid all over the paper and the pattern is printed over that ground in other colours.

"Sanitaries" are printed in oil colours and can, therefore, be sponged if necessary. If they are varnished, they can be washed or even scrubbed.

There is a class of paper largely used for ceilings called "Micas," from the fact that the pattern is printed with white mica powder, which has a sort of satin sheen. And there are other classifications too numerous to mention here.

Fig. 1.—Old Wallpapers should be Stripped off.
The old paper should first be thoroughly soaked and then stripped off either with the scraper or stripping knife.

Calculating Quantities.

When a pattern has been decided upon it is necessary to calculate the quantity required, and if the whole of, say, the ceiling or walls of a room are to be covered with one pattern, this calculation is comparatively simple.

English wallpapers are almost always made in pieces of about $11\frac{1}{2}$ yards long by 21 inches wide, and this fact is the basis of all our reckoning.

Two methods of measurement may be described. One is to measure the whole of the surfaces to be covered, and reduce these measurements to the total number of square yards.

The superficial area of a roll of paper is about 7 square yards; but we must make an allowance for the inevitable waste. So, if we take the total number of square yards to be covered, and divide that total by six, it will give us the required number of rolls, or "pieces" as they are called.

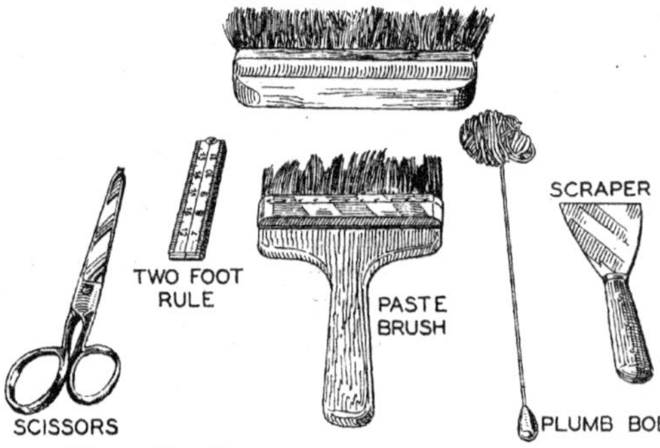

An Alternative Method.

Another method much favoured by some paperhangers is as follows. The height of the walls to be covered is measured and, if it is not more than $7\frac{1}{2}$ feet, it is safe to assume that each piece will cut four full lengths. If the height is more than 8 feet and not more than 10 feet, the rolls will each provide three full lengths.

Remembering that the lengths are all 21 inches wide, it is easy to calculate how many full lengths will be required. The total number of full lengths required is then divided by three or four as the case may be, and the resulting figure is the number of pieces required.

For the purposes of this kind of calculation, all short lengths required for over doors and above and below windows are ignored, as there will be some surplus from each piece that will suffice to cover these, but it is advisable to count those over the mantelpiece as full lengths.

Measuring Ceilings.

In measuring for ceilings, the same method may be adopted, except that, as ceiling lengths are generally longer than those required for walls, the dividing number may not be more than two, and is seldom more than three. The guiding principle to be observed is that all lengths hung shall be complete; broken lengths are quite inadmissible in correct paperhanging.

Let us assume, now, that we are to paper the walls of a room, that we have selected an appropriate pattern, and that a sufficient number of rolls have been purchased and are at hand. The room has been cleared of all pictures, hangings and portable articles of furniture.

Preparing the Surface.

The next operation is to prepare the surfaces to receive the paper. If they are bare plaster never before treated, preparation is simple. It consists in dusting down the walls and applying a coat of thin size, which is made by melting $\frac{1}{2}$ lb. of concentrated

Fig. 2.—The Tools required for Paperhanging.

PAPER HANGING

size powder in, say, a gallon of boiling water by stirring, and allowing the solution to cool before use.

The object of this sizing is not to stop all suction, but to reduce and equalise it.

If the surface has been previously distempered with ordinary size distemper, this must be thoroughly washed off, otherwise the paper will not adhere for long. After washing off the distemper, a coat of thin size must be applied.

If the walls or ceiling under treatment have been previously treated with water paint or washable distemper and that material is quite fast (which means impervious to moist rubbing), no preparation beyond a dusting or a swill down with water is called for. But if the old material is not fast, so much of it as is loose should be washed off and the surface should then be coated with weak size.

Stripping Old Papers.

Old papers should be stripped off. Provided that the old paper is quite firmly affixed, it is possible to paper over it, but this course is not advisable for three reasons.

One is that, although the old paper may appear fast, it may loosen when the paste of the new paper moistens it. Another is that, if new paper is applied over old, the joints of the underneath paper may show through. And, lastly, it is best to remove old papers for hygienic reasons, as the old paste, being a vegetable product, decays with the passage of time.

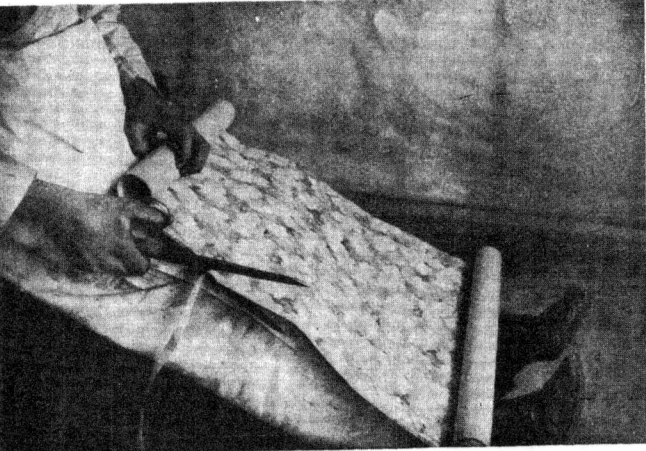

Fig. 3.—How to trim the Edges of Wallpaper.
This is done by alternately rolling with the left hand and cutting with the right. The roll is then replaced on the feet and the other edge trimmed the same.

Fig. 4.—Striking a Line on a Wall from which to begin Paper Hanging.

Old paper can be easily removed by first thoroughly soaking it with water and then stripping with a scraper or stripping knife. A washing down of the bared plaster will clear away any remaining traces of paper or paste not removed by the knife. Then a coat of thin size may be applied.

Repairing Cracks.

It may be that the walls contain cracks or have been damaged in some way. Such defects should be made good with either plaster of Paris, mixed with water and used immediately after mixing, or with Keene's cement. The cracks should be wetted before the plaster is inserted, and the face of the said plaster should be made quite smooth with the knife or trowel.

The Tools Required.

In paper hanging these are:

A large pair of scissors, which must be kept sharp and clean.

A paste brush (a part-worn whitewash brush is ideal for this purpose, or a special brush with rather short bristles can be purchased at most paint stores).

A paperhanger's brush (cheap types of these brushes are now available for amateur use).

A 2-foot rule.

A plumb bob (which is merely a length of string with a small weight at one end).

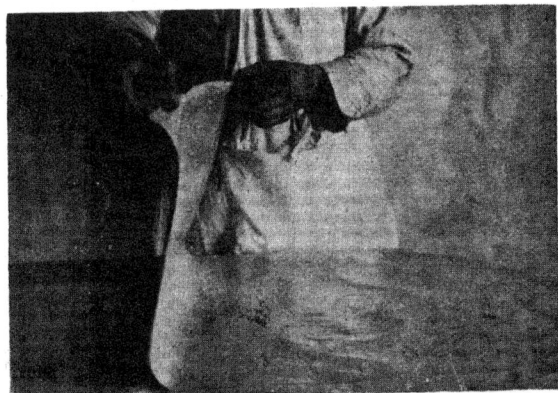

Fig. 5.—After Pasting take hold of the Corners between First Finger and Thumb and fold it over on itself, making sure that the Under and Over Edges coincide.

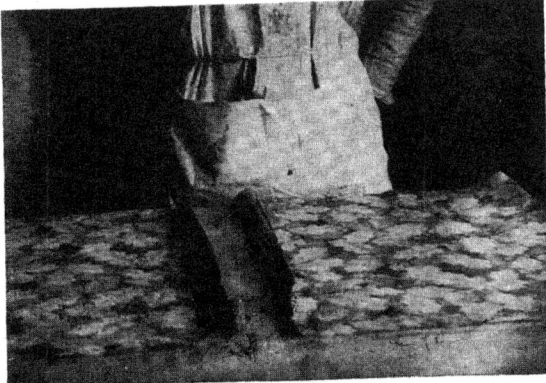

Fig. 6.—About an Inch at each End of the Length of Paper is left Unpasted.
This enables the paper to be handled without getting paste on the hands.

PAPER HANGING

Fig. 7.—THE FOLDED LENGTH OF PAPER IS CARRIED DRAPED OVER THE LEFT ARM FROM THE PASTEBOARD TO THE WALL.

Fig. 8.—IN TRIMMING THE BOTTOM EDGE MAKE A LINE BY DRAWING THE SCISSORS ALONG THE ANGLE OF THE WALL AND SKIRTING BOARD.
Then lift paper away slightly and cut with scissors.

A chalk line (which is a length of ordinary soft twine).

A table, a step-ladder, and a bucket.

Making Paste.

Some good paste will be required. Many quite satisfactory paste powders are obtainable, and making them up from the printed instructions on the package is a very simple operation.

Should it be desired to make up ordinary flour paste the following is one of several ways of preparing it.

Take 4 lbs. of flour, mix it into a perfectly smooth batter in a bucket by gradually adding cold water and constantly stirring. Then add more cold water to the total quantity of about a gallon. Then place the mixture over a fire or stove, constantly stirring until it boils, when it will, at once, thicken. Then remove it to a cool place, pour a little cold water on the surface to prevent skinning, and let it remain until quite cold. It is well worth while to strain the paste before use so as to remove any lumps there may be in it.

Trimming the Rolls.

Before the wallpaper is cut up, it is necessary to remove the selvedge edge. Many of the wallpaper stores do this for their customers by means of a machine. But, if the paper is untrimmed, the following procedure is usually followed.

Fig. 9.—PASTING THE PAPER.
Lay paper face downwards on the table. Paste the left end of paper first, and allow sheet to hang over the other end of the table.

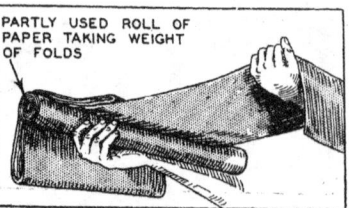

Fig. 11.—HOW TO PICK UP A LONG PASTED LENGTH OF PAPER.

Fig. 10.—AVOID PASTING THE TABLE.
Make sure the edge of the paper overhangs the edge of the table. This will prevent the paste from getting on the surface of the table, and will enable the paper to be kept clean.

Fig. 12.—NOTE HOW THE PASTED AND FOLDED PAPER IS HUNG FROM THE CENTRE OVER THE LEFT FOREARM.

Sitting on a chair, the worker extends his legs to their full extent, keeping the feet slightly apart. He places a roll on his feet, and takes hold of the end with his left hand. The edge is trimmed by means of the scissors held in the right hand, while the paper is drawn forward and re-rolled with the left. And this process of alternately rolling with the left hand and cutting with the right is continued until the whole of one edge of the roll is trimmed. The roll is then replaced on the feet and the other edge is trimmed in the same way.

For all good-class papers, both edges should certainly be trimmed. Cheap thin papers are sometimes only trimmed on one edge, but the writer prefers to trim both.

Cutting up.

In cutting up the rolls into the appropriate lengths, two allowances must be made: one for trimming top and bottom (2 or 3 inches in each case) and the other for matching the pattern.

Patterns are of two kinds: "set"

and "drop." "Set" patterns are those which match horizontally. "Drop" patterns match at different points on the two edges of the paper. And care must be taken to distinguish between the two types in cutting up the paper. When the pattern is of the "drop" kind, waste can sometimes be avoided by cutting alternate lengths from different rolls.

A number of lengths having been cut, they are placed in a pile, pattern side down on the table.

Striking Lines.

Before beginning to hang a wallpaper, it is best to make a pencil mark on the wall 21 inches from the window. Then take the plumb line (the length of string with a weight at the end) and draw it over a piece of coloured chalk. Pin it to the top of the wall so that it will hang exactly over the pencil mark. Then, pressing it tightly to the wall near the skirting board with the left hand, pull it away, higher up, with the right hand, and sharply release it. This will leave a line marked on the wall.

The object of striking this line is to obtain an exactly perpendicular line from which to work.

Now we return to the cut lengths on the table. Push the pile well back and draw the top one forward. The front edge of the paper should be exactly level with the front edge of the table and the right-hand end level with the end of the table.

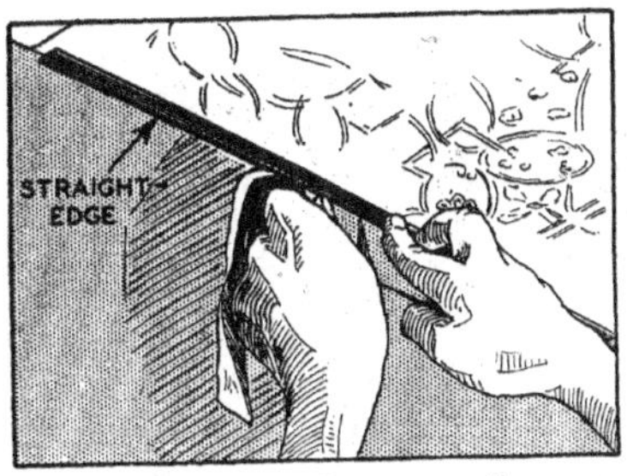

Pasting.

Then paste the length, working always outward from the centre to the edges so as to avoid getting any paste under those edges and on to the face of the paper. In pasting the back edge, insert the first finger of the left hand under the paper, lifting it slightly off the table just ahead of the brush. By so doing, the underlying length will be kept free from paste.

When all that portion of the length which is on the table is pasted, fold it in on itself, making sure that the upper fold is exactly over the lower.

Then draw this pasted and folded portion to the right, which will bring the remainder of the length on to the table. Now paste and fold this in exactly the same way. The two ends should then just about meet.

It will facilitate clean working if about an inch at each end is left unpasted. This will not matter because these ends will be cut off later in the final trimming on the wall.

All the time, a clean damp cloth should be available. With this, the worker should keep his hands, his scissors and the edge of the table scrupulously clean.

Hanging the Paper.

Take up the folded length, drape it over the left arm, and mount the ladder. The paper is now hung by holding the two top corners with the thumb and first finger of each hand, the second finger supporting the paper on the face side. The top half of the paper will then unfold itself by its own weight.

Now place the top edge of the paper against the wall in such a manner that there is an inch or two of excess at the top. See that the left hand perpendicular edge falls directly along the chalk line. That being done, run the fingers across the top of the paper to attach it to the wall.

Next, begin to brush (with the paperhanger's brush) the paper out, first down the centre and then from side to side, but making sure that the chalk line is being accurately followed.

Now pull the lower half of the length away from the wall, unfold it, and brush it out in the manner just described.

Trimming the Ends.

Run the point of the scissors along the top, thus making a line mark on the paper. Pull the paper away a little, cut it away at the mark, and brush the cut edge well back. Repeat this at the bottom, next to the skirting board.

The first length having been hung, the process is repeated all round the room, making sure, if the paper contains any sort of pattern, that the design is accurately matched at every joint.

The First Length.

The importance of hanging the first length

Fig. 13.—PAPERING A CEILING.
With the pasted sheet hanging on your left forearm, open the right-hand portion. Slip your right hand under the opened portion and offer it to the ceiling as shown in the above illustration.

Fig. 14.—THE NEXT STEP IN PAPERING A CEILING.
When the first portion has stuck you can proceed to brush the remainder of the paper to the ceiling. Holding the brush across the width of the paper, slowly walk down the scaffolding board.

Fig. 15.—A SIMPLE METHOD OF TRIMMING THE ENDS.
Hold a straight-edge against the corner and pull the paper away. The narrow strip will tear away quite easily and straight.

Fig. 16.—PAPERING A CEILING WITHOUT LADDERS AND BOARDS.

Fig. 17.—PAPERING A CEILING WITHOUT LADDERS AND BOARDS.

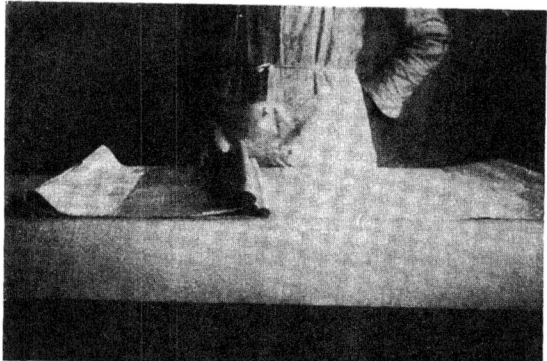

Fig. 18.—When folding a Ceiling Paper after Pasting, a Succession of Folds is formed.

Fig. 19.—Holding the folded Ceiling Paper while adjusting the End of the Starting Position.

correctly cannot be too much stressed. If it is not perfectly perpendicular, it will throw subsequent lengths wrong, so that the pattern, if any, will appear to be sloping up or down.

It is well to remember that the angles of a room are seldom quite straight. For that reason it is always advisable when approaching a corner to mark off and cut the paper into the angle. Before hanging the cut-off strip on the next wall, another line should be struck to work to. This will ensure a correct start on the new section of wall.

Panelling.

Where a wall is to be panelled the size of the panels should be determined and struck out in lines beforehand. The number of panels will be determined by personal taste and the positions in which the larger articles of furniture are to be placed. But it is a sound principle to have too few panels rather than too many. In the case of small rooms one panel to a wall is often enough, and even in large rooms three to the largest wall is generally quite sufficient.

Where there are to be three panels, it is seldom wise to have them all one size. A large centre

Fig. 20.—The End having been correctly applied to the Ceiling, the Worker then brushes out the Rest of the Length, releasing the Folds as he walks along the Plank.

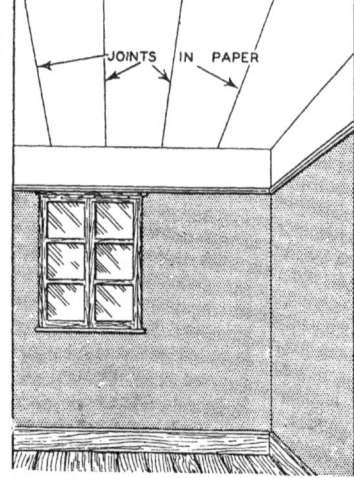

Fig. 21.—A Method of avoiding Joint Shadows in Ceiling Paper.

Hang the paper along the direction of the light with the laps facing the light.

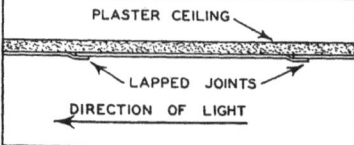

Fig. 22.—Another Method of avoiding Shadow Lines on a Ceiling.

Hang the paper so that the overlapping joints of the paper face the direction of the light.

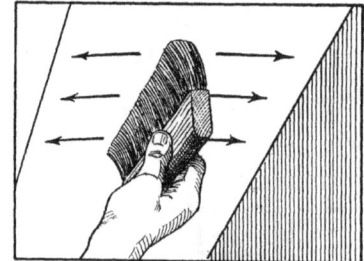

Fig. 23.—Method of brushing Paper to Ceiling

Work from centre to the edges.

and two flanking narrower panels is often a suitable arrangement. Several different arrangements are shown in the illustrations to the article on p. 53.

How Panels are Formed.

Panelling schemes are generally formed by hanging a plain or semi-plain paper to form the field of the panel and surrounding these, and dividing them from their neighbours, with what is called a "stiling" border. These borders are generally 7 or 10 inches wide. While the stiles are hung complete between the panels, they are often split in half for the top and bottom. Various arrangements are to be seen in Fig. 25, which also shows the various methods of "mitring" at the angles.

Cut-out Decorations.

Cut-out borders and built-up schemes are often used. In these goods the pattern is already punctured along its outline, and it is quite simple to tear off the selvedges with the fingers, after the paper has been pasted.

The paste used for these "cut-out" decorations should not be too thin. After fixing them lightly to the wall with the hand or brush, they should be pressed home with a soft clean rag, paying particular attention to the serrated edges.

PAPERING THE CEILING

In papering ceilings a rather different method is required.

A plank and two stepladders will be needed to form a scaffolding. Moreover, the lengths required will probably be longer than in the case of the walls, and therefore they will, in pasting, require to be folded rather differently. A succession of folds about 8 to 10 inches is a convenient form, as shown in the illustration.

The folded and pasted paper is carried on a spare roll in the left hand, and, when the worker has mounted the plank, he takes hold of the end of the paper in his right hand, applies it to the ceiling, and brushes it across so as to attach it properly. Then, walking along the plank, he brushes with the right hand while he allows the paper, upheld on the roll in his left hand, gradually to unfold.

This is not an easy thing to do correctly without considerable practice, and it is well to have an assistant who will hold up the pile of folded paper while his colleague does the fixing and brushing.

Right Place to Begin.

It is best to start papering a ceiling at the window side of the room, with the lengths running across the light. But even ceiling angles or plaster cornice edges are not always quite straight, and therefore it is best to strike a line through two marks made at each end, 21 inches from the ceiling angle or cornice, and work to this. The space between this line and the said angle or cornice can be filled in afterwards. The whole reason for the chalk lines is to begin on a perfectly straight line, and this is all-important if the job is to be neatly done.

Removing Whitewash from Ceilings.

This is at the best of times a messy job. To avoid ruining the wall finish and contents of the room, the walls, and such furniture as cannot be conveniently removed from the room, should be covered with dust sheets. These sheets should be attached to the top edge of the wall, close up to the angle of the ceiling, so as to afford the greatest possible protection. All carpets and similar furnishings should, of course, be taken up.

A Substitute for Dust Sheets.

If sufficient sheets completely to cover the walls are not easily procurable, sheets of brown paper of the type obtainable in rolls form can be used.

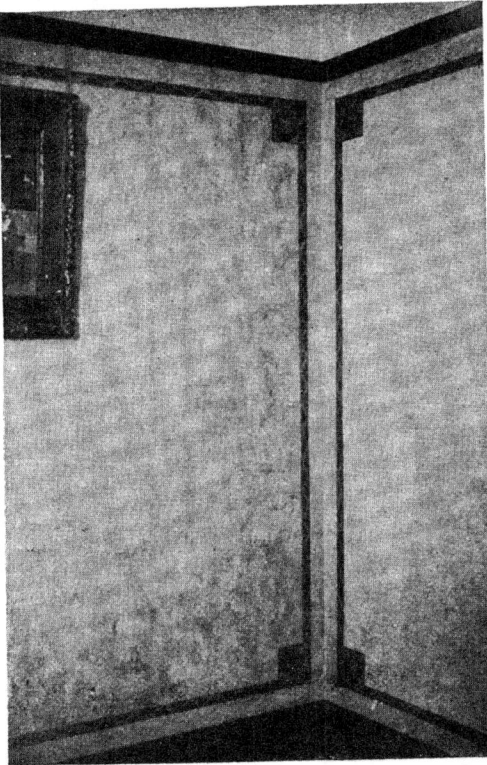

Fig. 24.—A Panelled Wallpaper Scheme. Showing half stile-border top and bottom with full width down corner of room. A square corner piece gives added effect.

Washing Down the Ceiling.

For the purpose of washing the ceiling, a large sponge is the best thing to use, or else a large whitewash brush.

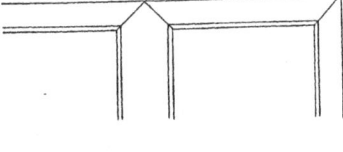

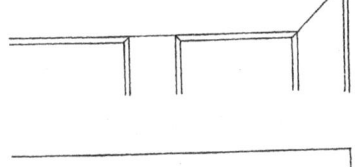

Fig. 25.—Various Methods of arranging and joining Stile Borders in Panelling.

The main point is to convey sufficient water to the ceiling. It is best to use hot water, because it has greater powers as a solvent of the glutinous binding of the whitewash, and also because it is more pleasant to use than cold water.

To Avoid Washing the Walls.

Start some little way from the walls to prevent too free an application of water from reaching the junction between the ceiling and the walls, and thus causing surplus water to get behind the protecting sheets and running down the wall, where it will cause unsightly marks which cannot be eradicated.

Use a Small Paint Brush when Dampering the Edges.

You can use as much water as you like over the centre area of the ceiling. When dealing with the edges it is a good plan to use a relatively small paint brush to apply the water, and then when the whitewash has become softened, finally remove it by gentle use of the scraper.

The Joints.

It can be taken as a good general rule that ceiling papers should be laid so that they run at right angles to the main window, and that the correct side to start laying the paper is from the window side.

Marking Guide Lines on a Ceiling.

It will be found a great help to mark a guide line on the ceiling to assist in placing the paper correctly. Such guide lines are easily marked with a length of string which has been suitably heated with a chalk of dark colour.

If your paper is 21 inches wide, mark off at one end of the ceiling a point 21 inches from the face of the wall, along which you will lay your first paper. One end of the chalked string is then lightly nailed on this point. The string is pulled taut at the other end of the room, the string pulled away from the ceiling and allowed to snap back into position, so that a chalk impression is left for you to follow when applying the paper.

The Essentials of Paper Hanging

The secret of good paper hanging largely consists of tasteful selection of the goods to be hung, careful planning and layout before hanging, and scrupulous cleanliness at every stage of the work. Given these conditions, a satisfactory result should be achieved.

Methods of Laying Concrete Crazy Paving

THE ordinary crazy paving stone used for garden paths and rock gardens is a natural stone quarried from mines or hill-sides. This stone may, however, be closely imitated by using concrete and cement mixtures under suitable conditions; moreover, the actual surface appearance, namely the texture and colour, can also be emulated.

One definite advantage of concrete crazy paving over the natural stone is that the former can be made with a perfectly flat surface, which is, of course, easier to walk upon than the natural stone. Moreover, the shapes of the artificial stone can be varied to suit one's actual requirements.

There is, also, the further advantage of cheapness, for the only cost is that of the materials.

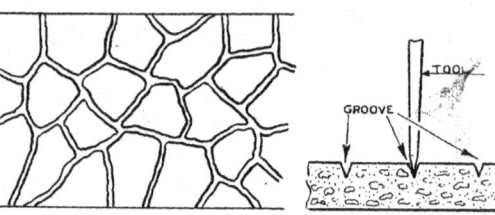

Fig. 1.—Showing Method of making Imitation Concrete Crazy Paving using a Pointed Tool to make Grooves in the Surface before the Concrete has Set Hard.

The Materials Used.

Although it is possible to save a certain amount of time by using the same material throughout for the crazy paving slabs, it is more economical to employ a somewhat coarser concrete mixture for the main body, and a finer cement mixture for the surface portion.

When selecting material for the concrete, it is advisable not to use any stones or other aggregate coarser than about 1 inch; that is to say, material that will pass through a 1-inch mesh sieve.

To form the main body concrete, one can either use about 5 parts of gravel to 1 part of Portland cement, or 3 parts of stones, chippings or similar aggregate, 2 parts of sand, and 1 part of cement.

For the surface layer a mixture of 2 to 3 parts sand and 1 part of cement is recommended.

If, however, it is desired to use the same material throughout, then one can use 4 parts of gravel and sand, graded up to ¼-inch or ⅜-inch size, and 1 part of cement. This gives a good natural stone surface colour and texture.

Estimating Quantity of Material Required.

When considering the subject of laying concrete crazing paving, the question of quantities of material and their cost will naturally arise. In order to assist the reader to arrive at these quantities the following information is given.

It will be necessary first to decide upon the proportions of sand, cement and aggregate which will be used for making the concrete.

We shall assume that the proportions used are as follows: Sand, 2 parts; cement 1 part and aggregate (stones) 3 parts. As it is the trade custom to purchase these materials in "loads," one load representing a cubic yard, it will be most useful if we state the superficial area of path which will be covered by 6 loads of concrete,

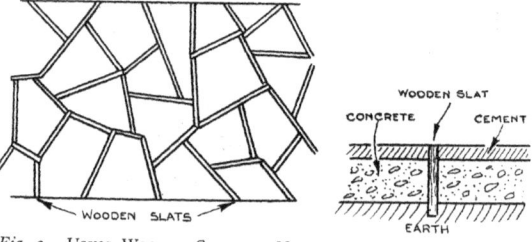

Fig. 2.—Using Wooden Slats as Moulds for making Separate Crazy Paving Slabs.

made up of 2 loads of sand, 1 load of cement and 3 loads of aggregate. Thus, with 2 inch thick concrete slabs of crazy paving, 6 loads of this mixture will cover 108 square yards.

Taking the width of the crazy paving path as 3 feet, a total length of 324 feet of path will easily be covered with the quantity of material mentioned.

Using 4 parts of gravel to 1 part of cement, then 5 loads of the resulting concrete will cover a length of path

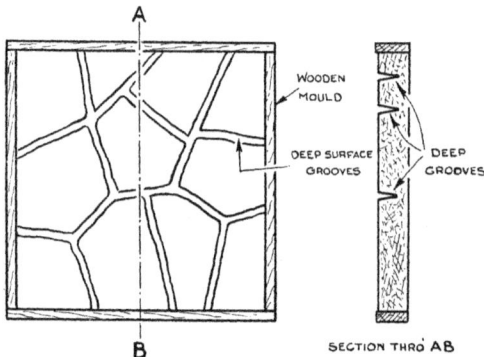

Fig. 3.—The Separate Broken Slab Method.

measuring 270 feet. From these figures the quantities for any other length of path are readily obtainable.

It may be of interest to remember that a square yard of crazy paving, 2 inches thick takes 1½ cubic feet of material.

Methods of Making the Slabs.

There are four different methods suitable for making concrete crazy paving which the home worker can employ. Two of these methods refer to making the paving on the actual site, so that it does not require moving again. The other two methods we shall describe are for paving which is afterwards transported to the site for fixing in position.

1. The Imitation Joint Method (Fig. 1).

Although not comparable in appearance with that of the separate slabs, this method is certainly a much quicker one to employ. Moreover, it has the merits of preventing grass and weeds from growing in the cracks—or their equivalents.

The site for the complete path should first be levelled to a depth of about 2 inches, leaving the edges square. It is not usually necessary to employ strips of wood to keep the edges intact, but a much straighter effect can be obtained thereby.

Next, fill the excavated site to within ½ inch of the top with the coarser concrete mixture, doing a section of the path at a time. Roughly level off the surface and, before it has quite set, pour over the finer cement mixture, thus filling up the last ½ inch, and leaving the surface level with the top of the ground.

Smooth off with a striking board, and then allow the material to set a little. The surface mixture should be in a pasty, but *not* a wet, condition for the next operation, namely, the *marking out of the slabs.*

A piece of pointed wood or metal should then be used to mark out the required slab effect on the surface and to a depth of about ⅜ inch. It will be found that during this operation a burr will be raised on either side of the edges; these burrs should be smoothed down. The path should then be allowed about three days in order to set hard, before it is used.

If the marking is properly carried out, the effect, as seen from a short distance away, will be that of real crazy paving. When, in time the crevasses become filled with dirt, the appearance will thereby be enhanced.

2. The Separate Slab Method (Fig. 2).

This method gives a path consisting of perfectly level and separate slabs of concrete, of irregular shapes, the spaces between them being filled with earth.

It is necessary first to dig out the site for the path to a depth of about 2 inches, tamping the earth down hard on the bottom of the recessed portion.

Next, obtain from the local builder or timber merchant a number of lengths of $\frac{1}{2} \times 2$-inch wooden slats, and cut these to different lengths in order to make the sides of the moulds for the concrete.

These slats should be fixed with their 2 in. sides vertical along the path site, arranging them so as to give the desired shapes of the finished slabs. The tops of these slats must all be level.

Next pour in the concrete mixture to within $\frac{1}{2}$ inch of the tops of the slats and, before the mixture has set, pour in the finer cement mixture for the surface layer. Smooth off the tops, leaving the edges of the wood slats level, and allow to set. When the cement is quite hard the wooden slats may be taken out, thus leaving a number of separate blocks of concrete with cement tops. The $\frac{1}{2}$-inch spaces between the blocks can then be filled in with sand or earth.

If the sides of the slats are greased lightly beforehand they will leave the concrete quite easily.

3. The Broken Slab Method (Fig. 3).

In this case the slabs are not formed *in situ*, as in the two preceding methods, but they are made in any convenient place and then transported to the site.

The concrete is poured into square moulds, the sides of the square being of about the same dimensions as the width of the path.

Fig. 4.—METHOD OF MOULDING SEPARATE SLABS, USING WOODEN SLATS IN SQUARE FRAME.
Below: The method of hinging the sides of the square frame.

Thus for a 3-foot path, the sides of the slabs would be about 2 feet 11 inches and 2 inches in thickness.

Before the concrete has properly set, the shapes of the slabs should be impressed deeply into the mixture, using a narrow strip of metal, or a pointed metal rod. The impressions should go at least 1 inch into the concrete; the deeper the better, so long as about $\frac{3}{4}$ inch of concrete is left at the bottoms of the grooves.

When the concrete is thoroughly hardened, turn the slab over on to a heap of earth or sand, and separate it into individual blocks with the aid of a heavy hammer; it will be found to crack at the bottoms of the grooves. The separate pieces can then be used after the manner of ordinary crazy paving.

4. The Separately Cast Slab Method (Fig. 4).

In this case a number of strips of wood are used to separate the slabs, using a square-shaped wooden mould as in the preceding example. Strips of wood of $\frac{3}{4} \times 2$ inches will be found suitable for the purpose, and to facilitate their removal, when the concrete has set, their sides should be black-leaded or greased.

If the square mould is made of hinged sides, with bolts or hooks and eyes to fasten them together, the finished slabs will be found much easier to remove.

An Attractive Form of Paving.

A particularly attractive form of imitation crazy paving suitable for pergola paths and similar walks, may be produced by moulding slabs of concrete to which powdered chalk, or barium sulphate has been added, afterwards breaking them into irregular slabs, in the manner previously explained. These irregular pieces should be laid in cement mortar which has been darkened by the addition of black oxide of manganese, in the proportions of 10 parts of the latter to 90 parts of cement, or 45 parts of cement and 45 parts of washed sand. This black mortar then makes a good filler for the joints between the slabs.

Another Inexpensive Method.

A fine surface colour and texture can be obtained, using any of the methods previously described, by the employment of a rich gravel and sand aggregate, using 4 parts of the latter to 1 part of cement. When the concrete has set, but before it is actually hard, the aggregate should be exposed by brushing the surface with a stiff brush, using plenty of water to remove the film of cement covering the material. This brings out the richness of colour of the aggregate.

FIXING LOOSE BEDSTEAD KNOBS

THE ornamental knobs on many metal bedsteads often become loose and need immediate attention.

There are two chief ways in which the knobs are fitted; in many cases the knob screws on to a screwed rod fixing in the bedstead frame; in other cases the knob has a screwed shank which screws into a hole in the frame.

Generally the cause of the trouble is due to the thread "stripping," so that the knob will no longer grip on the screwed rod; the seat of the trouble is usually to be found in the brass part.

The simplest and most effective remedy is to clean the underside of the knob and the screwed hole, then "tin" it in the usual way and proceed to build up the walls of the hole with a fairly thick layer of solder. Next file off the threads at the top or outer end of the screwed rod on the bedstead, then carefully screw the knob back into place. A little oil on the screwed rod will be a help, and if too much solder has been applied, scrape out a little with a pocket knife.

Similar treatment may be given to a screwed rod, but in this case it is very necessary to file the threads and make them quite bright before attempting to "tin" them.

When the necessary tools are available, a better plan is to drill out the hole in the knob and then bush it with a piece of thick brass tube soldered very securely into place. The tube must then be "tapped," or have a screw thread cut in it to suit the screwed rod.

Some knobs are made of thin metal spun to shape, and are often provided with an internal nut. This sometimes gets loose, and often is displaced when the knob is removed. The only way to refix the nut is to open the knob, which can be done by unsoldering the joint—if it can be found—or by cutting across the smallest part of the knob with a hacksaw. Before separating the parts, mark them, so that they can be reassembled properly. Next clean up the loose nut and "tin" the edges, then put it in its place and solder it there securely.

Do not file the sawn parts, but tin them carefully, put them together, and run the soldering iron around the joint to melt the solder inside. If this is all done carefully, the joint will scarcely be noticeable, but if necessary the knob can be repolished and lacquered.

Screw, Side and Top in Billiards

BILLIARDS on an undersize table has this advantage—all kinds of strokes are easier than they are on the full-size standard table. Range accounts for this in many shots, but there is also the consideration that strokes out of the ordinary are more amenable to the average performer, because the smaller balls are easier to do big things with.

A Simple Cannon—

In my first diagram, for example, I show a cannon, which, although of no outstanding difficulty, is nevertheless rather a teaser on a full-size table. The stroke, as Fig. 1 shows, is a cannon from white to red when the object-balls lie at a right angle, or nearly so, to the path of the cue-ball.

If you hit hard enough, it is not so very easy to miss this cannon, as the two object-balls are close enough to offer a biggish scoring target. But such a wild hit will leave nothing for your next shot, and as playing each stroke for position marks the difference between a billiard player and one who merely knocks the balls about, the importance of playing this cannon correctly needs no further stressing.

—and the Correct way to Play it.

The correct shot is a screw-cannon played thickly on white to cannon full and slowly on red and leave that ball well placed near the corner pocket, as indicated by the continuous line in diagram. To make this shot, you must know how to put screw on your ball. That is, how to make your ball run forward with backward spin on it.

Before telling you any more about this shot, you must allow me to remind you to chalk your cue.

Not only will the chalking help you to impart screw to your ball, but it will also prevent a miscue which might cut the cloth, particularly if of wool, although the cotton napless cloth is much less likely to be damaged in this manner.

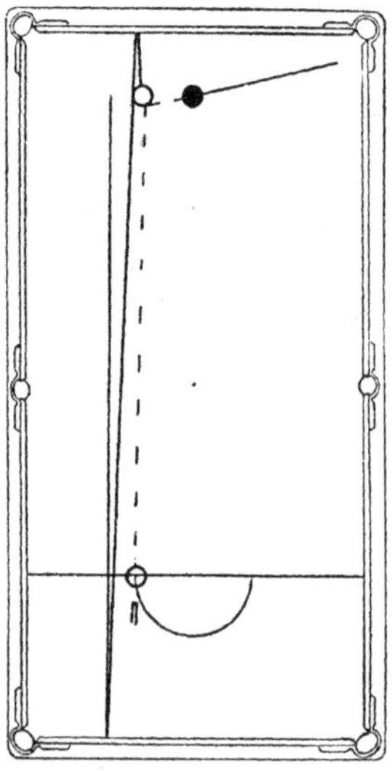

SCREW-BACK

To make your ball screw-back, strike it well below its centre, let your cue "get well hold of the ball," then check its forward momentum by clenching the hand holding the cue. By striking your ball in this manner you make it travel forward with backward twist on it.

The Effect of the Screw-back.

The effect of this is seen in the shot in the centre of Fig. 2. Red is on the centre-spot of the table, with the cue-ball directly behind it. The shot you want is to pot red in the facing middle-pocket and screw-back into the other. It is not an easy stroke by any means, but it is well within the cue-power of many amateurs, and learners will find it an admirable test-shot for the teaching of screw in a general way.

It is easy to get at the balls for replacing as successive strokes are practised, and while it may be a long

Fig. 1.—A Cannon from White to Red when Object-balls lie at a right angle to the Path of the Cue-ball.

The correct shot is a screw-cannon played thickly on white to cannon full and slowly on red and leave that ball well placed near the corner pocket as indicated by the continuous line.

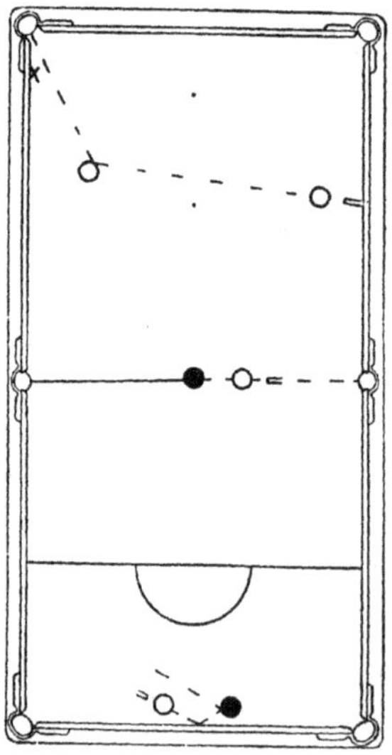

Fig. 2.—Three Methods of using Screw.

Top, widening the angle to send the ball into the top pocket; centre, potting the red in the facing middle pocket and screwing-back into the other; bottom, showing how screw takes effect if the cue-ball hits a cushion before contact with the object-ball.

time before the shot can be made as in the diagram, there is the constant gain that the practice is giving command of screw, perhaps the most fascinating movement the average amateur can impart to a billiard ball. Screw not only tells in direct screw-backs as in the diagram shot before us, but also in every shot which carries it.

Widening the Angle.

This is illustrated in the stroke shown at the spot-end of Fig. 2. Here the cross on the cushion indicates where your ball would go if struck in its centre, the contact with the object-ball being half-ball. But by putting screw on your ball, and hitting the object-ball in precisely the same place, your ball will be sent into the top-pocket, as shown by the dotted line in the diagram. This effect, known as "widening the angle," is ever present when screw is employed, taking effect in varying degree from the thinnest of ball-to-ball contacts to the full-ball screw-back in the centre of our diagram.

Screw also takes effect if the cue-ball hits a cushion before contact with the object-ball. An instance of this is shown at the baulk-end of Fig. 2. This is merely an indicative example, a shot instanced to show that if you strike the cushion in front of the object-ball with decided screw on your ball, the result of a full contact will bring your ball back.

When to use Slow Screw.

Slow screw, that is, the use of screw at slow strengths, is extremely useful in many positional shots. But it cannot be depended on if your ball has far to travel, as the screw rotation is soon lost as the ball revolves slowly over the cloth. Speed eliminates this. You can make screw shots, like the example in Fig. 1, at any range provided you put enough pace into the stroke.

The object of the shots so far instanced is to convey a general idea of the playing of the screw shot. By practising the shots as outlined, you will learn how to impart screw and the effect it has. The application of this knowledge in actual play is an inexhaustible source of entertainment, particularly when, as is usually the case, side is used in conjunction with screw. This brings us to the application and influence of side on a billiard ball, a subject so big and intricate that it almost has a literature of its own.

HOW TO PUT SIDE ON A BALL

In brief, with but one exception, we may say that side acts in the direction of its application. Fig. 3 explains this. Place your ball on the centre-spot of the baulk-line, strike it to the right and play a stroke straight along the line. Do not play too hard, but strike your ball briskly to make it spin forward. Then, as it strikes the cushion and the side takes effect, you will see your ball rebound into baulk. Play another shot, also straight along the line, but striking your ball to the

SCREW, SIDE AND TOP IN BILLIARDS

left instead of the right, and it will rebound from the cushion to the left.

What happens when a Side-laden Ball comes in contact with Object-ball.

This shows the influence side has on your ball after contact with a cushion. Precisely the same influence is exerted when a side-laden ball comes in contact with an object-ball. The angle of departure always veers towards the direction of the side employed. We see this in the stroke indicated at the other end of Fig. 3. By striking the object-ball without any side on your ball, you hit the top cushion where indicated by the continuous line. Left side on your ball, and an identical contact with the object-ball, spins your ball in the general direction of the dotted line to the left of the continuous line. Right side, of course, has the reverse effect, taking your ball away as indicated by the dotted line to the right. The effects of side in the above diagram shot are purposely exaggerated in order to be unmistakable.

When Side may cause the Ball to Swerve.

To an extent, particularly with a slow-moving ball running with the nap of a woollen cloth, side will cause your ball to swerve a little before contact with an object-ball some distance away. Fig. 4 explains this. By playing with very strong side at slow strength, it is quite possible to aim straight at the red on the spot and miss it altogether in the direction of the side imparted, right side in diagram shot. This effect is never apparent when the cue-ball moves rapidly, as the speed of the shot "keeps the ball straight," as they say in the billiard rooms.

One exception to the general action of Side.

The one great exception to the general action of side is seen when playing shots at slow strength directly against the nap of a woollen cloth. Then, for some inexplicable reason, the usual action of

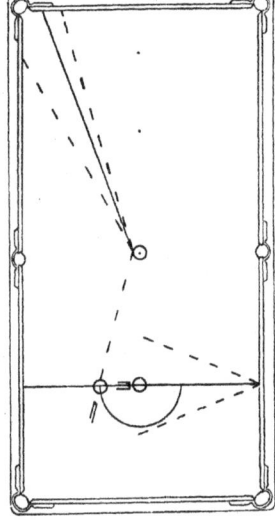

Fig. 3.—DIAGRAMS SHOWING THE EFFECT OF "SIDE."
The effects are purposely exaggerated so as to be unmistakable.

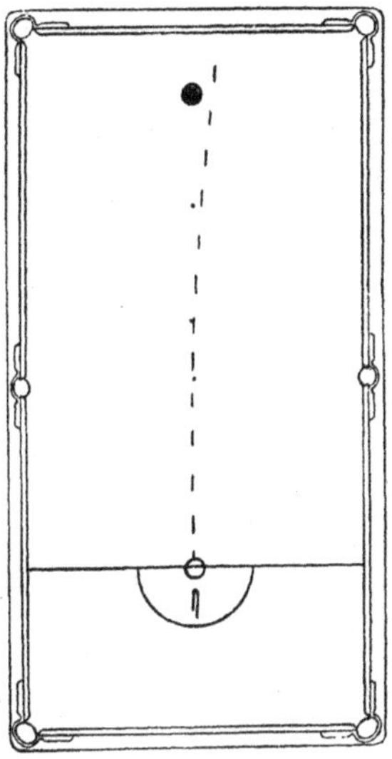

side on the run of a ball is completely reversed. This does not apply to strokes played on the napless cotton cloth.

By now the learner will know what is meant by screw and side, and understand their application and playing

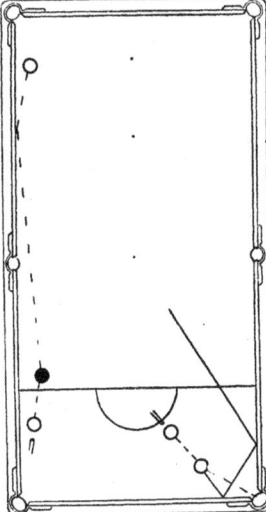

Fig. 5.—THE EFFECT OF "TOP."
When three balls are in a line as shown on the left strike your ball very high and hit the red almost full. Your ball will then run-through the red and dart away to make the cannon. The other stroke is a follow-through in-off played by striking your ball either centrally or very slightly above its centre and hitting the object-ball nearly full to the left.

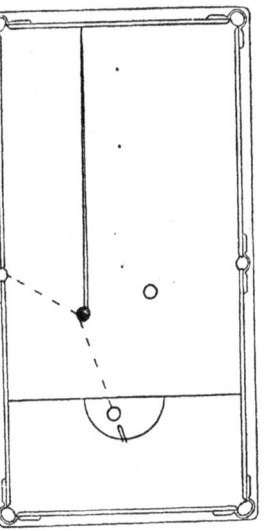

Fig. 4.—IN THE CASE OF A SLOW-MOVING BALL RUNNING WITH THE NAP OF A WOOLLEN CLOTH, SIDE WILL CAUSE THE BALL TO SWERVE.

Fig. 6.—AN IDEAL OPENING FOR AN ALL-ROUND BREAK.
Red offers a simple shot into one middle pocket, white into the other, the cue-ball being in hand. Having the cue ball in hand gives you the right to place your ball where you please in the baulk half-circle when playing from hand.

utility in a general way. But there is no substitute for the necessary practice to gain the requisite dexterity. This can only be attained cue in hand, and is suspiciously like drudgery for no particular purpose at first. But, to billiards, practising these strokes which give insight into ball movements is like practising scales at music. Tunes follow in music, and breaks follow at billiards. Whatever time is spent in mastering ball movements is repaid, when break-building is tackled, with abundant interest, added zest, and an infinity of extra enjoyment.

POINTS ABOUT "TOP"

The next ball movement to consider is "top." This is the direct reverse of "screw"; it is rotation imparted by striking your ball high above the centre, whereas "screw" comes from cue-contact below it. The effect of "top" is to give your ball powerful forward rotation which is indispensable for some follow-through shots.

Three Balls in a Direct Line.

Fig. 5 shows a shot in point. The cue-ball is a foot or so from red, which lies near the side cushion away up the table. All three balls are so nearly in a direct line that a fine cannon may be reckoned unplayable. But if you strike your ball very high, and hit red almost full, putting plenty of freedom and power into the shot, you will see your ball run-through the red and dart away to make the cannon.

Played correctly, the above shot will make your ball almost stop at the moment of thick contact with red, the pause is distinctly perceptible to the eye. Then, as the powerful "top" takes effect, your ball will spin smartly forward and away to make the cannon. Side is often used in conjunction with "top," when the general effect will be the same as described in the remarks on side.

Do not use "Top" needlessly.

It is a mistake to use "top" needlessly. Because

SCREW, SIDE AND TOP IN BILLIARDS

of its evident power in strokes like the example in Fig. 5, where its use is indispensable, it is easy to get into the habit of using "top" for all kinds of follow-through shots. This should be avoided, "top" tends to make the true run of the cue-ball difficult to estimate with complete accuracy.

When to avoid "Top."

Avoid it when, for instance, you want a follow-through in-off like the shot shown at the baulk-end of Fig. 5. This shot should be played by striking your ball either centrally or very slightly above its centre, and hitting the object-ball nearly full to the left.

If you swing your cue as you should, the impetus of the stroke will carry your ball through to the pocket. But a stroke played in this manner, with the object-ball as close as our other shot in Fig. 5, could not "carry the distance" for the long cannon.

MAKING BREAKS

Having dealt with the ball movements in common use, the application of them to the making of breaks is the next step. No better opening for an all-round break can be desired than the position shown in Fig. 6. Red offers a simple shot into one middle pocket, white into the other, the cue-ball being in hand. Here it is worth remembering that having the cue-ball in hand confers the one big advantage offered by English billiards, which is the right to place your ball where you please in the baulk half-circle when playing from hand. Never forget this when you are rather undecided whether to play for a pot, a cannon, or an in-off. After the pot or cannon you must play from where your ball stops rolling. After the in-off, you have the whole of the "D" in which to place it.

In-off Red into Middle Pocket.

Your first shot, from the diagram position, should be the in-off red as shown into the middle

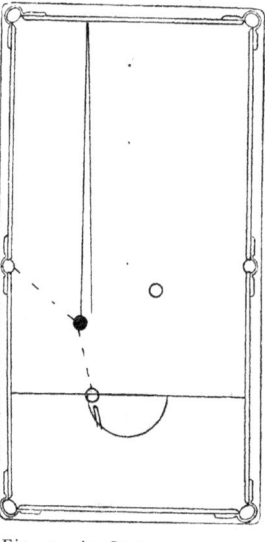

Fig. 7.—A LEAVE YOU ARE LIKELY TO GET WHEN PLAYING THE SHOT IN FIG. 6.

A little mistake in strength brings the red too close to the baulk line for the shot in Fig. 6 to be playable.

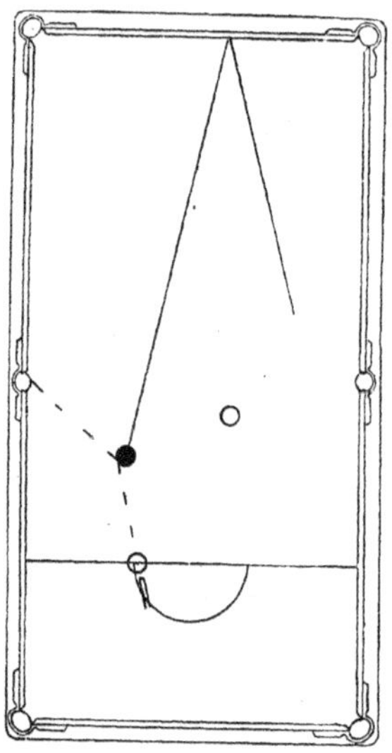

Fig. 8.—THIS IS AN EASY WAY OF SCORING AN IN-OFF, BUT IT WON'T LEAVE YOU ANYTHING.

The red ball is "cut away" across the table towards the side cushion.

pocket. This is a plain-ball shot, played by striking your ball centrally and hitting red half-ball. The shot is very easy to score, and ideal position will leave you another in-off of exactly the same kind. You should, after practice, reckon to leave yourself two

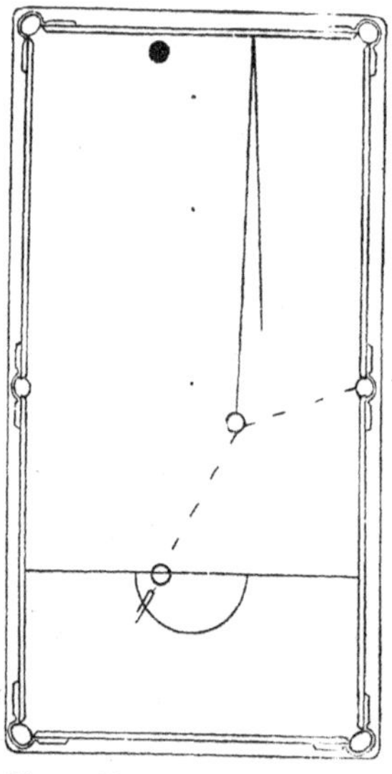

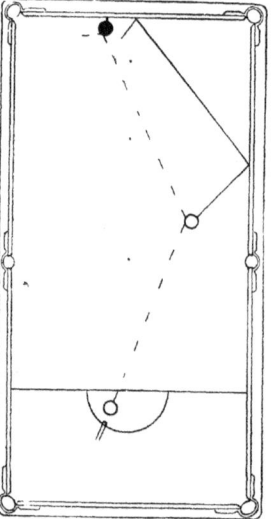

Fig. 9.—THE PROBLEM HERE IS TO "RESCUE" THE RED BALL IN AS FEW SHOTS AS POSSIBLE.

White offers a simple in-off into the right-hand middle pocket; red as a result of bad positional play has been left near the top cushion.

Fig. 10.—HOW A DROP-CANNON SHOULD BE HANDLED.

This is a cannon played to "drop" the balls into good position at the top of the table. Strike the first object-ball full enough to send it away towards the top cushion.

or three of these middle-pocket in-offs, but to make an appreciable sequence demands sufficient application to become an adept at red-ball play. Whether you undertake this or not, there is one thing connected with red-ball mid-pocket in-offs which ought always to be kept in mind.

Retaining Red Ball in Mid-table Position.

This is the necessity for retaining the red ball in mid-table position. Once it is played near the side cushion, your chance of leaving a feasible shot, either in-off or pot, is very greatly diminished. For instance, Fig. 7 shows a leave you are likely to get when playing the shot in Fig. 6. A little mistake in strength brings the red too close to the baulk-line for the shot in Fig. 6 to be playable.

Returning Red to its Original Position.

The score is the same, of course, in-off red in the middle pocket. But you must make it in a different manner. The correct shot is played by spotting your ball as in diagram, hitting it freely and rather above its centre, and striking red three-quarter full. This will make your ball run-through to the pocket, and return red to approximately its original position. It is worth remembering that this stroke was the backbone of George Gray's enormous runs off the red ball. He had such command of the shot that his middle-pocket in-offs seemed almost interminable.

What happens if Incorrect Shot is Played.

Notice how in Fig. 7 red travels straight up the table and back again, or very nearly so, veering, if anything, towards the middle of the table. That is the big thing in the shot; it retains the red ball in the lucrative mid-table scoring zone. Suppose, instead of playing the shot before us, you scored the in-off as shown in Fig. 8. This shot is very easy, it is perhaps the easiest way of scoring in the pocket, but what is the result? The red ball is "cut away" across the table towards the side cushion, and you have nothing much left for your next shot.

Importance of Playing on the Red Ball.

Why, you may ask, play all these shots on the red ball when the white offers a tempting shot in the middle pocket, as shown in Fig. 6? To begin with, you only score two points for in-off white against three for the same shot off red, so always give red the preferential playing treatment its value merits. There is also the important consideration that if red is pocketed, it is re-spotted on the table. But if white goes down, you lose it, and are left with only the red to play at.

Therefore, as a sound general rule, never play an in-off white except to rescue red from indifferent position. Sooner or later you will manœuvre red into difficulties. You will probably do so in a few shots, a first-class professional would keep plugging away at red, if he wished, until the "75 limit" stopped him. Eventually, however, the same problem will confront the beginner and the skilled adept. This is to utilise white to bring red back into the game, one of the key-moves in break-building, which we will now, therefore, deal with.

WHEN TO USE THE WHITE BALL

Utilising the white ball to bring the red into the game is the next thing to learn. Fig. 9 shows the position in which white is left, offering a simple in-off into the right-hand middle pocket. The red ball, as the result of a bad positional stroke, has been left near the top cushion. Our problem is how to "rescue" it in as few shots as possible.

We can only do this by manipulating white to leave good cannon position on red, and now see the advantage gained by not playing that tempting in-off white all the while a red-ball in-off was scorable. It is a mistake to play the in-off white to leave another shot of the same kind. Such play is as futile with white as it is profitable with red. Our stroke must be an in-off white played to leave cannon position from hand.

In-off White to leave Cannon Position from Hand.

How to do this is shown in Fig. 9, a very simple shot, which leaves the object-balls offering a "drop-cannon," that is, a cannon played to "drop" the balls into good position at the top of the table. Fig. 10 shows how this "drop-cannon" must be handled. The main thing is to be sure of striking the first object-ball full enough to send it away towards the top cushion.

NOTES ON CANNONS
The Drop-cannon.

It is very easy indeed to score the cannon by hitting white too thin, with the result that your ball is left between the other two, with nothing much to play at. Avoid this common error by practising the "drop-cannon" until

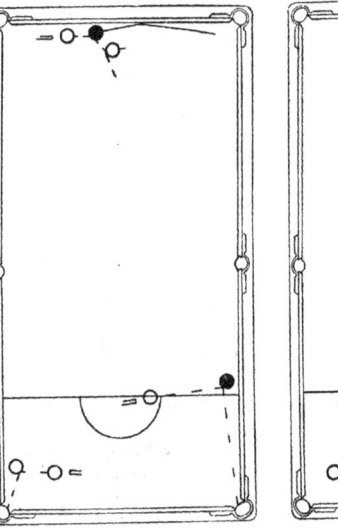

Fig. 11.—The Pot-red Cannon Movement.

The drop cannon has been played, leaving a simple cannon. If this cannon is played correctly it will leave an easy pot-red which you play to set up cannon position once more.

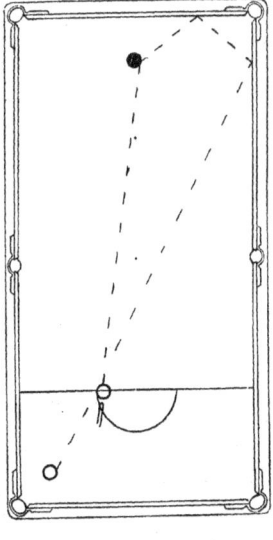

Fig. 12.—An all-round Cannon off several Cushions.

Red is on the spot, white is in baulk and the cue-ball is in hand. The cannon is played half-ball off red as shown and is a certainty if handled at all well.

you become accustomed to playing such cannons to bring the balls together. Dozens of diagrams of "drop-cannons" might be presented, but they all come out to the same thing in the end, which is to take the balls far enough up the table to leave them handy for break-building.

The Main Thing to Remember.

The big thing to remember is that red, always the key-ball in break-building (except the advanced refinement of close-cannon play), has to be spotted when pocketed, and that leaving white at the head of the table creates a scoring zone with the spotted red as its centre.

The Pot-red Cannon Movement.

The diagram shows that the completion of the cannon left by the "drop-cannon" leaves a simple pot-red in the top pocket. We play this and run the cue-ball through to return from the side cushion. Here, of course, we leave that spot-end position from which professionals score so freely. It is very evident that if you play the cannon in Fig. 11 correctly it will leave an easy pot-red, which you play to set up cannon position once more, from which you repeat the scoring movement.

Roughly, the above alternation of pot-red with cannon shows the method by which professionals keep the balls under such control that the best of them could score hundreds of points so cleverly that a plank laid across the centre of the table would make no difference to their break. Such perfection is not to be expected in home billiards, but it is interesting to see how far you can go with the pot-red cannon movement before you are beaten by an awkward run of the balls.

Keep on Practising.

This opens a prospect which defies detailed description. You get recreation from it by taking careful note of the lie of the balls in any of the innumerable positions likely to be left. It is a good plan to mark the position of the balls with a spot of tailor's pipe-clay. Do not use white chalk, as it leaves more of a permanent mark on the cloth than you want to be bothered with. Having marked the position, decide what leave you mean to get from it, play your shot, and see what happens. If execution and intention coincide, which they very seldom do, you can congratulate yourself and try some other shot in the same way.

The only Road to Billiard Proficiency.

But if, as is much more likely, you score your shot without leaving the position you had in mind, then you must stop and think out what has happened. Having done so, replace the balls, play the shot over again, and note the result. It may still be unsatisfactory. Repeated trials may prove that you are trying for the impossible, but the experience is invaluable. In fact, such serious practice is the only road to billiard proficiency.

An In-off Red played with Screw.

Break-building will not always run on the smooth lines of simple cannons and pot-reds, with half-ball in-offs to vary the game. Great cuemen can make it look like that, but average amateurs soon find the balls presenting all kinds of shots of varying difficulty. Two of these are indicated at the baulk-end of Fig. 11. On the left there is an in-off white played with screw and right side on your ball. It is not a difficult shot of its kind. After a few attempts you ought to see your ball pulled into the pocket by the strong side.

In-off into Baulk Pocket.

The other shot is hard to make. Red is just out of baulk and almost touching the side cushion. Cue-ball is in hand, and the shot you want is the in-off into the baulk pocket played as in diagram. This demands no small cue-power. Strike your ball low and hard with as much left side as you can possibly impart. Hit the red as full as you can without a kiss spoiling the shot. These directions will start you on the road to success, but you must expect to put in a lot of practice before you can call this shot your own.

All-round Cannon off Several Cushions.

Fig. 12 presents a type of shot not yet dealt with. It is an all-round cannon off several cushions. Red is on the spot, white is in baulk as shown, and the cue-ball is in hand. The cannon is played half-ball off red as shown, and is a certainty if handled at all well. But it is only a beginning, a mere indication of the possibilities of all-round cannon play. Side, strength, variation in ball-to-ball contact, all enter the problem and add to its interest.

How to Practise All-round Cannons.

For home billiards, it is excellent and instructive entertainment to take the position shown in Fig. 12 and vary it by gradually moving the white ball in successive stages clean across the table, keeping it near the baulk cushion the whole time. Play all-round cannons from hand at the different leaves thus presented, keeping red continually on the spot. This will teach you a great deal about the angles of the table, and help you with cushion-cannons whenever they occur in actual play.

When applying the knowledge gained from practice on the above lines, do not forget that all-round cannons vary considerably when the first object-ball is quite close to a cushion. You can gain an inkling into this by moving red from the spot to a point almost tight against the top cushion centre. Then, from this change of position, if you play some of the all-round cannons you have scored off the spotted red, you will soon appreciate the difference, particularly when side is used.

CLEANING AND PRESERVING A GALVANISED COLD WATER STORAGE CISTERN

THE cold water store tank is usually situated in the roof space of domestic buildings and approached by means of a trap-door in the top floor ceiling. Because of its remote and somewhat inaccessible position it is often in a dirty and neglected state, with 1 or 2 inches of sludge on the bottom, and the carcases of mice and birds even may be found.

Cleaning out Sludge.

To clean out, first shut the water supply off, or, if more convenient, tie the ball valve up to a stick placed across the top. Now open the draw-off taps and allow to run until the tank is emptied down to the level of the outlet pipe. Place a wooden plug in the end of the outlet pipe to prevent solids escaping down and possibly choking this pipe. Now, with a short domestic shovel and buckets, empty out the sludge; when as clean as possible by this means refill the tank with clean water, stir up well with a whitewash brush or similar tool and empty again; the last inch or two will have to be ladled out into buckets.

Old tanks of thin galvanised iron plate are often in a very rusty state, the galvanised surface having long ago disappeared. For that reason it is inadvisable to scrape the bottom with steel scrapers as it is quite possible to start leakages.

How to Increase the Life of the Tank.

A preservative coating will increase the life of an old galvanised tank. First well dry the surface by means of a painter's blow-lamp, and get rid of any loose dust. Replace plug in outlet pipe in case anything drops down.

Now make up a bitumastic paint in the following manner: Obtain some coal-tar pitch and melt it over a small gas flame in a paint kettle or similar utensil, taking care not to ignite it, add a little linseed oil, until consistency of stiff paint is obtained; a little resin and tallow is sometimes added. Test the paint on a piece of sheet iron or tin; when cold it should be hard and shiny, but with a degree of elasticity which will allow the metal to be bent without the coating scaling off. If the paint does not harden and remains sticky, add more pitch or resin, as such a coating would taint the water; if the paint shells off, add more linseed oil, or a little tallow, and test again. Having obtained the right degree of hardness apply hot with an old, but clean, paint brush of ample size to give quick application.

Applying the Preservative Composition.

The surfaces of the tank should be heated by means of a blow-lamp preceding the paint brush, taking care not to ignite the composition. First do all the angles, and brush well into the quirks and then the flat surfaces. Allow to stand for a few hours until set, remove the plug from outlet pipe and refill the tank.

If the tank is not provided with a cover, one should be made from tongue and grooved match boarding.

Dealing with Lead Lined Wooden Tanks.

If the tank is of timber with lead lining, care must be taken not to cut the lining when cleaning out with a sharp shovel. After cleaning and drying, a coat of caustic lime wash applied hot forms a protective coating against corrosive attack from soft water.

A bitumastic paint may be used, but it must be noted that in the event of such a tank leaking it would be a difficult propostion to solder it after it has been coated with such a composition. In the case of such a tank being perforated and difficulty is experienced in tracing the points of leakage for soldering, a bitumastic paint applied hot on the pre-warmed surfaces will often stop the leaks and give it another lease of life.

How to Make a Trolley Bookcase

The movable bookcase, shown in Fig. 1, has two partitioned shelves, a table top with two sliding flaps and a small drawer chest. It is mounted on a set of 3-inch rubber-tyred castors. At one end, at the level of the middle shelf, there is a flap which folds downwards and at the other end there is a hinged flap which covers a newspaper rack. This flap folds upwards. The sliding flaps beneath the table top may be extended from either side of the table top, and, as the drawer chest revolves, it is unnecessary to reverse the bookcase in order to make full use of the table top, drawers and writing flaps. If an unobstructed table top is required, the drawer chest may be removed.

General Arrangement.

Figs. 2 to 5 show the general arrangement and leading dimensions. The dotted lines in Fig. 5 indicate the alternative positions of the sliding flaps. The front of the drawers, it will be noticed, stands back from the edge of the table top in one position and is flush with it when reversed. The drawers may also be used in an endwise position. Each sliding flap has two ball catches on each side, as shown in Fig. 6. These catches limit the travel in the open and closed positions in both directions.

Materials.

The four legs are bought ready prepared as $30 \times 1\frac{3}{8}$ inches plain square pattern. The side rails consist of six pieces, each $22 \times 2 \times \frac{3}{4}$ inches, and the end rails, six pieces, each $14\frac{1}{2} \times 2 \times \frac{3}{4}$ inches. The twelve rails are planed to a finished sectional size of $1\frac{3}{4} \times \frac{1}{2}$ inches. The shelves, shelf partition, hinged and sliding flaps, and shelf brackets will require 18 square feet of $\frac{3}{4}$-inch board to be finished $\frac{1}{2}$-inch thick. The drawer sides and backs are made from $\frac{3}{8}$-inch material. Plywood, $\frac{1}{4}$ inch thick, is used for the drawer bottoms and supports the sliding flaps on the under side. The lower side and end rails are finished on top with a $\frac{1}{2}$-inch half-round moulding, which will absorb a length of 14 feet. The table top is finished $\frac{5}{8}$ inch thick.

Fig. 1.—The finished Bookcase with one Writing Flap extended.

The end flap on the left folds down after hinging its supporting brackets inwards. The flap on the right which hinges upwards covers a newspaper rack. The drawer chest revolves and both writing flaps may be extended on either side of the table top.

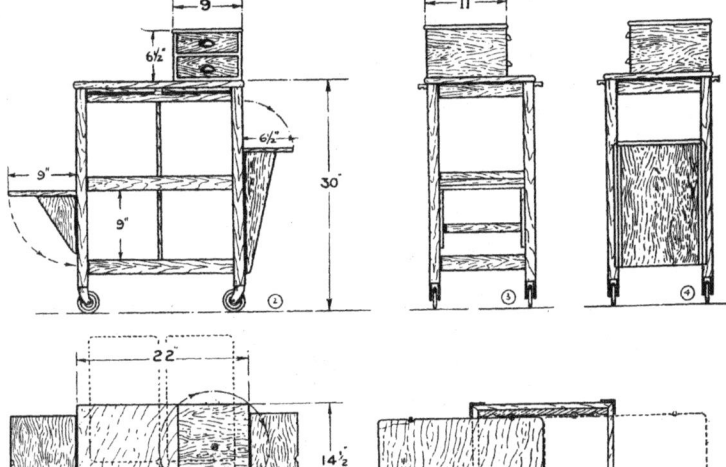

Figs. 2–6.—General arrangement and Leading Dimensions.

(2) Side view with leading dimensions. (3) End view with hinged flap. (4) End view with newspaper rack. (5) Plan showing positions of sliding and hinged flaps, alternative position of sliding flaps and revolving path of drawer chest. (6) Section showing sliding flap and ball catches.

Preparing the Legs.

Place the four legs together (Fig. 7) and support them in front of the bench. In Fig. 7 the legs rest on the open vice across which is placed a bench hook, that is, a piece of board with a fillet on top at one end and a fillet underneath at the other end. The legs are supported at the other end on a piece of square timber nailed or cramped with the bench holdfast.

Length of Leg and Mortise Positions.

With the try square and marking awl, or scriber, mark the legs for their finished length, which is 30 inches, less $3\frac{1}{4}$-inch allowance for the castors and $\frac{5}{8}$-inch for the table top, or $26\frac{1}{8}$ inches. Mark the sides of each leg "out" and "in." The sides marked "out" are to be cut for mortises and the "in" sides to be left plain.

Scribe the legs (Fig. 7) for the mortises of the long rails. The lower mortises are $1\frac{1}{2}$ inches from the bottom of the leg and each mortise is $1\frac{1}{4}$ inches from top to bottom. Measure 9 inches from the lower mortise and scribe two more lines $1\frac{3}{4}$ inches apart for the centre mortises and $1\frac{3}{8}$ inches from the top of the leg for the open top mortise (Fig. 11). Turn the legs over and scribe across for the short rail mortises (Fig. 8).

Width of Mortise.

Set the pins of the mortise gauge to mark the width of the mortises, which are the same as the finished thickness of the side and end rails, or $\frac{1}{2}$ inch. Each mortise is set out

HOW TO MAKE A TROLLEY BOOKCASE

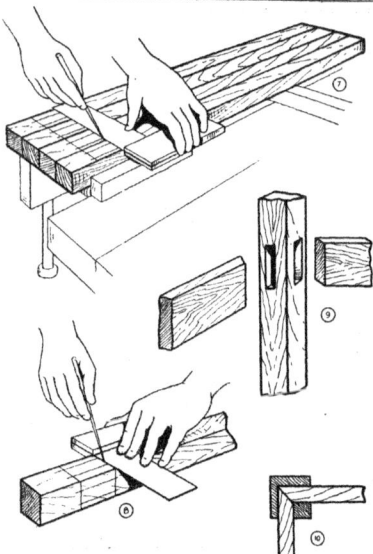

Figs. 7–10.—Details of the Legs.

(7) Marking out the leg mortises. (8) Transferring the mortise positions across to the adjacent face of the leg. (9) Portion of leg with mortises for the side and end rails which have bevelled ends. (10) Section of leg showing mitred ends of side and end rails meeting in the leg mortises.

¼ inch from the outer edge of the leg. Also each mortise is 1⅛ inches deep, so that it meets the corresponding mortise on the other side. The ends of the side and end rails are mitred (Fig. 9) and meet inside the leg mortises (Fig. 10).

Joints of Rails for Rack and Lower Shelf.

One pair of legs is marked for an extra mortise to take the rail at the top of the newspaper rack shown in Figs. 15, 16 and 19. The plywood back of the rack is screwed to this rail and the flap over the rack is hinged to it. This rail is 1¾ × 1¾ inches and is flush with the outer face of the leg, and is rebated on the lower edge for the ¼-inch plywood back of the rack. This rail is tenoned so that its mortises are in line with the other end rail mortises.

All the legs are marked for the notches of the rail shown in Figs. 3 and 23, which keeps the books in position on the lower shelf. The notches for this rail are also shown in Figs. 12 to 14. This rail is finished 1¼ × ¼ inches and is half-lapped at the ends.

First End Assembly.

Prepare the six side rails and mark them off for length together. Then cut and shoot the mitres. Do the same with the six end rails. Prepare the top rail of the newspaper rack. With a supply of glue ready to hand, assemble the short rails in one of the legs (Fig. 12), which has six mortises only. Drive on the other leg and then add the top rail, which is driven from the top, because the mortise is an open one (Figs. 11 and 13).

Second End Assembly.

The next operation is to assemble the newspaper rack end (Fig. 15). Assemble the five short rails to the legs in a similar manner to that shown in Figs. 12 and 13, when the end will appear as shown in Fig. 15. The rebate on the lower edge of the top rail of the rack is flush with the face of the rails below, which are recessed ¼ inch from the outer face of the leg. The plywood, when screwed into position (Fig. 16), has, therefore, a level bearing on all three end rails.

Figs. 15–22.—Details of Rack End Assembly.

(15) Newspaper rack end assembly. (16) Screwing on plywood back of newspaper rack. (17) Recess for butt hinge of flap. (18) Flap forming cover of newspaper rack. (19) Rack end assembly with dotted lines showing hinged flap. (20) Adding the rack end to complete the carcase assembly. (21) Fixing of shelf at corner. (22) Corner of carcase showing shelf fillets and notched corner of shelf for fitting round leg.

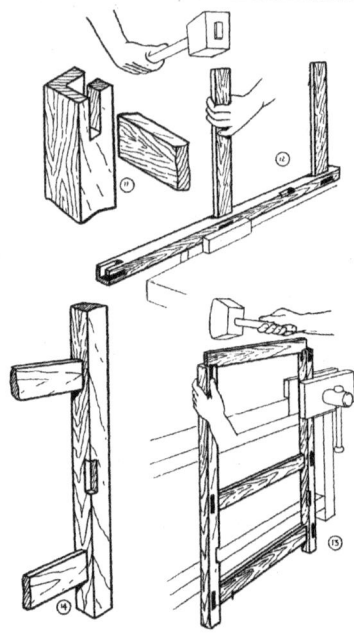

Figs. 11–14.—Details of End Assembly.

(11) Top of leg showing open mortises and bevelled end of top rail. (12) Assembling the short rails to a leg. (13) Knocking on the top rail of the end assembly. (14) Portion of end assembly showing notch for guard rail of lower shelf.

Top Rail Notches.

The front and back top rails differ from the other long rails in that they have two long notches the width and thickness of the sliding flaps, as shown in Fig. 20. The flaps are 8¾ inches wide and ½ inch thick and the notches are made 8⅞ inches long and 9⁄16 inch deep, which allows a 1⁄16-in. clearance all round.

Shelf Fillets.

It will now be convenient to add the fillets to all the rails which support the middle and bottom shelves, also the plywood undershelf of the sliding flaps. These fillets measure 1 inch from top to bottom and are ⅝-inch thick, so that when fixed they are flush with the underside of the rails and with the inside of the legs. They are butted between the legs and pinned or screwed to the rails (Figs. 22, 24, 27 and 28).

Carcase Assembly.

The bookcase is now assembled as shown in Fig. 20. The long rails are glued and driven into one end assembly which is laid on the floor. Then

HOW TO MAKE A TROLLEY BOOKCASE

the other assembly is added to it from above.

Middle Bearer and Shelves.

The carcase is now prepared for the reception of the bottom shelf, which is in two sections, as shown in Fig. 23. As each section is 10 × 13 inches it will require two pieces of board for each section, unless wide boards are available. This can be avoided by using plywood.

Turn the carcase upside down (Fig. 25) and fit a centre bearer. This bearer is 1¾ inches wide and the same depth as the shelf fillets, that is 1 inch. The bearer is half-lapped to the shelf fillets (Fig. 24) and screwed from underneath (Fig. 25). Each section of the shelf has a ⅝-inch bearing on the bearer between which is the ½-inch partition (Fig. 26). The partition is screwed from underneath.

Fitting Bearer and Partition.

Fix the centre bearer to the lower shelf. Then cut the partition to fit between the front and back rails, while for height it extends from the top of the lower shelf fillet to the underside of the table top. A straight-edge laid on top of the legs should, therefore, also touch the top of the partition. Before fixing the partition, add in the centre of each side of it a fillet of the same sectional size as the rail fillets, and in line with the other fillets of the middle shelf. Fix the partition by screwing it from underneath and driving in from the outside a small-headed nail or panel pin at the middle of each of the front and back rails.

Shelf Fitting.

The middle and bottom shelves are cut to fit between the side and end rails. They are also notched to fit round the inner corner of the legs (Figs. 21 and 22). Fix the shelves with small brass countersunk screws.

Sliding Flap Mounting.

The next stage of the construction is to make and mount the sliding flaps. Fig. 28 shows the position of the sliding flap, the plywood undershelf and fillets which support the plywood and carry one-half of the ball catches.

Make two pairs of fillets for supporting the plywood on the centre partition. The corresponding fillets on the side and end rails are already in position. Screw the plywood undershelves in position.

Ball Catch Mounting.

Make two pairs of ball catch fillets, ⅜-inch thick and ⅝-inch wide, and let into each four female portions of ball catches as shown in Fig. 6. Fix one pair of these fillets so that they are flush with the top and inner side of the legs (Fig. 28). The length of each fillet is the distance between the legs

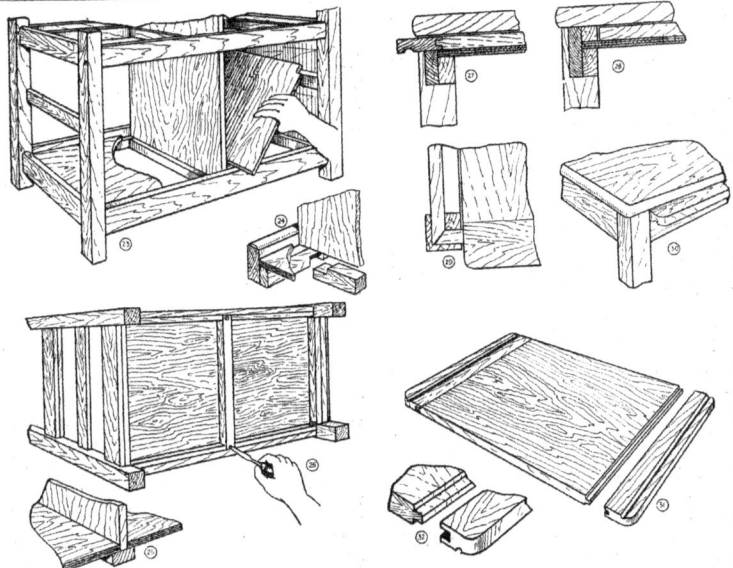

Figs. 23–32.—Some details of Shelves and Flap.

(23) Inserting a lower shelf section. (24) Half-lap at one end of centre cross bearer at bottom of carcase. (25) Screwing the cross bearer to the bottom shelf fillet from underneath. (26) Cross section of partition, shelves and cross bearer. (27) Lengthwise section of sliding flap and its supports. (28) Crosswise section of sliding flap and its supports. (29) Plan of portion of flap and cross-section of leg. (30) Flap showing projection in closed position. (31) Underside of flap with one clamped end removed. (32) Details of tongue and groove of clamped end of flap.

of the short end. The second pair of fillets are screwed to the top of the partition.

Sliding Flap Construction.

The sliding flaps are ½ inch thick and have clamped ends (Figs. 31 and 32). The width of the flap is the width between the ball catch fillets less ⅛ inch, so as to give 1/16 inch clearance each side. The length of the flap is 1 foot 4½ inches, so that it projects 1 inch each side when not in use. The clamped ends are grooved on the underside to form a finger-hold.

Lay the sliding flap on the plywood

Figs. 33–39.—Some Final Constructional Details.

(33) Drawer chest carcase and one drawer cut away to show the construction. (34) Tapped plate let into bottom of drawer chest and screw which engages with it. (35) The screw is normally engaged with the tapped plate under the drawer chest. The rounded end of the screw revolves in a hole in the table top. (36) Constructional details of newspaper rack. (37) Details of fixing of rack ends and front. (38) Method of attaching hinged flap at non-rack end. (39) Leg section showing position of hinged bracket, end rails, fillets and shelves.

undershelf and mark for the ball catches which are to be let into the edges of the flaps.

Table Top.

The boards for the table top are cut to the same overall dimensions as the carcase. The top is fixed by screwing it from the top to the side and end rails and partition. Care should be taken not to place a screw through the top of the leg, because, owing to it being cut for two open mortises, it may easily be split.

Drawer Chest Mounting.

Mark out the rectangle 9 × 11 inches on the table top occupied by the drawer chest, as shown in Fig. 5. Draw the diagonals so as to obtain the centre. Remove the sliding flap and bore a ⅜-inch hole, taking care not to penetrate the plywood undershelf. This hole is for a bolt end which engages with a tapped plate let into the underside of the drawer chest (Fig. 34). This metal fitting may be made by altering a shutter, or window screw, as sold by ironmongers. This screw consists of a tapped plate and a thumb screw. The thumb-piece is cut off and the end of the screw rounded over a hole bored so that the screw may be revolved with a piece of wire or skewer.

The table top is finished by covering it with leather cloth and concealing the tacks at the edges with a half-round moulding. The drawer chest (Fig. 33) is covered on the underside with baize.

Newspaper Rack.

The newspaper rack (Figs. 36 and 37) consists of two triangular ends and a sloping front. The ends are attached to the legs with fillets screwed to the outside of the end pieces and legs (Fig. 37). The sloping front is screwed to the ends and to a bottom rail which has a sloping front. This bottom rail (Fig. 36) is screwed through the plywood back of the rack to the end rail behind it.

The flap above the rack is the full width between the legs and one-half of the hinges are screwed to the top surface of the rail which has been specially provided. If required, the sides of the rack may be hinged in a similar manner to the brackets at the other end of the bookcase. In this instance the front of the rack is held between fillets in the ends and is removed by sliding it upwards.

Folding Flap with Hinged Brackets.

Constructional details of the hinged flap and brackets are shown in Figs. 38 and 39. A fillet is screwed to the middle end rail to which the hinges of the flap are screwed on the underside. The brackets are hinged to the legs (Fig. 39) so that the brackets fold inwards.

Fixing the Castors.

The final operation consists of turning the bookcase upside down and carefully marking the centre of the bottom of the legs and then boring for and fixing the castors.

It is suggested that the bookcase be wax polished.

REPLACING DAMAGED CASTORS

DAMAGE associated with castors must be considered under two headings; firstly, failure of the castor itself; secondly, breakdown of the leg or part of the furniture to which the castor is—or was—attached.

In either case, first provide safe access to the damage, by turning light furniture on to its side, or by raising a heavy piece and supporting it on blocks of wood, a strong box or anything convenient. Take care that the furniture stands firmly and that the opposite pair of legs are not unduly strained.

Failure of Castor.

Breakdown will probably be located at or near the centre pin and its junction with the socket, or plate. Repairs are generally impracticable, consequently remove the castor and obtain a new one.

The proper way of removal depends upon the style of the castor, of which there are—for all practical purposes—four types, apart from those used on metal bedsteads.

Old-style castors had a screwed pin and a plate which was fastened beneath the leg by three small screws. Removal is effected by taking out the small screws and turning the cap.

Much modern furniture has what is known as a spring-in-grip neck socket —the socket is driven into the woodwork and held by the serrated ring at the bottom; the castor proper is pushed into the socket and thereby expands the neck sufficiently to allow the head to pass. In some cases the castor can be removed from the socket by merely pulling vigorously, but in others the spring refuses to budge, and the socket must be pulled and levered bodily from its place.

Another variety is the plate castor—usually provided with ball bearings; this is simply fixed by four screws, which have only to be undone for removal of the castor.

The fourth category comprise the various socket castors, with square or conical cups or sockets that fit outside the leg and are fastened by screws through the sides.

Replacement of Castor.

Provided no damage has been done to the woodwork, replacement is merely a matter of screwing the castor into place, or inserting a new socket.

In most cases, however, the various holes for screws will be too large, and either a size larger screw, or a longer screw, must be used, or the holes should be fitted with plastic wood and the original screws replaced before the plastic wood hardens.

When this is done do not bring any weight on the castor for at least one hour, to allow time for the plastic wood to set.

Damaged Woodwork.

When the woodwork has been damaged, the castor generally gets off scatheless and can be used again. Damage is usually either a partial or complete breakage or a severe splintering of the end of the leg.

The latter trouble can be remedied easily and efficiently by first removing any dirt or badly crushed pieces that would prevent the splintered parts pushing back into place.

Next, inject some plastic wood solution or solvent, then follow it with plastic wood previously softened with solution. Force this thoroughly into the splintered parts and at once press them back into place. Cover the wood with several layers of paper saturated with grease, and bind the parts together very firmly with string. In the case of square sections, four pad pieces of wood should be prepared of such size that they bear evenly on the faces of the leg. Interpose a piece of greased paper between the pad and the leg, then bind or cramp together all the four pieces and leave for two or three hours or more for the plastic wood to harden. If carefully done this will effect an efficient repair, and is preferable to using glue.

Should any of the plastic solution be squeezed out on the faces of the work it should be wiped off before cramping or binding.

Traces of plastic wood on the faces of the work can be removed by scraping with a sharp knife and by judicious sandpapering; afterwards a touch of spirit stain and a rub of polish will obliterate all traces of the repair.

The castor may then be refixed as before, but small holes should be drilled for the entry of all screws before driving them home.

Socket castors that do not fit tightly should have plastic wood packed around the leg and the socket forced home while the plastic wood is still moist.

Protecting Water-pipes from Frost

In nine houses out of ten, the water-pipes are fixed to the interior faces of exterior walls, with the consequence that they are liable to freeze whenever wintry conditions prevail. In addition, the storage tank is usually placed in an exposed part of the roof, where a north wind may attack it with unpleasant results. In fact, the water supply is so arranged, generally, that few houses are safe whenever the temperature falls below freezing point.

The unfortunate householder has but one thing to do, and that is to accept the conditions as they are and make the best of them. How he can make the best of them we will now proceed to explain.

PRECAUTIONS TO TAKE BEFORE A COLD SPELL

In any campaign against the freezing of the water supply, the work should be divided into two clear-cut sections. The first should be undertaken long before a cold spell sets in, and the second, when it is actually in progress.

Encasing the Cold Water Storage Tank.

The cold water storage tank is usually situated in the roof. Normally, it is afforded very little protection and it has every chance of freezing. One thing to do is to wrap dozens of newspapers around and over it, tying them with string, so that they will not blow about or slip down, and then to cover them over with old hearthrugs, carpets, sacking, etc. This will make the tank fairly snug and it will considerably lessen the chances of freezing. Every part of the tank should be encased and the proper course is to afford the protection some time before winter sets in, so as to be on the safe side.

A Permanent Arrangement.

Although the newspapers and the rugs will serve their purpose well, they can only be regarded in the light of a temporary expedient and a more permanent arrangement is advised, whenever possible. Such an arrangement consists in encasing the tank with wood.

To do this, obtain some lengths of wood, 1 × 1 inch in section, and build a frame with them to fit round the tank and extend 3 or 4 inches beyond in each direction. That done, the sides and bottom are covered in with match-boarding. A lid will be necessary. This should be made to fit over the whole of the frame and it will be necessary to construct it with two faces, one 3 or 4 inches above the other. No hinges are necessary.

Fill the Spaces between Tank and Frame with Slag Wool.

In the spaces between the tank and the frame, and, also, between the two

Fig. 1.—Have you prepared your Tanks for the Winter?

Here is shown a storage tank in a jacket of paper and carpets. One corner of the carpet is turned up so that the paper may be seen. When it is replaced, the tank will be ready for the rigours of winter.

thicknesses of the lid, slag wool is packed fairly tightly. This is a bad conductor and the frost is effectively kept from the water. It may be added that the slag wool will last for years in good condition and no mice or other vermin will elect to make their homes in it.

Inspecting an Old Tank.

While considering the question of storage tanks, it will be advisable to examine the one that exists in the roof, if it has seen much service. Should it be on the point of decaying, it will probably be wise to scrap it and put in a new one, for during a frost, a considerable amount of contraction goes on, and this may easily cause a split, followed by an avalanche of water when the thaw comes.

An Immersion Heater.

If a new tank is fitted and electric current is available, it will be well to consider the advisability of providing an immersion heater. This is a piece of apparatus resembling a short rod which is fixed inside the tank. On the outside of the tank, it is connected up to the electric mains and a switch sets it in operation. Thus, if at any time there is a likelihood of the water freez-

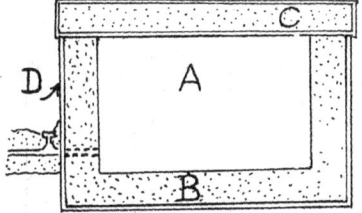

Fig. 2.—Diagram showing the principle of encasing a Tank.

A is the tank encased by the wooden box, D; B shows where the slag wool is packed; C is the double faced lid. Note that the tap on the outflow pipe has not been left exposed. Any other pipes leading to or from the tank should be treated in a similar manner.

ing in the tank, the switch is set on and the water is slightly heated. An hour now and again is all that is necessary, and a shillingsworth of current will make the tank absolutely safe during an ordinary spell of bad weather.

Lagging the Pipes.

Unfortunately, it is not sufficient to insulate the tank. The pipes that run up to it and those that come into the house from the main are, also, very vulnerable, especially those in the neighbourhood of the roof. A good plan is to wrap them in hair felt. Cut the felt in long strips, 3 or 4 inches wide, and wind them spirally around the pipes, tying them at intervals. The felt makes a neat job that is not unsightly.

Using Strips of Newspaper.

Should a cheaper method be wanted, bunch strips of newspaper round the pipes and cover them with any coarse material, such as hessian. Usually, it is necessary to draw the pipes away from the walls while the covering is being twisted round them, but this is not a difficult matter, nor does it add appreciably to the labour. Special care should be taken to make the covering particularly secure at corners and right-angle turns, because it is here that the pipes are most likely to freeze.

Water Fittings.

There is one thing more that should be done well in advance of a period of frost and that is to examine all the water fittings. See that every tap is supplied with an efficient washer and look at all the ball-cocks to note if they are functioning correctly. If any of these are faulty, have them repaired, since a tap or valve that does not work properly is a menace.

WHAT TO DO WHEN A FROST COMES

Now as to what to do when a frost is actually in progress. First, see once again that every tap will shut down tightly, and do not be tempted to leave one of them dripping all night.

The Danger of a Dripping Tap.

It is true that a movement in the column of water in the pipes is one way to lessen the chances of freezing, but it is a way of risking greater troubles. The dribbling water must run off somewhere and in trickling away it may easily solidify. If it does this, the exit pipe will become blocked, and, after that, the water will not be able to escape. It will overflow on to the floor, run through ceilings and cause endless damage. Moreover, it is a punishable offence to leave taps running.

PROTECTING WATER-PIPES FROM FROST

Precautions to take during the Daytime.

During the daytime, much can be done to keep the water on the move. Drain off a little water from all the taps and empty the flushing cistern in the lavatories every hour or so. If this is done with regularity, it ought to be impossible for the pipes to solidify, even in a severe frost.

Have the hot-water system at work and see that the pipes are charged with hot water at bedtime. There are several reasons why this should be done, but the chief is because the hot and the cold water pipes often run side by side.

What to Do at Night.

On retiring for the night, shut all windows that are anywhere near the pipes, not forgetting the one in the lavatory, and leave the doors of the warm living-rooms open.

Empty the Flushing Cistern.

The flushing cistern in the lavatory is a danger-point. Therefore, empty it just before going to bed, and before there has been time for much cold water to run in, fill it up with boiling water.

Add Common Salt to the Water.

Another good plan is to drop a large handful of common salt into the cold water. Salt water freezes at a lower temperature than ordinary water, and the cold must be much more intense to solidify the contents of the tank if it is charged with salt. While speaking of salt, it may be pointed out that it is an excellent plan to pour some boiling salt water down wash basins, sinks and all places where the exit is trapped, just before retiring for the night.

Oil Stove or Electric Fire.

Naturally a good deal can be done by placing some movable source of heat, during the night, at the positions where the pipes exist. For instance, an oil stove or a small electric fire will raise the temperature in the bath-room, lavatory or scullery, so that any freezing is impossible.

Bags Filled with Hot Sand are Useful.

A last suggestion. If it is very cold up in the roof and there are any right-angle bends in the pipes,

Fig. 3.—IF YOUR PIPES ARE LIKE THIS YOU NEED NOT WORRY ABOUT FROSTS.

Two pipes are seen side by side on the right, to the left of them is crumpled newspaper loosely wound round the pipes. This is in turn covered with canvas or hessian. Pipes completely covered in this manner are practically safe from the attacks of frost.

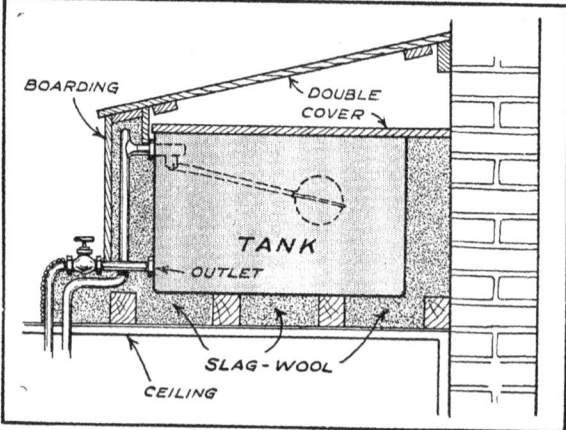

Fig. 4.—PROTECTING EXPOSED PIPES AND TANK FROM FROST.
Shows a store tank in the roof well insulated with a covering of slag wool boarded in round the tank.

Fig. 5.—SIMPLE PROTECTION FROM FROST.
Fit tank with wooden lid and cover the taps with felt.

place a hot water bottle on the corners, or, better still, fill small brown paper bags with very hot sand and put them on the bends, then cover up with pieces of sacking. There is no trouble in heating the sand if it is placed in an oven as soon as the evening meal has been prepared.

When Pipes should be Drained.

It naturally follows that if the stop-cock on the main supply is shut off and all of the house pipes are emptied, no freezing can take place. This plan provides perfect safety, but it often entails a considerable amount of labour,—more perhaps than the average householder is prepared to undertake at night, before retiring. Whether it should be attempted each evening during a frost or not is a matter for every person to decide, but the plan should be certainly followed, if the house is to be shut up for a few days during a cold period.

How to Empty Pipes.

To empty the pipes, shut off the stop-cock and open the lowest tap in the house. If the water will not run out freely, flush the tank in the lavatory. This will cause the level of the water in the storage tank to fall and the ball valve will be opened, in consequence. Air will then be admitted and it will force the column of water in the pipes out through the lowest tap. While this is being done, all the taps in the scullery and bath-room should be opened.

Naturally, the water will flow until the tank in the roof is emptied. If the tank is not encased with lagging, the best thing is to allow it all to run away; but if the tank is protected, this is unnecessary; moreover, it is a safeguard to have a full tank at hand. In such cases, turn off the exit tap which should be provided on all storage tanks.

It may be asked, "What should be done about the hot-water circuit?" Obviously, this must be drained as well, or, otherwise, there is a fear that the boiler might burst.

WHEN A PIPE FREEZES

When a cold snap occurs, a sharp look-out should be kept on the pipes, if there is any likelihood of them

Fig. 6.—Prevention is Better than Cure.
On severely cold nights, a pipe that is in a position where it is likely to freeze should be protected by setting an oil lamp close to it.

lead from the main, it is practically certain that the trouble exists between the spot where they leave the ground and where the tap is fitted. Usually, this is a short run of piping which is easily dealt with. Pour a kettle of boiling water on this length of piping, and, more than likely, the tap will immediately flow once again. Begin by showering the boiling water over and around the tap, because it is here that a stoppage is often set up. If a collection of cloths, rags and old dusters is arranged below the pipes, very little mess will be caused by the hot water.

How to Locate Frozen Point in case of Storage Tank Tap.

Now, if the tap that has failed is connected up to the storage tank, the work is not quite so straightforward. It may be possible to determine in which part of the piping the stoppage exists by noting whether other taps, leading from it, are still flowing. Anyway, the points most likely to freeze are those where there is a bend in the pipes, and, failing any better clues, these are the places where one's efforts should be directed. Pour hot water over them, or, if this is too messy, use a blow-pipe, but be very careful not to ignite any adjacent beams, joists or floor-boards. Hot water bottles and bags of very hot sand, as already mentioned, are helpful. It would be an exceptionally bad case that would not yield to one of these methods.

Is the Inflow Pipe to the Cistern Blocked?

Sometimes the taps will not flow because they have emptied the storage

Fig. 7.—Another method of preventing a Burst in the Coldest Weather.
Showing a bag filled with hot sand placed on a bend in a water pipe. Note how it is propped in position.

cistern and the inflow pipe to the cistern is blocked. A glance inside the tank will show whether this is the case or not. If it is, you may suspect that the trouble lies around the valve. Your best plan, in these circumstances, is to pour a kettle of boiling water over the valve arm, but hold the ball while doing so. The hot water will thaw the valve, and, if it is not supported, the ball will fall, seeing that there is no water on which it can float. If it is allowed to fall, it is quite possible that it will be seriously damaged.

The Hot Water Circuit.

It is hardly necessary to point out that, when the cold water pipes are frozen, it is highly dangerous to stoke the hot water circuit. As soon as it is found that the cold water taps will not run, the boiler fire should be allowed to die out, and, while this is occurring, no hot water ought to be taken from the taps.

freezing, and if they do freeze it is very necessary to act at once. A stoppage that is dealt with promptly is far more easily rectified than one that has run on for some hours.

How to Locate the Frozen Point when a Main Tap will not Flow.

The first thing is to try to locate where the freezing has occurred. It will be a very small area at the outset, but every hour may add appreciably to the extent. Suppose that it is a tap that will not flow. Trace the direction of the affected pipes and note from where they come. If they

COVERING A FLOOR WITH ODD PIECES OF LINOLEUM

LINOLEUM has the unfortunate habit of wearing in patches, and it is quite likely that you may find yours with a quantity of the material that is good in parts, but worn elsewhere. Probably there is not enough of one kind to cover a floor, when the worn areas are cut out, yet it seems a pity to waste what you have.

Proceed in this Way.

Take the used pieces that are sound and fit them together to cover one of your floors. It does not matter whether the pieces are made up of half a dozen different patterns, or whether some have no pattern at all. The only thing is that they should all be of about the same thickness.

As the floor will probably be covered by a rather large number of bits, it will be necessary to tack them down thoroughly, using a plentiful supply of nails. But as long as you drive them well home, the rest does not matter.

Fill in Cracks with Plastic Wood.

When the floor is entirely covered, it will present a somewhat remarkable appearance, but the job is not yet finished. First go over the lino and fill in the cracks with plastic wood; then, when it has hardened, rub them smooth with glasspaper. This will have the effect of making the surface appear as though it were all one piece.

Coat the Floor with Lino Paint.

The next step is to procure a tin of lino paint, which is made specially for floor covering. It can be bought at almost any good colourman's shop. Give the entire surface a coat of this, and when it has dried, follow with a second coat. You now have a floor covered with what appears to be new linoleum at a cost of about 3s.

Allow a Week to Harden.

It should be said that the floor ought to be given a week in which to harden before people walk on it, and that it is almost necessary to remove all the furniture from the room while the painting is proceeding.

The Decoration of Ceilings

Until recent years, the ceiling was not regarded as a particularly suitable surface for decoration, except in the very simplest and plainest ways.

Distemper, generally in plain white or cream, was the commonest form of treatment in dwelling-houses, although in larger and more important buildings paint was sometimes used. But even in such cases the colour was often quite plain and unbroken.

Change of Public Taste.

But of recent years the ceiling has been increasingly recognised for what it is, a most important part of every room, and a considerable variety of treatment is now apparent.

As, however, a plain distemper coating of white or cream is still sometimes required for the ceilings of sculleries, kitchens and bedrooms, readers are referred to the article on "Practical Methods of Distempering" which appears on p. 9.

A very frequent method of decorating ceilings is to cover them with a paper, and the technical process of paperhanging will be found described in the article on "Wallpapers and How to Hang Them" on p. 272.

Coloured Ceiling Papers.

But whereas the usual course in covering a ceiling with paper was, up to a few years ago, to use only one pattern, generally printed in white satin, coloured ceiling papers are now made in a profusion of designs and colourings. These are much more interesting and decorative than the all-white type.

We may note, too, another change. In the past, ceiling and wallpapers were sharply differentiated into two distinct classes. This is no longer so. Many of the plain, semi-plain and even the more lightly patterned papers, primarily intended for use on walls, can be applied to ceilings without any appearance of unfitness.

Panelling Schemes.

Nor is it any longer considered imperative that a ceiling should be papered all over with one uniform pattern. Panelling schemes are sometimes adopted and, where the ceiling consists structurally of one large unbroken surface, such arrangements lend an appearance of richness and restrained elaboration to what might otherwise be a rather monotonous feature.

In some of the houses now being

Fig. 1.—A Suggested Method of setting out a Ceiling for Panelling in Paper, Relief Material or Stencilling.

Fig. 2.—Arrangement of a Ceiling in One Large Panel with Corner Pieces.

This would be carried out in paper, relief material or paint.

erected in various parts of the country the old custom of incorporating both a sitting-room and a dining-room has been abandoned, and there is provided instead one long living-room running through the building from front to back. The long ceiling of such a room presents an ideal field for panelling, and such a treatment is often very attractive.

The ceiling may well be divided into two or, better still, three sections. Nor need they be of equal size. One large panel in the centre with two narrower ones at the end, or alternatively a narrow centre panel flanked by two larger ones will impart an extra note of variety.

Dividing the Ceiling.

The actual panels are covered with a

Fig. 3.—A Painted Ceiling can be shaded by means of a Glaze from the Edges or Corners towards the Centre.

suitable paper, generally semi-plain or carrying a pattern either small in detail or, if larger, of indeterminate outline, and printed in soft colours. The panels are surrounded and separated from each other by what are called "stiling" borders, which are made in 5-inch, 7-inch and 10-inch widths.

A further extension of this mode is to add additional cut-out ornaments at the corners of each panel, thus lessening the severity of an exactly square or rectangular layout. Indeed, so great is the variety of design, colouring and form of the paper decorations now available, that there is immense scope for ingenuity and individual taste in planning most pleasing schemes of ceiling ornamentation.

Relief Materials.

Rather more expensive, but also more permanent, ceiling coverings are the relief materials, such as Anaglypta, Lignomur, and the like, which are made from compressed material with the pattern raised or embossed. Although some of these goods can be obtained ready decorated, it is more usual to hang them in the plain and afterwards paint them in one or more colours. This latter method has the advantages that the material can be more freely handled without damage, and that the joints between the various pieces can be filled up and concealed before the final painting is done.

Here again, one pattern may be used over the whole surface or the ceiling may be cut up into divisions by means of mouldings or borders of the same kind of material.

THE DECORATION OF CEILINGS

decoration of the rest of the room. That does not mean that a ceiling must necessarily be in the same colour or even in a different shade of the same colour as the walls, but that it must be complementary to that colour.

Harmony in Colour.

Thus, if the prevailing tone of the walls is to be a warm fawn, the ceiling may be either pale cream or a delicate green. Or a pale blue ceiling would look well above brown walls. Or, yet again, a pale gold treatment of the ceiling would harmonise quite well with a general scheme, the prevailing note of which is jade green. In fact, the number of possible colour combinations has hardly any limit, save that of the ingenuity and taste of the worker.

Although dark coloured, and even black, ceilings are sometimes seen, they are only tolerable if the room is high, for it should be remembered that a dark colour so used will apparently reduce the height.

Light Colours Best.

It is generally advisable to confine the colouring to fairly pale shades, and that old rule of decoration which proceeds on the principle of working gradually upward from dark to light in a decorative scheme has much to commend it.

Also, it should be borne in mind that all colours look heavier in large masses than they do in small samples. Therefore, in deciding on the colours to be used, particularly for overhead work, it is well to choose a tint and then lighten it somewhat.

A painted ceiling may first be given the appropriate number of coats in, say, broken white (which means pure white just tinged with another colour). When the final coat is thoroughly dry, it can be shaded in any one of a number of ways with either a deeper shade of its own colour or with a contrasting tint.

Shading the Colours.

If the shading colour is mixed from ordinary paint pigments, it should be made thinner than for ordinary painting by the addition of extra turpentine.

The shading colour should be brushed on to the parts intended to be darkest, and then, by means of the stippler, this colour is graduated until it dies away into the ground colour.

Thus it may be laid on round the edges of the ceiling and shaded away towards the centre; or a circular patch may be laid in the centre and shaded off into the surrounding field of ground colour.

The Stippler.

The stippler is a special brush consisting of a square or oblong flat stock containing many bristles set at right angles and with a handle on the back. The stippling must be done as quickly as possible before the shading colour has time to set.

In addition to the two suggestions given above, there is a

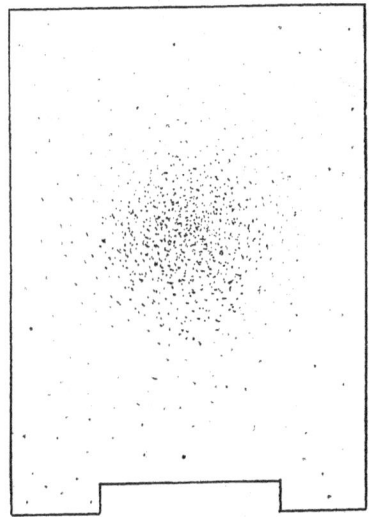

Fig. 4.—ANOTHER METHOD OF SHADING IS TO LAY ON A PATCH OF GLAZE IN THE CENTRE AND SHADE IT OFF TOWARDS THE SIDES.

Hanging Reliefs.

The various processes of hanging "reliefs" both on ceilings and other surfaces is fully described in a later article. Here it may suffice to say that the preparation of the surfaces to be covered is similar to that given in the article on "Wallpapers and How to Hang Them" on p. 272, while the paste to be used for hanging will require to be stronger. The addition of ¼ lb. of glue or size powder to each gallon of ordinary flour paste makes a suitable adhesive.

Shaded Work.

In addition to the methods already described of distempering, paperhanging and covering with relief materials, there are various treatments by means of paint or washable distemper, either plain or ornamented. Here, again, while plain white or cream work was at one time the almost invariable rule in domestic buildings, there is a decided change in modern taste, and not only are stronger colours being used, but shading and various forms of ornamentation are being successfully carried out.

Such treatments must always, of course, be in harmony with the

Fig. 5.—A CEILING PANELLED WITH RELIEF MATERIAL.
Also showing the application of relief ornaments to the frieze space.

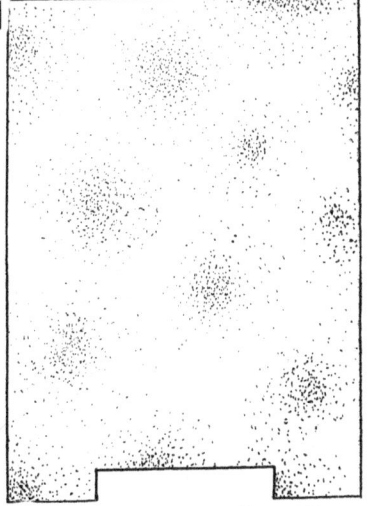

Fig. 6.—AN INTERESTING CLOUD EFFECT MAY BE OBTAINED BY APPLYING ISOLATED PATCHES OF GLAZE AND SHADING THEM INTO THEIR SURROUNDINGS.

THE DECORATION OF CEILINGS

third, which consists in applying the shading colour in isolated patches at more or less regular intervals over the whole of the ceiling, and softening these patches into the general ground colour. In this way all kinds of pleasing cloud effects may be produced.

Broken Colour Effects.

A more regular, but still very interesting effect, which avoids absolute plainness, is that known as broken colour.

In this case the whole surface is painted one uniform colour (again a "broken" white is quite suitable). When this is thoroughly hard and dry, it is coated all over with a contrasting colour, such as pale gold, pale green, etc., mixed rather thin. As this is applied by one worker, a colleague stipples it with a coarse rubber stippler, which is a brush in which the strands are of rubber strips instead of bristle.

The stippling colour must be mixed fairly thin, and no particular care need be taken in laying it on evenly, as the stippler will spread it, while at the same time producing a granulated or broken colour effect which allows the ground colour to show through.

A Home-made Stippler.

If it is not desired to go to the expense of purchasing a rubber stippler, a quite satisfactory substitute can be made by obtaining a flat piece of wood, say 6 inches square, covering one side of it with a sheet of rubber nailed at intervals of about an inch in each direction, and fixing some kind of handle on the other side. The result of the nailing is, of course, that the rubber protrudes between the nails.

If this home-made tool is struck against the glazing colour, it produces an effect rather different to, but equally as pleasing as, that made by the more orthodox rubber-stranded stippler.

We have already mentioned that the glazing colours used in this process should be of rather thin consistency. They can be made from ordinary coloured paint pigments, although some of these pigments make better glazes than others.

Special Glazes.

On the whole, the best course to adopt is to purchase a sufficient quantity of one of the several ready made glazing compounds specially made and sold for these purposes. Parso-Glaze is one of the best known. This is a scientifically compounded glaze made ready for use in a variety of colours, and it is much easier to manipulate than any glaze we can make ourselves, besides being clearer and more transparent in tone.

These specially made glazing compounds may be slightly more expensive than those made from ordinary painting colours, but the difference in cost is small, while the work produced with them is much superior.

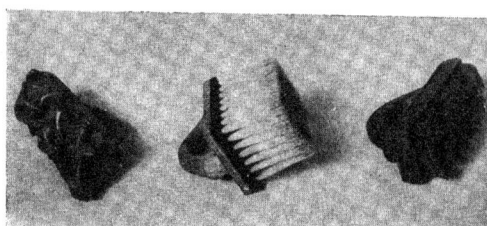

Fig. 7.—SOME USEFUL STIPPLERS.

That on the left is a home-made tool with a corrugated rubber face for producing broken colour effects. In the centre is a hair stippler for soft-shaded effects, while on the right is a stippler made of rubber strips which is also used for broken colour effects.

Stencilling.

Yet another method of decorating a ceiling is that which calls for the use of the stencil. The stencil is one of the most useful decorative devices ever invented, and although during recent years it has not been so widely used as formerly, it is undoubtedly coming into vogue again.

Anyone with even a small knowledge of drawing can easily make his or her own stencil plates. They are simply pieces of cartridge paper on which a suitable pattern is first traced and then cut through.

Cutting is best done with a sharp penknife, the paper being laid on a sheet of glass which enables the knife to make clean cuts. After the plate is made, it is given a coat of shellac knotting, which toughens it and enables it to be cleaned, from time to time, from the paint that might otherwise clog it.

Fig. 8.—A SIMPLE STENCILLED ORNAMENT APPLIED TO THE CENTRE OF A CEILING COULD BE CARRIED OUT IN ONE OR MORE COLOURS.

Fixing the Plate.

The stencil plate is temporarily attached to the surface to be decorated by means of small drawing pins, and the colour is stamped through with a stencil brush, the brush being very lightly charged with colour.

The paint used in stencilling is the ordinary kind, but containing no oil, it being thinned only with turpentine.

A ceiling painted all over in one pale uniform ground colour can be ornamented in innumerable ways by the judicious use of stencils.

Panels of regular or varying sizes, as described earlier for paper decoration, borders running all round the ceiling near its edge with rather larger units at the corners, bands running across the narrower width of the ceiling at intervals, isolated geometrical designs placed at intervals over the whole area—these are but a few of the forms, used either alone or in combination, with which ornaments, by means of stencilling, can be executed.

The same principle of restraint which has been recommended in the matter of colour should also be observed with regard to pattern. Over elaboration is always a mistake, but never more so than in the case of a ceiling.

Necessity for Careful Planning.

One thing, of course, is essential. The plan of the stencilling must be worked out before the actual execution begins, and all centres and lines must be accurately struck out by means of coloured chalk marks and lines on the ceiling itself. And these markings and lines must be accurately adhered to; for instance, a border that is not dead straight is always an offence to the eye, and never more so than on a ceiling, where the slightest crookedness is apparent at once.

Paint v. Washable Distemper.

One other note may be added. The groundwork for stencilling has been described as oil paint. The method is, however, equally applicable to a ceiling coated with washable distemper or water paint. But, for the actual stencilling itself, flat oil paint is recommended. Stencilling can be, and often is, done with washable distemper or water paint colours, but they are rather more liable to clog up the finer details of the plate than are oil colours. Therefore, the latter are to be preferred for this particular purpose. And, in any case, clean working is facilitated by cleaning the plate at intervals during the progress of the work. This can be done by carefully wiping off the accumulated paint with a rag dipped in turpentine.

Electric Christmas Tree Illumination

Fig. 1.—Some of the Electric Candles and Flower Lights on a Section of a Christmas Tree.

Fig. 2.—Some Finished Candles and Flower Lights. Note one candle painted in jazz colours.

NOTHING adds more to the charm and attractiveness of a Christmas tree than the flash of numerous small lights. The verdant background may be gaily decked with rainbow colours and sparkling ornaments, but the one thing that perhaps above all others makes the children dance with excitement is when the lights are switched on.

Outline of the System.

Most, if not all, commercial sets of lamps are wired in series, which means that if one lamp burns out the whole string is dead. The system used in this article has the lamps wired in parallel; thus a lamp can fail without affecting its neighbours. Small 4-volt screw-cap bulbs are used. They are held in threaded sockets; thus a replacement is the work of a few moments, while the holder is easily converted to a variety of uses.

The source of power can be either an accumulator or a mains transformer, thus the cost of maintaining the lights over a lengthy period is small.

Requirements.

Sheet tin, gauge 26–28.
Thin rubber flex.
Tinned copper wire, gauge 18.
Spring clips or crocodile grips.
Insulating tape.
Supply of small corks.
Supply of screw cap lamps (4-volt ·1 amp.).
Some artificial flowers.
Fancy paper and stiff cotton gauze.
Sealing wax.
Soldering outfit.

Making a Lamp Holder

Procure a short length of round wooden stick $\frac{11}{32}$-inch diameter; it will probably be necessary to reduce a piece of $\frac{1}{2}$-inch material to size with a piece of sandpaper. Wind a portion of the thick 18-gauge tinned wire tightly round the stick eight times, so

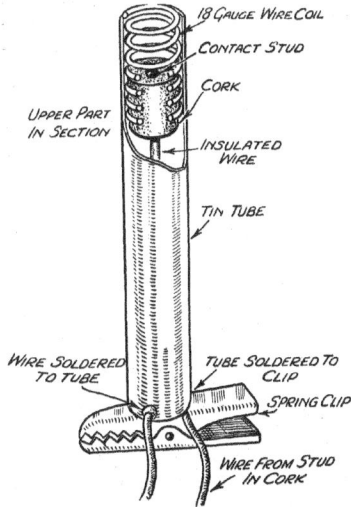

Fig. 3.—Details of the Construction of an Electric Candle for a Christmas Tree.

The method of winding the copper wire to make the lampholder is shown in Fig. 10.

that it resembles a coil spring (see Fig. 10), taking care to make the turns in an anti-clockwise direction. Now

slide the coil off the stick and screw a lamp into one end to see that it fits; the thread in the cap of the lamp should engage neatly with the turns in the coil of wire, and make a good fit.

Preparing the Piece of Cork.

Next file down a piece of cork so that it screws tightly into the other end of the wire coil and touches the end of the lamp cap when the end can be cut off to length just beyond the spiral. Having removed the piece of cork, make a slit in the side half way through, as in Fig. 5. Then prepare a short length of wire with a knob of solder on the end and the insulation removed, as shown in the figure. The bared flex can now be slipped into the slot and the cork then replaced in the wire coil. The plug should fit tightly, but to make it additionally secure paint the wire surrounding the cork with a *thick* solution of sealing wax dissolved in methylated spirits. This runs between the lampholder and the cork and; when it sets, makes the plug carrying the centre contact very firm.

The Electric Candles.

The lampholders described above are adapted in various ways, one of

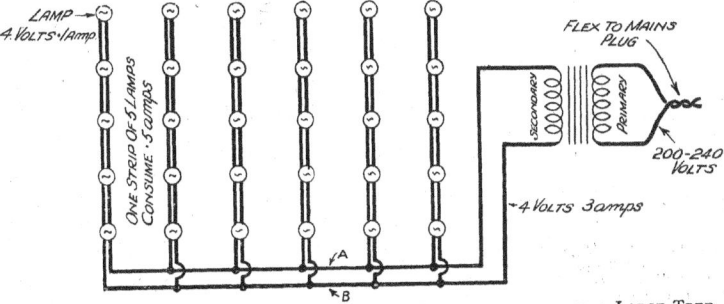

Fig. 4.—Wiring Diagram for Six Strips of Five Lights, Suitable for a Large Tree

The thirty lamps consume 3 amperes, and if it is not intended to use the lamps over long periods a 4-volt accumulator would be suitable. A better method, however, is to use A.C. in conjunction with a mains transformer such as is used in wireless ork.

ELECTRIC CHRISTMAS TREE ILLUMINATION

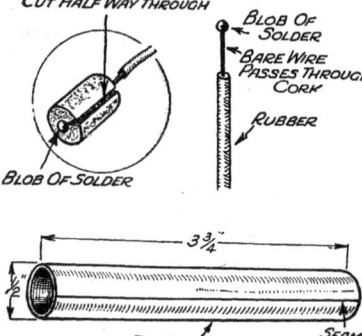

Fig. 5.—Showing Method of forming Centre Contact. Also dimensions for tin tube.

which is to make electric candles, as shown in Fig. 3. From a strip of tin 2¾ inches wide, cut off sufficient to wind round a piece of ½-inch steel rod and overlap about 3/16 inch; then, holding it with a pair of round-nose pliers, solder up the seam, as shown in Fig. 11. The tin cylinder is then soldered to the top of a spring clip as shown in Fig. 3, but care must be taken to leave a small portion of the base of the candle uncovered to permit the passage of the wire from the centre contact in the cork. A short length of insulated wire is then soldered to the outside of the tin cylinder.

One of the completed lampholders should now be introduced into the upper end of the candle; the wire coil should screw into place with the insulated wire from the centre contact passing freely down through the cylinder and out at the bottom. If in doubt as to the rigidity of the lampholder fix with a touch of solder to the top edge of it..

Finally, the finished candle should be enamelled

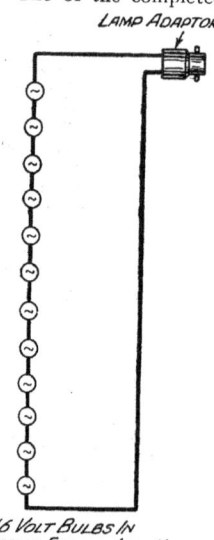

Fig. 9.—An Alternative Method.
16 volt bulbs with screw holders can be purchased and wired as shown above. Use 12 bulbs on a 200 volt circuit and 14 bulbs on a 230 volt circuit.

white and the clips bright yellow; some may be painted in jazz colours, like the one in Fig. 2.

Electric Flowers.

Fig. 8 shows how a lamp may be introduced into the centre of a flower. Note that here a slight addition is made to the lampholder, a second wire being soldered to the outside of the coil near the base (see Fig. 7); this is to provide the second contact. Suitable artificial flowers can be purchased or made up from coloured paper or gauze, a small ½-inch hole being cut in the centre to admit the lampholder, the petals being secured to the holder by binding with thread or stuck with a little fish glue. Fig. 8 shows two types of home-made flowers, while the two in Fig. 2 are made up with artificial flowers,

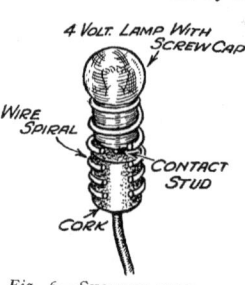

Fig. 6.—Showing how the Lamp fits into the Twisted Copper Wire.

the petals being stuck to the holder with seccotine.

Electric Fruits.

Pleasing effects can be obtained by taking a ping-pong ball and cutting out a ½-inch hole

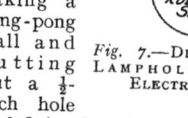

Fig. 7.—Details for the Lampholder of the Electric Flowers.

and fixing in a lamp and holder with the sealing wax solution described above. The outside surface of the ball being suitably tinted with thin colour to represent various types of fruit. When alight the thin white walls of the ball give an attractive translucent effect.

Wiring in Strips.

For convenience in attaching to the tree the lamps are wired up in strips of *five*, thus, as each lamp takes ·1 amps., the complete strip will consume half an ampere of current. The lamps are connected in parallel, that is the short centre contact wires are all connected to one main lead, while the outside contact wires are all joined to the other main lead. Fig. 7 shows how the

joints are made, the lead is bared for ½ inch and the end from the holder is twisted round and soldered, and a rubber sleeve or a piece of insulating tape is fitted over the joint.

Complete Wiring Diagram.

The complete wiring diagram (Fig. 4) shows thirty lamps arranged in six strips of five lights suitable for a large tree. When wiring a number of strips pleasing results may be obtained by having a row of candles, another of flowers, and yet another of fruit, and so on, each strip having similar type lamps but all strips being different.

Finally, each strip is joined up in parallel to two main leads from the power source, as shown in Fig. 7. Instead of permanently fixing the strips to the main lead wires small plugs and sockets, as used on wireless sets, can be used if desired.

The Source of Power.

If it is not intended to use the lamps over long periods a 4-volt accumulator will do admirably as a source of current supply. Many readers may wish to use the mains, and this is quite easily accomplished without the slightest danger as the voltage on the actual tree is only 4 volts, thus a shock is out of the question.

The Mains Transformer.

If the supply current is A.C. a suitable transformer must be used, and before purchasing one we must know the current consumption of the lamps. In the wiring diagram (Fig. 4) the thirty lamps consume 3 amperes, thus for such a series we want a transformer that will give 3 amps. at 4 volts. Wireless mains transformers giving 2–4 amps. at 4 volts can be purchased cheaply and these are admirably suited to our purpose. These transformers have two secondary windings,

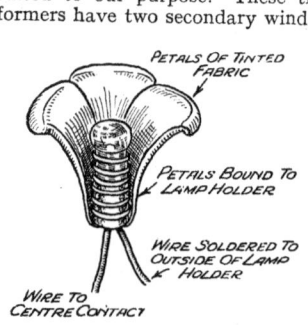

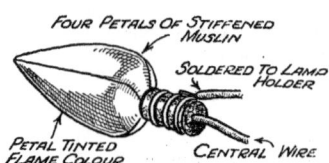

Fig. 8.—Two Types of Electric Flowers

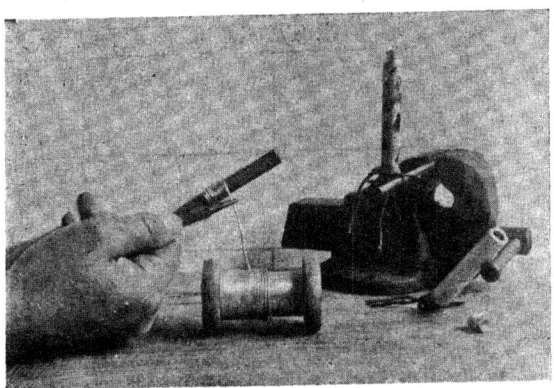

Fig. 10.—Twisting the Tinned Copper Wire to make the Lampholder.
A portion of the wire is wound tightly round a stick about eight times so that it resembles a coil spring.

Fig. 11.—Soldering the Seam of the Tin Cylinder forming the Candle.
Note the finished lampholder and the matchbox and the coil in the end of the candle in the foreground.

one for rectifier and the other to heat the filament of the valves; it is this latter-mentioned tapping which is required.

If the transformer only supplies 2 amps. then the lamps must be limited to four strips of five bulbs, while, should it be desired to light the full six strips off the 4 amps. tapping, then a stout 5 ohms resistance must be included in the circuit after it leaves the secondary of the transformer.

Other Transformers to Use.

A good bell transformer will light a small number of bulbs while a model electric railway transformer would light from 20–25 lamps, but a resistance would have to be used to reduce the voltage.

The Ferranti model railway transformer, for example, gives $2\frac{1}{2}$ amps. at 10 volts. A suitable resistance to reduce the voltage to 4 volts while supplying a load of $2\frac{1}{2}$ amps., *i.e.*, twenty-five lamps, would be 3 ohms.

Wiring up the Transformers.

Having obtained a transformer suited to the consumption of the lamps in the lighting set, screw it down to a baseboard and construct a small metal box to cover it; bore a couple of holes on opposite sides of the metal cover to admit the flex.

Connect the primary terminals, that is, the *input* pair, with 5-amp flex, to a supply plug, and use the same for the two main leads from the secondary which in turn supply the strips.

Using a Trickle Charger.

Some readers may possess a trickle charger for use with wireless accumulators, and this can be called into use to light the Xmas tree. If the charger has an output of $1\frac{1}{2}$ to 2 amps., then it can be connected up directly in circuit with the lamps which, of course, must be a suitable number so that their combined consumption is equal to the output of the charger.

When the trickle charger has only a small output of, say, $\frac{1}{2}$ to 1 amp., connect the lamp circuit to a small 4-volt accumulator and the charger to the same terminals of the cells so that they are charged while the lights are on. The drain on the cells will then be much less severe and they will maintain the lamps in use over a long period.

REPAIRING A HOLE IN LINOLEUM

It often happens that a hole wears in the linoleum under the leg of a table, a heavy chair, or a wardrobe. The weight of the piece of furniture seems first to crack the surface, then to render it into small pieces, and finally it disintegrates, leaving an unsightly hole. The rest of the floor may be perfectly good, and to buy fresh linoleum to cover it is considered an unwarrantable expense.

This is how the hole may be repaired, so as to appear almost, if not quite, unnoticeable. First look to see if the canvas backing is torn. If it is, lift up the strip of linoleum that is affected, trim away the torn part and stick a patch of new canvas or hessian over the hole, applying it to the under-surface. Then return the strip to the floor. Should the canvas be only slightly worn, there may be no need to do any trimming; it just depends on whether the patch can be put on smoothly. Let the patch be fully large for the hole that is being repaired.

Next, if the canvas backing is in good condition and not torn, do not trouble to lift the linoleum, but proceed as now suggested for step No. 2. This consists in obtaining a piece of waste linoleum or, better still, cork carpet. Flake off a quantity of the surface material and cut it into tiny pieces. If you have any disused grinding machine, such as a pepper mill, put the flakes in it and grind them into powder.

That done, make up some hot Scotch glue and mix a little of it with the powdered linoleum. The thing to aim at here is to make a putty with just sufficient glue to bind it.

The next step is to return to the hole, and while the linoleum is lying flat on the floor, to paint the canvas that is visible, together with the edges of the hole. Then take the putty just made, and force it on to the glued surface, paying particular attention that it binds well with the old edges.

When the hole is filled and before the new material has dried, level the surface with the blade of a knife and make quite certain that there are no depressions which will extend below the general level of the good lino.

At this point, the job must be left for a day or two, during which time the patch should be protected. As soon as the fresh material has thoroughly hardened, go over it with a piece of glasspaper and render it absolutely smooth.

Here it may be said that for very small holes, no larger than the size of a penny, it may be more convenient to use plastic wood than to make up a putty as here suggested.

In either case, the new surface may be finally coloured with oil paints to match the rest, if desired.

TIME, LABOUR AND MONEY-SAVING IDEAS

A HOLDER FOR VACUUM CLEANER PARTS

People who possess a vacuum cleaner are often at a loss to know where to keep the various accessories and interchangeable parts, such as the cleaning and polishing attachment, and the long flexible attachment and mouthpiece for curtains and upholsteries.

A holder for accessories similar to that illustrated can be made quite easily as follows. Take two odd pieces of floor board from the wood

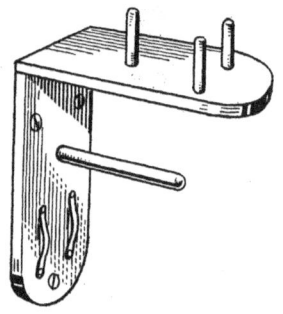

shed, smooth them down with glass-paper, and butt join them with glue and a couple of long screws. Then take 4 or 5 inches off an old broomstick and three slightly thinner pieces of curtain rod; taper their ends and drive them into holes previously bored in the bracket at suitable points. Smear some hot glue inside the holes before inserting the tapered ends.

If other accessories need accommodation, two or three flat springs screwed to the board beneath the projecting broom-handle will be useful. The holder should then be screwed to the wall in a convenient alcove or cupboard.

WEIGHTING TOOL HANDLES

It often occurs when a tool, such as a bradawl or a chisel, is thrown down in a hurry it will roll off the bench and fall to the floor. There is a risk that it may cut the foot of the worker or, in any case, it is likely that the hard surface will nick or dull the cutting edge. To prevent this it is a very good plan to weight the handles of certain tools. Bore a hole in the part of the handle that rests on the bench with a five-eighths cutting bit. Bore the hole only so far as the centre of the handle, but no farther, or the object will be defeated. Into the hole pour some melted lead which should not be so hot that it will burn the wood seriously. When the lead sets trim it off evenly with a fine rasp and finish with coarse sandpaper. Now, when a tool is thrown down hurriedly upon the bench, it will not roll over more than once and will come to rest leaded side downwards.

CLEANING DIRTY DRAINS

The easiest and quickest way of cleaning pipes and drains which have become choked with grease is to dissolve half a pound of caustic soda in a bucket of hot water and empty this down the sink. Afterwards flush with more hot water, and it will be found that pipes and drains have been rendered perfectly clean.

REMOVING MARKS FROM PAINT

The appearance of any painted surface may be very much improved by following a simple plan. Any marks or dirt smudges should first of all be taken away with soap and water and a rag. Do not rub at all hard as there is always a risk of cleaning away the paint from the wood. Now wipe very dry with a duster. When all the moisture has been removed take another rag, and on to it place a very little vaseline. Then apply this to the painted surface, rubbing in rather firmly. When all the paint has been treated, go over the surface with a soft rag, polishing gently. You will be surprised how nice the paint looks after it has been dealt with in this way. When vaseline has been applied it is not at all easy to make any marks on the paint, and this is a great advantage. Indeed, with any clean or newly-painted surface, it would pay to apply a little vaseline by way of protection.

TO PROTECT CROCKERY

Jugs, etc., are often cracked by being brought against the hard metal of the sink tap. A good way of preventing this is to fit half a hollow rubber ball

on the tap in the way shown. Make the hole in the rubber, which is to slip over the tap, of such a size that a good fit is the result.

THE TIGHT CANISTER LID

It sometimes happens that the lid of a tin canister is so firmly set that it proves extremely difficult to move. At such times here is a suggestion which will save a lot of trouble. An inch or so below the lid tie a piece of stout string, getting it as tight as possible and making the tying very secure. Now push a longish stick,—a pencil will do quite well—under the string. Start to twist the pencil, and this brings the band of string together even more closely, so that the top of the canister is drawn in a little and thus the lid is loosened.

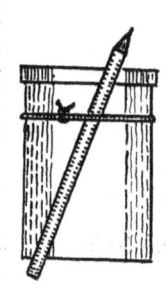

This simple hint may save endless time in struggling to remove a lid that has become tightly jammed.

WHAT TO DO WHEN TUBS SHRINK

When wooden tubs are allowed to become dry they often shrink and begin to let water. The only remedy is to make the wood swell out again so that all the cracks are filled. When the tub is large it is not easy to soak it and the swelling goes on slowly if water is poured in. An easy way of righting the matter is to fill the tub with bunched-up pieces of newspaper. Then pour water on to these so that they are made thoroughly damp. In the course of a few hours the moisture is absorbed by the tub, and it is then in order for use.

A SAW HINT

It is often necessary with a tenon saw to cut out grooves in wood to an exact depth. If the saw is employed in the ordinary way there is a risk of going too deeply. To prevent this the saw should be "blinded." Here two strips of metal are placed on either

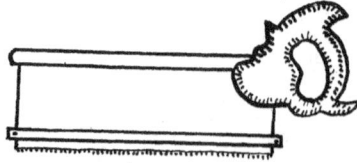

side of the saw in the way shown in the sketch. The strips are held together by bolts which are tightly screwed. In this way the metal strips can be adjusted to any position to prevent the saw cutting more deeply into the wood than is required.

RAFFIA-WORK
WITH SOME USEFUL EXAMPLES

RAFFIA-WORK is a craft which never loses its popularity, for the materials are cheap, the methods of using them are simple, and the results are so attractive.

Raffia can be used very similarly to wool; for instance, worked in formal patterns on canvas, the whole of the ground being covered, it is suitable for cushion-covers, bags, etc. If lightly varnished afterwards articles of this kind may be wiped over with a soaped flannel when soiled. (There is an attractive table-runner of this kind still "going strong" after ten years' daily use in the writer's home.)

Another method is to take a background of Madagascar matting (sometimes called raffia cloth), or coarse crash, stamp a bold embroidery transfer on it and proceed to embroider it, using raffia as if it were wool.

How Raffia is Sold.

Raffia is sold in a great variety of colours, in bundles of varying sizes, costing from 2d. upwards. Its quality varies very much. Sometimes it comes in broad strands of even width, at others you find the strands wide in the middle and narrow at the ends. Of course, when working formal all-over designs on canvas, completely covering the background (as in Fig. 1), all the strands must be of the same thickness or unevenness will result, so that sometimes one has to discard narrow strands. But they will not be wasted as they will be of use when embroidering flowers, etc., on crash or matting. The required width of the strand also varies with the texture of the canvas. This may be either single-thread or double-thread and fine or coarse, but it is essential that it should be fairly stiff, otherwise it will drag out of shape.

A TEA-COSY

Supposing for a start we take the tea-cosy in Fig. 1. An Italian pattern has been adapted for this, and it has the merit of being delightfully simple. Each stitch is worked over the same number of threads and every row is the same. So if you get the first row right all you have to do is to go on repeating it in the colours as directed.

Fig. 1.—A Delightfully Simple Tea-cosy in an Italian Pattern.

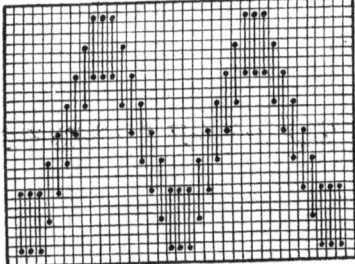

Fig. 2.—Chart for working the Tea-cosy.

The colours used in the original are dark green, light green, dark red, light red, orange, yellow and natural.

Fig. 3.—This Attractive Cushion should have a Coarse Brownish Crash Foundation and looks charming worked in Green, Orange, Blue, Yellow and Purplish-pink in the very Simplest Stitches.

The canvas used is brownish in colour and has ten double threads to the inch. (Single-thread canvas will do just as well.) If your canvas is coarser or finer it doesn't matter very much as long as you take care to use strands of raffia of appropriate width.

How to Make It.

You will probably want to make the cosy to fit a particular tea-pot, so your best plan is to cut a paper pattern and try this over the tea-pot, allowing room for the padding. Cut out two layers of cotton wadding for each side (without turnings) and two pieces of sateen for each side with ¼-inch turnings all round. (The colour of this should match one of the colours of raffia you will use.) Seam the two pieces of sateen together on the rounded edges, and turn out. Slip in the wadding. Turn in one raw edge of the lower edge of sateen and fell it over the other, *slightly* over the edge. Make the other side in the same way, then seam together by the outside edges, and the felled edges along the bottom should be on the outside.

The foundation is now ready for the raffia cover.

The measurements of the model cosy are: Width across, 11½ inches; height, 9 inches.

To Work the Raffia.

Place the paper pattern on the canvas and pencil all round it, but about ¼ inch away from the paper. (Of course, the lower edge will come on a row of holes.) Cut out with 1-inch turnings all round. This outer covering must be a little larger than the foundation.

Mark the Middle Hole of Bottom Row with a Pin.

Find the middle hole of the row near the bottom and mark with a pin. Take light red raffia and thread it in a coarse, blunt tapestry needle. About 12 inches is a good length for the strand, and it should be about ¼ inch wide.

Where to Begin Work.

Begin work in the hole to the right of the pin. Draw out the needle and raffia here. Take three upright stitches side by side (working to the left) over six double threads. After the third stitch bring out the needle three holes

Fig. 4.—This Plate Mat is 8 Inches Square worked in Dark Blue, Light Green, Orange, Yellow and Natural.

higher up. (This is halfway up the previous stitch.) * Make an upright stitch over six strands, then bring out the needle halfway down this stitch and repeat from * until you have five single stitches, then bring out the needle halfway down the last stitch and work three upright stitches as before.

Now work downwards to the bottom row again with single stitches (see Fig. 2). Work in this way to the pencil line at the left side. Darn in the raffia along the back of the work and return to the middle. Work from here to the right-hand line. You have now completed one row of the pattern.

The Order of the Colours worked upwards.

Now work upwards, repeating this row, but starting at the right hand. If preferred you can turn the canvas upside-down and work downwards. The following is the order of the colours worked *upwards*:—

1st row.—Light red.
2nd row.—Orange.
3rd row.—Yellow.
4th row.—Natural.
5th row.—Light green.
6th row.—Dark green.
7th row.—Dark red.

Of course, only work just up to the pencil line. Then fill in the spaces *below* the first line of the pattern with the appropriate colours.

Work both sides in the same way, then lay the work right side downwards on a thick blanket, place a wet cloth over it and press with a warm iron until dry. Press back all the turnings to the wrong side and cut down a little. Then seam the rounded edges together. Now take six strands of raffia of different colours and plait up in a triple plait. Sew this over the join at the rounded edges, making a loop at the top.

Place the raffia over the foundation and fell the sateen edge to the canvas all round. If liked, you can edge the bottom also with the plait.

LUNCHEON MATS

These are very practical, as if varnished they can be wiped over with a soaped flannel when soiled. The model mats are worked in dark blue, light green, orange, yellow and natural. These colours happen to harmonise with my luncheon china, but you will naturally choose a combination of colours which will suit your own special china. The foundation is the same as the tea-cosy, double thread canvas with ten threads to the inch. The plate mat is 8 inches square and the glass mat 4¾ inches.

The Plate Mat (Fig. 4).

Cut a piece of canvas 10 inches square. Crease the square lightly

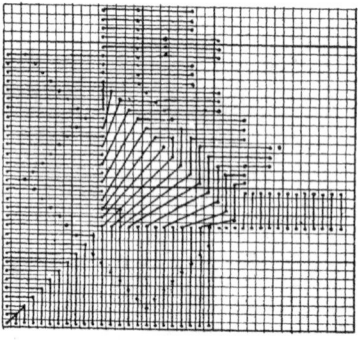

Fig. 5.—Chart for working the Plate Mat.

from corner to corner diagonally twice to get the centre and from the centre hole count thirty-seven holes diagonally (not including the centre hole). Thread a blunt tapestry needle with blue raffia and bring it out in the thirty-seventh hole. Count two holes up diagonally and put the needle through to the back, bring it out again on a straight line to the left of the thirty-seventh hole, but missing one hole. Now make an upright stitch over two double threads into the same hole as the first slanting stitch.

After this work to the left, starting every stitch on the same level (but not missing a hole), and making each stitch one hole higher than the previous one, until you have worked over nine threads, then work each stitch one hole lower until you have one stitch over two threads. Go along in this way until you have five complete pyramids; then miss a hole, bring out the needle and make a diagonal stitch into the same hole as before. Turn the mat round and work in the same way on the other three sides (Figs. 5 and 6).

Before beginning the very first strand of raffia make a small back-stitch in a part which will afterwards be worked over, and in starting subsequent strands darn in the needle along the backs of the stitches.

Care in Working.

Be very careful, as in the cosy, not to pull the raffia tightly. The holes should all be well filled and no canvas showing.

First work the Green Border.

Now work the green border. Bring out the raffia through the same hole as one of the shortest blue stitches. Make an upright stitch over nine threads, then work as in the blue border, but upside-down (or, if preferred, you can turn the mat round and work the opposite way). At each corner, after working a stitch over four threads, work one over two (this being one hole shorter than the previous one, both at the top and bottom). Now turn round and work along the other three sides in the same way.

Now work a Triangle in Each Corner.

Next take the orange raffia and work a triangle in each corner thus: bring out the raffia in the corner hole, then count eight holes up diagonally and make a diagonal stitch. Bring out the raffia again in the next left-hand hole (over a green stitch over five threads), and put it in again in the next diagonal hole. Now bring out over a green stitch over six threads, and put in again on the next diagonal hole. Bring out over a green stitch over seven threads and pull in again in the next diagonal hole. Miss one hole now over a green stitch and bring

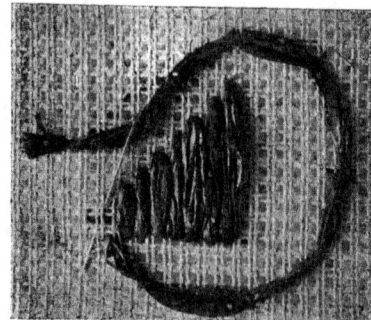

Fig. 6.—A Sample of the Stitch used on the Plate Mat.

out over the next stitch over five threads. Now go on and miss a hole in this way in the green border, but working into each hole diagonally. At last you will have a straight stitch over three threads. Then go to the first stitch and complete the triangle. Work this way in each corner.

Take the yellow raffia and work an inner border over four threads. When you come to the middle of the triangle turn round and work the opposite way, and fill in the little space with two stitches over two threads.

After this fill in the centre space with natural raffia.

Filling in the Centre.

1st row.—Start over the first right-hand yellow stitch on one of the straight sides. Work three upright stitches over six threads, then three over three threads and repeat to the end, finishing with three stitches over six strands.

2nd row.—Begin at the right hand, close to the yellow border, on a level with the top of the short stitches in the previous row. Then work groups of three stitches over six threads to the end.

Repeat the second row until the tallest stitches of the row leave only three threads between them and the border, then work like first row. Fill in any spaces with small stitches.

If you have worked evenly and have not drawn the raffia tightly the canvas will not be at all puckered.

Press the mat as described for the tea-cosy, then fill in a lining of sateen or casement cloth matching one of the colours of raffia. Thread blue raffia in a sharp-pointed crewel needle and work a kind of coarse seaming-stitch round the edges to cover the canvas threads.

The Glass Mat (Fig. 7).

Take a piece of canvas 6 inches square and round it work a border in blue similar to that on the mat, but the longest stitch should be only over eight threads instead of nine. Also, there should be only three pyramids. Work the green border to correspond, then make four orange triangles with no space left between them on the sides (Fig. 8). Work a border inside of yellow over four threads and fill in the centre with four diamonds in natural. Each diamond has five stitches, the longest being over six threads. Make up the mat in the same way as the larger one.

THE CUSHION

This attractive cushion has a coarse brownish crash foundation and looks charming worked in green, orange, blue, yellow and purplish-pink, in the very simplest stitches. The crinkly texture of raffia is very decorative and makes fine stitches unnecessary (Fig. 3).

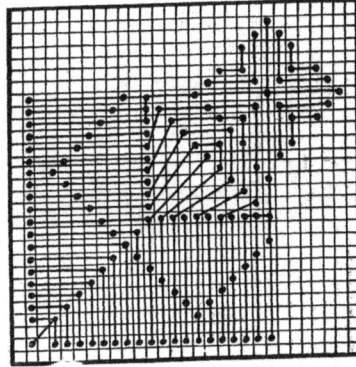

Fig. 8.—Chart for working the Glass Mat.

You'll need two squares of crash large enough to cover the foundation cushion you are going to use, also raffia in two shades of green, two of blue (one very dark), two of purplish-pink, and one each of yellow and orange. You won't need a whole bundle of each, and though two greens are essential, yet you can alter the other colours to suit your own taste.

The transfer is T.L.242 and costs 7d. from the Pattern Shop, 12 Southampton Street, Strand, W.C.2. Stamp this in the middle of one square of crash. First cut off the small spray and the number, though you may use them on the *back* of the crash to test the heat of the iron if you wish. The iron should be very hot when a thick material like crash is in question.

The Basket.

It is best when using raffia to pass

Fig. 7.—Attractive Design for a Glass Mat.

the needle up and down through the crash as if working in a frame, and to leave the raffia rather loose.

Use dark blue for the basket itself (or brown if you prefer). Take a strand just under ¼ inch in width and thread it in a coarse chenille needle (this has a long eye and a sharp point). Cover each upright line with a straight, single stitch, leaving it rather loose, then take a rather narrower strand and work the top and bottom bands in stroke stitches *across* to cover the spaces completely. Make these stitches about ⅜ inch long.

The Leaves.

All are worked in the same way, in slanting stitches taken from the outside edge to the centre line. The raffia should be just under ¼ inch in width. Use the two shades of green alternately—first a light leaf, then a dark one (Fig. 9).

The Flowers.

Long-and-short stitch is used for these, taking a long and a short stitch in turn from the outside edge to the edge of the inner ring. Use yellow, orange, two blues and two purplish-pinks for these and arrange them to contrast pleasantly, keeping the lightest shades to the top of the basket (Fig. 9).

Fill in each centre with four French knots—yellow and orange for the blues and purplish-pinks, and blue for the yellow and orange. *On no account pull the stitches tightly.*

The Leaves.

Use light green for the little leaves, just one stroke for each. The raffia should be rather wider than before, so that it spreads out to cover the leaf-space. Then work the line in

Fig. 9.—Detail for working the Leaves on the Cushion shown in Fig. 3.

outline-stitch with a narrow green strand.

Now place the work face downwards on a thick blanket with a wet cloth over. Press the crash very heavily with a hot iron but let it rest *very lightly* on the back of the raffia. Remove the wet cloth and press the crash until it is quite dry.

Make up the cover in the usual way, that is, stitching it together on three sides, and then, after turning it right side out and slipping it over the cushion, slip-stitching the open edges together.

But remember that the cover should always fit very tightly over the foundation.

Finish off the edges with a plait of raffia. Use nine colours and plait up into a triple plait. Sew this round the edges and add a tassel of the raffia at one lower corner.

A TRAVELLING WRITING CASE
Figs. 10 and 11

This handy travelling writing case makes a delightful present, and is both inexpensive and quickly worked. No transfer is needed as the design is so simple.

The original was carried out in Madagascar matting of natural colour, with raffia flowers in orange and two shades of red, and leaves of green suède. But cloth, arras cloth or linen could quite well be used for the foundation, and while still making the flowers of raffia, cloth could be used for the leaves.

Size of Matting Required.

Provide yourself with a piece of matting, cloth or other suitable material, 11½ inches wide and 25 inches long, a smaller piece 8 inches × 3 inches, a piece of sateen for lining, half a bundle each of brown, dark red, light red, orange and green raffia, a small piece of suède or cloth, sufficient to make a strap 10 inches long and 1½ inches wide and to cut out eleven small leaves, three round green wooden beads, two red beads and one yellow one, and a patent snap-fastener. If cloth is used, a piece of tailor's canvas will be needed for interlining, but not if the matting is used.

Turn back the edges of the large piece of matting for ½ inch all round and press them. (If using cloth, turn the edges over the canvas and tack them before pressing.) Now make a row of running in brown raffia close to the edge, taking stitches about ½ inch long, and leaving the same space between them. Return and cover the spaces left. Next make a similar row in dark

Fig. 10.—A Travelling Writing Case shown Closed. Cloth, arras cloth or linen could quite well be used for the foundation.

Fig. 11.—Travelling Writing Case shown Open.

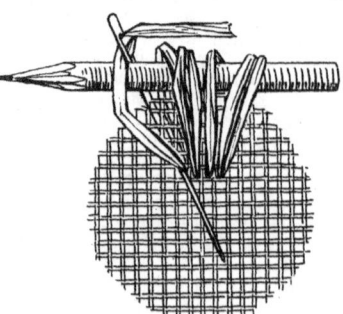

Fig. 12.—How to make the Flowers for the Travelling Writing Case.

red, but return with green, make a third row in green and return with orange. Fold the strip into three and crease well.

Take the smaller piece of matting, turn in the edges and line with sateen. Hold two strands of dark red raffia along one long edge and couch over them with brown.

To make the Flowers.

Start with the one for the pocket to get practice—they are all made in the same way.

Cut a circle of stiff muslin or buckram measuring 1¼ inches across. Draw a circle ½ inch across in the middle. Thread a broad strand of orange raffia in a coarse chenille needle (this has a big eye and a sharp point). Now work from the pencilled circle all round, taking loops about 1 inch long over a pencil. Work over and over so that the loops are very thick (Fig. 12). Fill in the centre with short loops in green.

Cut Two Leaves in Suède or Cloth.

Cut two leaves in suède or cloth 2¼ inches long × 1¼ inches wide, the shape of a little laurel leaf. Place these on the pocket in the position shown in the photograph and sew down in the middle with long stitches in green raffia. Work a short, thick stalk with green raffia, then place the flower over the leaves and turn up the loops near the stalks back on to the centre. Take the orange raffia and sew these loops down, then catch down the edges of the other loops.

Flowers for the Front of the Case.

Next make the flowers for the front of the case similarly. One 3 inches in diameter in light red, one 2½ inches in light red, two 2 inches across in light and dark red mixed, one in yellow 2¾ inches across, and another in yellow 2½ inches across. Be sure to get the loops very thick. Sew a bead in the centre of each, then work small green loops round the beads. Put green and yellow beads into red flowers and red ones into yellow flowers.

Now cut out Nine Leaves in Suède or Cloth.

Cut out nine leaves in suède or cloth. (If you have to buy this, one colour will do for all, but if you are using up odd bits two or three shades can be used). Cut to the shape of a laurel leaf, but of varying length, the longest being 3 inches and the shortest 2 inches. Arrange the leaves as shown, then take fine green sewing cotton and catch down the edges at intervals. With the same cotton, used double, work veinings in back-stitch down the middle, and one or two branching out at each side.

Sew Flowers Down with Cotton.

Place the flowers in position and sew them down with cotton round the bead, then take raffia to match and catch down the loops at intervals all round. The largest flower goes up in the left-hand corner, the next in size just below, and the others as shown.

The Pocket.

Tack the pocket to the front of the underpart of the case and catch down the edges all round with brown raffia over a strand of dark red. About 1½ inches from the right-hand make a downward row of invisible stitches to divide the pocket into two. Cut two short straps of suède 1½ inches wide, just long enough to secure the case when closed. One must be sewn at the top fold of the case under one of the leaves and the other on the lower edge of the flap inside. Fix the snap-fastener to fasten. Next fell in the lining and sew up the sides.

Take two strands of brown raffia, hold them exactly on the edge of the case and work over them in orange. All edges except the lower fold must be treated like this. Slip a writing-pad inside the case, and postcards, letters to be answered, book of stamps and pencil, inside the small pocket.

WHEN MOVING FROM ONE HOUSE TO ANOTHER

WHEN you are going to move from one house to another, make your plans systematically, for it is only by so doing that the ordeal will go through smoothly.

As soon as you can do so, write to three or four local firms for estimates for the move. Then lose no time in deciding which you intend to engage. If your change-over falls on a quarter-day, you should fix up with these people at least four weeks in advance.

Clear out all Cupboards, etc.

That done, begin preparing for the great day. First, go through all cupboards, wardrobes, chests, etc., and sort out the things that you ought to discard; then dispose of them. It is marvellous the number of unwanted books, papers, bottles, tins and similar things that accumulate.

In the previous two or three weeks, again go through the cupboards, wardrobes, etc., but clean them out and replace the articles tidily. Also clean out bookcases, china cabinets, etc.

Clean the Carpets and Roll up Linoleum.

A week before the move, clean the carpets and take them up; roll up the linoleum; take down the pictures and wash them, stacking them away in safety. Dismantle various fixtures which are to be taken with you, and do the same to such things as lamp shades, curtain poles, etc. Naturally, you will leave the living-rooms in order till the last.

Collapsible sheds and other things in the garden must be attended to. If plants are to be moved to the new house, this work ought not to be left to the last day, if it is possible to do it earlier.

If the old and the new house are within reasonable distance, it is well to engage a barrow, van or car to take over carpets, lino and garden materials before the actual move. Then you can re-lay the carpets and lino before the furniture is brought in. Do not re-lay the stair carpet, however.

People who Should be Told.

Three or four days before leaving, acquaint your friends and all business connections with the new address. Write to the local postal authorities and ask them to re-address all communications after a certain fixed time, which you will name. Also advise all tradesmen, especially those who call regularly on you for orders. Be quite certain that you stop the papers, the milk and the bread. In addition, send a note to the insurance company, respecting your fire and burglary policy. Usually, they will transfer the risk from one house to the other at no charge, unless you have purchased much new furniture, when an addition must be made to the premiums. Acquaint the gas, electricity and water companies of the exact time of your departure, and do the same with the local authority to whom you pay your rates.

All this concerns the old house, but the new premises must be considered in much the same way. Get into communication with the gas and electricity companies and arrange to have supplies ready for you as soon as you enter.

On the day of the move, be up early, have a good breakfast, and be ready for the men with the vans. Prepare some sandwiches and similar food to carry you through the day. You do not know when and where you will have the next meal.

Before Leaving.

(1) Turn off the water supply.
(2) Turn off the gas and electricity. Note the readings on the meters.
(3) Look round the house and garden when the last things have been carried out. Go to every cupboard, shelf, cellar and attic, to see that all has been taken.
(4) Close and catch all windows. Bolt all downstair doors that are on the outside of the house, but lock the front door.
(5) Forward the key to the landlord, before mid-day, if this applies.

On reaching the New House.

(1) Stand at the front door and instruct the men as they pass through with things, where they are to go. It will save a tremendous amount of bother if articles are placed in their correct rooms.
(2) Take note that beds, tables, wardrobes, bookcases and other articles are reassembled by the men, if this is part of the agreement.
(3) Notify any breakages to the foreman before he leaves.

If possible, before Entering the New House:

(1) See to the papering, whitewashing and painting, but leave any work on the staircase and hall until after the move.
(2) Have carpets and lino put down (again, not on the staircase or hall).
(3) Have blinds fixed up.
(4) Have the cistern cleaned out.
(5) Have the chimneys swept.
(6) Have fires lighted in several rooms the day before, in cold weather.
(7) Arrange for the telephone, if required.

An Attractive and [

The dolls' house has always been one of the most popular toys for a little girl. There are in our museums examples of such toys that delighted youngsters of past generations, and the fact that they are as popular in these days is shown by the enthusiasm aroused by the famous Queen's Dolls' House.

Apart from the pleasure it gives to the child, there is the additional advantage that it is a particularly interesting thing to make. There are so many little realistic touches that can be given, such as the addition of a garage, a garden, the furniture, and so on.

Actually, there is no limit to the work that can be put into a dolls' house, but as a practical matter it is better to keep it reasonably simple, because the child is not so much concerned with a scale model as with having fun by arranging furniture, dolls, and so on. The example in Fig. 1 has been designed as the happy compromise between a house of realistic appearance and a simplicity which makes for hard wear. It has four rooms, a lounge hall, and corresponding space above. The roofs in the actual model are a fixture, though one side could be made to hinge so that a convenient space is formed to hold batteries if it is desired to light the rooms with electricity. Plywood is used almost exclusively, this having the advantage of being very strong in comparison with its weight.

The Main Structure.

The sizes of the more important parts are given in Fig. 12. It is a good idea to begin by cutting out all of them. It certainly makes for economy in time and labour, though some may prefer to prepare the parts as the work proceeds, as it saves the tedium of a lot of cutting at one sitting.

The first parts needed are the top, bottom and two sides. There is no interior cutting in these parts. Trim them to the sizes given in Fig. 12, making sure that the edges are square and that the opposite pieces are the same size. Readers who have the ply cut by machine can leave edges just as they are from the saw, providing that they are cut true and that they are reasonably clean. The same applies when they are cut by hand, providing the saw is held perfectly upright.

Assembling.

The top and bottom are contained between the sides. It is advisable to ask a friend to hold the free end of the ply whilst the other end is being fixed. Glue the joining edges, and drive in nails at intervals of about 2 inches. Nails ¾ inch long are suitable. It is important that the nails enter the centre layer of the plywood beneath, and this necessitates some care in starting the nails in the right place, and in keeping them upright. Fairly fine nails are advisable, as thick ones may tend to separate the layers.

Having fixed the pieces together in the form of four sides of a box, the inner walls can be added. These are shown clearly in Fig. 3, one being fixed and the other ready for nailing. Two doorways have to be cut in each (Fig. 12). These are sawn easily with the fretsaw. The pieces sawn away can be used for the doors later.

Mark the Wall Positions.

It is obviously necessary that these inner walls are fixed at the correct distance from the sides, and that they are

Fig. 1.—View of the Attractive Four-

Fig. 3.—How the Inner Walls are added.

Fig. 2.—The Exterio[Plywood and Cove

LY-MADE DOLLS' HOUSE

...LS' HOUSE SHOWING THE FRONTS OPENED.

...OLLS' HOUSE MADE IN
...OLLS' HOUSE PAPER.

easy to see the exact position for the nails at the edges. To give the nail positions at the centre, pencil lines can be drawn joining these first nails on the outer surfaces of top and bottom. If any nails should run out of truth, withdraw them immediately, because a projecting nail may cause an injury.

Adding the Floors.

The floors of the two upper rooms are added next. Cut them to the sizes given in Fig. 12. They are fixed level with the bottom edges of the upper doorways, and, to ensure their being level, lines should be drawn from front to back in line with these edges. Corresponding lines should be drawn on the inner surfaces of the outer walls.

Glue the edges, and drive in nails at front and back, and then draw guiding lines so that nails can be driven in at the centre. There is no difficulty about putting in the nails through the inner walls, but when those through the outer walls are driven in, it is advisable to hold a fairly heavy weight underneath, as otherwise the nails may tend to spring. Fig. 4 shows the structure with the floors fixed.

The Staircase.

This is made up as a complete unit and fixed as a whole. It consists mainly of a centre part fretted out to represent the bannisters, with two sloping pieces as shown in Fig. 5. Sizes of the centre part are given in Fig. 12. The exact number of uprights is not important. The two flights meet at right angles, so that if a 45-degree set square is available this can be used to mark the flights from the front edge. Use the fretsaw to cut the shape, and trim the edges with glasspaper.

The two slopes are fixed one at each side of the centre piece as shown, nails being driven in through the latter. To give a neat finish the upper and lower ends can be bevelled. The treads are formed from short lengths of triangular moulding. This can be obtained ready made. It is cut up into short lengths, and glued down on to the slopes, the broad side downwards.

Before fixing the staircase, the centre upper floor is fixed. This does not run right through to the back, but stops a little way past the doors. Glue the edges, and fix it with nails driven in at an angle from the front and back. There is no need to put in centre nails.

Fixing the Staircase.

A view taken from the rear is shown in Fig. 6. Place the complete staircase in position, taking care that the bannisters are upright, and drive nails into it through the inner walls. The landing piece is then cut. It may be necessary to saw a little notch to fit round the bannister. It is nailed in, pencil lines being first drawn in as a guide. Fig. 7 shows the staircase from the front. A continuation of the bannister can be made to fit on the upper floor. This is shown clearly in Fig. 1.

Fig. 4.—THE TWO UPPER FLOORS ADDED.

AN ATTRACTIVE AND EASILY-MADE DOLLS' HOUSE

*Fig. 5.—*The Main Parts of the Staircase.

*Fig. 6.—*View of Staircase from Rear.

*Fig. 7.—*View of Staircase from Front.

*Fig. 8.—*Adding the End Roof Pieces.

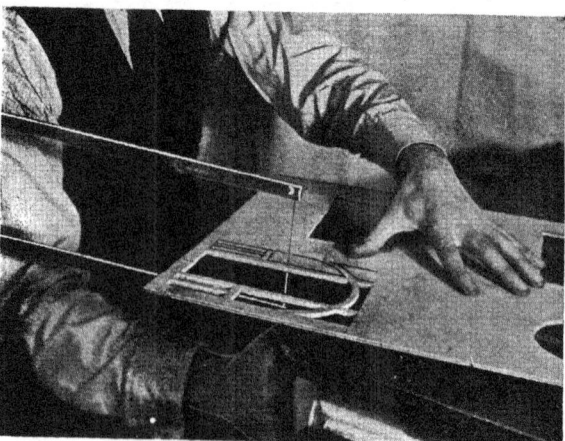

*Fig. 9.—*Fretting out the Front.

*Fig. 10.—*How the Porch is Made.

*Fig. 11.—*Covering the Fronts.
Note how edges are turned back.

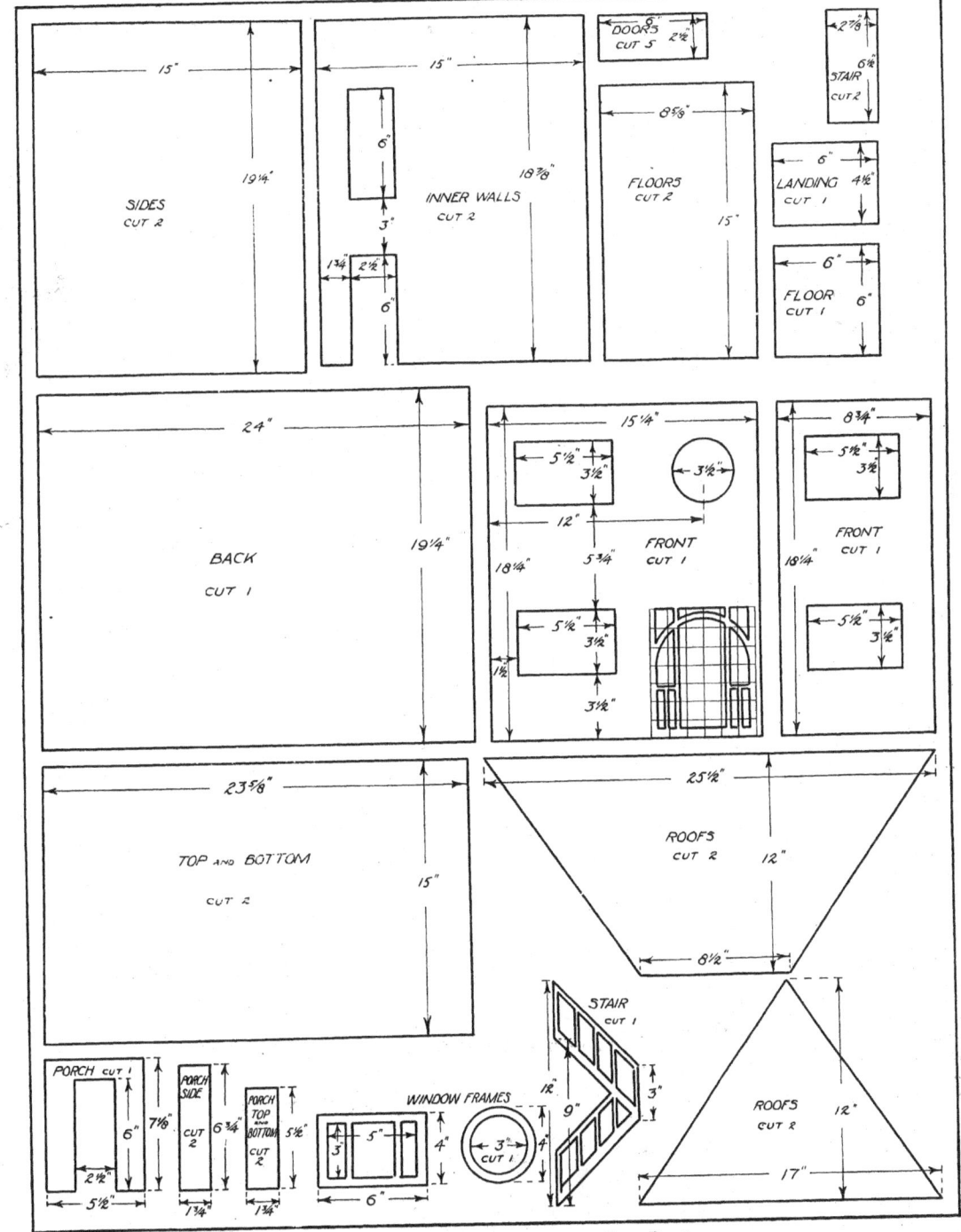

Fig. 12.—Showing the Sizes of the Main Parts.

The Roof.

Prepare the four pieces to the sizes in Fig. 12. Strictly, the sloping edges should be bevelled to make a close joint, but it really does not matter a great deal, because the paper covering hides the joints. The back roof could be ³⁄₁₆ inch narrower than the front, so that they are the same width when joined together.

Glue and nail these two pieces together, and place them in position. Before fixing, however, add a 1 × ¼-inch strip to the front edge of the house at the top. This piece can be seen in Fig. 2. The back also can be nailed on.

Ask a friend to hold the two roof pieces in position, and drive in nails along the edges. The short side pieces are easily added. Fig. 8 shows one of

AN ATTRACTIVE AND EASILY-MADE DOLLS' HOUSE

Fig. 13.—Cutting out the Windows.

Fig. 14.—The Roofs being covered.

them being placed in position. One or two nails can be driven in at an angle to hold them. To make them quite secure, pieces of sticky paper or *passe-partout* can be stuck over the angles.

The Fronts.

Fig. 9 shows the left-hand front being fretted out. The lines drawn across the diagram in Fig. 12 represent 1-inch squares, so that the shape can easily be drawn in. Compasses can be used for the curved member. After cutting, fit them against the house to make sure that they coincide.

The porch is made up as a separate box, and is fixed as a whole behind the fretted part. It is shown complete in Fig. 10. Notice that the sides are contained between the top and bottom, and that the back is fixed behind. The back is **cut away to form the door.** When fixing the porch, the bottom should be level with the top edge of the fretted front. This makes it stand up from the bottom edge, so enabling it to clear the bottom.

To provide a suitable surface for hinging, strips of wood are fixed against the outer edges of the fronts, and to the inner edges of the outer walls. These are seen in Fig. 1.

Covering.

A wide range of special dolls' house papers can be obtained ready printed. They represent bricks, tiles, slates, wall, ceiling and floors. Deal first with the fronts. Cut a sheet of brick paper large enough to allow a turnover all round, and lay it face downwards on the table. Brush a coat of thin glue or paste on the front, and lay the latter upon the paper. The projecting edges of the paper can then be glued and turned over, as shown in Fig. 11. Do the two opposite sides first, cut the corners and complete the remaining sides.

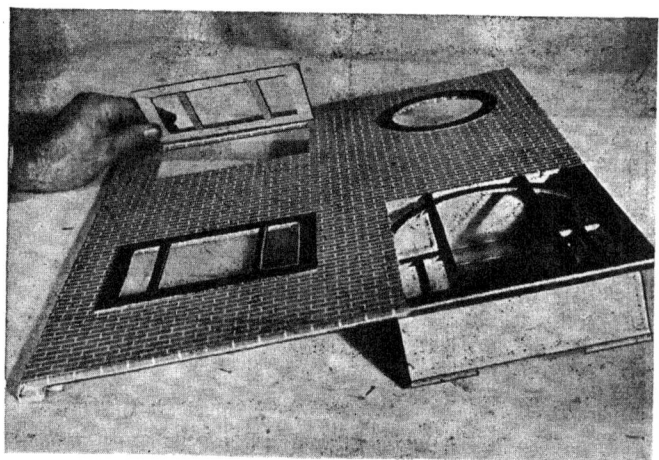

Fig. 15.—Fixing the Window Frames.

The windows are now dealt with. Hold the front against the light, as in Fig. 13, so that the window positions can be seen easily, and with a knife cut a line all round about ¾ inch from the edges. At each corner other mitre cuts can be made as shown. In the case of the circular window, a similar centre cut is made, and a series of cuts about ½ inch apart made all round up to the edge. In the case of the left-hand front it is advisable to cut away the part opposite the porch before fixing.

The chimneys are plain blocks of wood, 6 × 2 × 1 inch, with the lower ends cut off at 45 degrees. Brick paper is wrapped around them. Little flat projecting caps are glued on top.

Window Frames.

These can be conveniently cut in 1/16 inch plywood. Either paint or stain them, and nail them over the window openings as in Fig. 15. The glasses are laid in from the back, and glued in place by narrow strips of brown paper. Wallpaper can be pasted to the interior as desired, and realistic touches given by the addition of mantelpieces, shelves, and so on. The doors are hinged by means of strips of *passe-partout*.

Fitting an Electric Burglar Alarm

THE essential feature of a burglar alarm is reliability. Considerations of the initial cost of the alarm and installing it, within limits, should not wholly decide the particular type of alarm to be installed.

One of the best types of burglar alarms, commensurate with its cost, is one which is operated by a closed circuit relay.

Principle of Action of the Alarm.

The various alarm contacts which are fitted to doors, windows, and any places where illegal admission to the premises may be effected, are connected in series with the magnet coils of the relay. This circuit is energised with current from a battery of cells or a suitable transformer, when all the alarm contacts are closed.

When a door or window is opened, the alarm contact at this position opens the circuit, and the magnet coils of the relay are de-energised. The effect of opening the alarm circuit is to cause a pivoted soft iron armature, which is part of the mechanism of the relay, to close a local bell circuit which is supplied with current from a separate battery of cells, or from a bell transformer.

The bell will continue to ring until the relay mechanism is reset. In a similar manner, if the wiring of the alarm circuit is cut through at any part of the circuit, the relay will operate, and the alarm be given by the ringing of the bell.

The Materials and their Cost.

One high resistance closed circuit relay for battery operation, £2 10s., or, if required to work from a transformer, £4 4s.

Closed circuit contacts, 4s. 6d. each.

Two single-pole one-way bell switches, 1s. each.

One 4-volt, high capacity, low discharge rate accumulator, 16s., or 4 Edison Lelande cells, 15s.

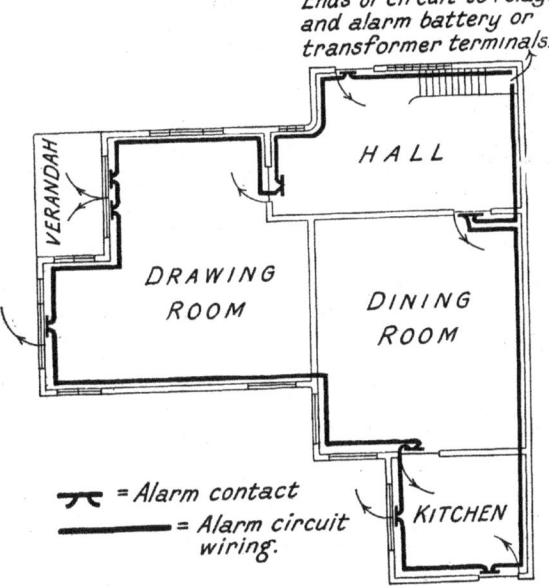

Fig. 1.—SUGGESTED POSITIONS AND WIRING CONNECTIONS OF ALARM CONTACTS FITTED ON THE GROUND FLOOR OF A DWELLING-HOUSE.

The alarm contacts are fitted at all positions where an entry into the premises may be made by opening a door or window. The wiring is run round the premises to the various contacts and connected to them. All the contacts are in series, so that in the event of any of the contacts being opened, or the wire being cut at any part of the circuit, the relay will operate and close the bell circuit.

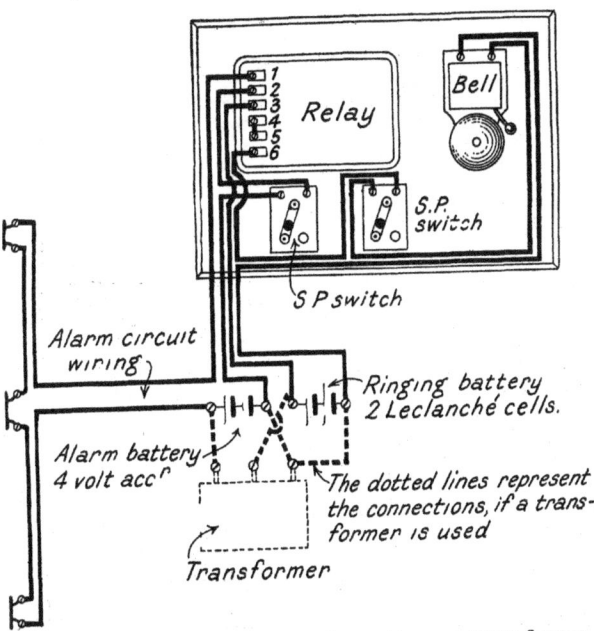

Fig. 2.—CONNECTIONS OF THE CLOSED CIRCUIT BURGLAR ALARM SYSTEM.

The alarm circuit is connected in circuit with the magnet coils of the relay. A switch is included in the circuit to open it when the system is not in use. Terminals 4 and 5 must be connected together so as to include in the ringing circuit, the short-circuiting blocks which open the circuit when the strut is used to set the relay. A switch is included in the ringing circuit to open it when the system is not in use.

Two No. 2 size Leclanché cells, 4s.

If a transformer is used for operating the alarm system instead of batteries, a bell transformer and a Wylex clock fuse connector, costing 10s. in all, will be required.

One 9 × 6½-inch polished wooden block, 1s.

Coil of single 1/.044-inch insulated bell wire, 2s., supply of staples, fixing screws for alarm contacts.

Selecting the Positions for the Alarm Contacts, Relay and Batteries.

Alarm contacts should be fitted to all windows which will open, and to doors which admit to principal rooms and the upper floors of the premises.

The batteries or transformer should be situated in a dry accessible position where admittance cannot be obtained without opening an alarm contact.

If a transformer is used, the main switch of the installation should not be accessible without opening an alarm contact.

The relay and bell should be fixed in an occupied bedroom, if the premises is a dwelling house, to prevent interference, and allow of setting the relay before retiring.

All occupied bedrooms having windows which are accessible from outside should be protected with alarm contacts, ventilation for these rooms being arranged without interference to the contact.

Fitting the Alarm Contacts to a Door.

Make a template of the metal base of the contact from a piece of stiff cardboard, this will be convenient for "marking off" on the various fixing surfaces.

Select a place on the architrave which is adjacent to the upper edge of the door, and also near to the edge which opens. The clearance between the architrave and the edge of the door at this place should not be excessive, or the contact will not

FITTING AN ELECTRIC BURGLAR ALARM

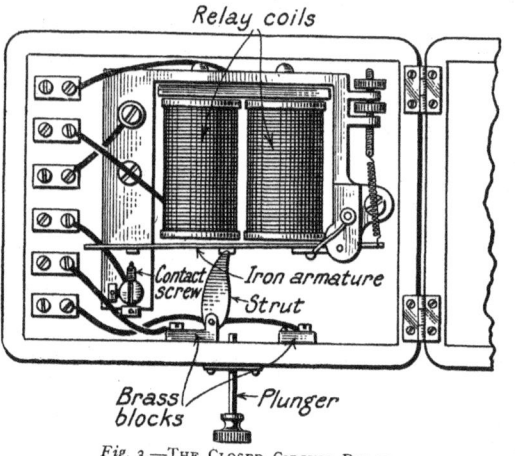

Fig. 3.—The Closed Circuit Relay

The relay consists of an electro-magnet with an armature pivoted at one end. Immediately beneath this is a strut, so fixed that if the plunger beneath it is pressed up it causes the strut to lift the armature adjacent to the magnet coils. It is retained in this position until the coils of the relay are energised, when the armature is attracted, causing the strut to be released. The strut now short-circuits the two brass blocks, which are included in the bell circuit. When an alarm contact is broken the relay coils are de-energised, and the armature falls back on the contact screw, completing the bell circuit. The bell will continue to ring until the strut is replaced.

close when the door is shut. If the clearance is excessive then the contact may be fitted to the door jamb near to the upper hinge.

The template is laid in position and the shape of the metal base of the contact marked off on the fixing surface. The wood is now slotted to a depth sufficient to accommodate the thickness of the metal base. The distance between the outer edges of the vulcanised fibre blocks is marked off on the face of the recess equidistant from the edges, and the wood between these marked lines is slotted to a depth sufficient to accommodate the fibre blocks and the wiring to the terminal screws. A ¼-inch hole is drilled from the upper surface of the architrave to the centre of the recess, to allow of the wiring to be threaded to the terminal screws of the contact.

When the contact is finally fixed in position, the metal ball will be in contact with the upper edge of the door, and press the contact springs together when the door is shut.

To prevent wear to the upper edge of the door at the point of contact of the metal ball, a recess may be cut at this point, and a small brass plate fixed in the recess, so that its upper face is flush with the edge of the door.

Fitting Contacts to Window.

A similar method will be adopted when fitting contacts to window frames, always making sure that the contacts will be closed when the windows are shut.

The contacts will be screwed down to their fixing surfaces when the wiring is connected to them.

Wiring the Alarm Circuit.

Assuming the premises to be an occupied dwelling house, the best run for the wiring in most cases would be round the picture rails, and across the upper edges of door architraves.

When running the

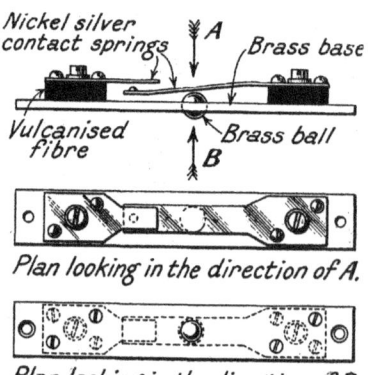

Fig. 4.—Details of an Alarm Contact.

Two heavy nickel silver springs are mounted on a brass base, but insulated from it with vulcanised fibre blocks. Each spring is provided with a terminal screw. The lower spring bears against the upper surface of a brass ball which is seated in a hole in the base. The hole has a slightly less diameter than the diameter of the ball.

When the contact is fitted in position to the door or window, the ball pushes the lower spring into contact with the upper. If the door or window is opened the ball is released and the springs are separated.

wiring from one room to the next, the upper surface of the architrave of the connecting door is drilled through from each room, the two holes converging at the recess which has previously been made to accommodate the alarm contact. This method will conceal the wiring and make a sightly job.

At each contact position sufficient wire should be allowed for connection to the terminal screws, and any slack wire can be packed neatly at the back of the recess.

The wiring should be secured at frequent intervals along the run with staples. The staples should be driven so as to just grip the wire without damaging it.

One end of the alarm circuit should be terminated at the position selected for the battery, and the other end at the relay.

Connecting the Alarm Contacts and Fixing them in their Positions.

The ends of the two wires at each contact position are cut to a suitable length, and the insulation stripped back for a distance of ½ inch, cleaning the bared ends. Slacken off the terminal screws of the contact and twist the bared ends of the wires round the shanks of the screws in the same direction as the screws will be tightened up, the wires should be under the washers. The screws are tightened up and the slack wire carefully packed at the back of the recess. The contact is now secured in the recess with ½-inch 6s countersunk head brass screws. The lower face of the brass base should be flush with the fixing surface, and when the door or window is closed, the contact should be closed.

Fixing the Relay, Bell, and Single Pole Switches.

The 9 × 6½-inch wooden block is fixed at the selected position. If the

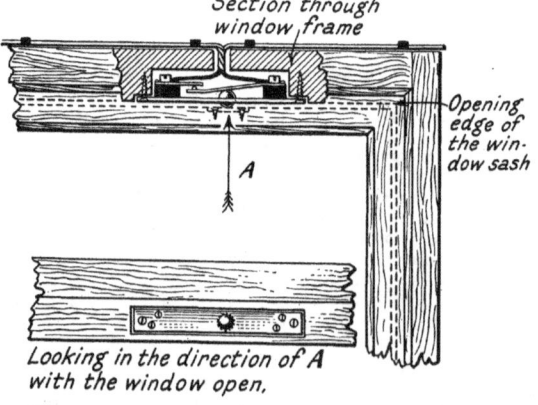

Fig. 5.—Alarm Contact fitted to a Casement Type Window Frame.

The head of the frame is slotted out to the correct depth to receive the alarm contact. The position of the slot should be near to the opening edge of the window sash, so that should the window be only partially opened the alarm contacts would open.

FITTING AN ELECTRIC BURGLAR ALARM

fixing surface is a brick wall, it should be drilled and plugged in two places.

The wooden block is drilled and countersunk, and secured in position with 2½-inch × 8ˢ countersunk head wood screws.

The side of the relay case is drilled to allow of the four connecting wires to pass through for connection to the terminals, and the base is drilled in two places for the screws, which will secure the relay to the wooden block.

The relay, bell, and switches are now screwed to the wooden block, the relay should be horizontal, so that when the strut is released by the pivoted iron armature, it will fall down on the brass short-circuiting blocks.

Wiring the Bell, Relay, Switches to the Alarm and Bell Circuits.

The alarm battery and the bell-ringing battery are placed in the selected positions. One end of the alarm circuit is connected to one terminal of the alarm battery, and another wire long enough to reach the relay position is connected to the other terminal of the battery. The ends of two wires are connected to their respective terminals of the bell-ringing battery, and together with the connecting wire from the alarm battery, and the free end of the wire from the alarm circuit, these four wires are run to the relay position. The wires are carefully stapled down to their fixing surface; do not damage the insulation of the wires with the staples.

The ends of these wires are connected to their correct terminals as indicated in the diagram of connections. Make sure that all the bared ends of the wires are clean and tightly gripped under the washers of the terminal screws.

Transformer used instead of Batteries.

The transformer and a Wylex clock connector are fixed in a convenient position near the main switch of the electrical installation, and connected to the main fuses as indicated in a previous article.

The two outer secondary terminals are connected in series with the alarm circuit, and one inner together with an outer terminal, supply the current to the bell-ringing circuit.

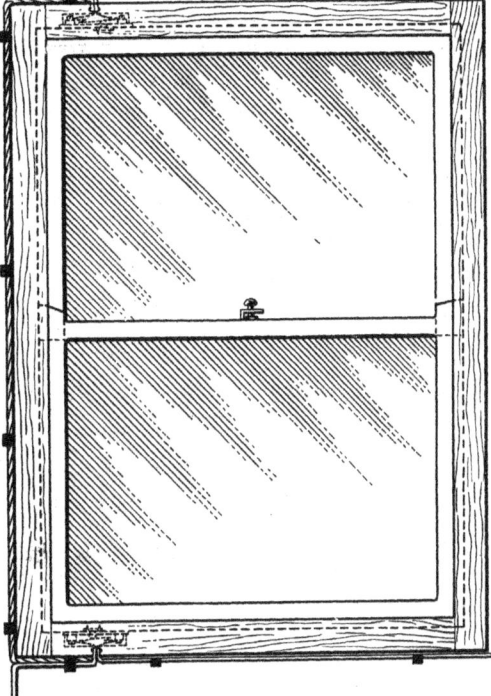

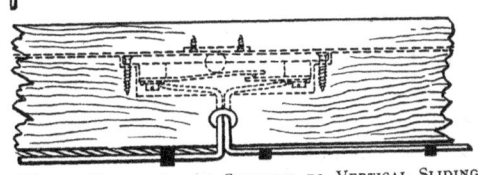

Fig. 7.—FITTING ALARM CONTACTS TO VERTICAL SLIDING SASH TYPE WINDOWS.

To protect this type of window it is necessary to fit two alarm contacts. One contact is fitted in the head, and the other contact fitted in the sill of the frame.

The surface of the wood is slotted out in each case, and the alarm contacts screwed down in position, so that when the window is closed, both the top and bottom contacts are closed. Holes are drilled through the head, and sill, from the front of the frame to the centre of the slots to accommodate the wiring to the contact terminals.

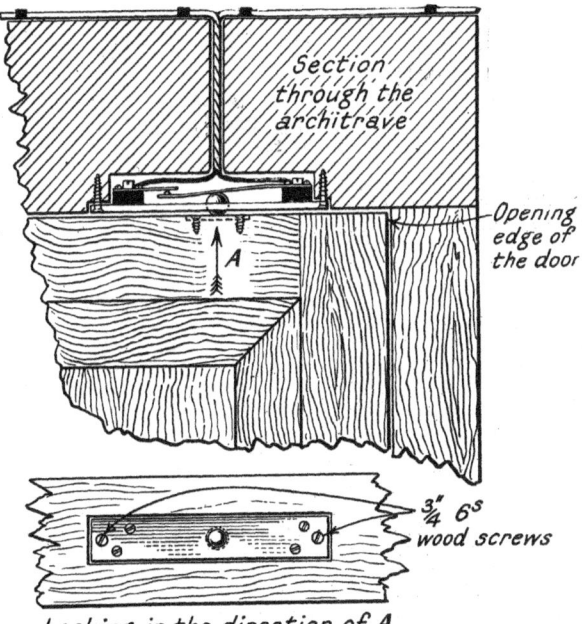

Fig. 6.—ALARM CONTACT FITTED TO THE ARCHITRAVE OF A DOOR.

The architrave is slotted to receive the contact so that when the door is closed, the ball pushes the lower spring into contact with the upper spring. A hole is drilled through the architrave, between the centre of the slot and the upper surface of the architrave, to allow of the wiring to pass through for connection to the terminal screws of the contact. The contact is secured in position with two ¾ inch 6ˢ countersunk head wood screws. The position of the slot should be near the opening edge of the door to ensure the alarm contacts opening when the door is only partially opened.

Testing the Alarm.

Close the two S. P. switches, set the relay with the strut engaged with the pivoted iron armature, and shut all windows and doors where the alarm contacts are fitted. Open one of the doors or windows; the relay magnet coils should now release the pivoted iron armature and the strut should fall across the brass short-circuiting blocks. The bell should continue to ring until the relay is reset. Close the door or window which was opened, and repeat the test until all the alarm contacts have been tested.

Charge the Batteries Periodically.

The accumulator and Leclanché battery will require periodical re-charging, and this duty should not be neglected.

FITTING AN ELECTRIC BURGLAR ALARM

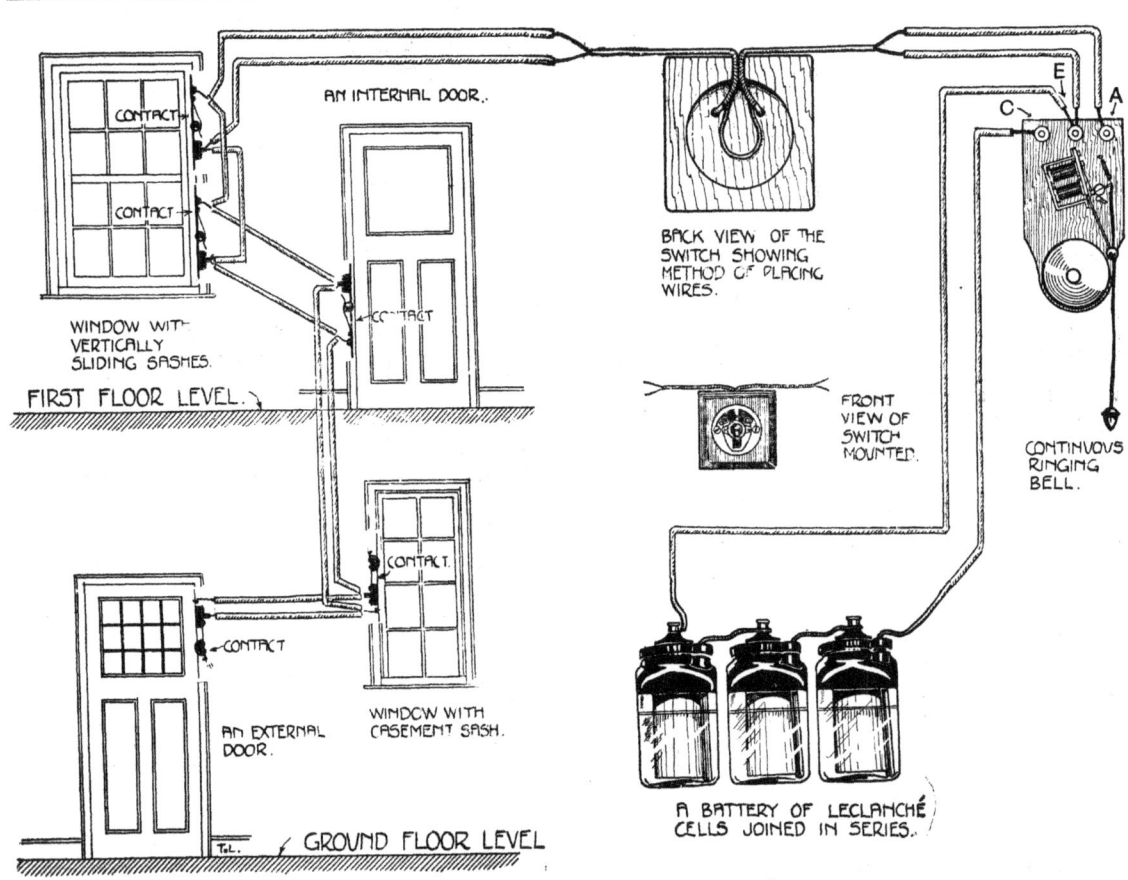

Fig. 8.—A Simple Form of Electric Burglar Alarm.
The components shown enlarged and the wires shown singly with covers taken off for purposes of clearness.

A SIMPLER FORM OF BURGLAR ALARM

The use of a closed circuit relay, although giving excellent results, may be considered by many people to be rather too costly. We give, therefore, in Fig. 8, details of a simpler form of Burglar Alarm which does not require a relay.

Materials Required.

The following materials will be required: Burglar alarm contacts, a continuous ringing type of bell having a gong of about 3 inches diameter, three Leclanché cells, a quantity of twin bell wire, a supply of staples, and an ordinary tumbler switch.

Method of Wiring.

The notes already given relating to the method of wiring and fixing the contacts, bell and batteries, apply equally well to the simpler system. It will be noticed that in Fig. 8 the position of the contacts on the doors and windows are slightly different from those shown in the previous illustrations. This, of course, does not affect the working of the alarm in any way, and either position can be adopted.

When fixing the wire it should be remembered to choose the paths that offer the most obscurity in conjunction with the shortest runs. Where it is possible to hide the wires under the floor or in the roof without disturbing the existing decorations, this should be done.

The Switch.

The switch by which the apparatus is set "on" and "off" should for preference be hidden in a cupboard if this can be arranged without involving too much extra wiring. In any case, it is a good plan to place it somewhere where it will not be easily noticed.

How to Test the Working of the System.

First of all close all doors and windows to which contacts have been fitted. Now gently pull the cord attached to the bell which will set the trigger. Place the switch in the "on" position, and then, when a door or window is opened, the bell should ring immediately and continue to do so until the switch is put in the "off" position and the cord on the bell is pulled.

This process should be repeated in turn with each door or window. Should it happen that the bell does not ring, examine all connections to contacts, etc., very carefully.

Do not fail to make periodic tests and to keep the battery in condition to ensure the satisfactory working of the alarm.

An alternative method, if you have A.C. mains in your house, is to use a transformer. See the article on p. 205 for details for using a transformer.

Five-Minute Christmas Decorations

To give a colourful and festive air to the Christmas table very cheaply and quickly, it is a good idea to cut your own one-day table mats and lampshades from holly or plain-coloured paper. By means of cunning folding, a decorative mat of the type shown in Fig. 1, or a gay lampshade like that in Fig. 2, is cut complete in less than five minutes at a negligible cost.

No knowledge whatever of drawing is needed. All you require is some sheets of Christmassy and other bright-coloured papers and a pair of scissors. As, usually, eight thicknesses of paper have to be cut at once, these scissors should be larger and sharper than those most households dedicate to paper cutting.

Round Mats are Prettiest.

Mats can be cut square or oblong if desired, but the round ones are usually prettiest, so begin by pencilling on your paper round a plate of the required size and cut out in this way several circles on which to start operations.

The pattern is a matter of the mood of the moment—or, rather, the chance of the moment, for part of the fascination of this cutting craft is that one never knows quite what result will be achieved until cutting is completed and the mat opened out for inspection.

How to Begin.

Begin as in Fig. 3 by folding the circles either two or three times in half, so as to get respectively four or eight thicknesses. Out of each folded edge of the triangle so achieved, cut any shapes in any positions that take your fancy, but do not let one cut run into another in any direction.

Fig. 4 shows how the curved edges of the folded shape have been pinked out in a series of little V's, and the folded edges then cut in several narrow oblong slashes, giving rather

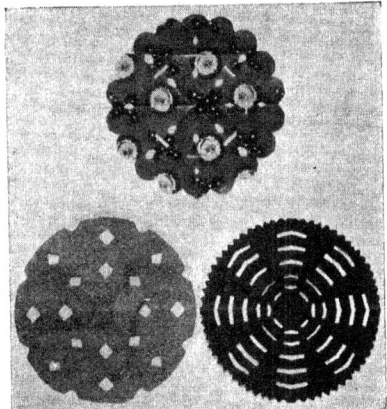

Fig. 1.—These attractive Table Mats are cut in a few slashes—and a few minutes.

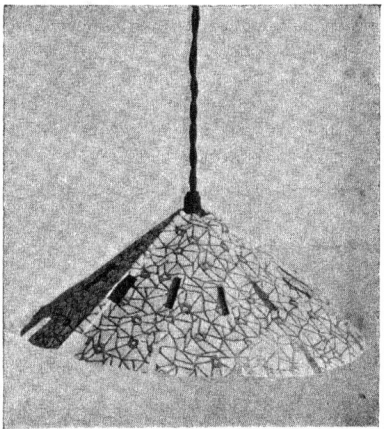

Fig. 2.—An attractive Lampshade that can be made almost at a moment's notice.

the effect of a Christmas tree. Open out this masterpiece and you have the very attractive result shown in the darkest of the three mats in Fig. 1.

The light plain mat in the same photograph was folded similarly in eight, but triangles cut out of its edges instead of the oblong slashes. The result, as you see, is a diamond pattern. The Santa Claus and holly-patterned mat in the same photograph combines oblong with diamond cuts.

In fact, the variety possible is endless, and, thanks to the multiple folding, charming results can be achieved in only three or four cuts, and the pattern obtainable is always perfectly symmetrical. The mat edges can be pinked, scalloped, or shaped in any other way desired.

Don't make the Cuts too Large.

Cuts may be plentiful but should not be large or they will weaken the paper too much, and make it liable to catch in cutlery, etc., and tear when in use on the Christmas table. It is a good plan to make all the mats for a table of the same paper, but of varying sizes and patterns. Bright green and bright red are the best colours in plain tints, as they are both gay and Christmassy. When patterned papers are used, the shaping of the edge is the most important thing, as interior cuts do not show up so well as on plain surfaces.

How to make the Mats Lie Flat.

If the mats will not lie flat after being folded, press them for a time under heavy books or iron them with a *warm* (not hot) iron.

Extra large mats, with a hole in the centre, and a slit from the edge to the hole, make the prettiest decorations for hanging lights fitted with opal shades, as in Fig. 2. Place the shade with its centre hole round the flex, overlap the cut edges sufficiently to take up any slack in the paper and pin or paste them together.

Both shades and mats are as handy for children's parties, club dances and other such functions as they are for the family dinner table on Christmas Day.

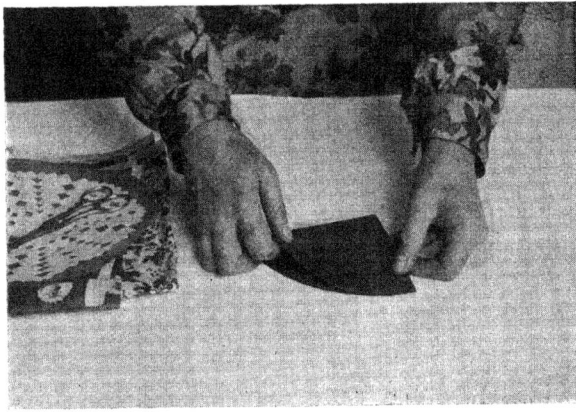

Fig. 3.—Folding a Circle of Paper preparatory to Cutting to make a Mat.

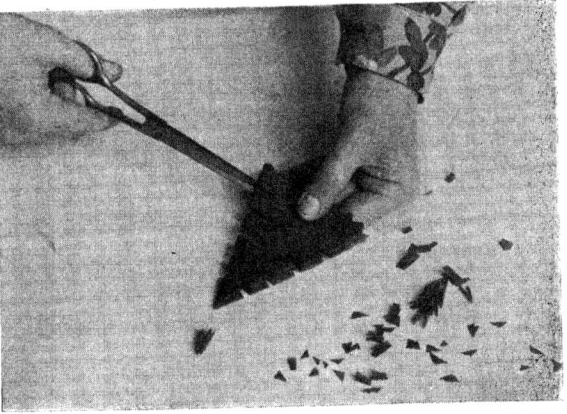

Fig. 4.—This Christmas Tree Shape, when opened, makes the Dark Mat shown in Fig. 1.

How to make a Window Seat

General Description.

The fitment shown in Fig. 1 consists of a comfortable seat for three persons with wide arm-rests at the ends. The seat has two lids which give access to a large locker for storing curtains, table-cloths and loose covers. Each arm-rest is another locker with a padded hinged lid. The upper shelves of the end cupboards are accessible both from the top and front, while the lower shelves have a sliding tray. The upper shelves and sliding trays have centre partitions.

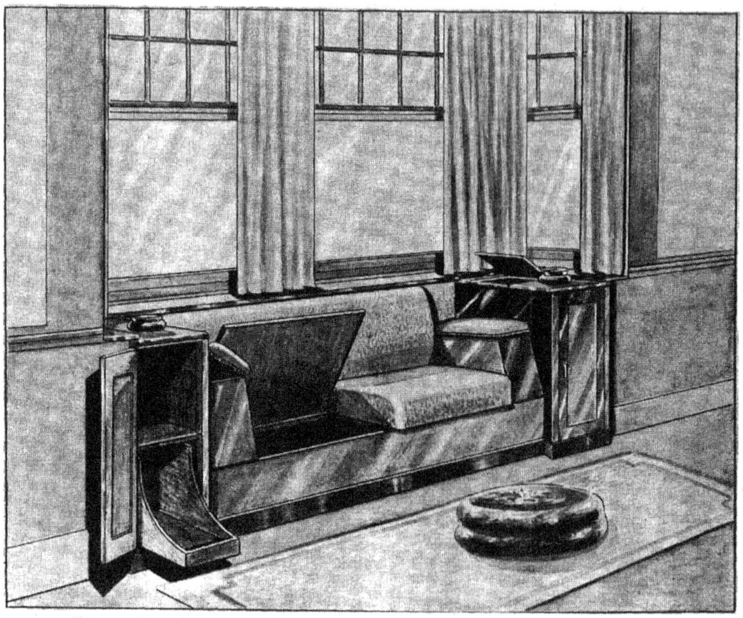

Fig. 1.—This Attractive Window Seat also forms a Locker with Two Lids.
The arm rests have hinged tops which give access to small side lockers. The upper shelf of the end cupboards is accessible from the top, also from the front. The bottom of each cupboard has a sliding tray. The whole assembly fits under the existing window shelf.

Dimensions.

The leading dimensions of the window seat are given in Figs. 2 to 4. These may be modified to suit any window recess, or the fitment may be placed under a window which is not recessed. In Fig. 2 the dimensions are based on a recess which is 8 feet 6 inches wide. The seat-board, or locker lid, is 11 inches high and allowance is made for a 5-inch cushion. The seat and end cupboards are 2 feet $8\frac{1}{2}$ inches from back to front. The tops of the cupboards fit under the existing shelf of the window recess. The fitment is designed to clear the existing skirting board, which is 10 inches high and stands out $\frac{1}{2}$ inch.

Material for End Cupboards.

The window seat is made of selected deal. For the cupboard uprights (Fig. 5) eight pieces each 2 feet 7 inches × $1\frac{1}{4}$ × $1\frac{3}{4}$ inches are required. Each pair of uprights is joined by three horizontal rails so that twelve rails are wanted in all. Each rail is 1 foot 4 inches × $\frac{5}{8}$ × $1\frac{3}{4}$ inches. Boards $\frac{5}{8}$ inch thick are used to cover the sides and top of the cupboard, also the shelves, sliding trays and partitions are made of similar material. About 78 square feet of this boarding is required altogether. The wall forms the back of the fitment.

Wood for Seat and Locker.

The front of the seat locker consists of a $\frac{7}{8}$-inch board 11 inches wide and 5 feet 10 inches long. On the back of it are three upright and one lengthwise battens each measuring $\frac{5}{8}$ × $1\frac{3}{4}$ inches, with a combined length of 8 feet. The seat or top of the locker requires 18 square feet of $\frac{7}{8}$-inch board, which includes a piece 8 inches wide under the seat back, also the fixed ends under the arm-rest lockers.

Running from back to front are three rectangular frames which support the top of the seat locker. These are made of $\frac{5}{8}$ × $1\frac{3}{4}$-inch batten and similar material is used for the three wall battens (Fig. 18), also the battens for the arm-rest lockers and seat lids, or a total length of 60 feet of $\frac{5}{8}$ × $1\frac{3}{4}$-inch batten. The front, top and side of the arm-rest lockers are made of $\frac{5}{8}$-inch board and will require 12 square feet of it.

Seat Back Material.

The upholstered seat back is made up on a wooden frame of $\frac{7}{8}$-inch material into which is rebated a $\frac{3}{8}$-inch panel. It is 5 feet 10 inches long and 1 foot 9 inches high. It is secured to

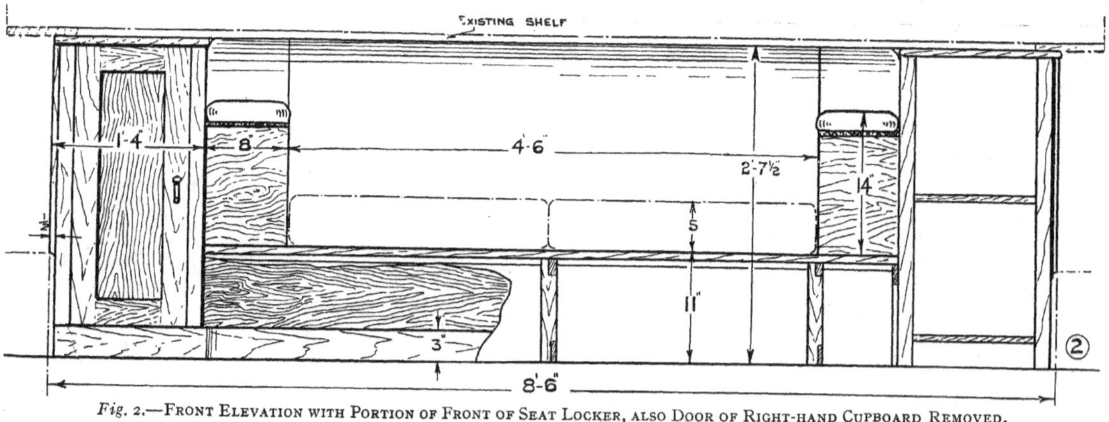

Fig. 2.—Front Elevation with Portion of Front of Seat Locker, also Door of Right-hand Cupboard Removed.
Leading dimensions are given above and in Figs. 3 and 4.

HOW TO MAKE A WINDOW SEAT

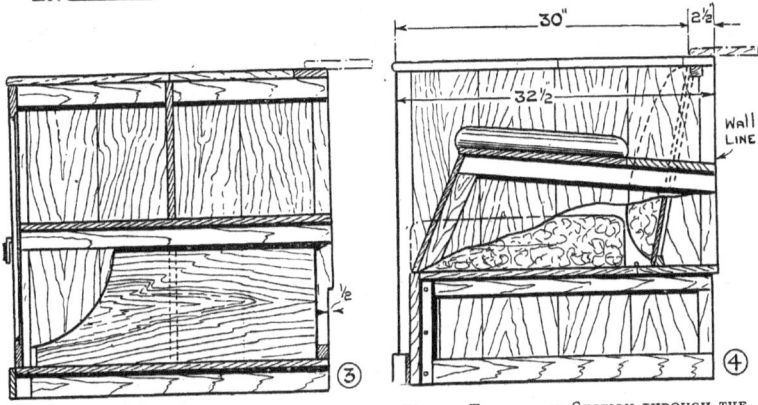

Fig. 3.—Transverse Section through an End Cupboard.

Fig. 4.—Transverse Section through the Arm Rest and Seat Lockers with Leading Dimensions.

Figs. 5-10.—Details of the Cupboard.

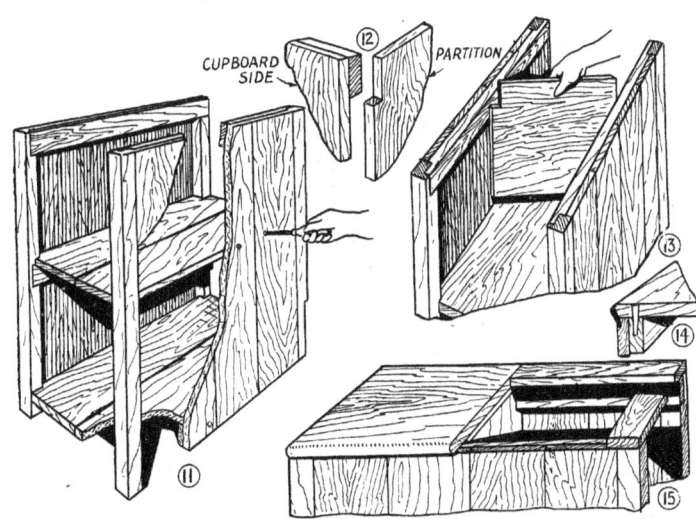

Figs. 11-15.—Further Details of the Cupboard

top and bottom fillets, which are made from 1½ × 1½-inch material.

The cupboard doors require 18 feet of 3 × ⅞-inch material and two plywood panels each measuring 24 × 8 inches.

Cupboard Frames.

The eight uprights of the cupboard frames are planed so that they are all the same width and thickness. They are marked out for length, which is the height of the existing window shelf 2 feet 7½ inches, less ⅝ inch, the thickness of the cupboard top, or 2 feet 6⅞ inches. The horizontal rails are each 1¾ inches deep. Set this dimension out at the ends and centre of each upright. The four uprights for the back of the cupboards are marked for laps 5/16 inch deep (Fig. 5), while the four front uprights have housings 1½ inches long (Figs. 5 and 7), so that the end grain of the rails is concealed. The back uprights are notched to clear the skirting (Fig. 6).

Cupboard Side Assemblies.

Each horizontal rail is marked out and cut for a lap 5/16 inch deep, or half its thickness at each end. Make up an end frame (Fig. 8). This is flush on the inside, and as the rails are ⅝ inch thick and the uprights are 1¼ inches thick, the recess on the outer side of ⅝ inch will be filled when the boards are added and screwed from the inside (Fig. 8). Having boarded a pair of cupboard sides, place them together in the vice (Fig. 9) and plane them as necessary so that they are the same size.

Cupboard Shelves.

Allowing for an ½-inch skirting, each cupboard is 15½ inches wide. The sides of the shelves touch the inside of the boarding and are, therefore, 1¼ inches less in width than the cupboard, or 14¼ inches wide. The shelves rest on the bottom and middle rails and are cut round the uprights (Fig. 11). The upper shelf is cut back ⅞ inch from the front to allow for the thickness of the door, and the bottom shelf is finished in a similar manner.

Each shelf is made up of two boards running lengthwise and joined on the underside with three small battens. Plane the shelves together in the vice to ensure that they are the same width. Then join the two sides of the cupboard by inserting the shelves and screwing them from the outside (Fig. 11).

Cupboard Partition and Top.

Measure the carcase for the top shelf centre partition (Fig. 13). This is cut to fit between the side boarding and is notched under the top rails. The partition is fixed by screwing it from the outside. Then make the fixed

315

HOW TO MAKE A WINDOW SEAT

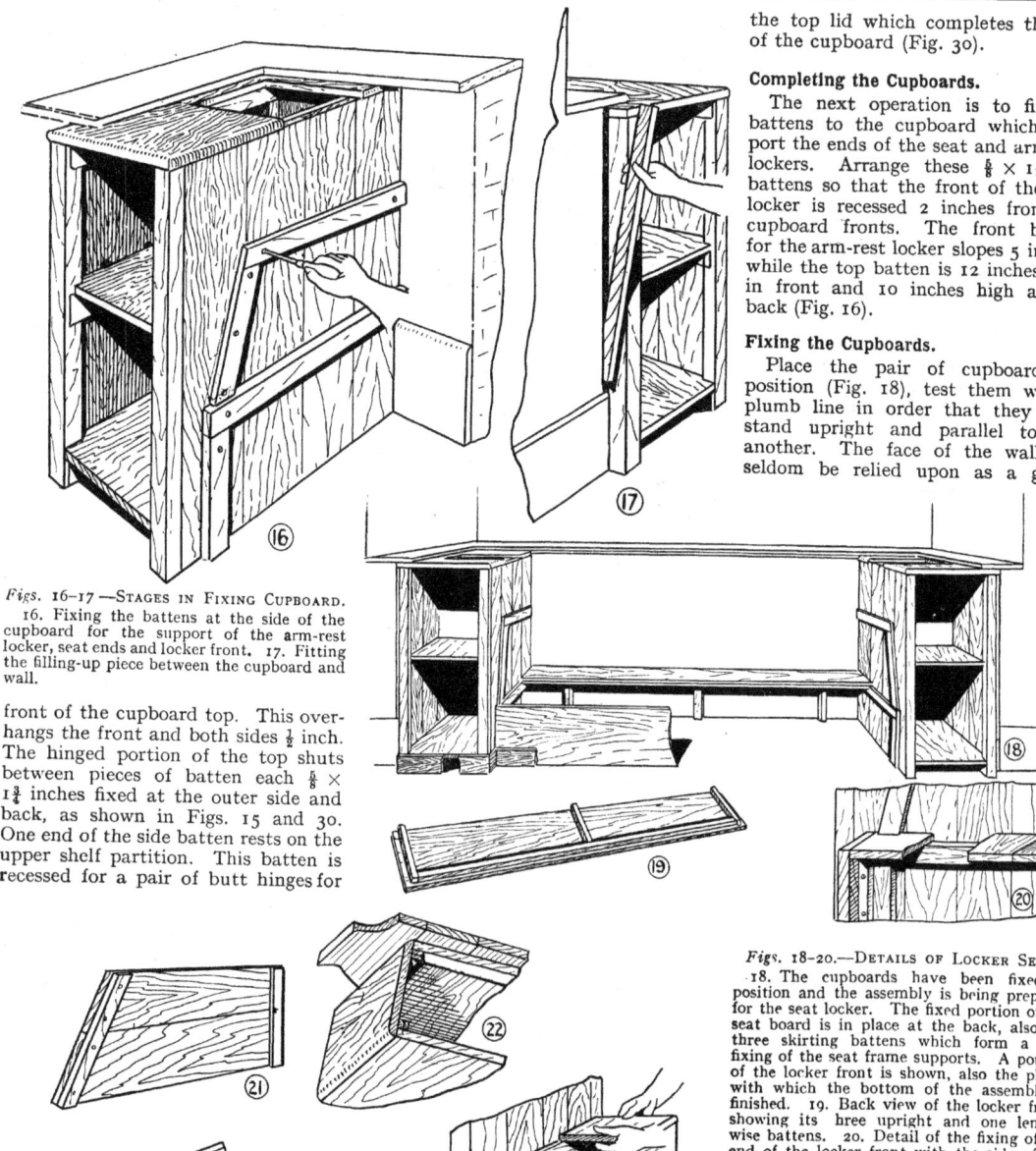

the top lid which completes the top of the cupboard (Fig. 30).

Completing the Cupboards.

The next operation is to fix the battens to the cupboard which support the ends of the seat and arm-rest lockers. Arrange these $\tfrac{5}{8} \times 1\tfrac{3}{4}$-inch battens so that the front of the seat locker is recessed 2 inches from the cupboard fronts. The front batten for the arm-rest locker slopes 5 inches, while the top batten is 12 inches high in front and 10 inches high at the back (Fig. 16).

Fixing the Cupboards.

Place the pair of cupboards in position (Fig. 18), test them with a plumb line in order that they shall stand upright and parallel to one another. The face of the wall can seldom be relied upon as a guide.

Figs. 16–17.—Stages in Fixing Cupboard.
16. Fixing the battens at the side of the cupboard for the support of the arm-rest locker, seat ends and locker front. 17. Fitting the filling-up piece between the cupboard and wall.

front of the cupboard top. This overhangs the front and both sides $\tfrac{1}{2}$ inch. The hinged portion of the top shuts between pieces of batten each $\tfrac{5}{8} \times 1\tfrac{3}{4}$ inches fixed at the outer side and back, as shown in Figs. 15 and 30. One end of the side batten rests on the upper shelf partition. This batten is recessed for a pair of butt hinges for

Figs. 18–20.—Details of Locker Seat.
18. The cupboards have been fixed in position and the assembly is being prepared for the seat locker. The fixed portion of the seat board is in place at the back, also the three skirting battens which form a rear fixing of the seat frame supports. A portion of the locker front is shown, also the plinth with which the bottom of the assembly is finished. 19. Back view of the locker front, showing its three upright and one lengthwise battens. 20. Detail of the fixing of the end of the locker front with the side of the cupboard.

The space between the wall and cupboard is filled with a piece of batten (Fig. 17). Each cupboard is fixed with two screws to the skirting through the end boarding.

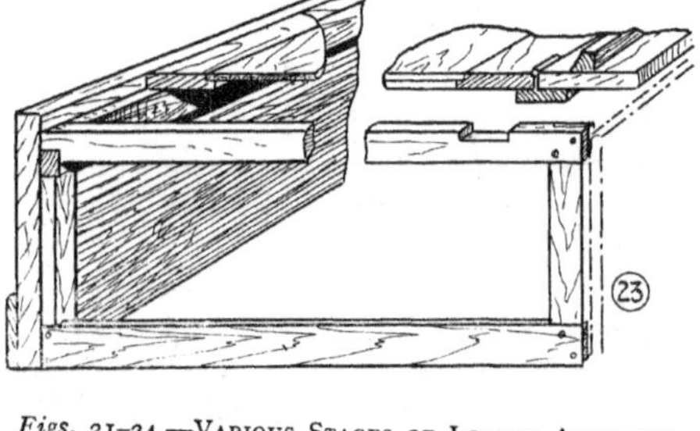

Seat Support Frames.

Three frames support the seat at each side of the lid openings and where the lids meet in the centre. These frames are lapped at the corners and touch the inside of the front of the locker and extend to the skirting (Fig. 23). These frames are made of $\tfrac{5}{8} \times 1\tfrac{3}{4}$-inch battens. The height of

Figs. 21–24.—Various Stages of Locker Assembly.
21. Battened side of the arm-rest locker. 22. View of arm-rest locker showing the rounded edges of the front. 23. Detail of seat support frame, framed and panelled locker lid and locker front. 24. Cut-away view showing arm-rest locker assembled on seat and against cupboard. The fixed rear portion of the locker top is being fitted.

HOW TO MAKE A WINDOW SEAT

each frame is 11 inches less the 7/8-inch lid, or 10 1/8 inches. The centre line of the end support is 8 inches from the cupboard. Mark out the skirting under the window for three battens, which are screwed against it (Fig. 18) and provide a rear fixing for the support frames.

Locker Front.

The position of the skirting battens above mentioned is copied and marked on the back of the locker front for a similar arrangement of battens, including a lengthwise one at the top. Cut the locker front to fit between the cupboards and fasten it to the cupboards through the end battens.

Rear Portion of Seat.

The back of the seat against the wall is 8 inches wide, and a 5/8 × 1 1/4-inch batten is screwed underneath the front edge projecting 1 inch so as to form a bearing for the lids. The position of this batten is marked out on the three support frames and a recess made (Fig. 23) for its reception.

Completing Fixed Portion of Seat.

Place the three support frames in position and fasten them to the battens of the locker front and skirting. Fix the rear portion of the seat. Cut two pieces of 7/8-inch board 8 inches wide for the bottoms of the arm-rest lockers. Fix these bottoms to the corresponding battens on the cupboard sides locker front and support frames. This board comes halfway across the support frame so that the other half is available as a lid support.

Seat Lids.

The opening in the locker top is measured for the pair of seat lids, which are made of 7/8-inch board battened on the underside, or they may be framed and panelled as shown in Fig. 23. The lid shuts flush with the inside and top of the locker front and is raised by means of a leather tab or flush handle. Or the lids may be an inch wider and overhang the front of the locker. In this instance

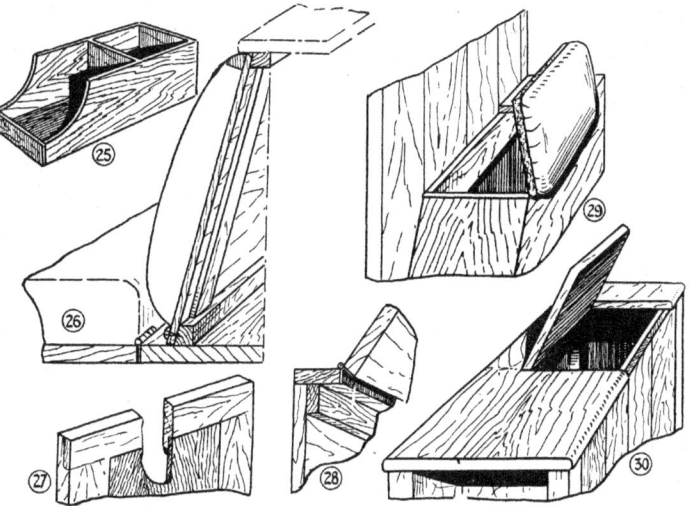

Figs. 25–30.—CONSTRUCTIONAL DETAILS OF VARIOUS PARTS.
25. Partitioned tray for bottom of cupboards. 26. Details of seat-back frame and retaining fillets. 27. Detail of panelled seat-back frame. 28. Detail of hinged top of cupboard. 29. Hinged and padded top of arm-rest locker. 30. Top of cupboard with lid open, which gives access to rear part of upper shelf.

the support frames are made the same height as the locker front.

Arm-rest Lockers.

The inner side of the arm-rest locker is formed by the cupboard. The other side and top of the locker are shown in Figs. 21, 22 and 24. The rear portion of the top is fixed and the front portion is hinged (Fig. 29). The front portion is padded and covered before fixing.

Cupboard Tray.

As the end cupboards measure 30 inches from front to back, access to the back of them is made convenient by the top lid already described and shown in Fig. 30, while the bottom has a tray (Fig. 25) which slides on it. This tray is moved by its front ledge, and is made so that it is 1/4 inch narrower than the cupboard door and 1/2 inch lower than the headroom between the shelves.

Seat Back.

Assuming that the existing window shelf projects 2 1/2 inches (Fig. 4) screw a fillet under it and against the wall. On the back of the seat-board screw a similar fillet 5 1/2 inches from the wall (Fig. 26). Both these fillets have bevelled fronts which agree with the slope of the setback frame. Stuff the seat back to a thickness of 4 inches. The upholstered back fits tightly between the seat and window shelf and is not otherwise fixed.

Cushions.

The cushions are made up to a thickness of 5 inches in front and 3 inches at the back so that the tops are parallel with those of the arm-rests.

Plinth.

A plinth 3 × 1/4 inches is fastened all round the base of the fitment, and a part of this can be seen in the diagram Fig. 18.

HOW TO BRONZE BRASS ARTICLES

It is first necessary to clean the articles thoroughly until they are quite free from grease and dirt. They should then be immersed in a solution made up as follows :—

Iron sulphate, 10 parts ; potassium permanganate, 2 parts ; hydrochloric acid, 1 part ; water, 200 parts.

Allow the objects to remain in the solution for about half a minute, then take them out and wash in warm clean water. Afterwards dry by rubbing lightly with fine softwood sawdust.

A good *reddish brown colour* may be obtained by immersing the articles in the following solution, heated to about 140° F. :—

Chromic acid solution, 1 part ; hydrochloric acid, 1 part ; potassium permanganate, 1 part ; iron sulphate, 5 parts ; water, 100 parts.

Allow the objects to remain in the solution for about a minute and then wash and dry as before.

A Luggage Hold-All for a Car

The luggage problem on the car is solved by the hold-all described below. No longer need you travel with unsightly packages of varying sizes strapped to the carrier, this container is remarkably light, weighing approximately 8 lbs., yet strong enough to support the weight of the owner. It is easily detachable, gives access to the contents while travelling without removal, and is absolutely watertight.

Materials Required.

20' 0" × 1½" × ⅜" machined deal.
5' 0" × 2" × ⅜" ,, ,,
15' 0" × 1" × ¼" ,, ,,
3' 0" × 1" × 1" deal quartering.
2' 7" × 1' 9"
2' 7" × 1' 5"
2' 7" × 1' 11" } ⅟₁₆" veneer plywood.
2' 7" × 2' 0"
(grain lengthwise).
2' 3" × 3' 0" × ⅛" plywood.
1" and ½" panel pins.
16' 0" × 1½" × ¼" machined deal } For
2' × 1" × 1" quadrant.   } the
8' × ⅜" × ⅜" quadrant.   } tray
2' 6" × 4' × ⅟₁₆" ply.
3 2" hinges
2 pairs strap bars } Chromium or
1 pair handles   } electro-plated.
1 trunk lock
2 spring clips
3½ yards × 50" black Rexine
4 straps 1" wide 2' long.

The Framing—the Ends.

From Figs. 2 and 4 you can see that the very thin plywood of which the case is made is held on a skeleton frame. The first step is to make the two ends A and B; they are cut from ⅛-inch ply and strips of 1 × ¼ inch are then glued and pinned round the edge to give rigidity. The curved corners are sawn off roughly with a bow-saw, the two sides are placed face to face and the rounded portions spokeshaved as one piece; this ensures an exact pair.

Fitting the Rails.

The rails E, F, H and J are cut to uniform length and a tongue sawn out as shown in the small sketch. Now place the tongued end in place on the edge of the completed side and mark the width of the groove; cut this away with a bow-saw and clean up with a chisel, taking care to make a tight fit. Having similarly fitted all these rails, proceed with G and K, only note that the ends of these are forked (see small sketch, Fig. 4); this is so that when the box is later sawn into two pieces one tongue will be in the side of the box while the other will form part of the lid.

Gluing Up.

Having cut all the rails and corresponding grooves in the side members, proceed to glue the frame together, pinning each joint with two panel pins, driving one into the tongue and another through the side piece into the shoulder of the rail.

When all the horizontal members are firm and the glue well set, proceed to cut and fit the three cross-pieces which form the base of the framework (see Fig. 4).

Fig. 3.—The finished Case and Tray before the Covering is added.

Fig. 2.—Here we see the completed Skeleton Frame in position.

Fig. 1.—The completed Luggage Hold-all in position on a Car.
It weighs approximately 8 lbs., is quickly detachable, and enables packages of all sizes to be easily carried.

The Lid Stiffening Member.

This is shown in Fig. 5, and the details of the joint can be seen in the small sketch attached. To get the correct angles for the shoulders on the tenon lay the three pieces of wood in position on the upturned surface of the side panel with the sloping piece resting on the two short uprights; while so placed a line should be marked across the two vertical pieces, this, then, gives the correct angle for the shoulders. The joint is best glued up and the curved edges spokeshaved off to the contour of the side afterwards.

Finally, approximately half the thickness of the upright is cut away so that the stiffening rib fits down on to the two upper horizontal rails as shown in Fig. 4. All that now remains to complete the skeleton frame is to fit and glue in the long top rail S (see Fig. 4).

The Top-Ply Covering.

The outside covering is in four pieces, the first to tackle is the top section with the curved corners. It should be cut roughly to size with a sharp knife, the two horizontal edges falling along a line running down the middle of the two upper rails, K and G. Fig. 9 shows how one edge is glued and pinned and then held firm with clamps, while the piece of ply is gradually bent over into position and clamped at the back. The piece of wood chosen for the top must have the top grain running from side to side of the case.

The Back and Front.

The back and front of the case are easily glued in position without the use of clamps; allow the sheets to project a little over the edge, then plane off flush when fixed. Finally the base is glued in position using

HOW TO MAKE A WINDOW SEAT

each frame is 11 inches less the ⅞-inch lid, or 10⅛ inches. The centre line of the end support is 8 inches from the cupboard. Mark out the skirting under the window for three battens, which are screwed against it (Fig. 18) and provide a rear fixing for the support frames.

Locker Front.

The position of the skirting battens above mentioned is copied and marked on the back of the locker front for a similar arrangement of battens, including a lengthwise one at the top. Cut the locker front to fit between the cupboards and fasten it to the cupboards through the end battens.

Rear Portion of Seat.

The back of the seat against the wall is 8 inches wide, and a ⅝ × 1¾-inch batten is screwed underneath the front edge projecting 1 inch so as to form a bearing for the lids. The position of this batten is marked out on the three support frames and a recess made (Fig. 23) for its reception.

Completing Fixed Portion of Seat.

Place the three support frames in position and fasten them to the battens of the locker front and skirting. Fix the rear portion of the seat. Cut two pieces of ⅞-inch board 8 inches wide for the bottoms of the arm-rest lockers. Fix these bottoms to the corresponding battens on the cupboard sides locker front and support frames. This board comes halfway across the support frame so that the other half is available as a lid support.

Seat Lids.

The opening in the locker top is measured for the pair of seat lids, which are made of ⅞-inch board battened on the underside, or they may be framed and panelled as shown in Fig. 23. The lid shuts flush with the inside and top of the locker front and is raised by means of a leather tab or flush handle. Or the lids may be an inch wider and overhang the front of the locker. In this instance

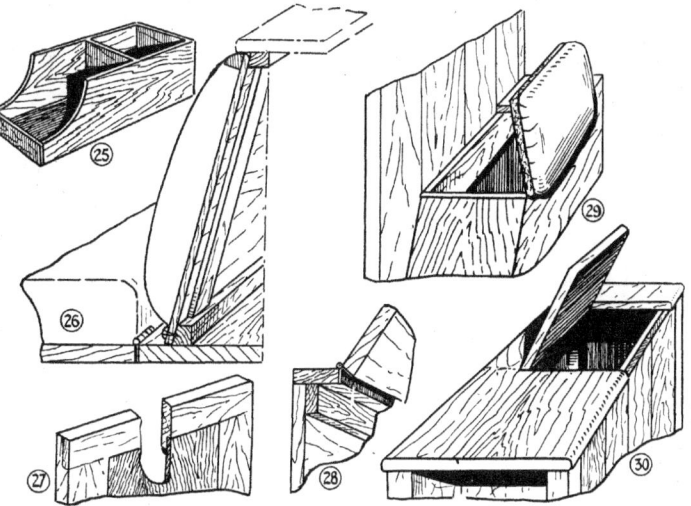

Figs. 25-30.—Constructional Details of Various Parts.
25. Partitioned tray for bottom of cupboards. 26. Details of seat-back frame and retaining fillets. 27. Detail of panelled seat-back frame. 28. Detail of hinged top of cupboard. 29. Hinged and padded top of arm-rest locker. 30. Top of cupboard with lid open, which gives access to rear part of upper shelf.

the support frames are made the same height as the locker front.

Arm-rest Lockers.

The inner side of the arm-rest locker is formed by the cupboard. The other side and top of the locker are shown in Figs. 21, 22 and 24. The rear portion of the top is fixed and the front portion is hinged (Fig. 29). The front portion is padded and covered before fixing.

Cupboard Tray.

As the end cupboards measure 30 inches from front to back, access to the back of them is made convenient by the top lid already described and shown in Fig. 30, while the bottom has a tray (Fig. 25) which slides on it. This tray is moved by its front ledge, and is made so that it is ⅛ inch narrower than the cupboard door and ½ inch lower than the headroom between the shelves.

Seat Back.

Assuming that the existing window shelf projects 2½ inches (Fig. 4) screw a fillet under it and against the wall. On the back of the seat-board screw a similar fillet 5½ inches from the wall (Fig. 26). Both these fillets have bevelled fronts which agree with the slope of the setback frame. Stuff the seat back to a thickness of 4 inches. The upholstered back fits tightly between the seat and window shelf and is not otherwise fixed.

Cushions.

The cushions are made up to a thickness of 5 inches in front and 3 inches at the back so that the tops are parallel with those of the arm-rests.

Plinth.

A plinth 3 × ¼ inches is fastened all round the base of the fitment, and a part of this can be seen in the diagram Fig. 18.

HOW TO BRONZE BRASS ARTICLES

It is first necessary to clean the articles thoroughly until they are quite free from grease and dirt. They should then be immersed in a solution made up as follows:—

Iron sulphate, 10 parts; potassium permanganate, 2 parts; hydrochloric acid, 1 part; water, 200 parts.

Allow the objects to remain in the solution for about half a minute, then take them out and wash in warm clean water. Afterwards dry by rubbing lightly with fine softwood sawdust.

A good *reddish brown colour* may be obtained by immersing the articles in the following solution, heated to about 140° F.:—

Chromic acid solution, 1 part; hydrochloric acid, 1 part; potassium permanganate, 1 part; iron sulphate, 5 parts; water, 100 parts.

Allow the objects to remain in the solution for about a minute and then wash and dry as before.

A Luggage Hold-All for a Car

The luggage problem on the car is solved by the hold-all described below. No longer need you travel with unsightly packages of varying sizes strapped to the carrier, this container is remarkably light, weighing approximately 8 lbs., yet strong enough to support the weight of the owner. It is easily detachable, gives access to the contents while travelling without removal, and is absolutely watertight.

Materials Required.

20′ 0″ × 1½″ × ⅜″ machined deal.
5′ 0″ × 2″ × ⅜″ ,, ,,
15′ 0″ × 1″ × ¼″ ,, ,,
3′ 0″ × 1″ × 1″ deal quartering.
2′ 7″ × 1′ 9″ ⎫
2′ 7″ × 1′ 5″ ⎬ ⅛″ veneer plywood.
2′ 7″ × 1′ 11″ ⎪
2′ 7″ × 2′ 0″ ⎭
(grain lengthwise).
2′ 3″ × 3′ 0″ × ⅛″ plywood.
1″ and ½″ panel pins.
16′ × 1½″ × ¼″ machined deal ⎫ For
2′ × 1″ × 1″ quadrant. ⎬ the
8′ × ⅜″ × ⅜″ quadrant. ⎭ tray
2′ 6″ × 4″ × 1/16″ ply.
3 2″ hinges
2 pairs strap bars ⎫ Chromium or
1 pair handles ⎬ electro-plated.
1 trunk lock ⎭
2 spring clips
3½ yards × 50″ black Rexine
4 straps 1″ wide 2′ long.

The Framing—the Ends.

From Figs. 2 and 4 you can see that the very thin plywood of which the case is made is held on a skeleton frame. The first step is to make the two ends A and B; they are cut from ⅛-inch ply and strips of 1 × ¼ inch are then glued and pinned round the edge to give rigidity. The curved corners are sawn off roughly with a bow-saw, the two sides are placed face to face and the rounded portions spokeshaved as one piece; this ensures an exact pair.

Fitting the Rails.

The rails E, F, H and J are cut to uniform length and a tongue sawn out as shown in the small sketch. Now place the tongued end in place on the edge of the completed side and mark the width of the groove; cut this away with a bow-saw and clean up with a chisel, taking care to make a tight fit. Having similarly fitted all these rails, proceed with G and K, only note that the ends of these are forked (see small sketch, Fig. 4); this is so that when the box is later sawn into two pieces one tongue will be in the side of the box while the other will form part of the lid.

Gluing Up.

Having cut all the rails and corresponding grooves in the side members, proceed to glue the frame together, pinning each joint with two panel pins, driving one into the tongue and another through the side piece into the shoulder of the rail.

When all the horizontal members are firm and the glue well set, proceed to cut and fit the three cross-pieces which form the base of the framework (see Fig. 4).

Fig. 3.—The finished case and tray before the covering is added.

Fig. 2.—Here we see the completed skeleton frame in position.

Fig. 1.—The completed luggage hold-all in position on a car.

It weighs approximately 8 lbs., is quickly detachable, and enables packages of all sizes to be easily carried.

The Lid Stiffening Member.

This is shown in Fig. 5, and the details of the joint can be seen in the small sketch attached. To get the correct angles for the shoulders on the tenon lay the three pieces of wood in position on the upturned surface of the side panel with the sloping piece resting on the two short uprights; while so placed a line should be marked across the two vertical pieces, this, then, gives the correct angle for the shoulders. The joint is best glued up and the curved edges spokeshaved off to the contour of the side afterwards.

Finally, approximately half the thickness of the upright is cut away so that the stiffening rib fits down on to the two upper horizontal rails as shown in Fig. 4. All that now remains to complete the skeleton frame is to fit and glue in the long top rail S (see Fig. 4).

The Top-Ply Covering.

The outside covering is in four pieces, the first to tackle is the top section with the curved corners. It should be cut roughly to size with a sharp knife, the two horizontal edges falling along a line running down the middle of the two upper rails, K and G. Fig. 9 shows how one edge is glued and pinned and then held firm with clamps, while the piece of ply is gradually bent over into position and clamped at the back. The piece of wood chosen for the top must have the top grain running from side to side of the case.

The Back and Front.

The back and front of the case are easily glued in position without the use of clamps; allow the sheets to project a little over the edge, then plane off flush when fixed. Finally the base is glued in position using

A LUGGAGE HOLD-ALL FOR A CAR

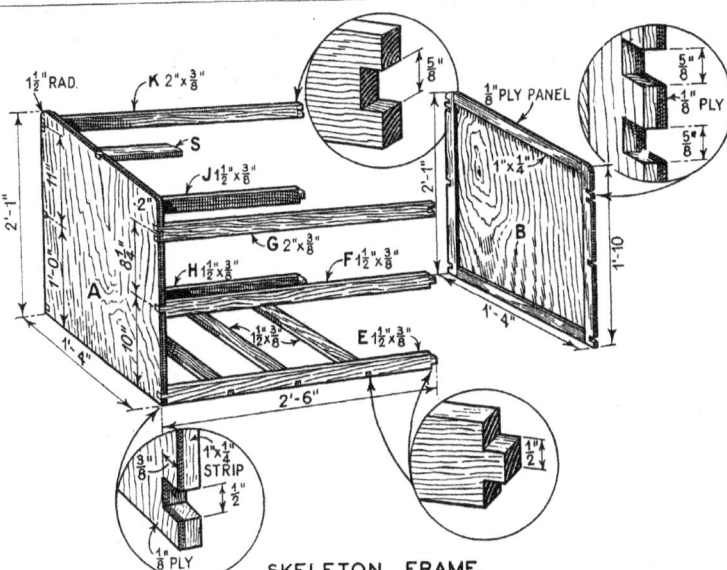

Fig. 4.—Details and Dimensions of the Skeleton Frame.

The case is made of very thin plywood and is held to a skeleton frame. The two ends A and B are cut from ⅛-inch ply, and strips of 1 × ¼-inch wood are then glued and pinned round the edge to give rigidity. The curved corners are sawn off roughly with a bow-saw, the two sides are placed face to face and the rounded portions spokeshaved as one piece.

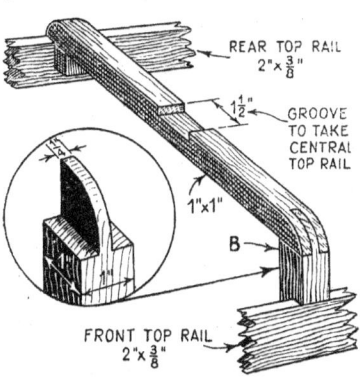

Fig. 5.—Details of the Lid Stiffening Member.

To get the correct angles for the shoulders on the tenon lay the three pieces of wood in position on the upturned surface of the side panel with the sloping piece resting on the two short uprights. While so placed, mark a line across the two vertical pieces, which will give the correct angle for the shoulders.

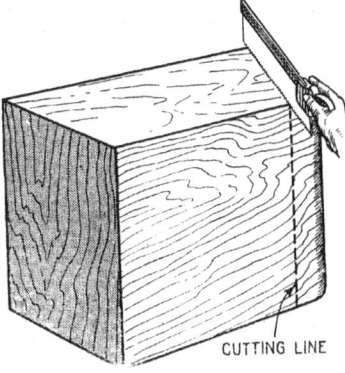

Fig. 6.—The Box is cut in two to form the Lid.

On each of the sides draw lines to fall midway between the tongues on the upper rails G and K, then continue these lines horizontally across the back and front; note the side lines will slope from the back. When the two pieces have been cut with a tenon saw clean up the sawn edges with a finely set smoothing plane or piece of No. 1 sandpaper.

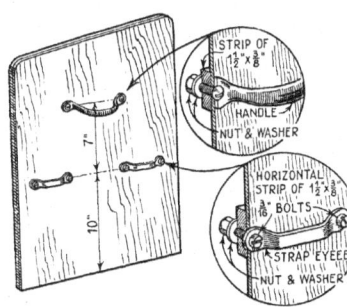

Fig. 7.—Details for Fitting the Handle and Strap Bars.

Fig. 8.—Details of the Support for the Tray.

1-inch panel pins round the edges and ½-inch ones across the central frame members.

Cutting the Box in Two.

The case now resembles a box without an opening. On each of the sides draw lines to fall midway between the tongues on the upper rails G and K, then continue these lines horizontally across the back and front; note the side lines will slope from the back slightly downwards towards the front. This slope is by design to facilitate the rain running away.

Now commence to saw along the line on one of the sides with a tenon saw (see Fig. 6), continue the cut right round the case until it is in two pieces. Then clean up the sawn edges with a finely set smoothing plane, or a piece of No. 1 sandpaper.

Fitting the Lip.

Fig. 11 shows a portion of a lip 1⅝ inches wide, fitted round the upper edge of the open box. It is glued and pinned to the upper framing, but notice that before attaching this strip of plywood a piece of 1/16-inch ply is sandwiched between the framing and the lip to throw it back sufficiently to allow the edge of the lid to clear when covered with the Rexine. The top edge of the ply should be cleaned up and slightly rounded.

The Hinges.

These must be fitted before attempting to cover the case, as small pieces have to be cut out of the top edge of the box and also from the corresponding side of the lid to allow for the thickness of the metal; note that there are three hinges.

The Covering.

A good quality Rexine stuck on with trimmers' paste or one of the special adhesives for the purpose makes the most successful covering. The box itself is best covered with three separate pieces, one taking the back and one end, the second piece covering the front and the remaining end, and finally a third piece on the bottom. The first two pieces should be cut long enough to bend 1½ inches round the extreme corners, and sufficiently wide to double 1½ inches under the base as well as turn over the lip of the box.

Mix the adhesive up to a thick paste and apply evenly to the back of the fabric, working it well in, and avoiding any small lumps.

When "tacky" lift it into position and smooth away all signs of creases with a dry cloth; press the Rexine well into the corners of the lip of the box with the handle of an old spoon. The second piece of material should overlap the first along the vertical edges, about ¾ inch, and the bottom piece must be cut on the small side so

A LUGGAGE HOLD-ALL FOR A CAR

Fig. 9.—Showing the Use of Clamps when fixing the $\frac{3}{16}$-inch Plywood in position.

Fig. 10.—Bolting on the Handles with $\frac{3}{16}$-inch Bolts. Note the piece of wood used to reinforce the plywood.

that it misses the edge by $\frac{1}{4}$ inch; it will then cover the turned over edges of the side and end pieces.

Covering the Lid.

One piece of Rexine should be cut large enough completely to cover the top, turning the ends well over the framing at the edge. Bend over the sides so that they lap over the ends of the lid about $\frac{1}{4}$ inch; cut out small vee-shaped pieces neatly to negotiate the corners. The small ends of the lid are covered last with two small pieces of material cut to the contour of the top edge so that it just overlaps the portion previously turned down from the edges of the main fabric.

Fitting the Handle and Strap Bars.

A chromium-plated handle (bathroom door type) is just what is required and this is bolted in position with $\frac{3}{16}$-inch bolts. A strip of wood $1\frac{1}{2} \times \frac{3}{8}$ inch must be glued on the inside of the case to reinforce the ply panel, and washers should be used under the nuts to prevent them cutting into the wood.

The strap bars or eyelets are fixed on in a similar manner, their position may vary with the type of carrier; they should be so placed that the straps when in position are quite vertical. They should not be more than 10 inches above the base of the case or it will be difficult to fix the hold-all rigid on the luggage grid.

The Lock and Clips.

The lock is attached to the back of a face plate and it will be necessary to cut away a small opening in the front of the case to

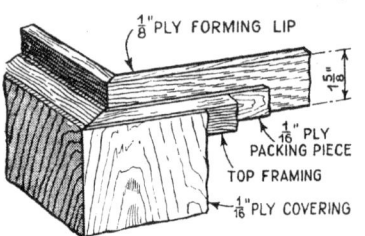

Fig. 11.—A portion of the Lip which is fitted round the Upper Edge of the Open Box.

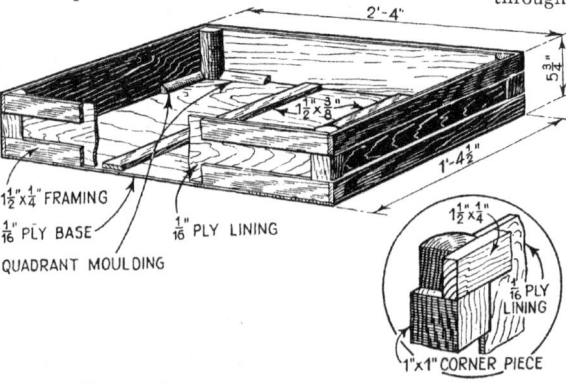

Fig. 12.—Constructional details for the Tray.

Fig. 13.—The Top Lid is fixed to the Case by means of three Hinges.

admit the rectangular metal case containing the lock itself. There are four screw holes in the plate, the upper two screws will go into the top framing rail but the lower two will require a short length of 4 inches of $\frac{3}{8}$-inch batten glued inside to the panel to take them. It is a good plan completely to frame the portion of the lock inside the case with $\frac{3}{8}$-inch batten and then glue over a small piece of $\frac{1}{16}$ inch; the lock is then entirely covered on the inside, thus preventing rain or dust penetrating through the keyhole. The hasp portion of the lock and the spring clips are simply secured with round-headed plated screws.

The Tray.

The construction of the tray is quite simple, as shown in Fig. 12.

The tray is supported inside the case on four small triangular pieces of wood glued at the correct level to the inside of each corner of the case (see Fig. 8).

Lining the Hold-all.

The lining used will probably vary with the taste of the reader. It is easily fixed in position by gluing the edges of the material to the framing of the case, and should hang quite loosely. The back, bottom, and front can be conveniently covered with one piece, and the lid can be similarly treated; the two ends requiring separate pieces of material. The tray can also be lined with one piece.

The Straps.

Four good straps, 2 feet long and 1 inch wide, black in colour, and fitted with plated buckles, can be procured at any good saddlers.

www.ingramcontent.com/pod-product-compliance
Lightning Source LLC
Chambersburg PA
CBHW080835230426
43665CB00021B/2850